New Comprehensive Mathematics for 'O' Level

Also from Stanley Thornes (Publishers) Ltd.

A Greer A FIRST COURSE IN STATISTICS
A Greer REVISION PRACTICE IN STATISTICS
A Greer C.S.E. MATHEMATICS — The Core Course
A Greer C.S.E. MATHEMATICS — The Special Topics
A Greer ARITHMETIC FOR COMMERCE
A Greer REVISION PRACTICE IN ARITHMETIC
A Greer REVISION PRACTICE IN ALGEBRA
A Greer REVISION PRACTICE IN NEW MATHEMATICS
A Greer REVISION PRACTICE IN GEOMETRY AND TRIGONOMETRY
A Greer REVISION PRACTICE IN MULTIPLE-CHOICE MATHS QUESTIONS
A Greer REVISION PRACTICE IN SHORT-ANSWER QUESTIONS IN O-LEVEL MATHEMATICS
Bostock and Chandler APPLIED MATHEMATICS I
Bostock and Chandler APPLIED MATHEMATICS II
Bostock and Chandler PURE MATHEMATICS I
Bostock and Chandler PURE MATHEMATICS II
Bostock and Chandler MATHEMATICS — THE CORE COURSE FOR A-LEVEL

A full list of books is available from the publishers including details of the MATHEMATICS FOR TECHNICIANS series by A Greer *and* G W Taylor.

New Comprehensive Mathematics for 'O' Level

2nd Edition

A. Greer

Formerly Senior Lecturer
Gloucestershire College of Arts and Technology

Stanley Thornes (Publishers) Ltd.

First published in 1979 by Stanley Thornes (Publishers) Ltd.,
Old Station Drive, Leckhampton, CHELTENHAM,
Glos. GL53 0DN

Reprinted 1980
Reprinted 1981
Reprinted with minor corrections 1982
2nd Edition 1983
Reprinted 1984
Reprinted 1985
Reprinted 1986

ISBN 0 85950159 0

Typeset by Alden Press, Oxford, London & Northampton and
Printed at The Bath Press, Avon

Preface

This book is an expanded edition of a Complete O-Level Mathematics. The contents include all the topics which appeared in that book often revised together with much new material.

Readers of the book will find it to be particularly suitable for the recently introduced Syllabus B of the University of London.

I have included revision material on Fractions and Decimals in response to many requests urging their inclusion. Also, to meet the requirements of various examining boards such topics as Polar Co-ordinates, Symmetry, Inequalities, Groups, Relations and Functions and Probability have been added. All relevant tables are also included. The resulting text now covers the O-Level mathematics requirements of all major examination boards and particularly the requirements of the University of London new Syllabus B.

The book is intended to be used as a revision course for those students seeking an O-Level qualification in Mathematics. Reference has been made to all the elementary aspects of the subject whenever this seemed desirable. The contents have been arranged in five broad categories: Arithmetic, Algebra, Geometry, Trigonometry and New Mathematics.

A very large number of graded exercises has been provided in each section of the work and I have indicated the order of difficulty of these exercises by using the notation A (easy), B (fairly easy), C (more difficult) and D (very difficult). The student should find it possible to work through the relatively easy problems (types A and B) thus gaining confidence in dealing with the harder questions which follow.

At the end of most chapters there are sets of objective type questions which have been called 'Self-Tests'.

The questions in the Miscellaneous Exercises have all been taken from recent examination papers. I am indebted to the University of London (L), the Associated Examining Board (A.E.B.) and the Joint Matriculation Board (J.M.B.) for permission to use questions taken from their examination papers.

Finally I would like to thank Mr. C. Eva for his invaluable work in correcting the manuscript and checking the answers to problems. It is probably too much to hope that despite the rigorous checking there are no errors and the publishers and myself would be pleased to hear from anyone who finds an error in either the text or in the answers to problems.

A. Greer   Gloucester

Note to the Second Edition

In response to several requests I have greatly expanded the topic of vectors to include the addition and subtraction of vector quantities and the parallelogram law. Also because of inflation, the topics on money such as exchange rates, wages, rates, etc. have become dated and these topics have been modified to bring them up to date. In addition, changes in Income Tax, Value Added Tax and the introduction of Mortgage Interest Relief At Source (MIRAS) have made it essential that these topics be altered to bring them into line with current practice.

I would like to take this opportunity to thank all of those who have written with constructive suggestions for improving the book and who have taken the trouble to report errors in the script and in the answers.

A. Greer   Gloucester, 1983

Contents

Chapter 1 Arithmetical Operations

SOME DEFINITIONS

The result obtained by adding numbers is called the *sum*. The sum of 4, 6 and 8 is $4 + 6 + 8 = 18$. The order in which numbers are added is not important.

$$4 + 6 + 8 = 6 + 4 + 8 = 8 + 4 + 6 = 18.$$

The *difference* of two numbers is the larger number minus the smaller number. The difference of 15 and 10 is $15 - 10 = 5$. The order in which we subtract is very important. $7 - 3$ is not the same as $3 - 7$.

The result obtained by multiplying numbers is called the *product*. The product of 8 and 7 is $8 \times 7 = 56$. The order in which we multiply is not important. $8 \times 7 = 7 \times 8$ and

$$3 \times 4 \times 6 = 4 \times 3 \times 6 = 6 \times 3 \times 4 = 72.$$

The result obtained by division is called the *quotient*. The quotient of $8 \div 4$ is 2. The order in which we divide *is* very important. $12 \div 3$ is not the same as $3 \div 12$.

SEQUENCE OF ARITHMETICAL OPERATIONS

Numbers are often combined in a series of arithmetical operations. When this happens a definite sequence must be observed.

(1) Brackets are used if there is any danger of ambiguity. The contents of the bracket must be evaluated before performing any other operation. Thus:

$$2 \times (7 + 4) = 2 \times 11 = 22$$
$$15 - (8 - 3) = 15 - 5 = 10$$

(2) Multiplication and division must be done before addition and subtraction. Thus:

$5 \times 8 + 7 = 40 + 7 = 47$ (not 5×15)

$8 \div 4 + 9 = 2 + 9 = 11$ (not $8 \div 13$)

$5 \times 4 - 12 \div 3 + 7 = 20 - 4 + 7 = 27 - 4 = 23$

So far we have used the standard operations of add, subtract, multiply and divide. However if we wished we could make up some operations of our own.

Suppose we have an operation shown by the symbol ‡ which means double the first number and add the second number. Then,

$$3 \ddagger 4 = 2 \times 3 + 4 = 6 + 4 = 10$$
$$5 \ddagger 3 = 2 \times 5 + 3 = 10 + 3 = 13$$

Exercise 1 — *Questions 1—4 and 11—14 type A, remainder B*

Find values for the following:

1) $3 + 5 \times 2$

2) $3 \times 6 - 8$

3) $7 \times 5 - 2 + 4 \times 6$

4) $8 \div 2 + 3$

5) $7 \times 5 - 12 \div 4 + 3$

6) $11 - 9 \div 3 + 7$

7) $3 \times (8 + 7)$

8) $2 + 8 \times (3 + 6)$

9) $17 - 2 \times (5 - 3)$

10) $11 - 12 \div 4 + 3 \times (6 - 2)$

The operation $*$ means divide the first number by 2 and add the second number. Use this operation to work out the following:

11) $2 * 4$ 13) $8 * 3$

12) $6 * 7$ 14) $10 * 2$

The operation † means add the first number to 3 times the second number. Use this operation to work out the following:

15) $8 \dagger 2$ 17) $2 \dagger 5$

16) $9 \dagger 4$ 18) $4 \dagger 3$

FACTORS AND MULTIPLES

If one number divides exactly into a second number the first number is said to be a factor of the second. Thus:

$$35 = 5 \times 7 \qquad \ldots 5 \text{ is a factor of } 35 \text{ and so is } 7.$$

$$240 = 3 \times 8 \times 10 \ldots 3, 8 \text{ and } 10 \text{ are all factors of } 240. \qquad \cdot$$

$$63 = 3 \times 21 = 7 \times 9$$

63 is said to be a *multiple* of any of the numbers 3, 7, 9 and 21 because each of them divides exactly into 63.

Every number has itself and 1 as factors. If a number has no other factors apart from these, it is said to be a *prime number*. Thus 2, 3, 7, 11, 13, 17 and 19 are all prime numbers.

A factor which is a prime number is called a *prime factor*.

LOWEST COMMON MULTIPLE (L.C.M.)

The L.C.M. of a set of numbers is the *smallest* number into which each of the given numbers will divide. Thus the L.C.M. of 3, 4, and 8 is 24 because 24 is the smallest number into which the numbers 3, 4 and 8 will divide exactly.

The L.C.M. of a set of numbers can usually be found by inspection.

HIGHEST COMMON FACTOR (H.C.F.)

The H.C.F. of a set of numbers is the greatest number which is a factor of each of the numbers. Thus 12 is the H.C.F. of 24, 36 and 60. Also 20 is the H.C.F. of 40, 60 and 80.

POWERS OF NUMBERS

The quantity $2 \times 2 \times 2 \times 2$ is written 2^4 and is called the fourth power of 2. The figure 4, which gives the number of 2's to be multiplied together is called the index (plural: indices).

$$5^6 = 5 \times 5 \times 5 \times 5 \times 5 \times 5 = 15\,625$$

$$7^3 = 7 \times 7 \times 7 = 343$$

Exercise 2 – *Question 7 type A, remainder B*

1) What numbers are factors of:
(a) 24   (b) 56   (c) 42?

2) Which of the following numbers are factors of 12:

2, 3, 4, 5, 6, 12, 18 and 24?

Which of them are multiples of 6?

3) Write down all the multiples of 3 between 10 and 40.

4) Express as a product of prime factors:
(a) 24   (b) 36   (c) 56   (d) 132

5) Write down the two prime numbers next larger than 19.

6) Find the L.C.M. of the following sets of numbers:
(a) 8 and 12   (b) 3, 4 and 5
(c) 2, 6 and 12   (d) 3, 6 and 8
(e) 2, 8 and 10   (f) 20 and 25
(g) 20 and 32   (h) 10, 15 and 40
(i) 12, 42, 60 and 70   (j) 18, 30, 42 and 48

7) Find the values of:
(a) 2^5 (b) 3^4 (c) 5^3
(d) 6^2 (e) 8^3

8) Find the H.C.F. of each of the following sets of numbers:
(a) 8 and 12   (b) 24 and 36
(c) 10, 15 and 30   (d) 26, 39 and 52
(e) 18, 30, 12 and 42
(f) 28, 42, 84, 98 and 112

SEQUENCES

A set of numbers which are connected by some definite law is called a series or a sequence of numbers. Each of the numbers in the series is called a term of the series. Here are some examples:

1, 3, 5, 7   . . . (each term is obtained by adding 2 to the previous term)

2, 6, 18, 54 . . . (each term is obtained by multiplying the previous term by 3)

EXAMPLE 1

Write down the next two terms of the following series:

112, 56, 28, . . .

The second term is found by dividing the first term by 2 and the third term is found by

2

dividing the second term by 2. Hence:

$$\text{Fourth term} = \frac{28}{2} = 14$$

$$\text{Fifth term} = \frac{14}{2} = 7$$

Exercise 3 — *All type A*

Write down the next two terms of each of the following series of numbers:

1) 3, 12, 48, . . .

2) 1, 4, 7, 10, . . .

3) 5, 11, 17, 23, . . .

4) 162, 54, 18, . . .

5) 6, 12, 24, . . .

SELF-TEST 1

In questions 1 to 15 state the letter (or letters) corresponding to the correct answer (or answers).

1) $3 + 7 \times 4$ is equal to:

a 40   **b** 31   **c** 84

2) $6 \times 5 - 2 + 4 \times 6$ is equal to:

a 52   **b** 42   **c** 18

3) $7 \times 6 - 12 \div 3 + 1$ is equal to:

a 40   **b** 39   **c** 21

4) $17 - 2 \times (6 - 4)$ is equal to:

a 30   **b** 1   **c** 13

5) $a * b$ means multiply the first number by 5 and subtract the second number multiplied by 3. $6 * 4$ is equal to:

a 2   **b** 26   **c** 18   **d** 6

6) $a \ddagger b$ means the product of 5 times the first number plus 2 times the second number. $3 \ddagger 5$ is equal to:

a 25   **b** 150   **c** 5   **d** 31

7) Which of the following is a prime number?

a 39   **b** 41   **c** 27   **d** 15

8) The product of 9 and 7 is:

a 16   **b** 63   **c** 2   **d** none of these

9) 2, 3 and 5 are the factors of:

a 6   **b** 15   **c** 10   **d** 30

10) 54 is a multiple of:

a 5   **b** 4   **c** 3   **d** none of these

11) The next two numbers in the sequence 5, 4, 6, 5, 7, 6, 8 are:

a 9 and 7   **b** 7 and 6   **c** 9 and 6

d 7 and 9

12) Consider the numbers 11, 21, 31, 77 and 112. Three of these numbers have a common factor. It is:

a 2   **b** 7   **c** 11   **d** 14

13) The L.C.M. of 2, 4, 6 and 5 is:

a 240   **b** 6   **c** 5   **d** 60

14) The H.C.F. of 20, 30 and 60 is:

a 2   **b** 20   **c** 10   **d** 60

Chapter 2 Fractions

VULGAR FRACTIONS

The circle in Fig. 2.1 has been divided into eight equal parts. Each part is called one-eighth of the circle and is written as $\frac{1}{8}$. The number 8 below the line shows how many equal parts there are and it is called the *denominator*. The number above the line shows how many of the equal parts are taken and it is called the *numerator*. If five of the eight equal parts are taken then we have taken $\frac{5}{8}$ of the circle.

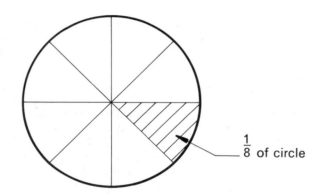

$\frac{1}{8}$ of circle

Fig. 2.1

From what has been said above we see that a fraction is always a part of something. The number below the line (the denominator) gives the fraction its name and tells us the number of equal parts into which the whole has been divided. The top number (the numerator) tells us the number of these equal parts that are to be taken. For example the fraction $\frac{3}{4}$ means that the whole has been divided into four equal parts and that three of these parts are to be taken.

The value of a fraction is unchanged if we multiply or divide both its numerator and denominator by the same amount.

$\frac{3}{5} = \frac{12}{20}$ (by multiplying the numerator (top number) and denominator (bottom number) by 4)

$\frac{2}{7} = \frac{10}{35}$ (by multiplying the numerator and denominator by 5)

$\frac{12}{32} = \frac{3}{8}$ (by dividing the numerator and denominator by 4)

$\frac{16}{64} = \frac{1}{4}$ (by dividing the numerator and denominator by 16)

EXAMPLE 1

Write down the fraction $\frac{2}{7}$ with a denominator (bottom number) of 28.

In order to make the denominator (bottom number) 28, we must multiply the original denominator of 7 by 4 because $7 \times 4 = 28$. Remembering that to leave the value of the fraction unchanged we must multiply both numerator (top number) and denominator (bottom number) by the same amount, then

$$\frac{2}{7} = \frac{2 \times 4}{7 \times 4} = \frac{8}{28}$$

Exercise 4 — *All type A*

Write down the following fractions with the denominator (bottom number) stated:

1) $\frac{3}{4}$ with denominator 28

2) $\frac{3}{5}$ with denominator 20

3) $\frac{5}{6}$ with denominator 30

4) $\frac{1}{9}$ with denominator 63

5) $\frac{2}{3}$ with denominator 12

6) $\frac{1}{6}$ with denominator 24

7) $\frac{3}{8}$ with denominator 64

8) $\frac{5}{7}$ with denominator 35

REDUCING A FRACTION TO ITS LOWEST TERMS

Fractions like $\frac{3}{8}$, $\frac{7}{16}$ and $\frac{3}{32}$ are said to be in their *lowest terms* because it is impossible to find a number which will divide exactly into both the top and bottom numbers. However, fractions like $\frac{9}{18}$, $\frac{8}{12}$ and $\frac{21}{24}$ are not in their lowest terms because they can be reduced further by dividing both the top and bottom numbers by some number which divides exactly into both of them. Thus,

$\frac{9}{18} = \frac{1}{2}$ (by dividing both top and bottom by 9)

$\frac{8}{12} = \frac{2}{3}$ (by dividing both top and bottom by 4)

$\frac{21}{24} = \frac{7}{8}$ (by dividing both top and bottom by 3)

Sometimes we can divide the top and bottom by the same number several times.

EXAMPLE 2

Reduce $\frac{210}{336}$ to its lowest terms.

$\frac{210}{336} = \frac{105}{168}$ (by dividing top and bottom by 2)

$= \frac{35}{56}$ (by dividing top and bottom by 3)

$= \frac{5}{8}$ (by dividing top and bottom by 7)

Hence $\frac{210}{336}$ reduced to its lowest terms is $\frac{5}{8}$.

Exercise 5 — *Questions 1–5 type A, remainder B*

Reduce the following fractions to their lowest terms:

1) $\frac{8}{16}$ 4) $\frac{15}{25}$ 7) $\frac{210}{294}$ 10) $\frac{210}{315}$

2) $\frac{9}{15}$ 5) $\frac{42}{48}$ 8) $\frac{126}{245}$

3) $\frac{8}{64}$ 6) $\frac{180}{240}$ 9) $\frac{132}{198}$

TYPES OF FRACTIONS

If the top number of a fraction is less than its bottom number the fraction is called a *proper fraction*. Thus $\frac{2}{3}$, $\frac{5}{8}$ and $\frac{3}{4}$ are all proper fractions. Note that a proper fraction has a value which is less than 1.

If the top number of a fraction is greater than its bottom number then the fraction is called an *improper fraction* or a *top heavy fraction*. Thus $\frac{5}{4}$, $\frac{3}{2}$ and $\frac{9}{7}$ are all top heavy, or improper, fractions. Note that all top heavy fractions have a value which is greater than 1.

Every top heavy fraction can be expressed as a whole number and a proper fraction. These are sometimes called *mixed numbers*. Thus $1\frac{1}{2}$, $5\frac{1}{3}$ and $9\frac{3}{4}$ are all mixed numbers. In order to convert a top heavy fraction into a mixed number it must be remembered that

$$\frac{\text{top number}}{\text{bottom number}} = \text{top number} \div \text{bottom number}$$

EXAMPLE 3

Express $\frac{15}{8}$ as a mixed number.

$$\frac{15}{8} = 1\frac{7}{8}$$

(because $15 \div 8 = 1$ and remainder 7)

From Example 3 we see that we convert a top heavy fraction into a mixed number by dividing the bottom number into the top number. Notice that the remainder becomes the top number in the fractional part of the mixed number. To change a mixed number into an improper fraction we multiply the whole number by the bottom number of the fractional part. To this we add the numerator of the fractional part and this sum then becomes the top number of the improper fraction. Its bottom number is the same as the bottom number of the fractional part of the mixed number.

EXAMPLE 4

Express $3\frac{5}{8}$ as a top heavy fraction.

$$3\frac{5}{8} = \frac{(8 \times 3) + 5}{8} = \frac{24 + 5}{8} = \frac{29}{8}$$

Exercise 6 — *All type A*

Express each of the following as a mixed number:

1) $\frac{7}{2}$ 3) $\frac{22}{10}$ 5) $\frac{21}{8}$

2) $\frac{8}{4}$ 4) $\frac{12}{11}$

Express each of the following as top heavy fractions:

6) $2\frac{3}{8}$ 8) $8\frac{2}{3}$ 10) $4\frac{3}{7}$

7) $5\frac{1}{10}$ 9) $6\frac{7}{20}$

LOWEST COMMON MULTIPLE (L.C.M.)

The L.C.M. of a set of numbers is the *smallest* number into which each of the given numbers will divide. Thus the L.C.M. of 4, 5 and 10 is 20 because 20 is the smallest number into which the numbers, 4, 5 and 10 will divide exactly.

The L.C.M. of a set of numbers can usually be found by inspection.

Exercise 7 — *Questions 1–7 type A, remainder B*

Find the L.C.M. of the following sets of numbers:

1) 4 and 6
2) 2, 6 and 10
3) 2, 4 and 12
4) 3, 4 and 8
5) 4, 8 and 10
6) 20 and 25
7) 10 and 32
8) 5, 15 and 40
9) 6, 42, 60 and 70
10) 18, 15, 42 and 48

LOWEST COMMON DENOMINATOR

When we wish to compare the values of two or more fractions the easiest way is to express the fractions with the same bottom number. This common denominator should be the L.C.M. of the denominators of the fractions to be compared and it is called the *lowest common denominator*.

EXAMPLE 5

Arrange the fractions $\frac{3}{4}, \frac{5}{8}, \frac{7}{10}$ and $\frac{11}{20}$ in order of size starting with the smallest.

The lowest common denominator of 4, 8, 10 and 20 is 40. Expressing each of the given fractions with a bottom number of 40 gives:

$$\frac{3}{4} = \frac{3 \times 10}{4 \times 10} = \frac{30}{40} \qquad \frac{5}{8} = \frac{5 \times 5}{8 \times 5} = \frac{25}{40}$$

$$\frac{7}{10} = \frac{7 \times 4}{10 \times 4} = \frac{28}{40} \qquad \frac{11}{20} = \frac{11 \times 2}{20 \times 2} = \frac{22}{40}$$

Therefore the order is:

$$\frac{22}{40}, \frac{25}{40}, \frac{28}{40}, \frac{30}{40} \quad \text{or} \quad \frac{11}{20}, \frac{5}{8}, \frac{7}{10} \text{ and } \frac{3}{4}$$

Exercise 8 — *All type A*

Arrange the following sets of fractions in order of size, beginning with the smallest:

1) $\frac{1}{2}, \frac{5}{6}, \frac{2}{3}, \frac{7}{12}$ 4) $\frac{3}{4}, \frac{5}{8}, \frac{3}{5}, \frac{13}{20}$

2) $\frac{9}{10}, \frac{3}{4}, \frac{6}{7}, \frac{7}{8}$ 5) $\frac{11}{16}, \frac{7}{10}, \frac{9}{14}, \frac{3}{4}$

3) $\frac{13}{16}, \frac{11}{20}, \frac{7}{10}, \frac{3}{5}$ 6) $\frac{3}{8}, \frac{4}{7}, \frac{5}{9}, \frac{2}{5}$

ADDITION OF FRACTIONS

The steps when adding fractions are as follows:

(1) Find the lowest common denominator of the fractions to be added.

(2) Express each of the fractions with this common denominator.

(3) Add the numerators of the new fractions to give the numerator of the answer. The denominator of the answer is the lowest common denominator found in (1).

EXAMPLE 6

Find the sum of $\frac{2}{7}$ and $\frac{3}{4}$.

First find the lowest common denominator (this is the L.C.M. of 7 and 4).

It is 28. Now express $\frac{2}{7}$ and $\frac{3}{4}$ with a bottom number of 28.

$$\frac{2}{7} = \frac{2 \times 4}{7 \times 4} = \frac{8}{28} \qquad \frac{3}{4} = \frac{3 \times 7}{4 \times 7} = \frac{21}{28}$$

Adding the top numbers of the new fractions:

$$\frac{2}{7} + \frac{3}{4} = \frac{8}{28} + \frac{21}{28} = \frac{29}{28} = 1\frac{1}{28}$$

A better way of setting out the work is as follows:

$$\frac{2}{7} + \frac{3}{4} = \frac{2 \times 4 + 3 \times 7}{28} = \frac{8 + 21}{28} = \frac{29}{28} = 1\frac{1}{28}$$

EXAMPLE 7

Simplify $\frac{3}{4} + \frac{2}{3} + \frac{7}{10}$.

The L.C.M. of the bottom numbers 4, 3 and 10 is 60.

$$\frac{3}{4} + \frac{2}{3} + \frac{7}{10} = \frac{3 \times 15 + 2 \times 20 + 7 \times 6}{60}$$

$$= \frac{45 + 40 + 42}{60}$$

$$= \frac{127}{60} = 2\frac{7}{60}$$

EXAMPLE 8

Add together $5\frac{1}{2}$, $2\frac{2}{3}$ and $3\frac{2}{5}$.

First add the whole numbers together, $5 + 2 + 3 = 10$. Then add the fractional parts in the usual way. The L.C.M. of 2, 3 and 5 is 30.

$$5\frac{1}{2} + 2\frac{2}{3} + 3\frac{2}{5} = 10 + \frac{15 \times 1 + 10 \times 2 + 6 \times 2}{30}$$

$$= 10 + \frac{15 + 20 + 12}{30}$$

$$= 10 + \frac{47}{30} = 10 + 1\frac{17}{30}$$

$$= 11\frac{17}{30}$$

Exercise 9 — *All type A*

Add together:

1) $\frac{1}{2} + \frac{1}{3}$

2) $\frac{2}{5} + \frac{9}{10}$

3) $\frac{3}{4} + \frac{3}{8}$

4) $\frac{3}{10} + \frac{1}{4}$

5) $\frac{1}{2} + \frac{3}{4} + \frac{7}{8}$

6) $\frac{1}{8} + \frac{2}{3} + \frac{3}{5}$

7) $1\frac{3}{8} + 3\frac{9}{16}$

8) $7\frac{2}{3} + 6\frac{3}{5}$

9) $3\frac{3}{8} + 5\frac{2}{7} + 4\frac{3}{4}$

10) $4\frac{1}{2} + 3\frac{5}{6} + 2\frac{1}{3}$

11) $7\frac{3}{8} + 2\frac{3}{4} + \frac{7}{8} + \frac{5}{16}$

12) $7\frac{2}{3} + \frac{2}{5} + \frac{3}{10} + 2\frac{1}{2}$

SUBTRACTION OF FRACTIONS

The method is similar to that used in addition. Find the common denominator of the fractions and after expressing each fraction with this common denominator, subtract.

EXAMPLE 9

Simplify $\frac{5}{8} - \frac{2}{5}$.

The L.C.M. of the bottom numbers is 40.

$$\frac{5}{8} - \frac{2}{5} = \frac{5 \times 5 - 8 \times 2}{40} = \frac{25 - 16}{40} = \frac{9}{40}$$

When mixed numbers have to be subtracted the best way is to turn the mixed numbers into top heavy fractions and then proceed in the way shown in Example 9.

EXAMPLE 10

Simplify $3\frac{7}{10} - 2\frac{3}{4}$.

$$3\frac{7}{10} - 2\frac{3}{4} = \frac{37}{10} - \frac{11}{4} = \frac{37 \times 2 - 11 \times 5}{20}$$

$$= \frac{74 - 55}{20} = \frac{19}{20}$$

EXAMPLE 11

Simplify $5\frac{2}{5} - 3\frac{7}{8}$.

$$5\frac{2}{5} - 3\frac{7}{8} = \frac{27}{5} - \frac{31}{8} = \frac{27 \times 8 - 31 \times 5}{40}$$

$$= \frac{216 - 155}{40} = \frac{61}{40} = 1\frac{21}{40}$$

Exercise 10 — *Questions 1–8 type A, remainder B*

Simplify the following:

1) $\frac{1}{2} - \frac{1}{3}$

2) $\frac{1}{3} - \frac{1}{5}$

3) $\frac{2}{3} - \frac{1}{2}$

4) $\frac{7}{8} - \frac{3}{8}$

5) $\frac{7}{8} - \frac{5}{6}$

6) $3\frac{1}{4} - 2\frac{3}{8}$

7) $3 - \frac{5}{7}$

8) $5 - 3\frac{4}{5}$

9) $5\frac{3}{8} - 2\frac{9}{10}$

10) $4\frac{7}{32} - 3\frac{9}{10}$

11) $1\frac{5}{16} - \frac{4}{5}$

COMBINED ADDITION AND SUBTRACTION

EXAMPLE 12

Simplify $5\frac{3}{8} - 1\frac{1}{4} + 2\frac{1}{2} - \frac{7}{16}$.

$$5\frac{3}{8} - 1\frac{1}{4} + 2\frac{1}{2} - \frac{7}{16} = \frac{43}{8} - \frac{5}{4} + \frac{5}{2} - \frac{7}{16}$$

$$= \frac{43 \times 2 - 5 \times 4 + 5 \times 8 - 7 \times 1}{16}$$

$$= \frac{86 - 20 + 40 - 7}{16}$$

$$= \frac{(86 + 40) - (20 + 7)}{16}$$

$$= \frac{126 - 27}{16} = \frac{99}{16} = 6\frac{3}{16}$$

Exercise 11 — *All type B*

Simplify the following:

1) $2\frac{1}{2} + 3\frac{1}{4} - 4\frac{3}{8}$ 3) $4\frac{3}{8} - 2\frac{1}{2} + 5$

2) $5\frac{1}{10} - 3\frac{1}{2} - 1\frac{1}{4}$ 4) $6\frac{1}{2} - 3\frac{1}{6} + 2\frac{1}{12} - 4\frac{3}{4}$

5) $1\frac{3}{16} - 2\frac{2}{5} + 3\frac{3}{4} + 5\frac{5}{8}$

6) $12\frac{7}{10} - 5\frac{1}{8} + 3\frac{3}{20} + 1\frac{1}{2}$

7) $2\frac{3}{16} - 2\frac{3}{10} + \frac{5}{8} + 1\frac{3}{4}$

8) $12\frac{3}{4} - 6\frac{7}{8} + 5\frac{21}{32} - 2\frac{13}{16}$

9) $3\frac{9}{20} + 1\frac{3}{8} - 2\frac{7}{10} + 1\frac{3}{4}$

10) $2\frac{9}{25} + 3\frac{4}{5} - 2\frac{7}{10} - \frac{3}{20}$

MULTIPLICATION

When multiplying together two or more fractions we first multiply all the top numbers together and then we multiply all the bottom numbers together. Mixed numbers must always be converted into top heavy fractions.

EXAMPLE 13

Simplify $\frac{5}{8} \times \frac{3}{7}$.

$$\frac{5}{8} \times \frac{3}{7} = \frac{5 \times 3}{8 \times 7} = \frac{15}{56}$$

EXAMPLE 14

Simplify $\frac{2}{5} \times 3\frac{2}{3}$.

$$\frac{2}{5} \times 3\frac{2}{3} = \frac{2}{5} \times \frac{11}{3} = \frac{2 \times 11}{5 \times 3} = \frac{22}{15} = 1\frac{7}{15}$$

EXAMPLE 15

Simplify $1\frac{3}{8} \times 1\frac{1}{4}$.

$$1\frac{3}{8} \times 1\frac{1}{4} = \frac{11}{8} \times \frac{5}{4} = \frac{11 \times 5}{8 \times 4} = \frac{55}{32} = 1\frac{23}{32}$$

Exercise 12 — *All type A*

Simplify the following:

1) $\frac{2}{3} \times \frac{4}{5}$ 4) $\frac{5}{9} \times \frac{11}{4}$ 7) $1\frac{2}{9} \times 1\frac{2}{5}$

2) $\frac{3}{4} \times \frac{5}{7}$ 5) $1\frac{2}{5} \times 3\frac{1}{2}$ 8) $1\frac{7}{8} \times 1\frac{4}{7}$

3) $\frac{2}{9} \times 1\frac{2}{3}$ 6) $2\frac{1}{2} \times 2\frac{2}{3}$

CANCELLING

EXAMPLE 16

Simplify $\frac{2}{3} \times 1\frac{7}{8}$.

$$\frac{2}{3} \times 1\frac{7}{8} = \frac{2}{3} \times \frac{15}{8} = \frac{2 \times 15}{3 \times 8} = \frac{30}{24} = \frac{5}{4} = 1\frac{1}{4}$$

The step to reducing $\frac{30}{24}$ to its lowest terms has been done by dividing 6 into both the top and bottom numbers.

The work can be made easier by *cancelling* before multiplication as shown below.

$$\frac{\overset{1}{\cancel{2}}}{\underset{1}{\cancel{3}}} \times \frac{\overset{5}{\cancel{15}}}{\underset{4}{\cancel{8}}} = \frac{1 \times 5}{1 \times 4} = \frac{5}{4} = 1\frac{1}{4}$$

We have divided 2 into 2 (a top number) and 8 (a bottom number) and also we have divided 3 into 15 (a top number) and 3 (a bottom number). You will see that we have divided the top numbers and the bottom numbers by the same amount. Notice carefully that we can only cancel between a top number and a bottom number.

EXAMPLE 17

Simplify $\dfrac{16}{25} \times \dfrac{7}{8} \times 8\dfrac{3}{4}$.

$$\dfrac{\overset{2}{\underset{5}{\cancel{16}}}}{\underset{5}{\cancel{25}}} \times \dfrac{7}{\underset{1}{\cancel{8}}} \times \dfrac{\overset{7}{\cancel{35}}}{\underset{2}{\cancel{4}}} = \dfrac{1 \times 7 \times 7}{5 \times 1 \times 2} = \dfrac{49}{10} = 4\dfrac{9}{10}$$

Sometimes in calculations with fractions the word 'of' appears. It should always be taken as meaning multiply. Thus:

$$\dfrac{4}{5} \text{ of } 20 = \dfrac{4}{\underset{1}{\cancel{5}}} \times \dfrac{\overset{4}{\cancel{20}}}{1} = \dfrac{4 \times 4}{1 \times 1}$$
$$= \dfrac{16}{1} = 16$$

Exercise 13 — *All type A*

Simplify the following:

1) $\dfrac{3}{4} \times 1\dfrac{7}{9}$

2) $5\dfrac{1}{5} \times \dfrac{10}{13}$

3) $1\dfrac{5}{8} \times \dfrac{7}{26}$

4) $1\dfrac{1}{2} \times \dfrac{2}{5} \times 2\dfrac{1}{2}$

5) $\dfrac{5}{8} \times \dfrac{7}{10} \times \dfrac{2}{21}$

6) $2 \times 1\dfrac{1}{2} \times 1\dfrac{1}{3}$

7) $3\dfrac{3}{4} \times 1\dfrac{3}{5} \times 1\dfrac{1}{8}$

8) $\dfrac{15}{32} \times \dfrac{8}{11} \times 24\dfrac{1}{5}$

9) $\dfrac{3}{4}$ of 16

10) $\dfrac{5}{7}$ of 140

11) $\dfrac{2}{3}$ of $4\dfrac{1}{2}$

12) $\dfrac{4}{5}$ of $2\dfrac{1}{2}$

DIVISION OF FRACTIONS

To divide by a fraction, all we have to do is to invert it (i.e. turn it upside down) and multiply. Thus:

$$\dfrac{3}{5} \div \dfrac{2}{7} = \dfrac{3}{5} \times \dfrac{7}{2} = \dfrac{3 \times 7}{5 \times 2} = \dfrac{21}{10} = 2\dfrac{1}{10}$$

EXAMPLE 18

Divide $1\dfrac{4}{5}$ by $2\dfrac{1}{3}$.

$$1\dfrac{4}{5} \div 2\dfrac{1}{3} = \dfrac{9}{5} \div \dfrac{7}{3} = \dfrac{9}{5} \times \dfrac{3}{7} = \dfrac{27}{35}$$

Exercise 14 — *All type A*

Simplify the following:

1) $\dfrac{4}{5} \div 1\dfrac{1}{3}$

2) $2 \div \dfrac{1}{4}$

3) $\dfrac{5}{8} \div \dfrac{15}{32}$

4) $3\dfrac{3}{4} \div 2\dfrac{1}{2}$

5) $2\dfrac{1}{2} \div 3\dfrac{3}{4}$

6) $5 \div 5\dfrac{1}{5}$

7) $3\dfrac{1}{15} \div 2\dfrac{5}{9}$

8) $2\dfrac{3}{10} \div \dfrac{3}{5}$

OPERATIONS WITH FRACTIONS

The sequence of operations when dealing with fractions is the same as those used with whole numbers. They are, in order:

(1) Work out brackets.
(2) Multiply and divide.
(3) Add and subtract.

EXAMPLE 19

Simplify $\dfrac{1}{5} \div \left(\dfrac{1}{3} \div \dfrac{1}{2}\right)$.

$$\dfrac{1}{5} \div \left(\dfrac{1}{3} \div \dfrac{1}{2}\right) = \dfrac{1}{5} \div \left(\dfrac{1}{3} \times \dfrac{2}{1}\right)$$
$$= \dfrac{1}{5} \div \dfrac{2}{3} = \dfrac{1}{5} \times \dfrac{3}{2} = \dfrac{3}{10}$$

EXAMPLE 20

Simplify $\dfrac{2\dfrac{4}{5} + 1\dfrac{1}{4}}{3\dfrac{3}{5}} - \dfrac{5}{16}$.

With problems of this kind it is best to work in stages as shown below:

$$2\dfrac{4}{5} + 1\dfrac{1}{4} = 3\dfrac{16 + 5}{20} = 3\dfrac{21}{20} = 4\dfrac{1}{20}$$

$$\dfrac{4\dfrac{1}{20}}{3\dfrac{3}{5}} = \dfrac{81}{20} \div \dfrac{18}{5} = \dfrac{81}{20} \times \dfrac{5}{18} = \dfrac{9}{8}$$

$$\dfrac{9}{8} - \dfrac{5}{16} = \dfrac{18 - 5}{16} = \dfrac{13}{16}$$

Exercise 15 — *All type B*

Simplify the following:

1) $3\frac{3}{14} + \left(1\frac{1}{49} \times \frac{7}{10}\right)$

2) $\frac{1}{4} \div \left(\frac{1}{8} \times \frac{2}{5}\right)$

3) $1\frac{2}{3} \div \left(\frac{3}{5} \div \frac{9}{10}\right)$

4) $\left(1\frac{7}{8} \times 2\frac{2}{5}\right) - 3\frac{2}{3}$

5) $\dfrac{2\frac{2}{3} + 1\frac{1}{5}}{5\frac{4}{5}}$

6) $3\frac{2}{3} \div \left(\frac{2}{3} + \frac{4}{5}\right)$

7) $\dfrac{5\frac{3}{5} - 3\frac{1}{2} \times \frac{2}{3}}{2\frac{1}{3}}$

8) $\frac{2}{5} \times \left(\frac{2}{3} - \frac{1}{4}\right) + \frac{1}{2}$

9) $\dfrac{3\frac{9}{16} \times \frac{4}{9}}{2 + 6\frac{1}{4} \times 1\frac{1}{5}}$

10) $\dfrac{\frac{5}{9} - \frac{7}{15}}{1 - \frac{5}{9} \times \frac{7}{15}}$

SELF-TEST 2

In questions 1 to 15, state the letter (or letters) corresponding to the correct answer (or answers).

1) When the fraction $\frac{630}{1470}$ is reduced to its lowest terms the answer is:

a $\frac{63}{147}$ b $\frac{3}{7}$ c $\frac{21}{49}$ d $\frac{9}{20}$

2) Which of the following fractions is equal to $\frac{4}{9}$?

a $\frac{12}{27}$ b $\frac{4}{36}$ c $\frac{36}{4}$ d $\frac{20}{90}$ e $\frac{52}{117}$

3) The fraction $\frac{3}{4}$ when written with denominator 56 is the same as:

a $\frac{3}{56}$ b $\frac{56}{12}$ c $\frac{42}{56}$ d $\frac{56}{42}$

4) The L.C.M. of 5, 15, 40 and 64 is:
a 960   b 192 000   c 640   d 64

5) The mixed number $3\frac{5}{6}$ is equal to:

a $\frac{15}{6}$ b $\frac{5}{18}$ c $\frac{15}{18}$ d $\frac{23}{6}$

6) The improper fraction $\frac{104}{14}$ when written as a mixed number in its lowest terms is equal to:

a $7\frac{3}{7}$ b $\frac{364}{49}$ c $7\frac{6}{14}$ d $\frac{52}{7}$

7) $\frac{1}{4} + \frac{2}{3} + \frac{3}{5}$ is equal to:

a $\frac{1}{2}$ b $\frac{1}{10}$ c $\frac{91}{60}$ d $1\frac{31}{60}$

8) $1\frac{3}{8} + 2\frac{5}{6} + 3\frac{1}{4}$ is equal to:

a $6\frac{4}{9}$ b $6\frac{15}{192}$ c $\frac{35}{24}$ d $\frac{21}{40}$ e $7\frac{11}{24}$

9) $1\frac{1}{8} + 2\frac{1}{6} + 3\frac{3}{4}$ is equal to:

a $6\frac{5}{18}$ b $7\frac{1}{24}$ c $1\frac{1}{24}$ d $7\frac{5}{24}$

10) $\frac{7}{8} \times \frac{3}{5}$ is equal to:

a $\frac{10}{13}$ b $\frac{4}{3}$ c $\frac{35}{24}$ d $\frac{21}{40}$

11) $\frac{5}{8} \times \frac{4}{15}$ is equal to one of the following, when the answer is expressed in its lowest terms:

a $\frac{20}{120}$ b $\frac{1}{6}$ c $\frac{32}{75}$ d $\frac{9}{23}$

12) $\frac{3}{4} \div \frac{8}{9}$ is equal to:

a $\frac{24}{36}$ b $\frac{2}{3}$ c $\frac{27}{32}$ d $\frac{3}{2}$

13) $6\frac{4}{9} \div 3\frac{2}{3}$ is equal to:

a $2\frac{2}{3}$ b $\frac{638}{27}$ c $\frac{58}{33}$ d $18\frac{8}{27}$

14) $3 \times \left(\frac{1}{2} - \frac{1}{3}\right)$ is equal to:

a $1\frac{1}{2} - \frac{1}{3}$ b $\frac{1}{2}$ c $3 \times \frac{1}{2} - 3 \times \frac{1}{3}$

15) $\frac{5}{8} + \frac{1}{2} \times \frac{1}{4}$ is equal to:

a $\frac{9}{32}$ b $\frac{3}{4}$ c $\frac{9}{16}$ d $\frac{3}{32}$

Chapter 3 The Decimal System

THE DECIMAL SYSTEM

The decimal system is an extension of our ordinary number system. When we write the number 666 we mean $600 + 60 + 6$. Reading from left to right each figure 6 is ten times the value of the next one.

We now have to decide how to deal with fractional quantities, that is, quantities whose values are less than one. If we regard 666.666 as meaning $600 + 60 + 6 + \frac{6}{10} + \frac{6}{100} + \frac{6}{1000}$ then the dot, called the decimal point, separates the whole numbers from the fractional parts. Notice that with the fractional, or decimal parts, e.g. .666, each figure 6 is ten times the value of the following one, reading from left to right. Thus $\frac{6}{10}$ is ten times as great as $\frac{6}{100}$, and $\frac{6}{100}$ is ten times as great as $\frac{6}{1000}$ and so on.

Decimals then are fractions which have denominators of 10, 100, 1000 and so on, according to the position of the figure after the decimal point.

If we have to write six hundred and five we write 605; the zero keeps the place for the missing tens. In the same way if we want to write $\frac{3}{10} + \frac{5}{1000}$ we write .305; the zero keeps the place for the missing hundredths. Also $\frac{6}{100} + \frac{7}{1000}$ would be written .067; the zero in this case keeps the place for the missing tenths.

When there are no whole numbers it is usual to insert a zero in front of the decimal point so that, for instance, .35 would be written 0.35.

Exercise 16 — *All type A*

Read off as decimals:

1) $\dfrac{7}{10}$

2) $\dfrac{3}{10} + \dfrac{7}{100}$

3) $\dfrac{5}{10} + \dfrac{8}{100} + \dfrac{9}{1000}$

4) $\dfrac{9}{1000}$

5) $\dfrac{3}{100}$

6) $\dfrac{1}{100} + \dfrac{7}{1000}$

7) $8 + \dfrac{6}{100}$

8) $24 + \dfrac{2}{100} + \dfrac{9}{10\,000}$

9) $50 + \dfrac{8}{1000}$

Read off the following with denominators (bottom numbers) 10, 100, 1000, etc.

10) 0.2

11) 4.6

12) 3.58

13) 437.25

14) 0.004

15) 0.036

16) 400.029

17) 0.001

18) 0.032 9

ADDITION AND SUBTRACTION OF DECIMALS

Adding or subtracting decimals is done in exactly the same way as for whole numbers. Care must be taken, however, to write the decimal points directly underneath one another. This makes sure that all the figures having the same place value fall in the same column.

EXAMPLE 1
Simplify $11.36 + 2.639 + 0.047$.

$$\begin{array}{r} 11.36 \\ 2.639 \\ 0.047 \\ \hline 14.046 \end{array}$$

EXAMPLE 2
Subtract 8.567 from 19.126.

$$\begin{array}{r} 19.126 \\ 8.567 \\ \hline 10.559 \end{array}$$

Exercise 17 — *All type A*

Write down the values of:

1) $2.375 + 0.625$

2) $4.25 + 7.25$

3) $3.196 + 2.475 + 18.369$

4) $38.267 + 0.049 + 20.3$

5) $27.418 + 0.967 + 25 + 1.467$

6) $12.48 - 8.36$

7) $19.215 - 3.599$

8) $2.237 - 1.898$

9) $0.876 - 0.064$

10) $5.48 - 0.069\,1$

MULTIPLICATION AND DIVISION OF DECIMALS

One of the advantages of decimals is the ease with which they may be multiplied or divided by 10, 100, 1000, etc.

EXAMPLE 3
Find the value of 1.4×10.

$$1.4 \times 10 = 1 \times 10 + 0.4 \times 10$$
$$= 10 + \frac{4}{10} \times 10 = 10 + 4 = 14$$

EXAMPLE 4
Find the value of 27.532×10.

$$27.532 \times 10 = 27 \times 10 + 0.5 \times 10$$
$$+ 0.03 \times 10 + 0.002 \times 10$$
$$= 270 + \frac{5}{10} \times 10 + \frac{3}{100}$$
$$\times 10 + \frac{2}{1000} \times 10$$
$$= 270 + 5 + \frac{3}{10} + \frac{2}{100}$$
$$= 275.32$$

In both of the above examples you will notice that the figures have not been changed by the multiplication; only the *positions* of the figures have been changed. Thus in Example 3, $1.4 \times 10 = 14$, that is the decimal point has been moved one place to the right. In Example 4, $27.532 \times 10 = 275.32$; again the decimal point has been moved one place to the right.

To multiply by 10, then, is the same as shifting the decimal point one place to the right. In the same way to multiply by 100 means shifting the decimal point two places to the right and so on.

EXAMPLE 5
$17.369 \times 100 = 1736.9$

The decimal point has been moved two places to the right.

EXAMPLE 6
$0.078\,95 \times 1000 = 78.95.$

The decimal point has been moved three places to the right.

Exercise 18 — *All type A*

Multiply each of the numbers in questions 1 to 6 by 10, 100 and 1000.

1) 4.1 6) $0.001\,753$

2) 2.42 7) $0.485\,3 \times 100$

3) 0.046 8) 0.009×1000

4) 0.35 9) 170.06×10

5) $0.148\,6$ 10) $0.563\,96 \times 10\,000$

When dividing by 10 the decimal point is moved one place to the left, by 100, two places to the left and so on. Thus,

$$154.26 \div 10 = 15.426$$

The decimal point has been moved one place to the left.

$$9.432 \div 100 = 0.094\,32$$

The decimal point has been moved two places to the left.

$$35 \div 1000 = 0.035$$

The decimal point has been moved three places to the left.

In the above examples note carefully that use has been made of zeros following the decimal point to keep the places for the missing tenths.

Exercise 19 — *All type A*

Divide each of the numbers in questions 1 to 5 by 10, 100 and 1000.

1) 3.6 6) $5.4 \div 100$

2) 64.198 7) $2.05 \div 1000$

3) 0.07 8) $0.04 \div 10$

4) 510.4 9) $0.008\,6 \div 1000$

5) 0.352 10) $627.428 \div 10\,000$

LONG MULTIPLICATION

EXAMPLE 7

Find the value of 36.5×3.504.

First disregard the decimal points and multiply
365 by 3504

```
          365
        3 504
      1 095 000
        182 500
          1 460
      1 278 960
```

Now count up the total number of figures
following the decimal points in both numbers
(i.e. $1 + 3 = 4$).   In the answer to the multiplication (the product), count this total
number of figures from the right and insert the
decimal point. The product is then 127.896 0
or 127.896 since the zero does not mean
anything.

Exercise 20 — *All type A*

Find the values of the following:

1) 25.42×29.23 4) 3.025×2.45

2) $0.361 8 \times 2.63$ 5) 0.043×0.032

3) 0.76×0.38

LONG DIVISION

EXAMPLE 8

Find the value of $19.24 \div 2.6$.

First convert the divisor (2.6) into a whole
number by multiplying it by 10. To compensate multiply the dividend (19.24) by 10 also
so that we now have $192.4 \div 26$. Now proceed
as in ordinary division.

```
26)192.4(7.4
   182          — this line  26 × 7
    10 4        — 4 brought down from
    10 4          above. Since  4  lies to
    . . .          the right of the decimal
                   point in the dividend
                   insert a decimal point
                   in the answer (the
                   quotient)
```

Notice carefully how the decimal point in the
quotient was obtained. The 4 brought down
from the dividend lies to the right of the decimal

point. Before bringing this down put a decimal
point in the quotient immediately following
the 7.

The division in this case is exact (i.e. there is no
remainder) and the answer is 7.4. Now let us
see what happens when there is a remainder.

EXAMPLE 9

Find the value of $15.187 \div 3.57$.

As before make the divisor into a whole number
by multiplying it by 100 so that it becomes
357. To compensate multiply the dividend also
by 100 so that it becomes 1518.7.
Now divide.

```
357)1518.7(4.254 06
    1428          — this line  357 × 4
     907          — 7 brought down
     714            from the dividend.
                     Since it lies to the
                     right of the decimal
                     point insert a
                     decimal point in
                     the quotient.
    1930          — bring down a zero
    1785            as all the figures in
    1450            the dividend have
    1428            been used up.
    2200          — Bring down a zero.
    2142            The divisor will not
      58            go into  220  so
                     place  0  in the
                     quotient and bring
                     down another zero.
```

The answer to 5 decimal places is 4.254 06.
This is not the correct answer because there is
a remainder. The division can be continued in
the way shown to give as many decimal places
as desired, or until there is no remainder.

DECIMAL PLACES

It is important to realise what is meant by an
answer given to so many decimal places. It is the
number of figures which follow the decimal
point which give the number of decimal places.
If the first figure to be discarded is 5 or more
then the previous figure is increased by 1.

Thus:

$85.768\,4 = 85.8$ correct to 1 decimal place

$\quad\quad\quad = 85.77$ correct to 2 decimal places

$\quad\quad\quad = 85.768$ correct to 3 decimal places

Notice carefully that zeros must be kept:

$0.007\,362 = 0.007$ correct to 3 decimal places

$\quad\quad\quad = 0.01$ correct to 2 decimal places

$7.601 = 7.60$ correct to 2 decimal places

$\quad\quad\quad = 7.6$ correct to 1 decimal place

If an answer is required correct to 3 decimal places the division should be continued to 4 decimal places and the answer corrected to 3 decimal places.

Exercise 21 — *All type B*

Find the value of:

1) $18.89 \div 14.2$ correct to 2 decimal places.

2) $0.039\,6 \div 2.51$ correct to 3 decimal places.

3) $7.21 \div 0.038$ correct to 2 decimal places.

4) $13.059 \div 3.18$ correct to 4 decimal places.

5) $0.1382 \div 0.0032$ correct to 1 decimal place.

SIGNIFICANT FIGURES

Instead of using the number of decimal places to express the accuracy of an answer, significant figures can be used. The number 39.38 is correct to 2 decimal places but it is also correct to 4 significant figures since the number contains four figures. The rules regarding significant figures are as follows:

(1) If the first figure to be discarded is 5 or more the previous figure is increased by 1.

$\quad 8.192\,5 = 8.193$ correct to 4 significant figures

$\quad\quad\quad = 8.19$ correct to 3 significant figures

$\quad\quad\quad = 8.2$ correct to 2 significant figures

(2) Zeros must be kept to show the position of the decimal point, or to indicate that the zero is a significant figure.

$24\,392 = 24\,390$ correct to 4 significant figures

$\quad\quad\quad = 24\,400$ correct to 3 significant figures

$0.085\,8 = 0.086$ correct to 2 significant figures

$425.804 = 425.80$ correct to 5 significant figures

$\quad\quad\quad = 426$ correct to 3 significant figures

Exercise 22 — *All type B*

Write down the following numbers correct to the number of significant figures stated:

1) $24.865\,82$ (i) to 6 (ii) to 4 (iii) to 2

2) $0.008\,357\,1$ (i) to 4 (ii) to 3 (iii) to 2

3) $4.978\,48$ (i) to 5 (ii) to 3 (iii) to 1

4) 21.987 to 2

5) 35.603 to 4

6) $28\,387\,617$ (i) to 5 (ii) to 2

7) $4.149\,76$ (i) to 5 (ii) to 4 (iii) to 3

8) $9.204\,8$ to 3

ROUGH CHECKS FOR CALCULATIONS

The worst mistake that can be made in a calculation is that of misplacing the decimal point. To place it wrongly, even by one place, makes the answer ten times too large or ten times too small. To prevent this occurring it is always worth while doing a rough check by using approximate numbers. When doing these rough checks always try to select numbers which are easy to multiply or which will cancel.

EXAMPLE 10

(1) 0.23×0.56.

For a rough check we will take 0.2×0.6.
Product roughly $= 0.2 \times 0.6 = 0.12$.
Correct product $= 0.128\,8$.

(The rough check shows that the answer is $0.128\,8$ not 1.288 or $0.012\,88$.)

(2) $173.3 \div 27.8$.

For a rough check we will take $180 \div 30$.
Quotient roughly $= 6$.
Correct quotient $= 6.23$.
(Note the rough check and the correct answer are of the same order.)

(3) $\dfrac{8.198 \times 19.56 \times 30.82 \times 0.198}{6.52 \times 3.58 \times 0.823}$.

Answer roughly $= \dfrac{8 \times 20 \times 30 \times 0.2}{6 \times 4 \times 1} = 40$.

Correct answer $= 50.94$.

(Although there is a big difference between the rough answer and the correct answer, the rough check shows that the answer is 50.94 and not 509.4.)

Exercise 23 — *All type B*

Find rough checks for the following:

1) $223.6 \times 0.004\,8$

2) 32.7×0.259

3) $0.682 \times 0.097 \times 2.38$

4) $78.41 \div 23.78$

5) $0.059 \div 0.002\,68$

6) $33.2 \times 29.6 \times 0.031$

7) $\dfrac{0.728 \times 0.006\,25}{0.028\,1}$

8) $\dfrac{27.5 \times 30.52}{11.3 \times 2.73}$

FRACTION TO DECIMAL CONVERSION

We found, when doing fractions, that the line separating the numerator and the denominator of a fraction takes the place of a division sign. Thus:

$$\frac{17}{80} \text{ is the same as } 17 \div 80$$

Therefore to convert a fraction into a decimal we divide the denominator into the numerator.

EXAMPLE 11

Convert $\dfrac{27}{32}$ to decimals.

$$\frac{27}{32} = 27 \div 32$$

```
32)27.0(0.843 75
   25 6
   ────
    1 40
    1 28
    ────
     120
      96
     ────
     240
     224
     ────
     160
     160
     ────
      ...
```

Therefore $\dfrac{27}{32} = 0.843\,75$.

EXAMPLE 12

Convert $2\dfrac{9}{16}$ into decimals.

When we have a mixed number to convert into decimals we need only deal with the fractional part. Thus to convert $2\frac{9}{16}$ into decimals we only have to deal with $\frac{9}{16}$.

$$\frac{9}{16} = 9 \div 16$$

```
16)9.0(0.562 5
   8 0
   ───
   1 00
     96
   ────
     40
     32
    ────
     80
     80
    ────
     ..
```

The division shows that $\frac{9}{16} = 0.562\,5$ and hence $2\frac{9}{16} = 2.562\,5$.

Sometimes a fraction will not divide out exactly as shown in Example 13

EXAMPLE 13

Convert $\dfrac{1}{3}$ to decimals.

$$\frac{1}{3} = 1 \div 3$$

15

$$3)\overline{1.0}\,(0.333$$
$$\underline{9}$$
$$10$$
$$\underline{9}$$
$$10$$
$$\underline{9}$$
$$1$$

It is clear that all we shall get from the division is a succession of threes.

This is an example of a recurring decimal and in order to prevent endless repetition the result is written $0.\dot{3}$. Therefore $\frac{1}{3} = 0.\dot{3}$.

Further examples of recurring decimals are:

$\frac{2}{3} = 0.\dot{6}$ (meaning $0.666\,6\ldots$ etc.)

$\frac{1}{6} = 0.1\dot{6}$ (meaning $0.166\,6\ldots$ etc.)

$\frac{5}{11} = 0.\dot{4}\dot{5}$ (meaning $0.454\,545\ldots$ etc.)

$\frac{3}{7} = 0.\dot{4}28\,57\dot{1}$ (meaning $0.428\,571\,428\,571\ldots$ etc.)

For all practical purposes we never need recurring decimals; what we need is an answer given to so many significant figures or decimal places. Thus:

$\frac{2}{3} = 0.67$ (correct to 2 decimal places)

$\frac{5}{11} = 0.455$ (correct to 3 significant figures)

Exercise 24 — *Questions 1—6 and 11—16 type A, remainder B*

Convert the following to decimals correcting the answers, where necessary, to 4 decimal places:

1) $\frac{1}{4}$ 5) $\frac{1}{2}$ 9) $1\frac{5}{6}$

2) $\frac{3}{4}$ 6) $\frac{2}{3}$ 10) $2\frac{7}{16}$

3) $\frac{3}{8}$ 7) $\frac{21}{32}$

4) $\frac{11}{16}$ 8) $\frac{29}{64}$

Write down the following recurring decimals correct to 3 decimal places:

11) $0.\dot{3}$ 15) $0.3\dot{5}$ 19) $0.\dot{3}2\dot{8}$

12) $0.\dot{7}$ 16) $0.\dot{2}\dot{3}$ 20) $0.\dot{5}67\dot{1}$

13) $0.1\dot{3}$ 17) $0.5\dot{2}$

14) $0.1\dot{8}$ 18) $0.\dot{3}\dot{8}$

CONVERSION OF DECIMALS TO FRACTIONS

We know that decimals are fractions with denominators 10, 100, 1000, etc. Using this fact we can always convert a decimal to a fraction.

EXAMPLE 14
Convert 0.32 to a fraction.

$$0.32 = \frac{32}{100} = \frac{8}{25}$$

When comparing decimals and fractions it is best to convert the fraction into a decimal.

EXAMPLE 15
Find the difference between $1\frac{3}{16}$ and 1.163 2.

$$1\frac{3}{16} = 1.187\,5$$

$$1\frac{3}{16} - 1.163\,2 = 1.187\,5 - 1.163\,2$$
$$= 0.024\,3$$

Exercise 25 — *Questions 1 and 2 type A, remainder B*

Convert the following to fractions in their lowest terms:

1) 0.2   3) 0.312 5   5) 0.007 5

2) 0.45   4) 2.55   6) 2.125

7) What is the difference between 0.281 35 and $\frac{9}{32}$?

8) What is the difference between $\frac{19}{64}$ and 0.295?

SELF-TEST 3

In questions 1 to 10 state the letter (or letters) corresponding to the correct answer (or answers).

1) The number 0.028 57 correct to 3 places of decimals is:

a 0.028   b 0.029   c 0.286   d 0.028 6

2) The sum of $5 + \frac{1}{100} + \frac{7}{1000}$ is:

a 5.17   b 5.017   c 5.0107   d 5.107

3) 13.006 3 × 1000 is equal to:

a 13.063   b 1300.63

c 130.063   d 13 006.3

4) 1.500 3 ÷ 100 is equal to:

a 0.015 003   b 0.150 03

c 0.153   d 1.53

5) 18.2 × 0.013 × 5.21 is equal to:

a 12.326 86   b 123.268 6

c 1.232 686   d 0.123 268 6

6) The number 158 861 correct to 2 significant figures is:

a 15   b 150 000   c 16   d 160 000

7) The number 0.081 778 correct to 3 significant figures is:

a 0.082   b 0.081

c 0.081 8   d 0.081 7

8) The number 0.075 538 correct to 2 decimal places is:

a 0.076   b 0.075   c 0.07   d 0.08

9) The number 0.16̇ correct to 4 significant figures is:

a 0.161 6   b 0.161 7

c 0.166 7   d 0.166 6

10) 0.017 ÷ 0.027 is equal to (correct to 2 significant figures):

a 0.63   b 6.3   c 0.063   d 63

11) 0.72 is equivalent to:

a $\dfrac{18}{25}$ b $\dfrac{7}{10}$ c $7\dfrac{1}{5}$ d $\dfrac{72}{1000}$

12) The value of 4.7 − 1.9 + 2.1 is:

a 5.9   b 0.7̇   c 8.7   d 1.7   e 4.9

13) 0.4 × 1.4 equals:

a 560   b 56   c 5.6

d 0.56   e 0.056

14) In the number 8.679 2 the value of the digit 7 is:

a 70   b $\dfrac{7}{10}$ c $\dfrac{7}{100}$ d 700   e $\dfrac{7}{1000}$

15) Given that 225 × 35 = 7875 then 22.5 × 0.35 is equal to:

a 787.5   b 7.875   c 0.787 5

d 0.078 75   e 0.007 875

Chapter 4 **The Electronic Calculator**

INTRODUCTION

A great deal of time and effort is often expended in arithmetic calculations even when logarithms are used. Much of this time and effort may be saved by using an electronic calculator. There are many types on the market but for most of us, a calculator which will add, subtract, multiply and divide is good enough.

The keyboard of a calculator has 10 number keys marked 0, 1, 2, 3, 4, 5, 6, 7, 8 and 9. There is also a decimal point. In the case of a simple calculator there are four function keys +, −, × and ÷ and also an = key. There is always a clear key, usually marked C, which is used to clear the display. Before each calculation it is safer to depress the C key.

EXAMPLE 1

To find the value of $9.632 + 18.564 - 12.768$.

Keyboard setting	Display
[9] [·] [6] [3] [2]	9.632
[+] [1] [8] [·] [5] [6] [4] [=]	28.196
[−] [1] [2] [·] [7] [6] [8] [=]	15.428

Hence $9.632 + 18.564 - 12.768 = 15.428$.

Note that when performing arithmetical operations the order of pressing the keys is always *Function* (+, −, × or ÷) *Number Equals*.

Some calculators do not require the use of the = key when the sequence is followed by one of the functions +, −, × or ÷. The sequence of operations is then,

Keyboard setting	Display
[9] [·] [6] [3] [2] [+]	9.632
[1] [8] [·] [5] [6] [4] [−]	28.196
[1] [2] [·] [7] [6] [8] [=]	15.428

Most calculators have an 8 figure display but the answer can be given to any number of significant figures up to 8. However, an answer to a calculation should not contain more significant figures than the least number of significant figures used amongst the given numbers.

EXAMPLE 2

Find the value of $7.231 \times 1.24 \times 1.3$ each number being correct to the number of significant figures shown.

Using a calculator,

$$7.231 \times 1.24 \times 1.3 = 11.656\,372$$

The least number of significant figures used amongst the given numbers is 2 (for the number 1.3). Hence the answer should only be stated correct to 2 significant figures.

$$\therefore \quad 7.231 \times 1.24 \times 1.3 = 12 \text{ correct to 2 significant figures}$$

EXAMPLE 3

Find the value of $\dfrac{0.728\,5 \times 0.062\,53}{0.028\,1}$ each number being correct to the number of significant figures shown.

Using a calculator,

$$\frac{0.728\,5 \times 0.062\,53}{0.028\,1} = 1.621\,106\,9$$

However, the least number of significant figures amongst the numbers used in the calculation is 3 (for the number 0.028 1). Hence the answer is 1.62, correct to 3 significant figures.

ROUGH CHECKS AND THE FEASIBILITY OF AN ANSWER

It was shown (on page 14) that an answer to a calculation can be checked by using approximate numbers. When using a calculator a rough check should always be made to make sure that the answer is feasible.

EXAMPLE 4

A calculator showed that

$$\frac{27.5 \times 31.32}{11.2 \times 2.94} = 26.16.$$

Is this answer feasible?

For purposes of a rough check we will take $27.5 \simeq 27$, $31.32 \simeq 30$, $11.2 \simeq 10$ and $2.94 \simeq 3$. (Note that the symbol $\simeq$ means 'is approximately equal to'.)

$$\text{Rough check} = \frac{27 \times 30}{10 \times 3} = 27.$$

Hence the answer is feasible because the rough check shows that the answer given is of the right size.

EXAMPLE 5

A calculator showed that

$$\frac{0.563 \times 0.621}{0.036\,2} = 0.966.$$

Is this answer feasible?

Performing a rough check: $\dfrac{0.5 \times 0.6}{0.03} = 10$.

Hence the given answer is not feasible and must be rejected. On performing the calculation again, the answer is found to be 9.66 which agrees with the rough check.

REARRANGING A PROBLEM TO EASE CALCULATION

It is sometimes necessary to change the order in which the arithmetic operations of a problem are performed so that the problem may be performed completely on the calculator.

EXAMPLE 6

Using a calculator, evaluate $\dfrac{84.3}{91.2} + \dfrac{76.51}{3.84}$.

If we proceed as shown the operations are:

Keyboard setting	Display
[8] [4] [·] [3]	
[÷] [9] [1] [·] [2] [=]	0.924 342 1

Write down display.

[7] [6] [·] [5] [1]	
[÷] [3] [·] [8] [4] [=]	19.924 479
[+] [0] [·] [9] [2] [4] [3] [4] [2] [1] [=]	
	20.848 821

Writing down a display in the middle of a calculation provides a fruitful source of error. It is better, if possible, to perform the calculation without writing down an intermediate result.

Our problem may be rewritten,

$$\frac{84.3}{91.2} + \frac{76.51}{3.84} = \left(\frac{84.3 \times 3.84}{91.2} + 76.51\right) \div 3.84$$

The operations are:

Keyboard setting	Display
[8] [4] [·] [3]	
[×] [3] [·] [8] [4] [=]	323.712
[÷] [9] [1] [·] [2] [=]	3.549 473 6
[+] [7] [6] [·] [5] [1] [=]	80.059 473 6
[÷] [3] [·] [8] [4] [=]	20.848 821

The answer is 20.8 correct to 3 significant figures.

OVERFLOW

If, as a result of a multiplication or addition the product or the sum contains more than 8 figures to the left of the decimal point then the machine will show the overflow indicator. To avoid this happening it pays to alternatively multiply and divide where this is possible.

EXAMPLE 7

Find the value of $\dfrac{289.53 \times 6548.79 \times 900.876}{87.63 \times 587.26}$.

If we perform the operations

[2] [8] [9] [·] [5] [3]
[×] [6] [5] [4] [8] [·] [7] [9] [=]
[×] [9] [0] [0] [·] [8] [7] [6] [=]

the overflow is brought into action.

However if we perform the operations like this:

[2] [8] [9] [·] [5] [3]
[÷] [8] [7] [·] [6] [3] [=]
[×] [6] [5] [4] [8] [·] [7] [9] [=]
[÷] [5] [8] [7] [·] [2] [6] [=]
[×] [9] [0] [0] [·] [8] [7] [6] [=]

we get the answer as $33\,192.229 = 33\,190$ correct to 4 significant figures.

Rough check $= \dfrac{300 \times 7000 \times 900}{90 \times 600}$

$= 35\,000$

Hence the answer shown in the display of the calculator is feasible.

CALCULATING POWERS OF NUMBERS

Powers of numbers are very easy to obtain using some calculators.

EXAMPLE 8

Find 6.358^9.

(The display is $16\,977\,927$)

gives the required operations. Note that the number of equal signs is always one less than the power of the number. (This method does not apply to all calculators. If it does not work for yours then perform the operations

$$6.358 \times 6.358 = \times 6.358 =$$

until nine multiplications have been performed.)

Since there are 4 significant figures in the number 6.358, the answer should only be stated to this degree of accuracy.

Hence $\qquad 6.358^9 = 16\,980\,000$

Rough check $= 6^9 = 10\,000\,000$ (approx.)

Hence the answer of $16\,980\,000$ is feasible.

Exercise 26 — *All type A*

In each of the following questions, each number is correct to the number of significant figures shown. Evaluate each of them and perform a rough check to test the feasibility of your answer.

1) 17.63×20.543

2) $11.26 + 3.178$

3) $15.92 - 7.63 + 2.184$

4) $25.14 \div 0.36$

5) $\dfrac{95.83 \times 6.14}{8.179\,5}$

6) $\dfrac{16.13 \times 270.52 \times 1.297\,5}{15.432 \times 139.68}$

7) $\dfrac{11.16}{7.34} + \dfrac{2.63}{8.71}$

8) $\dfrac{0.378\,6 \times 0.039\,7}{31.67 \times 1.265}$

9) $\dfrac{0.014\,6 \times 0.798\,3 \times 643.2}{33\,600 \times 11.82}$

10) $11.63 + \dfrac{17.63}{0.273}$

11) $\dfrac{12\,000 \times 280\,000}{19\,500 \times 26\,300}$

12) $\dfrac{0.004\,79 \times 0.000\,562}{0.056\,3 \times 0.002\,4}$

13) $(2.673)^5$

14) $(11.612)^7$

20

Chapter 5 Decimal Currency

THE BRITISH SYSTEM

The British system of decimal currency uses the pound as the basic unit. The only sub-unit used is the penny such that

$$100 \text{ pence } = 1 \text{ pound}$$

The abbreviation p is used for pence and the abbreviation £ is used for pounds. A decimal point is used to separate the pounds from the pence, for example

£3.58 meaning three pounds and fifty-eight pence

There are two ways of expressing amounts less than £1. For example 74 pence may be written as £0.74 or 74 p; 5 pence may be written as £0.05 or as 5 p.

ADDITION AND SUBTRACTION

The addition of sums of money is done in almost the same way as the addition of decimals. The exception occurs with the half-pence piece.

EXAMPLE 1
Add together £3.78, £5.23 and £8.19.

```
£3.78
£5.23
£8.19
──────
£17.20
```

Using a calculator:

| 3 | . | 7 | 8 | + | 5 | . | 2 | 3 |

| + | 8 | . | 1 | 9 | = |

The display is 17.2, which represents £17.20.

When amounts are given in pence it is best to write these as pounds. Thus 39 p is written £0.39, etc. The addition is then performed as previously described.

EXAMPLE 2
Subtract £2.36 from £3.08.

```
£3.08
£2.36
──────
£0.72
```

Using a calculator:

| 3 | . | 0 | 8 | − | 2 | . | 3 | 6 | = |

The display is 0.72 which represents £0.72 or 72 p.

Exercise 27 — *All type A*

1) Express the following amounts as pence:
£0.38, £0.63, £0.58.

2) Express the following as pence:
£2.16, £3.59, £17.68.

3) Express the following as pounds:
35 p, 78 p, 6 p, 3 p.

4) Express the following as pounds:
246 p, 983 p, 26 532 p.

5) Add the following sums of money together:
(a) £2.15, £3.28, £4.63
(b) £8.28, £109.17, £27.98, £70.15
(c) £0.17, £1.63, £1.71, £1.90
(d) 82 p, 71 p, 82 p
(e) 17 p, 27 p, 81 p, 74 p

6) Subtract the following:
(a) £7.60 from £9.84
(b) £3.49 from £11.42
(c) £18.73 from £87.35
(d) £0.54 from £1.32
(e) 54 p from £2.63½

MULTIPLICATION AND DIVISION

The multiplication and division of decimal currency are very similar to the methods used with decimal numbers.

EXAMPLE 3

Find the cost of 23 articles if each costs 27 p.

Now   27 p = £0.27

Cost of 23 articles @ £0.27

$$= 23 \times £0.27 = £6.21$$

Using a calculator:

| 0 | · | 2 | 7 | × | 2 | 3 | = |

The display is 6.21 which represents £6.21.

EXAMPLE 4

If 127 articles cost £15.24 find the cost of each article.

$$£15.24 \div 127 = £0.12 \text{ or } 12 \text{ p}$$

Using a calculator:

| 1 | 5 | · | 2 | 4 | ÷ | 1 | 2 | 7 | = |

The display is 0.12 which represents £0.12 or 12 p.

Exercise 28 — *All type B*

1) Find the cost of 12 articles costing 15 p each.

2) Find the cost of 85 articles costing 7 p each.

3) How much does 43 articles @ 39 p each cost?

4) What is the cost of 24 articles costing £7.03 each?

5) If 12 identical articles cost £1.56, how much does each cost?

6) If 241 identical articles cost £53.02, how much does each cost?

7) If 5000 articles cost £6600, find the cost of each article.

8) If 125 articles cost £271.25, what is the cost of each article?

SELF-TEST 5

In questions 1 to 6 state the letter (or letters) corresponding to the correct answer (or answers).

1) The cost of 4 articles at 72 p each is:
a £2.92   b £2.88   c £2.89
d £2.90   e £2.95

2) The cost of 2½ kg of tomatoes at 36 p per kg is:
a 90 p   b 86 p   c 100 p
d 72 p   e 84 p

3) The cost of 2 metres of material at £1.20 per metre and 3 metres at £1.50 per metre is:
a £6.90   b £13.50   c £6.60
d £7.10   e £2.70

4) The cost of 2000 articles at 25 p each is:
a £50 000   b £2500   c £5000
d £50   e £500

5) The change from £1 after buying 18 buttons at 3 p each is:
a 35 p   b 37 p   c 46 p
d 52 p   e 55 p

6) The cost of 200 articles at 3 p each is:
a £3.50   b £60.00   c £6.00
d £35.00   e £600.000

7) The cost of 5 plants at £1.25 each and 2 plants at £1.55 each is:

a £10.25   **b** £10.85   **c** £9.55
d £9.35   **e** £8.75

8) The change from £5 after buying 2 ties at £1.99 each is:

a £3.98   **b** £1.02   **c** £1.08
d £2.02   **e** £0.98

Chapter 6 Ratio and Proportion

A ratio is a comparison between two similar quantities. If the length of a certain ship is 120 metres and a model of it is 1 metre long then the length of the model is $\frac{1}{120}$th of the length of the ship. In making the model the dimensions of the ship are all reduced in the ratio of 1 to 120. The ratio 1 to 120 is usually written 1 : 120.

As indicated above a ratio may be expressed as a fraction and all ratios may be looked upon as fractions. Thus the ratio $2 : 5 = \frac{2}{5}$. The two terms of a ratio may be multiplied or divided without altering the value of the ratio. Hence $6 : 36 = 1 : 6 = \frac{1}{6}$. Again, $1 : 5 = 0.20$.

Before a ratio can be stated the units must be the same. We can state the ratio between 7 pence and £2 provided both sums of money are brought to the same units. Thus if we convert £2 to 200 p the ratio between the two amounts of money is 7 : 200.

EXAMPLE 1
Express the ratio 20 p to £4 in its simplest form.

$$£4 = 4 \times 100\,\text{p} = 400\,\text{p}$$

$$20 : 400 = \frac{20}{400} = \frac{1}{20}$$

EXAMPLE 2
Express the ratio $4 : \frac{1}{4}$ in its lowest terms.

$$4 : \frac{1}{4} = 4 \div \frac{1}{4} = 4 \times \frac{4}{1} = \frac{16}{1}$$

$$4 : \frac{1}{4} = 16 : 1$$

EXAMPLE 3
Two lengths are in the ratio 8 : 5. If the first length is 120 metres, what is the second length?

The second length $= \frac{5}{8}$ of the first length $= \frac{5}{8} \times 120 = 75$ metres.

EXAMPLE 4
Two amounts of money are in the ratio of 12 : 7. If the second amount is £21 what is the first amount?

First amount $= \frac{12}{7} \times £21 = £36$.

Exercise 29 — *Questions 1—7 type A, remainder B*

Express the following ratios as fractions in their lowest terms:

1) 8 : 3

2) 4 : 6

3) 12 : 4

4) 9 : 15

5) 8 : 12

6) Express the ratio of 30 p to £2 as a fraction in its lowest terms.

7) Express the ratio £5 : 80 p as a fraction in its lowest terms.

8) Two lengths are in the ratio 7 : 5. If the first length is 210 metres, what is the second length?

9) Two amounts of money are in the ratio 8 : 5. If the second amount is £120, what is the first amount?

10) Express $3 : \frac{1}{2}$ in its lowest terms.

PROPORTIONAL PARTS

The diagram (Fig. 6.1) shows a line AB whose length is 16 centimetres divided into two parts in the ratio 3 : 5. As can be seen in the diagram the line has been divided into a total of 8 parts.

The length AC contains 3 parts and the length BC contains 5 parts.

Each part is

$\frac{16}{8} = 2$ centimetres long; hence AC is $3 \times 2 = 6$ centimetres long and BC is $5 \times 2 = 10$ centimetres long.

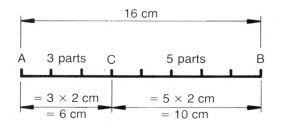

Fig. 6.1

We could tackle the problem in this way:

Total number of parts $= 3 + 5 = 8$ parts.

Length of each part $= \dfrac{16}{8} = 2$ centimetres.

Length of AC $= 3 \times 2 = 6$ centimetres.

Length of BC $= 5 \times 2 = 10$ centimetres.

EXAMPLE 5

Divide £1100 into two parts in the ratio 7 : 3.

Total number of parts $= 7 + 3 = 10$.

Amount of each part $= \dfrac{1100}{10} = £110$

Amount of first part $= 7 \times 110 = £770$

Amount of second part $= 3 \times 110 = £330$

EXAMPLE 6

An aircraft carries 2880 litres of fuel distributed in three tanks in the ratio 3 : 5 : 4. Find the quantity in each tank.

Total number of parts $= 3 + 5 + 4 = 12$.

Amount of each part $= \dfrac{2880}{12} = 240$ litres.

Amount of 3 parts $= 3 \times 240 = 720$ litres.

Amount of 4 parts $= 4 \times 240 = 960$ litres.

Amount of 5 parts $= 5 \times 240 = 1200$ litres.

The three tanks contain 720, 1200 and 960 litres.

Most calculators possess some method for retaining a constant value. On some, a constant key marked K is provided and we will assume that this is the case with our calculator. The operations are then

| 2 | 8 | 8 | 0 | ÷ | 1 | 2 | = | K |

| × | 3 | = | 5 | = | 4 | = |

Exercise 30 — *Questions 1—3 type A, remainder B*

1) Divide £800 in the ratio 5 : 3.

2) Divide £80 in the ratio 4 : 1.

3) Divide £120 in the ratio 5 : 4 : 3.

4) A sum of money is divided into two parts in the ratio 5 : 7. If the smaller amount is £200, find the larger amount.

5) An alloy consists of copper, zinc and tin in the ratios 2 : 3 : 5. Find the amount of each metal in 75 kilograms of the alloy.

6) A line is to be divided into three parts in the ratios 2 : 7 : 11. If the line is 840 millimetres long, calculate the length of each part.

7) Two villages have populations of 336 and 240 respectively. The two villages are to share a grant of £10 728 in proportion to their populations. Calculate how much each village receives.

8) Four friends contribute sums of money to a charitable organisation in the ratio of 2 : 4 : 5 : 7. If the largest amount contributed is £1.40, calculate the total amount contributed by the four people.

DIRECT PROPORTION

Two quantities are said to *vary directly*, or be in *direct proportion*, if they increase or decrease at the same rate. Thus the quantity of petrol used and the distance travelled by a motor car are in direct proportion. Again if we buy potatoes at 20 pence for 2 kilograms then we expect to pay 40 p for 4 kilograms and 10 p for 1 kilogram. That is if we double the amount bought then we double the cost; if we halve the amount bought we halve the cost.

In solving problems on direct proportion we can use either the unitary method or the fractional method. They are illustrated in Example 7.

EXAMPLE 7

If 25 kilograms of butter cost £17 how much does 8 kilograms cost?

(1) Using the unitary method:

25 kilograms cost £17 or 1700 pence

1 kilograms costs $\dfrac{1700}{25} = 68$ pence

25

8 kilograms cost 8×68

$$= 544 \text{ pence or } £5.44$$

(2) Using the fractional method:

Cost of 8 kilograms

$$= \frac{8}{25} \times 1700 = \frac{8 \times 1700}{25}$$

$$= 544 \text{ pence or } £5.44$$

Using a calculator:

| 8 | × | 1 | 7 | 0 | 0 | ÷ | 2 | 5 | = |

The display is 544 representing 544 p or £5.44.

EXAMPLE 8

A recipe for Boeuf Stroganoff quotes the following amounts to serve four people: 450 grams of rump steak, 3 tablespoons flour, 4 tablespoons butter, 50 grams of onion, 75 grams of mushrooms, 140 grams of sour cream. What amounts should be used for six people?

The quantities required and the number of people are in direct proportion. Hence the amounts must be increased in the ratio of $6:4$ or $3:2$.

Amount of rump steak

$$= \frac{3}{2} \times 450 = 675 \text{ grams}$$

Amount of flour $= \frac{3}{2} \times 3 = 4\frac{1}{2}$ tablespoons

Amount of butter $= \frac{3}{2} \times 4 = 6$ tablespoons

Amount of onion $= \frac{3}{2} \times 50 = 75$ grams

Amount of mushrooms

$$= \frac{3}{2} \times 75 = 112\frac{1}{2} \text{ grams}$$

Amount of sour cream

$$= \frac{3}{2} \times 140 = 210 \text{ grams}$$

Using a calculator:

6	÷	4	=	K	×	4	5	0	=
3	=	4	=	5	0	=	7	5	
=	1	4	0	=					

Exercise 31 — *All type A*

1) If 7 kilograms of apples cost £2.80, how much do 12 kilograms cost?

2) If 74 exercise books cost £5.92, how much do 53 cost?

3) If 40 articles cost £34.80, how much does 1 article cost? What is the cost of 55 articles?

4) Eggs cost 70 p per 10. How much will 25 eggs cost?

5) A car travels 205 kilometres on 20 litres of petrol. How much petrol is needed for a journey of 340 kilometres?

6) The ingredients for a cake which will serve 12 people are as follows: 55 grams of butter, 110 grams of castor sugar, 6 egg yolks, 120 grams plain flour and 3 tablespoons of milk. What quantities are needed to serve 4 people?

7) If 9 metres of carpet cost £21, how much will 96 metres cost?

8) A train travels 200 kilometres in 4 hours. How long will it take to complete a journey of 350 kilometres?

INVERSE PROPORTION

Suppose that 8 men working on a certain job take 10 days to complete it. If we double the number of men then we should halve the time taken. If we halve the number of men then the job will probably take twice as long. This is an example of inverse proportion.

EXAMPLE 9

20 men working in a factory produce 3000 articles in 12 working days. How long will it take 15 men to produce the 3000 articles?

The number of men is reduced in the ratio $\frac{15}{20} = \frac{3}{4}$.

Since this is an example of inverse proportion the number of days required must be increased in the ratio $\frac{4}{3}$.

Number of days required $= \frac{4}{3} \times 12$

$$= 16 \text{ days.}$$

Exercise 32 — *All type A*

1) A farmer employs 12 men to harvest his potato crop. They take 9 days to do the job. If he had employed 8 men how long would it have taken them?

2) 10 men produce 500 articles in 5 working days. How long would it take 15 men to produce the same amount?

3) Two gear wheels mesh together. One has 40 teeth and the other has 25 teeth. If the larger wheel makes 100 revolutions per minute how many revolutions per minute does the smaller wheel make?

4) A bag contains sweets. When divided amongst 8 children each child receives 9 sweets. If the sweets were divided amongst 12 children how many sweets would each receive?

5) 4 men can do a piece of work in 30 hours. How many men would be required to do the work in 6 hours?

FOREIGN EXCHANGE

Every country has its own monetary system. If there is to be trade and travel between any two countries there must be a rate at which the money of one country can be converted into money of the other country. This rate is called the *rate of exchange*.

FOREIGN MONETARY SYSTEMS AND EXCHANGE RATE, DECEMBER 1984

Country	Monetary Unit		Rate of Exchange	
Belgium	100 centimes	= 1 franc	BF 73.60	= £1
France	100 centimes	= 1 franc	F 11.22	= £1
Germany	100 pfennig	= 1 mark	DM 3.66	= £1
Greece	100 lepta	= 1 drachma	DR 164	= £1
Italy	100 centesimi	= 1 lira	Lira 2265	= £1
Spain	100 centimos	= 1 peseta	Ptas 203	= £1
Switzerland	100 centimes	= 1 franc	SWF 3.02	= £1
United States	100 cents	= 1 dollar	$1.20	= £1

The methods used for direct proportion are applicable to problems in foreign exchange.

EXAMPLE 10

If £1 = 203 Spanish pesetas, find to the nearest penny the value in British money of 1000 pesetas.

(1) Using the unitary method:

$$203 \text{ pesetas} = £1$$

$$1 \text{ peseta} = £\frac{1}{203}$$

$$1000 \text{ pesetas} = £\frac{1}{203} \times 1000$$

$$= £\frac{1000}{203} = £4.93$$

(2) Using the fractional method:

$$1000 \text{ pesetas} = £\frac{1000}{203} = £4.93$$

EXAMPLE 11

A tourist changes travellers cheques for £40 into French francs at 11.22 francs to the pound. How many francs does he get?

$$£40 = 40 \times 11.22 \text{ francs} = 449 \text{ francs}$$

Exercise 33 — *Questions 1–6 type A, remainder B*

Where necessary give the answers to 2 places of decimals.

Using the exchange rates given above find:

1) The number of German marks equivalent to £15.

2) The number of Spanish pesetas equivalent to £25.

3) The number of United States dollars equivalent to £32.

4) The number of pounds equivalent to 223 United States dollars.

5) The number of pounds equivalent to 8960 Italian lire.

6) The number of Belgian francs equivalent to £98.50.

7) A transistor set costs £26.30 in the United Kingdom. An American visitor wants to purchase a set but wishes to pay in United States dollars. What is the equivalent price in dollars?

8) A tourist changes travellers cheques for £50 into Greek currency at 164 drachma to the £1. He spends 6320 drachma and changes the remainder back into sterling at the same rate. How much did the tourist receive?

9) Calculate the rate of exchange if a bank exchanges 976 Swedish krona for £90.

10) A person on holiday in France changed £400 into francs at a rate of 10.50 francs to the £1. His hotel expenses were 250 francs per day for eight days and his other expenses were 1896 francs. On returning home he changed what francs he had left into sterling at a rate of 10.30 francs to the £1. Calculate:

(a) The number of francs received for the £400.
(b) The total expenses in francs.
(c) The number of francs left after paying these expenses.
(d) The amount in £'s obtained for the francs he had left. (Give your answer to the nearest pence.)

SELF-TEST 6

In questions 1 to 8 state the letter (or letters) corresponding to the correct answer (or answers).

1) In Holland there are 100 cents in a florin. There are 5 florins to a pound. How many pence is a 25 cent coin worth?

a 4   b $2\frac{1}{2}$ c 5
d 2   e 1

2) The ratio of A's share to B's share in the profits of a business is 5 : 4. If the total profit is £450 then A's share is:

a £90   b £200   c £225
d £250

3) If £120 is divided in the ratio 2 to 3 then the smaller share is:

a £48   b £80   c £72
d £60   e £40

4) The ratio of the shares of two partners A and B in the profits of a business is 5 : 3.

(a) How much will B receive when the profit is £1200?
   a £300   b £360   c £450   d £720

(b) How much will A receive when B receives £480?
   a £800   b £300   c £288   d £216

5) A car does 12 km per litre of petrol. How many complete litres of petrol will be needed to be sure of completing a journey of 100 km?

a 9   b 1200   c 8   d 12

6) If two men can paint a fence in 6 hours, how long will it take three men to paint it, assuming they all work at the same rate?

a 12 hours   b 3 hours   c 4 hours
d 9 hours

7) Change £150 into dollars when the exchange rate is £1 = $1.20.

a 180   b 120   c 450   d 125

8) Divide £1200 in the ratio 5 : 3.

a £240 and £960   b £800 and £400
c £1050 and £150   d £750 and £450

28

Chapter 7 Percentages

When comparing fractions it is often convenient to express them with a denominator of a hundred. Thus:

$$\frac{1}{2} = \frac{50}{100}$$

$$\frac{2}{5} = \frac{40}{100}$$

Fractions with a denominator of 100 are called *percentages*. Thus:

$$\frac{1}{4} = \frac{25}{100} = 25 \text{ per cent}$$

$$\frac{3}{10} = \frac{30}{100} = 30 \text{ per cent}$$

The sign % is usually used instead of the words per cent.

To convert a fraction into a percentage we multiply it by 100.

EXAMPLE 1

$$\frac{3}{4} = \frac{3}{4} \times 100\% = 75\%$$

$$\frac{17}{20} = \frac{17}{20} \times 100\% = 85\%$$

Using a calculator:

$$\boxed{1}\,\boxed{7}\,\boxed{\div}\,\boxed{2}\,\boxed{0}\,\boxed{\times}\,\boxed{1}\,\boxed{0}\,\boxed{0}\,\boxed{=}$$

The display is 85 which represents 85%.

Exercise 34 — *All type A*

Convert the following fractions to percentages:

1) $\frac{7}{10}$ 4) $\frac{4}{5}$ 7) $\frac{7}{10}$

2) $\frac{11}{20}$ 5) $\frac{31}{50}$ 8) $\frac{19}{20}$

3) $\frac{9}{25}$ 6) $\frac{1}{4}$

Decimal numbers may be converted into percentages by using the same rule. Thus:

$$0.3 = \frac{3}{10} = \frac{3}{10} \times 100 = 30\%$$

The same result is produced if we omit the intermediate step of turning 0.3 into a vulgar fraction and just multiply 0.3 by 100. Thus:

$$0.3 = 0.3 \times 100\% = 30\%$$

Using a calculator:

$$\boxed{0}\,\boxed{\cdot}\,\boxed{3}\,\boxed{\times}\,\boxed{1}\,\boxed{0}\,\boxed{0}\,\boxed{=}$$

The display is 30 which represents 30%.

EXAMPLE 2

$$0.56 = 0.56 \times 100\% = 56\%$$

$$0.683 = 0.683 \times 100\% = 68.3\%$$

Exercise 35 — *All type A*

Convert the following decimal numbers into percentages:

1) 0.7   4) 0.813   7) 0.819

2) 0.73   5) 0.927

3) 0.68   6) 0.333

To convert a percentage into a fraction we divide by 100.

EXAMPLE 3

$$45\% = \frac{45}{100} = 0.45$$

$$3.9\% = \frac{3.9}{100} = 0.039$$

Note that all we have done is to move the decimal point 2 places to the left.

Exercise 36 — *All type A*

Convert the following percentages into decimal fractions:

1) 32%   5) 31.5%   9) 3.95%

2) 78%   6) 48.2%   10) 20.1%

3) 6%   7) 2.5%

4) 24%   8) 1.25%

PERCENTAGE OF A QUANTITY

It is easy to find the percentage of a quantity if we first express the percentage as a fraction.

EXAMPLE 4

(1) What is 10% of 40?

Expressing 10% as a fraction it is $\frac{10}{100}$ and the problem then becomes: what is $\frac{10}{100}$ of 40?

$$10\% \text{ of } 40 = \frac{10}{100} \times 40 = 4$$

(2) What is 25% of £50?

$$25\% \text{ of } £50 = \frac{25}{100} \times £50 = £12.50$$

Using a calculator:

$$\boxed{2}\ \boxed{5}\ \boxed{\div}\ \boxed{1}\ \boxed{0}\ \boxed{0}\ \boxed{\times}\ \boxed{5}\ \boxed{0}\ \boxed{=}$$

The display is 12.5 which represents £12.50.

(3) 22% of a certain length is 55 cm. What is the complete length?

We have that 22% of the length = 55 cm.

$$1\% \text{ of the length} = \frac{55}{22} \text{ cm} = 2.5 \text{ cm}$$

Now the complete length will be 100%, hence:

Complete length = 100 x 2.5 cm = 250 cm.

Alternatively

$$22\% \text{ of the length} = 55 \text{ cm}$$

$$\text{Complete length} = \frac{100}{22} \times 55$$

$$= \frac{100 \times 55}{22} = 250 \text{ cm}$$

Using a calculator:

$$\boxed{1}\ \boxed{0}\ \boxed{0}\ \boxed{\div}\ \boxed{2}\ \boxed{2}\ \boxed{\times}\ \boxed{5}\ \boxed{5}\ \boxed{=}$$

The display is 249.9 which represents 250 cm.

(4) What percentage is 37 of 264? Give the answer correct to 5 significant figures.

$$\text{Percentage} = \frac{37}{264} \times 100$$

$$= \frac{37 \times 100}{264}$$

$$= 14.015\%$$

1) What is:
(a) 20% of 50
(b) 30% of 80
(c) 5% of 120
(d) 12% of 20
(e) 20.3% of 105
(f) 3.7% of 68?

2) What percentage is:
(a) 25 of 200
(b) 30 of 150
(c) 24 of 150
(d) 29 of 178
(e) 15 of 33?

Where necessary give the answer correct to 3 significant figures.

3) A girl scores 36 marks out of 60 in an examination. What is her percentage mark? If the percentage needed to pass the examination is 45% how many marks are needed to pass?

4) If 20% of a length is 23 cm what is the complete length?

5) Given that 13.3 cm is 15% of a certain length, what is the complete length?

6) What is:
(a) 9% of £80   (b) 12% of £110
(c) 75% of £250?

7) Express the following statements in the form of a percentage:
(a) 3 eggs are bad in a box containing 144 eggs.
(b) In a school of 650 pupils, 20 are absent.
(c) In a school of 980 pupils, 860 eat school lunches.

8) In a certain county the average number of children eating lunches at school was 29 336 which represents 74% of the total number of children attending school. Calculate the total number of children attending school in that county.

9) 23% of a consignment of bananas is bad. There are 34.5 kg of bad bananas. How many kilograms were there in the consignment?

10) A retailer accepts a consignment of 5000 ball point pens. He finds that 12% are faulty. How many faulty pens were there?

PERCENTAGE PROFIT AND LOSS

When a dealer buys or sells goods, the cost price is the price at which he buys the goods and the selling price is the price at which he sells the goods. If the selling price is greater than the cost price then a profit is made. The amount of profit is the difference between the selling price and the cost price. That is:

$$\text{Profit} = \text{selling price} - \text{cost price}$$

The profit per cent is always calculated on the cost price. That is:

$$\text{Profit \%} = \frac{\text{selling price} - \text{cost price}}{\text{cost price}} \times 100$$

If a loss is made the cost price is greater than the selling price. The loss is the difference between the cost price and the selling price. That is:

$$\text{Loss} = \text{cost price} - \text{selling price}$$

$$\text{Loss \%} = \frac{\text{cost price} - \text{selling price}}{\text{cost price}} \times 100$$

EXAMPLE 5

(1) A shopkeeper buys an article for £5.00 and sells it for £6.00. What is his profit per cent?

We are given:

$$\text{cost price} = £5 \quad \text{and} \quad \text{selling price} = £6$$

$$\text{Profit \%} = \frac{6 - 5}{5} \times 100$$

$$= \frac{1}{5} \times 100 = 20\%$$

Using a calculator:

$$\boxed{6} \boxed{-} \boxed{5} \boxed{\div} \boxed{5} \boxed{\times} \boxed{1} \boxed{0} \boxed{0} \boxed{=}$$

The display is 20 representing 20%.

(2) A dealer buys 20 articles at a total cost of £5. He sells them for 30 p each. What is his profit per cent?

Since £5 = 500 p,

$$\text{cost price per article} = \frac{500}{20} = 25\,\text{p}$$

$$\text{Profit \%} = \frac{30 - 25}{25} \times 100$$

$$= \frac{5}{25} \times 100 = 20\%$$

Using a calculator:

$$\boxed{2} \boxed{0} \boxed{\times} \boxed{0} \boxed{\cdot} \boxed{3} \boxed{-} \boxed{5} \boxed{\div} \boxed{5} \boxed{\times}$$
$$\boxed{1} \boxed{0} \boxed{0} \boxed{=}$$

The display is 20 representing 20%.

(3) A man buys a car for £1600 and sells it for £1200. Calculate his percentage loss.

$$\text{Loss} = \text{cost price} - \text{selling price}$$

$$= £1600 - £1200 = £400$$

$$\text{Loss \%} = \frac{400}{1600} \times 100 = 25\%$$

Exercise 38 — *Questions 1—4 type A, remainder type B*

1) A shopkeeper buys an article for 80 p and sells it for £1. Calculate the percentage profit.

2) Calculate the profit per cent when:

(a) Cost price is £1.50 and selling price is £1.80.

(b) Cost price is 30 p and selling price is 35 p.

3) Calculate the loss per cent when:

(a) Cost price is 75 p and selling price is 65 p.

(b) Cost price is £6.53 and selling price is £5.88.

4) The price of coal has increased from £30 to £33 per 1000 kilograms. What is the percentage increase in the price of coal?

5) A greengrocer buys a box of 200 oranges for £15. He sells them for 9 p each. Calculate his percentage profit.

6) A dealer buys 100 similar articles for £60 and sells them for 80 p each. Find his profit per cent.

7) A retailer buys 30 articles at 8 p each. Three are damaged and unsaleable but he sells the others at 10 p each. What is the profit per cent?

8) A car is bought for £1700 and sold for £1400. What is the loss per cent?

DISCOUNT

When a customer buys an article from a retailer for cash he will often ask the retailer for a *discount*. This discount, which is usually a percentage of the selling price, is the amount which the retailer will take off his selling price thus reducing his profit.

EXAMPLE 6

A radio is offered for sale at £60. A customer is offered a 10% discount for cash. How much does the customer actually pay?

$$\text{Discount} = 10\% \text{ of } £60$$

$$= \frac{10}{100} \times £60 = £6$$

Amount paid by customer

$$= £60 - £6 = £54$$

(*Alternatively:* since only 90% of the selling price is paid,

Amount customer pays

$$= 90\% \text{ of } £60 = \frac{90}{100} \times £60 = £54\Big)$$

Sometimes discounts are quoted as so much in the pound, for instance 5 p in the £1. If we remember that 5 p in the £1 is the same as 5% then the calculation of discounts is the same as that shown in Example 6.

EXAMPLE 7

How much will a girl pay for goods priced at £12.50 if a discount of 8 p in the £1 is offered for cash?

8 p in £1 is the same as 8%.

$$\text{Discount} = \frac{8}{100} \times £12.50 = £1.00$$

Amount paid by the girl
$$= £12.50 - £1.00 = £11.50$$

Since only 92% of the selling price is paid, using a calculator:

$$\boxed{9}\,\boxed{2}\,\boxed{\times}\,\boxed{1}\,\boxed{2}\,\boxed{\cdot}\,\boxed{5}\,\boxed{\div}\,\boxed{1}\,\boxed{0}\,\boxed{0}\,\boxed{=}$$

The display is 11.5 representing £11.50.

Exercise 39 — *All type A*

1) A chair marked for sale at £14 is sold for cash at a discount of 10%. What price did the customer pay?

2) A tailor charges £90 for a suit of clothes but allows a discount of 5% for cash. What is the cash price?

3) A grocer offers a discount of $2\frac{1}{2}\%$ to his customers provided their bills are paid within one week. If a bill of £21.75 is paid within one week, how much discount will the grocer allow?

4) A shop offers a discount of 5 p in the £1. How much discount will be allowed on a washing machine costing £170?

5) A furniture store offers a discount of 7 p in the £1 for cash sales. A customer buys a three piece suite priced at £570. How much will she actually pay?

PERCENTAGE CHANGE

An increase of 5% in a number means that the number has been increased by $\frac{5}{100}$ of itself.

Thus if the number is represented by 100, the increase is 5 and the new number is 105. The ratio of the new number to the old number is 105 : 100.

EXAMPLE 8

(1) An increase of 10% in salaries makes the wage bill for a factory £5500.
(a) What was the wage bill before the increase?
(b) What is the amount of the increase?

(a) If 100% represents the wage bill before the increase, then 110% represents the wage bill after the increase.
∴ Wage bill before the increase

$$= \frac{100}{110} \times £5500 = £5000$$

(b) The amount of the increase

$$= 10\% \text{ of } 5000$$

$$= \frac{10}{100} \times 5000 = £500$$

(2) By selling an article for £4.23 a dealer makes a profit of $12\frac{1}{2}\%$ on his cost price. What is his profit.

If 100% represents the cost price then $112\frac{1}{2}\%$ represents the selling price.

$$\therefore \text{Cost price} = \frac{100}{112\frac{1}{2}} \times £4.23 = \frac{200}{225} \times £4.23$$

$$= £3.76$$

$$\text{Profit} = \text{selling price} - \text{cost price}$$

$$= £4.23 - £3.76 = £0.47$$

A decrease of 5% in a number means that if the original number is represented by 100 then the decrease is 5 and the new number is 95. The ratio of the new number to the old number is 95 : 100.

EXAMPLE 9

An article was sold for £30 which was a loss on the cost price of 10%. What was the cost price?

If 100% represents the cost price then 90% represents the selling price.

$$\therefore \quad \text{Cost price} = \frac{100}{90} \times 30 = £33.33$$

Exercise 40 — *All type B*

1) Calculate the selling price when:
(a) cost price is £5.00 and profit per cent is 20%,
(b) cost price is £3.75 and profit per cent is 16%.

2) Calculate the cost price when:
(a) selling price is £20.00 and profit is 25%,
(b) selling price is 63 p and profit is $12\frac{1}{2}$%.

3) By selling an article for £10.80 a shop-keeper makes a profit of 8%. What should be the selling price for a profit of 20%?

4) (a) An article can be bought from a shop-keeper for a single cash payment of £74 or by 18 monthly instalments of £4.30. Calculate the extra cost of paying by instalments.
(b) By selling for £74 the shopkeeper made a profit of 25%. Find how much he paid for the article.

5) A shopkeeper marks an article to allow himself 25% profit on the cost price. If he sells it for £80 how much was the cost price?

6) If 8% of a sum of money is £2.40 find $9\frac{1}{2}$% of the sum.

7) The duty on an article is 20% of its value. If the duty is 60 p, find the value of the article.

8) When a sum of money is decreased by 10% it becomes £18. What was the original sum?

9) A man sells a car for £1275 thus losing 15% of what he paid for the car. How much did the car cost him?

10) Equipment belonging to a firm is valued at £15 000. Each year 10% of the value of the equipment is written off for depreciation. Find the value of the equipment at the end of two years.

SELF-TEST 7

In questions 1—15 state the letter (or letters) corresponding to the correct answer (or answers).

1) 35% is the same as:
a $\frac{35}{100}$ b $\frac{7}{20}$ c $\frac{35}{10}$ d 0.35

2) $\frac{11}{25}$ is the same as:
a 4.4%   b 44%   c 440%   d 25%

3) 30% of a certain length is 600 mm. The complete length is:
a 20 mm   b 200 mm   c 2000 mm
d 2 m

4) $\frac{9}{10}$ as a percentage is:
a 0.9%   b 9%   c 99%   d 90%

5) The word *discount* means:
a Money put down on an article bought on H.P.
b Money taken out of your wage.
c Money taken off the price of an article.
d Money owed to someone.

6) $\frac{3}{40}$ as a percentage is:
a 3%   b $7\frac{1}{2}$%   c 40%   d 75%   e 97%

7) A boy scored 70% in a test. If the maximum mark was 40, then the boy's mark was:
a 4   b 10   c 28   d 30   e 35

8) During a sale, a shop reduced the price of everything by 10%. What was the sale price of an article originally priced at £4.30?
a £0.43   b £3.40   c £3.87
d £3.97   e £4.73

9) For his holidays a man put aside 10% of his £150 weekly wage for 40 weeks in the year. How much did he save for his holiday?
a £600   b £300   c £150
d £1500   e £450

10) A special offer of 4 p off the normal selling price of 50 p for a packet of biscuits is made. What percentage reduction does this represent?
a 2%   b 25%   c 4%   d 8%   e 98%

11) In a sale, a discount of 10 p in the £1 is allowed off all marked prices. The price of a

33

pair of girl's shoes is marked at £6.50. For how much can the shoes be bought in the sale?

a £7.15   b £0.65   c £5.85   d £6

12) A girl bought a record for 75 p and sold it for 60 p.

(a) Her loss, as a percentage of the cost price, is:

    a 15%   b 20%   c 60%   d 75%

(b) For what price should she have sold the record to make a profit of 20% on her cost price of 75 p?

    a 95 p   b 90 p   c 80 p   d 72 p

(c) The shopkeeper from whom she bought the record made a profit of 50% on his cost price. How much did the record cost him?

a 25 p   b $37\frac{1}{2}$ p   c 50 p   d £1.25

13) When a dealer sells an article for £50 he makes a profit of 25%. The price he paid for the article is:

a £37.50   b £40.00   c £20   d £40.50

14) A dealer buys 40 articles at a total cost of £10.00. He sells them at 30 p each. His percentage profit is:

a $16\frac{2}{3}$%   b 20%   c 30%   d 25%

15) An article was sold for £60 which was a loss on the cost price of 10%. The cost price was therefore:

a £54.00   b £66.00   c £66.67

d £70.50

Chapter 8 Averages

AVERAGES

To find the average of a set of quantities, add the quantities together and divide by the number of quantities in the set. Thus,

$$\text{average} = \frac{\text{sum of the quantities}}{\text{number of quantities}}$$

EXAMPLE 1

(1) A boy makes the following scores at cricket: 8, 20, 3, 0, 5, 9, 15 and 12. What is his average score?

Average score

$$= \frac{8 + 20 + 3 + 0 + 5 + 9 + 15 + 12}{8}$$

$$= \frac{72}{8} = 9$$

(2) The oranges in a box have a mass of 4680 gm. If the average mass of an orange is 97.5 gm find the number of oranges in the box.

Total mass = average mass of an orange
× number of oranges in the box

∴ Number of oranges in the box $= \dfrac{4680}{97.5} = 48$

(3) Find the average age of a team of boys given that four of them are each 15 years 4 months old and the other three boys are each 14 years 9 months old.

Total age of 4 boys
   at 15 years 4 months = 61 years 4 months

Total age of 3 boys
   at 14 years 9 months =   44 years 3 months

Total age of 7 boys   = 105 years 7 months

$$\text{Average age} = \frac{105 \text{ years } 7 \text{ months}}{7}$$

$$= 15 \text{ years } 1 \text{ month}$$

(4) The average age of the teachers in a school is 39 years and their total age is 1170 years, whereas the pupils whose average age is 14 years have a total age of 6580 years. Find the average age of all the people in the school.

The first step is to find the number of teachers:

Number of teachers

$$= \frac{\text{total age of the teachers}}{\text{average age of the teachers}}$$

$$= \frac{1170}{39} = 30$$

We now find the number of pupils:

$$\text{Number of pupils} = \frac{6580}{14} = 470$$

We can now find the average age of all the people in the school:

Total age of all the people in the school
   = 1170 + 6580 = 7750 years

Total number of people in the school
   = 30 + 470 = 500

Average age of all the people in the school

$$= \frac{7750}{500} = 15.5 \text{ years}$$

Exercise 41 — *Questions 1—4 type A, 5—10 type B, remainder C*

1) Find the average of the following readings: 22.3 mm, 22.5 mm, 22.6 mm, 21.8 mm and 22.0 mm.

2) Find the average mass of 22 boxes if 9 have a mass of 12 kg, 8 have a mass of $12\frac{1}{2}$ kg and 5 have a mass of $11\frac{3}{4}$ kg.

3) 4 kg of apples costing 20 p per kg are mixed with 8 kg costing 14 p per kg. What is the average price per kg?

4) 30 litres of petrol costing 8 p per litre is mixed with 40 litres costing 9 p per litre. Find the average price of the mixture.

5) The average of nine numbers is 72 and the average of four of them is 40. What is the average of the other five?

6) The apples in a box have a mass of 240 kg. If the average mass of an apple is 120 g find the number of apples in the box.

7) Find the average age of a team of boys if 5 of them are each 15 years old and 6 of them are 14 years 1 month old.

8) A grocer sells 40 tins of soup at 8 p per tin, 50 at 9 p per tin and 60 tins at 10 p per tin. Find the average price per tin.

9) The average mark of 24 candidates taking an examination is 42. Find what the average mark would have been if one candidate, who scored 88, had been absent.

10) The average of three numbers is 58. The average of two of them is 49. Find the third number.

11) In a school, three classes took the same examination. Class A contained 30 pupils and the average mark for the class was 66. Class B contained 22 pupils and their average mark was 54. Class C contained 20 pupils. The average obtained by all the pupils together was 61.5. Calculate the average mark of Class C.

12) A farmer sent 50 sheep fleeces yielding a total of 168 kg of wool to a merchant. For one-third of the wool the farmer received 25 p per kg, for a quarter of the wool he received 20 p per kg and for the rest he received 15 p per kg. Calculate the total amount received by the farmer and the average price received for *each* fleece.

AVERAGE SPEED

The average speed is defined as *total distance travelled divided by the total time taken*. The unit of speed depends on the unit of distance and the unit of time. For instance, if the distance travelled is in kilometres (km) and the time taken is in hours (h) then the speed will be stated in kilometres per hour (km/h). If the distance is given in metres (m) and the time in seconds (s) then the speed is in metres per second (m/s).

EXAMPLE 2

(1) A car travels a total distance of 200 km in 4 hours. What is its average speed?

$$\text{Average speed} = \frac{\text{distance travelled}}{\text{time taken}} = \frac{200}{4}$$

$$= 50 \text{ km/h}$$

(2) A car travels 30 km at 30 km/h and 30 km at 40 km/h. Find its average speed.

Time taken to travel 30 km at 30 km/h

$$= \frac{30}{30} = 1 \text{ hour}$$

Time taken to travel 30 km at 40 km/h

$$= \frac{30}{40} = 0.75 \text{ hour}$$

Total distance travelled = 30 + 30 = 60 km.
Total time taken = 1 + 0.75 = 1.75 hour.

$$\therefore \quad \text{Average speed} = \frac{60}{1.75} = 34.3 \text{ km/h}$$

(3) A train travels for 4 hours at an average speed of 64 km/h. For the first 2 hours its average speed is 50 km/h. What is its average speed for the last 2 hours?

Total distance travelled in 4 hours
= average speed × time taken = 64 × 4
= 256 km

Distance travelled in first two hours
= 50 × 2 = 100 km

∴ Distance travelled in last two hours
= 256 − 100 = 156 km

Average speed for the last two hours

$$= \frac{\text{distance travelled}}{\text{time taken}} = \frac{156}{2} = 78 \text{ km/h}$$

Exercise 42 — *Questions 1–3 type A, remainder B*

1) A train travels 300 km in 4 hours. What is its average speed?

2) A car travels 200 km at an average speed of 50 km/h. How long does it take?

3) If a car travels for 5 hours at an average speed of 70 km/h how far has it gone?

4) For the first $1\frac{1}{2}$ hours of a 91 km journey the average speed was 30 km/h. If the average speed for the remainder of the journey was 23 km/h, calculate the average speed for the entire journey.

5) A motorist travelling at a steady speed of 90 km/h covers a section of motorway in 25 minutes. After a speed limit is imposed he finds that, when travelling at the maximum speed allowed he takes 5 minutes longer than before to cover the same section. Calculate the speed limit.

6) In winter a train travels between two towns 264 km apart at an average speed of 72 km/h. In summer the journey takes 22 minutes less than in the winter. Find the average speed in summer.

7) A train travels between two towns 135 km apart in $4\frac{1}{2}$ hours. If on the return journey the average speed is reduced by 3 km/h, calculate the time taken for the return journey.

8) A car travels 272 km at an average speed of 32 km/h. On the return journey the average speed is increased to 48 km/h. Calculate the average speed over the whole journey.

SELF-TEST 8

In the following questions state the letter (or letters) corresponding to the correct answer (or answers).

1) The average of 11.2, 11.3, 11.5, 11.1 and 11.2 is:

a 11.3   b 11.4   c 11.22   d 11.26

2) The average weight of two adults in a family is 81 kg and the average weight of the three children in the family is 23 kg. The average weight of the whole family is:

a 45.3 kg   b 46.2 kg   c 52.0 kg

d 20.8 kg

3) 50 litres of oil costing 8 p per litre is mixed with 70 litres of oil costing 9 p per litre. The average price of the mixture is about:

a 8.6 p   b 8.5 p   c 9.6 p   d 10.8 p

4) A grocer sells 20 tins of soup at 5 p per tin, 30 at 8 p per tin and 40 at 7 p per tin. The average price of the soup per tin is:

a $6\frac{2}{3}$ p   b $6\frac{8}{9}$ p   c 6 p   d $7\frac{1}{2}$ p

5) The average of three numbers is 116. The average of two of them is 98. The third number is:

a 18   b 107   c 110   d 152

6) An aeroplane flies non-stop for $2\frac{1}{4}$ hours and travels 1620 km. Its average speed in km/h is:

a 720   b 800   c 3645   d 364.5

7) A car travels 50 km at 50 km/h and 70 km at 70 km/h. Its average speed is:

a 60 km/h   b 65 km/h   c 58 km/h

d 62 km/h

8) A car travels for 3 hours at a speed of 45 km/h and for 4 hours at a speed of 50 km/h. It has therefore travelled a distance of:

a 27.5 km   b 95 km   c 335 km

d 353 km

9) A car travels 540 km at an average speed of 30 km/h. On the return journey the average speed is doubled to 60 km/h. The average speed over the entire journey is:

a 45 km/h   b 42 km/h   c 40 km/h

d 35 km/h.

10) A car travels between two towns 270 km apart in 9 hours. On the return journey the speed is increased by 10 km/h. The time taken for the return journey is:

a $6\frac{1}{2}$ hours   b $6\frac{3}{4}$ hours   c 2.7 hours

d $4\frac{1}{2}$ hours.

Chapter 9 Salaries, Household Bills, Rates and Taxes

Everyone who works for an employer receives a *wage* or *salary* in return for their labours. However the payment can be made in several different ways.

PAYMENT BY THE HOUR

Many people who work in factories, in the transport industry and in the building and construction industry are paid a certain amount of money for each hour that they work. Most employees work a basic week of so many hours and it is this basic week which fixes the hourly (or *basic*) rate of wages. The basic rate and the basic week are usually fixed by negotiation between the employer and the trades union which represents the workers.

EXAMPLE 1

A man works a basic week of 38 hours and his basic rate is £2.50 per hour. Calculate his total wage for the week.

$$38 \text{ hours at } £2.50 \text{ per hour}$$
$$= 38 \times £2.50 = £95.00$$

Hence the total wage for the week is £95.00.

EXAMPLE 2

A factory worker is paid £104 for a basic week of 40 hours. What is his hourly rate?

$$\text{Hourly rate} = \frac{£104}{40} = £2.60$$

Exercise 43 — *All type A*

Calculate the total pay in each of the following cases:

1) Basic rate   = £1.60 per hour.
   Basic week = 42 hours.

2) Basic rate   = £2.30 per hour.
   Basic week = 39 hours.

3) Basic rate   = £1.56 per hour.
   Basic week = 37 hours.

4) Basic rate   = £2.76 per hour.
   Basic week = 40 hours.

Calculate the hourly rate in each of the following cases:

5) Basic week   = 42 hours.
   Weekly wage = £94.08.

6) Basic week   = 39 hours.
   Weekly wage = £58.50.

7) Basic week   = 40 hours.
   Weekly wage = £64.00.

8) Basic week   = 44 hours.
   Weekly wage = £80.96.

OVERTIME

Hourly paid workers are usually paid extra money for working more hours than the basic week demands. These extra hours of work are called *overtime*.

Overtime is usually paid at one of the following rates:

(1) Time and a quarter — $1\frac{1}{4}$ times the basic rate.
(2) Time and a half — $1\frac{1}{2}$ times the basic rate.
(3) Double time — twice the basic rate.

EXAMPLE 3

A girl is paid a basic rate of £1.44 per hour. Find the rates of pay for overtime in the following cases: (1) time and a quarter; (2) time and a half; (3) double time.

(1) Overtime rate at time and a quarter
   $= 1\frac{1}{4} \times £1.44$
   $= 1.25 \times £1.44 = £1.80$

(2) Overtime rate at time and a half
   $= 1\frac{1}{2} \times £1.44$
   $= 1.5 \times £1.44 = £2.16$

(3) Overtime rate at double time
$$= 2 \times £1.44 = £2.88.$$

EXAMPLE 4

John Smith works a 42 hour week for which he is paid a basic wage of £75.60. He works 6 hours overtime at time and a half and 4 hours overtime at double time. Calculate his gross wage for the week.

$$\text{Basic hourly rate} = \frac{£75.60}{42} = £1.80$$

Overtime rate at time and a half
$$= 1\tfrac{1}{2} \times £1.80 = £2.70$$

Overtime rate at double time
$$= 2 \times £1.80 = £3.60$$

Gross wage
$$= £75.60 + 6 \times £2.70 + 4 \times £3.60$$
$$= £75.60 + £16.20 + £14.40 = £106.20$$

Exercise 44 — *All type B*

1) A shop girl works a 46 hour week for which she is paid £58.88. She works 4 hours overtime which is paid for at time and a quarter. How much did she earn that week?

2) Tom Brown works 54 hours in a certain week. His basic week is 42 hours for which he is paid £100.80. His overtime rate is time and a half. Calculate his gross wage for the week.

3) In an engineering firm employees work a basic week of 38 hours. Any overtime worked from Monday to Friday is paid for at time and a quarter. Overtime worked on Saturday is paid for at time and a half whilst on Sunday it is paid for at double time. If the basic rate is £2.48 per hour find the wages of a man who worked 6 hours overtime from Monday to Friday, 4 hours overtime on Saturday and 7 hours overtime on Sunday.

4) A man's basic wage for a 38 hour week is £121.60. In a certain week he earned £140.40 by working overtime. If he worked 5 hours overtime what is the overtime rate?

5) A man's basic hourly rate is £2.88. Overtime is paid for at time and a quarter. If the basic week is 40 hours, how many hours of overtime must he work in order to earn £136.80 for the week?

6) A man is paid a basic hourly rate of £3.20 for a 40 hour week. On weekdays he is paid at time and a half for overtime. If his wage for a certain week was £156.80, how many hours of overtime did he work?

COMMISSION

Shop assistants, salesmen and representatives are sometimes paid *commission* on top of their basic wage. This commission is usually a small percentage of the total value of the goods which they have sold.

EXAMPLE 5

A salesman is paid a commission of $2\tfrac{1}{2}\%$ on the value of the goods which he has sold. Calculate the amount of his commission if he sells goods to the value of £820 during a certain week.

$$\text{Commission} = 2\tfrac{1}{2}\% \text{ of } £820$$
$$= \frac{2.5}{100} \times £820 = £20.50$$

EXAMPLE 6

A shop assistant is paid a basic wage of £44 per week. In addition she is paid a commission of 2% of the value of the goods which she sells. During a certain week she sells goods worth £680. How much does she earn in the week?

$$\text{Commission} = 2\% \text{ of } £680$$
$$= \frac{2}{100} \times £680 = £13.60$$

Total wages for the week
$$= £44 + £13.60 = £57.60$$

Exercise 45 — *All type B*

1) A salesman sells £1300 of goods during a week. If he is paid a commission of 2% how much commission will he be paid?

2) Calculate the commission due to a car salesman if he sells a car for £3700 and his commission is 3%.

3) A sales assistant is paid a basic wage of £68 per week. In addition she is paid a commission of $2\tfrac{1}{2}\%$ on the value of the goods she sells. How much commission will she be paid on sales amounting to £1040 and what are her earnings for that week?

4) An agent selling agricultural machinery is paid a basic wage of £50 per week. In addition he is paid a commission of 3% on his sales. In one week he made sales totalling £6500. How much are his gross wages?

SALARIES

People like teachers, civil servants, secretaries and company managers are paid a definite amount for one year's work. It is unusual for them to be paid overtime, commission or a bonus. The annual salary is usually divided into twelve equal parts which are paid to the employee at the end of each month.

EXAMPLE 7

A teacher is employed at an annual salary of £4992. How much is he paid monthly?

Monthly salary $= £4992 \div 12 = £416$

Exercise 46 — *All type A*

Calculate the monthly payment for each of the following annual salaries:

1) £4320   3) £5712   5) £10 152
2) £3144   4) £7200

RATES

Every property in a town or city is given a *rateable value* which is fixed by the local district valuer. This rateable value depends upon the size, condition and position of the property.

The rates of a town or city are levied at so much in the £1 of rateable value, for instance, 125 p in the £1. The money brought in by the rates is used to pay for such things as education, police, libraries, etc.

In addition water rates are also payable at so much in the £1 to defray the cost of providing a water supply, sewerage and environmental services. The water rate is levied by the appropriate water authority, for instance, the Severn Trent Water Authority.

EXAMPLE 8

The rateable value of a house is £240. The local authority levies rates at 132.6 p in the £1 and the water authority levies water rates at 15.2 p in the £1. How much in rates will the householder pay per annum?

Amount of local rates
$= £240 \times 1.326 = £318.24$

Amount of water rates
$= £240 \times 0.152 = £36.48$

Total amount of the rates
$= £318.24 + £36.48$
$= £354.72$ per annum

EXAMPLE 9

A householder pays £180 in rates on property which has a rateable value of £150. What is the local rate?

For a rateable value of £150 rates paid are £180.

For a rateable value of £1 rates paid are $£\dfrac{180}{150} = £1.20.$

Hence the rates are levied at 120 p in the £1.

EXAMPLE 10

What rate should a council charge if they need to raise £4 510 000 from a total rateable value of £8 200 000?

Rates chargeable in the £1
$= \dfrac{4\,510\,000}{8\,200\,000} = 0.55.$

Hence the rates should be 55 p in the £1.

Most councils state on their rate demand the product of a penny rate. This is the amount that would be raised if the rate levied was 1 p in the £1, that is £0.01 in the £1.

EXAMPLE 11

The rateable value for a city is £9 350 000. What is the product of a penny rate?

Product of a penny rate
$= 9\,350\,000 \times 0.01 = £93\,500$

EXAMPLE 12

The cost of highways and bridges in a town is equivalent to a rate of 9.28 pence in the £1. If the rateable value of all the property in the town is £15 400 000 find how much money is available for spending on highways and bridges during the financial year.

Amount available
$= 9.28 \times 15\,400\,000$ pence
$= £\dfrac{9.28 \times 15\,400\,000}{100} = £1\,429\,120$

Exercise 47 — *All type A*

1) The rateable value of a house is £185. The local authority levies rates at 145.2 p in the £1 whilst the water authority levies a water rate of 14.8 p in the £1. How much, in total, will the householder pay in rates?

2) A householder pays £270 in rates when the rate levied is 150 p in the £1. What is the rateable value of the house?

3) A house is assessed at a rateable value of £135. The owner pays £121.50 in rates for the year. What is the rate in the £1?

4) What rate should a council charge if they need to raise £100 000 from a total rateable value of £320 000?

5) Calculate the total income from the rates of a town of rateable value £2 150 000 when the rates are 54 p in the £1.

6) A town of rateable value £772 000 needs to raise £70 400 from the rates. What local rate should be charged?

7) The rateable value of all the property in a city is £8 500 000. What is the product of a penny rate?

8) The rateable value for all the property in a city is £8 796 000. Calculate the product of a penny rate. How much must the rates be if the total expenses for the city for a year are £4 837 800?

9) The total rateable value for all the property in a city is £8 500 000. Calculate the total cost of public libraries if a rate of 4.6 pence in the £1 must be levied for the purpose.

10) The expenditure of a town is £900 000 and its rates are 87 pence in the £1. The cost of libraries is £30 000. What rate in the £1 is needed for the upkeep of the libraries?

INCOME TAX

Taxes are levied by the Chancellor of the Exchequer in order to produce income to pay for the Armed Services, the Civil Service, the National Health Services and other expenditures. The largest producer of revenue is *Income Tax*.

Every person who has an income above a certain minimum amount has to pay income tax to the Government. Tax is not paid on the whole income. Certain allowances are made as follows:

(1) an allowance, the amount of which varies according as to whether the taxpayer is a single person or a married man,
(2) allowances for dependent relatives, etc.,
(3) allowances for superannuation contributions, necessary expenses (such as cost of protective clothing), etc.

The residue of the income left after the allowances have been deducted is called the *taxable income*. The following example shows the method used in calculating income tax.

EXAMPLE 13

A man's salary is £5500 per year. His taxable income is found by deducting the following from his salary:

(1) A married man's allowance of £2795.
(2) Superannuation payments of £210.
(3) Allowable expenses £295.

He then pays tax at a standard rate of 30% Calculate his taxable income and the amount he has to pay in income tax.

To find the taxable income deduct the following from the salary of £5500.

Married man's allowance	=	£2795
Superannuation payments	=	£210
Expenses	=	£295
Total allowance		£3300

Taxable income = £5500 − £3300 = £2200

Total tax payable = 30% of £2200 = £660

P.A.Y.E.

Most people pay income tax by a method known as *Pay As You Earn* or P.A.Y.E. for short. The tax is deducted from their wage or salary before they receive it.

The tax payer and his employer receive a notice of coding which sets the allowances to which the person is entitled and sets his code number. The employer will then know from the tax tables supplied by the Inland Revenue the amount of tax to deduct from the wages of his employees. A typical Notice of Coding is shown overleaf.

Notice of Coding	
Coding allowance	**£**
Expenses	210
Personal	2795
Wife's earned income	—
Dependent relatives	—
Total allowances due	3005
Less	
Allowances given against other income	—
Income from property	—
Interest	85
Net allowance	2920
Less	
Tax unpaid for earlier years	—
Allowances given against pay	2920
Your code for 1983/84 is	**292H**

(Pension fund payments are deducted before tax is calculated and do not appear on the form.)

Exercise 48 — *All type A*

Use the following allowances for the questions in this exercise:

(1) Single person's allowance   £1785
(2) Married man's allowance   £2795
(3) Allowable expenses   relief in full
(4) Dependent relative   £100
(5) Pension fund payments   relief in full

1) A man's taxable income is £1200. If tax is paid at 35% find the amount paid in income tax.

2) When income tax is levied at 30% a man pays £240 in income tax. What is his taxable income?

3) Calculate the amount a single man, with no allowances except his single person's allowance, will pay in income tax when this is levied at 30%, if he earns £8000 per annum.

4) A married man with a dependent relative earns £6000 per annum. If he has no other allowances find the amount of tax he will pay when income tax is levied at 30%.

5) A married man has a dependent relative he helps to support and his pension fund payments amount to £420 per annum. If his annual salary is £7000, find the amount of Income Tax he will pay when this is levied at 30%.

VALUE ADDED TAX

Value added tax (or VAT) is a tax on goods and services which are purchased. Some goods and services bear no tax, for instance food and water. Services which are exempt are insurance, education and the postal service. The rate of tax varies from time to time.

EXAMPLE 14

A man buys a lawnmower which is priced at £40 plus VAT. How much will he pay for the mower if the rate of tax is 15%?

$$VAT = 15\% \text{ of } £40 = \frac{15}{100} \times £40 = £6$$

Total cost of the mower $= £40 + £6 = £46$

EXAMPLE 15

A person buys a table for £54 the price including VAT. If the rate of tax is 15%, what is the price of the table exclusive of VAT?

Let

100% be the price exclusive of VAT

then

115% is the price inclusive of VAT

Hence 115% represents £54

$$100\% \text{ represents } £54 \times \frac{100}{115} = £46.96$$

Exercise 49 — *All type A*

1) A man buys a washing machine whose price, exclusive of VAT, is £178. If VAT is charged at 15% how much did the man actually pay?

2) A chair is priced at £92 inclusive of VAT which is charged at 15%. What is the price exclusive of VAT?

3) A set of saucepans is priced at £18.40 inclusive of VAT. If VAT is charged at 15% calculate the price exclusive of VAT.

HIRE PURCHASE

When we purchase goods and pay for them by instalments we are said to have purchased them on *hire purchase*. Usually the purchaser pays a deposit and the balance of the purchase price plus interest is repaid in a number of instalments.

EXAMPLE 16

A woman buys some furniture for £280. A deposit of 25% is paid and interest at 12% per annum is charged on the outstanding balance. The balance is paid in 12 monthly instalments. Calculate how much each instalment will be.

Price of furniture = £280

Less deposit = £70 (25% of £280)

Outstanding balance
$$= £280 - £70 = £210$$

Plus interest at 12% on balance for 1 year
$$= 12\% \text{ of } £210 = £25.20$$

Total amount to be repaid
$$= £210 + £25.20 = £235.20$$

Amount of each instalment
$$= £\frac{235.20}{12} = £19.60$$

In Example 16, 12% would only be the true rate of interest if all of the outstanding balance was paid at the end of the year. However as each instalment is paid the amount outstanding is reduced and hence a larger proportion of each successive payment is interest. The true rate of interest is much higher than 12%; it is, in fact, about 22%.

BANK LOANS

Many people take out personal loans from a bank. The bank will calculate the interest for the whole period of the loan and the loan plus the interest is usually repaid in equal monthly payments.

EXAMPLE 17

A man borrows £300 from his bank. The bank charges 18% interest for the whole period of the loan. If the repayments are in 12 equal monthly instalments calculate the amount of each payment.

Interest = 18% of £300 = £54

Total amount to be repaid
$$= £300 + £54 = £354$$

Amount of each instalment
$$= £\frac{354}{12} = £29.50$$

Exercise 50 — *All type B*

1) A man buys a television set for £320. He pays a deposit of £50 and he is to pay the outstanding balance plus interest in 12 equal monthly instalments. If the interest is charged at 10% on the outstanding balance for the full period of the loan calculate the amount of the instalments.

2) A woman buys a suite of furniture for £320. A deposit of 20% is paid and interest at 12% per annum is charged on the outstanding balance for the full period of the loan. The balance is to be paid in 4 quarterly payments. How much is each payment?

3) A radio is priced at £84. It can be purchased on hire purchase by paying a deposit of £21 and 12 monthly instalments of £5.88. What rate of interest is being charged on the outstanding balance for the whole period of the loan?

4) A man borrows £250 from a bank who charge interest of 15% over the whole period of the loan. If the loan plus interest is to be repaid in 12 equal monthly instalments calculate the amount of the instalments.

5) A suite of furniture is priced at £240. Hire purchase terms are available which are: deposit 25% and 18 equal instalments of £11.80. Calculate the total hire purchase price and find the difference between the cash price and the hire purchase price.

6) An article of furniture can be purchased for £80 cash or by hire purchase. When purchased on the instalment system nine monthly repayments are required in which case interest at 18% per annum for nine months is added to the cash price. Calculate the amount of each instalment.

7) A bank lends a man £500. They charge interest at 12% per annum which is added to the amount of the loan. If the loan is repaid in 24 monthly instalments calculate the amount of each instalment.

GAS BILLS

Gas is charged according to the number of therms used (1 therm is 5.66 cubic metres of town gas or 2.83 cubic metres of natural gas). The gas corporation offers a choice of tariffs to its customers. The following are typical:

Tariff 1 A quarterly standing charge of £9.00
           A charge per therm of 30.5 p

Tariff 2 A quarterly standing charge of £17.50
           A charge per therm of 26.3 p per therm

The second tariff is intended for customers who use large quantities of gas in a year since it encourages the greater use of gas because of the lower charge per therm.

EXAMPLE 18

A householder has the choice of paying for his gas by either of the tariffs shown above. If he uses 110 therms per quarter which should he choose?

Tariff 1:

Cost of gas
$$= £9.00 + 110 \times 30.5\,p$$
$$= £9.00 + £33.55 = £42.55$$

Tariff 2:

Cost of gas
$$= £17.50 + 110 \times 26.3\,p$$
$$= £17.50 + £28.93 = £46.43$$

The customer should choose the first tariff as this will save him £3.88 per quarter.

ELECTRICITY BILLS

Electricity is charged according to the number of units used (1 unit is 1 kilowatt-hour). The electricity board offer its customers a choice of tariffs. The following are typical:

Tariff 1 (Flat rate)

| Lighting | 22.41 p per unit |
| Cooking, heating, etc. | 9.33 p per unit |

Tariff 2 (Two part)

A quarterly charge of £5.82

Cost per unit 5.17 p

Tariff 3 (Night rate)

A quarterly charge of £8.32

Cost per unit used between midnight and 8.00 a.m. 1.90 p

Cost per unit used at other times 5.35 p.

Tariff 1 is suitable when the amount of electricity used is small whilst Tariff 2 is suitable for the average household. Tariff 3 is suitable for households with central heating (storage heaters) which are switched on at night time.

EXAMPLE 19

A user of electricity estimates that he will use 2500 units during a quarter of which 1200 units will be used at night time. He has the choice of Tariffs 2 or 3 (see above). Which should he choose?

Tariff 2:

Cost of electricity
$$= £5.82 + 2500 \times 5.17\,p$$
$$= £5.82 + £129.25 = £135.07$$

Tariff 3:

Standing charge	£8.32
1300 units at 5.35 p per unit	£69.55
1200 units at 1.90 p per unit	£22.80
Total cost	£100.67

The householder should choose Tariff 3 because he will then save £34.40 per quarter.

TELEPHONE BILLS

The cost of using a telephone depends upon the number and type of the calls made. In addition there is a rental charge for the instrument itself. VAT is also charged as an addition to the user's bill. Charges for calls dialled direct are as follows at the time of going to press:

Standard Rate (Mon.—Fri. 8 a.m.—9 a.m. and 1 p.m.—6 p.m.) Price excludes VAT.

	Time allowed for 4.3 p
Local	2 minutes
up to 56 km	45 seconds
over 56 km	12.8 seconds
Channel Islands	12.8 seconds

EXAMPLE 20

A householder dialled 500 calls at 4.3 p per call in a certain quarter. The quarterly rental charge is £13.50. If VAT is charged at 15% find the total amount of the householder's telephone bill.

Quarterly rental charge	£13.50
500 calls at 4.3 p per call	
$= £0.043 \times 500$	£21.50
Total (exclusive of VAT)	£35.00
VAT at 15% $= \dfrac{15}{100} \times £35.00$	£5.25
Total including VAT	£40.25

Hence the total amount of the householder's telephone bill is £40.25.

Exercise 51 — *All type B*

1) A householder pays for his electricity by Tariff 1 (p. 44). If he uses 225 units for lighting and 470 units for cooking, etc., how much will he pay?

2) In a certain area electricity is charged for at a fixed rate of 6.9 p for every unit used. If a householder receives a bill for £50.37, how many units has she used ?

3) A customer uses 90 therms of gas in a quarter. He is charged 30.5 p per therm plus a standing charge of £9.00. How much is his gas bill?

4) A householder receives a gas bill for £114.69. He is charged 27.216 p per therm plus a standing charge of £20.70. How many therms has he used?

5) An electricity user consumes 4200 units in a quarter. He uses Tariff 3 (p. 44) and he uses 2300 of these units at night time. How much does he pay for electricity?

6) A householder has the choice of paying for his electricity as follows:

(a) at a fixed rate of 8.3 p per unit for each unit used,

(b) a standing charge of £5.82 plus 5.17 p per unit for each unit used.

If the householder estimates that he will use 650 units of electricity which method of payment should he choose?

7) A householder has a choice of Tariffs 2 or 3 (see p. 44) when paying for the electricity he consumes. If he uses 2800 units during the night and 1800 units during the day how much will he save by choosing Tariff 3?

8) A telephone bill is made up of the following charges:

Rental   £13.50 per quarter
Dialled units   603 at 4.3 p each

In addition VAT is charged at 15%. Calculate the total amount of the bill.

9) The telephone bill for a quarter is £35.30 which includes VAT at 15%. If the rental charge is £13.50 per quarter find the number of dialled calls if these are charged at 4.3 p each.

MORTGAGES

A person buying a house usually arranges a loan or *mortgage* from a Building Society. The Building Society usually requires a deposit of about 5 or 10% of the purchase price of the property. The balance of the purchase price plus the interest charged is paid back over a number of years. The interest rates of the Building Societies vary from time to time.

Prior to 1983, the borrower paid the Building Society the full amount of interest. He then received tax relief on this interest from the Inland Revenue. Now, however, under a scheme called Mortgage Interest Relief At Source (or MIRAS for short) the Building Society deducts the tax relief from the monthly repayments. Hence the borrower pays less to the Building Society but more in Income Tax, the decrease in mortgage repayments and the extra income tax being equal.

EXAMPLE 21

A Building Society quotes the repayments on a mortgage as £10.74 per month for 25 years per £1000 borrowed. What will be the monthly repayments on a mortgage of £8500.

Monthly repayments

$$= £\frac{8500}{1000} \times 10.74 = £91.29$$

Sometimes a combined mortgage and life insurance can be arranged. A life insurance policy is taken out for the value of the loan. Interest is paid on the loan for the whole period of the loan after which the money received from the insurance policy is used to repay it.

EXAMPLE 22

A person wishes to borrow £10 000 to buy a house, the loan being secured by an insurance policy for the 25 year period which costs £1.50 per £1000 per month. The Building Society charges interest at 10.25% but tax relief under MIRAS at 30% is deducted by the Society. Calculate the total monthly repayments to be paid by the borrower.

Annual interest payable to Society

    = 10.25% of £10 000 = £1025

Tax relief on interest

    = 30% of £1025 = £307.50

Annual amount payable to Society

    = £1025 − £307.50 = £717.50

Monthly repayments to Society

$$= £\frac{717.50}{12} = £59.79$$

Monthly insurance premiums

$$= £1.50 \times \frac{10\,000}{1000} = £15.00$$

Total monthly outgoings

$$= £59.79 + £15.00 = £74.79$$

Exercise 52 — *All type B*

1) A house is rented for £44.16 per week. Its rateable value is £174 and rates are levied at 108 p in the £1. What will be the weekly charge for rent and rates?

2) A flat is rented for £39.00 per week. Its rateable value is £162 and rates are charged at 120 p in the £1. What is the inclusive weekly charge for rent and rates?

3) A man borrows £12 000 from a Building Society in order to buy a house. The society charges £12.20 per month per £1000 borrowed. How much are the monthly payments?

4) A man borrows £6000 on a mortgage for 25 years. The mortgage costs £0.94 per £100 per month. What are his monthly repayments?

5) A person borrows £8000 from a Building Society to buy a house, the loan being covered by an insurance policy for the 10 year period which costs £7.95 per month per £1000. The Building Society charges interest at 10.25% per annum but deducts, under MIRAS, tax relief at 30% on the interest. Work out the total monthly outgoings of the borrower.

SELF-TEST 9

In questions 1 to 10 state the letter (or letters) corresponding to the correct answer (or answers).

1) A man's basic wage for a 35 hour week is £68.25. His overtime rate is 30 pence per hour more than his basic rate. If he works 6 hours of overtime in a certain week his wages for that week will be:

a £70.05   b £81.75   c £84   d £79.05

2) Office workers asked for a rise of 12% but were granted only 5% which brought their weekly wage up to £67.20. If the 12% rise had been granted their weekly wage would have been:

a £64   b £72   c £71.68   d £71.92

3) A man's basic pay for a 40 hour week is £80. Overtime is paid for at 25% above the basic rate. In a certain week he worked overtime and his total wage was £100. He therefore worked a total of:

a 48 hours   b 45 hours   c 50 hours
d 47 hours

4) A householder is charged for electricity as follows: the first 80 units are charged for at 6 p per unit and each subsequent unit used at 2.6 p per unit. If the electricity bill amounted to £16.24 the number of units used was:

a 600   b 550   c 440   d 520

5) A householder pays for his electricity by means of a fixed charge of £7.20 plus 2.4 p for each unit of electricity used. If he used 330 units of electricity his bill was:

a £7.92   b £15.12   c £16.10   d £8.52

6) The rateable value of a house is £150. If the rates are 80 p in the £1 the rates payable are:

a £150   b £12   c £120   d £140

7) In a certain city the total rateable value of all the property in the city is £8 000 000. The product of a penny rate is therefore:

a £80 000   b £8000   c £16 000
d £20 000

8) The cost of highways in a town is equivalent to a rate of 6.2 pence in the £1. If the rateable value of all property in the town is £3 500 000 then the cost of highways is:

a £21 700   b £22 000   c £220 000
d £217 000

9) The expenditure of a town is £300 000 and its rates are 75 pence in the £1. The cost of the library is £20 000. The rate needed for the upkeep of the library is:

a 4 p in the £1   b 5 p in the £1
c 8 p in the £1   d 7.5 p in the £1

10) When income tax was levied at 30% a man paid £90 in income tax. His taxable income was therefore:

a £30   b £27   c £270   d £300

Chapter 10 Simple Interest

SIMPLE INTEREST

Interest is the *profit return on investment*. If money is invested then interest is paid to the investor. If money is borrowed then the person who borrows the money will have to pay interest to the lender. The money which is invested or lent is called the *principal*. The percentage return is called the *rate per cent*. Thus interest at a rate of 12% means that the interest on a principal of £100 will be £12 per annum. The total formed by adding the interest to the principal is called the *amount*. The amount is therefore the total sum of money which remains invested after a period of time.

With simple interest the principal always stays the same no matter how many years the investment (or the loan) lasts.

EXAMPLE 1

How much interest does a man pay if he borrows £400 for one year at an interest rate of 12%?

$$\text{Interest} = 12\% \text{ of } £400$$

$$= \frac{12}{100} \times £400 = £48$$

If money is borrowed for two years the amount of interest payable will be doubled; for three years three times as much interest is payable; and so on.

The interest payable (or earned) depends upon:

(1) The amount borrowed or lent, i.e. the *principal*.
(2) The rate of interest charged, i.e. the *rate %*.
(3) The period of the loan, i.e. the *time* (in years).

To calculate the *simple interest* use the formula below:

$$I = \frac{PRT}{100}$$

where P stands for the principal
R stands for the rate per cent
T stands for the time in years

This formula can be transposed to give:

$$T = \frac{100I}{PR}$$

$$R = \frac{100I}{PT}$$

$$P = \frac{100I}{RT}$$

EXAMPLE 2

Find the simple interest on £500 borrowed for 4 years at 11%.

Here we have $P = £500$, $R = 11\%$ and $T = 4$ years.   Substituting these values in the simple interest formula gives:

$$I = \frac{500 \times 11 \times 4}{100} = 220$$

Thus the simple interest is £220.

EXAMPLE 3

£700 is invested at 4% per annum. How long will it take for the amount to reach £784?

The interest = £784 − £700 = £84.

We therefore have $I = 84$, $R = 4$ and $P = 700$ and we have to find T. Substituting these values in the simple interest formula gives:

$$T = \frac{100 \times 84}{700 \times 4} = 3$$

Hence the time taken is 3 years.

Simple interest tables (see p. 48) are sometimes used to find the amount of interest due at the end of a given period of time. The table shows the appreciation (the increase in value) of £1.

For instance:

£1 invested for 8 years at 11% per annum will become £1.88.

£1 invested for 15 years at 8% per annum will become £2.20.

47

TABLE OF SIMPLE INTEREST

Appreciation of £1 for periods from 1 year to 25 years

Year	5%	6%	7%	8%	9%	10%	11%	12%	13%	14%
1	1.050	1.060	1.070	1.080	1.090	1.100	1.110	1.120	1.130	1.140
2	1.100	1.120	1.140	1.160	1.180	1.200	1.220	1.240	1.260	1.280
3	1.150	1.180	1.210	1.240	1.270	1.300	1.330	1.360	1.390	1.420
4	1.200	1.240	1.280	1.320	1.360	1.400	1.440	1.480	1.520	1.560
5	1.250	1.300	1.350	1.400	1.450	1.500	1.550	1.600	1.650	1.700
6	1.300	1.360	1.420	1.480	1.540	1.600	1.660	1.720	1.780	1.840
7	1.350	1.420	1.490	1.560	1.630	1.700	1.770	1.840	1.910	1.980
8	1.400	1.480	1.560	1.640	1.720	1.800	1.880	1.960	2.040	2.120
9	1.450	1.540	1.630	1.720	1.810	1.900	1.990	2.080	2.170	2.260
10	1.500	1.600	1.700	1.800	1.900	2.000	2.100	2.200	2.300	2.400
11	1.550	1.660	1.770	1.880	1.990	2.100	2.210	2.320	2.430	2.540
12	1.600	1.720	1.840	1.960	2.080	2.200	2.320	2.440	2.560	2.680
13	1.650	1.780	1.910	2.040	2.170	2.300	2.430	2.560	2.690	2.820
14	1.700	1.840	1.980	2.120	2.260	2.400	2.540	2.680	2.820	2.960
15	1.750	1.900	2.050	2.200	2.350	2.500	2.650	2.800	2.950	3.100
16	1.800	1.960	2.120	2.280	2.440	2.600	2.760	2.920	3.080	3.240
17	1.850	2.020	2.190	2.360	2.530	2.700	2.870	3.040	3.210	3.380
18	1.900	2.080	2.260	2.440	2.620	2.800	2.980	3.160	3.340	3.520
19	1.950	2.140	2.330	2.520	2.710	2.900	3.090	3.280	3.470	3.660
20	2.000	2.200	2.400	2.600	2.800	3.000	3.200	3.400	3.600	3.800
21	2.050	2.260	2.470	2.680	2.890	3.100	3.310	3.520	3.730	3.940
22	2.100	2.320	2.540	2.760	2.980	3.200	3.420	3.640	3.860	4.080
23	2.150	2.380	2.610	2.840	3.070	3.300	3.530	3.760	3.990	4.220
24	2.200	2.440	2.680	2.920	3.160	3.400	3.640	3.880	4.120	4.360
25	2.250	2.500	2.750	3.000	3.250	3.500	3.750	4.000	4.250	4.500

EXAMPLE 4

Using the simple interest tables calculate the simple interest earned by £850 invested for 9 years at 10% per annum.

From the simple interest table, in 9 years at 10% p.a. £1 becomes £1.90. To find the amount accruing from £850 multiply 1.90 by £850.

Amount accruing
$$= 1.90 \times £850 = £1615$$

Interest earned
$$= £1615 - £850 = £765.$$

Exercise 53 — *Questions 1—8 type A, remainder type B*

1) Find the simple interest on £700 invested for 3 years at 6% per annum.

2) Find the simple interest on £500 invested for 6 months at 8% per annum.

3) In what length of time will £500 be the interest on £2500 which is invested at 5% per annum?

4) In what length of time will £16 be the simple interest on £480 invested at 8% per annum?

5) In what length of time will £75 be the simple interest on £500 invested at 6% per annum?

6) The interest on £600 invested for 5 years is £210. What is the rate per cent?

7) The interest on £200 invested for 4 months is £6. What is the rate per cent?

8) What principal is needed so that the interest will be £48 if it is invested at 3% per annum for 5 years?

9) Which receives the more interest per annum: £150 invested at 4% or £180 invested at $3\frac{1}{2}$%?
What is the annual difference?

10) A man invests £700 at 6% per annum and £300 at 8% per annum. What is his total annual interest on these investments?

11) A man deposited £350 in a bank and £14 interest was added at the end of the first year. The whole amount was left in the bank for

a second year at the same rate of interest. Find the amount of interest on the £364 paid in the second year.

12) Using the simple interest table on p. 48, calculate the simple interest earned in each of the following cases:

(a) £350 invested at 6% p.a. for 9 years.
(b) £500 invested at 11% p.a. for 5 years.
(c) £2500 invested at 8% p.a. for 16 years.
(d) £7000 invested at 13% p.a. for 11 years.
(e) £900 invested at 9% p.a. for 21 years.

SELF-TEST 10

In questions 1 to 10 state the letter (or letters) corresponding to the correct answer (or answers).

1) The simple interest on £500 for 4 years at 7% per annum is:

a £1400   **b** £14 000   **c** £20   **d** £140

2) The simple interest on £800 invested at 8% per annum for 6 months is:

a £48   **b** £32   **c** £64   **d** £60

3) The simple interest on £800 invested for 5 years was £240. The rate of interest per annum was therefore:

a 6%   **b** 5%   **c** 3%   **d** 7%

4) The simple interest on £800 invested at 5% per annum over a number of years amounted to £160. The cash was therefore invested for:

a 7 years   **b** 5 years   **c** 4 years
d 6 years

5) The simple interest on £400 invested for 4 months was £12. The rate of interest per annum is:

a 36%   **b** 4.8%   **c** 7%   **d** 9%

6) A man invests £700 at 5% per annum and £300 at 6% per annum. The entire investment has an interest rate of:

a $5\frac{1}{2}$%   **b** 5.3%   **c** 11%   **d** 53%

7) A man invests £9000 at 10% per annum and £1000 at 8% per annum. His return on the complete investment is:

a 18%   **b** 2%   **c** 10%   **d** 9.8%

8) What sum of money must be invested to give £30 simple interest if the rate is 6% per annum and the time is 2 years?

a £250   **b** £300   **c** £400   **d** £360

9) A sum of money is invested at 8% per annum for 4 years and the simple interest is £160. The amount of money invested is:

a £500   **b** £640   **c** £320   **d** £1280

10) A sum of money was invested at 5% per annum for 4 years. The total amount lying to the credit of the investor at the end of the 4 years was £600. The amount originally invested was:

a £800   **b** £600   **c** £500   **d** £400

Chapter 11 Compound Interest

Compound interest is different from simple interest in that the interest which is added to the principal also attracts interest. If money is invested at compound interest, the interest due at the end of each year is added to the principal for the next year.

EXAMPLE 1

Find the amount of money gained from an investment of £800 for 3 years at 10% per annum compound interest.

Interest on £800 for 1 year at 10%
$$= 10\% \text{ of } £800 = £80$$

Add this interest to the original principal of £800.

New principal = £880.

Interest on £880 for 1 year at 10%
$$= 10\% \text{ of } £880 = £88$$

Add this interest to the principal of £880.

New principal = £968.

Interest on £968 for 1 year at 10%
$$= 10\% \text{ of } £968 = £96.80$$

Amount accruing at the end of 3 years
$$= £968 + £96.80 = £1064.80$$

Although all problems on compound interest can be worked out by the method of Example 1, the work is tedious and time consuming particularly if the period is lengthy. Here is a formula which will allow you to calculate the compound interest:

$$A = P\left(1 + \frac{R}{100}\right)^n$$

where A stands for the amount of money accruing after n years
P stands for the principal
R stands for the rate per cent per annum
n stands for the number of years for which the money is invested

You will have to make use of logarithms or a calculator when using this formula (see Chapters 4 and 23).

EXAMPLE 2

Calculate the interest earned on £750 invested at 12% per annum for 8 years.

Here we have $P = £750$, $R = 12\%$ and $n = 8$ years. Substituting these values in the compound interest formula we have

$$A = 750 \times \left(1 + \frac{12}{100}\right)^8 = 750 \times (1.12)^8$$

number	log
1.12	0.049 2
	× 8
	0.393 6
750	2.875 1
	3.268 7

Antilog of 3.268 7 = 1857.

Hence the amount accruing after 8 years is £1857.

The interest earned is £1857 − £750 = £1107.

Using a calculator:

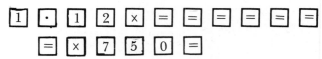

The display is 1856.972 which represents £1856.97.

Exercise 54 — *All type C*

Use the compound interest formula and the log tables to calculate the compound interest earned in each of the following:

1) £250 invested for 5 years at 8% per annum.

2) £400 invested for 7 years at 9% per annum.

3) £1200 invested for 12 years at 10% per annum.

50

4) £2500 invested for 15 years at 11% per annum.

5) £5000 invested for 6 years at 7% per annum.

6) How much interest is earned when £800 is invested at 9% per annum simple interest for 6 years? How much would have been earned if the money had been invested at compound interest?

7) A man borrowed £1200 for 8 years at 11% compound interest. How much will he have to repay?

8) Find to the nearest dollar the amount accruing when $970 is invested for 10 years at 12% compound interest.

COMPOUND INTEREST TABLES

In business, compound interest tables are used to find the amount of interest due at the end of a given period of time. Part of such a table is shown below.

Amount accruing

$$= 1.340 \times £750 = £1005$$

Interest earned

$$= £1005 - £750 = £255$$

Exercise 55 — *All type B*

Using the compound interest table below calculate the compound interest earned in each of the following:

1) £350 invested for 6 years at 7% per annum.

2) £500 invested for 5 years at 11% per annum.

3) £2500 invested at 5% per annum for 10 years.

4) £7000 invested for 7 years at 13% per annum.

5) £900 invested for 10 years at 9% per annum.

Years	5%	6%	7%	8%	9%	10%	11%	12%	13%	14%
1	1.050	1.060	1.070	1.080	1.090	1.100	1.110	1.120	1.130	1.140
2	1.103	1.124	1.145	1.166	1.188	1.210	1.232	1.254	1.277	1.300
3	1.158	1.191	1.225	1.260	1.295	1.331	1.368	1.405	1.443	1.482
4	1.216	1.262	1.311	1.360	1.412	1.464	1.518	1.574	1.603	1.689
5	1.276	1.338	1.403	1.469	1.539	1.611	1.685	1.762	1.842	1.925
6	1.340	1.419	1.501	1.587	1.677	1.772	1.870	1.974	2.082	2.195
7	1.407	1.504	1.606	1.714	1.828	1.949	2.076	2.211	2.353	2.502
8	1.477	1.594	1.718	1.851	1.993	2.144	2.304	2.476	2.658	2.853
9	1.551	1.689	1.838	1.999	2.172	2.358	2.558	2.773	3.004	3.252
10	1.629	1.791	1.967	2.159	2.367	2.594	2.839	3.106	3.395	3.707

The table shows the appreciation (the increase in value) of £1. For instance £1 invested for 5 years at 9% interest will become £1.539. Example 3 shows how the table is used in compound interest calculations.

EXAMPLE 3

Using the compound interest table find the amount of compound interest earned by £750 invested for 6 years at 5% per annum.

From the table in 6 years at 5%, £1 becomes £1.340.

To find the amount accruing from £750 we multiply 1.340 by £750.

DEPRECIATION

A business will own a number of assets such as machinery, typewriters, motor transport, etc. These assets reduce in value, i.e. *depreciate*, all the time. Each year the depreciation has to be calculated and charged as a business expense. A number of ways exist for calculating the depreciation. The commonest way is to use the reducing balance method in which the depreciation is calculated as a percentage of the book value of the assets at the beginning of the year.

EXAMPLE 4

A small business buys a centre lathe costing £2000. It decides to calculate the depreciation each year as 20% of its value at the beginning of the year. Calculate the book value after three complete years.

Cost of lathe
$$= £2000$$

Depreciation first year (20%)
$$= £400 \quad (20\% \text{ of } £2000)$$

Book value at start of second year
$$= £1600$$

Depreciation second year (20%)
$$= £320 \quad (20\% \text{ of } £1600)$$

Book value at start of third year
$$= £1280$$

Depreciation third year (20%)
$$= £256 \quad (20\% \text{ of } £1280)$$

Book value at end of third year
$$= £1024$$

Hence the lathe is reckoned to be worth £1024 at the end of the third year.

Although all problems with the reducing balance method of depreciation can be worked out by using the method of Example 4, it is much quicker to use the depreciation formula, which is very similar to the compound interest formula. It is:

$$A = P\left(1 - \frac{R}{100}\right)^n$$

where A stands for the book value after n years
        P stands for the initial cost of the asset
        R stands for the rate of depreciation
        n stands for the number of years

EXAMPLE 5

A business buys new machinery costing £12 000. It decides to calculate the depreciation each year at 25% of its value at the beginning of the year. Calculate the book value at the end of 4 years.

We are given that $P = £12\,000$, $R = 25\%$ and $n = 4$ years.   Substituting these values in the formula we have

$$A = 12\,000 \times \left(1 - \frac{25}{100}\right)^4$$

$$= 12\,000 \times 0.75^4$$

We must use logarithms for this calculation.

number	log
0.75^4	$\bar{1}.875\,1$
	$\times\ 4$
	$\bar{1}.500\,4$
$12\,000$	$4.079\,2$
	$3.579\,6$

The antilog of 3.579 6 is 3798 and hence the book value of the machinery at the end of 4 years is £3798.

Exercise 56 — *All type C*

1) A firm buys office machinery at a cost of £15 000. It is decided to calculate the depreciation each year as 15% of the book value at the beginning of the year. Calculate the book value at the end of 5 years.

2) The value of a machine depreciates each year by 12% of its value at the beginning of the year. If it cost £8000 when new calculate its value at the end of 7 years.

3) It is estimated that a machine costing £20 000 has a life of 10 years. It is decided to calculate the depreciation each year as $12\frac{1}{2}\%$ of the book value at the beginning of the year. Find the value of the machine at the end of the 10 years.

4) A machine which cost £5500 depreciates by 15% of the reducing balance. How much is the machine worth at the end of 5 years?

5) A lorry cost £6000 when new. 20% is written off its book value at the end of each year. Find its book value after 8 years.

SELF-TEST 11

In questions 1 to 5 state the letter (or letters) corresponding to the correct answer (or answers).

1) £500 invested at 10% compound interest for 2 years becomes:

a £600   b £700   c £605   d £665.50

2) A sum of £x is invested for 3 years at 10% per annum compound and the value of the investment amounts to £1331 at the end of this period. Hence x is equal to:

a £1024   b £1100   c £1000   d £1361

3) £500 invested for x years at 11% per annum becomes £842.50. Hence x is:

a $\dfrac{842.50}{11}$ **b** $\dfrac{500}{11}$ **c** 5

d $\dfrac{842.50}{500}$

4) The value of a machine depreciates each year by 15% of its value at the beginning of the year. If it costs £16 000 when new its value at the end of 6 years is:

a £1067 **b** £2667 **c** £6034

d nothing

5) A car depreciates in value by 10% of its cost price each year. It cost £4000 when new. Its value after 4 years is:

a £2624 **b** £2500 **c** £1000 **d** £3000

Chapter 12 Investment and Bankruptcy

SHARES

Many people at some time or another will have money to invest. It could be deposited in a bank, a building society or in the National Savings Bank where it will earn a fixed rate of interest. It could also be invested in a company by buying some of its *shares*.

Companies obtain their capital by the issue of shares to the public. Shares have a nominal value of 25 p, £1, £5, etc., which cannot be divided into fractional amounts. If the company does well the price of the shares will appreciate to a value above the nominal price. On the other hand if the company does badly the price will fall below the nominal value. Shares can be bought and sold through the Stock Exchange. Companies issue different kinds of shares, two of the most important kinds being as follows:

Preference shares which carry a fixed rate of interest. The holders of these shares have first call on any profits the company may make in order that payments due to them can be made.

Ordinary shares, the dividends on which vary according to the amount of profit that the company makes. The directors of the company decide what dividend shall be paid.

The dividends payable on the shares are a percentage of the nominal value of the shares.

EXAMPLE 1
A man buys 200 Emperor 25 p shares at 44 p. How much does he pay for the shares?

25 p is the nominal value of the shares.

44 p is the price he actually pays for the shares.

$$\text{Amount paid} = 200 \times 44 \text{ p}$$
$$= 8800 \text{ p} = £88$$

EXAMPLE 2
Tom Jones sells 500 Tuxo £5 shares at £4. How much does he get?

£5 is the nominal value of the shares.

£4 is the price at which he sells the shares.

$$\text{Amount received} = 500 \times £4 = £2000$$

EXAMPLE 3
A man owns 300 Ludo shares. The company declares a dividend of 32 p per share. How much does he get in dividends?

$$\text{Amount payable} = 300 \times 32 \text{ p}$$
$$= 9600 \text{ p} = £96$$

EXAMPLE 4
A man holds 600 Snake 50 p shares which he bought for 35 p. The declared dividend is 8% of the nominal value of the shares. How much does he get in dividends and what is the yield per cent on his investment?

Dividend per share
$$= 8\% \text{ of } 50 \text{ p} = 4 \text{ p}$$

Amount obtained in dividends
$$= 600 \times 4 \text{ p} = 2400 \text{ p} = £24$$

Yield per cent
$$= \frac{\text{dividend per share}}{\text{price paid per share}} \times 100$$
$$= \frac{4}{35} \times 100 = 11.4\%$$

EXAMPLE 5
The paid up capital of a company consists of 50 000 6% preference shares of £1 each and 200 000 ordinary shares of 50 p each. The profits available for distribution are £11 973. What dividend can be paid to the ordinary shareholders? What is the dividend per cent?

Preference dividend
$$= 6\% \text{ of } £50 000 = £3000$$

Amount of profit remaining
$$= £11 973 - £3000 = £8973$$

Dividend per share
$$= £\frac{8973}{200 000} = £0.0448 \text{ or } 4.48 \text{ p}$$

Dividend per cent

$$= \frac{4.48}{50} \times 100 = 8.96\%$$

Exercise 57 — *All type C*

1) Find the cost of the following shares:
(a) 400 Oak £2 shares at 314 p.
(b) 900 Staite 50 p shares at 39 p.
(c) 280 Mako 25 p shares at 59 p.

2) Find the amount raised by selling the following shares:
(a) 180 Kneck 80 p shares at 97 p.
(b) 350 Truck £5 shares at 87 p.
(c) 490 Mill 50 p shares at 117 p.

3) Calculate the dividend received from the following investments:
(a) 300 Proof shares; dividend is 8 p per share.
(b) 450 Shock shares; dividend is 18 p per share.
(c) 750 Stairways shares; dividend is 85 p per share.

4) Calculate the amount of dividend received from the following investments:
(a) 300 Well 75 p shares; declared dividend is 10%.
(b) 500 Toomet £5 shares; declared dividend is 5%.
(c) 1200 Boom 50 p shares; declared dividend is 16%.

5) Calculate the yield per cent on the following investments:
(a) 200 Salto £3 shares bought at 250 p; declared dividend is 9%.
(b) 500 Melting 40 p shares bought at 85 p; declared dividend is 5%.
(c) 85 Penn £2 shares bought at 98 p; declared dividend is 3%.

6) Calculate the yearly income from 500 Imperial £2 shares at 150 p when a dividend of 8% is declared. What is the yield per cent on the money invested?

7) Find the cost, income and yield per cent from 900 £1 shares at 82 p when a dividend of 7% is declared.

8) 500 Flag 25 p shares are sold for £160. What is the cash value of each share?

9) How much profit does a man make when he sells 900 Emblem £3 shares for 390 p, having bought them for 265 p?

10) The paid up capital of a company consists of 100 000 8% preference shares of £2 each and 250 000 ordinary shares of £1 each. The profits available for distribution are £27 000. What is the dividend per cent that can be paid to the ordinary shareholders?

11) The issued capital of a company is 200 000 8% preference £1 shares, 150 000 6% £2 preference shares and 500 000 ordinary 25 p shares. If the profits available for distribution to the shareholders is £92 000, what dividend per cent is payable to the ordinary shareholders?

12) The paid up capital of a company consists of 90 000 7% preference £1 shares and 110 000 ordinary 50 p shares. If a dividend of 10% is declared, what is the profit of the company?

STOCK

Stock is issued by the Government and Local Authorities when they need cash. This stock is issued at a fixed rate of interest and it can be redeemed after a certain number of years. Stock is always issued in £100 units but an investor need not necessarily buy whole units of stock. The price of stock varies in the same way as does the price of shares.

If you look in the financial section of your newspaper you will see statements like this:

Treasury 5% 1986–89 52

This means that £100 worth of Treasury Stock, paying 5% interest and redeemable between 1986 and 1989, can be bought for £52.

EXAMPLE 6

How much 9% Treasury Stock at 70 can be bought for £280? How much in dividends are payable and what is the yield per cent?

£70 buys £100 stock

£280 buys $£\dfrac{100}{70} \times 280 = £400$ stock

Interest payable
$$= 9\% \text{ of } £400 = £36$$

Yield per cent
$$= \frac{\text{interest payable}}{\text{amount paid for stock}} \times 100$$
$$= \frac{36}{280} \times 100 = 12.86\%$$

BROKERAGE

Brokerage is the commission charged by a broker for the purchase or sale of stocks and shares. It is calculated as a percentage of the sum for which they are bought or sold.

When buying add the brokerage to the price paid.

When selling deduct the brokerage from the sum received.

EXAMPLE 7

Find the change in income resulting from selling £2500 5% stock at 105 and investing the proceeds in 3% stock at 55. Brokerage is $1\frac{1}{2}$%.

Original income per annum
$$= 5\% \text{ of } £2500 = £125$$

Amount received for stock sold
$$= £2500 \times \frac{105}{100} = £2625$$

Brokerage $= 1\frac{1}{2}\%$ of £2625 $=$ £39.37

Amount received for stock sold less brokerage
$$= £2625 - £39.37$$
$$= £2585.63$$

Amount available for reinvestment
$$= £2585.63 \times \frac{100}{101\frac{1}{2}} = £2547.41$$

Stock bought at 55 $= £2547.41 \times \dfrac{100}{55}$
$$= £4631.67$$

New income $= 3\%$ of £4631.67 $=$ £138.95

Change in income $=$ £138.95 $-$ £125
$$= £13.95$$

Exercise 58 — *All type B*

1) Calculate the amount of stock that can be bought in each case:

(a) £300 invested in 5% Crewe at 75.
(b) £250 invested in Treasury stock at 69.
(c) £700 invested in Devon at 120.

2) Calculate the amount of interest received each year from the following:

(a) £800 stock at $3\frac{1}{2}$%.
(b) £1200 stock at 5%.
(c) £500 stock at 4%.

3) Calculate the amount of 6% Cambridge stock that can be bought for £600 if the price is 88. What is the interest earned per annum and what is the yield per cent?

4) How much does it cost to buy £300 of Railway stock at 80?

5) What are the proceeds from selling £400 of Dorset 3% stock at 75?

6) A man sells £800 worth of Argentine stock at 30 and buys German 8% stock at 110. How much German stock does he buy?

7) Find the change in income which results from selling £4000 of 5% stock at 102 and investing the proceeds in 4% stock at 92. Brokerage is 2% on each transaction.

8) A 6% stock is quoted at 130. Allowing for brokerage at $1\frac{1}{2}$% calculate:

(a) How much stock can be bought for £2000.
(b) How much is realised by the sale of £2000 of this stock.
(c) The net income from £2000 stock less income tax at 35%.

BANKRUPTCY

A person or company is *insolvent* when the liabilities of the person or company exceed the assets. Under certain conditions the person or company may be declared *bankrupt*. In this case the creditors (the people who are owed money) may appoint a trustee to sell the debtor's (the person or company owing the money) assets. After expenses and certain prior claims have been met the remainder of the proceeds will be distributed amongst the creditors.

To do this a dividend is declared which is worked out as follows:

$$\text{Dividend} = \frac{\text{net assets}}{\text{total liabilities}}$$

EXAMPLE 8

A bankrupt has liabilities of £10 000 and assets of £2000. Find the dividend. How much will a creditor owed £3000 be paid?

$$\text{Dividend} = £\frac{2000}{10\,000}$$

$$= £0.20 \text{ in the } £1 \text{ or } 20\,\text{p in the } £1$$

This means that each creditor will receive 20 p for each £1 that he is owed.

Amount received by creditor owed

$$£3000 = £3000 \times £0.20 = £600$$

Secured creditors do not rank for claim in the same way as unsecured creditors. They have prior claim to assets (either general or specific — i.e. a factory building, piece of machinery etc.); this is their *security*.

It is not always the case that the full extent of a loan should be treated in this way. For instance a bank may have only part of its loan to a firm secured; in this case the balance of the claim ranks for dividend in the usual way. If however the security raises more than the amount of the claim, the residue is added to the assets thus increasing the amount of the dividend.

EXAMPLE 9

A company, declared bankrupt, owes £85 873 to fully secured creditors and £98 748 to unsecured creditors. If the assets of the company realise £150 786 net find the dividend payable to the unsecured creditors.

Net assets	£150 786
Secured creditors	£85 873
Available for dividend	£64 913

$$\text{Dividend} = £\frac{64\,913}{98\,748}$$

$$= £0.66 \text{ in the } £1 \text{ or } 66\text{ p in the } £1$$

Exercise 59 — *All type C*

1) Find the dividends payable in the following cases:

(a) Net assets £20 000.
    Creditors £50 000.
(b) Net assets £7532.
    Creditors £82 516
(c) Net assets £190 632.
    Creditors £567 826.

2) Find the amounts paid to the following creditors:

(a) Dividend 30 p in the £1.
    Creditor owed £7000.
(b) Dividend 8 p in the £1.
    Creditor owed £6378.
(c) Dividend 19 p in the £1.
    Creditor owed £15 678.

3) The total assets of a company are sold for £358 907 but the expenses incurred are £28 712. If the company owes £739 054 to unsecured creditors find the amount of the dividend which can be paid.

4) The liabilities of a man in bankruptcy are £25 832 to fully secured creditors and £48 798 to unsecured creditors. If his assets realise £35 746 net what dividend can be paid?

5) A bankrupt owed £8572 to his ordinary (unsecured) creditors and £1750 to his secured creditors. If the expenses of the winding up were £125 and a dividend of 20 p in the £1 was declared, how much were his assets?

SELF-TEST 12

In each of the following state the letter (or letters) corresponding to the correct answer (or answers).

1) A man buys 500 Empress 50 p shares at 40 p. He therefore pays for the shares:

a £50   b £250   c £40   d £200

2) A person sells 400 Tuxedo £2 shares for 150 p. He gets:

a £60   b £600   c £80   d £800

3) A man holds 500 Ladder 80 p shares which he bought for 70 p. The declared dividend is 8%. He therefore receives:

a £32   b £28   c £40   d £56

4) A person holds 800 Persona 50 p shares which he bought for 75 p. The declared dividend is 10%. The yield per cent on the shares is:

a 10%   b $6\frac{2}{3}$%   c 15%   d $7\frac{1}{2}$%

5) How much 8% stock at 75 can be bought for £150?

a £200   b £75   c £150   d £1200

6) Calculate the interest received per annum from £800 stock at 5%.

a £50   b £400   c £40   d £500

7) A man sells £600 French stock at 50 and buys Belgian stock at 40. How much Belgian stock does he buy?

a £600   b £1200   c £750   d £400

8) A bankrupt has liabilities of £7000 and assets of £3500. How much will a creditor owed £2000 be paid?

a £2000   b £1000   c £500   d £700

Miscellaneous Exercise

Exercise 60

This exercise is divided into two sections A and B. The questions in Section A are intended to be done very quickly, but those in Section B should take about 20 minutes each to complete. All the questions are of the type found in O Level examination papers.

SECTION A

1) Express $\frac{132}{150}$ as a percentage. (A.E.B. 1975)

2) Calculate the simple interest on £1250 for 2 years at 9% per annum. (A.E.B. 1975)

3) Calculate the mean (average) of the numbers 438, 440, 442 and 444. (A.E.B. 1975)

4) In a school the ratio of the number of pupils to the number of teachers is 18.2 : 1.
(a) Assuming that there is a whole number of teachers and a whole number of pupils, find the smallest possible number of pupils in the school.
(b) If the number of teachers and pupils together is 960, find the number of teachers. (A.E.B. 1975)

5) Evaluate $\dfrac{1.5 \times 0.021}{0.003 \times 1.75}$. (L)

6) Express as a single fraction in its lowest terms $(2\frac{1}{2} + 1\frac{1}{4}) \div 2\frac{1}{4}$. (L)

7) Find the average of five numbers if one of them is 11 and the average of the other four numbers is 6. (L)

8) Find the number of years for which £120 must be invested at $7\frac{1}{2}\%$ per annum simple interest to amount to £174. (L)

9) Calculate the compound interest on £1500 at 5% per annum for 2 years. (L)

10) A bank delivers £50 worth of 2 p pieces to a supermarket. Calculate the weight of these coins, in kilograms, if each coin weighs 6.92 g. (J.M.B.)

11) Find the remainder when 69 259 is divided by 79. (J.M.B.)

12) A greyhound runs 800 metres in 50 seconds. Calculate its average speed in km/h. (J.M.B.)

13) In an election where there were only two candidates, 27 180 votes were cast and the winner's majority was 3558. Find how many votes the loser received. (J.M.B.)

14) Evaluate $3\frac{1}{3} \div (1\frac{1}{5} \times \frac{1}{2})$. (L)

15) Divide 52.16 by 3.2. (L)

16) A scale model of an aircraft is made to a scale of 1 : 78. If the wing span of the model is 35 cm find the wing span of the actual aircraft. (L)

17) Find the difference between the simple and the compound interest on £1250 for 2 years at 8% per annum. (L)

18) An agent buys 3600 articles for £2000. He sells 3060 of them at a profit of 30% and the remainder at a loss of 10%. Find his profit and express it as a percentage of his outlay. (L)

19) Find 5% of £260. (A.E.B. 1975)

20) Round off 0.049 49:
(a) correct to three significant figures;
(b) correct to three decimal places. (A.E.B. 1975)

21) The value of a car, after each year's use, decreases by a fixed percentage of its value at the beginning of that year. If a car costs £2560 when new and its value after one year was £2080 by what percentage has the value decreased? Calculate its value after a further year's use. (L)

22) After prices have risen by 8% the new price of an article is £70.47. Calculate the original price. (L)

23) Articles are purchased at £2.50 per 100 and sold at 3 p each. Calculate the profit as a percentage of the purchase price. (L)

24) Calculate the exact cost of 375 toys at £3.21 each. (L)

25) Next year a man will receive a 12% wage increase and his weekly wage will then be £80.64. What is his present weekly wage? (L)

26) A motorway journey takes 3 hours at an average speed of 120 km/h. How long will it take if the average speed is reduced to 80 km/h. (J.M.B.)

27) On 1st Jan. a man's shares were worth £500. By 1st Feb. their value had fallen by 20% but on 1st March their value was 120% of their value on 1st Feb. Calculate the value of the shares:
(a) on 1st Feb.
(b) on 1st March. (J.M.B.)

28) Given that the Value Added Tax on goods supplied is 15% of their value, calculate the Value Added Tax on goods valued at £64. (J.M.B.)

29) A car travels 20 km at an average speed of 48 km/h and then for a further 15 minutes at an average speed of 40 km/h. Calculate the average speed for the entire journey. (J.M.B.)

30) (a) Calculate $\frac{3}{4} - \frac{2}{3}$.
(b) Calculate exactly 7.3×2.1.
(A.E.B. 1976)

31) The mean of five numbers is 15 and the mean of a further eight numbers is 2. Calculate the mean of all thirteen numbers. (A.E.B. 1976)

32) The number of people working for a company at the end of 1974 was 1210. This was an increase of 10% on the number working for the company at the beginning of 1974. How many people worked for the company at the beginning of 1974? (A.E.B. 1976)

33) A cup costs 24 p and a saucer costs 15 p. How much change should be given from £5 after purchasing 8 cups and 8 saucers. (L)

34) A train is travelling at a uniform speed of 90 km/h. Calculate the time, in seconds, it takes to travel 600 m. (L)

35) £979 is to be divided into three parts in the proportions $1 : \frac{1}{2} : \frac{1}{3}$. Calculate the value of the smallest part. (L)

36) By selling a chair for £10.35 a shopkeeper makes a profit of 15% on his cost price. Calculate his profit. (L)

37) Find the exact value of $\dfrac{45}{0.9} + \dfrac{6.6}{0.55}$. (L)

38) A man left $\frac{3}{8}$ of his money to his wife and half the remainder to his son. The rest was divided equally amongst his five daughters. Find what fraction of the money each daughter received. (L)

39) By selling an article for £18 a shopkeeper makes a profit of 44% on the cost price. At what price must it be sold in order to make a profit of 40%? (L)

40) On a train journey of 117 km, the average speed for the first 27 km was 45 km/h and for the rest of the journey the average speed was 37.5 km/h. Calculate the uniform speed at which the train would have to travel in order to cover the whole distance in the same time. (L)

41) In a sale, the price of a bed, after being reduced by 17%, is £49.80. Calculate the price before the reduction. (L)

42) Calculate the monthly cost of owning a house given that the expenditure is as follows: Mortgage repayments £20 per month; Insurances £32 per year; Rates £59 per half year. (A.E.B. 1974)

43) (a) Express 0.166 66 correct to 3 decimal places.
(b) Express 0.026 66 correct to 2 significant figures. (A.E.B. 1976)

44) Find the mean of 1972, 1976, 1977 and 1979. (A.E.B. 1976)

45) A man sells his car for £810 and as a result loses 10% of the price he paid for it. What price did he pay for it? (A.E.B. 1976)

46) Given that $\dfrac{42 \times 462}{77} = 252$, find the exact value of $\dfrac{4.2 \times 0.046\,2}{0.077}$. (A.E.B. 1976)

47) The entry fee for an examination was £2.50 in 1975 and it was raised to £3.20 in 1976. Express the increase in the fee as a percentage of the fee in 1975. (J.M.B.)

48) Calculate $7\frac{1}{2}$% of £160. (J.M.B.)

49) Find $\frac{3}{4}$ of $7\frac{1}{3}$. (J.M.B.)

50) Find the cost of taking 34 children on an outing at £2.65 each. (J.M.B.)

SECTION B

51) Since a city typist moved to the coast, both the railway and the bus fares for her journeys have increased. Each year for her rail travel she buys three quarterly season tickets, one monthly season ticket and two weekly season tickets. The quarterly tickets have increased from £45.50 each to £53.00 and the monthly tickets from £16.50 each to £19.70 each. The weekly tickets have increased from £4.60 each to £5.40 each. During each of the 45 weeks she travels, she takes ten bus rides, each of which has increased from 9 p to 12 p. Calculate:
(a) the original annual cost of her travel;
(b) the increase in annual cost;
(c) the increase in annual cost expressed as a percentage of the original annual cost, correct to 3 significant figures.   (L)

52) A borough council decides to increase the rates by 3 p in the pound. If the total rateable value of the borough is £820 000, find the extra amount raised by the increase. A householder, living in the borough finds that, as a result of the increase, his rates go up from £110.88 to £115.20. Calculate:
(a) the rateable value of his house;
(b) the number of pence in the pound at which the new rate is charged;
(c) by what percentage, correct to two significant figures, the original rate increased;
(d) the total amount of rates due from the whole borough at the increased rate.   (L)

53) A company which produces paving slabs uses 1 tonne of granite to produce 18 paving slabs. The costs of the company in 1972 were divided between cost of granite, cost of labour and costs of overheads in the proportion 7 : 5 : 2. In that year 5000 tonnes of granite were bought at £3.50 per tonne, and the paving slabs produced were sold at 42 p each. Calculate the company's total costs for 1972 and the percentage of profit made. In 1973 the company bought the same quantity of granite. The labour costs rose by 40% but the other costs remained unchanged. Calculate the selling price of each paving slab if the percentage profit made by the company remained the same in 1973 as in 1972.   (L)

54) A man wishes to make a journey from his home to a meeting near to a town A and finds that the journey will consist of three parts:
(i) A car journey of 48 km from his home to the nearest railway station which he hopes to cover in 45 minutes.
(ii) A journey on the 9.10 a.m. train from this station to town A, a distance of 315 km, over which the train normally averaged 90 km/h.
(iii) A 24 minute taxi ride from the railway station at A to his meeting place, over which he hopes to average 40 km/h.
Neglecting the time taken changing from car to train and train to taxi, calculate:
(a) the average speed of his car;
(b) the time at which the train would normally arrive at A;
(c) the distance between the railway station at A and the meeting place;
(d) the average speed over the journey from home to the meeting place, giving your answer to the nearest whole number.
All went according to plan on the actual journey except for the fact that the train had to reduce speed to an average of 18 km/h for 10 minutes before picking up speed again. Assuming that the train averages 90 km/h over the rest of its journey, calculate by how many minutes the train was late.   (A.E.B. 1975)

55) A shopkeeper purchased 1020 articles for £3570 and planned to sell the articles at a profit of 20%. He sold 700 at his planned selling price and then, in a sale, reduced the selling price by 10% and sold a further 170 articles in the sale. Later, in order to get the rest of the articles off his hands, he sold the remaining articles at a greatly reduced price. When he had sold all 1020 articles, he found that he had made a total profit of £282.60. Calculate:
(a) the cost price per article to the shopkeeper;
(b) the planned selling price per article set by the shopkeeper;
(c) the sale price per article;
(d) the greatly reduced price of each article;
(e) his overall percentage profit, giving the answer correct to one place of decimals.   (A.E.B. 1976)

56) The promoter of a football pools competition takes as expenses 30% of the total money staked each week. The remainder is then divided in the ratio 7 : 5 to provide the first pool and the second pool respectively. The first "dividend" is obtained by dividing the first pool by the number of first prize winners. The second dividend is obtained by dividing the second pool by the number of second prize winners.

Calculate:
(a) the first dividend in a week when there were 15 first prize winners and the total stake money was £90 000.
(b) the expenses taken by the promoter in another week when there were 56 second prize winners who each received a second dividend of £25.

In a third week there were p first prize winners who each received a first dividend of £1000. Given that there were q second prize winners, obtain an expression for the second dividend.

(J.M.B.)

57) In 1973 the cost of building a garage was divided between materials, labour and overheads in the ratio $10 : 13 : 2$ and the garage cost £240. Calculate the respective costs of materials, labour and overheads. In 1974 the cost of materials rose by 10%, the cost of labour by 15% and the costs of overheads by 15%. Calculate the percentage increase in the cost of the garage. What percentage of this increase is due to the increase in the cost of labour? (A.E.B. 1974)

58) In 1969, A, B and C started a business in which their investments were in the proportion $4 : 7 : 9$. They agreed to distribute the profits in proportion to their investments. Calculate the amount A received if £23 000 profit was made. In 1970 and thenceforward, they agreed to accept salaries from the profit before it was shared and then distribute the balance in proportion to their investments. The salaries were to be £4000, £3000 and £2500 respectively. The profit in 1970 was again £23 000.

Calculate:
(a) the total amount each person received in 1970;
(b) the percentage gain in A's return from the business in 1970 compared with 1969 correct to 1 decimal place. In 1971 B received £6500. Calculate the total profit for that year before any salaries were paid.

(L)

59) The first £5000 of a sum of money is taxed at 30% and the remainder, if any, is taxed at 40%. Calculate:
(a) the tax on £6805;
(b) the sum on which tax is £1110;
(c) the sum on which tax is £1710.   (L)

60) A City Treasurer estimated that the City would need a rate of 82.5 p in the £ in order to provide £68 887 500 and that the cost to the rates of Family and Community Service would be 8.6 p in the £. Calculate:
(a) the estimated product of a penny rate;
(b) the percentage of the rate devoted to Family and Community Service, giving the answer correct to one place of decimals.

The Government made a grant to the City equivalent to 25.2 p in the £ so reducing the rate. Calculate:
(c) the amount of money granted to the city, giving the answer correct to the nearest ten thousand pounds.

A householder whose rateable value was £180 paid this reduced rate plus an extra amount for the water rate. If his *half-yearly* payment was £57.92, calculate the *annual* amount paid as a water rate.   (L)

Chapter 13 Squares, Square Roots and Reciprocals

SQUARES OF NUMBERS

When a number is multiplied by itself the result is called the square of the number. The square of 9 is $9 \times 9 = 81$. Instead of writing 9×9 it is usual to write 9^2 which is read as the square of 9. Thus

$$12^2 = 12 \times 12 = 144$$
$$(1.3)^2 = 1.3 \times 1.3 = 1.69$$

The square of any number can be found by multiplication but a great deal of time and effort is saved by using printed tables. Either three or four figure tables may be used. In the three figure tables the squares of numbers are given correct to three significant figures, but in the four figure tables the squares are given correct to four significant figures. Hence the four figure table are more accurate. The tables are on page 430.

Although the tables only give the squares of numbers from 1 to 10 they can be used to find the squares of numbers outside this range. The method is shown in the examples which follow.

EXAMPLE 1

Find $(168.8)^2$.

$$
\begin{aligned}
(168.8)^2 &= 168.8 \times 168.8 \\
&= 1.688 \times 100 \times 1.688 \times 100 \\
&= (1.688)^2 \times 100^2
\end{aligned}
$$

From the tables of squares,

$$(1.688)^2 = 2.848$$

Hence

$$(168.8)^2 = 2.848 \times 100^2 = 28\,480$$

EXAMPLE 2

Find $(0.2388)^2$.

$$(0.2388)^2 = 2.388 \times \frac{1}{10} \times 2.388 \times \frac{1}{10}$$

$$= (2.388)^2 \times \frac{1}{100} = (2.388)^2 \div 100$$

From the tables $(2.388)^2 = 5.702$

Hence $(0.2388)^2 = 5.702 \div 100$

$$= 0.057\,02$$

EXAMPLE 3

Find the value of $\left(\dfrac{0.9}{0.15}\right)^2$.

$$\left(\frac{0.9}{0.15}\right)^2 = 6^2 = 36$$

Exercise 61 — *Questions 1—12 type A, remainder B*

Find the square of the following numbers.

1)	1.5	11)	23
2)	2.1	12)	40.6
3)	8.6	13)	3093
4)	3.15	14)	112.3
5)	7.68	15)	98.12
6)	5.23	16)	0.019
7)	4.263	17)	0.729 2
8)	7.916	18)	0.004 219
9)	8.017	19)	0.283 4
10)	8.704	20)	0.000 578 4

21) Find the value of $(3.142)^2$ correct to 2 places of decimals.

22) Find the values of:

(a) $\left(\dfrac{0.75}{0.15}\right)^2$ (b) $\left(\dfrac{0.8}{0.2}\right)^2$

(c) $\left(\dfrac{0.25}{2}\right)^2$ (d) $\left(\dfrac{0.36}{6}\right)^2$

SQUARE ROOTS

The square root of a number is the number whose square equals the given number. Thus since $5^2 = 25$, the square root of $25 = 5$.

The sign $\sqrt{}$ is used to denote a square root and hence we write $\sqrt{25} = 5$.

Similarly, since $9^2 = 81$, $\sqrt{81} = 9$.

The square root of a number can usually be found with sufficient accuracy by using the printed tables of square roots. There are two of these tables. One gives the square roots of numbers 1 to 10 and the other gives the square roots of numbers from 10 to 100. The reason for having two tables is as follows:

$$\sqrt{2.5} = 1.581$$
$$\sqrt{25} = 5$$

Thus there are two square roots for the same figures, depending upon the position of the decimal point. The square root tables (see pages 431 and 432) are used in the same way as the table of squares.

EXAMPLE 4

(1) $\sqrt{2.748} = 1.657$ (directly from the tables from 1 to 10).

(2) $\sqrt{92.65} = 9.626$ (directly from the tables from 10 to 100).

(3) To find $\sqrt{836.3}$.

Mark off the figures in pairs to the *left* of the decimal point. Each pair of figures is called a *period*. Thus 836.3 becomes 8'36.3. The first period is 8 so we use the table of square roots from 1 to 10 and look up $\sqrt{8.363} = 2.892$. To position the decimal point in the answer remember that for each period to the left of the decimal point in the original number there will be one figure to the left of the decimal point in the answer. Thus:

$$\frac{2\ \ 8\ .92}{8'36.\ \ 3}$$

$$\sqrt{836.3} = 28.92$$

(4) To find $\sqrt{173\,900}$.

Marking off in periods 173 900 becomes 17'39'00. The first period is 17 so we use the table of square roots from 10 to 100 and look up $\sqrt{17.3900} = 4.170$.

$$\frac{4\ \ 1\ \ 7.0}{17'39'00}$$

$$\sqrt{173\,900} = 417.0$$

(5) To find $\sqrt{0.000\,094\,31}$.

In the case of numbers less than 1 mark off the periods to the right of the decimal point. 0.000 094 31 become 0.00'00'94'31. Apart from the zero pairs the first period is 94 so we use the tables from 10 to 100 to look up $\sqrt{94.31} = 9.712$. For each zero pair in the original number there will be one zero following the decimal point in the answer. Thus:

$$\frac{0.0\ \ 0\ \ 9\ \ 712}{0.00'00'94'31}$$

$$\sqrt{0.000\,094\,31} = 0.009\,712$$

(6) To find $\sqrt{0.073\,65}$.

Marking off in periods to the right of the decimal point 0.073 65 becomes 07'36'50. Since the first period is 07 we use the tables between 1 and 10 and look up $\sqrt{7.365} = 2.714$.

$$\frac{0\ \ 2\ \ 7\ \ 14}{0.07'36'50}$$

$$\sqrt{0.073\,65} = 0.271\,4$$

Exercise 62 — *Questions 1–12 type A, remainder B*

Find the square roots of the following numbers:

1) 3.4	13) 900
2) 8.19	14) 725.3
3) 5.264	15) 7142
4) 9.239	16) 89 000
5) 7.015	17) 3945
6) 3.009	18) 893 400 000
7) 35	19) 0.153 7
8) 89.2	20) 0.001 698
9) 53.17	21) 0.039 47
10) 82.99	22) 0.000 783 1
11) 79.23	23) 0.001 978
12) 50.01	

THE SQUARE ROOT OF A PRODUCT

The square root of a product is the product of the square roots. For example

$$\sqrt{4 \times 9} = \sqrt{4} \times \sqrt{9} = 2 \times 3 = 6$$

Also, $\sqrt{25 \times 16 \times 49}$

$$= \sqrt{25} \times \sqrt{16} \times \sqrt{49}$$
$$= 5 \times 4 \times 7 = 140$$

Exercise 63 — *All type A*

Find the values of the following:

1) $\sqrt{4 \times 25}$ 5) $\sqrt{16 \times 25 \times 36}$

2) $\sqrt{9 \times 25}$ 6) $\sqrt{4 \times 9 \times 25}$

3) $\sqrt{49 \times 49}$ 7) $\sqrt{36 \times 49 \times 64}$

4) $\sqrt{16 \times 36}$ 8) $\sqrt{4 \times 16 \times 25 \times 49 \times 81}$

THE SQUARE ROOT OF A FRACTION

To find the square root of a fraction, find the square roots of the numerator and denominator separately as shown in Example 5.

EXAMPLE 5

Find the square root of $\dfrac{16}{25}$.

$$\sqrt{\frac{16}{25}} = \frac{\sqrt{16}}{\sqrt{25}} = \frac{4}{5}$$

If the numbers under a square root sign are connected by a plus or a minus sign then we cannot find the square root by the methods used for products and quotients. We cannot say that $\sqrt{9 + 16} = \sqrt{9} + \sqrt{16} = 3 + 4 = 7$. We must add before finding the square root. Thus:

$$\sqrt{9 + 16} = \sqrt{25} = 5$$
and $\quad \sqrt{25 - 9} = \sqrt{16} = 4$

Exercise 64 — *Questions 1–5 type A, remainder B*

Find the square roots of the following:

1) $\dfrac{4}{9}$ 6) $\dfrac{12}{27}$ 11) $25 + 144$

2) $\dfrac{9}{16}$ 7) $\dfrac{100}{256}$ 12) $169 - 25$

3) $\dfrac{25}{49}$ 8) $\dfrac{125}{245}$ 13) $25 - 16$

4) $\dfrac{36}{81}$ 9) $\dfrac{48}{75}$ 14) $43 + 38$

5) $\dfrac{81}{100}$ 10) $\dfrac{10}{360}$ 15) $65 - 29$

ITERATIVE METHOD OF FINDING A SQUARE ROOT

When a calculating machine, which does not have a square root key, is available the square root of a real number may be found by using the following iterative formula:

$$x_{n+1} = \left(\frac{a}{x_n} + x_n \right) \div 2$$

where a is the number whose square root is to be found.

EXAMPLE 6

Using an iterative method find $\sqrt{9.61}$.

Now $\sqrt{9.61} \simeq 3$, so we use $x_0 = 3$.

$$x_1 = \left(\frac{9.61}{3} + 3 \right) \div 2 = 3.102$$

Now $(3.102)^2 = 9.622$, hence x_1 is a near approximation to $\sqrt{9.61}$. Continuing:

$$x_2 = \left(\frac{9.61}{3.102} + 3.102 \right) \div 2 = 3.100$$

Now $(3.100)^2 = 9.61$ exactly.

Hence $\qquad \sqrt{9.61} = 3.100$

EXAMPLE 7

Using an iterative method find $\sqrt{28.72}$.

Now $\sqrt{28.72} \simeq 5$.

$$x_1 = \left(\frac{28.72}{5} + 5 \right) \div 2 = 5.372$$

$$x_2 = \left(\frac{28.72}{5.372} + 5.372 \right) \div 2 = 5.359$$

x_2 is the value of $\sqrt{28.72}$ correct to 4 significant figures.

Exercise 65 — *All type B*

Using two iterations find the values of:

1) $\sqrt{1.72}$ 3) $\sqrt{8.61}$ 5) $\sqrt{76.22}$

2) $\sqrt{3.84}$ 4) $\sqrt{12.61}$ 6) $\sqrt{90.41}$

RECIPROCALS OF NUMBERS

The reciprocal of a number is $\dfrac{1}{\text{number}}$.

Thus the reciprocal of $5 = \dfrac{1}{5}$

and the reciprocal of 21.3 is $\dfrac{1}{21.3}$.

The table of reciprocals of numbers is used in much the same way as the table of squares of numbers, except that the proportional parts are subtracted and not added. The table on page 433, gives the reciprocals of numbers from 1 to 10 in decimal form.

From the tables:

the reciprocal of $\quad 6 = 0.1667$

the reciprocal of $\quad 3.157 = 0.3168$

The method of finding the reciprocals of numbers less than 1 or greater than 10 is shown in Example 8.

EXAMPLE 8

(1) To find the reciprocal of 639.2.

$$\frac{1}{639.2} = \frac{1}{6.392} \times \frac{1}{100}$$

From the table of reciprocals we find that the reciprocal of 6.392 is 0.1565.

$$\frac{1}{639.2} = 0.1565 \times \frac{1}{100}$$

$$= \frac{0.1565}{100} = 0.001565$$

(2) To find the reciprocal of 0.03982.

$$\frac{1}{0.03982} = \frac{1}{3.982} \times \frac{100}{1}$$

From the table of reciprocals we find the reciprocal of 3.982 to be 0.2512.

$$\frac{1}{0.03982} = 0.2512 \times 100 = 25.12$$

Exercise 66 — *Questions 1—5 type A,*
remainder B

Find the reciprocals of the following numbers:

1) 3.4	6) 35	11) 0.1537
2) 8.19	7) 89.2	12) 0.001698
3) 5.264	8) 53.17	13) 0.03947
4) 9.239	9) 900	14) 0.0007831
5) 7.015	10) 7142	15) 0.001978

USE OF TABLES IN CALCULATIONS

Calculations may often be speeded up by making use of the tables of squares, square roots and reciprocals.

EXAMPLE 9

Find the value of $\sqrt{(8.135)^2 + (12.36)^2}$.

By using the table of squares

$$\sqrt{(8.135)^2 + (12.36)^2}$$
$$= \sqrt{66.18 + 152.8}$$

By using the table of square roots

$$= \sqrt{218.98} = 14.80$$

EXAMPLE 10

Find the value of

$$\frac{1}{\sqrt{7.517}} + \frac{1}{(3.625)^2}.$$

By using the square and square root tables

$$\frac{1}{\sqrt{7.517}} + \frac{1}{(3.625)^2}$$

$$= \frac{1}{2.741} + \frac{1}{13.14}$$

By using the reciprocal table

$$= 0.3649 + 0.0761$$

$$= 0.4410$$

Exercise 67 — *Questions 1—6 type B,*
remainder C

Find the values of:

1) $\dfrac{1}{(15.28)^2}$ 3) $\dfrac{1}{(250)^2}$

2) $\dfrac{1}{(0.1372)^2}$ 4) $\dfrac{1}{\sqrt{8.406}}$

5) $\dfrac{1}{\sqrt{18.73}}$

6) $\dfrac{1}{\sqrt{0.01798}}$

7) $\dfrac{1}{(30.15)^2 + (8.29)^2}$

8) $\dfrac{1}{(11.26)^2 + (8.18)^2}$

9) $\sqrt{(2.65)^2 + (5.16)^2}$

10) $\sqrt{(11.18)^2 - (5.23)^2}$

11) $\dfrac{1}{8.2} + \dfrac{1}{9.9}$

12) $\dfrac{1}{0.732\,5} - \dfrac{1}{0.981\,7}$

13) $\dfrac{1}{\sqrt{7.517}} + \dfrac{1}{(8.209)^2} + \dfrac{1}{0.074\,9}$

14) $\dfrac{1}{71.36} + \dfrac{1}{\sqrt{863.5}} + \dfrac{1}{(7.589)^2}$

15) By means of tables, or otherwise, find correct to 3 decimal places the value of:

$$\dfrac{3}{2.5} + \dfrac{4}{3.5}$$

16) Given that $\dfrac{1}{18.27} = 0.054\,734\,5$ correct to 6 significant figures find the reciprocal of 3.654 correct to 5 significant figures.

SELF-TEST 13

In the following questions state the letter (or letters) corresponding to the correct answer (or answers).

1) 80^2 is equal to:
a 64   b 640   c 6400   d 6.4

2) 700^2 is equal to:
a 490 000   b 49 000   c 4900   d 490

3) 0.8^2 is equal to:
a 6.4   b 0.64   c 0.064   d 0.006 4

4) 0.09^2 is equal to:
a 0.081   b 0.008 1   c 0.81
d 0.000 81

5) $\sqrt{0.25}$ is equal to:
a 0.5   b 0.05   c 0.158   d 0.005

6) $\sqrt{0.036}$ is equal to:
a 0.6   b 0.06   c 0.189 7
d 0.018 97

7) $\sqrt{0.004\,9}$ is equal to:
a 0.7   b 0.07   c 0.221 4   d 0.022 14

8) $\sqrt{1690}$ is equal to:
a 130   b 13   c 41.11   d 411.1

9) $\sqrt{810}$ is equal to:
a 28.46   b 90   c 9   d 284.6

10) $\sqrt{12\,100}$ is equal to:
a 1100   b 110   c 347.9   d 3479

11) $\dfrac{1}{12.5}$ is equal to:

a 8   b 0.08   c 0.8   d 0.008

12) $\dfrac{1}{0.25}$ is equal to:

a 40   b 4   c 0.4   d 400

13) $\dfrac{1}{0.020}$ is equal to:

a 5   b 0.5   c 500   d 50

14) $\dfrac{1}{250}$ is equal to:

a 0.4   b 0.04   c 0.000 4   d 0.004

15) $18.3^2 - 8.3^2$ is equal to:
a 100   b 266   c 26.6   d 10

16) If $h = \dfrac{1}{u} + \dfrac{1}{v}$ then when $u = 37.17$ and $v = 1.477$ the value of h is:
a 0.703 9   b 0.945 7   c 0.094 57
d 0.070 39

17) If $p = b \sqrt{\dfrac{c}{q}}$ then when $b = 12$, $c = 4$ and $q = 16$ then p is equal to:
a 7.59   b 75.9   c 6   d 60

18) An approximate value of $\sqrt{2562.8}$ is:
a 16.2   b 50.6   c 520   d 162

19) $\dfrac{1}{0.3128}$ is equal to:

a 0.319 7   b 3.197   c 31.97
d 0.031 97

20) $(30.16)^2 + \dfrac{1}{0.047\,8}$ is equal to:

a 93.06   b 111.89   c 930.5
d 1119

Chapter 14 Directed Numbers

INTRODUCTION

Directed numbers are numbers which have either a plus or a minus sign attached to them such as $+7$ and -5. In this chapter we shall study the rules for the addition, subtraction, multiplication and division of directed numbers. We need these rules in connection with logarithms which will be dealt with in Chapter 23.

POSITIVE AND NEGATIVE NUMBERS

Fig. 14.1 shows part of a centigrade thermometer. The freezing point of water is $0°C$ (nought degrees celsius). Temperatures above freezing point may be read off the scale directly and so may those below freezing. We now have to decide on a method for showing whether a temperature is above or below zero. We may say that a temperature is 6 degrees above zero or 5 degrees below zero but these statements are not compact enough for calculations. Therefore we say that a temperature of $+6°$ is a temperature which is $6°$ above zero and a temperature of 5 degrees below zero would be written $-5°$. We have thus used the signs $+$ and $-$ to indicate a change of direction.

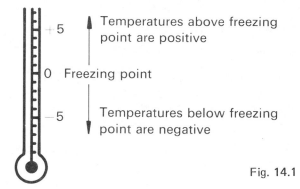

Fig. 14.1

Again if starting from a given point, distances measured to the right are regarded as being positive then distances measured to the left are regarded as being negative. As stated in the introduction, numbers which have a sign attached to them are called directed numbers. Thus $+7$ is a positive number and -7 is a negative number.

THE ADDITION OF DIRECTED NUMBERS

In Fig. 14.2 a movement from left to right (i.e. in the direction 0A) is regarded as positive, whilst a movement from right to left (i.e. in the direction 0B) is regarded as negative.

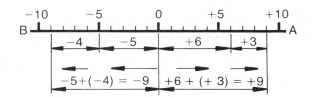

Fig. 14.2

To find the value of $+6+(+3)$
Measure 6 units to the right of 0 (Fig. 14.2) and then measure a further 3 units to the right. The final position is 9 units to the right of 0. Hence,

$$+6+(+3) = +9$$

To find the value of $-5+(-4)$
Again in Fig. 14.2, measure 5 units to the left of 0 since -5 is the opposite of $+5$. Then measure a further 4 units to the left. The final position is 9 units to the left of 0. Hence,

$$-5+(-4) = -9$$

From these results we obtain the rule:

To add several numbers together whose signs are the same add the numbers together. The sign of the sum is the same as the sign of each of the numbers.

To simplify the writing used when adding directed numbers the brackets may be omitted and the $+$ sign may also be omitted when it means "add". When the first number is positive it is usual to omit its $+$ sign.

1) $+5+(+9) = +14$.

More often this is written $5+9 = 14$.

2) $-7 + (-9) = -16$.

More often this is written $-7 - 9 = -16$.

3) $-7 - 6 - 4 = -17$.

Exercise 68 — *All type A*

Find the values of the following:

1) $+8 + 7$ 5) $-9 - 6 - 5 - 4$

2) $-7 - 5$ 6) $3 + 6 + 8 + 9$

3) $-15 - 17$ 7) $-2 - 5 - 8 - 3$

4) $8 + 6$ 8) $9 + 6 + 5 + 3$

THE ADDITION OF NUMBERS HAVING DIFFERENT SIGNS

To find the value of $-4 + 11$

Measure 4 units to the left of 0 (Fig. 14.3) and from this point measure 11 units to the right. The final position is 7 units to the right of 0. Hence,

$$-4 + 11 = 7$$

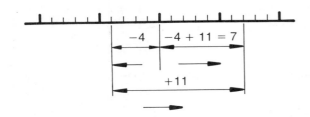

Fig. 14.3

To find the value of $8 - 15$

Measure 8 units to the right of 0 (Fig. 14.4) and from this point measure 15 units to the left. The final position is 7 units to the left of 0. Hence,

$$8 - 15 = -7$$

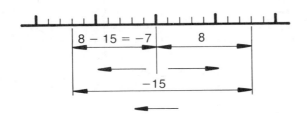

Fig. 14.4

From these results we obtain the rule:

To add two numbers together whose signs are different, subtract the numerically smaller from the larger. The sign of the result will be the same as the sign of the numerically larger number.

EXAMPLE 1

(1) $-12 + 6 = -6$

(2) $11 - 16 = -5$

When dealing with several numbers having mixed signs add the positive and negative numbers together separately. The set of numbers is then reduced to two numbers, one positive and the other negative, which are added in the way shown above.

EXAMPLE 2

$$-16 + 11 - 7 + 3 + 8$$
$$= -23 + 22 = -1$$

Exercise 69 — *All type A*

Find the values for the following:

1) $6 - 11$ 5) $-8 + 9 - 2$

2) $7 - 16$ 6) $15 - 7 - 8$

3) $-5 + 10$ 7) $23 - 21 - 8 + 2$

4) $12 - 7$ 8) $-7 + 11 - 9 - 3 + 15$

SUBTRACTION OF DIRECTED NUMBERS

To find the value of $-4 - (+7)$

To represent $+7$ we measure 7 units to the right of 0 (Fig. 14.5). Therefore to represent $-(+7)$ we must reverse direction and measure 7 units to the left of 0 and hence $-(+7)$ is the same as -7. Hence,

$$-4 - (+7) = -4 - 7 = -11$$

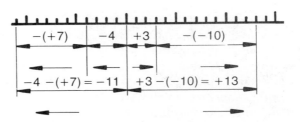

Fig. 14.5

To find the value of $+3-(-10)$

To represent -10 we measure 10 units to the left of 0 (Fig. 14.5). Therefore to represent $-(-10)$ we measure 10 units to the right of 0 and hence $-(-10)$ is the same as $+10$. Hence,

$$+3-(-10) = 3+10 = 13$$

The rule is:

To subtract a directed number change its sign and add the resulting number.

EXAMPLE 3

(1) $-10-(-6) = -10+6 = -4$

(2) $7-(+8) = 7-8 = -1$

(3) $8-(-3) = 8+3 = 11$

Exercise 70 — *All type A*

Find the values for the following:

1) $8-(+6)$ 5) $-4-(-5)$

2) $-5-(-8)$ 6) $-2-(+3)$

3) $8-(-6)$ 7) $-10-(-5)$

4) $-3-(-7)$ 8) $7-(-9)$

MULTIPLICATION OF DIRECTED NUMBERS

Now $5+5+5 = 15$

That is, $3 \times 5 = 15$

Thus two positive numbers multiplied together give a positive product.

Now $(-5)+(-5)+(-5) = -15$

$$3 \times (-5) = -15$$

Thus a positive number multiplied by a negative number gives a negative product.

Suppose, now, that we wish to find the value of $(-3) \times (-5)$. We can write (-3) as $-(+3)$ and hence:

$$(-3) \times (-5) = -(+3) \times (-5)$$
$$= -(-15) = +15$$

Thus a negative number multiplied by a negative number gives a positive product.

We may summarise the above results as follows:

$(+) \times (+) = (+)$ $(-) \times (+) = (-)$

$(+) \times (-) = (-)$ $(-) \times (-) = (+)$

and the rule is:

The product of two numbers with like signs is positive whilst the product of two numbers with unlike signs is negative.

EXAMPLE 4

(1) $7 \times 4 = 28$

(2) $7 \times (-4) = -28$

(3) $(-7) \times 4 = -28$

(4) $(-7) \times (-4) = 28$

Exercise 71 — *All type A*

Find the values of the following:

1) $7 \times (-6)$ 5) $(-2) \times (-4) \times (-6)$

2) $(-6) \times 7$ 6) $(-2)^2$

3) 7×6 7) $3 \times (-4) \times (-2) \times 5$

4) $(-7) \times (-6)$ 8) $(-3)^2$

DIVISION OF DIRECTED NUMBERS

The rules for division must be very similar to those used for multiplication, since if $3 \times (-5) = -15$,   then

$$\frac{-15}{3} = -5. \quad \text{Also} \quad \frac{-15}{-5} = 3.$$

The rule is:

When dividing, numbers with like signs give a positive quotient and numbers with unlike signs give a negative quotient.

The rule may be summarised as follows:

$(+) \div (+) = (+)$ $(+) \div (-) = (-)$

$(-) \div (+) = (-)$ $(-) \div (-) = (+)$

EXAMPLE 5

(1) $\dfrac{20}{4} = 5$ (3) $\dfrac{-20}{4} = -5$

(2) $\dfrac{20}{-4} = -5$ (4) $\dfrac{-20}{-4} = 5$

(5) $\dfrac{(-9) \times (-4) \times 5}{3 \times (-2)} = \dfrac{36 \times 5}{-6}$

$$= \frac{180}{-6} = -30$$

1) $6 \div (-2)$

2) $(-6) \div 2$

3) $(-6) \div (-2)$

4) $6 \div 2$

5) $(-10) \div 5$

6) $1 \div (-1)$

7) $(-4) \div (-2)$

8) $(-3) \div 3$

9) $8 \div (-4)$

10) $\dfrac{(-6) \times 4}{(-2)}$

11) $\dfrac{(-8)}{(1) \times (-4) \times (-2)}$

12) $\dfrac{(-3) \times (-4) \times (-2)}{3 \times 4}$

13) $\dfrac{4 \times (-6) \times (-8)}{(1-3) \times (-2) \times (-4)}$

14) $\dfrac{5 \times (-3) \times 6}{10 \times 3}$

TYPES OF NUMBERS

Whole numbers are called *natural numbers*. They are also called *counting numbers*. Thus the numbers $1, 2, 3, \ldots 17, 18, 19, \ldots$ etc. are natural or counting numbers.

Integers are whole numbers but they include zero and negative numbers. Thus, $-15, -8, 0, 2$ and 137 are all integers.

Rational numbers are numbers which can be expressed as a vulgar fraction. Thus 0.625 is a rational number because it can be written $\frac{5}{8}$. Recurring decimals are all rational because they can be converted into fractions. Thus:

$$0.\dot{1} = \frac{1}{9}$$

$$0.0\dot{1} = \frac{1}{99}$$

$$0.\dot{7}\dot{3} = \frac{73}{99}$$

$$0.00\dot{7}\dot{3} = \frac{73}{9900}$$

$$0.\dot{6}4\dot{7} = \frac{647}{999} \text{ etc.}$$

Irrational numbers cannot be expressed as a fraction. Consider $\sqrt{2}$. Since $1 \times 1 = 1$ and $2 \times 2 = 4$ the value of $\sqrt{2}$ lies between 1 and 2. Some fractions are very close to the exact value of $\sqrt{2}$, for instance:

$$\frac{7}{5} \times \frac{7}{5} = \frac{49}{25} = 1.96$$

$$\frac{71}{50} \times \frac{71}{50} = \frac{5041}{2500} = 2.016\,4$$

$$\frac{707}{500} \times \frac{707}{500} = \frac{499\,849}{250\,000} = 1.999\,396$$

However, it is impossible to find a fraction, which when multiplied by itself gives exactly 2. Hence $\sqrt{2}$ is an irrational number. Similarly $\sqrt{3}$, $\sqrt{5}$ and $\sqrt{7}$ are all irrational numbers. Not all square roots are irrational numbers. For instance $\sqrt{9}$ is not irrational because it equals 3. $\sqrt{2.25} = 1.5$ and hence $\sqrt{2.25}$ is rational because $1.5 = \frac{3}{2}$.

Imaginary numbers. Numbers like $\sqrt{-1}$, $\sqrt{-4}$, $\sqrt{-11}$, etc. have no real meaning. $1 \times 1 = 1$ and $(-1) \times (-1) = 1$ and hence it is impossible to find the value of $\sqrt{-1}$. Similarly, it is not possible to find $\sqrt{-4}$ or the square root of any negative number. The square root of a negative number is said to be an imaginary number. Numbers which are not imaginary are said to be *real*. Thus $\sqrt{16} = 4$ and $\sqrt{1.849\,6} = 1.36$ are *real rational numbers*. A number like $\sqrt{13}$ is called a *real irrational number*.

1) Which of the following are positive integers?
$5, -8, \frac{2}{3}, 1\frac{1}{2}, 2.75$ and 198.

2) Which of the following are negative integers?
$8\frac{1}{2}, -9, 7, -\frac{1}{3}$ and $-4\frac{3}{4}$.

3) Which of the following are rational and which are irrational?
$1.57, \frac{1}{4}, -5.625, \sqrt{9}, \sqrt{15}, 6.76$ and $-3\frac{1}{2}$.

4) Which of the following are real numbers?
$9.578\,2, -7.38, \sqrt{8}, \sqrt{-4}, 7\frac{2}{3}$ and $\sqrt{-5}$.

SEQUENCES OF NUMBERS

A set of numbers connected by some definite law is called a *sequence* or a *series*. Some examples are:

$3, 1, -1, -3$ (each number is 2 less than the preceding number).

$1, 4, 9, 16$ (squares of successive integers: $1^2 = 1$, $2^2 = 4$, etc.)

$2, 1, \frac{1}{2}, \frac{1}{4}$ (each number is $\frac{1}{2}$ of the preceding number).

Exercise 74 — *All type A*

Write down the next two terms of each of the following sequences:

1) $1, 4, 7, 10 \ldots$

2) $5, 11, 17, 23, \ldots$

3) $2, 0, -2, -4, \ldots$

4) $-5, -3, -1, 1, \ldots$

5) $\frac{3}{4}, \frac{1}{4}, \frac{1}{12}, \frac{1}{36}, \ldots$

6) $16, 25, 36, 49, \ldots$

7) $2, -2, 2, -2, \ldots$

8) $1.2, 1.44, 1.728, \ldots$

9) $3, -1.5, 0.75, -0.375, \ldots$

10) $1.1, -1.21, 1.331, \ldots$

SELF-TEST 14

In the following questions state the letter (or letters) corresponding to the correct answer (or answers).

1) $(-2) \times (-3)$ is equal to:

a -6 b $+6$ c -5 d $+5$

2) The value of $(+4)(-2) - (-2)$ is:

a -6 b -4 c $+4$ d $+6$

3) The value of $(-3)^2$ is:

a $+6$ b -6 c -9 d $+9$

4) $(-4) \times (-3)$ is equal to:

a -7 b $+7$ c -12 d $+12$

5) The value of $-6 - (-6)$ is:

a -12 b 0 c 12 d 36

6) Which of the following is a rational number?

a $\sqrt{6}$ b $\sqrt{3}$ c $\sqrt{2}$ d $\sqrt{4}$

7) The next number in the series $3, -1, \frac{1}{3}, -\frac{1}{9}$ is:

a $-\frac{1}{27}$ b $\frac{1}{27}$ c $\frac{2}{9}$ d $-\frac{2}{9}$

8) One of the following is an irrational number. Which?

a -5 b $\sqrt{-6}$ c $\sqrt{5}$ d $\sqrt{9}$

Chapter 15 Basic Algebra

INTRODUCTION

The methods of algebra are an extension of those used in arithmetic. In algebra we use letters and symbols as well as numbers to represent quantities. When we write that a sum of money is £50 we are making a *particular statement* but if we write that a sum of money is £P we are making a *general statement.* This general statement will cover any number we care to substitute for P.

USE OF SYMBOLS

The following examples will show how verbal statements can be translated into algebraic symbols. Notice that we can choose any symbol we like to represent the quantities concerned.

(1) The sum of two numbers.
Let the two numbers be x and y.
Sum of the two numbers = x + y.

(2) Three times a number.
Let the number be N.
Three times the number = 3 × N.

(3) One number divided by another number.
Let one number be a and the other number be b.
One number divided by another number
$= \dfrac{a}{b}$.

(4) Five times the product of two numbers.
Let the two numbers be m and n.
5 times the product of the two numbers
$= 5 \times m \times n$.

Exercise 75 – *All type A*

Translate the following into algebraic symbols:

1) Seven times a number, x.

2) Four times a number x minus three.

3) Five times a number x plus a second number, y.

4) The sum of two numbers x and y divided by a third number, z.

5) Half of a number, x.

6) Eight times the product of three numbers, x, y and z.

7) The product of two numbers x and y divided by a third number, z.

8) Three times a number, x, minus four times a second number, y.

SUBSTITUTION

The process of finding the numerical value of an algebraic expression for given values of the symbols that appear in it is called *substitution.*

EXAMPLE 1

If $x = 3$, $y = 4$ and $z = 5$ find the values of:

(a) $2y + 4$ (b) $3y + 5z$

(c) $8 - x$ (d) $\dfrac{y}{x}$

(e) $\dfrac{3y + 2z}{x + z}$.

Note that multiplication signs are often missed out when writing algebraic expressions so that, for instance, $2y$ means $2 \times y$. These missed multiplication signs must reappear when the numbers are substituted for the symbols.

(a) $2y + 4 = 2 \times 4 + 4 = 8 + 4 = 12$

(b) $3y + 5z = 3 \times 4 + 5 \times 5$
$= 12 + 25 = 37$

(c) $8 - x = 8 - 3 = 5$

(d) $\dfrac{y}{x} = \dfrac{4}{3} = 1\dfrac{1}{3}$

(e) $\dfrac{3y + 2z}{x + z} = \dfrac{3 \times 4 + 2 \times 5}{3 + 5}$
$= \dfrac{12 + 10}{8} = \dfrac{22}{8} = 2\dfrac{3}{4}$

If $a = 2$, $b = 3$ and $c = 5$ find the values of the following:

1) $a + 7$ 10) $4c + 6b$

2) $c - 2$ 11) $8c - 7$

3) $6 - b$ 12) $a + 2b + 5c$

4) $6b$ 13) $8c - 4b$

5) $9c$ 14) $2 \div a$

6) ab 15) $\dfrac{ab}{8}$

7) $3bc$ 16) $\dfrac{abc}{6}$

8) abc 17) $\dfrac{2c}{a}$

9) $5c - 2$ 18) $\dfrac{5a + 9b + 8c}{a + b + c}$

POWERS

The quantity $a \times a \times a$ or aaa is usually written as a^3. a^3 is called the third power of a. The number 3 which indicates the number of a's to be multiplied together is called the *index* (plural: *indices*).

$$2^4 = 2 \times 2 \times 2 \times 2 = 16$$
$$y^5 = y \times y \times y \times y \times y$$

EXAMPLE 2
Find the value of b^3 when $b = 5$.

$$b^3 = 5^3 = 5 \times 5 \times 5 = 125$$

When dealing with expressions like $8mn^4$ note that it is only the symbol n which is raised to the fourth power. Thus:

$$8mn^4 = 8 \times m \times n \times n \times n \times n$$

EXAMPLE 3
Find the value of $7p^2 q^3$ when $p = 5$ and $q = 4$.

$$7p^2 q^3 = 7 \times 5^2 \times 4^3 = 7 \times 25 \times 64$$
$$= 11\,200$$

Exercise 77 — *All type A*

If $a = 2$, $b = 3$ and $c = 4$ find the values of the following:

1) a^2 5) $ab^2 c^3$ 9) $\dfrac{3a^4}{c^2}$

2) b^4 6) $5a^2 + 6b^2$ 10) $\dfrac{c^5}{ab^3}$

3) ab^3 7) $a^2 + c^2$

4) $2a^2 c$ 8) $7b^3 c^2$

ADDITION OF ALGEBRAIC TERMS

Like terms are numerical multiples of the same algebraic quantity. Thus:

$$7x, \ 5x \ \text{and} \ -3x$$

are three like terms.

An expression consisting of like terms can be reduced to a single term by adding the numerical coefficients together. Thus:

$$7x - 5x + 3x = (7 - 5 + 3)x = 5x$$
$$3b^2 + 7b^2 = (3 + 7)b^2 = 10b^2$$
$$-3y - 5y = (-3 - 5)y = -8y$$
$$q - 3q = (1 - 3)q = -2q$$

Only like terms can be added or subtracted. Thus $7a + 3b - 2c$ is an expression containing three unlike terms and it cannot be simplified any further. Similarly with $8a^2 b + 7ab^3 + 6a^2 b^2$ which are all unlike terms.

It is possible to have several sets of like terms in an expression and each set can then be simplified:

$$8x + 3y - 4z - 5x + 7z - 2y + 2z$$
$$= (8 - 5)x + (3 - 2)y + (-4 + 7 + 2)z$$
$$= 3x + y + 5z$$

MULTIPLICATION AND DIVISION OF ALGEBRAIC QUANTITIES

The rules are exactly the same as those used with directed numbers:

$$(+x)(+y) = +(xy) = +xy = xy$$
$$5x \times 3y = 5 \times 3 \times x \times y = 15xy$$
$$(x)(-y) = -(xy) = -xy$$
$$(2x)(-3y) = -(2x)(3y) = -6xy$$
$$(-4x)(2y) = -(4x)(2y) = -8xy$$
$$(-3x)(-2y) = +(3x)(2y) = 6xy$$

$$\frac{+x}{+y} = +\frac{x}{y} = \frac{x}{y}$$

$$\frac{-3x}{2y} = -\frac{3x}{2y}$$

$$\frac{-5x}{-6y} = +\frac{5x}{6y} = \frac{5x}{6y}$$

$$\frac{4x}{-3y} = -\frac{4x}{3y}$$

When *multiplying* expressions containing the same symbols, indices are used:

$$m \times m = m^2$$

$$3m \times 5m = 3 \times m \times 5 \times m = 15m^2$$

$$(-m) \times m^2 = (-m) \times m \times m = -m^3$$

$$5m^2 n \times 3mn^3$$
$$= 5 \times m \times m \times n \times 3 \times m \times n \times n \times n$$
$$= 15m^3 n^4$$

$$3mn \times (-2n^2)$$
$$= 3 \times m \times n \times (-2) \times n \times n = -6mn^3$$

When *dividing* algebraic expressions, cancellation between numerator and denominator is often possible. Cancelling is equivalent to dividing both numerator and denominator by the same quantity:

$$\frac{pq}{p} = \frac{p \times q}{p} = q$$

$$\frac{3p^2 q}{6pq^2} = \frac{3 \times p \times p \times q}{6 \times p \times q \times q} = \frac{3p}{6q} = \frac{p}{2q}$$

$$\frac{18x^2 y^2 z}{6xyz} = \frac{18 \times x \times x \times y \times y \times z}{6 \times x \times y \times z} = 3xy$$

Exercise 78 — *All type A*

Simplify the following:

1) $7x + 11x$

2) $7x - 5x$

3) $3x - 6x$

4) $-2x - 4x$

5) $-8x + 3x$

6) $-2x + 7x$

7) $8a - 6a - 7a$

8) $5m + 13m - 6m$

9) $6b^2 - 4b^2 + 3b^2$

10) $6ab - 3ab - 2ab$

11) $14xy + 5xy - 7xy + 2xy$

12) $-5x + 7x - 3x - 2x$

13) $-4x^2 - 3x^2 + 2x^2 - x^2$

14) $3x - 2y + 4z - 2x - 3y + 5z + 6x + 2y - 3z$

15) $3a^2 b + 2ab^3 + 4a^2 b^2 - 5ab^3 + 11b^4 + 6a^2 b$

16) $1.2x^3 - 3.4x^2 + 2.6x + 3.7x^2 + 3.6x - 2.8$

17) $pq + 2.1qr - 2.2rq + 8qp$

18) $2.6a^2 b^2 - 3.4b^3 - 2.7a^3 - 3a^2 b^2 - 2.1b^3 + 1.5a^3$

19) $2x \times 5y$

20) $3a \times 4b$

21) $3 \times 4m$

22) $\frac{1}{4}q \times 16p$

23) $x \times (-y)$

24) $(-3a) \times (-2b)$

25) $8m \times (-3n)$

26) $(-4a) \times 3b$

27) $8p \times (-q) \times (-3r)$

28) $3a \times (-4b) \times (-c) \times 5d$

29) $12x \div 6$

30) $4a \div (-7b)$

31) $(-5a) \div 8b$

32) $(-3a) \div (-3b)$

33) $4a \div 2b$

34) $4ab \div 2a$

35) $12x^2 yz^2 \div 4xz^2$

36) $(-12a^2 b) \div 6a$

37) $8a^2 bc^2 \div 4ac^2$

38) $7a^2 b^2 \div 3ab$

39) $a \times a$

40) $b \times (-b)$

41) $(-m) \times m$

42) $(-p) \times (-p)$

43) $3a \times 2a$

44) $5X \times X$

45) $5q \times (-3q)$

46) $3m \times (-3m)$

47) $(-3pq) \times (-3q)$

48) $8mn \times (-3m^2n^3)$

49) $7ab \times (-3a^2)$

50) $2q^3r^4 \times 5qr^2$

51) $(-3m) \times 2n \times (-5p)$

52) $5a^2 \times (-3b) \times 5ab$

53) $m^2n \times (-mn) \times 5m^2n^2$

BRACKETS

Brackets are used for convenience in grouping terms together. When removing brackets each term within the bracket is multiplied by the quantity outside the bracket:

$$3(x + y) = 3x + 3y$$

$$5(2x + 3y) = 5 \times 2x + 5 \times 3y = 10x + 15y$$

$$4(a - 2b) = 4 \times a - 4 \times 2b = 4a - 8b$$

$$m(a + b) = ma + mb$$

$$3x(2p + 3q) = 3x \times 2p + 3x \times 3q = 6px + 9qx$$

$$4a(2a + b) = 4a \times 2a + 4a \times b = 8a^2 + 4ab$$

When a bracket has a minus sign in front of it, the signs of all the terms inside the bracket are changed when the bracket is removed. The reason for this rule may be seen from the following example:

$$-3(2x - 5y) = (-3) \times 2x + (-3) \times (-5y)$$
$$= -6x + 15y$$

$$-(m + n) = -m - n$$

$$-(p - q) = -p + q$$

$$-2(p + 3q) = -2p - 6q$$

When simplifying expressions containing brackets first remove the brackets and then add the like terms together:

$$(3x + 7y) - (4x + 3y) = 3x + 7y - 4x - 3y$$
$$= -x + 4y$$

$$3(2x + 3y) - (x + 5y) = 6x + 9y - x - 5y$$
$$= 5x + 4y$$

$$x(a + b) - x(a + 3b) = ax + bx - ax - 3bx$$
$$= -2bx$$

$$2(5a + 3b) + 3(a - 2b) = 10a + 6b + 3a - 6b$$
$$= 13a$$

Exercise 79 — *Questions 1–20 type A*
remainder B

Remove the brackets in the following:

1) $3(x + 4)$ 9) $-(3p - 3q)$

2) $2(a + b)$ 10) $-(7m - 6)$

3) $3(3x + 2y)$ 11) $-4(x + 3)$

4) $\frac{1}{2}(x - 1)$ 12) $-2(2x - 5)$

5) $5(2p - 3q)$ 13) $-5(4 - 3x)$

6) $7(a - 3m)$ 14) $2k(k - 5)$

7) $-(a + b)$ 15) $-3y(3x + 4)$

8) $-(a - 2b)$ 16) $a(p - q - r)$

17) $4xy(ab - ac + d)$

18) $3x^2(x^2 - 2xy + y^2)$

19) $-7P(2P^2 - P + 1)$

20) $-2m(-1 + 3m - 2n)$

Remove the brackets and simplify:

21) $3(x + 1) + 2(x + 4)$

22) $5(2a + 4) - 3(4a + 2)$

23) $3(x + 4) - (2x + 5)$

24) $4(1 - 2x) - 3(3x - 4)$

25) $5(2x - y) - 3(x + 2y)$

26) $\frac{1}{2}(y - 1) + \frac{1}{3}(2y - 3)$

27) $-(4a + 5b - 3c) - 2(2a + 3b - 4c)$

28) $2x(x - 5) - x(x - 2) - 3x(x - 5)$

29) $3(a - b) - 2(2a - 3b) + 4(a - 3b)$

30) $3x(x^2 + 7x - 1) - 2x(2x^2 + 3) - 3(x^2 + 5)$

SELF-TEST 15

In questions 1 to 38 the answer is either 'true' or 'false', state which.

1) The sum of two numbers can be represented by the expression $a + b$.

2) The expression $a - b$ represents the difference of two numbers a and b.

3) The product of 8 and x is $8 + x$.

4) 3 times a number minus 7 can be written as $3x - 7$.

5) Two numbers added together minus a third number and the result divided by a fourth number may be written as $(a + b - c) \div d$.

6) The value of $3a + 7$ when $a = 5$ is 36.

7) The value of $8x - 3$ when $x = 3$ is 21.

8) The value of $3b - 2c$ when $b = 4$ and $c = 3$ is 6.

9) The value of $8ab \div 3c$ when $a = 6$, $b = 4$ and $c = 2$ is 32.

10) The quantity $a \times a \times a \times a$ is written a^3.

11) The quantity $y \times y \times y$ is written y^3.

12) $a^3 b^2$ is equal to $a \times a \times a \times b \times b$.

13) The value of a^4 when $a = 3$ is 81.

14) When $x = 2$, $y = 3$ and $z = 4$ the value of $2x^2 y^3 z$ is 258.

15) $5x + 8x$ is equal to $13x^2$.

16) $3x + 6x$ is equal to $9x$.

17) $8x - 5x$ is equal to 3.

18) $7x - 2x$ is equal to $5x$.

19) $15xy + 7xy - 3xy - 2xy$ is equal to $17xy$.

20) $8a \times 5a$ is equal to $40a$.

21) $9x \times 5x$ is equal to $45x^2$.

22) $(-5x) \times (-8x) \times 3x$ is equal to $120x^3$.

23) $a^2 b$ is the same as ba^2.

24) $5x^3 y^2 z$ is the same as $5y^2 zx^3$.

25) $8a^3 b^2 c^4$ and $16a^3 b^3 c^3$ are like terms.

26) $6x^2 \div (-3x)$ is equal to $3x$.

27) $(-5pq^2) \times (-8p^2 q)$ is equal to $40p^3 q^3$.

28) $a^2 b^2 \times (-a^2 b^2) \times 5a^2 b^2$ is equal to $5a^2 b^2$.

29) $3(2x + 7)$ is equal to $6x + 7$.

30) $5(3x + 4)$ is equal to $15x + 20$.

31) $4(x + 8)$ is equal to $4x + 32$.

32) $-(3x + 5y)$ is equal to $-3x + 5y$.

33) $-(2a + 3b)$ is equal to $-2a - 3b$.

34) $4x(3x - 2xy)$ is equal to $12x^2 - 8x^2 y$.

35) $-8a(a - 3b)$ is equal to $-8a^2 - 24ab$.

36) $3(x - y) - 5(2x - 3y)$ is equal to $12y - 7x$.

37) $2x(x - 2) - 3x(x^2 - 5)$ is equal to $-3x^3 + 2x^2 - 19x$.

38) $3a(2a^2 + 3a - 1) - 2a(3a^2 + 3)$ is equal to $9a^2 + 3a$.

76

Chapter 16 Factorisation

FACTORISING

The expression $3x + 3y$ has the number 3 common to both terms.

$3x + 3y = 3(x + y)$; 3 and $(x + y)$ are said to be *the factors of* $3x + 3y$.

To factorise $2x + 6$ we note that 2 is common to both terms. We place 2 outside the bracket. To find the terms inside the bracket divide each of the terms making up the expression by 2. Thus:

$$2x + 6 = 2(x + 3)$$

$$5x^2 - 10x = 5x(x - 2)$$

Exercise 80 — *All type B*

Factorise the following:

1) $4x + 4y$
2) $5x - 10$
3) $4x - 6xy$
4) $mx - my$
5) $5a - 10b + 15c$
6) $3y - 9y^2$
7) $ab^3 - ab$
8) $3x^2 - 6x$
9) $7a - 14b$
10) $36a^2 - 9a$

HIGHEST COMMON FACTOR (H.C.F.)

The H.C.F. of a set of algebraic expressions is the highest expression which is a factor of each of the given expressions. To find the H.C.F. we therefore select the lowest power of each of the quantities which occur in *all* of the expressions and multiply them together. The method is shown in the following examples.

EXAMPLE 1
(1) Find the H.C.F. of $ab^2c^2, a^2b^3c^3, a^2b^4c^4$.

Each expression contains the quantities a, b and c. To find the H.C.F. choose the *lowest* power of each of the quantities which occur in the three expressions and multiply them together. The lowest power of a is a, the lowest power of b is b^2 and the lowest power of c is c^2. Thus:

$$\text{H.C.F.} = ab^2c^2$$

(2) Find the H.C.F. of $x^2y^3, x^3y^2z^2, xy^2z^3$.

We notice that only x and y appear in all three expressions. The quantity z appears in only two of the expressions and cannot therefore appear in the H.C.F. To find the H.C.F. choose the lowest powers of x and y which occur in the three expressions and multiply them together. Thus:

$$\text{H.C.F.} = xy^2$$

(3) Find the H.C.F. of $3m^2np^3, 6m^3n^2p^2, 24m^3p^4$.

Dealing with the numerical coefficients 3, 6 and 24 we note that 3 is a factor of each of them. The quantities m and p occur in all three expressions, their lowest powers being m^2 and p^2. Hence:

$$\text{H.C.F.} = 3m^2p^2$$

More difficult algebraic expressions may be factorised by finding the H.C.F. of all the terms making up the expression.

EXAMPLE 2
Find the factors of $m^2n - 2mn^2$.

The H.C.F. of m^2n and $2mn^2$ is mn.

$\therefore \qquad m^2n - 2mn^2 = mn(m - 2n)$

$\left(\text{since} \quad \dfrac{m^2n}{mn} = m \quad \text{and} \quad \dfrac{2mn^2}{mn} = 2n \right).$

EXAMPLE 3
Find the factors of $3x^4y + 9x^3y^2 - 6x^2y^3$.

The H.C.F. of $3x^4y, 9x^3y^2$ and $6x^2y^3$ is $3x^2y$.

$\therefore \qquad 3x^4y + 9x^3y^2 - 6x^2y^3$

$\qquad = 3x^2y(x^2 + 3xy - 2y^2)$

$$\left(\text{since } \frac{3x^4 y}{3x^2 y} = x^2, \quad \frac{9x^3 y^2}{3x^2 y} = 3xy\right.$$

$$\left.\text{and } \frac{6x^2 y^3}{3x^2 y} = 2y^2\right).$$

EXAMPLE 4

Find the factors of $\dfrac{ac}{x} + \dfrac{bc}{x^2} - \dfrac{cd}{x^3}$.

The H.C.F. of $\dfrac{ac}{x}$, $\dfrac{bc}{x^2}$ and $\dfrac{cd}{x^3}$ is $\dfrac{c}{x}$

$$\therefore \quad \frac{ac}{x} + \frac{bc}{x^2} - \frac{cd}{x^3} = \frac{c}{x}\left(a + \frac{b}{x} - \frac{d}{x^2}\right)$$

$$\left(\text{since } \frac{ac}{x} \div \frac{c}{x} = a, \quad \frac{bc}{x^2} \div \frac{c}{x} = \frac{b}{x}\right.$$

$$\left.\text{and } \frac{cd}{x^3} \div \frac{c}{x} = \frac{d}{x^2}\right).$$

Exercise 81 — *Questions 1–12 type B, remainder C*

Find the H.C.F. of the following:

1) $p^3 q^2, p^2 q^3, p^2 q$

2) $a^2 b^3 c^3, a^3 b^3, ab^2 c^2$

3) $3mn^2, 6mnp, 12m^2 np^2$

4) $2ab, 5b, 7ab^2$

5) $3x^2 yz, 12x^2 yz, 6xy^2 z^3, 3xyz^2$

Factorise the following:

6) $x^2 y^2 - axy + bxy^2$

7) $5x^3 - 10x^2 y + 15xy^2$

8) $9x^3 y - 6x^2 y^2 + 3xy^5$

9) $\dfrac{x}{3} - \dfrac{y}{6} + \dfrac{z}{9}$

10) $I_0 + I_0 \alpha t$

11) $2a^2 - 3ab + b^2$

12) $x^3 - x^2 + 7x$

13) $\dfrac{m^2}{pn} - \dfrac{m^3}{pn^2} + \dfrac{m^4}{p^2 n^2}$

14) $\dfrac{x^2 y}{2a} - \dfrac{2xy^2}{5a^2} + \dfrac{xy^3}{a^3}$

15) $\dfrac{l^2 m^2}{15} - \dfrac{l^2 m}{20} + \dfrac{l^3 m^2}{10}$

16) $\dfrac{a^3}{2x^3} - \dfrac{a^2 b}{4x^4} - \dfrac{a^2 c}{6x^3}$

78

THE PRODUCT OF TWO BINOMIAL EXPRESSIONS

A binomial expression consists of *two terms*. Thus $3x + 5$, $a + b$, $2x + 3y$ and $4p - q$ are all binomial expressions.

To find the product of $(a + b)(c + d)$ consider the diagram (Fig. 16.1).

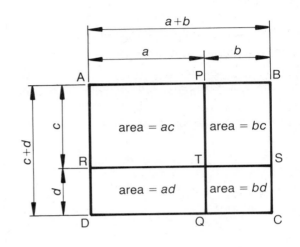

Fig. 16.1

In Fig. 16.1 the rectangular area ABCD is made up as follows:

$$ABCD = APTR + TQDR + PBST + STQC$$

i.e. $(a + b)(c + d) = ac + ad + bc + bd$

It will be noticed that the expression on the right hand side is obtained by multiplying each term in the one bracket by each term in the *other* bracket. The process is illustrated below where each pair of terms connected by a line are multiplied together.

$$(a + b)(c + d) = ac + ad + bc + bd$$

$$\begin{aligned}(3x + 2)(x + 4) &= (3x)(x) + (3x)(4) \\ &\quad + (2)(x) + (2)(4) \\ &= 3x^2 + 12x + 2x + 8 \\ &= 3x^2 + 14x + 8\end{aligned}$$

$$\begin{aligned}(2p - 3)(3p - 4) &= (2p)(3p) + (2p)(-4) \\ &\quad + (-3)(3p) + (-3)(-4) \\ &= 6p^2 - 8p - 9p + 12 \\ &= 6p^2 - 17p + 12\end{aligned}$$

Exercise 82 — *All type B*

Remove the brackets from the following:

1) $(x + 1)(x + 3)$

2) $(2x + 5)(x + 3)$

3) $(5x - 2)(2x + 4)$

4) $(a + 3)(a - 6)$

5) $(3x + 1)(2x - 5)$

6) $(x - 2)(x - 3)$

7) $(4x - 1)(2x - 3)$

8) $(x - 1)(x + 1)$

9) $(2x - 3)(2x + 3)$

10) $(x - 4)(2x + 5)$

FACTORISING BY GROUPING

To factorise the expression $ax + ay + bx + by$ first group the terms in pairs so that each pair of terms has a common factor. Thus:

$$ax + ay + bx + by = (ax + ay) + (bx + by)$$
$$= a(x + y) + b(x + y)$$

Now notice that in the two terms $a(x + y)$ and $b(x + y)$, $(x + y)$ is a common factor. Hence,

$$a(x + y) + b(x + y) = (x + y)(a + b)$$
$$\therefore \quad ax + ay + bx + by = (x + y)(a + b)$$

Similarly,

$$np + mp - qn - qm = (np + mp) - (qn + qm)$$
$$= p(n + m) - q(n + m)$$
$$= (n + m)(p - q)$$

Exercise 83 — *All type C*

Factorise the following:

1) $ax + by + bx + ay$

2) $mp + np - mq - nq$

3) $a^2c^2 + acd + acd + d^2$

4) $2pr - 4ps + qr - 2qs$

5) $4ax + 6ay - 4bx - 6by$

6) $ab(x^2 + y^2) - cd(x^2 + y^2)$

7) $mn(3x - 1) - pq(3x - 1)$

8) $k^2l^2 - mnl - k^2l + mn$

FACTORS OF QUADRATIC EXPRESSIONS

A quadratic expression is an expression in which the highest power of the symbol used is 2. Thus:

$$x^2 - 5x + 7 \quad \text{and} \quad 3a^2 + 2a - 5$$

are both quadratic expressions.

(a) Factorising when the coefficient of the squared term is 1.

$$(x + 3)(x + 2) = x^2 + 5x + 6$$

Note that the factors of 6 are 3 and 2. The coefficient of x is 5 which equals the factors of 6 added together (i.e. $3 + 2 = 5$). This example gives a clue as to how we factorise quadratic expressions.

EXAMPLE 5

(1) Factorise $x^2 + 7x + 12$.

We see that $12 = 4 \times 3$ and that $7 = 4 + 3$.

Hence $(x^2 + 7x + 12) = (x + 4)(x + 3)$

(2) Factorise $x^2 - 2x - 3$.

We see that $-3 = (-3) \times 1$ and that $-3 + 1 = -2$.

Hence $x^2 - 2x - 3 = (x - 3)(x + 1)$

(b) Factorising where the coefficient of the squared term is not 1. In this case we find all the possible factors of the first and last terms. Then by trying all the possible combinations, the combination of factors which gives the correct middle term is found.

EXAMPLE 6

Factorise $12x^2 + 11x - 15$.

Factors of $12x^2$		Factors of -15	
$12x$	x	-15	$+1$
$6x$	$2x$	$+1$	-15
$3x$	$4x$	-5	$+3$
		$+5$	-3

The combinations of these factors are:

$$(12x - 15)(x + 1) = 12x^2 - 3x - 15$$
which is incorrect

$$(12x + 1)(x - 15) = 12x^2 - 179x - 15$$
which is incorrect

$$(12x - 5)(x + 3) = 12x^2 + 31x - 15$$
which is incorrect

$$(12x + 5)(x - 3) = 12x^2 - 31x - 15$$
which is incorrect

$$(6x - 15)(2x + 1) = 12x^2 - 24x - 15$$
which is incorrect

$$(6x + 1)(2x - 15) = 12x^2 - 88x - 15$$
$$\text{which is incorrect}$$
$$(6x - 5)(2x + 3) = 12x^2 + 8x - 15$$
$$\text{which is incorrect}$$
$$(6x + 5)(2x - 3) = 12x^2 - 8x - 15$$
$$\text{which is incorrect}$$
$$(3x - 15)(4x + 1) = 12x^2 - 57x - 15$$
$$\text{which is incorrect}$$
$$(3x + 1)(4x - 15) = 12x^2 - 41x - 15$$
$$\text{which is incorrect}$$
$$(3x - 5)(4x + 3) = 12x^2 - 11x - 15$$
$$\text{which is incorrect}$$
$$(3x + 5)(4x - 3) = 12x^2 + 11x - 15$$
$$\text{which is correct}$$

Hence

$$12x^2 + 11x - 15 = (3x + 5)(4x - 3)$$

Exercise 84 — Questions 1–8 type C, remainder D

Factorise the following quadratic expressions:

1) $x^2 + 5x + 6$ 　　　9) $2x^2 - 7x + 5$

2) $x^2 + 6x + 8$ 　　　10) $2x^2 + 13x + 15$

3) $x^2 - 7x + 10$ 　　　11) $3x^2 + x - 2$

4) $x^2 - 11x + 30$ 　　　12) $3x^2 - 8x - 28$

5) $x^2 - x - 2$ 　　　13) $2x^2 - 5x - 3$

6) $x^2 - 2x - 15$ 　　　14) $10x^2 + 19x - 15$

7) $x^2 + 2x - 8$ 　　　15) $6x^2 + x - 35$

8) $x^2 + x - 12$

(c) Where the factors form a perfect square.

$$(a + b)^2 = (a + b)(a + b)$$
$$= a^2 + ab + ab + b^2$$
$$= a^2 + 2ab + b^2$$
$$(a - b)^2 = (a - b)(a - b)$$
$$= a^2 - ab - ab + b^2$$
$$= a^2 - 2ab + b^2$$

The square of a binomial expression therefore consists of:

$$(\text{first term})^2 + 2 \times (\text{first term})$$
$$\times (\text{second term}) + (\text{last term})^2$$

EXAMPLE 7

(1) Factorise $9a^2 + 12ab + 4b^2$.

$$9a^2 = (3a)^2 \qquad 4b^2 = (2b)^2$$
$$2 \times 3a \times 2b = 12ab$$
$$\therefore \qquad 9a^2 + 12ab + 4b^2 = (3a + 2b)^2$$

(2) Factorise $16x^2 - 40x + 25$.

$$16x^2 = (4x)^2 \quad 25 = 5^2$$
$$2 \times 4x \times 5 = 40x$$
$$\therefore \qquad 16x^2 - 40x + 25 = (4x - 5)^2$$

(d) Where the factors form the difference of two squares.

$$(a + b)(a - b) = a^2 + ab - ab - b^2$$
$$= a^2 - b^2$$

Hence the factors of $a^2 - b^2$ are the sum and difference of the square roots of each of the squares.

EXAMPLE 8

(1) Factorise $x^2 - 1$.

$$x^2 = (x)^2 \quad \text{and} \quad 1 = (1)^2$$

Hence $x^2 - 1 = (x + 1)(x - 1)$.

(2) Factorise $9x^2 - 16$.

$$9x^2 = (3x)^2 \quad \text{and} \quad 16 = 4^2$$

Hence $9x^2 - 16 = (3x + 4)(3x - 4)$.

Exercise 85 — All type B

Factorise the following:

1) $x^2 + 2x + 1$ 　　　6) $x^2 - 4x + 4$

2) $x^2 - 2x + 1$ 　　　7) $4x^2 - 1$

3) $x^2 + 4x + 4$ 　　　8) $a^2 - b^2$

4) $9x^2 + 6x + 1$ 　　　9) $1 - x^2$

5) $25x^2 - 20x + 4$ 　　　10) $121x^2 - 64$

In questions 11 to 17 complete the bracket which has been left blank.

11) $x^2 - x - 6 = (x + 2)(\qquad)$

12) $x^2 - 12x + 35 = (x - 5)(\qquad)$

13) $6x^2 + 31x + 40 = (3x + 8)(\qquad)$

14) $10x^2 - 31x + 15 = (2x - 5)(\qquad)$

15) $x^2 + 2x + 1 = (\quad)^2$

16) $x^2 - 2x + 1 = (\quad)^2$

17) $9p^2 - 25 = (3p + 5)(\quad)$

MORE DIFFICULT FACTORISATION

Many algebraic expressions need a combination of several of the methods of factorising discussed previously. The following examples show the methods that should be adopted.

EXAMPLE 9

(1) Factorise $(3p - q)^2 + 2r(3p - q)$.

The H.C.F. is $(3p - q)$.

$\therefore (3p - q)^2 + 2r(3p - q) = (3p - q)(3p - q + 2r)$

(2) Factorise $a^2 - b^2 + 2a + 2b$.

$$a^2 - b^2 + 2a + 2b = (a^2 - b^2) + (2a + 2b)$$
$$= (a + b)(a - b) + 2(a + b)$$
$$= (a + b)(a - b + 2)$$

[since the H.C.F. is $(a + b)$].

(3) Factorise $2x^3 - 50xy^2$.

The H.C.F. is $2x$.

$$\therefore \quad 2x^3 - 50xy^2 = 2x(x^2 - 25y^2)$$
$$= 2x(x + 5y)(x - 5y)$$

(4) Factorise $4(a - b) - c(b - a)$.

The term $-c(b - a)$ may be written

$$(-1) \times (-c) \times (-1)(b - a) = +c(-b + a)$$
$$= +c(a - b).$$

The expression is unaltered because $(-1) \times (-1) = 1$.

$$\therefore \quad 4(a - b) - c(b - a) = 4(a - b) + c(a - b)$$
$$= (a - b)(4 + c)$$

(5) Factorise $a^2 - b^2 - a - b$.

$$a^2 - b^2 - a - b = (a^2 - b^2) - (a + b)$$
$$= (a + b)(a - b) - (a + b)$$
$$= (a + b)(a - b - 1)$$

[since the H.C.F. is $(a + b)$].

Exercise 86 — *Questions 1–15 type C, remainder D*

Factorise the following:

1) $(a - b)^2 - 2x(a - b)$

2) $3(x + y) + (x + y)^2$

3) $5(3m - n)^2 - 5a(3m - n)$

4) $x^2 - y^2 + x - y$

5) $a^2 - b^2 - 3a - 3b$

6) $3x^2 - 3y^2 - 2x - 2y$

7) $2m^2 - 2n^2 + 4m + 4n$

8) $\pi R^2 + 2\pi Rh$

9) $4y^3 - 9a^2 y$

10) $\pi l R^2 - \pi l r^2$

11) $20x^3 - 45xy^2$

12) $\frac{2}{3}\pi r^3 + \frac{1}{3}\pi r^2 h$

13) $a^2 - 2ab - 2bc + ac$

14) $(x - 1)^2 - 4y^2$

15) $xy(2p - 3) - y(2p - 3)$

16) $a^2 - b^2 - (a + b)$

17) $18p^3 - 2p$

18) $3(x - y)^2 - 2(y - x)$

19) $8(x - y)^2 - 4(y - x)$

20) $a^2 - b^2 - 3(b - a)$

SELF-TEST 16

In questions 1 to 30 the answer is either 'true' or 'false', state which.

1) The H.C.F. of $a^2 bc^3$ and ab^2 is ab.

2) The H.C.F. of $x^2 y^3 z$ and $x^2 yz^2$ is $x^2 y^3 z^2$.

3) The H.C.F. of $a^3 b^2 c^2$, $a^2 b^3 c^3$ and $ab^4 c^4$ is $ab^2 c^2$.

4) The factors of $a^2 x^3 + bx^2$ are $x^2(a^2 x + b)$.

5) The factors of $3a^3 y + 6a^2 x + 9a^4 z$ are $3a(a^2 y + 2ax + 3a^3 z)$.

6) The factors of $\dfrac{bz}{y} - \dfrac{cz}{y^2} + \dfrac{dz}{y^3}$ are $\dfrac{z}{y}\left(b - \dfrac{c}{y} + \dfrac{d}{y^2}\right)$.

7) One factor of $a^2 b^3 - a^3 b^4 + ab^2$ is $(ab - a^2 b^2 + 1)$. The other factor is ab^2.

8) $(2p + 5)(3p - 7)$ is equal to $6p^2 + 29p - 35$.

9) $(3x + 7)(2x - 7)$ is equal to $6x^2 - 7x + 49$.

10) $(5x + 2)(3x - 8)$ is equal to $15x^2 - 34x - 16$.

11) $(2x + 3)^2$ is equal to $4x^2 + 6x + 9$.

12) $(3x + 5)^2$ is equal to $9x^2 + 30x + 25$.

13) $(7x - 2)^2$ is equal to $49^2 - 28x - 4$.

14) $(3x - 4)^2$ is equal to $9x^2 - 24x + 16$.

15) $(2x - 3)(2x + 3)$ is equal to $4x^2 - 9$.

16) $(5x - 2)(5x + 2)$ is equal to $25x^2 + 4$.

17) $x^2 + 5x + 6$ is equal to $(x + 3)(x + 2)$.

18) $x^2 - 8x + 15$ is equal to $(x + 3)(x + 5)$.

19) $x^2 - 9x + 14$ is equal to $(x - 2)(x - 7)$.

20) $x^2 - 2x - 15$ is equal to $(x + 3)(x - 5)$.

21) $x^2 + 2x - 35$ is equal to $(x - 5)(x + 7)$.

22) $9x^2 - 3x - 12$ is equal to $(3x + 4)(3x - 3)$.

23) $8x^2 - 10x - 25$ is equal to $(2x - 5)(4x + 5)$.

24) $25x^2 + 10x - 3$ is equal to $(5x - 1)(5x + 3)$.

25) $(3x + 2)^2$ is equal to $9x^2 + 12x + 4$.

26) $4x^2 - 12x + 9$ is equal to $(2x - 3)^2$.

27) $25x^2 - 10x - 1$ is equal to $(5x - 1)^2$.

28) $49x^2 + 70x + 25$ is equal to $(7x + 5)^2$.

29) $4x^2 - 25$ is equal to $(2x + 5)(2x - 5)$.

30) $9x^2 - 49$ is equal to $(3x - 7)(3x + 7)$.

Chapter 17 **Algebraic Fractions**

MULTIPLICATION AND DIVISION OF FRACTIONS

As with ordinary arithmetic fractions, numerators can be multiplied together, as can denominators, in order to form a single fraction. Thus:

$$\frac{a}{b} \times \frac{c}{d} = \frac{a \times c}{b \times d} = \frac{ac}{bd}$$

and

$$\frac{3x}{2y} \times \frac{p}{4q} \times \frac{r^2}{s} = \frac{3x \times p \times r^2}{2y \times 4q \times s} = \frac{3xpr^2}{8yqs}$$

Factors which are common to both numerator and denominator may be *cancelled*. It is important to realise that this cancelling means dividing the numerator and denominator by the same quantity. For instance,

$$\frac{8ab}{3mn} \times \frac{9n^2m}{4ab^2}$$

$$= \frac{\overset{2}{\cancel{8}} \times \cancel{a} \times \cancel{b} \times \overset{3}{\cancel{9}} \times \cancel{n} \times n \times \cancel{m}}{\cancel{3} \times \cancel{m} \times \cancel{n} \times \cancel{4} \times \cancel{a} \times \cancel{b} \times b} = \frac{6n}{b}$$

and

$$\frac{7ab}{8mn^2} \times \frac{3m^2n^3}{2ab^3} \times \frac{16an}{63bm}$$

$$= \frac{\cancel{7} \times \cancel{a} \times \cancel{b} \times \cancel{3} \times m \times \cancel{m} \times \cancel{n} \times \cancel{n} \times n \times \cancel{16} \times a \times n}{\cancel{8} \times \cancel{m} \times \cancel{n} \times \cancel{n} \times \cancel{2} \times \cancel{a} \times b \times b \times b \times \underset{3}{\cancel{63}} \times \cancel{b} \times \cancel{m}}$$

$$= \frac{an^2}{3b^3}$$

To divide by a fraction invert it and then multiply.

EXAMPLE 1

Simplify $\dfrac{ax^2}{by} \div \dfrac{a^2}{b^2y^2}$.

$$\frac{ax^2}{by} \div \frac{a^2}{b^2y^2} = \frac{ax^2}{by} \times \frac{b^2y^2}{a^2} = \frac{bx^2y}{a}$$

Exercise 87 — *All type B*

Simplify the following:

1) $\dfrac{a}{bc^2} \times \dfrac{b^2c}{a}$

2) $\dfrac{3pq}{r} \times \dfrac{qs}{2t} \times \dfrac{3rs}{pq^2}$

3) $\dfrac{2z^2y}{3ac^2} \times \dfrac{6a^2}{5zy^2} \times \dfrac{10c^3}{3y^2}$

4) $\dfrac{3pq}{5rs} \div \dfrac{p^2}{15s^2}$

5) $\dfrac{6ab}{5cd} \div \dfrac{4a^2}{7bd}$

Before attempting to simplify, factorise where this is possible and then cancel factors which are common to both numerator and denominator. Remember that the contents of a bracket may be regarded as a single term. Hence the expressions $(x - y)$, $(b + c)$ and $(x - 3)$ may be regarded as single terms.

EXAMPLE 2

(1) Simplify $\dfrac{x^2 - x}{x - 1}$.

$$x^2 - x = x(x - 1)$$

Hence, $\dfrac{x^2 - x}{x - 1} = \dfrac{x(x - 1)}{(x - 1)} = x$

(2) Simplify $\dfrac{3x - 12}{4x^2 - 8} \times \dfrac{2x^2 - 4}{9x - 36}$.

Factorising where this is possible:

$$\frac{3x - 12}{4x^2 - 8} \times \frac{2x^2 - 4}{9x - 36}$$

$$= \frac{3(x - 4)}{4(x^2 - 2)} \times \frac{2(x^2 - 2)}{9(x - 4)} = \frac{1}{6}$$

(3) Simplify $\dfrac{3xy - 6x + y - 2}{y^2 - 4}$.

Now,

$$3xy - 6x + y - 2 = (3xy - 6x) + (y - 2)$$
$$= 3x(y - 2) + (y - 2)$$
$$= (y - 2)(3x + 1)$$

also $y^2 - 4 = (y + 2)(y - 2)$.

$\therefore \quad \dfrac{3xy - 6x + y - 2}{y^2 - 4} = \dfrac{(y - 2)(3x + 1)}{(y + 2)(y - 2)}$

$$= \dfrac{3x + 1}{y + 2}$$

(4) Simplify $\dfrac{4x^2 - 9}{4x^2 + 12x + 9}$.

Now $4x^2 - 9 = (2x + 3)(2x - 3)$,

and $4x^2 + 12x + 9 = (2x + 3)^2$.

$\therefore \dfrac{4x^2 - 9}{4x^2 + 12x + 9} = \dfrac{(2x + 3)(2x - 3)}{(2x + 3)^2} = \dfrac{2x - 3}{2x + 3}$

Exercise 88 — *Questions 1 and 2 type B, remainder C*

Simplify the following:

1) $\dfrac{3x - 6}{5x - 10}$

2) $\dfrac{4m - 2}{3m^2 - 15} \times \dfrac{5m^2 - 25}{8m - 4}$

3) $\dfrac{2az + 6bz}{6az + 3bz} \times \dfrac{8a + 4b}{az + bz} \times \dfrac{2az + 4bz}{3a + 9b}$

4) $\dfrac{2m - 5}{3m + 2} \div \dfrac{4m^2 - 10m}{9m^2 + 6m}$

5) $\dfrac{3x + 3y}{2x^2 + 4xy} \div \dfrac{6x + 6y}{4x}$

6) $\left(\dfrac{3x + 6}{2x + 6} \times \dfrac{5x}{3x^2 + 6x} \right) \div \dfrac{2x + 8}{x^2 + 3x}$

7) $\dfrac{a^2 - b^2}{a + b}$

8) $\dfrac{3a - 2b}{9a^2 - 12ab + 4b^2}$

9) $\dfrac{3x + 2}{12x^2 + 23x + 10}$

10) $\dfrac{4x + 7}{8x^2 + 2x - 21}$

11) $\dfrac{2x - 1}{2x^2 + 5x - 3}$

12) $\dfrac{a^2 - b^2 + 2a + 2b}{a - b + 2}$

13) $\dfrac{2a^3 - 18ax^2}{2a + 6x}$

14) $\dfrac{(2x - y)^2 + 3a(2x - y)}{3a - y + 2x}$

ADDITION AND SUBTRACTION OF FRACTIONS

The method for algebraic fractions is the same as for arithmetical fractions, that is:

(1) Find the L.C.M. of the denominators.

(2) Express each fraction with the common denominators.

(3) Add or subtract the fractions.

EXAMPLE 3

(1) Simplify $\dfrac{a}{2} + \dfrac{b}{3} - \dfrac{c}{4}$.

The L.C.M. of 2, 3, and 4 is 12.

$$\dfrac{a}{2} + \dfrac{b}{3} - \dfrac{c}{4} = \dfrac{6a}{12} + \dfrac{4b}{12} - \dfrac{3c}{12}$$

$$= \dfrac{6a + 4b - 3c}{12}$$

(2) Simplify $\dfrac{2}{x} + \dfrac{3}{2x} + \dfrac{4}{3x}$.

The L.C.M. of x, $2x$ and $3x$ is $6x$.

$$\dfrac{2}{x} + \dfrac{3}{2x} + \dfrac{4}{3x} = \dfrac{12 + 9 + 8}{6x} = \dfrac{29}{6x}$$

The sign in front of a fraction applies to the fraction as a whole. The line which separates the numerator and denominator acts as a bracket.

EXAMPLE 4

Simplify $\dfrac{m}{12} + \dfrac{2m + n}{4} - \dfrac{m - 2n}{3}$.

The L.C.M. of 12, 4 and 3 is 12.

$\therefore \qquad \dfrac{m}{12} + \dfrac{2m + n}{4} - \dfrac{m - 2n}{3}$

$$= \dfrac{m + 3(2m + n) - 4(m - 2n)}{12}$$

$$= \dfrac{m + 6m + 3n - 4m + 8n}{12}$$

$$= \dfrac{3m + 11n}{12}$$

Exercise 89 — *All type B*

Simplify the following:

1) $\dfrac{x}{3}+\dfrac{x}{4}+\dfrac{x}{5}$

2) $\dfrac{5a}{12}-\dfrac{7a}{18}$

3) $\dfrac{2}{q}-\dfrac{3}{2q}$

4) $\dfrac{3}{y}-\dfrac{5}{3y}+\dfrac{4}{5y}$

5) $\dfrac{3}{5p}-\dfrac{2}{3q}$

6) $\dfrac{3x}{2y}-\dfrac{5y}{6x}$

7) $3x-\dfrac{4y}{5z}$

8) $1-\dfrac{2x}{5}+\dfrac{x}{8}$

9) $3m-\dfrac{2m+n}{7}$

10) $\dfrac{3a+5b}{4}-\dfrac{a-3b}{2}$

11) $\dfrac{3m-5n}{6}-\dfrac{3m-7n}{2}$

12) $\dfrac{x-2}{4}+\dfrac{2}{5}$

13) $\dfrac{x-5}{3}-\dfrac{x-2}{4}$

14) $\dfrac{3x-5}{10}+\dfrac{2x-3}{15}$

LOWEST COMMON MULTIPLE (L.C.M.) OF ALGEBRAIC TERMS

In arithmetic the L.C.M. of two or more given numbers is the smallest number into which the given numbers will divide.

EXAMPLE 5

Find the L.C.M. of 12, 40 and 45.

$$12 = 2^2 \times 3; \quad 40 = 2^3 \times 5; \quad 45 = 3^2 \times 5$$

$$\text{L.C.M.} = 2^3 \times 3^2 \times 5 = 360$$

(Note that in finding the L.C.M. we have selected the highest power of each of the prime factors which occur in any of the given *numbers*.)

To find the L.C.M. of a set of algebraic expressions we select the highest power of each factor which occurs in any of the *expressions*.

EXAMPLE 6

(1) Find the L.C.M. of $a^3 b^2$, abc^3, $ab^3 c$.

The highest powers of a, b and c which occur in any of the given expressions are a^3, b^3 and c^3.

$$\therefore \quad \text{L.C.M.} = a^3 b^3 c^3$$

(2) Find the L.C.M. of $5a^4 b^4$, $10a^2 b^3$, $6a^4 b$.

The L.C.M. of the numerical coefficients 5, 10 and 6 is 30. The highest powers of a and b which occur are a^4 and b^4. Hence:

$$\text{L.C.M.} = 30a^4 b^4$$

(3) Find the L.C.M. of $(x+4)^2$, $(x+4)(x+1)$.

Since the contents of a bracket may be regarded as a single symbol.

$$\text{L.C.M.} = (x+4)^2 (x+1)$$

(4) Find the L.C.M. of $(a+b)$, (a^2-b^2).

We note that a^2-b^2 factorises to give $(a+b)(a-b)$.

$$\therefore \quad \text{L.C.M.} = (a+b)(a-b)$$

If the denominators factorise then this must be done before attempting to find the L.C.M. of the denominators.

EXAMPLE 7

(1) Express as a single fraction in its lowest terms:

$$\frac{1}{x-1}+\frac{2x}{1-x^2}.$$

Now $1-x^2 = (1+x)(1-x)$.

We can rewrite $\dfrac{1}{x-1}$ as

$$\frac{(-1)\times 1}{(-1)\times(x-1)} = -\frac{1}{1-x}$$

$$\therefore \quad \frac{1}{x-1}+\frac{2x}{1-x^2} = -\frac{1}{1-x}+\frac{2x}{(1+x)(1-x)}$$

The L.C.M. of $(1-x)$ and $(1+x)(1-x)$ is $(1+x)(1-x)$.

$$\therefore \quad \frac{-1}{1-x}+\frac{2x}{(1+x)(1-x)} = \frac{-1(1+x)+2x}{(1+x)(1-x)}$$

$$= \frac{-1-x+2x}{(1+x)(1-x)}$$

$$= \frac{x-1}{(1+x)(1-x)}$$

$$= -\frac{1}{1+x}$$

(2) Simplify $\dfrac{2x}{x^2+x-6}+\dfrac{1}{x-2}.$

$$\frac{2x}{x^2+x-6}+\frac{1}{x-2} = \frac{2x}{(x+3)(x-2)}+\frac{1}{x-2}$$

$$= \frac{2x+(x+3)}{(x+3)(x-2)}$$

$$= \frac{3x+3}{(x+3)(x-2)}$$

$$= \frac{3(x+1)}{(x+3)(x-2)}$$

Exercise 90 — *Questions 1–4 type A, 5 and 6 type B, remainder C*

Find the L.C.M. of the following:

1) $4, 12x$

2) $3x, 6y$

3) $2ab, 4a, 6b$

4) ab, bc, ac

5) $3m^2pq, 9mp^2q, 12mpq, 3mn^2$

6) $5a^2b^3, 10ab^4, 2a^2b^3$

7) $(m-n)^2, (m-n)$

8) $(x+3)^2, (x+3), (x+1)$

9) $(x-1), (x^2-1)$

10) $(9a^2-b^2), (3a+b), (3a-b)$

Simplify:

11) $\dfrac{4}{x-5} - \dfrac{15}{x(x-5)} - \dfrac{3}{x}$

12) $\dfrac{3}{2x-1} - \dfrac{2x}{4x^2-1}$

13) $\dfrac{5x}{x^2-x-6} - \dfrac{2}{x+2}$

14) $\dfrac{7}{x^2+3x-10} - \dfrac{2}{x^2+5x} - \dfrac{2}{x^2-2x}$

15) $\dfrac{x+2}{x+3} - \dfrac{x-2}{x-3}$

16) $\dfrac{3x}{x^2-y^2} - \dfrac{x+3}{(x+y)^2}$

SELF-TEST 17

In the questions below state the letter (or letters) corresponding to the correct answer (or answers).

1) $\dfrac{a^2-a}{a-1}$ is equal to:

a a **b** a^2-1 **c** a^2 **d** $1-a^2$

2) $\dfrac{2x-6}{4x^2-8x} \times \dfrac{3x^2-6x}{4x-16}$ is equal to:

a $\dfrac{3x-9}{8x-32}$ **b** $\dfrac{1}{4}$ **c** $\dfrac{3(x-3)}{8(x-4)}$ **d** 0

3) $\dfrac{9x^2-25}{9x^2-9x-10}$ is equal to:

a $\dfrac{1-5x}{1-9x}$ **b** $\dfrac{3x+5}{3x+2}$ **c** $\dfrac{5}{2}$ **d** 2

4) $\left(\dfrac{6y+12}{4y+12} \times \dfrac{5y}{3y^2+6y}\right) \div \dfrac{4y+16}{2y^2+6y}$ is equal to:

a $\dfrac{5y}{4y+16}$ **b** $\dfrac{1}{4}$ **c** $\dfrac{75}{(3y+2)(2y+3)}$

d $\dfrac{5y}{4(y+4)}$

5) The L.C.M. of a^4b^3, ab^2c^4 and ab^3c^3 is:

a abc **b** ab^2 **c** $a^4b^3c^4$ **d** $a^6b^8c^7$

6) The L.C.M. of $(x+3)^2, (x+2)(x+3)$ and $(x+2)^2$ is:

a $(x+3)^3(x+2)^3$ **b** $(x+3)^2(x+2)^2$

c $(x+2)(x+3)$ **d** $x+5$

7) The L.C.M. of $a^2+2ab+b^2$ and a^2-b^2 is:

a $2a^2b^2$ **b** $(a^2-b^2)(a^2+2ab+b^2)$

c $2a^3b^3$ **d** $(a-b)(a+b)^2$

8) $\dfrac{6m-2n}{2}$ is equal to:

a $\dfrac{3m-2n}{2}$ **b** $6m-n$ **c** $3m-2n$

d $3m-n$

9) $t - \dfrac{3-t}{2} + \dfrac{3+t}{2}$ is equal to:

a t **b** $2t$ **c** $3+2t$ **d** $4t$

10) $\dfrac{x}{x^2-1} - \dfrac{2x}{x-1}$ is equal to:

a $\dfrac{1-2x}{x-1}$ **b** $\dfrac{x(3-2x)}{x^2-1}$

c $\dfrac{x(2x+1)}{1-x^2}$ **d** $\dfrac{1}{x-1} + 2$

11) $\dfrac{3x-7}{3} - \dfrac{2x-5}{2}$ is equal to:

a -12 **b** -2 **c** $\dfrac{1}{6}$ **d** $-\dfrac{29}{6}$

12) $\dfrac{5x-10}{5} - \dfrac{3x-6}{3}$ is equal to:

a 0 **b** -4 **c** $2x-4$ **d** $2x$

Chapter 18 Operations with Numbers

Given any two numbers, there are various ways of operating on them apart from the familiar operations of adding, subtracting, dividing and multiplying. The method is shown in Examples 1 and 2.

EXAMPLE 1

If $a * b$ means $\sqrt{ab}$ find the value of $4 * 9$.

Here we have $a = 4$ and $b = 9$.

Hence $\qquad 4 * 9 = \sqrt{4 \times 9} = 6$

EXAMPLE 2

If $a * b$ means $\frac{1}{2}(2a - b)$ find the value of $5 * 2$.

Here $a = 5$ and $b = 2$.

Hence $5 * 2 = \frac{1}{2}(2 \times 5 - 2)$

$\qquad = \frac{1}{2}(10 - 2) = \frac{1}{2} \times 8 = 4$

Exercise 91 — *All type B*

1) If $a * b$ means $2a + b$ find the value of $3 * 1$.

2) If $x * y$ means $3x - 2y$ find the value of $2 * 5$.

3) If $a * b$ means $\frac{1}{4}(a - b)$ find the value of $5 * 3$.

4) If $a * b$ means $(a + b)^2$ find the value of $2 * 3$.

5) If $x * y$ means $\sqrt{xy}$ find the value of $9 * 16$.

6) If $a * b$ means $\sqrt{a^2 - b^2}$ find the value of $5 * 3$.

7) If $p * q$ means $\frac{1}{2}(p^2 + q^3)$ find the value of $4 * 2$.

8) If $a * b$ means $(a - b^2)^2$ find the value of $3 * (-2)$.

9) If $a * b$ means $(a^3 + b)^2$ find the value of $(-5) * 3$.

10) If $m * n$ means $m^2 - 2mn + n^3$ find the value of $2 * 3$.

Chapter 19 Equations

INTRODUCTION

Fig. 19.1 shows a pair of scales which are in balance. That is each scale pan contains exactly the same number of grams. Therefore

$$x + 2 = 7$$

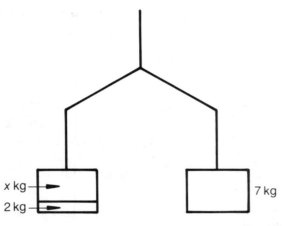

Fig. 19.1

This is an example of an equation. To solve the equation we have to find a value for x such that the scales remain in balance. Now the only way to keep the scales in balance is to add or subtract the same amount from each pan. If we take 2 kilograms from the left hand pan then we are left with x kilograms in this pan, but we must also take 2 kilograms from the right hand pan to maintain balance. That is,

$$x + 2 - 2 = 7 - 2$$
$$x = 5$$

Therefore x is 5 kilograms.

We now take a second example as shown in Fig. 19.2. In the left hand pan we have three packets exactly the same, whilst in the right hand pan there is 6 kg. How many kilograms are there in each packet?

If we let there be x kilograms in each packet then there are $3x$ kilograms in the three packets. Therefore we have the equation:

$$3x = 6$$

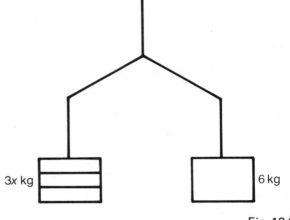

Fig. 19.2

We can maintain the balance of the scales if we multiply or divide the quantities in each scale by the same amount. In our equation if we divide each side by three we have

$$\frac{3x}{3} = \frac{6}{3}$$

Cancelling the threes on the left hand side we have

$$x = 2$$

and hence each packet contains 2 kilograms.

From these two examples we can say:

(1) An equation expresses balance between two sets of quantities.

(2) We can add or subtract the same amount from each side of the equation without destroying the balance.

(3) We can multiply or divide each side of the equation by the same amount without destroying the balance.

SIMPLE EQUATIONS

Simple equations contain only the first power of the unknown quantity. Thus

$$7t - 5 = 4t + 7$$

$$\frac{5x}{3} = \frac{2x + 5}{2}$$

are both examples of simple equations. After an equation is solved, the solution should be checked by substituting the result in each side of the equation separately. If each side of the equation then has the same value the solution is correct.

SOLVING SIMPLE EQUATIONS

Equations requiring multiplication and division.

EXAMPLE 1

(1) Solve the equation $\dfrac{x}{6} = 3$.

Multiplying each side by 6, we get

$$\frac{x}{6} \times 6 = 3 \times 6$$

$$x = 18$$

Check: When $x = 18$, L.H.S. $= \dfrac{18}{6} = 3$

R.H.S. $= 3$

Hence the solution is correct.

(2) Solve the equation $5x = 10$.

Dividing each side by 5, we get

$$\frac{5x}{5} = \frac{10}{5}$$

$$x = 2$$

Check: When $x = 2$, L.H.S. $= 5 \times 2 = 10$

R.H.S. $= 10$

Hence the solution is correct.

Equations requiring addition and subtraction.

EXAMPLE 2

(1) Solve $x - 4 = 8$.

If we add 4 to each side, we get

$$x - 4 + 4 = 8 + 4$$

$$x = 12$$

The operation of adding 4 to each side is the same as transferring -4 to the R.H.S. but in so doing the sign is changed from a minus to a plus. Thus,

$$x - 4 = 8$$

$$x = 8 + 4$$

$$x = 12$$

Check: When $x = 12$, L.H.S. $= 12 - 4 = 8$

R.H.S. $= 8$

Hence the solution is correct.

(2) Solve $x + 5 = 20$.

If we subtract 5 from each side, we get

$$x + 5 - 5 = 20 - 5$$

$$x = 15$$

Alternatively moving $+5$ to the R.H.S.

$$x = 20 - 5$$

$$x = 15$$

Check: When $x = 15$, L.H.S. $= 15 + 5 = 20$

R.H.S. $= 20$

Hence the solution is correct.

Equations containing the unknown quantity on both sides.

In equations of this kind group all the terms containing the unknown quantity on one side of the equation and the remaining terms on the other side.

EXAMPLE 3

(1) Solve $7x + 3 = 5x + 17$.

Transferring $5x$ to the L.H.S. and $+3$ to the R.H.S.

$$7x - 5x = 17 - 3$$

$$2x = 14$$

$$x = \frac{14}{2}$$

$$x = 7$$

Check: When $x = 7$,

L.H.S. $= 7 \times 7 + 3 = 52$

R.H.S. $= 5 \times 7 + 17 = 52$

Hence the solution is correct.

(2) Solve $3x - 2 = 5x + 6$.

$$3x - 5x = 6 + 2$$

$$-2x = 8$$

$$x = \frac{8}{-2}$$

$$x = -4$$

Check: When $x = -4$,

$$\text{L.H.S.} = 3 \times (-4) - 2 = -14$$
$$\text{R.H.S.} = 5 \times (-4) + 6 = -14$$

Hence the solution is correct.

Equations containing brackets.

When an equation contains brackets remove these first and then solve as shown previously.

EXAMPLE 4

(1) Solve $2(3x + 7) = 16$.

Removing the bracket,

$$6x + 14 = 16$$
$$6x = 16 - 14$$
$$6x = 2$$
$$x = \frac{2}{6}$$
$$x = \frac{1}{3}$$

Check: When $x = \frac{1}{3}$,

$$\text{L.H.S.} = 2 \times \left(3 \times \frac{1}{3} + 7\right) = 2 \times (1 + 7)$$
$$= 2 \times 8 = 16$$
$$\text{R.H.S.} = 16$$

Hence the solution is correct.

(2) Solve $3(x + 4) - 5(x - 1) = 19$.

Removing the brackets,

$$3x + 12 - 5x + 5 = 19$$
$$-2x + 17 = 19$$
$$-2x = 19 - 17$$
$$-2x = 2$$
$$x = \frac{2}{-2}$$
$$x = -1$$

Check: When $x = -1$,

$$\text{L.H.S.} = 3 \times (-1 + 4) - 5 \times (-1 - 1)$$
$$= 3 \times 3 - 5 \times (-2)$$
$$= 9 + 10 = 19$$
$$\text{R.H.S.} = 19$$

Hence the solution is correct.

Equations containing fractions.

When an equation contains fractions, multiply each term of the equation by the L.C.M. of the denominators.

EXAMPLE 5

(1) Solve $\dfrac{x}{4} + \dfrac{3}{5} = \dfrac{3x}{2} - 2$.

The L.C.M. of the denominators 2, 4 and 5 is 20.

Multiplying each term by 20 gives,

$$\frac{x}{4} \times 20 + \frac{3}{5} \times 20 = \frac{3x}{2} \times 20 - 2 \times 20$$
$$5x + 12 = 30x - 40$$
$$5x - 30x = -40 - 12$$
$$-25x = -52$$
$$x = \frac{-52}{-25}$$
$$\therefore \qquad x = \frac{52}{25}$$

The solution may be verified by the check method shown in the previous examples.

(2) Solve the equation

$$\frac{x - 4}{3} - \frac{2x - 1}{2} = 4.$$

In solving equations of this type remember that the line separating the numerator and denominator acts as a bracket. The L.C.M. of the denominators 3 and 2 is 6. Multiplying each term of the equation by 6,

$$\frac{x - 4}{3} \times 6 - \frac{2x - 1}{2} \times 6 = 4 \times 6$$
$$2(x - 4) - 3(2x - 1) = 24$$
$$2x - 8 - 6x + 3 = 24$$
$$-4x - 5 = 24$$
$$-4x = 24 + 5$$
$$-4x = 29$$
$$x = \frac{29}{-4}$$
$$x = -\frac{29}{4}.$$

90

Exercise 92 — *Questions 1–19 type A, remainder B*

Solve the equations:

1) $x + 2 = 7$

2) $t - 4 = 3$

3) $2q = 4$

4) $x - 8 = 12$

5) $q + 5 = 2$

6) $3x = 9$

7) $\dfrac{y}{2} = 3$

8) $\dfrac{m}{3} = 4$

9) $2x + 5 = 9$

10) $5x - 3 = 12$

11) $6p - 7 = 17$

12) $3x + 4 = -2$

13) $7x + 12 = 5$

14) $6x - 3x + 2x = 20$

15) $14 - 3x = 8$

16) $5x - 10 = 3x + 2$

17) $6m + 11 = 25 - m$

18) $3x - 22 = 8x + 18$

19) $0.3d = 1.8$

20) $1.2x - 0.8 = 0.8x + 1.2$

21) $2(x + 1) = 8$

22) $5(m - 2) = 15$

23) $3(x - 1) - 4(2x + 3) = 14$

24) $5(x + 2) - 3(x - 5) = 29$

25) $3x = 5(9 - x)$

26) $4(x - 5) = 7 - 5(3 - 2x)$

27) $\dfrac{x}{5} - \dfrac{x}{3} = 2$

28) $\dfrac{x}{3} + \dfrac{x}{4} + \dfrac{x}{5} = \dfrac{5}{6}$

29) $\dfrac{m}{2} + \dfrac{m}{3} + 3 = 2 + \dfrac{m}{6}$

30) $3x + \dfrac{3}{4} = 2 + \dfrac{2x}{3}$

31) $\dfrac{3}{m} = 3$

32) $\dfrac{5}{x} = 2$

33) $\dfrac{4}{t} = \dfrac{2}{3}$

34) $\dfrac{7}{x} = \dfrac{5}{3}$

35) $\dfrac{4}{7}y - \dfrac{3}{5}y = 2$

36) $\dfrac{1}{3x} + \dfrac{1}{4x} = \dfrac{7}{20}$

37) $\dfrac{x + 3}{4} - \dfrac{x - 3}{5} = 2$

38) $\dfrac{2x}{15} - \dfrac{x - 6}{12} - \dfrac{3x}{20} = \dfrac{3}{2}$

39) $\dfrac{2m - 3}{4} = \dfrac{4 - 5m}{3}$

40) $\dfrac{3 - y}{4} = \dfrac{y}{3}$

MAKING EXPRESSIONS

It is important to be able to translate information into symbols thus making up algebraic expressions. The following examples will illustrate how this is done.

EXAMPLE 6

(1) Find an expression which will give the total mass of a box containing x articles if the box has a mass of 7 kg and each article has a mass of 1.5 kg.

The total mass of x articles is $1.5x$

$\therefore$ Total mass of the box of articles is $1.5x + 7$

(2) If x apples can be bought for 6 pence write down the cost of y apples.

If x apples cost 6 pence then 1 apple costs $\dfrac{6}{x}$ pence.

Hence y apples cost $\dfrac{6}{x} \times y = \dfrac{6y}{x}$ pence.

Exercise 93 — *Questions 1 and 2 type A, remainder B*

1) A boy is x years old now. How old was he 5 years ago?

2) Find the total cost of 3 pencils at a pence each and 8 pens at b pence each.

3) A man works x hours per weekday except Saturday when he works y hours. If he works z hours on Sunday how many hours does he work per week?

4) What is the perimeter of a rectangle l mm long and b mm wide?

5) A man A has £a and a man B has £b. If A gives B £x how much will each have?

6) How many minutes are there between x minutes to 10 o'clock and 12 o'clock?

7) Find in pounds the total cost of a gramophone costing £Y and n records costing X pence each.

8) m articles are bought for x pence. Find the cost in pounds of buying n articles at the same rate.

9) In one innings a batsman hit a sixes, b fours and c singles. How many runs did he score?

10) A factory employs M men, N boys and P women. If a man earns £x per week, a boy £y per week and a woman £z per week what is the total wage bill per week?

CONSTRUCTION OF SIMPLE EQUATIONS

It often happens that we are confronted with mathematical problems that are difficult or impossible to solve by arithmetical methods. We then represent the quantity that has to be found by a symbol. Then by constructing an equation which conforms to the data of the problem we can solve it to give us the value of the unknown quantity. It is stressed that both sides of the equation must be in the same units.

EXAMPLE 7

(1) The perimeter of a rectangle is 56 cm. If one of the two adjacent sides is 4 cm longer than the other, find the dimensions of the rectangle.

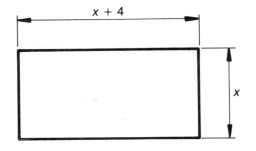

Fig. 19.3

As shown in Fig. 19.3:

Let x cm = length of the shorter side

Then $(x + 4)$ cm = length of the longer side

Total perimeter $= x + (x + 4) + x + (x + 4)$

$= (4x + 8)$ cm

But the total perimeter = 56 cm.

∴

$$4x + 8 = 56$$
$$4x = 48$$
$$x = 12$$

Hence the shorter side is 12 cm long and the longer side is $12 + 4 = 16$ cm long.

(2) 20 articles are bought. Some cost £2 whilst the others cost £3. If £52 is spent in all, how many of each kind of article are bought?

Let x be the number of articles bought at £2.

Then $(20 - x)$ articles are bought at £3 each.

Total amount spent $= £[2x + 3(20 - x)]$

$= £(60 - x)$

But the total amount spent is £52

∴

$$60 - x = 52$$
$$x = 8$$

Hence 8 articles are bought for £2 each and 12 articles for £3 each.

Exercise 94 — *All type B*

1) I think of a number. If I subtract 8 from it and multiply this difference by 3 the result is 21. What is the number I thought of?

2) 15 articles are bought. Some cost 5p each and the remainder cost 8 p each. If the total amount spent is 90 p, how many of each are bought?

3) A room is 3 metres longer than its width. If its perimeter is 126 metres, find the dimensions of the room.

4) 18 books are bought by a library. Some cost £2 and the remainder cost £2.50. How many of each are bought if the total cost is £40?

5) Find the number, which when added to the numerator and denominator of the fraction $\frac{5}{7}$ gives a new fraction which is equal to $\frac{4}{5}$.

6) Find three consecutive whole numbers whose sum is 48.

7) £380 is divided between A and B. If A receives £144 more than B, how much does each receive?

8) Two numbers, when added, total 9. 5 times the first number minus 4 times the second number also equals 9. What are the two numbers?

9) The sides of a triangle are x cm, $(x-4)$ cm and $(x+2)$ cm long respectively. If its perimeter is 46 cm, find the length of each side.

10) The three angles of a triangle are $(x-20)°$, $50°$ and $(2x+30)°$. Find the magnitude of each angle, given that the sum of the angles of a triangle is $180°$.

SELF-TEST 19

In questions 1 to 25 the answer is either 'true' or 'false'.

1) If $\dfrac{x}{7} = 3$ then $x = 21$.

2) If $\dfrac{x}{5} = 10$ then $x = 2$.

3) If $\dfrac{x}{4} = 16$ then $x = 64$.

4) If $5x = 20$ then $x = 4$.

5) If $3x = 6$ then $x = 18$.

6) If $x - 5 = 10$ then $x = 5$.

7) If $x + 8 = 16$ then $x = 2$.

8) If $x + 7 = 14$ then $x = 21$.

9) If $x + 3 = 6$ then $x = 3$.

10) If $x - 7 = 14$ then $x = 21$.

11) If $3x + 5 = 2x + 10$ then $x = 3$.

12) If $2x + 4 = x + 8$ then $x = 4$.

13) If $5x - 2 = 3x - 8$ then $x = -6$.

14) If $3x - 8 = 2 - 2x$ then $x = 10$.

15) If $2(3x + 5) = 18$ then $x = 1$.

16) If $2(x + 4) - 5(x - 7) = 7$ then $x = 12$.

17) If $6y = 10(8 - y)$ then $y = 15$.

18) If $\dfrac{5}{y} = 10$ then $y = 2$.

19) If $\dfrac{8}{y} = 4$ then $y = 2$.

20) If $\dfrac{x}{3} + \dfrac{x}{4} = \dfrac{2x}{5} - 11$ then $x = 60$.

21) If $\dfrac{x}{2} - 1 = \dfrac{x}{3} - \dfrac{1}{2}$ then $x = 3$.

22) If $\dfrac{3}{x+5} = \dfrac{4}{x-2}$ then $x = 26$.

23) If $\dfrac{3}{x-6} = \dfrac{2}{x-4}$ then $x = -2$.

24) If $\dfrac{x-4}{2} - \dfrac{x-3}{3} = 4$ then $x = 10$.

25) If $\dfrac{2x-3}{2} - \dfrac{x-6}{5} = 3$ then $x = 3$.

In questions 26 to 40 state the letter (or letters) corresponding to the correct answer (or answers).

26) If $3(2x - 5) - 2(x - 3) = 3$ then x is equal to:

a 3   b 6   c $\dfrac{5}{4}$ d $\dfrac{11}{4}$

27) If $2(x + 6) - 3(x - 4) = 1$ then x is equal to:

a 25   b 17   c 23   d -7

28) If $\dfrac{x-5}{3} = \dfrac{x+2}{2}$ then x is equal to:

a 16   b -16 c 7   d -7

29) If $3(x - 2) - 5(x - 7) = 12$ then x is equal to:

a $-8\frac{1}{2}$ b $8\frac{1}{2}$ c -7 d 0

30) If $\dfrac{3-2y}{4} = \dfrac{2y}{6}$ then y is equal to:

a $\dfrac{18}{20}$ b $\dfrac{9}{10}$ c 3   d -3

31) The cost of electricity is obtained as follows: A fixed charge of £a, rent of a meter £b and a charge of c pence for each unit of electricity supplied. The total cost of using n units of electricity is therefore:

a £$(a + b + nc)$ b £$(100(a + b) + nc)$

c $[100(a + b) + nc]$ pence

d £$\left(a + b + \dfrac{nc}{100}\right)$

32) At a factory p men earn an average wage of $£a$, q women earn an average wage of $£b$ and r apprentices earn an average wage of $£c$. The average wage for all these employees is:

a $£(a + b + c)$

b $£\left(\dfrac{a}{p} + \dfrac{b}{q} + \dfrac{c}{r}\right)$

c $£\dfrac{(ap + bq + cr)}{a + b + c}$

d $£\left(\dfrac{ap + bq + cr}{p + q + r}\right)$

33) A dealer ordered N tools from a manufacturer. The manufacturer can produce p tools per day but $x\%$ of these are faulty and unfit for sale. The number of days it takes the manufacturer to complete the order is:

a $\dfrac{N}{p(100 - x)}$

b $\dfrac{100N}{p(100 - x)}$

c $\dfrac{N}{p(1 - x)}$

d $\dfrac{p(100 - x)}{N}$

34) A shopkeeper pays $£c$ for x kg of apples. He sells them for b pence per kg. His percentage profit is therefore:

a $\dfrac{bx - c}{c}$

b $\dfrac{bx - 100c}{100c}$

c $\dfrac{100(bx - c)}{c}$

d $\dfrac{bx - 100c}{c}$

35) A man walked for t hours at v km per hour and then cycled a distance of x km at c km per hour. His average speed for the whole journey was:

a $\dfrac{vt + x}{t + c}$

b $\dfrac{vt + x}{t}$

c $\dfrac{c(vt + x)}{ct + x}$

d $\dfrac{vt + x}{t + \dfrac{x}{c}}$

36) The cost of hiring a bus is $£60$. If nine of the seats are unoccupied the cost per person is $£1$ more than each person would have to pay if all the seats were full. If n is the number of seats in the bus then:

a $\dfrac{60}{n} - \dfrac{60}{n - 9} = 1$

b $\dfrac{60}{n - 9} - \dfrac{60}{n} = 1$

c $\dfrac{60}{n} = n$

d $\dfrac{60}{n - 9} = n$

37) At the beginning of term a student bought x books at a total cost of $£22$. A few days later he bought three more books for a further expenditure of $£4$. He found that this purchase had reduced the average cost per book by 20 pence. An equation from which x can be found is:

a $\dfrac{26}{x} = 20$

b $\dfrac{26}{x + 3} = 0.20$

c $\dfrac{22}{x} - \dfrac{26}{x + 3} = 0.20$

d $\dfrac{26}{x + 3} - \dfrac{22}{x} = 0.20$

38) The smallest of three consecutive even numbers is m. Twice the square of the largest is greater than the sum of the squares of the other two numbers by 244. Hence:

a $2(m + 2)^2 = (m + 1)^2 + m^2 + 244$

b $2(m + 2)^2 - (m + 1)^2 + m^2 = 244$

c $2(m + 4)^2 = (m + 2)^2 + m^2 + 244$

d $2(m + 4)^2 - (m + 2)^2 + m^2 = 244$

39) A bill for $£74$ was paid with $£5$ and $£1$ notes, a total of 50 notes being used. If x is the number of $£5$ notes used then:

a $x + 5(50 - x) = 74$

b $5x + (50 - x) = 74$

c $5x + (74 - x) = 50$

d $x + 5(74 - x) = 50$

40) A householder can choose to pay for his electricity by one of the two following methods:
(1) a basic charge of $£1.60$ together with a charge of 0.5 pence for each unit of electricity used;
(2) a basic charge of $£2.60$ together with a charge of 0.4 pence for each unit of electricity used.
The number of units N for which the bill would be the same by either method may be found from the equation

a $1.60 + 0.5N = 2.60 + 0.4N$

b $1.60N + 50 = 2.60N + 40$

c $160 + 0.5N = 260 + 0.4N$

d $160N + 50 = 260N + 40$

Chapter 20 Formulae

EVALUATING FORMULAE

A formula is an equation which *describes the relationship* between two or more quantities. The statement that $E = IR$ is a formula for E in terms of I and R. The value of E may be found by simple arithmetic after substituting the given values of I and R.

EXAMPLE 1

If $E = IR$ find the value of E when $I = 6$ and $R = 4$.

Substituting the given values of I and R and remembering that multiplication signs are omitted in formulae, we have:

$$E = IR = 6 \times 4 = 24$$

EXAMPLE 2

The formula for the surface area of a sphere is $A = 4\pi r^2$ where $\pi = 3.142$ and r is the radius of the sphere. Find the surface area of a sphere whose radius is 8.

Substituting the given values

$$A = 4 \times 3.142 \times 8^2 = 804.4$$

Exercise 95 — *All type B*

1) If $v = u + at$ find v when $u = 5$, $a = 3$ and $t = 4$.

2) If $P = \dfrac{RT}{V}$ find P when $R = 48$, $T = 20$ and $V = 6$.

3) If $C = \pi D$ find C when $\pi = 3.142$ and $D = 6$.

4) If $I = \dfrac{PRT}{100}$ find I when $P = 700$, $R = 12$ and $T = 3$.

5) If $P = \dfrac{1}{n}$ find P when $n = 5$.

6) If $K = \dfrac{WV^2}{2g}$ find K when $W = 64$, $V = 20$ and $g = 32$.

7) If $A = \frac{1}{2}BH$ find A when $B = 6$ and $H = 7$.

8) If $S = 90(n - 4)$ find S when $n = 6$.

9) If $P = 3r^4$ find P when $r = 5$.

10) If $y = \dfrac{3t}{c}$ find y when $t = 12$ and $c = 6$.

FORMULAE AND EQUATIONS

Suppose that we are given the formula $M = \dfrac{P}{Q}$ and that we have to find the value of Q given the values of M and P. We can do this by substituting the given values and solving the resulting equation for Q.

EXAMPLE 3

Find Q from the equation $M = \dfrac{P}{Q}$ if $M = 3$ and $P = 6$.

Substituting the given values we have:

$$3 = \frac{6}{Q}$$

$$3Q = 6 \quad \text{(multiplying each side by } Q\text{)}$$

$$Q = 2 \quad \text{(dividing each side by 3)}$$

EXAMPLE 4

Find T from the formula $D = \dfrac{T + 2}{P}$ when $D = 5$ and $P = 3$.

Substituting the given values:

$$5 = \frac{T + 2}{3}$$

$$15 = T + 2 \quad \text{(multiplying each side by 3)}$$

$$13 = T \quad \text{(subtracting 2 from each side)}$$

Hence $T = 13$.

Exercise 96 — *All type B*

1) Find n from the formula $P = \dfrac{1}{n}$ when $P = 2$.

2) Find R from the formula $E = IR$ when $E = 20$ and $I = 4$.

3) Find B from the formula $A = BH$ when $A = 12$ and $H = 4$.

4) Find c from the formula $H = abc$ when $H = 40$, $a = 2$ and $b = 5$.

5) Find P from the formula $I = \dfrac{PRT}{100}$ when $I = 20$, $R = 5$ and $T = 4$.

6) Find D from the formula $C = \pi D$ when $\pi = 3.142$ and $C = 27$.

7) Find r from the formula $A = \pi rl$ when $\pi = 3.142$, $A = 96$ and $l = 12$.

8) Find W from the formula $K = Wa + b$ when $K = 30$, $b = 6$ and $a = 4$.

TRANSPOSITION OF FORMULAE

Consider, again, the formula $M = \dfrac{P}{Q}$. M is called the *subject* of the formula. We may be given several corresponding values of M and Q and we want to find the corresponding values of P. We could, of course, find these by using the methods shown in Examples 3 and 4 but considerable time and effort would be spent in solving the resulting equations. Much of this time and effort would be saved if we could express the formula with P as the subject, because then we need only substitute the given values of M and Q in the rearranged formula.

The process of rearranging a formula so that one of the other symbols becomes the subject is called *transposing the formula*. The rules used in transposition are the same as those used in solving equations. The methods used are as follows:

Symbols connected as a product

EXAMPLE 5

(1) Transpose the formula $F = ma$ to make a the subject.

Divide both sides by m, then:

$$\frac{F}{m} = \frac{ma}{m}$$

$$\frac{F}{m} = a$$

or

$$a = \frac{F}{m}$$

(2) Make h the subject of the formula $V = \pi r^2 h$.

Divide both sides by πr^2, then:

$$\frac{V}{\pi r^2} = \frac{\pi r^2 h}{\pi r^2}$$

$$\frac{V}{\pi r^2} = h$$

or

$$h = \frac{V}{\pi r^2}$$

Symbols connected as a quotient

EXAMPLE 6

(1) Transpose $x = \dfrac{y}{b}$ for y.

Multiply both sides by b, then:

$$x \times b = \frac{y}{b} \times b$$

$$bx = y$$

or

$$y = bx$$

(2) Transpose $M^3 = \dfrac{3x^2 w}{p}$ for p.

Multiply both sides by p, then:

$$M^3 p = 3x^2 w$$

Divide both sides by M^3, then:

$$\frac{M^3 p}{M^3} = \frac{3x^2 w}{M^3}$$

$$p = \frac{3x^2 w}{M^3}$$

Symbols connected by a plus or minus sign

Remember that when a term is transferred from one side of a formula to the other its sign is changed.

EXAMPLE 7

(1) Transpose $x = 3y + 5$ for y.

Subtract 5 from both sides of the equation,

$$x - 5 = 3y$$

Divide both sides by 3,

$$\frac{x - 5}{3} = y$$

or

$$y = \frac{x - 5}{3}$$

(2) Transpose $w = H + Cr$ for r.

Subtract H from both sides, then:

$$w - H = Cr$$

Divide both sides by C,

$$\frac{w - H}{C} = r$$

or

$$r = \frac{w - H}{C}$$

Formulae containing brackets

EXAMPLE 8

(1) Transpose $y = a + \dfrac{x}{b}$ for x.

Subtract a from both sides, then:

$$y - a = \frac{x}{b}$$

Multiply both sides by b,

$$b(y - a) = x$$

or

$$x = b(y - a)$$

(2) Transpose $l = a + (n - 1)d$ for n.

Subtract a from both sides, then:

$$l - a = (n - 1)d$$

Divide both sides by d,

$$\frac{l - a}{d} = n - 1$$

add 1 to each side,

$$\frac{l - a}{d} + 1 = n$$

or

$$n = \frac{l - a}{d} + 1$$

(3) Transpose $y = \dfrac{ab}{a - b}$ for a.

Multiply both sides by $a - b$,

$$y(a - b) = ab$$

Remove the brackets as a is on both sides,

$$ay - yb = ab$$

Group the terms containing a on the L.H.S. and other terms on the R.H.S.

$$ay - ab = yb$$

Factorising the L.H.S.

$$a(y - b) = yb$$

Divide both sides by $y - b$,

$$a = \frac{yb}{y - b}$$

(4) Transpose $Q = \dfrac{w(H - h)}{T - t}$ for t.

Multiply both sides by $(T - t)$,

$$Q(T - t) = w(H - h)$$

Divide both sides by Q,

$$T - t = \frac{w(H - h)}{Q}$$

Take t to the R.H.S. so that it becomes positive and take $\dfrac{w(H - h)}{Q}$ to the L.H.S.

$$T - \frac{w(H - h)}{Q} = t$$

or

$$t = T - \frac{w(H - h)}{Q}$$

Formulae containing roots

In tackling formulae containing square roots it must be remembered that when a term containing a root is squared, all that happens is that the root sign disappears. Thus,

$$(\sqrt{H})^2 = H$$
$$(\sqrt{gh})^2 = gh$$

EXAMPLE 9

(1) Transpose $d = \sqrt{2hr}$ for r.

Squaring both sides,

$$d^2 = (\sqrt{2hr})^2$$
$$d^2 = 2hr$$

Dividing both sides by $2h$,

$$\frac{d^2}{2h} = r$$

or

$$r = \frac{d^2}{2h}$$

(2) Transpose $d = \sqrt{\dfrac{b(x - b)}{c}}$ for x.

Squaring both sides,

$$d^2 = \frac{b(x-b)}{c}$$

Multiplying both sides by c,

$$cd^2 = b(x-b)$$

Dividing both sides by b,

$$\frac{cd^2}{b} = x - b$$

Adding b to both sides,

$$\frac{cd^2}{b} + b = x$$

or

$$x = \frac{cd^2}{b} + b$$

(3) Transpose $y = \dfrac{3t}{\sqrt{c}}$ for c.

Multiplying both sides by $\sqrt{c}$,

$$y\sqrt{c} = 3t$$

Dividing both sides by y,

$$\sqrt{c} = \frac{3t}{y}$$

Squaring both sides

$$c = \left(\frac{3t}{y}\right)^2$$

or

$$c = \frac{3t}{y} \times \frac{3t}{y} = \frac{9t^2}{y^2}$$

Exercise 97 — *Questions 1—12 and 15—18*
type B, 13, 14, 19—28, 33, 34
type C, remainder D

Transpose the following:

1) $C = \pi d$ for d

2) $S = \pi dn$ for d

3) $PV = c$ for V

4) $A = \pi r l$ for l

5) $v^2 = 2gh$ for h

6) $I = PRT$ for R

7) $x = \dfrac{a}{y}$ for y

8) $I = \dfrac{E}{R}$ for R

9) $x = \dfrac{u}{a}$ for u

10) $P = \dfrac{RT}{V}$ for T

11) $d = \dfrac{0.866}{N}$ for N

12) $S = \dfrac{ts}{T}$ for t

13) $H = \dfrac{PLAN}{33\,000}$ for L

14) $V = \dfrac{\pi d^2 h}{4}$ for h

15) $p = P - 14.7$ for P

16) $v = u + at$ for t

17) $n = p + cr$ for r

18) $y = ax + b$ for x

19) $y = \dfrac{x}{5} + 17$ for x

20) $H = S + qL$ for q

21) $a = b - cx$ for x

22) $D = B - 1.28d$ for d

23) $V = \dfrac{2R}{R-r}$ for r

24) $C = \dfrac{E}{R+r}$ for E

25) $S = \pi r(r + h)$ for h

26) $H = wS(T - t)$ for T

27) $C = \dfrac{N-n}{2p}$ for N

28) $T = \dfrac{12(D-d)}{L}$ for d

29) $V = \dfrac{2R}{R-r}$ for R

30) $P = \dfrac{S(C-F)}{C}$ for C

31) $V = \sqrt{2gh}$ for h

32) $w = k\sqrt{d}$ for d

33) $t = 2\pi\sqrt{\dfrac{l}{g}}$ for l

34) $t = 2\pi \sqrt{\dfrac{W}{gf}}$ for f

35) $P - mg = \dfrac{mv^2}{r}$ for m

36) $Z = \sqrt{\dfrac{x}{x+y}}$ for x

37) $k = \dfrac{3n+2}{n+1}$ for n

38) $a = \dfrac{3}{4t+5}$ for t

39) $v^2 = 2k\left(\dfrac{1}{x} - \dfrac{1}{a}\right)$ for x

40) $d = \dfrac{2(S - an)}{n(n-l)}$ for a

41) $c = 2\sqrt{2hr - h^2}$ for r

42) $x = \dfrac{dh}{D-d}$ for d

43) $\dfrac{D}{d} = \sqrt{\dfrac{f+p}{f-p}}$ for f

SELF-TEST 20

In the following questions state the letter (or letters) corresponding to the correct answer (or answers).

1) The value of $\dfrac{ab - c^2}{a^2 - bc}$ when $a = 2$, $b = -2$ and $c = -3$ is:

a -6.5 b 6.5 c -3.5 d 3.5

2) The value of $x^2 + y^2 + z^2 - 3yz$ when $x = -2$, $y = 3$ and $z = -4$ is:

a 25 b -47 c -7 d 65

3) The value of $(2a - 5b)^2 + 8ab$ when $a = 3$ and $b = -2$ is:

a 208 b -32 c 304 d 16

4) The value of $\dfrac{x}{y^2} - \dfrac{y}{z^2} - \dfrac{z}{x^2}$ when $x = -2$, $y = 3$ and $z = -4$ is:

a $-\dfrac{149}{144}$ b $\dfrac{85}{144}$ c $-\dfrac{203}{144}$ d $\dfrac{139}{144}$

5) The value of $ab(b - 2c) - 3abc$ when $a = 3$, $b = -4$ and $c = 1$ is:

a -36 b 60 c -60 d 108

6) If $v = u - at$ then t is equal to:

a $\dfrac{v-u}{a}$ b $\dfrac{u-v}{a}$ c $\dfrac{-v}{au}$ d $\dfrac{u}{av}$

7) If $a = b + t\sqrt{x}$ then x is equal to:

a $\dfrac{(a-b)^2}{t}$ b $\dfrac{t}{(a-b)^2}$ c $\dfrac{t^2}{(a-b)^2}$

d $\dfrac{(a-b)^2}{t^2}$

8) If $x = 2y - \dfrac{w}{v}$ then v is equal to:

a $\dfrac{w}{2y-x}$ b $\dfrac{2y-x}{w}$ c $\dfrac{-w}{x-2y}$

d $\dfrac{-w}{2y-x}$

9) If $y = \dfrac{1 - t^2}{1 + t^2}$ then t is equal to:

a $\left(\dfrac{1-y}{y+1}\right)^2$ b $\sqrt{\dfrac{1-y}{y+1}}$ c $\sqrt{\dfrac{1-y}{2}}$

d $\dfrac{(1-y)^2}{4}$

10) If $F = \dfrac{W(v - u)}{gt}$ then u is equal to:

a $v - \dfrac{WF}{gt}$ b $\dfrac{Fgt}{W} - v$

c $v - \dfrac{Fgt}{W}$ d $Fgt - Wv$

11) If $y = \dfrac{1 - 3x}{1 + 5x}$ then x is equal to:

a $\dfrac{1-y}{8}$ b $\dfrac{1-y}{2}$ c $\dfrac{1-y}{5y+3}$ d $\dfrac{1-y}{5y-3}$

12) If $A = 2\pi R(R + H)$ then H is equal to:

a $A - 2\pi R^2$ b $\dfrac{A}{2\pi R} - R$

c $R - \dfrac{A}{2\pi R}$ d $\dfrac{A - 2\pi R^2}{2\pi R}$

13) If $S = 90(2n - 4)$ then n is equal to:

a $\dfrac{S}{180} + 4$ b $\dfrac{S}{180} - 2$ c $\dfrac{S}{180} + 2$

d $\dfrac{S + 360}{180}$

14) If $k = \dfrac{3n + 2}{n + 1}$ then n is equal to:

a $\dfrac{2-k}{k-3}$ b $\dfrac{k-2}{3-k}$ c $\dfrac{1}{k-3}$ d $\dfrac{1}{3-k}$

15) If $T = 2\pi\sqrt{\dfrac{R-H}{g}}$ then R is equal to:

a $\dfrac{T^2}{2\pi} + \dfrac{H}{g}$
b $\dfrac{gT^2}{2\pi} + H$

c $\dfrac{gT^2 + 2\pi H}{2\pi}$
d $\dfrac{gT^2}{4\pi^2} + H$

16) If $K = \dfrac{Wv^2}{2g}$ then v is equal to:

a $\sqrt{\dfrac{K}{2g} - W}$
b $\sqrt{2Kg - W}$

c $\sqrt{\dfrac{2Kg}{W}}$
d $\sqrt{2KgW}$

17) If $H = wS(T - t)$ then t is equal to:

a $\dfrac{H}{wS} - T$
b $\dfrac{H - wST}{wS}$
c $\dfrac{T - H}{wS}$

d $\dfrac{wST - H}{wS}$

18) If $y = \dfrac{ab}{a - b}$ then b is equal to:

a $\dfrac{ya}{a + 1}$
b $\dfrac{ya}{a - 1}$
c $\dfrac{ya}{a + y}$

d $\dfrac{ya}{a - y}$

19) If $a = \sqrt{\dfrac{b}{b + c}}$ then b is equal to:

a $\dfrac{a^2 c}{1 + a^2}$
b $\dfrac{a^2 c}{1 - a^2}$
c $\dfrac{c}{1 + a^2}$

d $\dfrac{c}{1 - a^2}$

20) If $x = \sqrt{\dfrac{a^2 - b^2}{ay}}$ then b is equal to:

a $a - x^2 ay$
b $\sqrt{x^2 ay - a^2}$
c $\sqrt{a^2 - x^2 ay}$
d $\sqrt{a(a - x^2 y)}$

Chapter 21 Simultaneous Equations

Consider the two equations:

$$2x + 3y = 13 \qquad [1]$$
$$3x + 2y = 12 \qquad [2]$$

Each equation contains the unknown quantities x and y. The solutions of the equations are the values of x *and* y which satisfy both equations. Equations such as these are called *simultaneous equations*.

ELIMINATION METHOD IN SOLVING SIMULTANEOUS EQUATIONS

The method will be shown by considering the following examples.

EXAMPLE 1

(1) Solve the equations:

$$3x + 4y = 11 \qquad [1]$$
$$x + 7y = 15 \qquad [2]$$

If we multiply equation [2] by 3 we shall have the same coefficient of x in both equations:

$$3x + 21y = 45 \qquad [3]$$

We can now eliminate x by subtracting equation [1] from equation [3]

$$3x + 21y = 45 \qquad [3]$$
$$3x + 4y = 11 \qquad [1]$$
$$17y = 34$$
$$y = 2$$

To find x we substitute for $y = 2$ in either of the original equations. Thus, substituting for $y = 2$ in equation [1],

$$3x + 4 \times 2 = 11$$
$$3x + 8 = 11$$
$$3x = 11 - 8$$
$$3x = 3$$
$$x = 1$$

Hence the solutions are:

$$x = 1 \quad \text{and} \quad y = 2$$

To check these values substitute them in equation [2]. There is no point in substituting them in equation [1] because this was used in finding the value of x. Thus,

$$\text{L.H.S.} = 1 + 7 \times 2 = 15 = \text{R.H.S.}$$

Hence the solutions are correct since the L.H.S. and R.H.S. are equal.

(2) Solve the equations:

$$5x + 3y = 29 \qquad [1]$$
$$4x + 7y = 37 \qquad [2]$$

The same coefficient of x can be obtained in both equations if equation [1] is multiplied by 4 (the coefficient of x in equation [2]) and equation [2] is multiplied by 5 (the coefficient of x in equation [1]).

Multiplying equation [1] by 4,

$$20x + 12y = 116 \qquad [3]$$

Multiplying equation [2] by 5,

$$20x + 35y = 185 \qquad [4]$$

Subtracting equation [3] from equation [4],

$$23y = 69$$
$$y = 3$$

Substituting for $y = 3$ in equation [1],

$$5x + 3 \times 3 = 29$$
$$5x + 9 = 29$$
$$5x = 20$$
$$x = 4$$

Hence the solutions are:

$$y = 3 \quad \text{and} \quad x = 4$$

Check in equation [2],

$$\text{L.H.S.} = 4 \times 4 + 7 \times 3$$
$$= 16 + 21 = 37 = \text{R.H.S.}$$

(3) Solve the equations:

$$7x + 4y = 41 \qquad [1]$$
$$4x - 2y = 2 \qquad [2]$$

In these equations it is easier to eliminate y because the same coefficient of y can be obtained in both equations by multiplying equation [2] by 2.

Multiplying equation [2] by 2,

$$8x - 4y = 4 \qquad [3]$$

Adding equations [1] and [3],

$$15x = 45$$
$$x = 3$$

Substituting for $x = 3$ in equation [1],

$$7 \times 3 + 4y = 41$$
$$21 + 4y = 41$$
$$4y = 20$$
$$y = 5$$

Hence the solutions are:

$$x = 3 \quad \text{and} \quad y = 5$$

Check in equation [2],

$$\text{L.H.S.} = 4 \times 3 - 2 \times 5$$
$$= 12 - 10 = 2 = \text{R.H.S.}$$

(4) Solve the equations:

$$\frac{2x}{3} - \frac{y}{4} = \frac{7}{12} \qquad [1]$$

$$\frac{3x}{4} - \frac{2y}{5} = \frac{3}{10} \qquad [2]$$

It is best to clear each equation of fractions before attempting to solve.

In equation [1] the L.C.M. of the denominators is 12. Hence by multiplying equation [1] by 12,

$$8x - 3y = 7 \qquad [3]$$

In equation [2] the L.C.M. of the denominators is 20. Hence by multiplying equation [2] by 20,

$$15x - 8y = 6 \qquad [4]$$

We now proceed in the usual way. Multiplying equation [3] by 8,

$$64x - 24y = 56 \qquad [5]$$

Multiplying equation [4] by 3,

$$45x - 24y = 18 \qquad [6]$$

Subtracting equation [6] from equation [5],

$$19x = 38$$
$$x = 2$$

Substituting for $x = 2$ in equation [3],

$$8 \times 2 - 3y = 7$$
$$16 - 3y = 7$$
$$-3y = -9$$
$$y = 3$$

Hence the solutions are:

$$x = 2 \quad \text{and} \quad y = 3$$

Since equation [3] came from equation [1] we must do the check in equation [2].

$$\text{L.H.S.} = \frac{3 \times 2}{4} - \frac{2 \times 3}{5} = \frac{6}{4} - \frac{6}{5}$$
$$= \frac{30 - 24}{20} = \frac{6}{20} = \frac{3}{10} = \text{R.H.S.}$$

Exercise 98 — *Questions 1–5 type B, remainder C*

Solve the following equations for x and y and check the solutions:

1) $3x + 2y = 7$
    $x + y = 3$

2) $4x - 3y = 1$
    $x + 3y = 19$

3) $x + 3y = 7$
    $2x - 2y = 6$

4) $7x - 4y = 37$
    $6x + 3y = 51$

5) $4x - 6y = -2.5$
    $7x - 5y = -0.25$

6) $\dfrac{x}{2} + \dfrac{y}{3} = \dfrac{13}{6}$

    $\dfrac{2x}{7} - \dfrac{y}{4} = \dfrac{5}{14}$

7) $\dfrac{x}{8} - y = -\dfrac{5}{2}$

    $3x + \dfrac{y}{3} = 13$

8) $\dfrac{x-2}{3} + \dfrac{y-1}{4} = \dfrac{13}{12}$

    $\dfrac{2-x}{2} + \dfrac{3+y}{3} = \dfrac{11}{6}$

9) $\dfrac{x}{3} - \dfrac{y}{2} + 1 = 0$

    $6x + y + 8 = 0$

10) $3x - 4y = 5$
    $2x - 5y = 8$

11) $x - y = 3$

    $\dfrac{x}{5} - \dfrac{y}{7} = \dfrac{27}{35}$

12) $3x + 4y = 0$
    $2x - 2y = 7$

PROBLEMS INVOLVING SIMULTANEOUS EQUATIONS

In problems which involve two unknowns it is first necessary to form two separate equations from the given data. The equations may then be solved as shown previously.

EXAMPLE 2

(1) A bill for £74 was paid with £5 and £1 notes, a total of 50 notes being used. Find how many £5 notes were used.

Let x be the number of £5 notes and y be the number of £1 notes. Then

$$x + y = 50 \qquad [1]$$

The total value of x £5 notes is £$5x$ and the value of y £1 notes is £y. Hence the total value of x £5 notes and y £1 notes is £$(5x + y)$ and this must equal £74. Hence

$$5x + y = 74 \qquad [2]$$

Subtracting equation [1] from equation [2],

$$4x = 24$$
$$x = 6$$

Therefore six £5 notes were used.

(2) Find two numbers such that their sum is 108 and their difference is 54.

Let x and y be the two numbers.

Then their sum is $x + y$ and their difference is $x - y$. Hence,

$$x + y = 108 \qquad [1]$$
$$x - y = 54 \qquad [2]$$

adding equations [1] and [2],

$$2x = 162$$
$$x = 81$$

Substituting for x in [1],

$$81 + y = 108$$
$$y = 108 - 81$$
$$y = 27$$

(3) A foreman and 7 men together earn £520 per week whilst 2 foremen and 17 men together earn £1220 per week. Find the weekly wages of a foreman.

Let a foreman earn £x per week and a man earn £y per week.

$$\therefore \qquad x + 7y = 520 \qquad [1]$$
$$2x + 17y = 1220 \qquad [2]$$

Multiplying equation [1] by 2,

$$2x + 14y = 1040 \qquad [3]$$

Subtracting equation [3] from equation [2]

$$3y = 180$$
$$y = 60$$

Substituting for $y = 60$ in equation [1],

$$x + 7 \times 60 = 520$$
$$x + 420 = 520$$
$$x = 100$$

Hence a foreman earns £100 per week.

Exercise 99 — *Questions 1 and 2 type B, 3—8 type C, remainder D*

1) Find two numbers such that their sum is 27 and their difference is 3.

2) A bill for £123 was paid with £5 and £1 notes a total of 59 notes being used. Find how many £5 notes were used.

3) £x is invested at 6% and £y is invested at 8%. The annual income from these investments is £23.20. If £x had been invested at 8% and £y at 6% the annual income would have been £21.60. Find x and y.

4) An alloy containing 8 cm³ of copper and 7 cm³ of tin has a mass of 121 g. A second alloy containing 9 cm³ of copper and 11 cm³ of tin has a mass of 158 g. Find the densities of copper and tin in g/cm³.

5) A motorist travels x km at 40 km/h and y km at 50 km/h. The total time taken is $2\frac{1}{2}$ hours. If the time taken to travel $6x$ km at 30 km/h and $4y$ km at 50 km/h is 14 hours find x and y.

6) 500 tickets were sold for a concert, some at 40 p each and the remainder at 25 p each. The money received for the dearer tickets was £70 more than for the cheaper tickets. Find the number of dearer tickets which were sold.

7) The ages of A and B are in the ratio 4 : 3. In eight years' time the ratio of their ages will be 9 : 7. Find their present ages. If n years ago, A was three times as old as B, find the value of n.

8) The organisers of a charity concert sold tickets at two different prices. If they had sold 112 of the dearer tickets and 60 of the cheaper ones they would have received £45.60 but if they had sold 96 of the dearer tickets and 120 of the cheaper ones they would have received £52.80. Find the price of the dearer tickets.

9) Two numbers are in the ratio $5 : 7$. When 15 is added to each the ratio changes to $5 : 6$. Calculate the two numbers.

10) A man bought a number of 3 p stamps and also sufficient 4 p stamps to make his total expenditure 120 p. If, instead of the 3 p stamps, he had bought three times as many 2 p stamps he would have needed 9 fewer 4 p stamps than before for his expenditure to be 120 p. Find how many 3 p stamps he bought.

SELF-TEST 21

In the following questions state the letter (or letters) which correspond to the correct answer (or answers).

1) In the simultaneous equations:

$$2x + 3y = 17$$
$$3x + 4y = 24$$

x is equal to 4. Hence the value of y is:

a $\dfrac{25}{3}$ b 75   c 3   d 4

2) In the simultaneous equations:
$$2x - 3y = -16$$
$$5y - 3x = 25$$

x is equal to -5. Hence the value of y is:

a 2   b -2 c $\dfrac{26}{3}$ d 0

3) By eliminating x from the simultaneous equations:
$$2x - 5y = 8$$
$$2x - 3y = -7$$
the equation below is obtained:

a $-8y = 1$ b $-2y = 15$
c $-8y = 15$ d $-2y = 1$

4) By eliminating y from the simultaneous equations:
$$3x - 4y = -10$$
$$x + 4y = 8$$

the equation below is obtained:

a $2x = -18$ b $4x = -18$
c $2x = -2$ d $4x = -2$

5) By eliminating x from the simultaneous equations:

$$3x + 5y = 2$$
$$x + 3y = 7$$

the equation below is obtained:

a $4y = -19$ b $8y = 9$
c $4y = 19$ d $4y = 5$

6) By eliminating y from the simultaneous equations:

$$2x - 4y = 3$$
$$3x + 8y = 7$$

the equation below is obtained:

a $7x = 13$ b $x = -1$
c $x = 1$ d $7x = 10$

7) The solutions to the simultaneous equations:

$$2x - 5y = 3$$
$$x - 3y = 1 \quad \text{are:}$$

a $x = 4, y = 1$ b $y = 4, x = 1$
c $y = 4, x = 13$ d $x = 4, y = 3$

8) The solutions to the simultaneous equations:

$$3x - 2y = 5$$
$$4x - y = 10 \quad \text{are:}$$

a $x = -3, y = 22$ b $x = -3, y = -22$
c $x = 3, y = 2$ d $x = 3, y = -2$

9) Two numbers, x and y, are such that their sum is 18 and their difference is 12. The equations below will allow x and y to be found:

a $x + y = 18$ b $x + y = 18$
  $y - x = 12$ $x - y = 12$
c $x - y = 18$ d $y - x = 18$
  $x + y = 12$ $x + y = 12$

10) A bill for 40 pence is paid by means of 5 pence and 10 pence pieces. Seven coins were used in all. If x is the number of 5 pence pieces used and y is the number of 10 pence pieces used then:

a $x + y = 7$ b $x + y = 7$
  $x + 2y = 40$ $5x + 10y = 40$
c $x - y = 7$ d $x - y = 7$
  $x + y = 40$ $5x + 10y = 40$

104

11) A motorist travels x km at 50 km/h and y km at 60 km/h. The total time taken is 5 hours. If his average speed is 56 km/h then:

a $50x + 60y = 5$
$\quad\ x + \quad y = 280$

b $6x + 5y = 1500$
$\quad x + \ y = 280$

c $\dfrac{x}{50} + \dfrac{y}{60} = 5$
$\quad\ \dfrac{x + y}{5} = 56$

d $50x + 60y = 5$
$\quad\ x + \quad y = 280$

12) 300 tickets were sold for a concert some at 20 p each and the remainder at 30 p each. The cash received for the cheaper tickets was £10 more than that received for the dearer tickets. Therefore:

a $\quad x + \quad y = 300$
$\quad 20x - 30y = 10$

b $\quad x + \quad y = 300$
$\quad 20x - 30y = 1000$

c $\ x + \ y = 300$
$\quad 2x - 3y = 100$

d $\ x + \ y = 300$
$\quad 2x + 3y = 1$

Chapter 22 Quadratic Equations

INTRODUCTION

An equation of the type $ax^2 + bx + c = 0$ is called a *quadratic equation*. The constants a, b and c can have any numerical values. Thus:

$$x^2 - 36 = 0$$

in which $a = 1$, $b = 0$ $c = -36$.

$$5x^2 + 7x + 8 = 0$$

in which $a = 5$, $b = 7$ and $c = 8$.

$$2.5x^2 - 3.1x - 2 = 0$$

in which $a = 2.5$, $b = -3.1$ and $c = -2$.

These are all examples of quadratic equations. A quadratic equation may contain only the square of the unknown quantity, as in the first of the above equations, or it may contain both the square and the first power as in the remaining two equations.

EQUATIONS OF THE TYPE $ax^2 + c = 0$

When $b = 0$, the standard quadratic equation $ax^2 + bx + c = 0$ becomes $ax^2 + c = 0$. The methods of solving such equations are shown in the examples which follow.

EXAMPLE 1

(1) Solve the equation $x^2 - 16 = 0$.

Since
$$x^2 - 16 = 0$$
$$x^2 = 16$$

Taking the square root of both sides
$$x = \pm\sqrt{16}$$
and
$$x = \pm 4$$

It is necessary to insert the double sign before the value obtained for x since $+4$ and -4 when squared both give 16. This means that there are two solutions which will satisfy the given equation. The solution $x = \pm 4$ means that either $x = +4$ or $x = -4$.

The solution to a quadratic equation always consists of a pair of numbers (i.e., there are always two solutions although it is possible for both solutions to have the same numerical value).

(2) Solve the equation $2x^2 - 12 = 0$.

Since
$$2x^2 - 12 = 0$$
$$2x^2 = 12$$
$$x^2 = 6$$
$$x = \pm\sqrt{6}$$
and
$$x = \pm 2.45$$

(by using the square root tables to find $\sqrt{6}$).

(3) Solve the equation $2x^2 + 18 = 0$.

Since
$$2x^2 + 18 = 0$$
$$2x^2 = -18$$
$$x^2 = -9$$
and
$$x = \pm\sqrt{-9}$$

The square root of a negative quantity has no arithmetic meaning and it is called an imaginary number. The reason is as follows:

$$(-3)^2 = 9 \qquad (+3)^2 = 9$$
$$\therefore \qquad \sqrt{9} = \pm 3$$

Hence it is not possible to give a meaning to $\sqrt{-9}$. The equation $2x^2 + 18 = 0$ is said, therefore, to have imaginary roots.

SOLUTION BY FACTORS

If the product of two factors is zero, then one factor or the other factor must be zero or they may both be zero. Thus if $ab = 0$, then either $a = 0$ or $b = 0$ or both $a = 0$ and $b = 0$.

We make use of this fact in solving quadratic equations.

EXAMPLE 2

(1) Solve the equation:

$$(2x + 3)(x - 5) = 0$$

Since the product of the two factors $(2x + 3)$ and $(x - 5)$ is zero then,

either $\quad 2x + 3 = 0 \quad$ giving $\quad x = -\dfrac{3}{2}$

or $\qquad x - 5 = 0 \quad$ giving $\quad x = 5$

The solutions are $\quad x = -\frac{3}{2} \quad$ or $\quad x = 5$.

(2) Solve the equation $\quad x^2 - 5x + 6 = 0$.

Factorising, $\quad (x - 3)(x - 2) = 0$

either $\qquad x - 3 = 0 \quad$ giving $\quad x = 3$

or $\qquad x - 2 = 0 \quad$ giving $\quad x = 2$

The solutions are $\quad x = 3 \quad$ or $\quad x = 2$.

(3) Solve the equation $\quad 6x^2 + x - 15 = 0$.

Factorising $\quad (2x - 3)(3x + 5) = 0$

either $\quad 2x - 3 = 0 \quad$ giving $\quad x = \dfrac{3}{2}$

or $\qquad 3x + 5 = 0 \quad$ giving $\quad x = -\dfrac{5}{3}$

The solutions are $\quad x = \dfrac{3}{2} \quad$ or $\quad x = -\dfrac{5}{3}$.

(4) Solve the equation $\quad x^2 - 5x = 0$.

Factorising $\quad x(x - 5) = 0$

either $\qquad\qquad x = 0$

or $\qquad x - 5 = 0 \quad$ giving $\quad x = 5$

The solutions are $\quad x = 0 \quad$ and $\quad x = 5 \quad$ (note that it is incorrect to say that the solution is $x = 5$. The solution $x = 0$ must be stated also).

Exercise 100 — *All type C*

Solve the following quadratic equations:

1) $x^2 - 25 = 0$

2) $x^2 - 8 = 0$

3) $x^2 - 16 = 0$

4) $3x^2 - 48 = 0$

5) $5x^2 - 80 = 0$

6) $7x^2 - 21 = 0$

7) $(x - 5)(x - 2) = 0$

8) $(3x - 4)(x + 3) = 0$

9) $x(x + 7) = 0$

10) $3x(2x - 5) = 0$

11) $m^2 + 4m - 32 = 0$

12) $x^2 + 9x + 20 = 0$

13) $m^2 = 6m - 9$

14) $x^2 + x - 72 = 0$

15) $3x^2 - 7x + 2 = 0$

16) $14q^2 = 29q - 12$

17) $9x + 28 = 9x^2$

18) $x^2 - 3x = 0$

19) $y^2 + 8y = 0$

20) $4a^2 - 4a - 3 = 0$

SOLUTION BY FORMULA

The standard form of the quadratic equation is

$$ax^2 + bx + c = 0$$

It can be shown that the solution of this equation is

$$x = \frac{-b \pm \sqrt{b^2 - 4ac}}{2a}$$

Note that the whole of the numerator including $-b$ is divided by $2a$. The formula is used when factorisation is not possible.

EXAMPLE 3

(1) Solve the equation:

$$3x^2 - 8x + 2 = 0$$

Comparing with $\quad ax^2 + bx + c = 0 \quad$ we have $a = 3, \quad b = -8 \quad$ and $\quad c = 2$. Substituting these values in the formula,

$$x = \frac{-(-8) \pm \sqrt{(-8)^2 - 4 \times 3 \times 2}}{2 \times 3}$$

$$= \frac{8 \pm \sqrt{64 - 24}}{6}$$

$$= \frac{8 \pm \sqrt{40}}{6}$$

$$= \frac{8 \pm 6.325}{6}$$

either

$$x = \frac{8 + 6.325}{6} \quad \text{or} \quad \frac{8 - 6.325}{6}$$

$$= \frac{14.325}{6} \quad \text{or} \quad \frac{1.675}{6}$$

$$= 2.39 \quad \text{or} \quad 0.28$$

(2) Solve the equation:

$$-2x^2 + 3x + 7 = 0$$

Where the coefficient of x^2 is negative it is best to make it positive by multiplying both sides of the equation by (-1). This is equivalent to changing the sign of each of the terms. Thus,

$$2x^2 - 3x - 7 = 0$$

This gives $a = 2$, $b = -3$ and $c = -7$.

$$x = \frac{-(-3) \pm \sqrt{(-3)^2 - 4 \times 2 \times (-7)}}{2 \times 2}$$

$$= \frac{3 \pm \sqrt{9 + 56}}{4}$$

$$= \frac{3 \pm \sqrt{65}}{4}$$

$$= \frac{3 \pm 8.063}{4}$$

either

$$x = \frac{11.063}{4} \quad \text{or} \quad x = \frac{-5.063}{4}$$

$$= 2.766 \quad \text{or} \quad -1.266$$

Exercise 101 — *All type B*

Solve the following equations:

1) $4x^2 - 3x - 2 = 0$

2) $x^2 - x - 1 = 0$

3) $3x^2 + 7x - 5 = 0$

4) $7x^2 + 8x - 2 = 0$

5) $5x^2 - 4x - 1 = 0$

6) $2x^2 - 7x = 3$

7) $x(x + 4) + 2x(x + 3) = 5$

8) $5x(x + 1) - 2x(2x - 1) = 20$

9) $x(x + 5) = 66$

10) $(2x - 3)^2 = 13$

EQUATIONS GIVING RISE TO QUADRATIC EQUATIONS

EXAMPLE 4

(1) Solve the simultaneous equations:

$$3x - y = 4 \qquad [1]$$
$$x^2 - 3xy + 8 = 0 \qquad [2]$$

From equation [1],

$$y = 3x - 4$$

Substituting for y in equation [2],

$$x^2 - 3x(3x - 4) + 8 = 0$$
$$x^2 - 9x^2 + 12x + 8 = 0$$
$$-8x^2 + 12x + 8 = 0$$
$$8x^2 - 12x - 8 = 0$$

Dividing throughout by 4,

$$2x^2 - 3x - 2 = 0$$
$$(2x + 1)(x - 2) = 0$$

either $2x + 1 = 0$ giving $x = -\dfrac{1}{2}$

or $x - 2 = 0$ giving $x = 2$

when $x = -\dfrac{1}{2}$, $y = 3 \times \left(-\dfrac{1}{2}\right) - 4 = -5\frac{1}{2}$

when $x = 2$, $y = 3 \times 2 - 4 = 2$.

Thus the solutions are:

$$x = -\frac{1}{2}, \quad y = -5\tfrac{1}{2} \quad \text{or} \quad x = 2, \quad y = 2$$

(2) Solve the simultaneous equations:

$$x - 6y - 5 = 0 \qquad [1]$$
$$xy - 6 = 0 \qquad [2]$$

From equation [1],

$$x = 6y + 5$$

Substituting for x in equation [2],

$$(6y + 5)y - 6 = 0$$
$$6y^2 + 5y - 6 = 0$$
$$(3y - 2)(2y + 3) = 0$$

either $3y - 2 = 0$ giving $y = \dfrac{2}{3}$

or $2y + 3 = 0$ giving $y = -\dfrac{3}{2}$

when $y = \dfrac{2}{3}$, $x = 6 \times \dfrac{2}{3} + 5 = 9$

when $y = -\dfrac{3}{2}$, $x = 6 \times \left(-\dfrac{3}{2}\right) + 5 = -4$

Thus the solutions are:

$$x = 9, \quad y = \dfrac{2}{3} \quad \text{or} \quad x = -4, \quad y = -\dfrac{3}{2}$$

Exercise 102 — *All type D*

Solve the following simultaneous equations:

1) $x + y = 3$
   $xy = 2$

2) $x - y = 3$
   $xy + 10x + y = 150$

3) $x^2 + y^2 - 6x + 5y = 24$
   $x + y = 9$

4) $x + y = 12$
   $2x^2 + 3y^2 = 7xy$

5) $2x^2 - 3y^2 = 20$
   $2x + y = 6$

6) $x^2 + y^2 = 34$
   $x + 2y = 13$

7) $3x + 2y = 13$
   $xy = 2$

8) $-3x + y + 15 = 0$
   $2x^2 + 4x + y = 0$

PROBLEMS INVOLVING QUADRATIC EQUATIONS

EXAMPLE 5

(1) The area of a rectangle is 6 square metres. If the length is 1 metre longer than the width find the dimensions of the rectangle.

Let x metres be the width of the rectangle.

Then the length of the rectangle is $(x + 1)$ metres. Since the area is length x breadth, then

$$x(x + 1) = 6$$
$$x^2 + x - 6 = 0$$
$$(x + 3)(x - 2) = 0$$

either $x + 3 = 0$ giving $x = -3$

or $x - 2 = 0$ giving $x = 2$

The solution cannot be negative and hence $x = 2$. Hence the width is 2 metres and the length is $(2 + 1) = 3$ metres.

(2) Two square rooms have a total floor area of 208 square metres. One room is 4 metres longer each way than the other. Find the floor dimensions of each room.

Let the smaller room have sides of x metres. The area of this room is then x^2 square metres.

The larger room will then have sides of $(x + 4)$ metres and its floor area is
$(x + 4)(x + 4) = (x + 4)^2$ square metres.

Hence
$$x^2 + (x + 4)^2 = 208$$
$$x^2 + x^2 + 8x + 16 = 208$$
$$2x^2 + 8x - 192 = 0$$

Dividing through by 2,
$$x^2 + 4x - 96 = 0$$
$$(x + 12)(x - 8) = 0$$

either $x + 12 = 0$ giving $x = -12$

or $x - 8 = 0$ giving $x = 8$

The negative value of x is not possible hence $x = 8$.

The floor dimensions of the two rooms are 8 metres by 8 metres and 12 metres by 12 metres.

(3) A rectangular room is 4 metres wider than it is high and it is 8 metres longer than it is wide. The total area of the walls is 512 square metres. Find the width of the room.

Let the height of the room be x metres. Then the width of the room is $(x + 4)$ metres and the length of the room is
$x + 4 + 8 = (x + 12)$ metres.

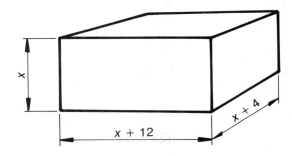

Fig. 22.1

These dimensions are shown in Fig. 22.1.

The total wall area is $2x(x+12)+2x(x+4)$.

Hence $2x(x+12)+2x(x+4)=512$

Dividing both sides of the equation by 2,

$$x(x+12)+x(x+4)=256$$
$$x^2+12x+x^2+4x=256$$
$$2x^2+16x=256$$

Dividing both sides of the equation by 2 again,

$$x^2+8x=128$$
$$x^2+8x-128=0$$
$$(x+16)(x-8)=0$$

either $x+16=0$ giving $x=-16$

or $x-8=0$ giving $x=8$

Thus the height of the room is 8 metres. Its width is $(x+4)=8+4=12$ metres.

(4) The smallest of three consecutive positive numbers is m. Three times the square of the largest is greater than the sum of the squares of the other two numbers by 67. Find m.

The three numbers are m, $m+1$ and $m+2$.

Three times the square of the larger number is $3(m+2)^2$.

The sum of the squares of the other two numbers is $m^2+(m+1)^2$.

$$\therefore \qquad 3(m+2)^2-[m^2+(m+1)^2]=67$$
$$3(m^2+4m+4)-[m^2+m^2+2m+1]=67$$
$$3m^2+12m+12-[2m^2+2m+1]=67$$
$$3m^2+12m+12-2m^2-2m-1=67$$
$$m^2+10m+11=67$$
$$m^2+10m-56=0$$
$$(m-4)(m+14)=0$$

either $m-4=0$ giving $m=4$

or $m+14=0$ giving $m=-14$

Since m must be positive its value is 4.

Exercise 103 — *Questions 1–7 type C, remainder D*

1) Find the number which when added to its square gives a total of 42.

2) A rectangle is 72 square metres in area and its perimeter is 34 metres. Find its length and breadth.

3) Two squares have a total area of 274 square centimetres and the sum of their sides is 88 centimetres. Find the side of the larger square.

4) The area of a rectangle is 4 square metres and its length is 3 metres longer than its width. Find the dimensions of the rectangle.

5) Part of a garden consists of a square lawn with a path 1.5 metres wide around its perimeter. If the lawn area is two-thirds of the total area find the length of a side of the lawn.

6) The largest of three consecutive positive numbers is n. The square of this number exceeds the sum of the other two numbers by 38. Find the three numbers.

7) The length of a rectangle exceeds its breadth by 4 centimetres. If the length were halved and the breadth increased by 5 cm the area would be decreased by 35 square centimetres. Find the length of the rectangle.

8) In a certain fraction the denominator is greater than the numerator by 3. If 2 is added to both the numerator and denominator, the fraction is increased by $\frac{6}{35}$. Find the fraction.

9) A piece of wire which is 18 metres long is cut into two parts. The first part is bent to form the four sides of a square. The second part is bent to form the four sides of a rectangle. The breadth of the rectangle is 1 metre and its length is x metres. If the sum of the areas of the square and rectangle is A square metres show that:

$$A=16-3x+\frac{x^2}{4}$$

If $A=9$, calculate the value of x.

10) One side of a rectangle is d cm long. The other side is 2 cm shorter. The side of a square is 2 cm shorter still. The sum of the areas of the square and rectangle is 148 square centimetres. Find an equation for d and solve it.

11) The exchange rate in 1964 was x dollars to £1. An American tourist remembered that in 1952 he needed $1\frac{1}{2}$ dollars more for each £1 he received in exchange. Using these facts only write down expressions for the number of pounds he received for a 100 dollar note: (a) in 1964 (b) in 1952.

In 1952 he received £12 less for his 100 dollars than in 1964. Form an equation in x and show that it may be reduced to the form $2x^2+3x-25=0$. Solve this equation for x.

12) A garage owner bought a certain number of litres of petrol for £156. If petrol costs x pence per litre write down an expression for the number of litres of petrol he received. When the price per litre was increased by a penny he found that he received 100 litres fewer for the same sum of money. Form an equation for x and show it reduces to $x^2 + x - 156 = 0$. Calculate the original price of the petrol per litre.

13) Two rectangular rooms each have an area of 240 square metres. If the length of one of the rooms is x metres and the other room is 4 metres longer, write down the width of each room in terms of x. If the widths of the rooms differ by 3 metres form an equation in x and show that this reduces to $x^2 + 4x - 320 = 0$. Solve this equation and hence find the difference between the perimeters of the rooms.

SELF-TEST 22

In the following questions state the letter (or letters) corresponding to the correct answer (or answers).

1) If $(2x - 3)(3x + 4) = 0$ then x is equal to:

a $-\dfrac{3}{2}$ or $\dfrac{4}{3}$ b $-\dfrac{2}{3}$ or $\dfrac{3}{4}$

c $\dfrac{2}{3}$ or $-\dfrac{3}{4}$ d $\dfrac{3}{2}$ or $-\dfrac{4}{3}$

2) If $(5x + 2)(3x - 2) = 0$ then x is equal to:

a $-\dfrac{2}{5}$ or $\dfrac{2}{3}$ b $-\dfrac{2}{5}$ or $-\dfrac{2}{3}$

c $\dfrac{5}{2}$ or $-\dfrac{3}{2}$ d $\dfrac{2}{5}$ or $-\dfrac{2}{3}$

3) If $(2x + 5)(4x - 7) = 0$ then x is equal to:

a $-\dfrac{2}{5}$ or $\dfrac{4}{7}$ b $-\dfrac{5}{2}$ or $\dfrac{7}{4}$

c $-\dfrac{5}{2}$ or $-\dfrac{7}{4}$ d $\dfrac{2}{5}$ or $-\dfrac{4}{7}$

4) If $x(2x - 5) = 0$ then x is equal to:

a $\dfrac{5}{2}$ b $-\dfrac{5}{2}$ c 0 or $\dfrac{5}{2}$ d 0 or $-\dfrac{5}{2}$

5) If $x^2 - 25 = 0$ then x is equal to:

a 0 b 5 c ± 5

6) If $3x^2 - 27 = 0$ then x is equal to:

a 9 b 3 c ± 3

7) If $x^2 - 5x - 2 = 0$ then x is equal to:

a $\dfrac{-5 \pm \sqrt{33}}{2}$ b $\dfrac{5 \pm \sqrt{33}}{2}$

c $\dfrac{-5 \pm \sqrt{17}}{2}$ d $\dfrac{5 \pm \sqrt{17}}{2}$

8) If $3x^2 + 2x - 3 = 0$ then x is equal to:

a $\dfrac{2 \pm \sqrt{40}}{6}$ b $\dfrac{-2 \pm \sqrt{40}}{6}$

c $\dfrac{2 \pm \sqrt{32}}{6}$ d $\dfrac{-2 \pm \sqrt{36}}{6}$

9) If $x^2 + 9x + 7 = 0$ then x is equal to:

a $\dfrac{9 \pm \sqrt{109}}{2}$ b $\dfrac{9 \pm \sqrt{53}}{2}$

c $\dfrac{-9 \pm \sqrt{109}}{2}$ d $\dfrac{-9 \pm \sqrt{53}}{2}$

10) If $x^2 - 7x + 3 = 0$ then x is equal to:

a $\dfrac{7 \pm \sqrt{37}}{2}$ b $\dfrac{7 \pm \sqrt{61}}{2}$

c $\dfrac{-7 \pm \sqrt{37}}{2}$ d $\dfrac{-7 \pm \sqrt{61}}{2}$

11) If $\dfrac{3}{x - 3} - \dfrac{2}{x - 1} = 5$ then:

a $5x^2 - 21x + 24 = 0$

b $5x^2 - 21x + 12 = 0$

c $x - 14 = 0$ d $x - 2 = 0$

12) If $\dfrac{2}{x + 1} - 3 = \dfrac{1}{x - 2}$ then:

a $3x^2 + 2x + 11 = 0$

b $-3x^2 - 2x - 11 = 0$

c $3x^2 - 4x - 1 = 0$

d $-3x^2 + 4x + 1 = 0$

Chapter 23 Indices and Logarithms

LAWS OF INDICES

The laws of indices are as shown below.

MULTIPLICATION

When multiplying powers of the same quantity together *add* the indices.

$$x^6 \times x^7 = x^{6+7} = x^{13}$$
$$y^2 \times y^3 \times y^4 \times y^5 = y^{2+3+4+5} = y^{14}$$

DIVISION

When dividing powers of the same quantity *subtract* the index of the denominator (bottom part) from the index of the numerator (top part).

$$\frac{x^5}{x^2} = x^{5-2} = x^3$$

$$\frac{a^3 \times a^4 \times a^8}{a^5 \times a^7} = \frac{a^{3+4+8}}{a^{5+7}}$$

$$= \frac{a^{15}}{a^{12}} = a^{15-12} = a^3$$

$$\frac{3y^2 \times 2y^5 \times 5y^4}{6y^3 \times 4y^4} = \frac{30y^{2+5+4}}{24y^{3+4}}$$

$$= \frac{30y^{11}}{24y^7} = \frac{5y^{11-7}}{4} = \frac{5y^4}{4}$$

POWERS

When raising the power of a quantity to a power *multiply* the indices together.

$$(3x)^3 = 3^{1 \times 3} \times x^{1 \times 3} = 3^3 x^3 = 27x^3$$
$$(a^2 b^3 c^4)^2 = a^{2 \times 2} b^{3 \times 2} c^{4 \times 2} = a^4 b^6 c^8$$
$$\left(\frac{3m^3}{5n^2}\right)^2 = \frac{3^2 m^{3 \times 2}}{5^2 n^{2 \times 2}} = \frac{9m^6}{25n^4}$$

NEGATIVE INDICES

A negative index indicates the reciprocal of the quantity.

$$a^{-1} = \frac{1}{a}$$

$$5x^{-3} = \frac{5}{x^3}$$

$$a^2 b^{-2} c^{-3} = \frac{a^2}{b^2 c^3}$$

FRACTIONAL INDICES

The numerator of a fractional index indicates the power to which the quantity must be raised; the denominator indicates the root which is to be taken.

$$x^{\frac{2}{3}} = \sqrt[3]{x^2}$$
$$ab^{\frac{3}{4}} = a \times \sqrt[4]{b^3}$$
$$a^{\frac{1}{2}} = \sqrt{a}$$

(Note that for square roots the number indicating the root is usually omitted.)

$$\sqrt{64a^6} = (64a^6)^{\frac{1}{2}} = (8^2 a^6)^{\frac{1}{2}}$$
$$= 8^{2 \times \frac{1}{2}} a^{6 \times \frac{1}{2}} = 8a^3$$

ZERO INDEX

Any quantity raised to the power of zero is equal to 1.

$$a^0 = 1$$
$$\left(\frac{x}{y}\right)^0 = 1$$

EXAMPLE 1

(1) $\left(\dfrac{1}{3}\right)^{-4} = \dfrac{1^{-4}}{3^{-4}} = \dfrac{3^4}{1^4} = 81$

(2) $4^{\frac{5}{2}} = (2^2)^{\frac{5}{2}} = 2^{\frac{2}{1} \times \frac{5}{2}}$

$$= 2^5 = 32$$

(3) $\sqrt{9x^2} = (3^2 x^2)^{\frac{1}{2}} = 3^{\frac{2}{1} \times \frac{1}{2}} x^{\frac{2}{1} \times \frac{1}{2}}$

$\qquad = 3^1 x^1 = 3x$

EXAMPLE 2

If $3^{p+4} = 9^{p-2}$ find the value of p.

$$3^{p+4} = (3^2)^{p-2}$$
$$3^{p+4} = 3^{2p-4}$$

Since $(p+4)$ and $(2p-4)$ are both powers of 3, they must be equal.

$\therefore \qquad p + 4 = 2p - 4$

$\qquad\qquad p = 8$

Exercise 104 — *Questions 1—7 type A,*
8—15 type B, remainder C

Simplify the following:

1) $3^5 \times 3^2 \times 3^7$

2) $b^2 \times b^4 \times b^5 \times b^8$

3) $\dfrac{5^7}{5^2}$

4) $\dfrac{2^3 \times 2^4 \times 2^7}{2^2 \times 2^5}$

5) $(7^2)^3$

6) $(3x^2 y^3)^4$

7) $(a^2 b^3 c)^5$

8) $\left(\dfrac{5a^3}{2b^2}\right)^7$

9) Find the values of: 10^{-1}, 2^{-5}, 3^{-4} and 5^{-2}.

10) Find the values of: $4^{\frac{1}{2}}$, $8^{\frac{1}{3}}$, $32^{\frac{1}{5}}$.

11) Express as powers of 3: 9^2, 27^4, 81^3.

12) Express as powers of x: $\sqrt[3]{x}$, $\sqrt[5]{x^3}$, $\sqrt[7]{x^4}$.

13) Find the value of: $32^{\frac{1}{5}} \times 25^{\frac{1}{2}} \times 27^{\frac{1}{3}}$.

14) Find the values of: $(\frac{1}{5})^0$, $125^{-\frac{1}{3}}$, $(1\,000\,000)^{\frac{1}{3}}$.

15) Find the value of $\sqrt{\dfrac{p}{q}}$ when $p = 64^{\frac{2}{3}}$ and $q = 3^{-2}$.

16) If $3^m = 9$, find m.

17) If $2^{x+1} = 4^x$ find x.

18) If $5^{2x+3} = 125^{x+5}$, find x.

19) Find the value of p for which $3^{2p-1} = 243$.

20) Find the value of x if $(2^{2x})(4^{x+1}) = 64$.

NUMBERS IN STANDARD FORM

A number expressed in the form $A \times 10^n$, where A is a number between 1 and 10 and n is an integer is said to be in standard form.

EXAMPLE 3

$$50\,000 = 5 \times 10\,000 = 5 \times 10^4$$
$$0.003 = \frac{3}{1000} = \frac{3}{10^3} = 3 \times 10^{-3}$$

Exercise 105 — *All type B*

Express each of the following in standard form:

1) 8000   5) 0.035

2) 92,500   6) 0.7

3) 893   7) 0.000 365

4) 5,600,000   8) 0.007 12

LOGARITHMS

Any positive number can be expressed as a power of 10. For instance:

$$1000 = 10^3$$
$$74 = 10^{1.869\,2}$$

These powers of 10 are called *logarithms to the base 10.*

That is: number $= 10^{\text{logarithm}}$

The log tables at the end of this book give the logarithms of numbers between 1 and 10.

Thus, $\log 5.176 = 0.714\,0$

To find the logarithms of numbers outside this range we make use of numbers in standard form and the multiplication law of indices. For example:

$$324.3 = 3.243 \times 10^2$$
$$\log 3.243 = 0.510\,9$$
$$324.3 = 10^{0.510\,9} \times 10^2$$
$$= 10^{2.510\,9}$$

$\therefore \qquad \log 324.3 = 2.510\,9$

A logarithm therefore consists of two parts:

(1) A whole number part called the *characteristic*.

(2) A decimal part called the *mantissa* which is found directly from the log tables.

For a number, 10 or greater, the characteristic is found by subtracting 1 from the number of figures to the left of the decimal point in the given number.

In the number 825.7 the characteristic is 2.

$\therefore \qquad \log 825.7 = 2.916\,8$

In the number 18 630 the characteristic is 4.

$\therefore \qquad \log 18\,630 = 4.270\,2$

NEGATIVE CHARACTERISTICS

$$0.632\,1 = 6.321 \times 10^{-1}$$

$$\log 6.321 = 0.800\,8$$

$$0.632\,1 = 10^{0.800\,8} \times 10^{-1}$$

$$= 10^{-1 + 0.800\,8}$$

The characteristic is therefore -1 and the mantissa is $0.800\,8$. However writing $-1 + 0.800\,8$ for the logarithm of $0.632\,1$ would be awkward and we therefore write:

$$\log 0.632\,1 = \bar{1}.800\,8$$

Note that the minus sign has been written above the characteristic but it must be clearly understood that

$$\bar{2}.735\,6 = -2 + 0.735\,6$$

and $\qquad \bar{4}.067\,3 = -4 + 0.067\,3$

All numbers between 0 and 1 have negative characteristics which are found by adding 1 to the number of zeros following the decimal point.

In the number 0.073 58 the characteristic is $\bar{2}$.

$\therefore \qquad \log 0.073\,58 = \bar{2}.866\,8$

In the number 0.000 612 3 the characteristic is $\bar{4}$.

$\therefore \qquad \log 0.000\,612\,3 = \bar{4}.787\,0$

ANTI-LOGARITHMS

The table of *antilogs* at the end of this book contains the numbers which correspond to the given logarithms. In using these tables remember that only the decimal part of the log is used.

EXAMPLE 4

(1) To find the number whose log is 2.531 2. Using the mantissa .531 2, we find 3398 as the number corresponding. Since the characteristic is 2 the number must be 339.8. (Note that $\log 339.8 = 2.531\,2$.)

(2) To find the number whose log is $\bar{3}.617\,8$. Using the mantissa .617 8 we find 4148 as the number corresponding. Since the characteristic is $\bar{3}$ the number must be 0.004 148. (Note that $\log 0.004\,148 = \bar{3}.617\,8$.)

Exercise 106 — *All type A*

Write down the logarithms of the following numbers:

1) 7.263	7) 70.01
2) 8.197	8) 176 300
3) 63.25	9) 0.178 6
4) 716.4	10) 0.006 341
5) 1823	11) 0.068 91
6) 78 640	12) 0.000 718 2

Write down the antilogs of the following:

13) 2.618 3	17) $\bar{1}.234\,5$
14) 1.735 8	18) $\bar{2}.600\,8$
15) 0.628 8	19) $\bar{4}.631\,8$
16) 3.105 8	20) $\bar{3}.555\,7$

RULES FOR THE USE OF LOGARITHMS
MULTIPLICATION

Find the logs of the numbers and *add* them together. The antilog of the sum gives the required answer.

EXAMPLE 5

$19.63 \times 0.067\,34 \times 0.918\,7$

	number	logarithm
	19.63	1.292 9
	0.067 34	$\bar{2}.828\,3$
	0.918 7	$\bar{1}.963\,2$
Answer =	1.215	0.084 4

DIVISION

Find the log of each number. Then *subtract* the log of the denominator (bottom number) from the log of the numerator (top number).

EXAMPLE 6

$$\frac{17.63}{0.038\,62}$$

number	logarithm
17.63	1.246 3
0.038 62	$\overline{2}$.586 8
Answer = 456.6	2.659 5

EXAMPLE 7

$$\frac{0.617\,8 \times 20.31}{136.5 \times 0.092\,73}$$

In problems where there is multiplication and division a table layout like the one below is helpful.

Numerator		Denominator	
number	logarithm	number	logarithm
0.617 8	$\overline{1}$.790 8	136.5	2.135 1
20.31	1.307 7	0.092 73	$\overline{2}$.967 2
numerator	1.098 5	denominator	1.102 3
denominator	1.102 3		
Answer = 0.991 3	$\overline{1}$.996 2		

POWERS

Find the log of the number and *multiply* it by the index denoting the power.

EXAMPLE 8

$$(0.317\,8)^3$$

$$\log (0.317\,8)^3 = 3 \times \log 0.317\,8$$
$$= 3 \times \overline{1}.502\,2 = \overline{2}.506\,6$$

By finding the antilog of $\overline{2}.506\,6$

$$(0.317\,8)^3 = 0.032\,11$$

EXAMPLE 9

$$\frac{(0.763\,1)^4 \times 18.26}{0.916\,2}$$

The table layout shown below is helpful when powers or roots form part of the calculation.

number	operator	logarithm
$(0.763\,1)^4$	$4 \times \overline{1}.882\,6$	$\overline{1}$.530 4
18.26		1.261 5
		0.791 9
0.916 2		$\overline{1}$.962 0
Answer = 6.759		0.829 9

ROOTS

Find the logarithm of the number and *divide* it by the number denoting the root.

EXAMPLE 10

$$\sqrt[3]{0.731\,8}$$

$$\log 0.731\,8 = \overline{1}.864\,4$$

$$\log \sqrt[3]{0.731\,8} = \frac{\overline{1}.864\,4}{3}$$

We must make the negative characteristic exactly divisible by 3 so we write:

$$\frac{\overline{1}.864\,4}{3} = \frac{\overline{3} + 2.864\,4}{3} = \overline{1}.954\,8$$

(Note that $\overline{3} + 2.864\,4 = \overline{1}.864\,4$)

Hence $\sqrt[3]{0.731\,8} = 0.901\,2$

Exercise 107 — *All type C*

Use logs to find the values of:

1) 37.16×9.234

2) $11.14 \times 1.783 \times 28.42$

3) $158.2 \times 0.778\,3$

4) $0.087\,39 \times 0.118\,8$

5) $\dfrac{186.4}{27.93}$

6) $\dfrac{0.917\,8}{0.034\,82}$

7) $\dfrac{2.418}{0.006\,134}$

8) $\dfrac{0.158\,9}{29.48}$

115

9) $\dfrac{178.2 \times 0.006\,342}{11.43 \times 0.736\,2}$

10) $\dfrac{765\,8 \times 0.000\,116\,4}{178.2 \times 26.43}$

11) $(9.763)^4$

12) $(27.14)^3$

13) $(0.563\,2)^3$

14) $(0.013\,25)^2$

15) $(0.299\,8)^2 \times 17.63$

16) $\dfrac{(0.516\,2)^2}{0.063\,17}$

17) $\dfrac{46\,327 \times (0.618\,2)^3}{19.17 \times (2.483)^2}$

18) $\sqrt[3]{17.63}$

19) $\sqrt[4]{1.289}$

20) $\sqrt[3]{0.061\,82}$

21) $\sqrt[5]{0.761\,9}$

22) $\sqrt[3]{0.000\,782\,8}$

USE OF LOGARITHMS IN EVALUATING FORMULAE

EXAMPLE 11

(1) A positive number is given by the formula

$$y = \dfrac{3t}{\sqrt{c}}$$

(i) Use tables to calculate y when $t = 7.32$ and $c = 205$.

(ii) If t may take any value from 5 to 8 (inclusive) and c may take any value from 100 to 225 (inclusive), calculate the greatest possible value of y.

(i) Substituting the given values $t = 7.32$ and $c = 205$,

$$y = \dfrac{3 \times 7.32}{\sqrt{205}} = \dfrac{21.96}{14.32}$$

by using the square root tables.

Using the log tables:

number	log
21.96	1.341 6
14.32	1.155 9
Answer = 1.533	0.185 7

Hence $y = 1.533$.

116

(ii) The greatest possible value of y will occur when t has its greatest possible value and c has its least possible value. Hence, when $t = 8$ and $c = 100$,

$$y = \dfrac{3 \times 8}{\sqrt{100}} = \dfrac{24}{10} = 2.4$$

(2) Calculate the value of y from the formula

$$y^3 = \dfrac{ab}{a - b}$$

when $a = 0.649$ and $b = 0.022$.

Since

$$y^3 = \dfrac{ab}{a - b}$$

$$y = \sqrt[3]{\dfrac{ab}{a - b}}$$

Substituting the given values $a = 0.649$ and $b = 0.022$,

$$y = \sqrt[3]{\dfrac{0.649 \times 0.022}{0.649 - 0.022}} = \sqrt[3]{\dfrac{0.649 \times 0.022}{0.627}}$$

Using the log tables:

number	log
0.649	$\overline{1}.812\,2$
0.022	$\overline{2}.342\,4$
0.649 × 0.022	$\overline{2}.154\,6$
0.627	$\overline{1}.797\,3$
0.649 × 0.022 ÷ 0.627	$\overline{2}.357\,3$
	÷ 3
Answer = 0.283 4	$\overline{1}.452\,4$

Hence $y = 0.283\,4$.

(Note that we can only use logs when numbers are to be multiplied or divided. They must never be used when numbers are to be added or subtracted.)

WRITING FORMULAE IN LOGARITHMIC FORM

When working with formulae it is often useful to write the equation connecting the quantities in logarithmic form.

EXAMPLE 12

(1) Write the equation $P = \dfrac{RT}{V}$ in logarithmic form.

We are given that $P = R \times T \div V$

$\therefore \quad \log P = \log R + \log T - \log V$

Note that multiplication signs become plus signs and division signs become minus signs.

(2) Write the equation $t = 2\pi\sqrt{\dfrac{W}{gf}}$ in logarithmic form.

Writing the equation in index form it becomes:

$$t = 2\pi\left(\frac{W}{gf}\right)^{1/2} = \frac{2\pi W^{1/2}}{g^{1/2} f^{1/2}}$$
$$= 2\pi W^{1/2} g^{-1/2} f^{-1/2}$$

$$\therefore \quad \log t$$
$$= \log 2 + \log \pi + \tfrac{1}{2}\log W - \tfrac{1}{2}\log g - \tfrac{1}{2}\log f$$

(3) Express as a formula without logarithms:

$$\log y = 3 - n \log x$$

The expressions on the R.H.S. must all be made logarithms and since $\log 1000 = 3$,

$$\log y = \log 1000 - n \log x$$
$$\therefore \qquad y = \frac{1000}{x^n}$$

SOLVING LOGARITHMIC EQUATIONS

The methods are shown in the following examples.

EXAMPLE 13

(1) If $\log x^2 - \log 10 = 1$ find x.

Now $\log x^2 = 2 \log x$ and $\log 10 = 1$

$$\therefore \qquad 2 \log x - 1 = 1$$
$$\therefore \qquad 2 \log x = 2$$
$$\therefore \qquad \log x = 1$$

Since the anti-log of 1 is 10,

$$x = 10$$

(2) If $VT^n = C$ find the value of n when $V = 12$, $T = 3$ and $C = 108$.

Substituting the given values in the equation,

$$12 \times 3^n = 108$$

Taking logs of both sides

$$\log 12 + n \log 3 = \log 108$$

Since $\log 12 = 1.0792$; $\log 3 = 0.4771$ and $\log 108 = 2.0334$ we have,

$$1.0792 + 0.4771n = 2.0334$$
$$\therefore \qquad 0.4771n = 0.9542$$

$$\therefore \qquad n = \frac{0.9542}{0.4771}$$
$$\therefore \qquad n = 2$$

Exercise 108 — *All type C*

1) Evaluate the formula $1.73 \times \sqrt[3]{d^2}$ when $d = 2.8$.

2) Find D from the formula $D = 1.2 \times \sqrt{dL}$ when $d = 12$ and $L = 0.756$.

3) Find the value of the expression:
$$0.25 \times (d - 0.5)^2 \times \sqrt{S}$$
when $d = 4.33$ and $S = 5.12$.

4) Find the value of the expression:
$$\frac{p_1 v_1 - p_2 v_2}{c - 1}$$
when $v_1 = 28.6$, $v_2 = 32.2$, $p_1 = 18.5$, $p_2 = 13.5$ and $c = 1.42$.

5) Find P from the formula:
$$P = \sqrt{\frac{x^2 - y^2}{2xy}}$$
when $x = 5.531$ and $y = 3.469$.

6) If $A = PV^n$ find A when $P = 0.9314$, $V = 0.6815$ and $n = \tfrac{1}{2}$.

7) Calculate M from the formula:
$$M^3 = \frac{3x^2 w}{p}$$
when $x = 0.3512$, $w = 1.664$ and $p = 2.308$.

8) Given that $x = \dfrac{dh}{D - d}$ find x when $d = 0.638$, $h = 0.516$ and $D = 0.721$.

9) Find the value of R from the equation:
$$R = k\sqrt{\frac{P}{H^2}}$$
when $k = 65.2$, $P = 81.3$ and $H = 22.7$.

10) Transpose the formula:
$$y = \frac{Wl^3}{48EI}$$
to make I the subject and find its value when $y = 0.346$, $W = 10\,300$, $l = 122$ and $E = 30 \times 10^6$.

11) If $N = 10^x$ find N when x is:
(a) 3   (b) $\tfrac{1}{2}$ (c) $\tfrac{1}{3}$

12) Solve the following equations for x:

(a) $10^{2x} = 320.2$ (b) $3^{3x} = 9$
(c) $5 \times 2^x = 100$ (d) $\log x^2 = 4$
(e) $2 \log x - 1 = 3$

13) If $pv^n = C$ find n when $p = 80$, $v = 3.1$ and $c = 329.2$.

14) If $\log x^4 - \log 100 = 1$ find x.

15) Find x if
$$\log x^2 = \log \sqrt{16} - \log 2 + \log 3^2.$$

SELF-TEST 23

State the letter (or letters) corresponding to the correct answer (or answers) to all questions except Question 8.

1) If $2^x = 32$ then x is equal to:

a 5   b $\sqrt{32}$ c 16   d $\dfrac{1}{5}$

2) The product of 2.5×10^4 and 8×10^{-5} is:

a 1.8   b 2.0   c 5.5   d 105

3) $(x^{1/2})^3 \times \sqrt{x^9}$ is equal to:

a $x^{9/2}$ b x^5 c $x^{11/2}$ d x^6

4) The cube root of $0.036\,03$ is:

a 0.330 3   b 0.033 03   c 0.600 2
d 6.002

5) $(8x^3)^{-1/3}$ is equal to:

a $8x$ b $\dfrac{8}{x}$ c $2x$ d $\dfrac{1}{2x}$

6) $(3x^3)^2$ is equal to:

a $3x^5$ b $9x^5$ c $3x^6$ d $9x^6$

7) $\sqrt{9p^4} \div \dfrac{1}{2}p^2$ is equal to:

a 6   b 3   c $6p^4$ d $3p^4$

8) Write down $0.097\,63$ in standard form:

a 97.63×10^3 b 9.763×10^2
c 9.763×10^{-2} d 97.63×10^{-3}

9) If $a = 1.2 \times 10^7$ and $b = 3.2 \times 10^6$ then $\sqrt{a^2 + b^2}$ is equal to:

a 1.242×10^6 b 1.242×10^7
c 2.098×10^7 d 2.098×10^6

10) If $\sqrt{3} = 1.732$ correct to three decimal places then $\sqrt{27}$, correct to two decimal places, is equal to:

a 2.99   b 5.19   c 5.20   d 8.98

11) The cube root of 27×10^{-6} is:

a 3×10^{-3} b 5.20×10^{-3}
c 3×10^{-2} d 5.20×10^{-2}

12) $(5 \times 7^3) \times (3 \times 7^5)$ is equal to:

a 8×7^8 b 15×7^8 c 8×7^{15}
d 15×7^{15}

13) $\sqrt{16a^4 b^{16}}$ is equal to:

a $8a^2 b^4$ b $4a^2 b^4$ c $4a^2 b^8$ d $8a^2 b^8$

14) If $\log y = -2$ then y is equal to:

a -100 b -0.01 c 0.1   d 0.01

15) The largest of the numbers $\dfrac{1}{7}$, 1.3×10^{-1}, 0.12 and 1.4×10^{-2} is:

a $\dfrac{1}{7}$ b 1.3×10^{-1} c 0.12
d 1.4×10^{-2}

16) The value of $32^{-3/5}$ is:

a 19.2   b $\dfrac{1}{8}$ c 8   d -19.2

17) $\dfrac{5 \times 10^{-6}}{0.001}$ is equal to:

a 5×10^{-9} b 5×10^{-4} c 5×10^{-3}
d 5×10^{-2}

18) The value of $\left(\dfrac{1}{9}\right)^{-1/2}$ is:

a -9 b $-\dfrac{1}{18}$ c $-\dfrac{1}{3}$ d 3

19) $8 \times 10^{-3} \times 1.25 \times 10^4$ is equal to:

a 1   b 10   c 100   d 2

20) The value of $10^{1.324\,3}$ is:

a 13.243   b 0.132 43   c 2.110
d 21.10

21) The value of $10^{0.301\,0} \times 10^{0.477\,1}$ is:

a 6   b 60   c 0.778 1   d 7.781

22) The value of $(10^{1.431\,4})^{1/3}$ is:

a 4.771   b 0.477 1   c 3   d 30

23) The value of $10^{-1.770\,9}$ is:

a $-0.177\,09$ b -17.709
c 0.169 4   d 0.016 94

24) $\bar{2}.8 \div 6$ is equal to:

a $\bar{2}.6$ b -2.6 c $\bar{1}.8$ d -1.8

25) $\bar{8}.2 \div 3$ is equal to:

a $\bar{2}.4$ b $\bar{3}.4$ c -3.4 d -2.4

Chapter 24 **Arithmetical and Geometrical Series**

SERIES

A set of numbers which are connected by some definite law is called a *series* or *progression*.

Each of the numbers forming the set is called a term of the series. The following sets of numbers are examples of series:

1, 3, 5, 7 . . . (each term is obtained by adding 2 to the previous term);

1, 3, 9, 27 . . . (each term is three times the preceding term).

SERIES IN ARITHMETICAL PROGRESSION

A series in which each term is obtained by adding or subtracting a constant amount is called an arithmetical progression (often abbreviated to A.P.) Thus in the series 1, 4, 7, 10 . . . the difference between each term and the preceding one is 3. The difference between one term and the preceding term is called the *common difference*. Thus for the above series the common difference is 3. Some further examples of series in A.P. are 0, 5, 10, 15 . . . (common difference is 5) 6, 8, 10, 12 . . . (common difference is 2).

GENERAL EXPRESSION FOR A SERIES IN A.P.

Let the first number in the series be a and the common difference be d. The series can then be written as:

$$a, a + d, a + 2d, a + 3d \ldots$$

The first term is a.

The second term is $a + d$.

The third term is $a + 2d$.

The fourth term is $a + 3d$.

Notice that the coefficient of d is always one less than the number of the term. Thus:

the 8th term is $a + 7d$

the 19th term is $a + 18d$.

EXAMPLE 1

(1) Find the 9th and 18th terms of the series 1, 5, 9 . . . .

The 1st term is 1 and hence $a = 1$.

The common difference is 4 and hence $d = 4$.

The 9th term $= a + 8d = 1 + 8 \times 4 = 33$.

The 18th term $= a + 17d = 1 + 17 \times 4 = 69$.

(2) The 5th term of a series in A.P. is 19 and the 11th term is 43. Find the 20th term.

The 5th term is $a + 4d = 19$ [1]

The 11th term is $a + 10d = 43$ [2]

Subtracting equation [1] from [2]

$$6d = 24$$
$$d = 4$$

Substituting for d in equation [1]

$$a + 4 \times 4 = 19$$
$$a = 3$$

The 20th term is $a + 19d = 3 + 19 \times 4 = 79$.

(3) Find the number of the term which is 65 in the series 2, 5, 8 . . . .

Here $a = 2$ and $d = 3$.

Let the nth term be 65 then:

$$a + (n - 1)d = 65$$
$$2 + 3(n - 1) = 65$$
$$3(n - 1) = 63$$
$$n - 1 = 21$$
$$n = 22$$

Hence the 22nd term is 65.

(4) Insert five arithmetic means between 2 and 26.

This question poses the problem of finding five numbers between 2 and 26 such that 2 ? ? ? ? ? 26 forms a series in A.P.

The 1st term is 2 hence $a = 2$.
The 7th term is 26 hence $a + 6d = 26$.

$$2 + 6d = 26$$
$$6d = 24$$
$$d = 4$$

2nd term is $a + d = 2 + 4 = 6$.
3rd term is $a + 2d = 2 + 8 = 10$.
4th term is $a + 3d = 2 + 12 = 14$.
Similarly the 5th term is 18 and the 6th term is 22.
The series is 2, 6, 10, 14, 18, 22, 26.

SUM OF A SERIES IN A.P.

The sum of a series in A.P. is

$$S = \frac{n}{2}(a + l)$$

where n = the number of terms in the series
a = the 1st term in the series
l = the last term in the series

EXAMPLE 2
Find the sum of the series 5, 9, 13 . . . if the series consists of 12 terms.

We have

$$a = 5 \quad \text{and} \quad d = 4 \quad \text{with} \quad n = 12$$
$$l = a + 11d = 5 + 44 = 49$$

Hence the sum is

$$S = \frac{12}{2}(5 + 49) = 6 \times 54 = 324$$

Exercise 109 — *All type A*

1) Find the 10th term of the series 1, 4, 7, 10 . . .

2) Find the 8th term of the series 5, 11, 17 . . .

3) The 3rd term of a series in A.P. is 32 and the 7th term is 16. Find the 12th term.

4) The 7th term of a series in A.P. is 32 and the 15th term is 72. Find the 24th term.

5) Find the number of the term which is 47 in the series 2, 5, 8 . . .

6) Insert six arithmetic means between 7 and 42.

7) Find the sum of the series 8, 11, 14 . . . If there are 10 terms in the series.

8) Find the sum of the series in arithmetical progression which has a 1st term of 60 and a 9th and last term of 96.

9) A series in A.P. has its 5th term equal to 25 and its 9th term equal to 41. If the series has 14 terms calculate its sum.

10) A series in A.P. has a sum of 120. If its 3rd term is 7 and its 7th term is 15 find the number of terms in the series.

SERIES IN GEOMETRICAL PROGRESSION

A series in which each term is obtained from the preceding term by multiplying or dividing by a constant quantity is called a *geometric progression* or simply a G.P. The constant quantity is called the *common ratio* for the series. In the series 1, 2, 4, 8, 16 . . . , each successive term is formed by multiplying the preceding term by 2. The series is therefore in G.P. with a common ratio of 2.

Some further examples of series in G.P. are:
2, 10, 50, 250 . . . (common ratio of 5),
8, 24, 72, 216 . . . (common ratio of 3),
24, 12, 6, 3 . . . (common ratio of $\frac{1}{2}$).

GENERAL EXPRESSION FOR A SERIES IN G.P.

Let the first term be a and the common ratio be r. The series can be represented by a, ar, ar^2, ar^3 . . .

The first term is a.

The second term is ar.

The third term is ar^2.

The fourth term is ar^3.

Notice that the index of r is always one less than the number of the term in the series.

Thus the 9th term is ar^8 (the index of r is 8) the 20th term is ar^{19} (the index of r is 19).

EXAMPLE 3
(1) Find the 7th term of the series 2, 6, 18 . . .

The 1st term is 2 and the common ratio is 3, that is $a = 2$ and $r = 3$.

The 7th term is $ar^6 = 2 \times 3^6 = 1458$.

(2) The 1st term of a series in G.P. is 19 and the 6th term is 27. Find the 10th term.

The first term is $a = 19$.

The sixth term is $ar^5 = 27$.   [1]

Substituting for a in [1],

$$19r^5 = 27$$

$$r = \sqrt[5]{\frac{27}{19}} = 1.073$$

The tenth term is $ar^9 = 19 \times 1.073^9 = 35.75$.

(3) Insert four geometric means between 1.8 and 11.2. This is equivalent to putting four terms between 1.8 and 11.2 so that the six numbers form a series in G.P.

Thus   1.8, ?, ?, ?, ?, 11.2   must be a G.P.

The first term is $a = 1.8$.

The sixth term is $ar^5 = 11.2$.   [1]

Substituting for a in [1],

$$1.8r^5 = 11.2$$

$$r = \sqrt[5]{\frac{11.2}{1.8}} = 1.442$$

Hence the second term is

$$ar = 1.8 \times 1.442 = 2.596$$

The third term is

$$ar^2 = 1.8 \times 1.442^2 = 2.596 \times 1.442$$

$$= 3.774$$

The fourth term is

$$ar^3 = 3.774 \times 1.442 = 5.399$$

The fifth term is

$$ar^4 = 5.399 \times 1.442 = 7.785$$

The required series is 1.8, 2.596, 3.774, 5.399, 11.2.

SUM OF A SERIES IN G.P.

The sum of a series in G.P. is

$$S = \frac{a(r^n - 1)}{r - 1}$$

which is a convenient form if r is greater than 1.

If r is less than 1 it is better to use the following expression:

$$S = \frac{a(1 - r^n)}{1 - r}$$

In both expressions:

    a = the first term in the series

    r = the common ratio

    n = the number of terms in the series

EXAMPLE 4

(1) Find the sum of the series 2, 6, 18 . . . which has six terms.

Since the common ratio, r, is 3 (obtained from $\frac{6}{2}$ or $\frac{18}{6}$) we shall use the expression:

$$S = \frac{a(r^n - 1)}{r - 1}$$

In this problem $a = 2$ and $n = 6$. Substituting these two values in the expression for S we get,

$$S = \frac{2 \times (3^6 - 1)}{3 - 1} = \frac{2 \times (729 - 1)}{2} = 728$$

(2) Find the sum of the series 71.2, 65.50, 60.26 . . . which has eight terms.

Here $r = \frac{65.50}{71.20} = 0.92$

Hence we shall use the expression:

$$S = \frac{a(1 - r^n)}{1 - r}$$

Since $a = 71.2$ and $r = 0.92$ we have:

$$S = \frac{71.2 \times (1 - 0.92^8)}{1 - 0.92} = \frac{71.2 \times (1 - 0.513\,2)}{0.08}$$

$$= \frac{71.2 \times 0.486\,8}{0.08} = 433.25$$

Exercise 110 — *All type A*

1) In a series in G.P. the first term is 5 and the common ratio is 2. Find the eighth and fourteenth terms.

2) Find the seventh term of the series 3, 12, 48 . . . .

3) Find the eighth term of the series 1.1, 1.21, 1.331 . . . .

4) Find the sixth term of the series 14.6, 11.826, 9.579 . . . .

5) The first term in a series in G.P. is 24 and the fifth term is 39. Find the eleventh term.

6) The third term in a series in G.P. is 17 and the seventh term is 42. Find the ninth term.

7) Insert six geometric means between 9.2 and 27.6.

8) Find the sum of the series 9.8, 6.86, 4.802 . . . which has eight terms.

9) Find the sum of the series 5, 8, 12.8 . . . which has seven terms.

10) The first term of a series in G.P. is 3.4 and the fifth term is 19.8. If the series has ten terms find its sum.

SELF-TEST 24

State the letter corresponding to the correct answer.

1) In the series 1.5, 1.25, 1.00, . . . the common difference is:

a 1.25   b 1.2   c 0.25   d $-$ 0.25

2) In the series $\frac{1}{16}, \frac{1}{8}, \frac{1}{4}, \ldots$ the common ratio is:

a $\frac{1}{16}$ b $\frac{1}{2}$ c 2   d $-$ 2

3) The eighth term of a geometric progression whose first term is m and whose common ratio is a is given by:

a $m + 8a$ b $m + 7a$ c ma^7 d ma^8

4) The fifth term of an arithmetic progression whose first term is p and whose common difference is q is given by:

a $p + 5q$ b $p + 4q$ c pq^5

d pq^4

5) The sum of the series 3, 1, $-$ 1, to 10 terms is:

a 60   b 1025   c $-$ 1025

d $-$ 60

Chapter 25 **The Remainder Theorem, etc.**

LONG MULTIPLICATION

The long multiplication of algebraic terms is sometimes required. The method is shown in Example 1.

EXAMPLE 1

Multiply $(x^2 - 3x + 2)$ by $(2x + 5)$.

$$
\begin{aligned}
(x^2 - 3x + 2)(2x + 5) &= 2x(x^2 - 3x + 2) + 5(x^2 - 3x + 2) \\
&= 2x^3 - 6x^2 + 4x + 5x^2 - 15x + 10 \\
&= 2x^3 - x^2 - 11x + 10
\end{aligned}
$$

If desired, the work may be set out as follows:

$$
\begin{array}{l}
\quad x^2 - 3x + 2 \\
\quad\quad\; 2x + 5 \\
\hline
2x^3 - 6x^2 + 4x \qquad \text{[multiplying } (x^2 - 3x + 2) \text{ by } 2x] \\
\quad\quad\; 5x^2 - 15x + 10 \quad \text{[multiplying } (x^2 - 3x + 2) \text{ by } 5] \\
\hline
2x^3 - x^2 - 11x + 10 \quad \text{[adding like terms together]}
\end{array}
$$

Notice that in long multiplication by this method, like terms are placed directly beneath each other in order to facilitate their addition.

LONG DIVISION

The way in which long division is done is shown in Example 2.

EXAMPLE 2

Simplify $\dfrac{2x^3 - 13x^2 + 11x + 6}{2x - 3}$.

$$
\begin{array}{r}
x^2 - 5x - 2 \\
2x - 3 \,\big)\, 2x^3 - 13x^2 + 11x + 6 \\
\underline{2x^3 - 3x^2} \;\ldots\; x^2(2x - 3) = 2x^3 - 3x^2 \\
-10x^2 + 11x \\
\underline{-10x^2 + 15x} \;\ldots\; -5x(2x - 3) = -10x^2 + 15x \\
-4x + 6 \\
\underline{-4x + 6} \;\ldots\; -2(2x - 3) = -4x + 6 \\
\cdot \;\; \cdot \;\; \cdot
\end{array}
$$

Start off by dividing $2x$ into $2x^3$. The result is x^2. Place x^2 in the answer and multiply $2x - 3$ by x^2 to give $2x^3 - 3x^2$. Subtracting $2x^3 - 3x^2$ from $2x^3 - 13x^2$ gives $-10x^2 + 11x$. Now divide $2x$ into $-10x^2$. The result is $-5x$. Place $-5x$ in the answer and bring down $+11x$. Multiply $2x - 3$ by $-5x$ to give $-10x^2 + 15x$. Subtracting $-10x^2 + 15x$ from $-10x^2 + 11x$ gives $-4x$. Next divide $2x$ into $-4x$. The result is -2 which is placed in the answer. Bring down $+6$ and multiply $2x - 3$ by -2 giving $-4x + 6$. Subtracting $-4x + 6$ from $-4x + 6$ gives zero and hence the division is finished.

Note that in this case there is no remainder.

Hence $\dfrac{2x^3 - 13x^2 + 11x + 6}{2x - 3} = x^2 - 5x - 2$

EXAMPLE 3

Divide $3x^4 + 6x^3 - 2x^2 + 3x - 8$ by $x - 2$ and state the remainder.

$$x - 2 \,)\,3x^4 + 6x^3 - 2x^2 + 3x - 8 \,(\,3x^3 + 12x^2 + 22x + 47$$
$$\underline{3x^4 - 6x^3}$$
$$12x^3 - 2x^2$$
$$\underline{12x^3 - 24x^2}$$
$$22x^2 + 3x$$
$$\underline{22x^2 - 44x}$$
$$47x - 8$$
$$\underline{47x - 94}$$
$$86$$

Hence the remainder is 86.

THE REMAINDER THEOREM

An expression like $5x^4 + 7x^3 - 3x^2 + 2x - 9$ is called a *polynomial* expression. Suppose we wish to find the remainder when this expression is divided by $(x - 3)$. This could be done by long division as shown in Example 3, but the work is speeded up by using the *remainder theorem*.

The remainder theorem states that when a polynomial expression is divided by $(x - a)$ the remainder is obtained by writing a for x in the given expression.

Thus to find the remainder when $5x^4 + 7x^3 - 3x^2 + 2x - 9$ is divided by $(x - 3)$ all we have to do is to substitute $x = 3$ in the given polynomial expression. Hence

$$\text{remainder} = 5 \times 3^4 + 7 \times 3^3 - 3 \times 3^2$$
$$+ 2 \times 3 - 9 = 564$$

EXAMPLE 4

Find the value of k if the remainder when the polynomial $3x^4 + kx^3 - 6x^2 + 5x + 8$ is divided by $(x - 2)$ is 74.

Substituting $x = 2$ in the expression we have

$$\text{remainder} = 3 \times 2^4 + k \times 2^3 - 6 \times 2^2$$
$$+ 5 \times 2 + 8 = 42 + 8k$$

Therefore
$$42 + 8k = 74$$
$$8k = 32$$
$$k = 4$$

The remainder theorem may also be used to help factorise polynomial expressions. If the remainder is zero when a polynomial expression is divided by $(x - a)$ then $(x - a)$ is a factor of the expression.

EXAMPLE 5

(1) Show that $(x - 5)$ is a factor of $x^3 + 3x^2 - 2x - 190$. Substituting $x = 5$ in the given expression we have,

$$\text{remainder} = 5^3 + 3 \times 5^2 - 2 \times 5 - 190 = 0$$

Since the remainder is zero when $x = 5$ is substituted in the given expression then $(x - 5)$ is a factor of it.

(2) Show by using the remainder theorem that $(2x - 3)$ is a factor of $2x^2 - 11x + 12$.

We may write $(2x - 3)$ as $2(x - 1.5)$ and hence $(2x - 3)$ is a factor if the remainder is zero when $x = 1.5$ is substituted in $2x^2 - 11x + 12$.

$$\text{Remainder} = 2 \times 1.5^2 - 11 \times 1.5 + 12 = 0$$

Hence $(2x - 3)$ is a factor of $2x^2 - 11x + 12$.

Exercise 111 — *All type A*

1) Multiply $(2x^3 - 5x - 3)$ by $(2x - 4)$.

2) Multiply $(4x^3 - 2x^2 + 7x - 3)$ by $(x + 5)$.

3) Divide $(2x^3 - 7x^2 + 11x - 10)$ by $(x - 2)$.

4) Divide $(6x^4 - 7x^3 + 16x^2 - 13x + 3)$ by $(2x - 1)$.

5) Find the remainder when $x^4 + 5x^2 - 7x + 8$ is divided by $x - 5$.

6) Find the remainder when $16x^4 - 8x^3 + 4x^2 - 2x + 3$ is divided by $2x - 5$.

7) Find the value of k if the remainder is 60 when $2x^4 + kx^3 - 11x^2 + 4x + 12$ is divided by $x - 3$.

8) Show that $(x + 3)$ and $(x - 2)$ are both factors of $x^3 - 7x + 6$. What is the third factor?

9) Find the values of p and q if $(x - 1)$ and $(x + 2)$ are both factors of $px^3 + 4x^2 + qx - 6$.

10) Show that $x - 2$ is a factor of $x^3 - 7x^2 + 14x - 8$ and find the other factors.

EQUATIONS AND IDENTITIES

A *conditional equation* is satisfied by *only* a certain number of values of the variable. Thus the equation

$$x^2 - 3x + 2 = 0$$

is satisfied *only* by $x = 2$ and $x = 1$. No other values will satisfy this equation.

An *identity* is an equation which is satisfied by *all* values of the variable. Thus:

$$x(x + 2) = x^2 + 2x$$

is true for *all* values of x and hence it is an identity.

The symbol $\equiv$ is usually used to show that the equation is an identity. Thus:

$$(x - 4)(x + 3) \equiv x^2 - x - 12$$

From the definition of an identity it is clear

that the coefficients of like terms on the two sides of the equation must be identical. Thus if:

$$3x^2 - 7x + 8 \equiv Ax^2 + Bx + C$$

then $A = 3$, $B = -7$ and $C = 8$.

EXAMPLE 6

If, for all values of x,

$$(x - 2)(x - 3) \equiv (x - 1)(x - 4) + A(x - 2)$$
$$- B(x - 4)$$

find the values of A and B.

Removing brackets,

$$x^2 - 5x + 6 \equiv x^2 - 5x + 4 + Ax - 2A - Bx + 4B$$
$$\equiv x^2 + x(-5 + A - B) + (4 - 2A + 4B)$$

Since the equation is an identity we may equate the coefficients of like terms. Hence,

$$-5 = -5 + A - B$$

$$\therefore \qquad A - B = 0 \qquad\qquad [1]$$

$$6 = 4 - 2A + 4B$$

$$\therefore \qquad 2A - 4B = -2 \qquad\qquad [2]$$

Solving these two simultaneous equations gives:

$$A = 1 \quad \text{and} \quad B = 1$$

Exercise 112 — *All type A*

1) If $x^2 + 3x + 7 \equiv Ax^2 + Bx + C$, find the values of A, B and C.

2) If, for all values of x,

$$x(4x + 5) = Ax(2x + 5) + Bx$$

find the values of A and B.

3) If $(x - 1)(x - 2) \equiv x^2 + Ax + B$, find the values of A and B.

4) If $x(3x - 7)(2x + 3) \equiv Ax^3 + Bx^2 + Cx + D$, find the values of A, B, C and D.

5) If $(2x - 3)(x - 4) = Ax^2 + B(x - 1) + C(x - 2)$ find the values of A, B and C.

Miscellaneous Exercise

EXERCISE 113

This exercise is divided into two sections A and B. The questions in Section A are intended to be done very quickly, but those in Section B should take about 20 minutes each to complete. All the questions are of the type found in O Level examination papers.

SECTION A

1) Express 35.7×10^{-3} in the form $A \times 10^n$ where $1 \leqslant A < 10$ and n is an integer.
(A.E.B. 1975)

2) Factorise completely $2\pi r^2 - 6\pi r h^2$.
(A.E.B. 1975)

3) Solve the equations:
(a) $x^2 + 4x = 0$
(b) $y^2 - 4 = 0$
(A.E.B. 1975)

4) If $5x = 7y$ state the ratio of x to y.
(A.E.B. 1975)

5) Solve the simultaneous equations:

$$3x + 2y = 4 \qquad [1]$$
$$x + 2y = 0 \qquad [2]$$
(A.E.B. 1975)

6) (a) Write down from your tables the square root of 50.
(b) Hence write down the value of $\sqrt{500\,000}$.
(A.E.B. 1975)

7) Solve the equation $9x^2 - 4 = 0$. (J.M.B.)

8) Given the formula $y = mx + c$, obtain a formula for x in terms of y, m and c. (J.M.B.)

9) Use tables to evaluate $\sqrt{(2.8)^2 + (4.5)^2}$.
(J.M.B.)

10) Factorise completely:
(a) $3x^2 + 12$
(b) $3x^2 + 12x$
(c) $3x^2 + 12x + 9$.
(J.M.B.)

11) Find the value of:

$$(3.48)^2 + 2(3.48)(1.52) + (1.52)^2 \qquad \text{(L)}$$

12) If x is a real number, find correct to 2 decimal places the positive value of x which satisfies the equation:

$$2x^2 - x - 4 = 0 \qquad \text{(L)}$$

13) The positive numbers I, n, E, R and r are connected by the formula $I = \dfrac{nE}{nR + r}$.
Express n in terms of I, E, R and r. (L)

14) The real numbers x and y are related by:

$$y = \frac{4}{5}(x - 18)$$

(a) When $x = 4$, find the value of y.
(b) Find the value of x when $y = 6$. (L)

15) (a) Write down the expansion of $(x + y)^2$.
(b) Given that $x^2 + y^2 = 37$ and $x + y = 7$, find the value of xy. (L)

16) Evaluate:
(a) the positive square root of $(49)^3$.
(b) $\dfrac{0.28}{3.142 \times 0.83}$ correct to 2 significant figures. (L)

17) The positive numbers r and A are connected by the formula $r = \sqrt{\dfrac{A}{4\pi}}$.

(a) Find the value of r when $A = 154$ (take π as $3\frac{1}{7}$).
(b) Express A in terms of r and π. (L)

18) Simplify $\dfrac{1}{x - 1} - \dfrac{1}{x + 1}$. (J.M.B.)

19) Using mathematical tables calculate the value of $\dfrac{(6.23)^2 \times 8.75}{0.326}$. (J.M.B.)

20) Given that 2 kg of apples and 5 oranges cost 79 p and that 1 kg of apples and 9 oranges cost 59 p, calculate the cost of an orange. (J.M.B.)

21) Make x the subject of the formula $p = \dfrac{k}{\sqrt{x}}$. (A.E.B. 1975)

22) State two possible values of x for which $x^2 - 5x - 6 = 0$. (A.E.B. 1975)

23) Use tables to calculate $(0.5948)^{\frac{1}{3}}$ correct to 3 significant figures. (A.E.B. 1976)

24) Make K the subject of the formula
$$p = \sqrt{\frac{K-1}{K+1}}.$$
(L)

25) Solve the equation $3x^2 - 8x + 2$, giving the roots correct to 2 decimal places. (L)

26) Solve for x, the simultaneous equations:
$$x - 2y = 1 \qquad [1]$$
$$xy - y = 8 \qquad [2]$$
(L)

27) Use tables to evaluate $\dfrac{\sqrt{905.5}}{0.0879}$. (L)

28) Calculate the value of $\dfrac{y + y^{-\frac{1}{2}}}{y^{\frac{1}{3}}}$ when $y = 64$. (L)

29) Factorise completely the expression $2x^3 - 9x^2 + 10x - 3$ given that $x - 3$ is one of the factors. (L)

30) Simplify $\dfrac{1}{(x+1)(x+2)} + \dfrac{1}{x+2}$. (J.M.B.)

31) Solve the equation $\dfrac{3x+2}{x+2} = x$. (J.M.B.)

32) Factorise $(3x+4)^2 - 9$. (J.M.B.)

33) Given that $x + 3y$ is five times $2y - 3x$, find $\dfrac{x}{y}$. (J.M.B.)

34) Find the value of p which satisfies the equation:
$$0.2(p-15) + 0.3(p+20) = 8 \quad \text{(J.M.B.)}$$

35) Factorise completely $2 - 10x - 12x^2$. (J.M.B.)

36) Find the value of $\frac{2}{3}[(9.7)^2 - (5.3)^2]$. (A.E.B. 1973)

37) Find the value of q which satisfies the equations:
$$3p - 4q - 11 = 0 \qquad [1]$$
$$5p + 9q + 13 = 0 \qquad [2]$$
(A.E.B. 1973)

38) Find the value of p for which $2^{p+3} = 4^p$. (A.E.B. 1973)

39) Given that $\dfrac{1}{a} + \dfrac{1}{b} = \dfrac{1}{c}$, use reciprocal tables to calculate the value of b when $a = -0.35$ and $c = 0.4666$. (A.E.B. 1973)

40) Simplify $\dfrac{2w^2 + w - 6}{4w^2 - 9}$. (A.E.B. 1973)

41) Given that $x = (x-b)(x+d)$ express b in terms of x and d. (A.E.B. 1973)

42) Calculate the exact value of $\dfrac{0.185\,82}{3.26}$ and express the answer in the form $B \times 10^{-n}$, where B is a number between 1 and 10 and n is an integer. (L)

43) Solve the simultaneous equations:
$$xy = 42 \qquad [1]$$
$$x - 4y = 17 \qquad [2]$$
(L)

44) Express as a single fraction
$$\frac{5}{x^2 - 1} - \frac{2}{(x-1)^2}.$$
(L)

45) Without using tables evaluate:
(a) $8^{\frac{4}{3}}$ (b) $(-\frac{1}{2})^{-2}$ (c) $(3\frac{1}{2})^0$. (L)

46) Factorise completely:
(a) $27 - 3x^2$ (b) $3 + 2x - 8x^2$. (L)

47) Solve the equation:
$$\tfrac{1}{5}(x-2) - \tfrac{1}{7}(x+3) = 1 \qquad \text{(L)}$$

48) Simplify $\dfrac{4x+6}{4x^2-9}$. (L)

49) Make x the subject of the formula
$$y = \frac{p+x}{1-px}.$$
(L)

50) Without using tables, evaluate:
(a) $(\frac{8}{27})^{-\frac{1}{3}}$ (b) $\sqrt[3]{0.027}$ (c) $25^{\frac{3}{2}}$. (L)

51) The value of y which satisfies the equation $4(y-4) = 20$ is:

a 1   b 24   c 6   d 9   e 4

52) Five times a certain number plus six is equal to seven times the number plus one. If the number is m what is the correct algebraic statement?

a $5m + 6 = 7 + m + 1$

b $5 \times m + 6 = 7 + m + 1$

c $5 + m + 6 = 7 \times m + 1$

d $5 + m + 6 = 7 + m + 1$

e $5m + 6 = 7m + 1$

53) When $100I = PTR$, then:

(a) When $P = 5$, $T = 6$ and $R = 7$, then I is:

   a 21 000   **b** 2100   **c** 210   **d** 21

   e 2.1

(b) When $I = 42$, $P = 560$ and $R = 2\frac{1}{2}$, then T is:

   a $\frac{1}{3}$ **b** $2\frac{1}{2}$ **c** 3   **d** $3\frac{1}{3}$

   e none of these

(c) R is equal to:

   a $100IPT$ **b** $100I - PT$ **c** $\dfrac{PT}{100I}$

   d $\dfrac{100I}{PT}$ **e** $\dfrac{PTI}{100}$

54) If $(x + 3)(x - 1) = 0$ then the value of x is:

a 3 or -1 **b** 3 or 1   **c** -3 or -1

d -3 or 1   **e** 3 or 0

55) $(2x + y) - (x - 2y)$ is equal to:

a $3x - y$ **b** $x + 3y$ **c** $x - 3y$

d $3x + y$ **e** $x - y$

56) $(2x + y)(x - 2y)$ is equal to:

a $2x^2 - 2y^2$ **b** $2x^2 + 2y^2$

c $2x^2 + 3xy + 2y^2$ **d** $2x^2 + 3xy - 2y^2$

e $2x^2 - 3xy - 2y^2$

57) Which one of the following is not equal to $\frac{1}{2}pq$?

a $\dfrac{pq}{2}$ **b** $p \times \dfrac{q}{2}$ **c** $\frac{1}{2}qp$

d $\dfrac{1}{2p} \times q$ **e** $q \times \dfrac{p}{2}$

58) $(3a^2)^3$ is equal to:

a $3a^6$ **b** $9a^6$ **c** $18a$ **d** $27a^3$

e $27a^6$

59) The value of $64^{\frac{1}{3}}$ is:

a 2   **b** 8   **c** 16   **d** 4   **e** $21\frac{1}{3}$

60) $x - 2$ and $x + 3$ are factors of:

a $2x + 1$ **b** $x^2 - 9$ **c** $x^2 - 6$

d $x^2 - x - 6$ **e** $x^2 + x - 6$

61) If $\log 5 = 0.699\,0$ then $\log 0.05$ is:

a $\overline{2}.699\,0$ **b** $\overline{1}.699\,0$ **c** $0.699\,0$

d $1.699\,0$ **e** $2.699\,0$

62) The number 36 700 written in standard form is:

a 36.7×10^3 **b** 3.67×10^5 **c** 3.67×10^4

d $3.670\,0$ **e** 367×10^2

63) If $\log \overline{1}.360\,0$ is divided by 4 the answer is:

a $\overline{1}.090\,0$ **b** $\overline{1}.340\,0$ **c** $\overline{1}.840\,0$

d $\overline{1}.590\,0$ **e** $\overline{1}.680\,0$

64) If $X = Pr + Q$ then r is:

a $X - Q - P$ **b** $\dfrac{X}{P + Q}$ **c** $\dfrac{Q - X}{P}$

d $\dfrac{X - Q}{P}$ **e** $\dfrac{X - P}{Q}$

65) If $a * b$ is $\sqrt{ab}$ the value of $4 * 9$ is:

a 7   **b** 36   **c** 6   **d** 49   **e** 5

SECTION B

66) In a factory, x metal hooks and $(x + 4)$ plastic hooks are produced every minute. Write down expressions for the times, in seconds, to produce one metal hook and one plastic hook respectively.

If a metal hook takes $1\frac{1}{4}$ seconds longer to produce than a plastic hook, form an equation in x and solve it.

Calculate the total number of hooks produced altogether in 8 minutes.   (L)

67) Of the series:

(i) $2 - \frac{1}{2} + \frac{1}{8} - \ldots$
(ii) $2 - \frac{1}{2} + 1 - \ldots$
(iii) $2 - \frac{1}{2} - 3 - \ldots$

one is an arithmetic progression (A.P.), one is a geometric progression (G.P.) and one is neither.

(a) State which is the A.P. and calculate its common difference.

(b) State which is the G.P. and calculate its common ratio.

(c) Calculate the sum of the first 20 terms of the A.P.

(d) The 25th term of the G.P. is equal to 2^n. Find the value of n.   (L)

68) In the following questions

$$a = \frac{1}{x - 1} \quad \text{and} \quad b = \frac{1}{2x + 3}.$$

(a) Find the value of $3a + b$ when $x = 4$.

(b) Use logarithms to evaluate $\sqrt[3]{5a}$ when $x = 7.911$.

(c) Express $a - 2b$ as a single fraction in its simplest terms.

(d) When $a + b = \frac{1}{6}$, prove that x satisfies the equation:
$$2x^2 - 17x - 15 = 0$$
Solve this equation for x, giving your answers correct to one decimal place.
(A.E.B. 1976)

69) (a) Use logarithms to evaluate
$$\frac{(11.31)^4}{5432 \times 0.978\,5}.$$

(b) Two variable quantities x and y are connected by the relation $y = a + bx^2$, where a and b are constants. Given that $y = 16\frac{1}{2}$ when $x = 2$ and $y = 9\frac{1}{2}$ when $x = 1\frac{1}{2}$, calculate the values of a and b. Find the value of y when $x = 5$ and the values of x when $y = 1\frac{1}{4}$. (A.E.B. 1977)

70) When the price of admission to a discothèque rises by $5\,\mathrm{p}$, the takings rise from £37.50 to £40 but the attendance drops by 50. Given that the new price of admission is x pence obtain expressions in terms of x for:

(a) the old price of admission,
(b) the old attendance,
(c) the new attendance.

Hence obtain an equation for x and solve it.
(J.M.B.)

71) (a) One square has a side of length p cm and a second square has a side of length q cm. Their perimeters differ by 20 cm and their areas differ by 110 cm². Form two equations that show the relationship between p and q and hence find the values of p and q.

(b) Given that
$$\log_{10}(x^2 + 5) - \log_{10}(x + 2) = 1$$

show that $x^2 - 10x - 15 = 0$ and hence find the positive value of x correct to 3 significant figures.
(A.E.B. 1977)

72) Given that $\dfrac{6 - 3y}{2y + 1} = x$:

(a) Find y in terms of x.
(b) Express $2x + 3$ as a single fraction in terms of y.
(c) Calculate the values of y for which $x = 2y$. (L)

73) (a) Solve the equations:
$$2x^2 + xy - y^2 = 8 \qquad [1]$$
$$3x + y = 7 \qquad [2]$$

(b) If, for all values of x,
$$(x - 4)(x - 2) = (x - 3)(x - 5) - A(x - 3) - B(x - 4)$$
where A and B are numerical constants, find the values of A and B.
(L)

74) (a) Use logarithms to evaluate
$$\sqrt[3]{\frac{5.761}{24 \times 4.368}}.$$

(b) If $\log_{10} 2 = 0.301\,03$ and $\log_{10} 3 = 0.477\,12$ find, correct to five decimal places:
(i) $\log_{10} 6$
(ii) $\log_{10} 9$
(iii) $\log_{10} 1.5$.

(c) Without using tables find the value of x if $2^x = 4^{x-4}$. (L)

75) (a) Solve the equations:
$$x^2 + 3y^2 + xy - x = 18 \qquad [1]$$
$$2x + 3y = 7 \qquad [2]$$

(b) Given that $(x - k)$ is a factor of $2x^2 + kx - k - 2$, find the two possible values of k and hence find the other factor in each case. (L)

129

Chapter 26 **Mensuration**

THE METRIC SYSTEM OF LENGTH

The metric system is essentially a decimal system. The standard unit of length is the metre but for some purposes the metre is too large a unit and it is therefore split up into smaller units as follows:

$$1 \text{ metre (m)} = 10 \text{ decimetres (dm)}$$
$$= 100 \text{ centimetres (cm)}$$
$$= 1000 \text{ millimetres (mm)}$$

When dealing with large distances the metre is too small a unit and large distances are measured in kilometres.

$$1 \text{ kilometre (km)} = 1000 \text{ metres}$$

Since the metric system is essentially a decimal system we can easily convert from one unit to another by simply moving the decimal point the required number of places.

EXAMPLE 1

Convert 3.792 m into centimetres.

$$1 \text{ m} = 100 \text{ cm}$$
$$3.792 \text{ m} = 100 \times 3.792 \text{ cm}$$
$$= 379.2 \text{ cm}$$

EXAMPLE 2

Convert 98 375 mm into metres.

$$1000 \text{ mm} = 1 \text{ m}$$
$$1 \text{ mm} = \frac{1}{1000} \text{ m}$$
$$98\,375 \text{ mm} = \frac{98\,375}{1000} \text{ m} = 98.375 \text{ m}$$

Sometimes you may have difficulty in deciding whether to multiply or divide when converting from one unit to another. If you remember that when converting to a smaller unit you multiply and when converting to a larger unit you divide, this difficulty will disappear.

THE METRIC SYSTEM FOR MASS

The standard unit of mass is the kilogram which is suitable for most purposes connected with weights and measures. However for some purposes the kilogram is too large a unit and the gram is then used. For very small masses the milligram is used.

$$1 \text{ kilogram (kg)} = 1000 \text{ grams (g)}$$
$$1 \text{ gram} = 1000 \text{ milligrams (mg)}$$

For very large masses the tonne is used, such that

$$1 \text{ tonne} = 1000 \text{ kg}$$

EXAMPLE 3

Convert 5397 mg into grams.

$$1000 \text{ mg} = 1 \text{ g}$$
$$1 \text{ mg} = \frac{1}{1000} \text{ g}$$
$$5397 \text{ mg} = \frac{5397}{1000} \text{ g} = 5.397 \text{ g}$$

EXAMPLE 4

Convert 2.56 kg into grams.

$$1 \text{ kg} = 1000 \text{ g}$$
$$2.56 \text{ kg} = 1000 \times 2.56 \text{ g} = 2560 \text{ g}$$

EXAMPLE 5

Convert 5.4 tonnes into kilograms.

$$5.4 \text{ tonnes} = 5.4 \times 1000 \text{ kg}$$
$$= 5400 \text{ kg}$$

Exercise 114 — *All type A*

1) Convert to metres:

(a) 5.63 km   (b) 0.68 km
(c) 17.698 km   (d) 592 cm
(e) 68 cm   (f) 6895 mm
(g) 73 mm   (h) 4597 cm
(i) 798 mm   (j) 5 mm

2) Convert to kilometres:

(a) 9753 m   (b) 259 m
(c) 58 m   (d) 2985 cm
(e) 790 685 mm

3) Convert to centimetres:

(a) 4.68 m   (b) 0.782 m
(c) 5.16 km   (d) 3897 mm
(e) 88 mm

4) Convert to millimetres:

(a) 1.234 m   (b) 0.58 km
(c) 25.8 cm   (d) 389 cm
(e) 0.052 m

5) Convert to kilograms:

(a) 530 g   (b) 35 000 g
(c) 2473 mg   (d) 597 600 mg

6) Convert into grams:

(a) 56 000 mg   (b) 96 mg
(c) 8.63 kg   (d) 0.081 kg
(e) 584 mg

7) Convert 18 200 kg into tonnes.

8) Convert 19.4 tonnes into kilograms.

SI UNITS

The Système International d'Unités (the international system of units) is essentially a metric system. It is based upon six fundamental units which are:

Length — the metre (abbreviation m)
Mass — the kilogram (kg)
Time — the second (s)
Electric current — the ampere (A)
Luminous Intensity — the candela (cd)
Temperature — the Kelvin (K)

Where possible, multiples and sub-multiples should be of the form 10^{3n} where n is an integer. Thus 5000 metres should be written as 5 kilometres and not as 50 hectometres. Double prefixes are not permitted in the SI system. For example 1000 km cannot be written as 1 kkm but only as 1 Mm. Again, 0.000 006 km cannot be written as 6 μkm but only as 6 mm.

EXAMPLE 6

(1) Express 203 560 kg as the highest multiple possible.

$$203\,560 \text{ kg} = 203\,560 \times 10^3 \text{ gram}$$
$$= 203.560 \times 10^3 \times 10^3 \text{ gram}$$
$$= 203.560 \times 10^6 \text{ gram}$$
$$= 203.560 \text{ mega gram}$$
$$= 203.560 \text{ Mg}$$

(It is usually better to use 203.560 Mg rather than 0.203 560 Gg). Note that 203.560 Mg is also written 203.560 tonnes.

(2) A measurement is taken as 0.000 000 082 m. Express this measurement as a standard submultiple of a metre.

$$0.000\,000\,082 \text{ m} = \frac{82}{1\,000\,000\,000} \text{ m}$$
$$= \frac{82}{10^9} \text{ m} = 82 \times 10^{-9} \text{ m}$$
$$= 82 \text{ nm}$$

(It is better to use 82 nm rather than 0.082 pm).

For many applications some of the above units are too small or too large and hence multiples and sub-multiples are often needed. These multiples and sub-multiples are given special names which are shown here on the right:

Multiplication Factor	Prefix		Symbol
1 000 000 000 000	10^{12}	tera	T
1 000 000 000	10^9	giga	G
1 000 000	10^6	mega	M
1 000	10^3	kilo	k
100	10^2	hecto	h
10	10^1	deca	da
0.1	10^{-1}	deci	d
0.01	10^{-2}	centi	c
0.001	10^{-3}	milli	m
0.000 001	10^{-6}	micro	μ
0.000 000 001	10^{-9}	nano	n
0.000 000 000 001	10^{-12}	pico	p
0.000 000 000 000 001	10^{-15}	femto	f
0.000 000 000 000 000 001	10^{-18}	atto	a

Express each of the following as a standard multiple or sub-multiple.

1) 8000 m

2) 15 000 kg

3) 3800 km

4) 1 891 000 kg

5) 0.007 m

6) 0.000 001 3 m

7) 0.028 kg

8) 0.000 36 km

9) 0.000 064 kg

10) 0.003 6 A

Express each of the following in the form $A \times 10^n$ where A is a number between 1 and 10 and n is an integer.

11) 53 km

12) 18 kg

13) 3.563 Mg

14) 18.76 Gg

15) 70 mm

16) 78 mg

17) 358 pm

18) 18.2 μm

19) 270.6 Tm

20) 253 μg

UNITS OF AREA

The area of a plane figure is measured by seeing how many square units it contains. 1 square metre (abbreviation: m^2) is the area contained in a square whose side is 1 metre. Similarly 1 square centimetre (abbreviation: cm^2) is the area contained in a square having a side of 1 cm.

EXAMPLE 7

(1) Figure 26.1 shows the cross-section of a girder. Find its area in square centimetres. The section may be split up into two rectangles and a parallelogram as shown.

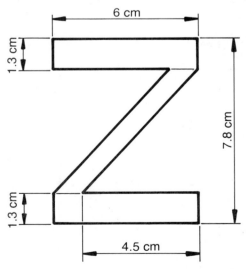

Fig. 26.1

area of rectangle $= 6 \times 1.3$

$= 7.8$ cm^2

area of parallelogram $= 1.5 \times 5.2$

$= 7.8$ cm^2

area of section $= 7.8 + 7.8 + 7.8$

$= 23.4$ cm^2

(2) A quadrilateral has the dimensions shown in Fig. 26.2. Find its area.

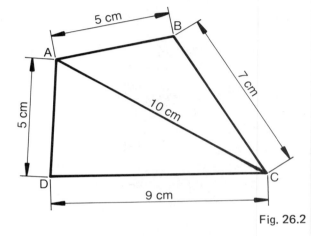

Fig. 26.2

The quadrilateral is made up to the triangles ABC and ACD. To find their areas we use the formulae given on the opposite page.

To find the area of $\triangle$ ABC,

$$s = \frac{5 + 7 + 10}{2} = 11$$

Area of $\triangle$ ABC

$= \sqrt{s(s-a)(s-b)(s-c)}$

$= \sqrt{11 \times (11-5) \times (11-7) \times (11-10)}$

$= \sqrt{11 \times 6 \times 4 \times 1}$

$= \sqrt{264} = 16.25$ cm^2

To find the area of $\triangle$ ACD,

$$s = \frac{5 + 9 + 10}{2} = 12$$

Area of $\triangle$ ACD

$= \sqrt{s(s-a)(s-b)(s-c)}$

$= \sqrt{12 \times (12-5) \times (12-9) \times (12-10)}$

$= \sqrt{12 \times 7 \times 3 \times 2}$

$= \sqrt{504} = 22.45$ cm^2

$\therefore$ area of quadrilateral

$=$ area of $\triangle$ ABC $+$ area of $\triangle$ ACD

$= 16.25 + 22.45 = 38.70$ cm^2

AREAS OF PLANE FIGURES

The following table gives the areas and perimeters of some simple geometrical shapes.

Figure	Diagram	Formulae
Rectangle	b, l	Area $= l \times b$ Perimeter $= 2l + 2b$
Parallelogram	h, b	Area $= b \times h$
Triangle	B, c, a, h, A, b, C	Area $= \frac{1}{2} \times b \times h$ Area $= \sqrt{s(s-a)(s-b)(s-c)}$ where $s = \dfrac{a+b+c}{2}$
Trapezium	a, h, b	Area $= \frac{1}{2} \times h \times (a + b)$
Circle	r	Area $= \pi r^2$ Circumference $= 2\pi r$ ($\pi = 3.142$ or $\frac{22}{7}$)
Sector of a circle	$\theta°$, r	Area $= \pi r^2 \times \dfrac{\theta}{360}$ Length of arc $= 2\pi r \times \dfrac{\theta}{360}$

133

(3) The cross-section of a block of metal is shown in Fig. 26.3. Find its area.

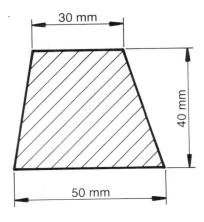

Fig. 26.3

Area of trapezium $= \frac{1}{2} \times 40 \times (30 + 50)$

$\qquad\qquad\qquad = \frac{1}{2} \times 40 \times 80$

$\qquad\qquad\qquad = 1600 \text{ mm}^2$

(4) A hollow shaft has an outside diameter of 3.25 cm and an inside diameter of 2.5 cm. Calculate the cross-sectional area of the shaft (Fig. 26.4).

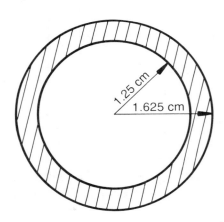

Fig. 26.4

Area of cross-section

$= $ area of outside circle $-$ area of inside circle

$= \pi \times 1.625^2 - \pi \times 1.25^2$

$= \pi(1.625^2 - 1.25^2)$

$= 3.142 \times (2.640 - 1.563)$

$= 3.142 \times 1.077$

$= 3.388 \text{ cm}^2$

(5) Calculate:
(a) the length of arc of a circle whose radius is 8 m and which subtends an angle of 56° at the centre, and
(b) the area of the sector so formed.

Length of arc $= 2\pi r \times \dfrac{\theta°}{360}$

$\qquad\qquad\quad = 2 \times \pi \times 8 \times \dfrac{56}{360}$

$\qquad\qquad\quad = 7.82 \text{ m}$

Area of sector $= \pi r^2 \times \dfrac{\theta°}{360}$

$\qquad\qquad\quad = \pi \times 8^2 \times \dfrac{56}{360}$

$\qquad\qquad\quad = 31.28 \text{ m}^2$

Exercise 116 — *All type A*

1) The area of a rectangle is 220 mm². If its width is 25 mm find its length.

2) A sheet metal plate has a length of 147.5 mm and a width of 86.5 mm. Find its area in m².

3) Find the areas of the sections shown in Fig. 26.5.

(a) (all dimensions in mm)

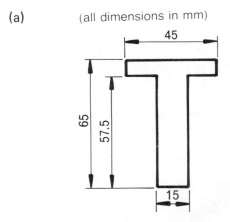

(b)

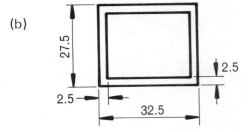

Fig. 26.5

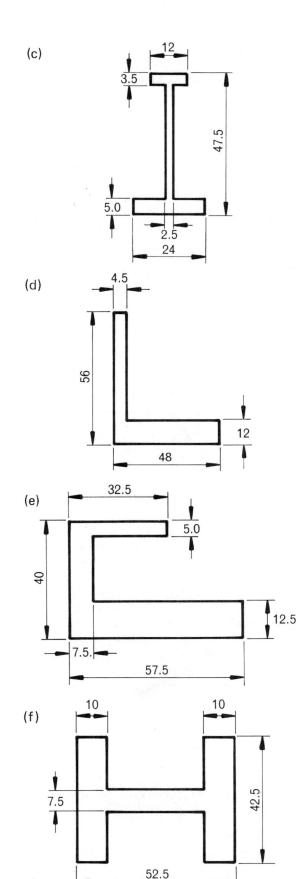

(c)

(d)

(e)

(f)

4) Find the area of a triangle whose base is 7.5 cm and whose altitude is 5.9 cm.

5) A triangle has sides 4 cm, 7 cm and 9 cm long. What is its area?

6) A triangle has sides 37 mm, 52 mm and 63 mm long. What is its area in cm² ?

7) Find the area of the shape shown in Fig. 26.6.

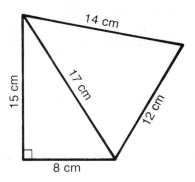

Fig. 26.6

8) Find the areas of the quadrilateral shown in Fig. 26.7.

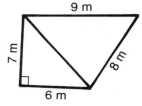

Fig. 26.7

9) What is the area of a parallelogram whose base is 7 cm long and whose vertical height is 4 cm?

10) Determine the length of the side of a square whose area is equal to that of a parallelogram with a base of 3 m and a vertical height of 1.5 m.

11) Find the area of a trapezium whose parallel sides are 75 mm and 82 mm long respectively and whose vertical height is 39 mm.

12) The parallel sides of a trapezium are 12 cm and 16 cm long. If its area is 220 cm², what is its altitude?

13) Find the areas of the shaded portions in each of the diagrams of Fig. 26.8.

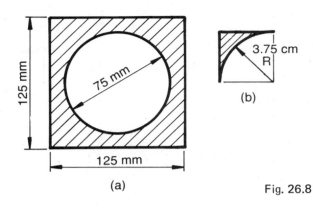

(a)

3.75 cm

R

(b)

Fig. 26.8

14) Find the circumference of circles whose radii are:

(a) 3.5 mm   (b) 13.8 m   (c) 4.2 cm

15) Find the diameter of circles whose circumferences are:

(a) 34.4 mm   (b) 18.54 cm

(c) 195.2 m

16) A ring has an outside diameter of 3.85 cm and an inside diameter of 2.63 cm. Calculate its area.

17) A hollow shaft has a cross-sectional area of 8.68 cm^2. If its inside diameter is 0.75 cm, calculate its outside diameter.

18) Find the area of the plate shown in Fig. 26.9.

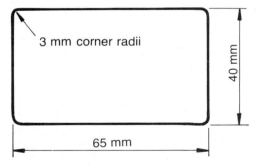

3 mm corner radii

40 mm

65 mm

Fig. 26.9

19) How many revolutions will a wheel make in travelling 2 km if its diameter is 700 mm?

20) If r is the radius and θ is the angle subtended at the centre by an arc find the length of arc when:

(a) $r = 2$ cm, $\theta = 30°$

(b) $r = 3.4$ cm, $\theta = 38°40'$

21) If l is the length of an arc, r is the radius and θ is the angle subtended by the arc, find θ when:

(a) $l = 9.4$ cm, $r = 4.5$ cm

(b) $l = 14$ mm, $r = 79$ mm

22) If an arc 7 cm long subtends an angle of 45° at the centre what is the radius of the circle?

23) Find the areas of the following sectors of circles:

(a) radius 3 m, angle of sector 60°.

(b) radius 2.7 cm, angle of sector 79°45'.

(c) radius 7.8 cm, angle of sector 143°42',

24) Calculate the area of the cross-section shown in Fig. 26.10.

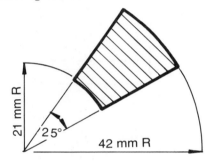

21 mm R

25°

42 mm R

Fig. 26.10

UNIT OF VOLUME

The volume of a solid figure is measured by seeing how many cubic units it contains. A cubic metre is the volume inside a cube which has a side of 1 metre. Similarly a cubic centimetre is the volume inside a cube which has a side of 1 centimetre. The standard abbreviations for units of volume are:

cubic metre   m^3

cubic centimetre cm^3

cubic millimetre mm^3

EXAMPLE 8

(1) How many cubic centimetres are contained in 1 cubic metre?

$$1 \text{ m} = 10^2 \text{ cm}$$

$$1 \text{ m}^3 = (10^2 \text{ cm})^3 = 10^6 \text{ cm}^3$$

$$= 1\,000\,000 \text{ cm}^3$$

(2) A tank contains 84 000 000 cubic millimetres of liquid. How many cubic metres does it contain?

$$1 \text{ mm} = 10^{-3} \text{ m}$$

$$1 \text{ mm}^3 = (10^{-3} \text{ m})^3 = 10^{-9} \text{ m}^3$$

$$84\,000\,000 \text{ mm}^3 = 84\,000\,000 \times 10^{-9} \text{ m}^3$$

$$= 8.4 \times 10^7 \times 10^{-9} \text{ m}^3$$

$$= 8.4 \times 10^{-2} \text{ m}^3$$

$$= \frac{8.4}{10^2} = 0.084 \text{ m}^3$$

UNIT OF CAPACITY

The capacity of a container is usually measured in litres (ℓ), such that

$$1 \text{ litre} = 1000 \text{ cm}^3$$

EXAMPLE 9

A tank contains 30 000 litres of liquid. How many cubic metres does it contain?

$$30\,000 \text{ litres} = 30\,000 \times 1\,000 \text{ cm}^3$$

$$= 3 \times 10^7 \text{ cm}^3$$

$$1 \text{ cm} = 10^{-2} \text{ m}$$

$$1 \text{ cm}^3 = (10^{-2} \text{ m})^3 = 10^{-6} \text{ m}^3$$

$$\therefore \quad 3 \times 10^7 \text{ cm}^3 = 3 \times 10^7 \times 10^{-6} \text{ m}^3$$

$$= 3 \times 10 = 30 \text{ m}^3$$

Exercise 117 — *All type A*

Convert the following volumes into the units stated:

1) 5 m³ into cm³.

2) 0.08 m³ into mm³.

3) 18 m³ into mm³.

4) 830 000 cm³ into m³.

5) 850 000 mm³ into m³.

6) 78 500 cm³ into m³.

7) A tank contains 5000 litres of petrol. How many cubic metres of petrol does it contain?

8) A small vessel contains 2500 mm³ of oil. How many litres does it contain?

9) A tank holds, when full, 827 m³ of water. How many litres does it hold?

10) A container holds 8275 cm³ when full. How many litres does it hold?

EXAMPLE 10

A steel section has the cross-section shown in Fig. 26.11. If it is 9 m long calculate its volume and total surface area.

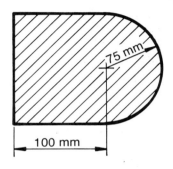

Fig. 26.11

To find the volume we use the formulae given on page 138.

Area of cross-section

$$= \tfrac{1}{2} \times \pi \times 75^2 + 100 \times 150$$

$$= 23\,836 \text{ mm}^2$$

$$= \frac{23\,836}{(1000)^2} = 0.023\,836 \text{ m}^2$$

Volume of solid

$$= 0.023\,836 \times 9$$

$$= 0.214\,5 \text{ m}^3$$

To find the surface area:

Perimeter of cross-section

$$= \pi \times 75 + 2 \times 100 + 150$$

$$= 585.5 \text{ mm}$$

$$= \frac{585.5}{1000} = 0.585\,5 \text{ m}$$

Lateral surface area

$$= 0.585\,5 \times 9 = 5.270 \text{ m}^2$$

Surface area of ends

$$= 2 \times 0.024 = 0.048 \text{ m}^2$$

Total surface area

$$= 5.270 + 0.048$$

$$= 5.318 \text{ m}^2$$

VOLUMES AND SURFACE AREAS

The following table gives volumes and surface areas of some simple solids.

Figure	Volume	Surface Area
Any solid having a uniform cross-section	Cross-sectional area × length of solid	Curved surface + ends, i.e. (perimeter of cross-section × length of solid) + (total area of ends)
Cylinder	$\pi r^2 h$	$2\pi r(h + r)$
Cone	$\frac{1}{3}\pi r^2 h$ (h is the vertical height)	$\pi r l$ (l is the slant height)
Frustum of a cone	$\frac{1}{3}\pi h(R^2 + Rr + r^2)$	Curved surface area (h is the vertical height) $= \pi l(R + r)$ Total surface area $= \pi l(R + r) + \pi R^2 + \pi r^2$ (l is the slant height)
Sphere	$\frac{4}{3}\pi r^3$	$4\pi r^2$
Pyramid	$\frac{1}{3}Ah$	Sum of the areas of the triangles forming the sides plus the area of the base area of base $= A$

THE TETRAHEDRON

A tetrahedron is a pyramid which has a triangular base (Fig. 26.12). Hence it possesses four triangular faces.

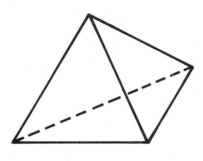

Tetrahedron

Fig. 26.12

EXAMPLE 11

A tetrahedron has a base with sides 8 cm, 7 cm and 9 cm long respectively. Its altitude is 5 cm. Calculate its volume.

Using the formula

$$A = \sqrt{s(s-a)(s-b)(s-c)}$$

to find the area of the base we have:

$a = 8$ cm, $b = 7$ cm and $c = 9$ cm

$$s = \frac{a+b+c}{2} = \frac{8+7+9}{2} = 12 \text{ cm}$$

$$A = \sqrt{12 \times (12-8) \times (12-7) \times (12-9)}$$

$$= \sqrt{12 \times 4 \times 5 \times 3} = 26.83 \text{ cm}^2$$

The volume of the tetrahedron is:

$$V = \tfrac{1}{3}Ah = \tfrac{1}{3} \times 26.83 \times 5 = 44.72 \text{ cm}^3$$

Exercise 118 — *Questions 1—10 type B, remainder type C*

1) A steel ingot whose volume is 2 m³ is rolled into a plate 15 mm thick and 1.75 m wide. Calculate the length of the plate in m.

2) A block of lead 1.5 m × 1 m × 0.75 m is hammered out to make a square sheet 10 mm thick. What are the dimensions of the square?

3) Calculate the volume of a metal tube whose bore is 50 mm and whose thickness is 8 mm if it is 6 m long.

4) The volume of a small cylinder is 180 cm³. If the radius of the cross-section is 25 mm find its height.

5) A steel ingot is in the shape of a cylinder 1.5 m diameter and 3.5 m long. How many metres of square bar of 50 mm side can be rolled from it?

6) A cone has a diameter of 70 mm and a height of 100 mm. What is its volume?

7) Calculate the diameter of a cylinder whose height is the same as its diameter and whose volume is 220 cm³.

8) An ingot whose volume is 2 m³ is to be made into ball bearings whose diameters are 12 mm. Assuming 20% of the metal in the ingot is wasted, how many ball bearings will be produced from the ingot?

9) The washer shown in Fig. 26.13 has a square of side l cut out of it. If its thickness is t find an expression for the volume, V, of the washer. Hence find the volume of a washer when $D = 6$ cm, $t = 0.2$ cm and $l = 4$ cm.

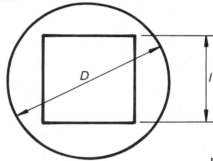

Fig. 26.13

10) A water tank with vertical sides has a horizontal base in the shape of a rectangle with semi-circular ends as illustrated in Fig. 26.14. The total inside length of the tank is 7 m, its width 4 m and its height 2 m.

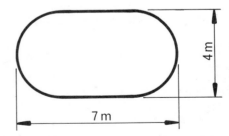

Fig. 26.14

Calculate:
(a) the surface area of the vertical walls of the tank in m²,
(b) the area of the base in m²,
(c) the number of litres of water in the tank when the depth of water is 1.56 m.

11) A tank 1 m long and 60 cm wide, internally, contains water to a certain depth. An empty tank 40 cm long, 30 cm wide and 25 cm deep, internally, is filled with water from the first tank. If the depth of water in the first tank is now 35 cm, what was the depth at first?

12) Figure 26.15 represents a bird cage in the form of a cylinder surmounted by a cone. The diameter of the cylinder is 35 cm and its height is 25 cm. The total volume of the bird cage is 31 178 cm³. Calculate:

(a) the total height of the bird cage,
(b) the surface area of the cover for the cage (except the base).

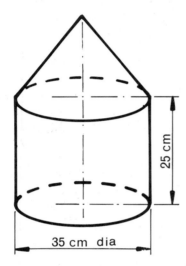

Fig. 26.15

13) A solid iron cone is 12 cm in height and the radius of the circular base is 4 cm. It is placed on its base in a cylindrical vessel of internal radius 5 cm. Water is poured into the cylinder until the depth of water is 16 cm. The cone is then removed. Find by how much the water level falls.

14) A rolling mill produces steel sheet 1.2 m wide and 3 mm thick. If the length of sheeting produced per hour is 2 km and the steel has a density of 7.75 grams per cubic centimetre, find in kilograms the mass of steel produced per hour.

15) A measuring jar is in the form of a vertical cylinder which is graduated so that the volume of liquid in the jar can be read directly in cubic centimetres. The internal radius of the jar is 2.4 cm. Find to the nearest millimetre the distance between the two marks labelled

200 cm³ and 300 cm³. When the jar is partly full of water, a steel sphere of radius 1.8 cm is lowered into the jar and completely immersed in the water without causing the water to overflow. Find in millimetres the distance the water-level rises in the jar.

16) A cylindrical tank, open at the top, is made of metal 75 mm thick. The internal radius of the tank is 1.2 m and the internal depth of the tank is 1.9 m. The tank stands with its plane base horizontal. Calculate:

(a) the number of litres of liquid in the tank when it is $\frac{4}{5}$ full,
(b) the area of the external curved surface of the tank,
(c) the area of the plane surface of metal at the base of the tank.

17) A cylindrical can whose height is equal to its diameter has a capacity of 9 litres. Find the height of the can. If the diameter is halved and the height altered so that the can still has a capacity of 9 litres, find the ratio of the original curved surface area to the final curved surface area.

18) A cheese is made in the form of a cylinder of radius 21 cm and height 45 cm. The slice shown in Fig. 26.16 (where AB is 13.5 cm and lies along the axis of the cylinder and where $\angle XAY = 30°$) has a mass of 1.3 kg. Calculate the mass of the whole cheese in kg.

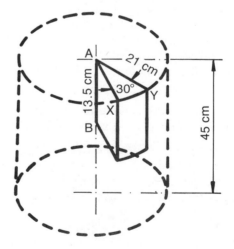

Fig. 26.16

19) The diagram (Fig. 26.17) shows a section through a chemical flask consisting of a spherical body of internal radius r cm with a cylindrical neck of internal radius $\frac{1}{6} r$ cm and a length

140

r cm. Show that when filled to the brim the flask will hold approximately $\dfrac{77r^3}{18}$ cm³. (The volumes enclosed by the sphere and cylinder overlap — between the dotted lines — but this fact may be ignored.)

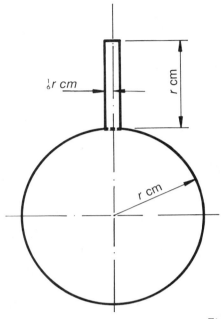

Fig. 26.17

20) A cylindrical can is filled with water. It has a capacity of 300 cm³ and is 6.5 cm high. Calculate its radius. The water is now poured into another container which has a square horizontal base of side 8 cm and vertical sides. Calculate the depth of water in this container. Calculate also the area of this container which is in contact with the water.

21) A pyramid has a rectangular base 8 cm long and 5 cm wide. Its altitude is 7 cm. Calculate the volume of the pyramid.

22) A piece of steel is in the form of a tetrahedron whose base is a right-angled triangle. The sides forming the right-angle are 5 cm and 6 cm long respectively. If the height of the tetrahedron is 7 cm, calculate its volume. If the tetrahedron is melted down, calculate the length of bar of diameter 20 mm that can be made from it, assuming no waste.

DENSITY AND RELATIVE DENSITY

The density of a substance is its mass per unit volume.

Thus

$$\text{density} = \frac{\text{mass}}{\text{volume}}$$

or

$$\text{mass} = \text{volume} \times \text{density}$$

EXAMPLE 12

(1) A block of lead has a volume of 800 cm³. What is its mass if the density of lead is 11.4 g/cm³?

Mass = volume × density

= 800 × 11.4 = 9120 g = 9.12 kg

(2) A steel pipe 3 m long has an internal radius of 15 mm and an external radius of 18 mm. If steel has a density of 7.7 g/cm³ calculate (to the nearest gram) the mass of the pipe.

Converting all the dimensions to centimetres, internal radius = 1.5 cm, external radius = 1.8 cm and the length = 3000 cm.

Volume of pipe

= cross-sectional area × length

= $\pi(1.8^2 - 1.5^2) \times 300$

= $\pi \times 0.99 \times 300$

= 933 cm³

Mass = volume × density

= 933 × 7.7

= 7184 g

= 7.184 kg

The relative density is the number of times a substance is heavier than water, volume for volume.

$$\text{Relative density} = \frac{\text{density of substance}}{\text{density of water}}$$

Since the density of water is 1 g/cm³ the density of a substance in g/cm³ is numerically equal to the relative density.

EXAMPLE 13

(1) The flask shown in Fig. 26.18 is completely filled with oil whose relative density is 0.8. Find the mass of oil in the flask.

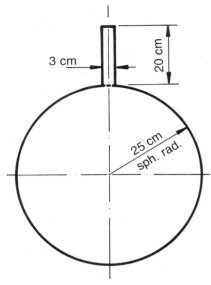

3 cm

20 cm

25 cm
sph. rad.

Fig. 26.18

Volume of the sphere

$$= \frac{4}{3} \pi \times 25^3 = 65\,450 \text{ cm}^3$$

Volume of the cylinder

$$= \pi \times 1.5^2 \times 20 = 141 \text{ cm}^3$$

Volume of the flask

$$= 65\,450 + 141 = 65\,591 \text{ cm}^3$$

Since the relative density is 0.8, the density of the oil is 0.8 g/cm³. Hence:

mass of the oil $=$ volume $\times$ density

$$= 65\,591 \times 0.8$$

$$= 52\,473 \text{ g}$$

$$= 52.473 \text{ kg}$$

Exercise 119 — *Questions 1—3 type B, remainder type C*

1) The density of aluminium is 2590 kg/m³. Find the mass of a piece of aluminium which has a volume of 2 m³.

2) A lead sheet is 1.5 m × 0.75 m × 3 mm thick. If lead has a density of 11.4 g/cm³ find the mass of the sheet.

3) A cast iron pipe has an external diameter of 75 mm and an internal diameter of 63 mm. If it is 5 m long and the density of cast iron is 7.5 g/cm³, what is the mass of the pipe?

4) The diagram (Fig. 26.19) represents the vertical cross-section of a horizontal feeding trough 2 m long and closed at both ends. The

trough is made from sheet metal. Calculate in square metres the total area of sheet metal required. If the metal is 4 mm thick and it has a density of 7.7 g/cm³ find the mass of the sheet metal.

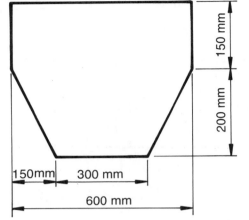

150 mm

200 mm

150mm   300 mm

600 mm

Fig. 26.19

5) The diagram (Fig. 26.20) shows the end view of a metal block of uniform cross-section. The block is 90 mm long and has a mass of 2.898 kg. Calculate the volume of the block and hence find the density in g/cm³ of the metal from which it is made.

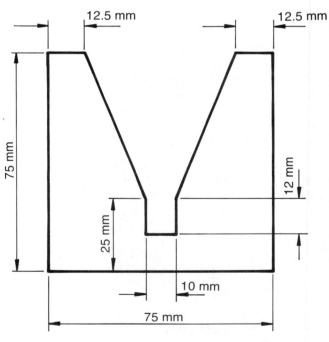

12.5 mm   12.5 mm

75 mm

25 mm

12 mm

10 mm

75 mm

Fig. 26.20

6) A porcelain crucible is in the form of a thick hemi-spherical shell. The radius of the internal hemi-sphere is 5 cm and the thickness

of the shell is 1 cm. If the crucible weighs 720 g calculate the density of porcelain.

7) Figure 26.21 shows the cross-section of a steel girder 2 m long. If steel has a density of 7.7 g/cm³ calculate the mass of the girder in kg.

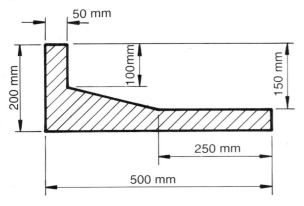

Fig. 26.21

8) A test tube consists of a cylindrical part of internal diameter 2.4 cm and a hemispherical base of internal diameter 2.4 cm. It is placed so that the axis of the cylinder is vertical and liquid is poured into the test tube so that the greatest depth of liquid is 9.5 cm. If the relative density of the liquid is 0.7 find the mass of liquid in the test tube.

9) An iron weight is found to be 15 g too light and to correct this a cylindrical hole of diameter 1.60 cm is made in the base and the iron removed is replaced by lead. Given that 1 cm³ of iron has a mass of 7.14 g and 1 cm³ of lead has a mass of 11.34 g, calculate the depth of the hole, giving your answer correct to the nearest mm.

10) A bowl is made by cutting in half a hollow sphere of external diameter 50 cm and made of metal 2.5 cm thick. If the bowl is filled with liquid of relative density 0.95 calculate the total mass of liquid in the bowl. The bowl when empty has a mass of 97 kg. Find the relative density of the metal from which the bowl is made.

THE FLOW OF WATER

Suppose that water is flowing through a pipe whose cross-sectional area is A square metres at a speed of v metres per second. If the pipe is running full, the discharge from the pipe per second is the volume of a cylinder of cross-section A and length v. That is, the discharge per second is Av cubic metres per second.

EXAMPLE 14

(1) Water is flowing through a pipe whose bore is 75 mm at a speed of 2 metres per second. Calculate the discharge from the pipe:

(a) in cubic metres per second,
(b) in litres per minute.

(a) Bore of pipe = 75 mm = 0.075 m

Area of pipe = $\pi \times (0.037\,5)^2 = 0.004\,4$ m³

Discharge from pipe
    = speed of flow × area of pipe
    = $2 \times 0.004\,4 = 0.008\,8$ m³/s

(b) Since 1 m = 100 cm

Discharge from pipe = $0.008\,8 \times 100^3$
                    = 8800 cm³/s

Since 1 ℓ = 1000 cm³

Discharge from pipe
    = $\dfrac{8800}{1000} = 8.8$ ℓ/s
    = $8.8 \times 60 = 528$ ℓ/min

(2) Water is being pumped through a pipe of 10 cm diameter so that it discharges 1250 litres per minute. Calculate the speed of flow of the water in metres per second. The pipe is used to empty a swimming bath containing 800 cubic metres of water. How long does it take, in hours, to empty the bath?

Area of the pipe = $\pi \times 5^2 = 25\pi$ cm².

Volume of water discharged per second
    = 1250 ℓ = 1 250 000 cm³

Speed of flow = $\dfrac{\text{discharge}}{\text{area}} = \dfrac{1\,250\,000}{25\pi}$

    = 15 920 cm/min

    = 159.2 m/min

    = $\dfrac{159.2}{60} = 2.65$ m/s

Time taken to empty bath = $\dfrac{\text{volume}}{\text{discharge}}$

Volume = 800 m³

Discharge = 1 250 000 cm³/min
          = 1.25 m³/min

143

Time taken to empty bath

$$= \frac{800}{1.25} = 640 \text{ min}$$

$$= \frac{640}{60} = 10.67 \text{ hours}$$

Exercise 120 — *Questions 1–3 type A, remainder type B*

1) Water is flowing through a pipe whose bore is 15 cm at a speed of 3 metres per second. Calculate the discharge from the pipe in cubic metres per second.

2) The discharge of water from a pipe is 500 cubic centimetres per second. The bore of the pipe is 10 cm. Calculate the speed of flow of the water.

3) Water is pumped through a pipe so that it discharges 10 litres per minute. It is used to empty a tank containing 3 m³ of water. How long does it take to empty the tank?

4) A rectangular swimming bath with vertical sides is 25 m long and 10 m wide and its rectangular base slopes uniformly from a depth of 1 m at the shallow end to 3 m at the deep end. If the bath contains 400 cubic metres of water find the distance of the water level below the top of the bath. The water is emptied from the bath through a pipe at a rate of 1.5 cubic metres per second. Find the time taken to empty the bath.

5) Water is poured into a cylindrical reservoir 10 m in diameter at the rate of 3000 litres per minute. Find at what rate the level of the water in the reservoir rises.

6) A large reservoir was replenished with 28 000 m³ of water flowing through three inlet pipes whose diameters were 0.8 m, 1 m and 1.3 m, and the speeds at which water flowed through them were 2 m/s, 1.5 m/s and 1 m/s. Calculate the time taken to replenish the reservoir.

7) A rectangular block of lead is 40 cm long, 35 cm wide and 25 cm high. The metal is to be used in the manufacture of lead pipe of internal diameter 5 cm and external diameter 10 cm. Calculate in metres, the length of pipe manufactured. If water is to be pumped through the pipe at a rate of 15 000 litres per minute calculate, in m/s, the speed of water flowing through the pipe.

8) A swimming bath is 20 m long and 7 m wide. The depth of water increases uniformly from 1.2 m at the shallow end to 2.2 m at the deep end. Calculate the number of cubic metres of water in the bath. This water is pumped into the cleaning plant through a cylindrical pipe whose internal diameter is 20 cm at 4000 litres per minute. Calculate the speed in metres per second at which the water is moving through the pipe.

SIMILAR SOLIDS

Two solids are similar if the ratios of their corresponding linear dimensions are equal. The two cones shown in Fig. 26.22 are similar if

$$\frac{h_1}{h_2} = \frac{r_1}{r_2}$$

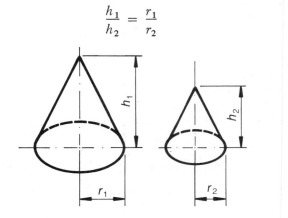

Fig. 26.22

The two cylinders shown in Fig. 26.23 are similar since

$$\frac{150}{75} = \frac{100}{50}$$

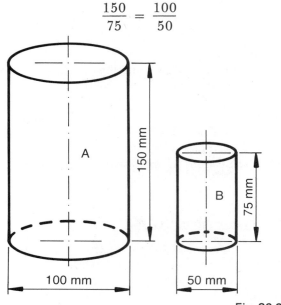

Fig. 26.23

The surface areas of similar solids are proportional to the squares of their linear dimensions.

(1) If two spheres having radii r_1 and r_2 have surface areas A_1 and A_2 respectively, then

$$\frac{A_1}{A_2} = \left(\frac{r_1}{r_2}\right)^2$$

(2) The ratio of the surface areas of the two cones shown in Fig. 26.22 is:

$$\frac{A_1}{A_2} = \frac{r_1{}^2}{r_2{}^2} = \frac{h_1{}^2}{h_2{}^2}$$

(3) The ratio of the surface areas of the two cylinders shown in Fig. 26.23 is:

$$\frac{A_1}{A_2} = \frac{100^2}{50^2} = \frac{150^2}{75^2} = \frac{4}{1}$$

EXAMPLE 15

Find the surface area of a sphere 120 mm radius. What is the surface area of a sphere 60 mm radius?

Surface area of 120 mm radius sphere
$$= 4\pi r^2 = 4\pi \times 120^2 = 180\,956 \text{ mm}^2$$

If A_1 = surface area of 120 mm sphere and A_2 = surface area of 60 mm sphere

$$\frac{A_2}{A_1} = \frac{60^2}{120^2} = \frac{1}{4}$$

$$A_2 = \frac{1}{4} \times A_1 = \frac{180\,956}{4} = 45\,239 \text{ mm}^2$$

The volumes of similar solids are proportional to the cubes of their corresponding linear dimensions.

(1) If two spheres of radii r_1 and r_2 have volumes V_1 and V_2 respectively, then

$$\frac{V_1}{V_2} = \frac{r_1{}^3}{r_2{}^3}$$

(2) The ratio of the volumes of the two cones shown in Fig. 26.22 is:

$$\frac{V_1}{V_2} = \frac{r_1{}^3}{r_2{}^3} = \frac{h_1{}^3}{h_2{}^3}$$

(3) The ratio of the volumes of the two cylinders shown in Fig. 26.23 is:

$$\frac{V_1}{V_2} = \frac{100^3}{50^3} = \frac{150^3}{75^3} = \frac{8}{1}$$

Since mass is proportional to volume

$$\frac{M_1}{M_2} = \frac{V_1}{V_2}$$

where M_1 and M_2 are the masses of two similar solids made of material of the same density and whose volumes are V_1 and V_2 respectively.

EXAMPLE 16

(1) The volume of a cone of height 135 mm is 1090 mm³. Find the volume of a cone whose height is 72 mm.

Let V_1 and V_2 be the volumes of the two cones. Then:

$$\frac{V_2}{V_1} = \frac{h_2{}^3}{h_1{}^3}$$

$$\frac{V_2}{1090} = \frac{72^3}{135^3}$$

$$V_2 = 1090 \times \frac{72^3}{135^3} = 165.4 \text{ mm}^3$$

(2) A cone 90 mm high has a mass of 8 kg. A frustum of this cone is formed by cutting off the top 20 mm of the cone as shown in Fig. 26.24. Find the mass of the frustum.

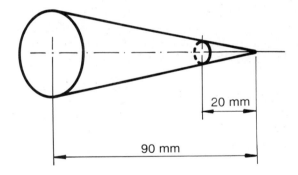

20 mm

90 mm

Fig. 26.24

To solve this problem we note that:

mass of frustum = mass of original cone
                 − mass of piece cut off

Let M_1 be mass of original cone and M_2 be mass of piece cut off.

$$\frac{M_2}{M_1} = \frac{20^3}{90^3}$$

$$M_2 = \frac{20^3}{90^3} \times M_1 = \frac{20^3}{90^3} \times 8 = 0.088 \text{ kg}$$

Mass of frustum $= 8 - 0.088 = 7.912 \text{ kg}$

Exercise 121 — *All type B*

1) Two spheres have radii 3 cm and 5 cm respectively. Find their volumes.

2) A spherical cap has a height of 2 cm and a volume of 8 cm³. A similar cap has a height of 3 cm. What is its volume?

3) The volume of a cone of height 14.2 cm is 210 cm³. Find the height of a similar cone whose volume is 60 cm³.

4) Find the surface area of a metal sphere whose radius is 73 mm. What is the area of a sphere whose radius is 29 mm?

5) The curved surface of a cone has an area of 20.5 cm². What is the curved surface area of a similar cone whose height is 1.5 times as great as the first cone?

6) Find the mass of a hemi-spherical bowl of copper whose external and internal diameters are 24 cm and 16 cm respectively. The density of copper is 8.9 g/cm³. What is the mass of a similar bowl whose external diameter is 20 cm?

7) A metal pyramid has a square base of side 3 cm and it has a mass of 70 kg. What is the mass of a similar pyramid whose base is a square of side 6 cm. If the height of the first pyramid is 8 cm what is the height of the second pyramid?

8) A solid cylinder has a radius of r cm. The length of the cylinder is $3r$ cm and the *total* surface area is 308 cm². Taking π to be $\frac{22}{7}$ calculate the value of r. A second cylinder has a radius of $2x$ cm and a height of $6x$ cm. If its surface area is 254 cm² what is the value of x?

9) A cone is 100 mm high and has a radius of 20 mm. Find its volume. A frustum of this cone is formed by cutting off the top 20 mm. Find the volume of the frustum.

10) In a scale model of a school the area of the assembly hall is $\frac{1}{100}$ of the actual area. Calculate the ratio of the volume of the model hall to the volume of the actual hall.

NETS

Suppose that we have to make a cube out of thin sheet metal. We need a pattern giving us the shape of the metal needed to make the cube. As shown in Fig. 26.25, the pattern consists of six squares. The shape which can be folded to make a cube is called the *net* of the cube. (Engineers call the net the *development*.)

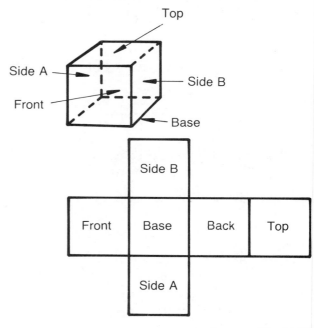

Fig. 26.25

It is possible for there to be more than one net for a solid object. For instance, the cube in Fig. 26.25 can be made from the net shown in Fig. 26.26.

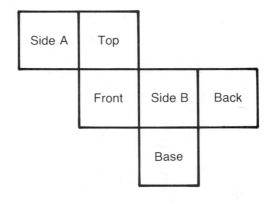

Fig. 26.26

EXAMPLE 17

Sketch the net of the triangular prism shown in Fig. 26.27. As can be seen from Fig. 26.28, the net consists of three rectangles representing the base and the two sides and two triangles representing the two ends.

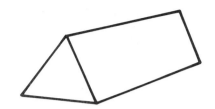

Fig. 26.27

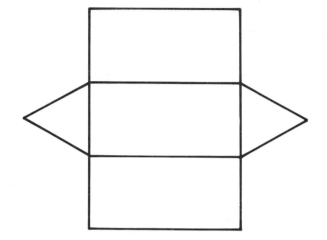

Fig. 26.28

NETS OF CURVED SURFACES

The net for a cylinder without a top and bottom is shown in Fig. 26.29. The length of the net is equal to the circumference of the cylinder.

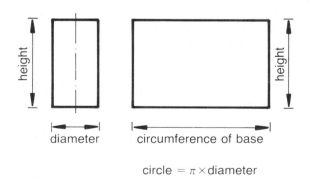

circle $= \pi \times$ diameter

Fig. 26.29

EXAMPLE 18
Draw the net for the cone shown in Fig. 26.30.

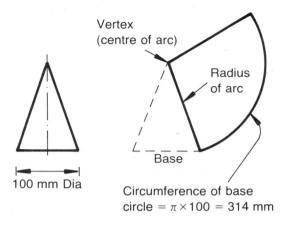

Circumference of base
circle $= \pi \times 100 = 314$ mm

Fig. 26.30

The net is in the form of a sector of a circle. Note that the arms of the sector are equal to the slant height of the cone and that the length of the arc is equal to the circumference of the base circle of the cone.

Exercise 122 — *All type B*

Sketch the nets for the following solids:

1) A cuboid 8 cm long, 3 cm wide and 4 cm high.

2) A triangular prism whose ends are right-angled triangles of base 3 cm and height 4 cm and whose length is 6 cm.

3) A pyramid with a square base of side 5 cm and a height (altitude) of 8 cm.

4) A cube with an edge of 4 cm.

5) A cylinder with a height of 5 cm and a diameter of 3 cm.

6) A cone with a vertical height of 8 cm and a base diameter of 7 cm.

7) The diagrams (Fig. 26.31) show the nets of various solids. Name each solid.

(a)

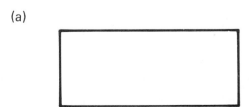

(b)

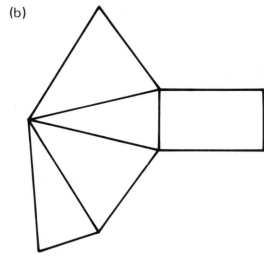

(c)

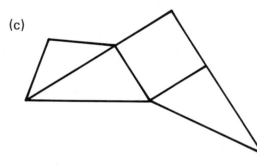

(d)

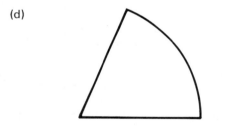

Fig. 26.31

SELF-TEST 26

In the following questions state the letter (or letters) corresponding to the correct answer (or answers).

1) An area is 30 000 square centimetres. Hence it is:
a 3000 m²   b 300 m²   c 3 m²
d 30 m²

2) An area is 5 m². Hence it is:
a 50 cm²   b 500 cm²   c 5000 cm²
d 50 000 cm²

3) An area is 2000 mm². Hence it is:
a 2 cm²   b 20 cm²   c 0.2 cm²
d 200 cm²

4) An area is 600 000 mm². Hence it is:
a 6000 m²   b 600 m²   c 6 m²
d 0.6 m²

5) An area is 0.3 m². Hence it is:
a 30 mm²   b 300 mm²
c 30 000 mm²   d 300 000 mm²

6) An area is 20 km². It is therefore:
a 2000 m²   b 20 000 m²
c 20 000 000 m²   d 200 000 m²

7) A rectangular plot of ground is 4 km long and 8 km wide. Its area is therefore:
a 32 Mm²   b 32 km²   c 32 000 m²
d 0.32 Mm²

8) A triangle has an altitude of 100 mm and a base of 50 mm. Its area is:
a 2500 mm²   b 5000 mm²   c 25 cm²
d 50 cm²

9) A parallelogram has a base 10 cm long and a vertical height of 5 cm. Its area is:
a 25 cm²   b 50 cm²   c 2500 mm²
d 5000 mm²

10) A trapezium has parallel sides whose lengths are 18 cm and 22 cm. The distance between the parallel sides is 10 cm. Hence the area of the trapezium is:
a 400 cm²   b 200 cm²   c 3960 cm²
d 495 cm²

11) The area of a circle is given by the formula:
a $2\pi r^2$ b $2\pi r$ c πr^2 d πr

12) The circumference of a circle is given by the formula:
a πr^2 b $2\pi r$ c πr d πd

13) A ring has an outside diameter of 8 cm and an inside diameter of 4 cm. Its area is therefore:
a $\pi(8^2 - 4^2)$ b $8\pi - 4\pi$
c $\pi(8 + 4)(8 - 4)$ d $\pi(4^2 - 2^2)$

14) A wheel has a diameter of 70 cm. The number of revolutions it will make in travelling 55 km is:
a 25 000   b 50 000   c 5000   d 2500

15) An arc of a circle is 22 cm and the radius of the circle is 140 cm. The angle subtended by the arc is:

a 90°   b 9°   c 180°   d 18°

16) A sector of a circle subtends an angle of 120°. If the radius of the circle is 42 cm then the area of the sector is:

a 88 cm²   b 1848 cm²   c 3696 cm²

d 176 cm²

17) A tank has a volume of 8 m³. Hence the volume of the tank is also:

a 800 cm³   b 8000 cm³   c 80 000 cm³

d 8 000 000 cm³

18) A solid has a volume of 200 000 mm³. Hence the volume of the solid is also:

a 2000 cm³   b 200 cm³   c 20 cm³

d 20 000 cm³

19) The capacity of a container is 50 litres. Hence its capacity is also:

a 50 000 cm³   b 5000 cm³   c 0.5 m³

d 0.05 m³

20) The area of the curved surface of a cylinder of radius r and height h is:

a $2\pi rh$ b $2\pi r^2 h$ c πrh d $\pi r^2 h$

21) The volume of a cylinder of radius r and height h is:

a $2\pi rh$ b $2\pi r^2 h$ c πrh d $\pi r^2 h$

22) The total surface area of a closed cylinder whose radius is r and whose height is h is:

a $\pi rh + 2\pi r^2$ b $\pi r(h + 2r)$

c $2\pi rh + 2\pi r^2$ d $2\pi r(h + r)$

23) A small cylindrical container has a diameter of 280 mm and a height of 50 mm. It will hold:

a 3.08 ℓ   b 30.8 ℓ   c 6.16 ℓ   d 61.6 ℓ

24) A cone has height of 90 mm and a diameter of 140 mm. Hence, the volume of the cone is:

a 462 cm³   b 19 800 mm³

c 462 000 mm³   d 19.8 cm³

25) A test tube whose overall length is h and whose radius is r has a hemi-spherical end. A formula for its volume is:

a $\pi r^2 \left(\frac{2}{3}r + h\right)$ b $\pi r^2 \left(h - \frac{1}{3}r\right)$

c $2\pi r(r + h)$ d $\pi r^2 (2 + h - r)$

26) The mass of an object is:

a $\dfrac{density}{volume}$ b $\dfrac{volume}{density}$

c volume × density

27) The density of a material is:

a $\dfrac{volume}{mass}$ b $\dfrac{mass}{volume}$

c mass × volume

28) A block of lead has a volume of 80 cm³. If its mass is 880 g, the density of lead is:

a 0.09 g/cm³   b 11 g/cm³

c 90 kg/m³   d 11 000 kg/m³

29) The relative density of a substance is 0.8. Hence its density is:

a 0.8 g/cm³   b 8 g/mm³

c 800 kg/m³   d 80 kg/m³

30) A flask contains 500 litres of oil whose relative density is 0.7. The mass of oil in the flask is:

a 350 kg   b 35 kg   c 3500 kg

d 3.5 kg

31) Water is flowing through a pipe at a speed of 5 m/s. If the bore of the pipe has an area of 2000 cm², the discharge from the pipe per second is:

a 10 000 cm³   b 1 000 000 cm³

c 0.010 m3   d 1000 ℓ

32) A tank contains 2000 litres of water. It is emptied by means of a pipe through which the water discharges at 4 m³/min. The time taken to empty the tank is:

a 30 seconds   b 500 min   c 5 min

d 8 min

33) Two cylinders are similar. Cylinder A has a radius of 8 cm and cylinder B has a radius of 4 cm. Therefore:

a $\dfrac{\text{Surface area of A}}{\text{Surface area of B}} = \dfrac{4}{1}$

b $\dfrac{\text{Surface area of A}}{\text{Surface area of B}} = \dfrac{2}{1}$

c $\dfrac{\text{Volume of A}}{\text{Volume of B}} = \dfrac{4}{1}$

d $\dfrac{\text{Volume of A}}{\text{Volume of B}} = \dfrac{8}{1}$

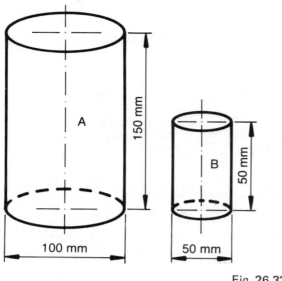

Fig. 26.32

34) Figure 26.32 shows two cylinders. Therefore:

a $\dfrac{\text{Volume of A}}{\text{Volume of B}} = \dfrac{8}{1}$

b $\dfrac{\text{Volume of A}}{\text{Volume of B}} = \dfrac{12}{1}$

c $\dfrac{\text{Volume of A}}{\text{Volume of B}} = \dfrac{27}{1}$

35) A metal hemi-sphere has a diameter of 50 cm. A second hemisphere made of the same metal has a diameter of 25 cm. If the second hemisphere has a mass of 600 kg, the mass of the first hemisphere is:

a 1200 kg   b 2400 kg   c 4800 kg

Chapter 27 Graphs

In newspapers, business reports and government publications use is made of pictorial illustrations to present and compare quantities of the same kind. These diagrams help the reader to understand what deductions can be drawn from the quantities represented in the diagrams. The most common form of diagram is the *graph*.

AXES OF REFERENCE

To plot a graph we take two lines at right angles to each other (Fig. 27.1). These lines are called the axes of reference. Their intersection, the point O, is called the origin.

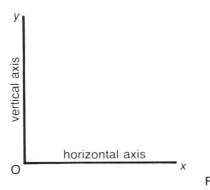

Fig. 27.1

SCALES

The number of units represented by a unit length along an axis is called the *scale*. For instance 1 cm could represent 2 units. The scales need not be the same on both axes.

CO-ORDINATES

Co-ordinates are used to mark the points of a graph. In Fig. 27.2 values of x are to be plotted against values of y. The point P has been plotted so that $x = 8$ and $y = 10$. The values of 8 and 10 are said to be the rectangular co-ordinates of the point P. We then say that P is the point (8, 10).

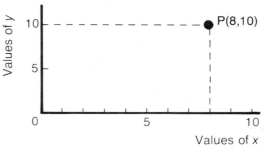

Fig. 27.2

DRAWING A GRAPH

Every graph shows a relation between two sets of numbers. The table below gives corresponding values of x and y.

x	0	2	4	6	8
y	0	4	16	36	64

To plot the graph we first draw the two axes of reference. Values of x are always plotted along the horizontal axis and values of y along the vertical axis. We next choose suitable scales. In Fig. 27.3 we have chosen 1 cm = 2 units along the horizontal axis and 1 cm = 10 units along the vertical axis. On plotting the graph we see that it is a smooth curve which passes through all the plotted points.

When a graph is either a straight line or a smooth curve we can use the graph to deduce corresponding values of x and y between those given in the table.

To find the value of y corresponding to $x = 3$, find 3 on the horizontal axis and draw a vertical line to meet the graph at point P (Fig. 27.3). From P draw a horizontal line to meet the vertical axis and read off the value which is 9. Thus when $x = 3$, $y = 9$.

To find the value of x corresponding to $y = 25$ find 25 on the vertical axis and draw a horizontal line to meet the graph at point Q. From Q draw a vertical line to meet the horizontal axis and read off this value which is 5. Thus when $y = 25$, $x = 5$.

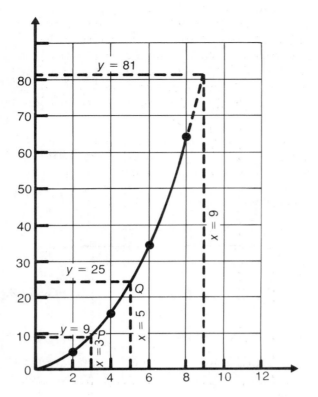

Fig. 27.3

As before we draw two axes at right-angles to each other, indicating the day on the horizontal axis. Since the temperatures range from 15 °C to 22 °C we can make 14 °C (say) our starting point on the vertical axis. This will allow us to use a larger scale on that axis which makes for greater accuracy in plotting the graph.

On plotting the points (Fig. 27.4) we see that it is impossible to join the points by means of a smooth curve. The best we can do is to join the points by means of a series of straight lines. The rise and fall of temperatures do not follow any mathematical law and the graph shows this by means of the erratic line obtained. However the graph does present in pictorial form the variations in temperature and at a glance we can see that the 1st, 3rd and 6th June were cool days whilst the 2nd and 5th were warm days.

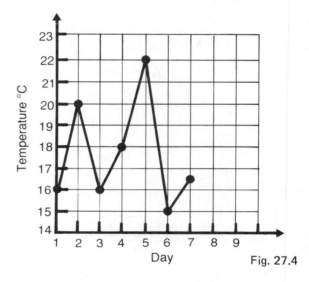

Fig. 27.4

Using a curve in this way to find values which are not given in the table is called *interpolation*. If we extend the curve so that it follows the general trend we can estimate values of x and y which lie *just beyond* the range of the given values. Thus in Fig. 27.3 by extending the curve we can find the probable value of y when $x = 9$. This is found to be 81. Finding a probable value in this way is called *extrapolation*.

An extrapolated value can usually be relied upon, but in certain cases it may contain a substantial amount of error. Extrapolated values must therefore be used with care.

It must be clearly understood that interpolation can only be used if the graph is a smooth curve or a straight line. It is no use applying interpolation in the graph of the next example.

EXAMPLE 1

The following table gives the temperature at 12.00 noon on seven successive days. Plot a graph to illustrate this information.

Day	June	1	2	3	4	5	6	7
Temp °C			16	20	16	18	22	15	16.5

Exercise 123 — *All type A*

1) The table below gives particulars of the amount of steel delivered to a factory during successive weeks. Plot a graph to show this with the week number on the horizontal axis.

Week number	1	2	3
Amount delivered (kg)	25 000	65 000	80 000

Week number	4	5
Amount delivered (kg)	30 000	50 000

2) The table below gives corresponding values of x and y. Plot a graph and from it estimate the value of y when $x = 1.5$ and the value of x when $y = 30$.

x	0	1	2	3	4	5
y	3	5	11	21	35	63

3) The areas of circles for various diameters is shown in the table below. Plot a graph with diameter on the horizontal axis and from it estimate the area of a circle whose diameter is 18 cm.

Diameter (cm)	5	10	15	20	25
Area (cm²)	19.6	78.5	176.6	314.2	492.2

4) The values in the table below are corresponding values of two quantities i and v.

v	15	25	35	50	70
i	1.1	2.0	2.5	3.2	3.9

Plot a graph with i horizontal and find v when $i = 3.0$.

5) An electric train starts from A and travels to its next stop 6 km from A. The following readings were taken of the time since leaving A (in minutes) and the distance from A (in km).

Time	$\frac{1}{2}$	1	$1\frac{1}{2}$	2	$2\frac{1}{2}$	3
Distance	0.10	0.34	0.8	1.46	2.46	3.50
Time	$3\frac{1}{2}$	4	$4\frac{1}{2}$	5	$5\frac{1}{2}$	6
Distance	4.34	5.0	5.44	5.74	5.92	6.0

Draw a graph of these values taking time horizontally. From the graph estimate the time taken to travel 2 km from A.

GRAPHS OF SIMPLE EQUATIONS

Consider the equation:

$$y = 2x + 5$$

We can give x any value we please and so calculate a corresponding value for y. Thus,

when $x = 0$ $y = 2 \times 0 + 5 = 5$

when $x = 1$ $y = 2 \times 1 + 5 = 7$

when $x = 2$ $y = 2 \times 2 + 5 = 9$ and so on.

The value of y therefore depends on the value allocated to x. We therefore call y the *dependent variable*. Since we can give x any

value we please, we call x the *independent variable*. It is usual to mark the values of the independent variable along the horizontal axis and this axis is frequently called the *x*-axis. The values of the dependent variable are then marked off along the vertical axis which is often called the *y*-axis.

In plotting graphs representing equations we may have to include co-ordinates which are positive and negative. To represent these on a graph we make use of the number scales used in directed numbers (Fig. 27.5).

Positive values of y are measured upwards above the origin.

Positive values of x are measured to the right of the origin.

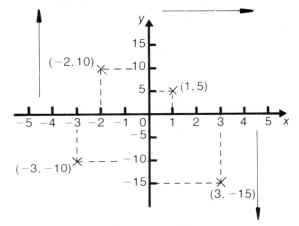

Negative values of x are measured to the left of the origin.

Negative values of y are measured downwards below the origin.

Fig. 27.5

EXAMPLE 2

(1) Draw the graph of $y = 2x - 5$ for values of x between -3 and 4.

Having decided on some values for x we calculate the corresponding values for y by substituting in the given equation. Thus,

when $x = -3$,

$$y = 2 \times (-3) - 5 = -6 - 5 = -11$$

For convenience the calculations are tabulated as shown below.

x	-3	-2	-1	0
$2x$	-6	-4	-2	0
-5	-5	-5	-5	-5
$y = 2x - 5$	-11	-9	-7	-5

x	1	2	3	4
$2x$	2	4	6	8
-5	-5	-5	-5	-5
$y = 2x - 5$	-3	-1	1	3

A graph may now be plotted using these values of x and y (Fig. 27.6). The graph is a straight line.

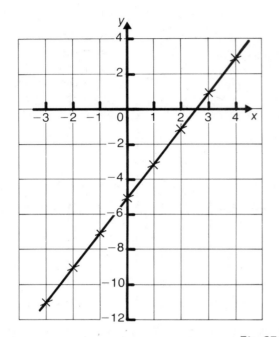

Fig. 27.6

Equations of the type $y = 2x - 5$, where the highest powers of the variables, x and y, is the first are called equations of the *first degree*.

All equations of this type give graphs which are straight lines and hence they are often called *linear equations*. In order to draw graphs of linear equations we need only take two points. It is safer, however, to take three points, the third point acting as a check on the other two.

(2) By means of a graph show the relationship between x and y in the equation $y = 5x + 3$. Plot the graph between $x = -3$ and $x = 3$.

Since this is a linear equation we need only take three points.

x	-3	0	$+3$
$y = 5x + 3$	-12	3	$+18$

The graph is shown in Fig. 27.7.

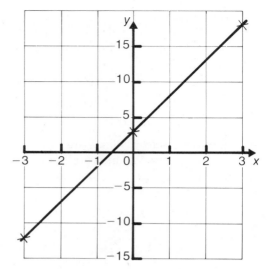

Fig. 27.7

THE EQUATION OF A STRAIGHT LINE

Every linear equation may be written in the standard form:

$$y = mx + c$$

Hence $y = 2x - 5$ is in the standard form with $m = 2$ and $c = -5$.

The equation $y = 4 - 3x$ is in standard form if we rearrange it to give $y = -3x + 4$. We then see that $m = -3$ and $c = 4$.

THE MEANING OF m AND c IN THE EQUATION OF A STRAIGHT LINE

The point B is any point on the straight line shown in Fig. 27.8 and it has the co-ordinates x and y. Point A is where the line cuts the y-axis and it has co-ordinates $x = 0$ and $y = c$.

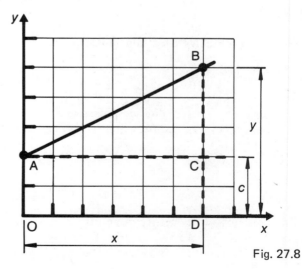

Fig. 27.8

$\dfrac{BC}{AC}$ is called the gradient of the line

now

$$BC = \dfrac{BC}{AC} \times AC = AC \times \text{gradient of the line}$$

$$y = BC + CD = BC + AO$$

$$= AC \times \text{gradient of the line} + AO$$

$$= x \times \text{gradient of the line} + c$$

But $\qquad\qquad y = mx + c$

Hence it can be seen that:

$$m = \text{gradient of the line}$$

$$c = \text{intercept on the } y\text{-axis}$$

Figure 27.9 shows the difference between positive and negative gradients.

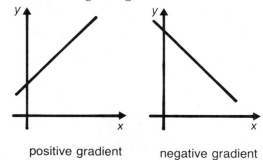

positive gradient   negative gradient

Fig. 27.9

EXAMPLE 3

(1) Find the law of the straight line shown in Fig. 27.10.

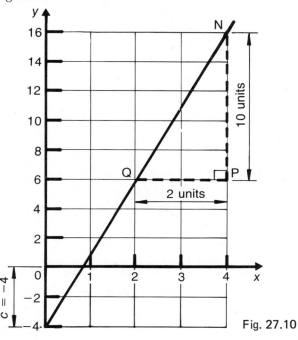

Fig. 27.10

Since the origin is at the intersection of the axes, c is the intercept on the y axis. From Fig. 27.10 it will be seen that $c = -4$. We now have to find m. Since this is the gradient of the line we draw $\triangle QNP$ making the sides reasonably long since a small triangle will give very inaccurate results. Using the scales of x and y we see that $QP = 2$ units and $PN = 10$ units.

$$\therefore \qquad m = \dfrac{NP}{QP} = \dfrac{10}{2} = 5$$

$\therefore$ The standard equation of a straight line $y = mx + c$ becomes $y = 5x - 4$.

(2) Find the values of m and c if the straight line $y = mx + c$ passes through the point $(-1, 3)$ and has a gradient of 6.

Since the gradient is 6 we have $m = 6$

$$\therefore \qquad\qquad y = 6x + c$$

Since the line passes through the point $(-1, 3)$ we have $y = 3$ when $x = -1$. By substitution,

$$3 = 6 \times (-1) + c$$

$$3 = -6 + c$$

$$\therefore \qquad\qquad c = 9$$

Hence $\qquad\qquad y = 6x + 9$

(3) Find the law of the straight line shown in Fig. 27.11.

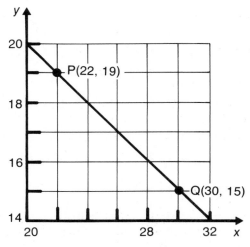

Fig. 27.11

It will be seen from Fig. 27.11 that the *origin is not at the intersection of the axes*. In order to determine the law of the straight line we use

155

two simultaneous equations as follows: Choose two convenient points P and Q and find their co-ordinates (these two points should be as far apart as possible to get maximum accuracy). If a point lies on a line then the x and y values of that point must satisfy the equation:

$$y = mx + c$$

at point P, $\quad x = 22 \quad$ and $\quad y = 19$

$$\therefore \qquad 19 = 22m + c \qquad [1]$$

at point Q, $\quad x = 30 \quad$ and $\quad y = 15$

$$15 = 30m + c \qquad [2]$$

Subtracting equation [2] from equation [1],

$$4 = -8m$$

$$\therefore \qquad m = \frac{-4}{8}$$

$$m = -0.5$$

Substituting $\quad m = -0.5 \quad$ in equation [1],

$$19 = 22 \times (-0.5) + c$$

$$19 = -11 + c$$

$$c = 30$$

Thus the equation of the line shown in Fig. 27.11 is:

$$y = -0.5x + 30$$

(4) Find the values of m and c if the straight line $\quad y = mx + c \quad$ passes through the points $(3, 4)$ and $(7, 10)$.

$$y = mx + c$$

The first point has co-ordinates $\quad x = 3, \quad y = 4$.

Hence, $\qquad 4 = 3m + c \qquad [1]$

The second point has co-ordinates $\quad x = 7,$ $y = 10.$ Hence,

$$10 = 7m + c \qquad [2]$$

Subtracting equation [1] from equation [2],

$$6 = 4m$$

$$\therefore \qquad m = 1.5$$

Substituting for $\quad m = 1.5 \quad$ in equation [1],

$$4 = 4.5 + c$$

$$\therefore \qquad c = -0.5$$

The equation of the straight line is

$$y = 1.5x - 0.5$$

EXPERIMENTAL DATA

One of the most important applications of the straight-line equation is the determination of an equation connecting two quantities when values have been obtained from an experiment.

EXAMPLE 4

In an experiment carried out with a lifting machine the effort E and the load W were found to have the values given in the table below:

W (kg)	15	25	40	50	60
E (kg)	2.75	3.80	5.75	7.00	8.20

Plot these results and obtain the equation connecting E and W which is thought to be of the type $\quad E = aW + b$.

If E and W are connected by an equation of the type $\quad E = aW + b \quad$ then the graph must be a straight line. Note that when plotting the graph, W is the independent variable and must be plotted on the horizontal axis. E is the dependent variable and must be plotted on the vertical axis.

On plotting the points (Fig. 27.12) it will be noticed that they deviate only slightly from a straight line. Since the data are experimental we must expect errors in measurement and observation and hence slight deviations from a straight line must be expected. Although the straight line will not pass through some of the points an attempt must be made to ensure an even spread of the points above and below the line.

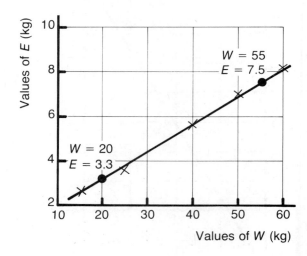

Fig. 27.12

To determine the equation we choose two points which lie on the straight line. Do not use any of the experimental results from the table unless they happen to lie exactly on the line. Choose the points as far apart as is convenient because this will help the accuracy of your result.

The point $W = 55, E = 7.5$ lies on the line. Hence,

$$7.5 = 55a + b \qquad [1]$$

The point $W = 20, E = 3.3$ also lies on the line. Hence,

$$3.3 = 20a + b \qquad [2]$$

Subtracting equation [2] from equation [1],

$$4.2 = 35a$$
$$a = 0.12$$

Substituting for $a = 0.12$ in equation [2],

$$3.3 = 20 \times 0.12 + b$$
$$b = 0.9$$

The required equation connecting E and W is therefore

$$E = 0.12W + 0.9$$

Exercise 124 — Questions 1—8 type A, remainder type B

Draw graphs of the following simple equations:

1) $y = x + 2$ taking values of x between -3 and 2.

2) $y = 2x + 5$ taking values of x between -4 and 4.

3) $y = 3x - 4$ taking values of x between -4 and 3.

4) $y = 5 - 4x$ taking values of x between -2 and 4.

The following equations represent straight lines. State in each case the gradient of the line and the intercept on the y-axis.

5) $y = x + 3$ 7) $y = -5x - 2$

6) $y = -3x + 4$ 8) $y = 4x - 3$

9) Find the values of m and c if the straight line $y = mx + c$ passes through the point $(-2, 5)$ and has a gradient of 4.

10) Find the values of m and c if the straight line $y = mx + c$ passes through the point $(3, 4)$ and the intercept on the y-axis is -2.

In the following find the values of m and c if the straight line $y = mx + c$ passes through the given points:

11) $(-2, -3)$ and $(3, 7)$

12) $(1, 1)$ and $(2, 4)$

13) $(-2, 1)$ and $(3, -9)$

14) $(-3, 13)$ and $(1, 1)$

15) $(2, 17)$ and $(4, 27)$

16) The following table gives values of x and y which are connected by an equation of the type $y = ax + b$. Plot the graph and from it find the values of a and b.

x	2	4	6	8	10	12
y	10	16	22	28	34	40

17) The following observed values of P and Q are supposed to be related by the linear equation $P = aQ + b$, but there are experimental errors. Find by plotting the graph the most probable values of a and b.

Q	2.5	3.5	4.4	5.8
P	13.6	17.6	22.2	28.0

Q	7.5	9.6	12.0	15.1
P	35.5	47.4	56.1	74.6

18) In an experiment carried out with a machine the effort E and the load W were found to have the values given in the table below. The equation connecting E and W is thought to be of the type $E = aW + b$. By plotting the graph check if this is so and hence find a and b.

W (kg)	10	30	50	60	80	100
E (kg)	8.9	19.1	29	33	45	54

19) A test on a metal filament lamp gave the following values of resistance (R ohms) at various voltages (V volts).

V	62	75	89	100	120
R	100	117	135	149	175

These results are expected to agree with an equation of the type $R = mV + c$ where m and c are constants. Test this by drawing the graph and find suitable values for m and c.

20) During an experiment to verify Ohm's Law the following results were obtained.

E (volts)	0	1.0	2.0	2.5	3.7
I (amperes)	0	0.24	0.5	0.63	0.92

E (volts)	4.1	5.9	6.8	8.0
I (amperes)	1.05	1.48	1.70	2.05

Plot these values with I horizontal and find the equation connecting E and I.

NON-LINEAR EQUATIONS WHICH CAN BE REDUCED TO THE LINEAR FORM

Many non-linear equations can be reduced to the linear form by making a suitable substitution.

Consider the equation $y = ax^2 + b$. Let $z = x^2$ so that the given equation becomes $y = az + b$. If we now plot values of z against values of y we shall obtain a straight line because $y = az + b$ is of the standard linear form.

EXAMPLE 5

The fusing current I amperes for wires of various diameters d mm is as shown in the table below.

d (mm)	5	10	15	20	25
I (amperes)	6.25	10	16.25	25	36.25

Construct another table showing values of d^2 against I and verify graphically that d and I are connected by a law of the form

$$I = ad^2 + b$$

where a and b are constants. Use your graph to estimate:

(a) Values for a and b.
(b) The value of I when $d = 12.5$ mm.
(c) The value of d when $I = 22$ amperes.

Drawing up the new table:

d^2	25	100	225	400	625
I	6.25	10	16.25	25	36.25

From the graph (Fig. 27.13) we see that the points lie on a straight line and hence we have verified that $I = ad^2 + b$. Note that I is the dependent variable and is plotted on the vertical axis and that d^2 is the independent variable and is plotted on the horizontal axis.

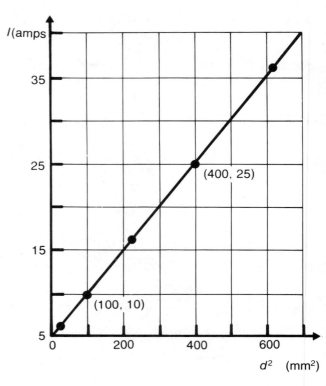

Fig. 27.13

(a) To find the values of a and b choose two points which lie on the line and find their co-ordinates.

The point $(400, 25)$ lies on the line,

$$\therefore \qquad 25 = 400a + b \qquad [1]$$

The point $(100, 10)$ lies on the line,

$$\therefore \qquad 10 = 100a + b \qquad [2]$$

Subtracting equation [2] from equation [1],

$$15 = 300a$$
$$a = 0.05$$

Substituting $a = 0.05$ in equation [2],

$$10 = 100 \times 0.05 + b$$
$$b = 5$$

Therefore the law is:

$$I = 0.05d^2 + 5$$

(b) When $d = 12.5$,

$$I = 0.05 \times (12.5)^2 + 5 = 12.81$$

Hence when $d = 12.5$ mm, $I = 12.81$ amperes.

158

(c) When $I = 22$,

$$22 = 0.05d^2 + 5$$
$$17 = 0.05d^2$$
$$d = \sqrt{\frac{17}{0.05}} = 18.43$$

$\therefore$ When $I = 22$ amperes, $d = 18.43$ mm.

EXAMPLE 6

Two variables P and Q are connected by an equation of the type

$$P = a\sqrt{Q} + b$$

where a and b are constants. When $Q = 9$, $P = 5$ and when $Q = 25$, $P = 8$. Draw a graph which shows the relationship between P and $\sqrt{Q}$. Use your graph to estimate:

(a) Probable values of a and b.
(b) The value of Q when $P = 7$.
(c) The value of P when $Q = 20$.

Drawing up a table to show corresponding values of P and $\sqrt{Q}$:

$\sqrt{Q}$	3	5
P	5	8

(a) The graph is plotted in Fig. 27.14. Since $\sqrt{Q}$ is the independent variable it is plotted horizontally. The gradient may be found by drawing the right angled triangle ABC, from which

$$a = \frac{BC}{AC} = \frac{3}{2} = 1.5$$

To find the value of b, take any point on the line AB and find its co-ordinates. Thus D(4, 6.5) lies on the line AB. Now substitute these values of P and Q in the equation

$$P = 1.5\sqrt{Q} + b$$
$$6.5 = 1.5 \times 4 + b$$
$$6.5 = 6 + b$$
$$b = 0.5$$
$$\therefore \qquad P = 1.5\sqrt{Q} + 0.5$$

(b) When $P = 7$,

$$7 = 1.5\sqrt{Q} + 0.5$$
$$\sqrt{Q} = \frac{7 - 0.5}{1.5} = 4.333$$
$$Q = (4.333)^2 = 18.77$$

(c) When $Q = 20$,

$$P = 1.5 \times \sqrt{20} + 0.5$$
$$= 1.5 \times 4.472 + 0.5$$
$$= 7.208$$

Note that the method used here to find a and b is an alternative to the simultaneous equation method shown in Example 5.

Exercise 125 — *All type C*

1) A car travelling along a straight road passed a post P, and T seconds after passing P its

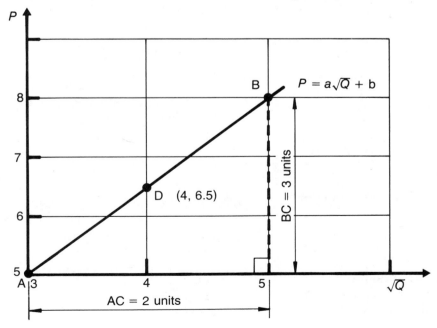

Fig. 27.14

distance (D metres) from P was estimated. The following results were obtained:

T	2	3	$3\frac{1}{2}$	$4\frac{1}{2}$	5	$5\frac{1}{2}$	6
D	46	68	82	117	138	161	186

Construct another table showing values of T^2 against D, and verify graphically that T and D are connected approximately by a law of the form

$$D = aT^2 + b$$

where a and b are constants.

Use your graph to estimate:

(a) values for a and b,
(b) the time when the car was 175 m past P, giving your answer correct to the nearest tenth of a second,
(c) the distance travelled from $T = 4$ to $T = 5$.

[*Scales*: take 2 cm to represent 20 m on the D-axis and 5 units on the T^2-axis.]
(A.E.B. 1974)

2) Two variables, X and Y, are connected by a law of the form

$$\sqrt{Y} = aX + b$$

where a and b are constants. When $X = 2.5$, $Y = 48$ and when $X = 15$, $Y = 529$. Draw a graph of X against $\sqrt{Y}$ and use your graph to estimate values for a and b. Also use your graph to estimate:

(a) the value of X when $Y = 441$,
(b) the percentage increase in Y as X increases from 6 to 12.

[*Scales*: take 2 cm to represent 2 units on the X-axis and 2 units on the $\sqrt{Y}$-axis.]
(A.E.B. 1976)

3) The prototype of a new car was tested on a straight road to find the resistance (R newtons) to the motion of the car at various speeds (V km/h). The following results were obtained:

V	13	30	42	50	60	65
R	1080	1240	1440	1580	1840	1960

Construct another table giving values of V^2 against R. Plot a graph of V^2 against R and show that V and R are connected by a law of the form

$$R = aV^2 + b$$

where a and b are constants.

[*Scales*: take 2 cm to represent 500 units on the V^2-axis and 100 units on the R-axis.]

Use your graph to estimate:

(a) probable values of a and b,
(b) the speed at which the resistance was 1500 newtons,
(c) the percentage increase in the resistance as the speed increased from 25 km/h to 50 km/h.
(A.E.B. 1976)

4) In a laboratory experiment a heavy spring was suspended vertically from a horizontal beam. A mass of M kilograms was hung on the lower end of the spring which was stretched and then released. The time of oscillation, T seconds, of the mass was measured and the experiment was repeated for various values of M. The following results were obtained:

M	0.13	0.25	0.37	0.50	0.63	0.71	0.85
T	1.8	2.0	2.2	2.4	2.6	2.7	2.9

Construct a new table showing M against T^2 and by plotting these new values on a graph show that M and T^2 are connected by a law of the form

$$T^2 = aM + b$$

where a and b are constants.

[*Scales*: take 2 cm to represent 0.1 kg on the M-axis and take 2 cm to represent 1 unit on the T^2-axis.]

Use your graph to estimate:

(a) values of a and b,
(b) the value of M for which $T = 2.5$,
(c) the percentage increase in T as M increases from 0.4 to 0.8. (A.E.B. 1975)

GRAPHS OF QUADRATIC FUNCTIONS

The expression $ax^2 + bx + c$ where a, b and c are constants is called *a quadratic function of x*. When plotted, quadratic functions always give a smooth curve known as a parabola.

EXAMPLE 7

Plot the graph of $y = 3x^2 + 10x - 8$ between $x = -6$ and $x = 4$.

A table may be drawn up as follows giving corresponding values of y for chosen values of x.

x	-6	-5	-4	-3	-2	-1
$3x^2$	108	75	48	27	12	3
$10x$	-60	-50	-40	-30	-20	-10
-8	-8	-8	-8	-8	-8	-8
y	40	17	0	-11	-16	-15

x	0	1	2	3	4
$3x^2$	0	3	12	27	48
$10x$	0	10	20	30	40
-8	-8	-8	-8	-8	-8
y	-8	5	24	49	80

The graph is shown in Fig. 27.15 and it is a smooth curve. Equations which are non-linear always give a graph which is a smooth curve.

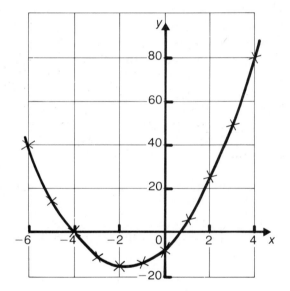

Fig. 27.15

Note that the gradient of curve is explained on page 179.

SOLUTION OF EQUATIONS

An equation may be solved by means of a graph. The following examples show the method.

EXAMPLE 8

(1) Plot the graph of $y = 6x^2 - 7x - 5$ between $x = -2$ and $x = 3$. Hence solve the equation $6x^2 - 7x - 5 = 0$.

A table is drawn up as follows.

x	-2	-1	0	1	2	3
y	33	8	-5	-6	5	28

The curve is shown in Fig. 27.16. To solve the equation $6x^2 - 7x - 5 = 0$ we have to find the values of x when $y = 0$. That is, we have to find the values of x where the graph cuts the x-axis. These are points A and B in Fig. 27.16 and hence the solutions are

$$x = -0.5 \quad \text{or} \quad x = 1.67$$

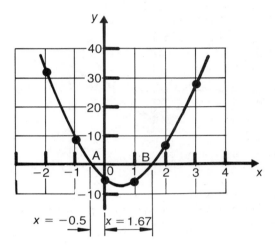

Fig. 27.16

(2) Plot the graph of $y = 2x^2 - x - 6$ and hence solve the equations:

(a) $2x^2 - x - 6 = 0$
(b) $2x^2 - x - 4 = 0$
(c) $2x^2 - x - 9 = 0$.

Take values of x between -4 and 6.

To plot $y = 2x^2 - x - 6$ draw up a table of values as shown below:

x	-4	-3	-2	-1	0
y	30	15	4	-3	-6

x	1	2	3	4	5	6
y	-5	0	9	22	39	60

(a) The graph is plotted as shown in Fig. 27.17. The curve cuts the x-axis, i.e. where $y = 0$, at the points where $x = -1.5$ and $x = 2$. Hence the solutions of the equation $2x^2 - x - 6 = 0$ are,

$$x = -1.5 \quad \text{or} \quad x = 2$$

161

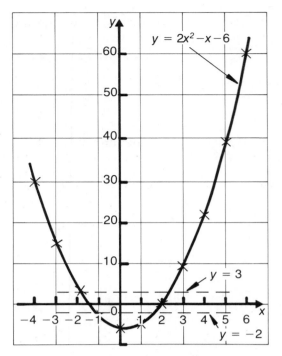

Fig. 27.17

(b) The equation $2x^2 - x - 4$ may be written in the form

$$2x^2 - x - 6 = -2$$

Hence if we find the values of x when $y = -2$ we shall obtain the solutions required. These are where the line $y = -2$ cuts the curve (see Fig. 27.17). The solutions are therefore

$$x = -1.18 \quad \text{or} \quad 1.69$$

(c) The equation $2x^2 - x - 9 = 0$ may be written in the form

$$2x^2 - x - 6 = 3$$

Hence by drawing the line $y = 3$ and finding where it cuts the curve we shall obtain the solutions. They are:

$$x = -1.89 \quad \text{or} \quad 2.36$$

Exercise 126 — *Questions 1–5 type A,*
6–9 type B, remainder type C.

Plot the graphs of the following equations:

1) $y = 2x^2 - 7x - 5$ between $x = -4$ and $x = 12$.

2) $y = x^2 - 4x + 4$ between $x = -3$ and $x = 3$.

3) $y = 6x^2 - 11x - 35$ between $x = -3$ and $x = 5$.

4) $y = 3x^2 - 5$ between $x = -2$ and $x = 4$.

5) $y = 1 + 3x - x^2$ between $x = -2$ and $x = 3$.

By plotting suitable graphs solve the following equations:

6) $x^2 - 7x + 12 = 0$ (take values of x between 0 and 6).

7) $x^2 + 16 = 8x$ (take values of x between 1 and 7).

8) $x^2 - 9 = 0$ (take values of x between -4 and 4).

9) $3x^2 + 5x = 60$ (take values of x between -6 and 4.

10) Plot the graph of $y = x^2 + 7x + 3$ taking values of x between -12 and 2. Hence solve the equations:
(a) $x^2 + 7x + 3 = 0$ (b) $x^2 + 7x - 2 = 0$
(c) $x^2 + 7x + 6 = 0$

11) Draw the graph of $y = 1 - 2x - 3x^2$ between $x = -4$ and $x = 4$. Hence solve the equations:
(a) $1 - 2x - 3x^2 = 0$ (b) $3 - 2x - 3x^2 = 0$
(c) $9x^2 + 6x = 6$

12) Draw the graph of $y = x^2 - 9$ taking values of x between -5 and 5. Hence solve the equations:
(a) $x^2 - 9 = 0$ (b) $x^2 - 5 = 0$
(c) $x^2 + 6 = 0$

INTERSECTING GRAPHS

Equations may also be solved graphically by using intersecting graphs. The method is shown in the following example.

EXAMPLE 9

Plot the graph of $y = 2x^2$ and use it to solve the equation $2x^2 - 3x - 2 = 0$. Take values of x between -2 and 4.

The equation $2x^2 - 3x - 2 = 0$ can be solved graphically by the method used in earlier examples, but the alternative method shown here is often preferable. The equation $2x^2 - 3x - 2 = 0$ may be written in the form

162

$2x^2 = 3x + 2$. We now plot on the same axes and to the same scales the graphs

$$y = 2x^2 \quad \text{and} \quad y = 3x + 2$$

x	-2	-1	0	1	2	3	4
$y = 2x^2$	8	2	0	2	8	18	32
$y = 3x + 2$	-4		2				14

Note that to plot $y = 3x + 2$ we need only three points since this is a linear equation. The graphs are shown plotted in Fig. 27.18.

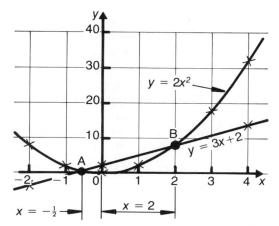

Fig. 27.18

At the points of intersection of the curve and the line (points A and B in Fig. 27.18) the y value of $2x^2$ is the same as the y value of $3x + 2$. Therefore at these points the equation $2x^2 = 3x + 2$ is satisfied. The required values of x may now be found by inspection of the graph. They are at A, where $x = -\frac{1}{2}$ and at B, where $x = 2$. The required solutions are therefore $x = -\frac{1}{2}$ or $x = 2$.

GRAPHICAL SOLUTIONS OF SIMULTANEOUS EQUATIONS

The method is shown in the following examples.

EXAMPLE 10

(1) Solve graphically

$$y - 2x = 2 \qquad [1]$$

$$3y + x = 20 \qquad [2]$$

Equation [1] may be written as:

$$y = 2 + 2x$$

Equation [2] may be written as:

$$y = \frac{20 - x}{3}$$

Drawing up the following table we can plot the two equations on the *same axes*.

x	-3	0	3
$y = 2 + 2x$	-4	2	8
$y = \dfrac{20 - x}{3}$	7.7	6.7	5.7

The solutions of the equations are the co-ordinates of the point where the two lines cross (that is, point P in Fig. 27.19). The co-ordinates of P are $x = 2$ and $y = 6$. Hence the solutions of the given equations are

$$x = 2 \quad \text{and} \quad y = 6$$

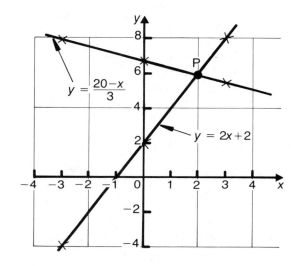

Fig. 27.19

(2) Draw the graph of $y = (3 + 2x)(3 - x)$ for values of x from $-1\frac{1}{2}$ to 3. On the same axes, and with the same scales, draw the graph of $3y = 2x + 14$. From your graphs determine the values of x for which $3(3 + 2x)(3 - x) = 2x + 14$.

To plot the graph of $y = (3 + 2x)(3 - x)$ we draw up the following table.

x	$-1\frac{1}{2}$	-1	$-\frac{1}{2}$	0
$y = (3 + 2x)(3 - x)$	0	4	7	9

x	$\frac{1}{2}$	1	$1\frac{1}{2}$	2	$2\frac{1}{2}$	3
$y = (3 + 2x)(3 - x)$	10	10	9	7	4	0

The equation $3y = 2x + 14$ may be rewritten as

$$y = \frac{2x + 14}{3}$$

163

To draw this graph we need only take three points since it is a linear equation.

x	-1	1	3
$y = \dfrac{2x + 14}{3}$	4	$5\frac{1}{3}$	$6\frac{2}{3}$

The graphs are shown in Fig. 27.20. Since the equation $3(3 + 2x)(3 - x) = 2x + 14$ may be rewritten to give

$$(3 + 2x)(3 - x) = \frac{2x + 14}{3}$$

the co-ordinates where the curve and the line intersect give the solutions which are:

$$x = -1 \quad \text{and} \quad x = 2.17$$

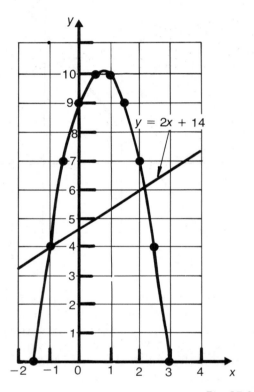

Fig. 27.20

Exercise 127 — *Questions 1–5 type B, remainder type C*

1) Plot the graph of $y = 3x^2$ taking values of x between -3 and 4. Hence solve the following equations:

(a) $3x^2 = 4$ (b) $3x^2 - 2x - 3 = 0$
(c) $3x^2 - 7x = 0$

2) Plot the graph of $y = x^2 + 8x - 2$ taking values of x between -12 and 2. On the same axes, and to the same scale, plot the graph of $y = 2x - 1$. Hence find the values of x which satisfy the equation $x^2 + 8x - 2 = 2x - 1$.

Solve graphically the following simultaneous equations:

3) $2x - 3y = 5$; $x - 2y = 2$

4) $7x - 4y = 37$; $6x + 3y = 51$

5) $\dfrac{x}{2} + \dfrac{y}{3} = \dfrac{13}{6}$; $\dfrac{2x}{7} - \dfrac{y}{4} = \dfrac{5}{14}$

6) If $y = x^2(15 - 2x)$ construct a table of values of y for values of x from -1 to $1\frac{1}{2}$ at half-unit intervals. Hence draw the graph of this function. Using the same axes and scales draw the straight line $y = 10x + 10$. Write down and simplify an equation which is satisfied by the values of x where the two graphs intersect. From your graph find the approximate value of the two roots of this equation.

7) Write down the three values missing from the following table which gives values of $2x^3 + x + 3$ for values of x from -2 to 2.

x	-2.0	-1.5	-1.0	-0.5
$2x^3 + x + 3$	-15.0	-5.25		2.25

x	0	0.5	1.0	1.5	2.0
$2x^3 + x + 3$		3.75	6.0		21.0

Using the same axes draw the graphs of $y = 2x^3 + x + 3$ and $y = 9x + 3$. Use your graphs to write down:

(a) the range of values of x for which $2x^3 + x + 3$ is less than $9x + 3$;
(b) the solution of the equation $2x^3 + x + 3 = 5$. Write down and simplify the equation which is satisfied by the values of x at the points of intersection of the two graphs.

8) Write down the three values missing from the following table which gives values, correct to two decimal places, of $6 - \dfrac{10}{2x + 1}$ for values of x from 0.25 to 5.

x	0.25	0.5	1	1.5
$6 - \dfrac{10}{2x + 1}$	-0.67	1.00	2.67	3.50

x	2	3	3.5	4	4.5	5
$6 - \dfrac{10}{2x + 1}$		4.57		4.89		5.09

Using the same axes draw the graphs of $y = 6 - \dfrac{10}{2x + 1}$ and $y = x + 1$. Use your graphs to solve the equation $2x^2 - 9x + 5 = 0$.

9) If $y = \dfrac{x + 10}{x + 1}$ construct a table of values of y when $x = 0, 1, 2, 3, 4, 5$. Draw the graph of this function and also using the same axes and scales draw the graph of $y = x - 1$. Write down, and simplify, an equation which is satisfied by the value of x where the graphs intersect. From your graphs find the approximate value of the root of this equation.

10) Calculate the values of $\dfrac{x^2}{4} + \dfrac{24}{x} - 12$ which are omitted from the table below.

x	2	2.5	3	3.5	4
$\dfrac{x^2}{4} + \dfrac{24}{x} - 12$		-0.84		-2.08	

x	4.5	5	5.5	6
$\dfrac{x^2}{4} + \dfrac{24}{x} - 12$	-1.60	-0.95	-0.07	1.00

Draw the graph of $y = \dfrac{x^2}{4} + \dfrac{24}{x} - 12$ from $x = 2$ to $x = 6$. Using the same scales and axes draw the graph of $y = \dfrac{x}{3} - 2$. Write down, but do not simplify, an equation which is satisfied by the values of x where the graphs intersect. From your graphs find approximate values for the two roots of this equation.

SELF-TEST 27

In questions 1 to 20 the answer is either "true" or "false", state which.

1) The intersection of the two axes of reference, used when plotting a graph, is called the origin.

2) When a graph is a straight line it means that there is a definite law connecting the two quantities which are plotted.

3) When a graph is a smooth curve it means that there is not a definite law connecting the two quantities which are plotted.

4) Interpolation means using a graph to find values which are not given in the table from which the graph is drawn.

5) In order to extrapolate the graph is extended just beyond the range of the values from which the graph was plotted.

6) The co-ordinates of the point shown in Fig. 27.21 are $(3, 5)$.

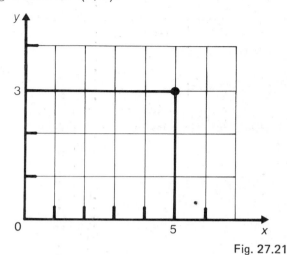

Fig. 27.21

7) The co-ordinates of the point shown in Fig. 27.22 are $(2, 3)$.

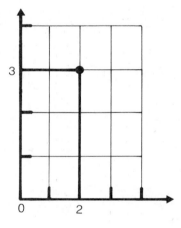

Fig. 27.22

8) When the co-ordinates of a point are stated as $(3, 6)$ it means that $x = 3$ and $y = 6$.

9) When the co-ordinates of a point are stated as $(-2, 4)$ it means that $y = -2$ when $x = 4$.

10) The equation $y = 3x + 7$ will give a graph which is a curve.

11) The equation $y = 3 - 5x$ will give a graph which is a straight line.

12) The equation $p = \dfrac{5}{q}$ will give a graph which is a straight line.

13) The equation $y = 8 - \dfrac{3}{x}$ will give a graph which is a straight line.

14) The equation $y = 3 + x^2$ will give a graph which is a curve.

15) The equation $y = 3 - 2x^3$ will give a graph which is a curve.

16) When drawing the graph of $y = 5x^2 + 7x + 8$ values of y are plotted on the vertical axis.

17) When drawing the graph of $M = q^2 + 3$ values of q are plotted on the vertical axis.

18) When $r = 3s + 7$, r is called the independent variable.

19) When $q = 7p - 8$, p is called the independent variable.

20) When $V = 8r^3$, V is called the dependent variable.

In questions 21 to 28 state the letter (or letters) which correspond to the correct answer (or answers).

21) The graph of $y = 3 + 2x$ will look like one of the following diagrams (Fig. 27.23).

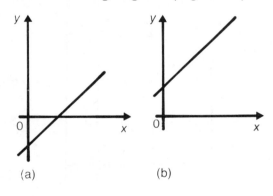

(a) (b)

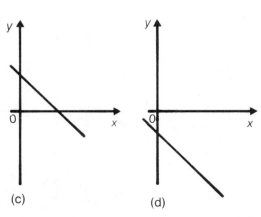

(c) (d)

Fig. 27.23

22) The graph of $y = 5 - 3x$ will look like one of the following diagrams (Fig. 27.24).

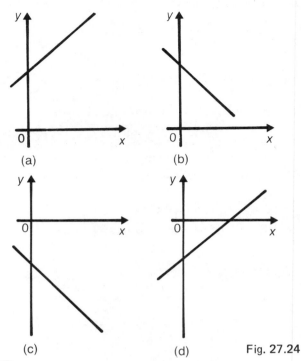

(a) (b)

(c) (d) Fig. 27.24

23) A straight line passes through the points $(0, 1)$ and $(2, 7)$. The law of the line is therefore:

a $y = 3x + 1$ b $y = 3x - 1$

c $y = \frac{3}{7}x + 1$ d $y = \frac{3}{7}x - 1$

24) The law of the line shown in Fig. 27.25 is:

a $y = 2x + 5$ b $y = 5 - 2x$

c $y = 2x + 1$ d $y = \frac{1}{2}x + \frac{1}{2}$

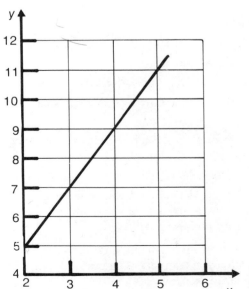

Fig. 27.25

25) The graph showing the relationship between two quantities S and T is a straight line. Values of S are indicated on the horizontal axis. The gradient of the graph is 5 and the intercept on the vertical axis is 3. Hence the law of the line is:

a $S = 5T + 3$ **b** $T = 5S + 3$

c $S = 3T + 5$ **d** $T = 3S + 5$

26) Figure 27.26 shows the graphs of $y = x^2 - 3x + 2$ and $y = 3x + 6$, plotted on the same axes. The solutions of the equation $x^2 - 6x - 4 = 0$:

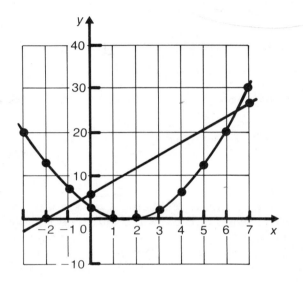

Fig. 27.26

a cannot be found from the graphs,

b are -0.6 and 6.6,

c are 4 and 25,

d are -0.6 and 4 and 6.6 and 25.

27) You are given the graph of $y = 2x^2 + x - 15$. From the graph the solutions of the equation $2x^2 - 11x + 15 = 0$

are required. Hence, on the same axes, you would plot:

a $y = 30 - 12x$ **b** $y = 10x - 30$

c $y = 12x - 30$ **d** $y = 10x + 30$

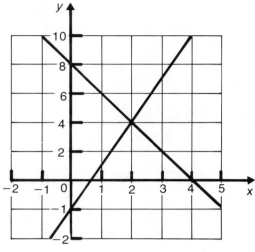

Fig. 27.27

28) Figure 27.27 shows the graphs of $y = 3x - 2$ and $y = 8 - 2x$, plotted on the same axes. The solutions of the simultaneous equations $3x - y = 2$ and $2x + y = 8$:

a cannot be found from the graphs,

b are $x = 2$ and $y = 4$,

c are $x = 4$ and $y = 2$,

d are $x = 4$ and $y = -2$.

29) Two variables X and Y are connected by an equation of the type $Y = \dfrac{a}{X^2} + b$. In order to obtain a straight line graph one of the following is plotted.

a Y against X **b** Y against X^2

c Y^2 against X **d** Y against $\dfrac{1}{X^2}$

Chapter 28 **Variation**

DIRECT VARIATION

The statement that y is proportional to x (often written $y \propto x$) means that the graph of y against x is a straight line passing through the origin (Fig. 28.1). If the gradient of this line is k, then $y = kx$. The value of k is called the constant of proportionality. Thus, the ratio of y to x is equal to the constant of proportionality and y is said to *vary directly as* x. Hence direct variation means that if x is doubled then y is also doubled, if x is halved then y is halved and so on. Some examples of direct variation are as follows:

(1) The circumference of a circle is directly proportional to its diameter.

(2) The volume of a cone of given radius is directly proportional to its height.

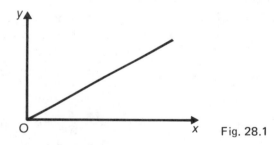

Fig. 28.1

Most problems on direct variation involve first finding the constant of proportionality from information given in the problem as shown in the following example.

EXAMPLE 1

If y is directly proportional to x and $y = 2$ when $x = 5$, find the value of y when $x = 6$.

Since $y \propto x$ then $y = kx$.

We are given that when $y = 2$, $x = 5$. Hence,

$$2 = k \times 5 \quad \text{or} \quad k = \frac{2}{5}$$

$$\therefore \qquad y = \frac{2}{5} x$$

when $x = 6$,

$$y = \frac{2}{5} \times 6 = \frac{12}{5}$$

The volume of a sphere is given by the equation $V = \frac{4}{3}\pi r^3$. From this equation we see that V varies directly as the cube of r (that is $V \propto r^3$) and the constant of proportionality is $\frac{4}{3}\pi$.

If y is proportional to x^2 ($y \propto x^2$) the graph of y against x^2 is a straight line passing through the origin. If the gradient of this line is k then $y = kx^2$.

Similarly if $y \propto \sqrt{x}$ then $y = k\sqrt{x}$.

EXAMPLE 2

The surface area of a sphere, A square millimetres, varies directly as the square of its radius, r millimetres. If the surface area of a sphere 2 mm radius is 50.24 mm² find the surface area of a sphere whose radius is 4 mm.

Since $A \propto r^2$ then $A = kr^2$.

We are given that $A = 50.24$ when $r = 2$. Hence:

$$50.24 = k \times 2^2 \quad \text{or} \quad k = \frac{50.24}{2^2} = 12.56$$

$$\therefore \qquad A = 12.56r^2$$

when $r = 4$,

$$A = 12.56 \times 4^2 = 200.96 \text{ mm}^2$$

INVERSE VARIATION

If y is inversely proportional to x then the graph of y against $\dfrac{1}{x}$ is a straight line passing through the origin (Fig. 28.2). If the gradient of this line is k, then,

$$y = k \times \frac{1}{x} = \frac{k}{x}$$

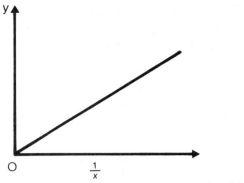

Fig. 28.2

EXAMPLE 3

The electrical resistance, R ohms, of a wire of given length is inversely proportional to the square of the diameter of the wire, d mm. If R is 4.25 ohms when d is 2 mm find the value of R when $d = 3$ mm.

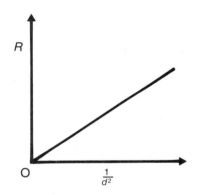

Fig. 28.3

Since R is inversely proportional to d^2 (Fig. 28.3)

$$R \propto \frac{1}{d^2}$$

$$R = \frac{k}{d^2}$$

when $R = 4.25$, $d = 2$, hence:

$$4.25 = \frac{k}{2^2}$$

$$k = 4.25 \times 2^2 = 17$$

$$\therefore \quad R = \frac{17}{d^2}$$

when $d = 3$,

$$R = \frac{17}{3^2} = 1.9 \text{ ohms}$$

Exercise 128 — *All type A*

1) Express the following with an equal sign and a constant:

(a) y varies directly as x^2.
(b) U varies directly as the square root of V.
(c) S varies inversely as T^3.
(d) h varies inversely as the cube root of m.

2) If $y = 2$ when $x = 4$ write down the value of y when $x = 9$ for the following:

(a) y varies directly as the square of x.
(b) y varies inversely as the square root of x.
(c) y varies inversely as x.

3) If S varies inversely as T^3 and $S = 54$ when $T = 3$ find the value of T when $S = 16$.

4) If U varies directly as $\sqrt{V}$ and $U = 2$ when $V = 9$ find the value of V when $U = 4$.

5) The surface area of a sphere, V mm^2, varies directly as the square of its diameter, d mm. If the surface area is to be doubled by what ratio must the diameter be altered.

JOINT VARIATION

The volume of a cylinder varies directly as two dimensions: its height and the square of its radius. Hence the volume is directly proportional to the *product* of its height and the square of its radius. Written as an equation the statement becomes:

$$V = khr^2$$

Again, the constant k can be found from information given in the problem.

EXAMPLE 4

A certain law in physics connecting three quantities p, v and t states that p varies directly as t and inversely as v. If it is known that $p = 800$ when $t = 300$ and $v = 36$ calculate the value of v when $p = 700$ and $t = 350$.

We are given $p \propto t$ and $p \propto \dfrac{1}{v}$

$$\therefore \qquad p = \frac{kt}{v}$$

Since $p = 800$ when $t = 300$ and $v = 36$,

$$800 = \frac{k \times 300}{36}$$

169

$$\therefore \qquad k = \frac{800 \times 36}{300} = 96$$

$$\therefore \qquad p = \frac{96t}{v}$$

To find v when $p = 700$ and $t = 350$ substitute these values in the last equation. Thus,

$$700 = \frac{96 \times 350}{v}$$

$$v = \frac{96 \times 350}{700}$$

$$\therefore \qquad v = 48$$

VARIATION AS THE SUM OF TWO PARTS

The function $(ax + bx^2)$ is the sum of two quantities:

ax which varies directly as x, and

bx^2 which varies directly as x^2.

An alternative description would describe the function $(ax + bx^2)$ as that function which varies partly as x and partly as x^2.

It is important to be able to recognise whether problems involve joint variation or variation as the sum of two parts.

EXAMPLE 5

(1) A quantity p is the sum of two terms, one of which is constant, whilst the other varies inversely as the square of q. When $q = 1$, $p = -1$ and when $q = 2$, $p = 2$. Find the positive value of q when $p = 2\frac{3}{4}$.

If a and b are constants

$$p = a + \frac{b}{q^2} \quad \text{(see Fig. 28.4)}$$

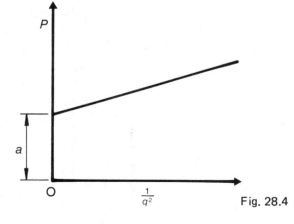

Fig. 28.4

In order to evaluate a and b we use the information given in the question. Thus when $q = 1$, $p = -1$

$$\therefore \qquad -1 = a + \frac{b}{1^2}$$

or $\qquad -1 = a + b \qquad\qquad [1]$

when $q = 2$, $p = 2$

$$\therefore \qquad 2 = a + \frac{b}{2^2}$$

or $\qquad 2 = a + \frac{b}{4}$

$\qquad 8 = 4a + b \qquad\qquad [2]$

Subtracting equation [1] from [2],

$$9 = 3a$$

$$\therefore \qquad a = 3$$

Substituting for $a = 3$ in equation [1],

$$-1 = 3 + b$$

$$\therefore \qquad b = -4$$

$$\therefore \qquad p = 3 - \frac{4}{q^2}$$

when $p = 2\frac{3}{4}$, $\quad 2\frac{3}{4} = 3 - \frac{4}{q^2}$

$$\frac{4}{q^2} = \frac{1}{4}$$

$$q^2 = 16$$

$$q = \pm 4$$

Since only the positive value of q is required

$$q = 4$$

Exercise 129 — *All type B*

1) The mass of a solid cone varies jointly as the square of the radius of the base and as the height. If a cone has a mass of 15 g, a height of 5 mm and a radius of 3 mm find the radius of a second cone made from the same material which has a mass of 32 g and a height of 6 mm.

2) It is known that P varies inversely as the square of Q. Corresponding pairs of values are shown in the following table:

P	t	$t+1$
Q	5	4

Calculate the value of t.

170

3) If y varies directly as x^3 and $y = 25$ when $x = 10$, calculate the value of y when $x = 6$.

4) Draw a neat sketch graph of the function $y = \dfrac{p}{x}$, giving p the value which will make y equal to 4 when $x = 3$. State this value of p. You are not required to draw the graph accurately but simply to show its position and give a general idea of its shape.

5) A quantity C is the sum of two parts. The first part varies directly as the cube of t; the second part varies inversely as the square of t. Given that $C = 74$ when $t = 1$ and $C = 34$ when $t = 2$, find the value of C when $t = 3$.

6) A quantity P is the difference between two parts. The first part is constant and the second varies inversely as the square of Q. If $P = 1$ when $Q = 2$ and $P = 6$ when $Q = 3$, find the positive value of Q when $P = 7\frac{3}{4}$.

7) It is given that y is inversely proportional to the square of $(x + 3)$. If $y = 9$ when $x = 1$, find the possible values of x when $y = 1$.

8) The velocity, v metres per second, of a body moving in a straight line is at any given instant given by the sum of two terms, one of which is proportional to the time t seconds which has elapsed since the body started moving and the other is proportional to the square of the time t. Given that $v = 68$ when $t = 1$ and $v = 104$ when $t = 2$, form an equation for v in terms of t. Use your equation to calculate the value of t when the body comes to rest.

9) For a certain series of experiments it is known that a quantity F is directly proportional to h and the square root of P, and inversely proportional to the square of d. If $d = 8$, $h = 40$ and $P = 1000$ when $F = 12$, calculate the value of P when $F = 8$, $d = 10$ and $h = 30$.

10) Three quantities E, D and H are connected so that E varies directly as H and inversely as the square of root of D. If $E = 5$ when $H = 10$ and $D = 16$ find the value of D when $E = 20$ and $H = 4$.

SELF-TEST 28

In questions 1 to 15 the answer is either 'true' or 'false', state which.

1) The graph in Fig. 28.5 shows y plotted against $\sqrt{x}$. Hence y is proportional to $\sqrt{x}$.

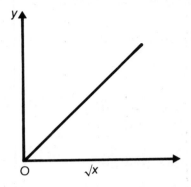

Fig. 28.5

2) The graph in Fig. 28.6 shows y plotted against x^2. Therefore $y = kx^2$ where k is a constant.

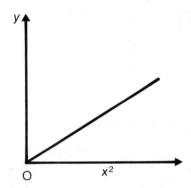

Fig. 28.6

3) The graph in Fig. 28.7 shows y plotted against $\dfrac{1}{x}$. Therefore $y = kx$.

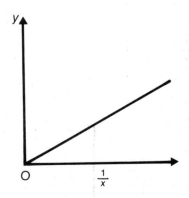

Fig. 28.7

4) If V is proportional to r^2 and V is 6 when r is 2 then $V = 1.5r^2$.

5) If Q is inversely proportional to $\sqrt{x}$ then $Q = \dfrac{k}{\sqrt{x}}$.

6) If y is inversely proportional to d^3 and y is $\frac{3}{8}$ when d is 2 then $y = 3d^3$.

7) If M varies directly as p and inversely as q^2 then $M = \dfrac{kp}{q^2}$.

8) If y varies directly as the square root of v and inversely as u then $y = ku\sqrt{v}$.

9) A quantity F varies directly as m and inversely as p. If $m = 6$ and $p = 3$ when $F = 4$ then $F = 2pm$.

10) The graph shown in Fig. 28.8 means that y is the sum of two parts.

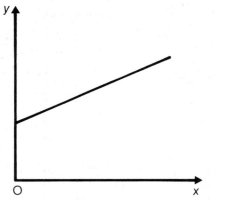

Fig. 28.8

11) In Fig. 28.8 $y = kx + c$ where k and c are constants.

12) In Fig. 28.9, the graph indicates that the quantity Q is the difference between two parts, the first being a constant and the second varying directly with x^2.

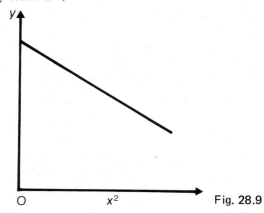

Fig. 28.9

13) A quantity M is the sum of two parts. The first part varies directly as the square of p and the second part as the cube of p. Hence $M = k_1p^2 + k_2p^3$ where k_1 and k_2 are constants.

14) The graph in Fig. 28.10 represents the relationship $y = \dfrac{k}{x}$.

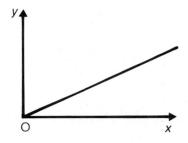

Fig. 28.10

15) A quantity C is the sum of two parts. The first part varies directly as the square root of m and the second part varies inversely as the square of m. Hence $C = \dfrac{k\sqrt{m}}{m^2}$ where k is a constant.

In questions 16 to 24 state the letter (or letters) which correspond to the correct answer (or answers).

16) In Fig. 28.11:

a $y = kx^2$ **b** $y = \dfrac{k}{x^2}$

c $y = k_1 + k_2x^2$ **d** $y = k_1 + \dfrac{k_2}{x^2}$

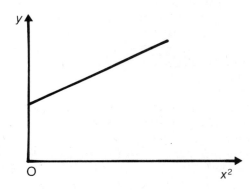

Fig. 28.11

17) In Fig. 28.12 if k_1 and k_2 are positive, then:

a $y = k_1 + k_2\sqrt{x}$ **b** $y = k_1 - k_2\sqrt{x}$

c $y = k_1\sqrt{x}$ **d** $y = \dfrac{k_1}{\sqrt{x}}$

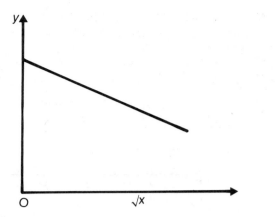

Fig. 28.12

18) If y varies as x^2 and $y = 25$ when $x = 10$ then the value of y when $x = 2$ is:

a 1   **b** 16   **c** 625   **d** 0.062 5

19) If R varies inversely as $\sqrt{p}$ and $R = 2$ when $p = 4$, then the value of R when $p = 16$ is:

a $\frac{1}{4}$ **b** 4   **c** 1   **d** 8

20) A quantity M varies directly as d^2 and inversely as q. When $M = 6$, $d = 2$ and $q = 2$. Thus when $d = 4$ and $q = 8$ the value of M is:

a 96   **b** $\frac{1}{96}$ **c** $\frac{1}{6}$ **d** 6

21) A quantity P is the difference of two parts. The first part varies directly as r and the second part varies inversely as r^2. If k_1 and k_2 are positive, an expression for P is:

a $P = k_1 r + k_2 r^2$ **b** $P = k_1 r - k_2 r^2$

c $P = k_1 r + \dfrac{k_2}{r^2}$ **d** $P = k_1 r - \dfrac{k_2}{r^2}$

22) A quantity y is the sum of two parts. The first part is a constant and the second part varies directly as $\sqrt{x}$. If C and k are positive, an expression for y is:

a $y = C(1 + \sqrt{x})$ **b** $y = C(1 - \sqrt{x})$

c $y = C + k\sqrt{x}$ **d** $y = C - k\sqrt{x}$

23) A quantity m is the sum of two parts, one of which is constant and the other varies inversely as the square of p. When $p = 2$, $m = 5$ and when $p = 1$, $m = 14$. Hence an expression for m is:

a $m = 2 + \dfrac{12}{p^2}$ **b** $m = 2 - \dfrac{12}{p^2}$

c $m = 2 + 12p^2$ **d** $m = 2 - 12p^2$

24) The electrical resistance, R, of a wire varies directly as the length, l, and inversely as the square of the diameter d. A formula giving d in terms of l, R and a constant of variation, k, is:

a $d = \dfrac{kl}{R}$ **b** $d = \sqrt{\dfrac{kl}{R}}$ **c** $d = \dfrac{R}{kl}$

d $d = \sqrt{\dfrac{R}{kl}}$

Chapter 29 Inequalities

An *inequality* is a statement that one number or quantity is greater than a second number or quantity.

If we want to say that n is greater than 5 we write,

$$n > 5$$

Similarly, if x is less than 3 we write,

$$x < 3$$

If x is greater or equal to 7 we write,

$$x \geqslant 7$$

Similarly, if y is less or equal to 2 we write,

$$y \leqslant 2$$

Note that the arrow always points to the smaller quantity.

SOLUTIONS OF INEQUALITIES

If $x < 4$, what values of x could there be for the inequality to be true? There are very many different values which will make it true. Some of these are $3, 0, -1\frac{1}{2}, -3$, but there are very many values all of which are less than 4. However if x has to be a positive whole number then only 1, 2 and 3 are possible solutions.

The solution to an inequality like $x < 4$ can be shown on a number line (Fig. 29.1). The empty circle at the end of the arrowed line shows that $x = 4$ is not included as a possible value of x.

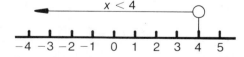

Fig. 29.1

Figure 29.2 shows the solution for $x \geqslant -2$. The solid circle at the end of the arrowed line shows that -2 is included as a possible value for x.

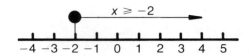

Fig. 29.2

EXAMPLE 1

Solve the inequality $3x > 12$.

$$3x > 12$$
$$x > 4 \quad \text{(Dividing each side by 3)}$$

The process is similar to solving a simple equation and the solution can be shown on a number line (Fig. 29.3).

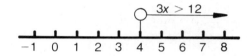

Fig. 29.3

EXAMPLE 2

Solve the inequality $2x + 5 \geqslant 11$.

$$2x + 5 \geqslant 11$$
$$2x \geqslant 6 \quad \text{(Subtracting 5 from each side)}$$
$$x \geqslant 3 \quad \text{(Dividing both sides by 2)}$$

Figure 29.4 shows the solution on a number line.

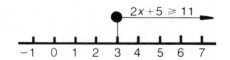

Fig. 29.4

EXAMPLE 3

Solve the inequality $7x + 4 \geqslant 3x + 12$.

$$7x + 4 \geqslant 3x + 12$$
$$7x - 3x \geqslant 12 - 4$$
$$4x \geqslant 8$$
$$x \geqslant 2$$

Figure 29.5 shows the solution on a number line.

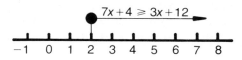

Fig. 29.5

EXAMPLE 4

If x has to be one of the numbers $0, 1, 2, 3, 4,$ 5 or $6,$ find the solution for $x < 5$ and $x \geqslant 3.$

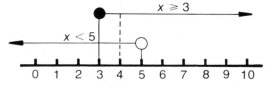

Fig. 29.6

Representing both inequalities on a number line we see (Fig. 29.6) that the solution is that x must equal 3 or $4,$ because the arrow lines representing the independent solution for each inequality overlap.

EXAMPLE 5

If x must be a whole number between 0 and 10 inclusive find the solution for the pair of inequalities $x \leqslant 2$ and $x \geqslant 5.$

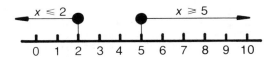

Fig. 29.7

From Fig. 29.7 we see that there are no numbers which make both the given inequalities true. This is because the arrow lines representing the two independent inequalities do not overlap.

Note that the inequalities $x \leqslant 2$ and $x \geqslant 5$ are sometimes written $2 \geqslant x \geqslant 5.$

Exercise 130 — *All type B*

Solve the following inequalities and represent the solutions on number lines:

1) $2x > 4$ 2) $x - 4 > 3$

3) $x + 5 > 7$ 5) $6x + 11 \leqslant 25 - x$

4) $3x - 4 \leqslant 2$ 6) $3x + 22 \geqslant 8x - 18$

Use number lines to find solutions for the following pairs of inequalities. In each case x must be one of the numbers $0, 1, 2, 3, 4,$ $5, 6, 7$ and $8.$

7) $x < 3$ and $x > 1$

8) $x < 0$ and $x > 6$

9) $x > 3$ and $x < 8$

10) $x \geqslant 0$ and $x \leqslant 7$

GRAPHS OF LINEAR INEQUALITIES

EXAMPLE 6

(1) Illustrate on a graph the solution of the inequality $3y + 6x < 8.$

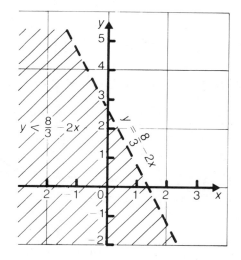

Fig. 29.8

First express the inequality in the form

$$3y < 8 - 6x$$

$$y < \frac{8}{3} - 2x$$

Next draw the graph of $y = \frac{8}{3} - 2x$ as shown in Fig. 29.8. The solution of the inequality $y < \frac{8}{3} - 2x$ is the shaded portion below the straight line representing the equation $y = \frac{8}{3} - 2x.$ Since the solution does not include points on the line $y = \frac{8}{3} - 2x,$ this is shown dotted.

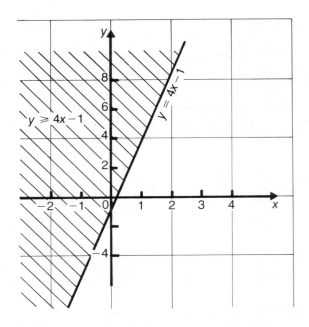

Fig. 29.9

(2) Show graphically the solution of the inequality $y \geqslant 4x - 1$.

The solution is the shaded portion of Fig. 29.9 which lies above the straight line representing the equation $y = 4x - 1$. Since the solution includes all the points lying on the line $y = 4x - 1$, this is shown by a full line.

(3) Show graphically the solution for the inequality $x \geqslant 4$.

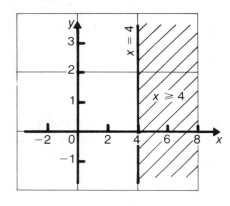

Fig. 29.10

The graph of the straight line $x = 4$ is parallel to the y-axis and 4 units from it (Fig. 29.10). The solution is given by the shaded part of the diagram.

176

(4) Illustrate on a graph the inequality $y < 2$. The graph of the straight line $y = 2$ is parallel to the x-axis and 2 units above it (Fig. 29.11). The solution is shown by the shaded portion of the diagram.

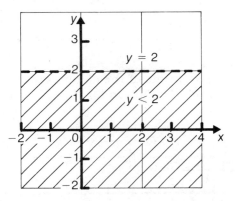

Fig. 29.11

Exercise 131 — *All type B*

Illustrate graphically the solutions for the following inequalities:

1) $x > 2$

2) $x \leqslant 3$

3) $x \geqslant -2$

4) $y > 0$

5) $y \leqslant 4$

6) $y \geqslant 1$

7) $y > 2$

8) $x + y \geqslant 2$

9) $y < 3x + 4$

10) $y + x - 1 < 0$

11) $3x + 2y - 5 \geqslant 0$

12) $4x + 2y + 6 \geqslant 0$

When several inequalities are graphed simultaneously on the same axes, their common solution is shown by the overlapping of the different shaded areas. The common area is usually a triangle, a quadrilateral or some kind of polygon.

EXAMPLE 7

Shade the region $y \geqslant 2x$, $y \leqslant 4$, $4x + 3y \geqslant 12$.

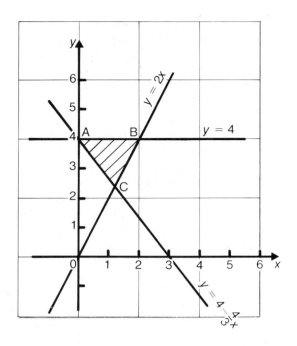

Fig. 29.12

In Fig. 29.12, the lines $y = 2x$, $y = 4$ and $y = 4 - \frac{4}{3}x$ have been drawn on the same axes. The region which contains the common solution is $\triangle$ ABC, which has been shaded in the diagram.

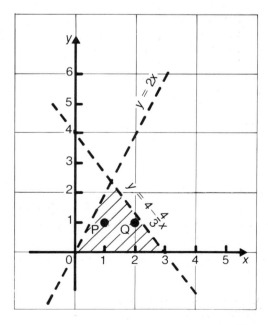

Fig. 29.13

EXAMPLE 8

If $y < 2x$, $4x + 3y < 12$, $y > 0$ and $x > 0$ and if x and y are both integers, find the two possible values of $(x + y)$.

In Fig. 29.13, the solution is contained in the shaded triangle. Since x and y are both integers (i.e. whole numbers), only the points P and Q meet the given conditions.

At P,

$$x = 1 \quad \text{and} \quad y = 1$$
$$\therefore \qquad x + y = 1 + 1 = 2$$

At Q,

$$x = 2 \quad \text{and} \quad y = 1$$
$$\therefore \qquad x + y = 2 + 1 = 3$$

Exercise 132 — *All type C*

Shade the following regions:

1) $x \geqslant 0$, $y \geqslant 0$, $x + y \geqslant 10$

2) $x \geqslant 0$, $y \geqslant 0$, $2x + 3y \leqslant 12$, $5x + 2y \leqslant 20$

3) $x \geqslant 2$, $y \geqslant 1$, $x + y \leqslant 6$, $x \leqslant 4$, $y \leqslant 3$

4) $y \geqslant 4$, $x \leqslant 3$, $y \leqslant 2x$

5) $y \leqslant 3$, $x \geqslant 0$, $y + 2x \leqslant 5$, $y - x \geqslant 0$

6) Draw the graph of $y = x^2 - 5x + 4$ for values of x from -1 to 6. On the same axes draw the line $y = 4$. Use these graphs to find the range of values for which $x^2 - 5x + 4 < 4$.

SELF-TEST 29

State the letter corresponding to the correct answer.

1) x has to be a whole number such that $0 \leqslant x \leqslant 10$. The solution for $x < 4$ and $x \geqslant 7$ is:

a 5   **b** 7   **c** no solution   **d** 5, 6 or 7

2) x has to be a whole number such that $0 \leqslant x \leqslant 6$. The solution for $x \leqslant 5$ and $x \geqslant 3$ is:

a no solution   **b** $x > 6$ **c** $x \leqslant 3$

d 3, 4, 5

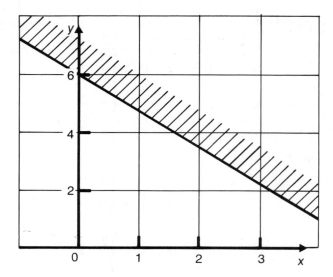

Fig. 29.14

3) The shaded portion of Fig. 29.14 represents the solution of the inequality:

a $y \leqslant 6 - \frac{4}{3}x$ **b** $y < 6 - \frac{4}{3}x$

c $y \geqslant 6 - \frac{4}{3}x$ **d** $y > 6 - \frac{4}{3}x$

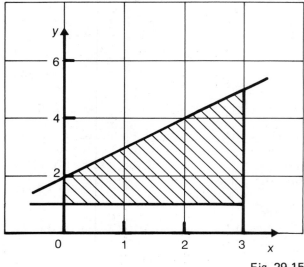

Fig. 29.15

4) The shaded region of Fig. 29.15 represents the solution of the inequalities:

a $y > x + 2$, $y > 1$, $0 < x < 3$
b $y \geqslant x + 2$, $y \geqslant 1$, $0 \leqslant x \leqslant 3$
c $y \leqslant x + 2$, $y \geqslant 1$, $0 \leqslant x \leqslant 3$
d $y < x + 2$, $y > 1$, $0 < x < 3$

5) The solution of the inequalities $y > 2$, $y < x + 3$, $0 < x < 4$ is represented by the shaded region in Fig. 29.16.

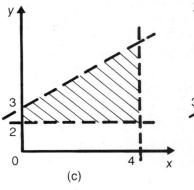
(a)

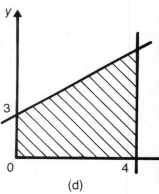
(b)

(c)

(d)

Fig. 29.16

Chapter 30 **The Differential Calculus**

THE GRADIENT OF A CURVE

In mathematics and science we often need to know the rate of change of one variable with respect to another. For instance, speed is the rate of change of distance with respect to time and acceleration is the rate of change of speed with respect to time.

Consider the graph $y = x^2$ part of which is shown in Fig. 30.1. As the values of x increase so do the values of y, but they do not increase at the same rate. A glance at the portion of the curve shown in Fig. 30.1 shows that the values of y increase faster when x is large because the gradient of the curve is increasing.

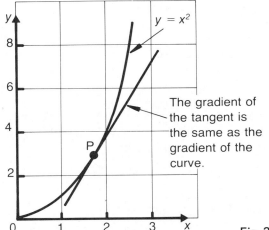

Fig. 30.1

To find the rate of change of y with respect to x at a particular point we need to find the gradient of the curve at that point. If we draw a tangent to the curve at the point, the gradient of the tangent will be the same as the gradient of the curve.

EXAMPLE 1
(1) Draw the curve of $y = x^2$ and find the gradient of the curve at the points where $x = 2$ and $x = -2$.

To draw the curve the table below is drawn up

x	-3	-2	-1	0	1	2	3
$y = x^2$	9	4	1	0	1	4	9

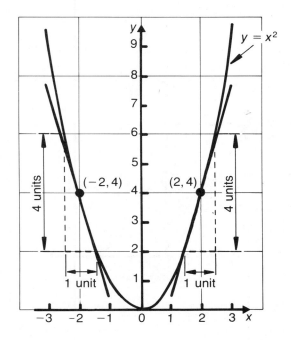

Fig. 30.2

The point where $x = 2$ is the point $(2, 4)$. We draw a tangent at this point as shown in Fig. 30.2. Then by constructing a right-angled triangle the gradient is found to be $\frac{4}{1} = 4$.

This gradient is positive since the tangent slopes upwards from left to right.

A positive value of the gradient indicates that y is increasing as x increases.

The point where $x = -2$ is the point $(-2, 4)$.

By drawing the tangent at this point and constructing a right-angled triangle as shown in Fig. 30.2, the gradient is found to be

$$\frac{-4}{1} = -4$$

The gradient is negative because the tangent slopes downwards from left to right.

A negative value of the gradient indicates that y is decreasing as x increases.

179

(2) Draw the graph of $y = x^2 - 3x + 7$ between $x = -4$ and $x = 4$ and hence find the gradient of the curve at the points $x = -3$ and $x = 2$.

To plot the curve draw up the following table.

x	-4	-3	-2	-1	0	1	2	3	4
y	35	25	17	11	7	5	5	7	11

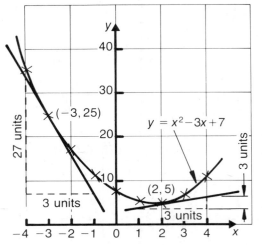

Fig. 30.3

At the point where $x = -3$, $y = 25$.

At the point $(-3, 25)$ draw a tangent to the curve as shown in Fig. 30.3. The gradient is found by drawing a right-angled triangle (which should be as large as possible for accuracy) as shown and measuring its height and base. Hence

gradient at the point

$$(-3, 25) = -\frac{27}{3} = -9$$

At the point where $x = 2$, $y = 5$. Hence by drawing a tangent and a right-angled triangle at the point $(2, 5)$,

$$\text{gradient at point } (2, 5) = \frac{3}{3} = 1$$

(3) Draw the graph of $y = x^2 + 3x - 2$ taking values of x between $x = -1$ and $x = 4$. Hence find the value of $y = x^2 + 3x - 2$ where the gradient of the curve is 7.

To plot the curve the following table is drawn up

x	-1	0	1	2	3	4
y	-4	-2	2	8	16	26

The curve is shown in Fig. 30.4.

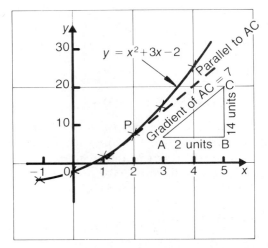

Fig. 30.4

To obtain a line whose gradient is 7 we draw the $\triangle$ ABC making (for convenience) AB = 2 units to the scale on the x-axis and BC = 14 units to the scale on the y-axis. Hence:

$$\text{gradient of AC} = \frac{\text{BC}}{\text{AB}} = \frac{14}{2} = 7$$

Using set-squares we draw a tangent to the curve so that the tangent is parallel to AC. As can be seen this tangent touches the curve at the point P where $x = 2$. Hence the gradient of the curve is 7 at the point where $x = 2$.

Exercise 133 — *All type C*

1) Draw the graph of $y = 3x^2 + 7x + 3$ and find the gradient of the curve at the points where $x = -2$ and $x = 2$.

2) Draw the graph of $y = 2x^2 - 5$ for values of x between -2 and 3. Find the gradient of the curve at the points where $x = -1$ and $x = 2$.

3) Draw the curve of $y = x^2 - 3x + 2$ from $x = 2.5$ to $x = 3.5$ and find its gradient at the point where $x = 3$.

4) For what values of x is the gradient of the curve $y = \dfrac{x^3}{3} + \dfrac{x^2}{2} - 33x + 7$ equal to 3? In drawing the curve take values of x between -8 and 6.

180

5) If $y = (1 + x)(5 - 2x)$ copy and complete the table below

x	-2	$-1\frac{1}{2}$	-1	0	$\frac{1}{2}$	1	$1\frac{1}{2}$	2	3
y	-9			0	5		6	5	3	-4

Hence draw the graph of $y = (1 + x)(5 - 2x)$. Find the value of x at which the gradient of the curve is -2.

6) If $y = x^2 - 5x + 4$ find by plotting the curve between $x = 4$ and $x = 12$ the value of x at which the gradient of the curve is 11.

DIFFERENTIATION

It is possible to find the gradient of a curve at *any* point by graphical means. However this method is often inconvenient and not very accurate. Hence the gradient of a curve is usually found by *differentiation*.

The gradient of a curve at any point on the curve is given by its derived function. Thus if

$$y = x^n$$

then it can be shown that the derived function is

$$\frac{dy}{dx} = nx^{n-1}$$

This formula is true for all values of n including fractional and negative indices. The expression $\frac{dy}{dx}$, compares the rate of change of y with that of x and it must be realised that $\frac{dy}{dx}$ is not a fraction in the ordinary sense. The d in dy is not a multiple (compare with $\cos y$ or $\log y$) and dy cannot be separated from its denominator dx.

The process of finding $\frac{dy}{dx}$ is called differentiation.

EXAMPLE 2

(1) If $y = x^3$, $\frac{dy}{dx} = 3x^2$.

(2) If $y = \dfrac{1}{x}$ then $y = x^{-1}$ and

$\dfrac{dy}{dx} = -x^{-2} = -\dfrac{1}{x^2}$.

(3) If $y = \sqrt{x}$ then $y = x^{1/2}$ and
$\dfrac{dy}{dx} = \dfrac{1}{2}x^{-1/2} = \dfrac{1}{2x^{1/2}} = \dfrac{1}{2\sqrt{x}}$.

(4) If $y = \sqrt[5]{x^2}$ then $y = x^{2/5}$ and
$\dfrac{dy}{dx} = \dfrac{2}{5}x^{-3/5} = \dfrac{2}{5x^{3/5}} = \dfrac{2}{5 \cdot \sqrt[5]{x^3}}$.

When a power of x is multiplied by a constant, the constant remains unchanged by the process of differentiation. Hence if:

$$y = ax^n$$

$$\frac{dy}{dx} = nax^{n-1}$$

EXAMPLE 3

(1) If $y = 3x^4$, $\dfrac{dy}{dx} = 3 \times 4x^3 = 12x^3$.

(2) If $y = 2x^{1.3}$, $\dfrac{dy}{dx} = 2 \times 1.3x^{0.3} = 2.6x^{0.3}$.

(3) If $y = \dfrac{3}{4}\sqrt[3]{x} = \dfrac{3}{4}x^{1/3}$.

$\dfrac{dy}{dx} = \dfrac{3}{4} \times \dfrac{1}{3}x^{-2/3} = \dfrac{1}{4}x^{-2/3} = \dfrac{1}{4 \cdot \sqrt[3]{x^2}}$

(4) If $y = \dfrac{4}{x^2} = 4x^{-2}$.

$\dfrac{dy}{dx} = 4 \times (-2)x^{-3} = -8x^{-3} = -\dfrac{8}{x^3}$

When a numerical constant is differentiated the result is zero. Since $x^0 = 1$, we can write the numerical constant 4 as $4 \times x^0$. Then differentiating with respect to x we get

$$4 \times 0x^{-1} = 0$$

To differentiate an expression containing a sum of terms we differentiate each individual term separately.

EXAMPLE 4

(1) If $y = 3x^2 + 2x + 3$.

$\dfrac{dy}{dx} = 3 \times 2x^1 + 2 \times 1x^0 + 0 = 6x + 2$

(2) If $y = ax^3 + bx^2 + cx + d$ where a, b, c and d are constants.

$$\frac{dy}{dx} = 3ax^2 + 2bx + c$$

(3) If $y = \sqrt{x} + \dfrac{1}{\sqrt{x}} = x^{1/2} + x^{-1/2}$.

$$\frac{dy}{dx} = \frac{1}{2}x^{-1/2} + \left(-\frac{1}{2}\right)x^{-3/2}$$

$$= \frac{1}{2\sqrt{x}} - \frac{1}{2\sqrt{x^3}}$$

(4) If $s = \dfrac{t^3 + t^2 + 2t}{t}$

then $s = \dfrac{t^3}{t} + \dfrac{t^2}{t} + \dfrac{2t}{t} = t^2 + t + 2$

$$\frac{ds}{dt} = 2t + 1$$

Exercise 134 — *All type A*

Differentiate the following:

1) $y = x^2$

2) $y = x^7$

3) $y = 4x^3$

4) $y = 6x^5$

5) $s = 0.5t^3$

6) $A = \pi R^2$

7) $y = x^{1/2}$

8) $y = 4x^{3/2}$

9) $y = 2\sqrt{x}$

10) $y = 3\sqrt[3]{x^2}$

11) $y = \dfrac{1}{x^2}$

12) $y = \dfrac{1}{x}$

13) $y = \dfrac{3}{5x}$

14) $y = \dfrac{2}{x^3}$

15) $y = \dfrac{1}{\sqrt{x}}$

16) $y = \dfrac{2}{\sqrt[3]{x}}$

17) $y = \dfrac{5}{x \cdot \sqrt{x}}$

18) $s = \dfrac{3\sqrt{t}}{5}$

19) $K = \dfrac{0.01}{H}$

20) $y = \dfrac{5}{x}$

21) $y = 4x^2 - 3x + 2$

22) $s = 3t^3 - 2t^2 + 5t - 3$

23) $q = 2u^2 - u + 7$

24) $y = 5x^4 - 7x^3 + 3x^2 + 5$

25) $s = 7t^3 - 3t^2 + 7$

26) $y = \dfrac{x + x^3}{\sqrt{x}}$

27) $y = \dfrac{3 + x^2}{x}$

28) $y = \sqrt{x} + \dfrac{1}{\sqrt{x}}$

29) $y = x^3 + \dfrac{3}{\sqrt{x}}$

30) $s = t^{1.3} - \dfrac{1}{4t^{2.3}}$

31) $y = \dfrac{3x^3}{5} - \dfrac{2x^2}{7} - \sqrt{x}$

32) $y = 0.08 + \dfrac{0.01}{x}$

33) $y = 31x^{1.5} - 2.4x^{0.6}$

34) $y = \dfrac{x^3}{2} - \dfrac{5}{x} + 3$

35) $s = 10 - 6t + 7t^2 - 2t^3$

THE GRADIENT OF A CURVE BY THE CALCULUS

It has been shown previously that $\dfrac{dy}{dx}$ represents the general expression for the gradient of a curve at any point.

EXAMPLE 5

(1) If $y = x^2 - 5x + 7$ find the gradient of the curve at the points where $x = -3$ and $x = 2$.

Since

$$y = x^2 - 5x + 7$$

$$\frac{dy}{dx} = 2x - 5$$

when $x = -3$, $\dfrac{dy}{dx} = 2 \times (-3) - 5 = -11$.

Hence the gradient of the curve when $x = -3$ is -11.

When $x = 2$, $\dfrac{dy}{dx} = 2 \times 2 - 5 = -1$

Hence when $x = 2$, the gradient of the curve is -1.

(2) If $y = x^3 - 3x^2 + 7$, find the values of x at which the gradient of the curve is 24.

Since

$$y = x^3 - 3x^2 + 7$$

$$\frac{dy}{dx} = 3x^2 - 6x$$

When the gradient of the curve is 24, $\frac{dy}{dx} = 24$

hence

$$3x^2 - 6x = 24$$

$$3x^2 - 6x - 24 = 0$$

$$x^2 - 2x - 8 = 0$$

$$(x - 4)(x + 2) = 0$$

$$x = 4 \text{ or } -2$$

The gradient of the curve is 24 when $x = 4$ and $x = -2$.

Exercise 135 — *All type A*

1) Find the gradient of the curve $y = 2x^2 - 5x + 3$ at the point $(1, 0)$.

2) Find the gradient of the curve $y = x^2 + 2x - 3$ at the point where $x = 2$.

3) Find the gradient of the curve $y = \frac{1}{x} + 5$ at the point $(2, 5.5)$.

4) Find the value of x where the gradient of the curve $y = x^2 + 2x + 7$ is 8.

5) Find the co-ordinates of the points on the curve $y = x^3 - 2x^2 + 3x - 5$ where its gradient is 2.

6) The curve $y = x^2 + \frac{A}{x}$ has a gradient of 7 when $x = 4$. Calculate the value of A.

7) Prove that the curve $y = 4x - \frac{32}{x^2}$ crosses the x-axis at the point where $x = 2$. Calculate the gradient of the curve at this point.

TURNING POINTS

At the points P and Q (Fig. 30.5) the tangent to the curve is parallel to the x-axis. The points P and Q are called *turning points*. The

turning point at P is called a *maximum* turning point and the turning point at Q is called a *minimum* turning point. It will be seen from Fig. 30.5 that the value of y at P is not the greatest value of y nor is the value of y at Q the least. The terms maximum and minimum values apply only to the values of y at the turning points and not to the values of y in general.

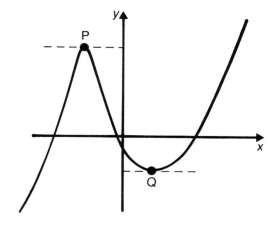

Fig. 30.5

EXAMPLE 6

(1) Plot the graph of $y = x^3 - 5x^2 + 2x + 8$ for values of x between -2 and 6. Hence find the maximum and minimum values of y.

To plot the graph we draw up a table in the usual way.

x	-2	-1	0	1
$y = x^3 - 5x^2 + 2x + 8$	-24	0	8	6

x	2	3	4	5	6
$y = x^3 - 5x^2 + 2x + 8$	0	-4	0	18	56

The graph is shown in Fig. 30.6. The maximum value occurs at the point P where the tangent to the curve is parallel to the x-axis. The minimum value occurs at the point Q where again the tangent to the curve is parallel to the x-axis. From the graph the maximum value of y is 8.21 and the minimum value of y is -4.06.

Notice that the value of y at P is not the greatest value of y nor is the value of y at Q the least. However, the values of y at P and Q are called the maximum and minimum values of y respectively.

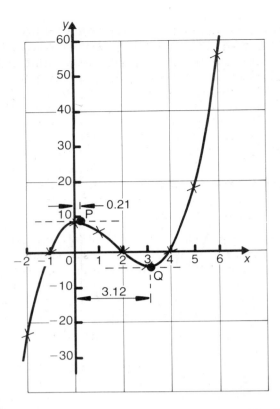

Fig. 30.6

its length $= 36 - 2x$

its breadth $= 24 - 2x$

its height $= x$

The volume of the box is

$$V = \text{length} \times \text{breadth} \times \text{height}$$

$\therefore \qquad V = x(36 - 2x)(24 - 2x)$

We now have to plot a graph of this equation and so we draw up the table below:

x	1	2	3	4
$36 - 2x$	34	32	30	28
$24 - 2x$	22	20	18	16
V	748	1280	1620	1792

x	5	6	7	8
$36 - 2x$	26	24	22	20
$24 - 2x$	14	12	10	8
V	1820	1728	1540	1280

The graph is shown in Fig. 30.8 and it can be seen that the maximum volume is 1825 cm^3 which occurs when $x = 4.71$ cm.

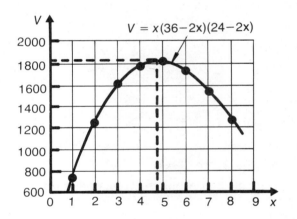

Fig. 30.8

(2) A small box is to be made from a rectangular sheet of metal 36 cm by 24 cm. Equal squares of side x cm are cut from each of the corners and the box is then made by folding up the sides. Prove that the volume V of the box is given by the expression $V = x(36 - 2x)(24 - 2x)$. Find the value of x so that the volume may be a maximum and find this maximum volume.

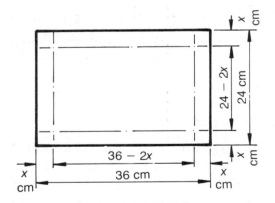

Fig. 30.7

Referring to Fig. 30.7 we see that after the box has been formed

Exercise 136 — *Questions 1–3 type B, remainder C*

1) Find the minimum value of the curve $y = 3x^2 + 2x - 3$. Plot the graph for values of x between -2 and 3.

2) Find the maximum value of the curve $y = -x^2 + 5x + 7$. Plot the graph for values of x between -2 and 4.

3) Plot the graph of $y = x^3 - 9x^2 + 15x + 2$ taking values of x from 0 to 7. Hence find the maximum and minimum values of y.

184

4) Draw the graph of $y = x^2 - 3x$ from $x = -1$ to $x = 4$ and use your graph to find:

(a) the least value of y;
(b) the two solutions of the equation $x^2 - 3x = 1$;
(c) the two solutions of the equation $x^2 - 2x - 1 = 0$.

5) Draw the graph of $y = (x - 1)(4 - x)$ for values of x from 0 to 5. From your graph find the greatest value of $(x - 1)(4 - x)$.

6) Write down the three values missing from the following table which gives values of $\frac{1}{2}(3x^2 - 5x - 1)$ for values of x from -2 to 3.

x	-2	-1.5	-1	-0.5
$\frac{1}{2}(3x^2 - 5x - 1)$	10.50	6.63		1.13

x	0	0.5	1
$\frac{1}{2}(3x^2 - 5x - 1)$		-1.38	-1.50

x	1.5	2	2.5	3.0
$\frac{1}{2}(3x^2 - 5x - 1)$		-0.88	2.63	5.50

Draw the graph of $y = \frac{1}{2}(3x^2 - 5x - 1)$ and from it find the minimum value of $\frac{1}{2}(3x^2 - 5x - 1)$ and the value of x at which it occurs.

7) A piece of sheet metal 20 cm × 12 cm is used to make an open box. To do this, squares of side x cm are cut from the corners and the sides and ends folded over. Show that the volume of the box is

$$V = x(20 - 2x)(12 - 2x)$$

By taking values of x from 1 cm to 5 cm in 0.5 cm steps, plot a graph of V against x and find the value of x which gives a maximum volume. What is the maximum volume of the box?

8) An open tank which has a square base of x metres has to hold 200 cubic metres of liquid when full. Show that the height of the tank is $\frac{200}{x^2}$ and hence prove that the surface area of the tank is given by $A = \left(x^2 + \frac{800}{x}\right)$ square metres. By plotting a graph of A against x find the dimensions of the tank so that the surface area is a minimum. (Take values of x from 3 to 9.)

9) A rectangular parcel of length x metres, width k metres and height k metres is to be sent through the post. The total length and girth (i.e. the distance round) of the parcel is to be exactly 2 metres. Show that the volume of the parcel is

$$V = \frac{x}{16}(2 - x)^2$$

Draw a graph of V against x for values of x from 0.3 to 1 in steps of 0.1 and hence find the dimensions of the parcel which has the greatest possible volume.

10) A farmer uses 100 m of hurdles to make a rectangular cattle pen. If he makes a pen of length x metres show that the area enclosed is $(50x - x^2)$ square metres. Draw the graph of $y = 50x - x^2$ for values of x between 0 and 50 and use your graph to find:

(a) the greatest possible area that can be enclosed,
(b) the dimensions of the pen when the area enclosed is 450 square metres.

MAXIMUM AND MINIMUM VALUES USING THE CALCULUS

In Fig. 30.9 the point P is a maximum turning point and the point Q is a minimum turning point. At both P and Q the tangent to the curve is parallel to the x-axis and hence at both points

$$\frac{dy}{dx} = 0$$

By using the fact that $\frac{dy}{dx} = 0$ at a turning point, we can find the turning points without drawing a graph.

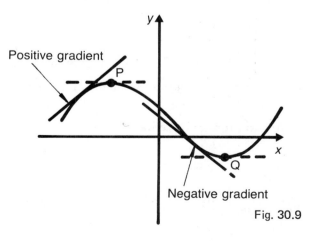

Fig. 30.9

185

EXAMPLE 7

(1) Find the maximum and minimum values of $y = x^3 - 6x^2 + 9x + 2$.

$$y = x^3 - 6x^2 + 9x + 2$$

$$\frac{dy}{dx} = 3x^2 - 12x + 9$$

At a turning point $\frac{dy}{dx} = 0$. Hence at a turning point

$$3x^2 - 12x + 9 = 0$$

$$x^2 - 4x + 3 = 0$$

$$(x - 3)(x - 1) = 0$$

$$x = 1 \text{ or } 3$$

Hence the turning points occur when $x = 1$ and $x = 3$. It now remains for us to determine which of these values of x makes y a maximum and which makes y a minimum. From Fig. 30.9 we see that the gradient of the curve is *negative* just before a *minimum* turning point and it is *positive* just before a *maximum* turning point. Therefore if we take a value of x just slightly less than the value of x at the turning point and substitute this value in the expression for $\frac{dy}{dx}$ we can discover which turning point is a maximum and which is a minimum.

When $x = 1$: Take x slightly less than 1, say 0.9. Substituting this value in the expression for $\frac{dy}{dx}$:

$$\frac{dy}{dx} = 3 \times 0.9^2 - 12 \times 0.9 + 9 = 0.63$$

This value of $\frac{dy}{dx}$ is positive and hence when $x = 1$ we have a maximum turning point. The maximum value of y is

$$y = 1^3 - 6 \times 1^2 + 9 \times 1 + 2 = 6$$

When $x = 3$: Take x as slightly less than 3, say 2.9. Substituting for $x = 2.9$ in the expression for $\frac{dy}{dx}$. We have:

$$\frac{dy}{dx} = 3 \times 2.9^2 - 12 \times 2.9 + 9 = -0.57$$

This value of $\frac{dy}{dx}$ is negative and hence when

$x = 3$ we have a minimum turning point. The minimum value of y is

$$y = 3^3 - 6 \times 3^2 + 9 \times 3 + 2 = 2$$

(2) The total area of the surface of a solid cylinder is 132 cm^2. If the height of the cylinder is h cm and its radius is r cm, show that $h = \frac{21}{r} - r$. Hence calculate the value of r for which the volume of the cylinder is a maximum. $\left(\text{Take } \pi = \frac{22}{7} \right)$.

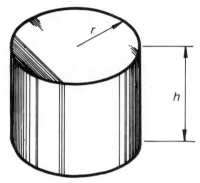

Fig. 30.10

From Fig. 30.10 the surface area of the solid cylinder is

$$A = 2\pi r^2 + 2\pi rh$$

Since the surface area is 132 cm^2

$$2\pi r^2 + 2\pi rh = 132$$

$$2\pi rh = 132 - 2\pi r^2$$

$$h = \frac{132}{2\pi r} - \frac{2\pi r^2}{2\pi r}$$

$$h = \frac{21}{r} - r$$

The volume of the cylinder is

$$V = \pi r^2 h$$

Substituting for h,

$$V = \pi r^2 \left(\frac{21}{r} - r \right)$$

$$V = 21\pi r - \pi r^3$$

$$\frac{dV}{dr} = 21\pi - 3\pi r^2$$

For a maximum or a minimum $\frac{dV}{dr} = 0$

$$\therefore \qquad 21\pi - 3\pi r^2 = 0$$
$$3\pi r^2 = 21\pi$$
$$r^2 = 7$$
$$r = \pm\sqrt{7}$$

Only the positive value applies and hence $r = \sqrt{7}$. This must give a maximum volume since the minimum value of the volume must be zero (i.e. a cylinder having a very large radius and practically no height or vice versa).

Exercise 137 — *Questions 1–4 type B,*
remainder C

1) Find the maximum and minimum values of:
(a) $y = 2x^3 - 3x^2 - 12x + 4$
(b) $y = x^3 - 3x^2 + 4$
(c) $y = -6x^2 + x^3$

2) Given that $y = 60x + 3x^2 - 4x^3$, calculate:
(a) the gradient of the tangent to the curve of y at the point where $x = 1$;
(b) the value of x for which y has its maximum value;
(c) the value of x for which y has its minimum value.

3) Calculate the co-ordinates of the points on the curve $y = x^3 - 3x^2 - 9x + 12$ at each of which the tangent to the curve is parallel to the x-axis.

4) A curve has the equation $y = 8 + 2x - x^2$. Find:
(a) the value of x for which the gradient of the curve is 6;
(b) the value of x which gives the maximum value of y;
(c) the maximum value of y.

5) The curve $y = 2x^2 + \dfrac{k}{x}$ has a gradient of 5 when $x = 2$. Calculate:
(a) the value of k;
(b) the minimum value of y.

6) From a rectangular sheet of metal measuring 12 cm by 7.5 cm equal squares of side x are cut from each of the corners. The remaining flaps are then folded upwards to form an open box. Prove that the volume of the box is given by $V = 90x - 39x^2 + 4x^3$. Find the value of x such that the volume is a maximum.

7) An open rectangular tank of height h metres with a square base of side x metres is to be constructed so that it has a capacity of 500 cubic metres. Prove that the surface area of the four walls and the base will be $\left(\dfrac{2000}{x} + x^2\right)$ square metres. Find the value of x for this expression to be a minimum.

8) The volume of a cone is given by the formula $V = \frac{1}{3}\pi r^2 h$, where h is the height of the cone and r its radius. If $h = 6 - r$, calculate the value of r for which the volume is a maximum.

9) A box without a lid has a square base of side x cm and rectangular sides of height h cm. It is made from 108 cm^2 of sheet metal of negligible thickness. Prove that $h = \dfrac{108 - x^2}{4x}$ and that the volume of the box is $(27x - \frac{1}{4}x^3)$. Hence calculate the maximum volume of the box.

10) A cylindrical tank, with an open top, is to be made to hold 300 cubic metres of liquid. Find the dimensions of the tank so that its surface area shall be a minimum.

SELF-TEST 30

In questions 1 to 25 the answer is either 'true' or 'false', state which.

1) In Fig. 30.11 the gradient of the curve at the point where $x = 1$ is 4.

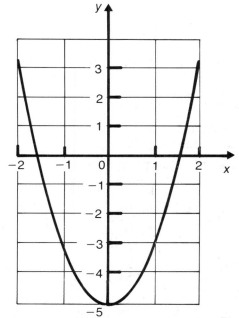

Fig. 30.11

2) In Fig. 30.11 the gradient of the curve at the point where $x = -1$ is 4.

3) In Fig. 30.11 the gradient of the curve at the point where $x = -1.5$ is -6.

4) In Fig. 30.11, the value of x is 0.5 when the gradient of the curve is 2.

5) In Fig. 30.11, the value of $x = -1$ when the gradient of the curve is -4.

6) If $y = x^4$ then $\frac{dy}{dx} = 4x^3$.

7) If $y = \frac{1}{x^2}$ then $\frac{dy}{dx} = 2x$.

8) If $y = \frac{1}{x^3}$ then $\frac{dy}{dx} = -\frac{3}{x^4}$.

9) If $y = \sqrt[3]{x^2}$ then $\frac{dy}{dx} = \frac{2}{3\sqrt[3]{x}}$.

10) If $y = \sqrt[4]{x^3}$ then $\frac{dy}{dx} = -\frac{3}{4\sqrt[4]{x}}$.

11) If $y = \frac{8}{x^4}$ then $\frac{dy}{dx} = -\frac{32}{x^5}$.

12) If $y = 7x^2 - 4x + 3$ then $\frac{dy}{dx} = 14x - 4$.

13) If $y = \frac{3 + x^3}{x}$ then $\frac{dy}{dx} = -3$.

14) If $y = \frac{5 + x^4}{x^2}$ then $\frac{dy}{dx} = 2x - \frac{10}{x^3}$.

15) If $y = x^2 - 7x + 5$, the gradient of the curve at the point where $x = 2$ is -3.

16) If $y = x^2 - 7x + 5$, the point where the gradient is 10 is $x = 8.5$.

17) If $y = 2x - \frac{16}{x^2}$, the gradient of the curve at the point where $x = 2$ is -2.

18) If $y = 2x - \frac{32}{x^2}$, the gradient of the curve at the point where $x = 2$ is 10.

19) If $y = x^2 + 3x - 2$, the turning point on the curve occurs when $x = -1.5$.

20) If $y = x^3 - 5x^2 - 8x + 3$, then there will be two turning points on the curve.

21) The turning points in question 20 occur when $x = -1.5$ and $x = 4$.

22) In question 21, the turning point at $x = 4$ is a minimum.

23) The minimum value of the curve of $y = 2x^2 - 8x + 3$ is -5.

24) The maximum value of the curve of $y = -x^2 + 8x + 7$ is 23.

25) The greatest value of $(x - 2)(4 - x)$ is 7.

In questions 26 to 34 state the letter (or letters) corresponding to the correct answer (or answers).

26) In the curve (Fig. 30.12), the gradient of the curve at the point where $x = -2$ is:

a -6 **b** 6 **c** $-\frac{1}{6}$ **d** $\frac{1}{6}$

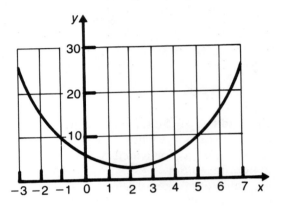

Fig. 30.12

27) In the curve (Fig. 30.12) the gradient of the curve at the point where $x = 3$ is:

a -2 **b** 2 **c** $-\frac{1}{2}$ **d** $\frac{1}{2}$

28) If $y = \frac{3x^3 - 2x^2}{x}$, then $\frac{dy}{dx}$ is equal to:

a $9x^2 - 4x - \frac{1}{x^2}$ **b** $9x^2 - 4x + \frac{1}{x^2}$

c $6x - 2$ **d** $2 - 6x$

29) If $y = 5 \times \sqrt[3]{x^2}$, then $\frac{dy}{dx}$ is equal to:

a $\frac{15\sqrt{x}}{2}$ **b** $\frac{15}{2\sqrt{x}}$

c $\frac{10}{3 \times \sqrt[3]{x}}$ **d** $\frac{10 \times \sqrt[3]{x}}{3}$

30) If $y = 3x - \frac{30}{x}$ the gradient of the curve is 10.5 at the points where x is equal to:

a 2 **b** -2 **c** ± 2 **d** 5

188

31) The curve $y = x^2 - 4$ cuts the positive x-axis at a point P. The gradient of the curve at P is:

a 2   b − 2   c 4   d − 8

32) The maximum value of the function $y = 2x^3 - 21x^2 + 72x + 5$ is:

a 4   b 3   c 85   d 86

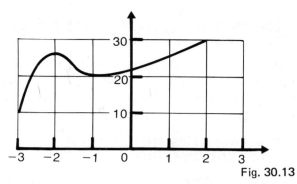

Fig. 30.13

33) The maximum value of the function shown in Fig. 30.13 is:

a − 2   b 25   c 2   d 30

34) The minimum value of the function shown in Fig. 30.13 is:

a − 3   b 10   c − 1   d 20

Chapter 31 Integration

INTEGRATION AS THE INVERSE OF DIFFERENTIATION

In Chapter 30, we discovered how to obtain the differential coefficients of various functions. Our objective in this chapter is to find out how to reverse the process. That is, being given the differential coefficient of a function we try to discover the original function.

If $\quad y = \dfrac{x^4}{4} \quad$ then $\quad \dfrac{dy}{dx} = x^3$.

We may write

$$dy = x^3 \, dx$$

The expression $x^3 \, dx$ is called *the differential of* $\dfrac{x^4}{4}$.

Reversing the process of differentiation is called *integration*. It is indicated by using the integration sign $\int$ in front of the differential. Thus if:

$$dy = x^3 \, dx$$

$$y = \int x^3 \, dx = \frac{x^4}{4}$$

Similarly if $\quad y = \dfrac{x^5}{5}$

$$\frac{dy}{dx} = x^4$$

$$dy = x^4 \, dx$$

Reversing the process

$$y = \int x^4 \, dx = \frac{x^5}{5}$$

If $\qquad y = \dfrac{x^{n+1}}{n+1}, \qquad \dfrac{dy}{dx} = x^n$

$$dy = x^n \, dx$$

$$y = \int x^n \, dx = \frac{x^{n+1}}{n+1}$$

$\dfrac{x^{n+1}}{n+1}$ is called *the integral of* $x^n \, dx$.

This rule applies to all indices, positive, negative and fractional except for

$$\int x^{-1} \, dx$$

THE CONSTANT OF INTEGRATION

We know that the differential of $\dfrac{x^2}{2}$ is $x \, dx$.

Therefore if we are asked to integrate $x \, dx$, $\dfrac{x^2}{2}$ is one answer but it is not the only possible answer because

$$\frac{x^2}{2} + 2, \frac{x^2}{2} + 5, \frac{x^2}{2} + 19$$

etc., are all expressions whose differential is $x \, dx$.

The general expression for $\int x \, dx$ is therefore $\dfrac{x^2}{2} + c$, where c is a constant known as the *constant of integration*. Every time we integrate the constant of integration must be added in.

$$\int x^n \, dx = \frac{x^{n+1}}{n+1} + c$$

EXAMPLE 1

(1) $\displaystyle\int x^5 \, dx = \frac{x^{5+1}}{5+1} + c = \frac{x^6}{6} + c$

(2) $\displaystyle\int x \, dx = \frac{x^{1+1}}{1+1} + c = \frac{x^2}{2} + c$

A constant coefficient may be taken outside the integral sign. Thus

$$\int 3x^2 \, dx = 3 \int x^2 \, dx = 3\frac{x^3}{3} + c = x^3 + c$$

The integral of a sum is the sum of their separate integrals.

EXAMPLE 2

(1) $\int (x^2 + x)\, dx.$

Integrating each term separately.

The integral of x^2 is $\dfrac{x^3}{3}$.

The integral of x is $\dfrac{x^2}{2}$.

$\therefore \qquad \int (x^2 + x)\, dx = \dfrac{x^3}{3} + \dfrac{x^2}{2} + c$

(2) $\int (5x^4 + 3x^2 + 2x - 6)\, dx$

$\qquad = x^5 + x^3 + x^2 - 6x + c$

(3) $\int (2x + 5)^2\, dx$

$\qquad = \int (4x^2 + 20x + 25)\, dx$

$\qquad = \dfrac{4x^3}{3} + \dfrac{20x^2}{2} + 25x + c$

$\qquad = \dfrac{4x^3}{3} + 10x^2 + 25x + c$

Exercise 138 — *All type B*

Integrate with respect to x:

1) x^2	9) $x^2 + x + 3$
2) x^8	10) $2x^3 - 7x - 4$
3) x	11) $x^2 - 5x + 2$
4) x^4	12) $3x^2 - 2x + 3$
5) $2x^2$	13) $(x - 2)(x - 1)$
6) $5x^4$	14) $(x + 3)^2$
7) $3x^4$	15) $(2x - 7)^2$
8) $5x^8$	

EVALUATING THE CONSTANT OF INTEGRATION

The value of the constant of integration may be found provided a corresponding pair of values of x and y are known.

EXAMPLE 3

The gradient of the curve which passes through the point $(2, 3)$ is given by x^2. Find the equation of the curve.

We are given $\dfrac{dy}{dx} = x^2$.

$\therefore \qquad y = \int x^2\, dx = \dfrac{x^3}{3} + c$

We are also given that when $x = 2$, $y = 3$. Substituting these values in

$$y = \dfrac{x^3}{3} + c$$

$$3 = \dfrac{2^3}{3} + c$$

$$3 = 2\tfrac{2}{3} + c$$

$\therefore \qquad c = \dfrac{1}{3}$

Hence the equation of the curve is

$$y = \dfrac{x^3}{3} + \dfrac{1}{3} = \dfrac{1}{3}(x^3 + 1)$$

Exercise 139 — *All type C*

1) The gradient of the curve which passes through the point $(2, 3)$ is given by x. Find the equation of the curve.

2) The gradient of the curve which passes through the point $(3, 8)$ is given by $(x^2 + 3)$. Find the value of y when $x = 5$.

3) It is known that for a certain curve $\dfrac{dy}{dx} = 3 - 2x$ and the curve cuts the x-axis where $x = 5$. Express y in terms of x. State the length of the intercept on the y-axis and find the maximum value of y, by plotting a suitable graph.

4) Find the equation of the curve which passes through the point $(1, 4)$ and is such that:

$$\dfrac{dy}{dx} = 2x^2 + 3x + 2$$

5) If $\dfrac{dp}{dt} = (3 - t)^2$ find p in terms of t given that $p = 3$ when $t = 2$.

THE DEFINITE INTEGRAL

It has been shown that

$$\int x^n\, dx = \dfrac{x^{n+1}}{n+1} + c$$

This expression is called an *indefinite integral* and it must contain an arbitrary constant.

For many purposes we require *definite integrals* which are written

$$\int_b^a x^n \, dx$$

The values of a and b are called the limits, a being the upper limit and b the lower limit.

The method of evaluating a definite integral is shown in the following examples.

EXAMPLE 4

(1) Find the value of $\int_2^3 x^2 \, dx$.

$$\int_2^3 x^2 \, dx = \left[\frac{x^3}{3}\right]_2^3$$

$$= \left(\text{value of } \frac{x^3}{3} \text{ when } x \text{ is put equal to } 3\right)$$

$$- \left(\text{value of } \frac{x^3}{3} \text{ when } x \text{ is put equal to } 2\right)$$

$$= \frac{3^3}{3} - \frac{2^3}{3} = \frac{27}{3} - \frac{8}{3} = \frac{19}{3} = 6\tfrac{1}{3}$$

(2) Find the value of $\int_1^2 (3x^2 - 2x + 5) \, dx$.

$$\int_1^2 (3x^2 - 2x + 5) \, dx = \left[x^3 - x^2 + 5x\right]_1^2$$

$$= (2^3 - 2^2 + 5 \times 2)$$
$$- (1^3 - 1^2 + 5 \times 1)$$
$$= 14 - 5 = 9$$

Exercise 140 — *All type C*

Evaluate the following definite integrals:

1) $\int_1^2 x^2 \, dx$

2) $\int_2^3 (2x + 3) \, dx$

3) $\int_0^2 (x^2 + 3) \, dx$

4) $\int_1^2 (3x^2 - 4x + 3) \, dx$

5) $\int_1^2 x(2x - 1) \, dx$

6) $\int_0^2 (x + 1)(x + 2) \, dx$

7) $\int_2^3 (x - 1)^2 \, dx$

8) $\int_2^4 (x - 1)(x - 3) \, dx$

AREA UNDER A CURVE

The general expression for finding the area bounded by a curve, the x-axis and the lines $x = a$ and $x = b$ (Fig. 31.1) is:

$$A = \int_a^b y \, dx$$

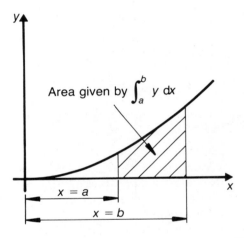

Area given by $\int_a^b y \, dx$

$x = a$

$x = b$

Fig. 31.1

EXAMPLE 5

Find the area bounded by the curve $y = x^3 + 3$, the x-axis and the lines $x = 1$ and $x = 3$.

$$A = \int_1^3 (x^3 + 3) \, dx$$

$$= \left[\frac{x^4}{4} + 3x\right]_1^3$$

$$= \left[\frac{3^4}{4} + 3 \times 3\right] - \left[\frac{1^4}{4} + 3 \times 1\right]$$

$$= 29\tfrac{1}{4} - 3\tfrac{1}{4} = 26 \text{ square units}$$

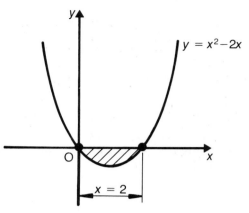

Fig. 31.2

Consider the curve $y = x^2 - 2x$ which is sketched in Fig. 31.2. The shaded area may be found by calculating the value of the definite integral

$$\int_0^2 (x^2 - 2x)\,dx$$

Thus:

$$A = \int_0^2 (x^2 - 2x)\,dx = \left[\frac{x^3}{3} - x^2\right]_0^2$$

$$= \left[\frac{2^3}{3} - 2^2\right] = \frac{8}{3} - 4$$

$$= -1\tfrac{1}{3} \text{ square units}$$

The negative result simply indicates that the shaded area lies below the x-axis.

Now suppose that we require the area bounded by the x-axis and the lines $x = -1$ and $x = 3$ (Fig. 31.3). We see that the required area consists of three parts labelled A, B and C in the diagram.

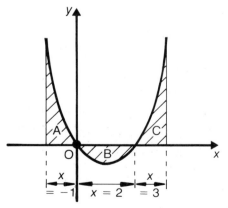

Fig. 31.3

The total area is found by finding areas A, B and C separately and adding them. Thus:

Area A

$$= \int_{-1}^0 (x^2 - 2x)\,dx = \left[\frac{x^3}{3} - x^2\right]_{-1}^0$$

$$= 0 - \left[\frac{(-1)^3}{3} - (-1)^2\right] = -\left[-\frac{1}{3} - 1\right]$$

$$= -\,[-1\tfrac{1}{3}] = 1\tfrac{1}{3}$$

Area B

$$= 1\tfrac{1}{3} \text{ (as found previously)}$$

Area C

$$= \int_2^3 (x^2 - 2x)\,dx = \left[\frac{x^3}{3} - x^2\right]_2^3$$

$$= \left(\frac{3^3}{3} - 3^2\right) - \left(\frac{2^3}{3} - 2^2\right)$$

$$= 0 - \left(\frac{8}{3} - 4\right) = 0 - (-1\tfrac{1}{3}) = 1\tfrac{1}{3}$$

Total area

$$= 1\tfrac{1}{3} + 1\tfrac{1}{3} + 1\tfrac{1}{3} = 4 \text{ square units}$$

If we attempt to find the area by $\int_{-1}^3 (x^2 - 2x)\,dx$ we get:

$$A = \int_{-1}^3 (x^2 - 2x)\,dx$$

$$= \left[\frac{x^3}{3} - x^2\right]_{-1}^3$$

$$= \left[\frac{3^3}{3} - 3^2\right] - \left[\frac{(-1)^3}{3} - (-1)^2\right]$$

$$= 0 - (-1\tfrac{1}{3}) = 1\tfrac{1}{3} \text{ square units}$$

which is the net area, i.e. $1\tfrac{1}{3} - 1\tfrac{1}{3} + 1\tfrac{1}{3}$.

Hence before attempting to find the area under a curve, the curve should be sketched so that the area (or areas) to be found can be seen.

GRAPHICAL INTEGRATION

The area under a graph may be found by one of several approximate methods. The simplest method is by counting the squares on the graph paper. Although it is a simple method it gives results which are as accurate as those obtained by more complicated methods.

EXAMPLE 6

Plot the graph of the function $y = 2x^2 - 7x + 8$ for values of x between 0 and 8. Hence, by counting squares find the area under the curve between $x = 2$ and $x = 6$.

x	0	1	2	3	4	5	6	7	8
y	8	3	2	5	12	23	38	57	80

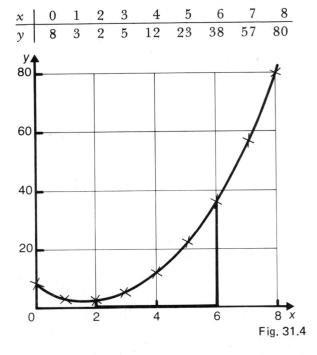

Fig. 31.4

The graph is drawn in Fig. 31.4. On the horizontal axis a scale of 1 large square = 2 units has been used and on the vertical axis the scale is 1 large square = 20 units. Hence, on the horizontal axis 1 small square = $\frac{2}{10}$ = 0.2 units and on the vertical axis 1 small square = $\frac{20}{10}$ = 2 units. Therefore, 1 small square represents an area = 0.2 × 2 = 0.4 square units (Fig. 31.5).

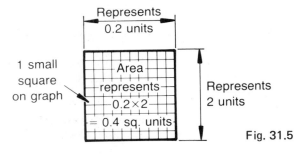

Fig. 31.5

To find the area between the graph, the x-axis and the lines $x = 2$ and $x = 6$ we count up the number of small squares in this region, judgement being exercised in the case of parts of small squares. The number of small squares is found to be about 145. Hence

$$\text{area required} = 145 \times 0.4$$

$$= 58 \text{ square units}$$

We are said to have found this area by *graphical integration*.

THE MID-ORDINATE RULE

This is one of the rules which may be used in graphical integration. Suppose that we desire to find the area of the figure shown in Fig. 31.6. We first divide the area up into a number of *equal* strips each of width b.

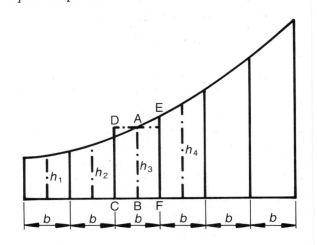

Fig. 31.6

Consider the third strip. Draw AB, the centre-line of the strip and through A draw a horizontal line as shown in the diagram. Then CDEF is a rectangle whose area is $b \times AB$. This rectangle CDEF has an area which is very nearly equal to the area of the third strip.

AB is called the *mid-ordinate* of the strip as it is mid-way between the vertical edges of the strip.

To find the area of the whole figure, the areas of the remaining strips are found in a similar way. All these areas are then added together to give the final result.

If the mid-ordinates are $h_1, h_2, h_3, \ldots$ etc., then

$$\text{area} = bh_1 + bh_2 + bh_3 + \ldots$$

$$= b(h_1 + h_2 + h_3 + \ldots)$$

$$= \text{width of strip} \times \text{sum of the mid-ordinates}$$

EXAMPLE 7

Find the area required in Example 6, by using the mid-ordinate rule.

194

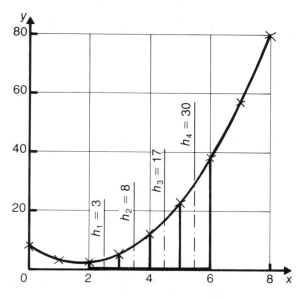

Fig. 31.7

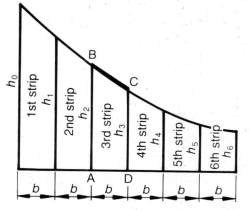

Fig. 31.8

The graph is shown in Fig. 31.7. Four strips have been used with a width of 1 unit each. The mid-ordinates of the strips can either be found by scaling the graph or they can be calculated as follows:

1st strip: mid-ordinate occurs at $x = 2.5$.

$$h_1 = 2 \times 2.5^2 - 7 \times 2.5 + 8 = 3$$

2nd strip: mid-ordinate occurs at $x = 3.5$.

$$h_2 = 2 \times 3.5^2 - 7 \times 3.5 + 8 = 8$$

and so on.

$$\begin{aligned} \text{Area} &= \text{width of strips} \times \text{sum of} \\ &\quad \text{the mid-ordinates} \\ &= 1 \times (3 + 8 + 17 + 30) \\ &= 58 \text{ square units} \end{aligned}$$

which is the same answer as was produced by counting the squares (see Example 6). The correct answer (produced by integration) is $58\frac{2}{3}$, so the areas produced by both our approximate methods are pretty accurate. When using the mid-ordinate rule the more strips that are used the more accurate will be the answer.

THE TRAPEZOIDAL RULE

This is the third method for finding the area under a curve. In order to find the area shown in Fig. 31.8 we divide the area up into a number of equal strips each of width b.

Consider the third strip. If we join BC then ABCD is a trapezium and its area is $b \times \frac{1}{2}(\text{AB} + \text{CD})$ which very nearly equals the area of the strip.

If the ordinates at the extremes of the strips are $h_0, h_1, h_2, \ldots$ etc., then the area of the first strip is

$$A_1 = b \times \tfrac{1}{2}(h_0 + h_1) = \tfrac{1}{2}bh_0 + \tfrac{1}{2}bh_1$$

The area of the second strip is

$$A_2 = b \times \tfrac{1}{2}(h_1 + h_2) = \tfrac{1}{2}bh_1 + \tfrac{1}{2}bh_2$$

The area of the third strip is

$$A_3 = b \times \tfrac{1}{2}(h_2 + h_3) = \tfrac{1}{2}bh_2 + \tfrac{1}{2}bh_3$$

and so on.

The total area is:

$$\begin{aligned} A &= A_1 + A_2 + A_3 + \ldots \\ &= \tfrac{1}{2}bh_0 + \tfrac{1}{2}bh_1 + \tfrac{1}{2}bh_1 \\ &\quad + \tfrac{1}{2}bh_2 + \tfrac{1}{2}bh_2 + \tfrac{1}{2}bh_3 + \ldots \\ &= \tfrac{1}{2}bh_0 + bh_1 + bh_2 + \ldots \\ &= b(\tfrac{1}{2}h_0 + h_1 + h_2 + \ldots) \\ &= \text{width of strips} \times (\tfrac{1}{2} \text{ the} \\ &\quad \text{sum of first and last ordinates} \\ &\quad + \text{sum of remaining ordinates}) \end{aligned}$$

This is known as the *trapezoidal rule*.

EXAMPLE 8

Find the area required in Example 6 by using the trapezoidal rule.

Using the values of y given in the table of Example 6 we have:

$$\begin{aligned} \text{Area} &= 1 \times [\tfrac{1}{2}(2 + 38) + 5 + 12 + 23] \\ &= 60 \text{ square units} \end{aligned}$$

This compares very well with the exact area of $58\frac{2}{3}$. A more accurate estimate may be obtained by taking more strips.

Exercise 141 — *All type C*

Find the areas under the following curves by integration or by using graphical methods:

1) Between the curve $y = x^3$, the x-axis and the lines $x = 5$ and $x = 3$.

2) Between the curve $y = 3 + 2x + 3x^2$, the x-axis and the lines $x = 1$ and $x = 2$.

3) Between the curve $y = x^2(2x - 1)$, the x-axis and the lines $x = 1$ and $x = 2$.

4) Between the curve $y = (x + 1)^2$, the x-axis and the lines $x = 1$ and $x = 3$.

5) Between the curve $y = 5x - x^3$, the x-axis and the lines $x = 1$ and $x = 2$.

SOLID OF REVOLUTION

If the area under a curve is rotated about the x-axis, the solid which results is called a *solid of revolution*. Any section of this solid by a plane perpendicular to the x-axis is a circle.

It can be shown that the volume of a solid of revolution (Fig. 31.9) is:

$$V = \int_a^b \pi y^2 \, dx$$

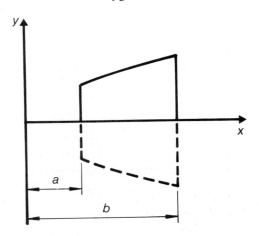

Fig. 31.9. When a curve is rotated about the x-axis the volume of the solid of revolution so produced is $\int_a^b \pi y^2 \, dx$

EXAMPLE 9

(1) The area between the curve $y = x^2$, the x-axis and the ordinates at $x = 1$ and $x = 3$ is rotated about the x-axis. Calculate the volume of the solid generated.

$$V = \int_1^3 \pi y^2 \, dx = \pi \int_1^3 (x^2)^2 \, dx = \pi \int_1^3 x^4 \, dx$$

$$= \pi \left[\frac{x^5}{5} \right]_1^3 = \pi \left[\frac{3^5}{5} - \frac{1^5}{5} \right] = \pi \left[\frac{243}{5} - \frac{1}{5} \right]$$

$$= 48.4\pi \text{ cubic units}$$

(2) The area between the curve $y^2 = 3x - 1$, the x-axis and the ordinates at $x = 2$ and $x = 5$ is rotated about the x-axis. Calculate the volume of the solid generated. (You may leave π as a factor in your answer.)

$$V = \int_2^5 \pi y^2 \, dx = \pi \int_2^5 (3x - 1) \, dx$$

$$= \pi \left[\frac{3x^2}{2} - x \right]_2^5$$

$$= \pi \left\{ \left[\frac{3 \times 5^2}{2} - 5 \right] - \left[\frac{3 \times 2^2}{2} - 2 \right] \right\}$$

$$= \pi(37.5 - 5) - (6 - 2)$$

$$= 28.5\pi \text{ cubic units}$$

Exercise 142 — *All type C*

Find the volume of solid of revolution when the areas under the following curves are rotated about the x-axis. Leave the answers as multiples of π.

1) $y = 2x^2$ between $x = 0$ and $x = 2$.

2) $y = \sqrt{x}$ between $x = 2$ and $x = 4$.

3) $y = \frac{1}{x^2}$ between $x = 1$ and $x = 3$.

4) $y = x + 2$ between $x = 0$ and $x = 4$.

5) $y = 2x + 5$ between $x = 1$ and $x = 3$.

6) The part of the curve $y = x(x + 2)$ between the ordinates $x = 1$ and $x = 2$ is rotated about the x-axis. Calculate the volume of the solid of revolution so formed.

7) The area bounded by the x-axis, the curve $y = 3x - \frac{2}{x}$ and the ordinates $x = 1$ and $x = 4$ is rotated about the x-axis. Calculate the volume of the solid generated.

196

8) The area between the curve $y^2 = 2x + 5$, the x-axis and the ordinates at $x = 1$ and $x = 3$ is rotated about the x-axis. Calculate the volume of the solid generated.

9) The curve represented by the equation $y = x^2 - 3x$ cuts the x-axis at two points A and B. The area bounded by the x-axis and the arc of the curve AB is rotated through a complete revolution about the x-axis. Calculate the volume generated.

10) The area bounded by the curve $y = x^3 - 6x^2$, the line $x = 1$ and the x-axis from $x = 0$ to $x = 1$ is rotated about the x-axis. Calculate the volume generated.

SELF-TEST 31

In the following questions state the letter (or letters) corresponding to the correct answer (or answers).

1) $\int x^2 \, dx$ is equal to:

a $\dfrac{x^3}{3}$ **b** $\dfrac{x^3}{3} + c$ **c** $2x$ **d** $2x + c$

2) $2\int x^2 \, dx$ is equal to:

a $\dfrac{2x^3}{3}$ **b** $\dfrac{2x^3}{3} + c$ **c** $4x$ **d** $x^3 + c$

3) $\int \dfrac{dx}{x^2}$ is equal to:

a $-\dfrac{2}{x}$ **b** $-\dfrac{2}{x} + c$ **c** $-\dfrac{1}{x}$ **d** $-\dfrac{1}{x} + c$

4) $\int \dfrac{1}{\sqrt{x}} \, dx$ is equal to:

a $\dfrac{1}{2\sqrt{x}} + c$ **b** $\dfrac{1}{2\sqrt{x}}$ **c** $2\sqrt{x} + c$

d $2\sqrt{x}$

5) $\int (3x^2 + 8x + 5) \, dx$ is equal to:

a $x^3 + 4x^2 + 5x + c$ **b** $x^3 + 4x^2 + 5x$
c $6x + 8 + c$ **d** $6x + 8$

6) $\int (x^2 + 2) \, dx$ is equal to:

a $\dfrac{x^3}{3} + 2x$ **b** $\dfrac{x^3}{3} + 2x + c$

c $2x + c$ **d** $2x$

7) $\int (x + 4)^2 \, dx$ is equal to:

a $2(x + 4) + c$ **b** $\dfrac{(x + 4)^3}{3} + c$

c $\dfrac{x^3}{3} + 4x^2 + 16x + c$ **d** $\dfrac{x^3}{3} + 16x + c$

8) $\int (2x - 3)^2 \, dx$ is equal to:

a $2(2x - 3) + c$ **b** $\dfrac{(2x - 3)^3}{3} + c$

c $\dfrac{4x^3}{3} - 9x + c$ **d** $\dfrac{4x^3}{3} - 6x^2 + 9x + c$

9) The equation of a curve is $y = x^2 + 3x + c$. The curve passes through the point $(2, 13)$. Hence c is equal to:

a 3   **b** -3 **c** -206 **d** 206

10) For a certain curve $\dfrac{dy}{dx} = 2x$ and the curve passes through the point $(4, 9)$. Hence the equation of the curve is:

a $y = x^2$ **b** $y = x^2 - 7$
c $y = x^2 - 65$ **d** $y = x^2 + 7$

11) In Fig. 31.10, the graph of $y = x^2 - 2$ is drawn. The shaded area is given by the expression:

a $\int_0^1 y \, dx$ **b** $\int_0^{-1} y \, dx$ **c** $\int_{-1}^1 y \, dx$

d $\int_{-1}^1 (x^2 - 2) \, dx$

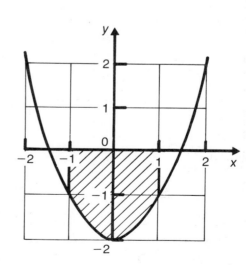

Fig. 31.10

12) The shaded area in Fig. 31.10 is:

a $-3\frac{1}{3}$ **b** $3\frac{1}{3}$ **c** $\frac{2}{3}$ **d** $-4\frac{2}{3}$

13) The integral $\int_{1}^{2} (6 + x - x^2)\, dx$ is equal to:

a $6\frac{1}{6}$ b $17\frac{1}{6}$ c $16\frac{1}{2}$ d $18\frac{1}{6}$

14) The area between the straight line $y = 13 - 2x$ and the curve $y = 2x^2 + 1$ is given by:

a $\displaystyle\int_{-3}^{2} (13 - 2x)\, dx - \int_{-3}^{2} (2x^2 + 1)\, dx$

b $\displaystyle\int_{-2}^{3} (13 - 2x)\, dx - \int_{-2}^{3} (2x^2 + 1)\, dx$

c $\displaystyle\int_{-2}^{3} (2x^2 + 1)\, dx - \int_{-2}^{3} (13 - 2x)\, dx$

d $\displaystyle\int_{-3}^{2} (2x^2 + 1)\, dx - \int_{-3}^{2} (13 - 2x)\, dx$

15) The shaded area shown in Fig. 31.11 is rotated about the x-axis. The volume of the solid of revolution so formed is:

a $\pi \displaystyle\int_{0}^{2} y\, dx$ b $\pi \displaystyle\int_{-2}^{2} y\, dx$

c $\pi \displaystyle\int_{0}^{2} y^2\, dx$ d $\pi \displaystyle\int_{-2}^{2} y^2\, dx$

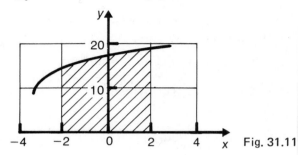

Fig. 31.11

Chapter 32 Time, Distance and Speed

AVERAGE SPEED

In Chapter 8 it was shown that

$$\text{Average speed} = \frac{\text{distance travelled}}{\text{time taken}}$$

If the distance is measured in metres and the time in seconds, then the speed is measured in metres per second (m/s). Similarly, if the distance is measured in kilometres and the time in hours, then the speed is measured in kilometres per hour (km/h).

EXAMPLE 1

(1) A car travels a distance of 100 km in 2 hours. What is the average speed?

$$\text{Average speed} = \frac{100 \text{ km}}{2 \text{ h}} = 50 \text{ km/h}$$

(2) A body travels a distance of 80 metres in 4 seconds. What is its average speed?

$$\text{Average speed} = \frac{80 \text{ m}}{4 \text{ s}} = 20 \text{ m/s}$$

DISTANCE—TIME GRAPHS

Since,

$$\text{distance} = \text{speed} \times \text{time}$$

If the speed is constant the distance travelled is proportional to time and a graph of distance against time will be a straight line passing through the origin. The gradient of this graph will represent the speed.

EXAMPLE 2

A man travels a distance of 120 km in 2 hours by car. He then cycles 20 km in 1½ hours and finally walks a distance of 8 km in 1 hour all at constant speed. Draw a graph to illustrate this journey and from it find the average speed for the entire journey.

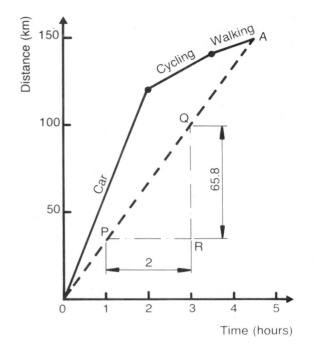

Fig. 32.1

The graph is drawn in Fig. 32.1 and it consists of three straight lines. The average speed is found by drawing the straight line OA and finding its gradient.

To find the gradient of OA we draw the right-angled triangle PQR, which, for accuracy, should be as large as possible.

$$\text{Gradient of OA} = \frac{\text{QR}}{\text{PR}} = \frac{65.8}{2} = 32.9$$

Hence average speed = 32.9 km/h.

Exercise 143 — All type B

1) A vehicle travels 300 km in 5 hours. Calculate its average speed.

2) A car travels 400 km at an average speed of 80 km/h. How long does the journey take?

3) A train travels for 5 hours at an average speed of 60 km/h. How far has it travelled?

4) A vehicle travels a distance of 250 km in a time of 5 hours. Draw a distance—time graph to depict the journey and from it find the average speed of the vehicle.

5) A car travels a distance of 120 km in 3 hours. It then changes speed and travels a further distance of 80 km in 2½ hours. Assuming that the two speeds are constant draw a distance—time graph. From the graph find the average speed of the journey.

6) A girl cycles a distance of 20 km in 100 minutes. She then rests for 20 minutes and then cycles a further 10 km which takes her 50 minutes. Draw a distance—time graph to represent the journey and from it find the average speed for the entire journey.

7) A man travels a distance of 90 km by car which takes him 1½ hours. He then cycles 18 km in a time of 1½ hours. He then rests for 15 minutes before continuing on foot during which he walks 8 km in 2 hours. By drawing a distance—time graph find his average speed for the entire journey assuming that he travels at constant speed for each of the three parts of the journey.

EXAMPLE 3

A cyclist sets out from a point A at a speed of 18 km/h. He cycles for 40 minutes and then rests for 10 minutes. He keeps this up for 2½ hours. A second cyclist sets out 1 hour later from A and cycles without resting at a speed of 25 km/h. When and where does the second cyclist overtake the first?

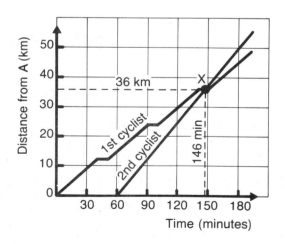

Fig. 32.2

As shown in Fig. 32.2 distance—time graphs are drawn on the same axes for both cyclists. Note that for the second cyclist zero distance travelled occurs at a time of 60 minutes. The co-ordinates of the point X, where the two graphs intersect, give the time and the distance from A where the second cyclist overtakes the first. From the graph the distance is 36 km from A and the time is 146 min after the first cyclist sets off.

EXAMPLE 4

Two towns A and B are 120 km apart. A motorist sets out from A at 9.00 a.m. and drives towards B at a constant speed of 60 km/h. At 9.30 a.m. a second motorist sets out from B and drives at a constant speed of 90 km/h towards A. How far from A will the two cars meet?

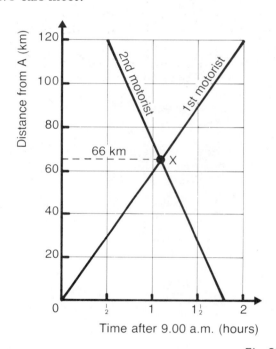

Fig. 32.3

The distance—time graphs for both motorists are drawn on the same axes as shown in Fig. 32.3. Since the speed of the first motorist is constant the graph is a straight line. If 9.00 a.m. is taken as zero time then this line passes through the origin.

At a time of ½ hour, the second motorist is at B, 120 km from A and as time progresses he gets nearer to A. Hence the distance—time graph for the second motorist slopes downwards from left to right.

The vertical co-ordinate of the point X, where the two graphs intersect, gives the distance from A where the two motorists meet. This distance is found, from the graph, to be 66 km.

Exercise 144 — *All type C*

1) A cyclist starts from a town A at 9.00 a.m. and cycles towards town B at an average speed of 15 km/h. At 10.00 a.m. a motorist starts to make the same journey but he travels at 60 km/h. When and where will the motorist overtake the cyclist?

2) A train left London for Newcastle (420 km) at 15.00 hours. It stopped at Grantham (180 km from London) for 12 minutes. It stopped again at York (315 km from London) for 12 minutes. Except for the halts it travelled at a steady 70 km/h. A second train left Newcastle for London at 15.30 hours. It travelled non-stop at 90 km/h.

(a) Draw a distance—time graph for the first train.
(b) What time did the first train reach Newcastle?
(c) On the same axes draw the distance—time graph for the second train.
(d) When and where did the two trains cross?

3) Figure 32.4 shows an incomplete distance—time graph for a squad of soldiers walking from A to B. Copy the graph.

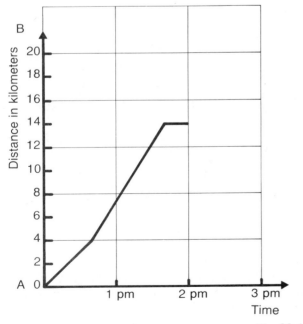

Fig. 32.4

(a) At what speed, in kilometres per hour, was the squad walking during the first 20 minutes?
(b) Up to 2 p.m. for how long did the squad rest?
(c) The squad started off again at 2 p.m. and, at the end of 3 hours and 40 minutes, it had walked a total distance of 22 km. On your copy of Fig. 32.4 complete the graph for the last 1 hour 40 minutes assuming that the squad walked at a uniform speed during this period.
(d) By drawing a suitable straight line on the graph find the average speed of the squad for the entire journey, including resting time.
(e) What was the fastest walking speed of the squad as shown by the complete graph?

4) A man leaves home at 9 a.m. and returns at 4.30 p.m. The graph (Fig. 32.5) shows his distances from home, in kilometres, at various times during the day.

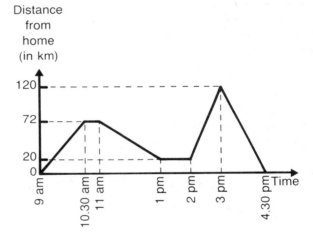

Fig. 32.5

(a) Calculate his average speed between 9 a.m. and 10.30 a.m.
(b) Find the total number of kilometres he travels between 9 a.m. and 4.30 p.m.
(c) How far is he from home at 2.45 p.m.?
(d) For how many hours during the day is he moving towards home?

5) A young man sets out at noon to cycle from P to Q, a distance of 200 km. He cycles at a steady 20 km/h for 4½ hours then stops and rests for 1 hour. He then cycles on and reaches Q at 22.00 hours. A motorist, using the same route, sets out from Q at 18.00 hours and

travels towards **P**. He maintains a steady speed of 60 km/h. On the same axes draw graphs of these two journeys using 1 cm = 1 hour horizontally and 1 cm = 40 km vertically.

(a) At what time do the motorist and cyclist pass each other?
(b) How far is the cyclist from **Q** when the motorist passes him?
(c) At what speed does the cyclist travel during the second part of his journey?
(d) At what times were the motorist and cyclist 20 km apart?

VELOCITY

Velocity is speed in a given direction, e.g. 50 km/h due North.

VELOCITY—TIME GRAPHS

If a velocity—time graph is drawn (Fig. 32.6), the area under the graph gives the distance travelled. The gradient of the curve gives the acceleration since acceleration is rate of change of velocity. If the velocity is measured in metres per second (m/s), the acceleration will be measured in metres per second per second (m/s^2).

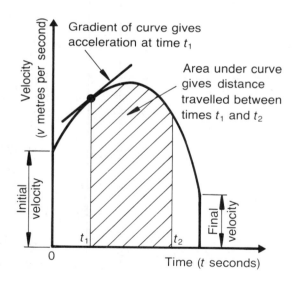

Fig. 32.6

If the acceleration is constant the velocity—time graph will be a straight line (Fig. 32.7). When the velocity is increasing the graph has a positive gradient (i.e. it slopes upwards to the right). If the velocity is decreasing (i.e. there is deceleration, sometimes called retardation) the graph has a negative gradient (i.e. it slopes downwards to the right).

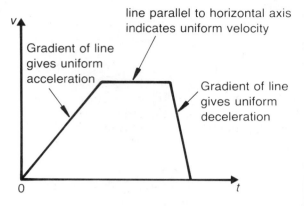

Fig. 32.7

EXAMPLE 5

A car, starting from rest, attains a velocity of 20 m/s after 5 seconds. It continues at this speed for 15 seconds and then slows down and comes to rest in a further 8 seconds. If the acceleration and retardation are constant, draw a velocity—time graph and from it, find:

(a) The acceleration of the car.
(b) The retardation of the car.
(c) The distance travelled in the total time of 28 seconds.

The velocity—time graph is drawn in Fig. 32.8.

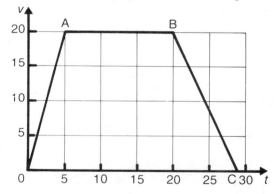

Fig. 32.8

(a) The acceleration is given by the gradient of the line OA.

$$\text{Acceleration} = \frac{20}{5} = 4 \text{ m/s}^2$$

(b) The retardation is given by the gradient of the line BC.

$$\text{Retardation} = \frac{20}{8} = 2.5 \text{ m/s}^2$$

202

(c) The distance travelled in the 28 seconds the car was travelling is given by the area of the trapezium OABC.

$$\text{Distance travelled} = 20 \times \tfrac{1}{2} \times (15 + 28)$$
$$= 20 \times \tfrac{1}{2} \times 43$$
$$= 430 \text{ m}$$

EXAMPLE 6

The table below gives the speed of a car, v metres per second, after a time of t seconds.

t	0	5	10	15	20	25
v	0	2.4	5.0	7.5	9.5	10.2

t	30	35	40	45	50	55
v	9.2	5.2	2.7	2.3	2.7	3.5

Draw a smooth curve to show how v varies with t. Use the graph:

(a) to find the speed of the car after 47 seconds,

(b) to find the times when the speed is 4 m/s,

(c) to find the acceleration after 15 seconds,

(d) to find the retardation after 35 seconds.

The graph is drawn in Fig. 32.9.

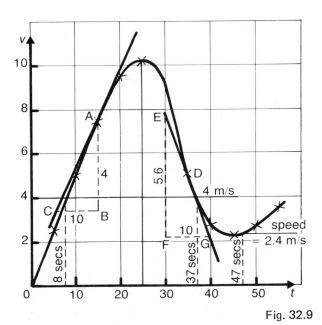

Fig. 32.9

(a) The speed after 47 seconds is read directly from the graph and it is found to be 2.4 m/s.

(b) The times when the speed is 4 m/s are also read directly from the graph and they are found to be 8 seconds and 37 seconds.

(c) To find the acceleration at a time of 15 seconds, draw a tangent to the curve at the point A and find its gradient by constructing the right-angled triangle ABC. The gradient $= \dfrac{4}{10} = 0.4$. Hence the acceleration is 0.4 m/s^2.

(d) To find the retardation at a time 35 seconds draw a tangent to the curve at the point D. Then by constructing the right-angled triangle EFG, retardation $= \dfrac{5.6}{10} = 0.56$ m/s^2. Note that the car is slowing down at this time and hence retardation occurs. This is also shown by the negative gradient of the tangent at the point D.

Exercise 145 — *Question 1—6 type B, remainder C*

1) Figure 32.10 shows a number of velocity—time diagrams. In each case state the distance travelled.

(a)

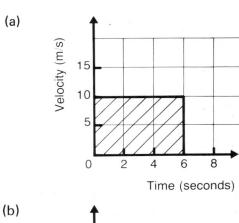

(b)

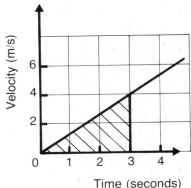

203

(c)

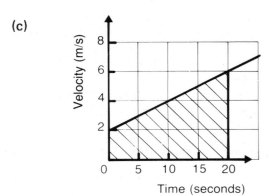

2) In Fig. 32.11 are shown some velocity—time graphs. For each write down the acceleration or retardation.

(a)

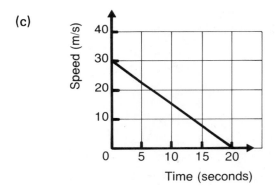

(b)

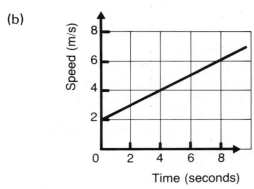

(d)

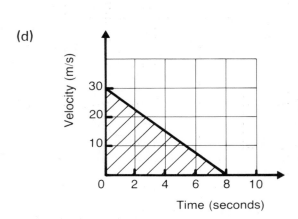

(c)

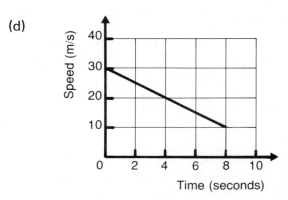

(e)

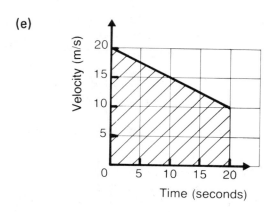

Fig. 32.10

(d)

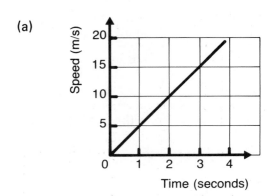

Fig. 32.11

3) Figure 32.12 shows the velocity—time graph for a vehicle travelling at a constant speed of 10 m/s. Find the total distance travelled in 15 s.

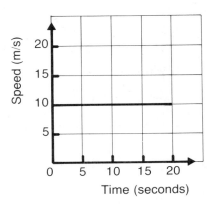

Fig. 32.12

4) The velocity—time graph shown in Fig. 32.13 shows a car travelling with constant acceleration.

(a) What is the acceleration?
(b) What is the initial speed?
(c) What is the distance travelled in 30 seconds?

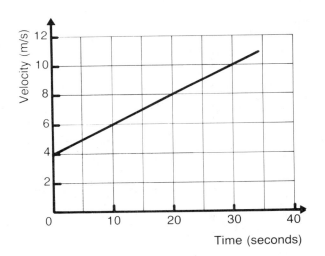

Fig. 32.13

5) From the velocity—time graph of Fig. 32.14, find:

(a) the acceleration,
(b) the retardation,
(c) the initial speed,
(d) the distance travelled in 20 seconds.

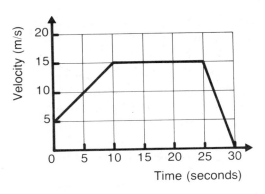

Fig. 32.14

6) Figure 32.15 shows a velocity—time diagram. Find:

(a) the acceleration after 5 seconds,
(b) the acceleration after 18 seconds,
(c) the acceleration after 40 seconds,
(d) the maximum speed reached,
(e) the total distance travelled in 50 seconds.

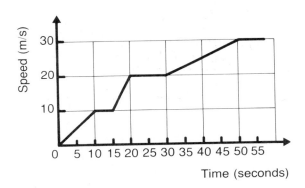

Fig. 32.15

7) A vehicle starting from rest attains a velocity of 16 m/s after it has been travelling for 8 seconds with uniform acceleration. It continues at this speed for 15 seconds and then it slows down, with uniform retardation, until it finally comes to rest in a further 10 seconds.

(a) Draw the velocity—time graph.
(b) Determine the acceleration of the vehicle.
(c) What is the retardation?
(d) From the diagram, find the distance travelled during the 33 seconds represented on the graph.

8) A car has an initial velocity of 5 m/s. It then accelerates uniformly for 6 seconds at $\frac{1}{2}$ m/s². It then proceeds with this speed for a further 25 seconds.

(a) Draw a velocity—time graph from this information.

(b) Calculate the distance travelled by the car in the time of 31 seconds.

9) The speed of a body, v metres per second, at various times, t seconds, is shown in the following table:

t	0	1	2	3	4	5	6	7	8
v	0	1	2	6	12	20	30	42	56

(a) Draw a graph showing how v varies with t. Horizontally take 1 cm to represent 1 second and vertically take 1 cm to represent 10 m/s.

(b) From the graph find the acceleration after times (i) 2 seconds, (ii) 6 seconds.

10) The graph, Fig. 32.16, shows how the speed of a vehicle varies over a period of 20 seconds. From the graph, find:

(a) the acceleration of the vehicle at a time of 4 seconds,

(b) the time at which the speed of the car is decreasing at the greatest rate,

(c) the distance travelled by the vehicle in the 20 seconds represented on the graph.

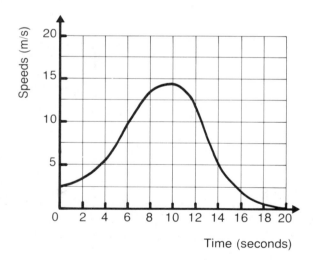

Fig. 32.16

VELOCITY AND ACCELERATION USING THE CALCULUS

Suppose that a body travels a distance of s metres in a time of t seconds. Since velocity is the rate of change of distance with respect to time, $\dfrac{ds}{dt}$ gives an expression for the instantaneous velocity at any time t seconds. If the velocity is v metres per second then

$$v = \frac{ds}{dt}$$

Acceleration is the rate of change of velocity with respect to time. Hence $\dfrac{dv}{dt}$ gives an expression for the instantaneous acceleration at any time t seconds. If the acceleration is a metres per second per second then

$$a = \frac{dv}{dt}$$

Note that $\dfrac{ds}{dt}$ and $\dfrac{dv}{dt}$ represent the *instantaneous* velocity and acceleration as opposed to the *average* velocity and acceleration which were used previously.

EXAMPLE 7

A body moves a distance of s metres in a time of t seconds so that $s = 2t^3 - 5t^2 + 4t + 5$. Find:

(a) its velocity after 3 seconds,
(b) its acceleration after 3 seconds,
(c) when its velocity is zero,
(d) when its acceleration is zero.

(a) $s = 2t^3 - 5t^2 + 4t + 5$

$$\frac{ds}{dt} = 6t^2 - 10t + 4$$

Since $v = \dfrac{ds}{dt}$, when $t = 3$

$$v = 6 \times 3^2 - 10 \times 3 + 4 = 28$$

Hence the velocity after 3 seconds is 28 m/s.

(b) $v = 6t^2 - 10t + 4$

$$\frac{dv}{dt} = 12t - 10$$

Since $a = \dfrac{dv}{dt}$, when $t = 3$

$$a = 12 \times 3 - 10 = 26$$

Hence the acceleration after 3 seconds is 26 m/s².

(c) When the velocity is zero, $\dfrac{ds}{dt} = 0$

$\therefore \quad 6t^2 - 10t + 4 = 0$

or $\quad 3t^2 - 5t + 2 = 0$

$(3t - 2)(t - 1) = 0$

$t = \dfrac{2}{3}$ or 1

Hence the velocity is zero when

$t = \dfrac{2}{3}$ seconds or when $t = 1$ second.

(d) When the acceleration is zero, $\dfrac{dv}{dt} = 0$

$\therefore \quad\quad\quad 12t - 10 = 0$

$t = \dfrac{5}{6}$

Hence the acceleration is zero when

$t = \dfrac{5}{6}$ seconds.

Exercise 146 — *All type C*

1) If $s = 10 + 50t - 2t^2$, where s metres is the distance travelled in t seconds by a body, what is the speed of the body after 2 seconds?

2) If $v = 5 + 24t - 3t^2$, where v metres per second is the speed of the body after t seconds, what is the acceleration of the body after 3 seconds?

3) A body moves s metres in a time t seconds so that $s = t^3 - 3t^2 + 8$. Find:

(a) its speed at the end of 3 seconds,
(b) when its speed is zero,
(c) its acceleration at the end of 2 seconds,
(d) when its acceleration is zero.

4) A body moves s metres in t seconds where $s = 3t^2$. Find the speed and acceleration after 3 seconds.

5) The distance moved by a body in t seconds is given in metres by $s = 2t^2 + 5t - 3$. Find:

(a) the initial velocity,
(b) the velocity after 3 seconds,
(c) the acceleration of the body.

It was shown previously that if a body travels s metres in time of t seconds then the velocity of the body is

$$v = \dfrac{ds}{dt}$$

Hence $\quad\quad s = \int v\ dt + c$

Therefore to find the distance travelled we integrate the expression for the velocity.

The acceleration of the body is

$$a = \dfrac{dv}{dt}$$

or $\quad\quad v = \int a\ dt + c$

Hence to find the velocity we integrate the expression for the acceleration

The area under a velocity–time graph represents the distance travelled, whilst the area under an acceleration–time graph represents the velocity.

EXAMPLE 8

(1) The velocity of a body, v metres per second, after a time of t seconds is given by

$$v = t^2 + 1$$

Find the distance travelled at the end of 2 seconds.

When $t = 0$ the distance travelled will be 0 metres. Hence the distance travelled at the end of 2 seconds is found by integrating the expression for v between the limits of 2 and 0.

$$s = \int_0^2 (t^2 + 1)\ dt$$

$$= \left[\dfrac{t^3}{3} + t \right]_0^2 = \dfrac{2^3}{3} + 2 = 4\tfrac{2}{3} \text{ metres}$$

(2) The acceleration of a moving body at the end of t seconds from the commencement of motion is $(9 - t)$ metres per second. Find the velocity and the distance travelled at the end of 2 seconds if the initial velocity is 5 metres per second.

$$v = \int a\ dt + c = \int (9 - t)\ dt + c$$

$$= 9t - \dfrac{t^2}{2} + c$$

The initial velocity is the velocity when $t = 0$. Hence when $t = 0$, $v = 5$

$$\therefore \quad 5 = 9 \times 0 - 0 + c \quad \text{or} \quad c = 5$$

$$\therefore \quad v = 9t - \frac{t^2}{2} + 5$$

When $t = 2$, $v = 9 \times 2 - \frac{2^2}{2} + 5$

$$= 21 \text{ metres per second.}$$

Now

$$s = \int v \, \mathrm{d}t = \int \left(9t - \frac{t^2}{2} + 5 \right) \mathrm{d}t + d$$

$$= \frac{9t^2}{2} - \frac{t^3}{6} + 5t + d$$

Unless information is given to the contrary it is always assumed that $s = 0$ when $t = 0$.

Hence $d = 0$

and $\quad s = \frac{9t^2}{2} - \frac{t^3}{6} + 5t$

When $t = 2$,

$$s = \frac{9 \times 2^2}{2} - \frac{2^3}{6} + 5 \times 2$$

$$= 26\tfrac{2}{3} \text{ metres}$$

Exercise 147 — *All type C*

1) The velocity of a body is $(t + 1)$ metres per second after a time of t seconds. Find the distance travelled at the end of 3 seconds.

2) The acceleration of a moving body at the end of t seconds from the commencement of motion is $(5 - t)$ m/s². If the initial velocity is 10 m/s find the velocity and distance travelled at the end of 3 seconds.

3) The acceleration of a moving body is constant at 15 m/s². If the initial velocity is 10 m/s, derive an expression for the distance moved in t seconds. Hence find the distance travelled at the end of 4 seconds.

4) The motion of a body is given by

$$\frac{\mathrm{d}s}{\mathrm{d}t} = 3t^2 - 2t + c$$

If the displacement of the particle is 5 m when $t = 1$ second and 2 m when $t = \frac{1}{2}$ second, find the displacement when $t = 2$ seconds.

5) A body moving along a straight path passes a fixed point O with a velocity of 12 m/s and t seconds later, when it is s metres from O its acceleration is $6t$. Find the velocity of the body when $t = 4$ and its distance from O at that instant.

6) The acceleration of a body is $(3t^2 + 5)$ m/s² after a time of t seconds. If its initial velocity is 8 m/s, find the distance travelled at the end of 4 seconds.

SELF-TEST 32

In the following questions state the letter corresponding to the correct answer.

1) An aeroplane flies non-stop for $2\frac{1}{4}$ hours and travels 1620 km. Its average speed in km/h is:

a 720 km/h   b 800 km/h

c 3645 km/h   d 364.5 km/h

2) A car travels 50 km at 50 km/h and 70 km at 70 km/h. Its average speed is:

a 60 km/h   b 65 km/h

c 58 km/h   d 62 km/h

3) A car travels for 3 hours at a speed of 45 km/h and for 4 hours at a speed of 50 km/h. It has therefore travelled a distance of:

a 27.5 km   b 95 km   c 335 km

d 353 km

4) A car travels 540 km at an average speed of 30 km/h. On the return journey the average speed is doubled to 60 km/h. The average speed over the entire journey is:

a 45 km/h   b 42 km/h   c 40 km/h

d 35 km/h.

5) A car travels between two towns 270 km apart in 9 hours. On the return journey the speed is increased by 10 km/h. The time taken for the return journey is:

a $6\frac{1}{2}$ hours   b $6\frac{3}{4}$ hours   c 2.7 hours

d $4\frac{1}{2}$ hours

6) Fig. 32.17 shows a distance–time graph. The average speed for the entire journey was:

a 50 km/h   b 60 km/h

c 45 km/h   d 45 km/min

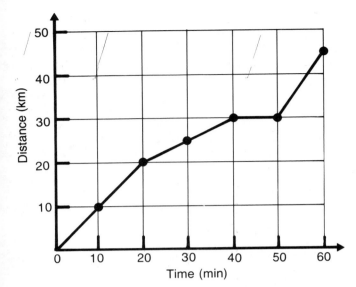

Fig. 32.17

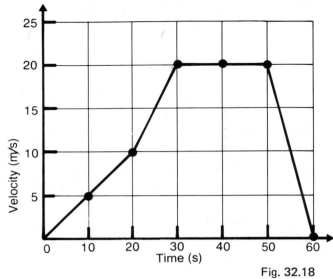

Fig. 32.18

7) Fig. 32.18 shows a velocity—time graph. The maximum acceleration is:

a 0.5 m/s²   b 2 m/s²

c 1 m/s²   d 1.5 m/s²

8) In Fig. 32.18 the distance travelled in the first 20 seconds is:

a 0.5 m/s²   b 2 m/s²

c 10 m   d 100 m

9) In Fig. 32.18, the retardation is:

a 0.5 m/s²   b 2 m/s²

c 1 m/s²   d 100 m/s²

10) The acceleration of a moving body at the end of t seconds is $(9 - t)$ m/s². If it starts from rest, the velocity at the end of 3 seconds is:

a 6 m/s   b 3 m/s   c 22.5 m/s   d 8 m/s

11) The acceleration of a body is $(3t^2 + 2)$ m/s² after a time of t seconds. Its initial velocity is 5 m/s. Hence at the end of 2 seconds the body will have travelled a distance of:

a 17 m   b 6 m   c 18 m   d 8 m

12) A particle moves s metres in a time t seconds so that $s = 2t^2 - 6t + 5$. Hence the distance the particle travels before it comes to rest is:

a 3 m   b 3.5 m   c 4 m   d 0.5 m

Miscellaneous Exercise

Exercise 148

This exercise is divided into two sections A and B. The questions in Section A are intended to be done very quickly, but those in Section B should take about 20 minutes each to complete. All the questions are of the type found in O Level examination papers.

SECTION A

1) A rectangular tank open at the top and constructed of thin sheet metal is 90 cm high. Its base measures 104 cm by 85 cm. Assuming that there is no overlap at the edges, calculate:

(a) the area, in cm^2, of sheet metal used in its construction,

(b) the capacity of the tank in litres, expressed to the nearest litre. (L)

2) The diameter of a cylindrical garden roller is 0.77 m. Calculate the number of complete revolutions it makes in rolling a stretch of ground 84.7 m long. If the roller is 1.33 m wide, find the area of ground rolled for every 100 revolutions. (L)

3) Express the area of a rectangle, 10 cm long by 6 cm wide, as a fraction of the area of a square with side 8 cm. (L)

4) Four circles of equal areas are cut from a square piece of wood of side 14 cm. If the area of wood left over is $109\frac{3}{8}$ cm^2, calculate the diameter of each circle and its circumference. (Take π as $3\frac{1}{7}$.) (L)

5) The area of a rectangle is 286 cm^2. If the larger side were decreased by 4 cm and the shorter side increased by 2 cm the area would be reduced by 16 cm^2. Calculate the dimensions of the original rectangle. (L)

6) A pile of 500 sheets of paper is 4 cm thick. Calculate the thickness, in mm, of each sheet of paper. (Give your answer in the form $A \times 10^n$ where A is a number between 1 and 10 and n is a whole number.) (A.E.B. 1974)

7) Figure 1 shows part of the graphs of $2x + y = 4$ and $2x + 5y = 10$. Indicate clearly the region defined by $y \geqslant 0$, $2x + y \geqslant 4$, $2x + 5y \leqslant 10$. (J.M.B.)

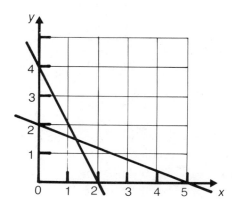

Fig. 1

8) How many square centimetres are there in a square metre?

a 100   b 1000

c 10 000   d 100 000

e 1 000 000

9) Four packets have weights marked: 2 kg, 250 g, 500 g, $3\frac{1}{2}$ kg. Their total weight in kilograms is:

a 5.25   b 6   c 6.25

d 13   e 75.55

10) If the perimeter of a square is 36 cm then the area of the square in square centimetres is:

a 9   b 6   c 36   d 81

e 36^2

11) A rectangular sheet of metal is L metres long, W centimetres wide and T millimetres thick. If the sheet has a mass of M kilograms find a formula for M given that 1 cm^3 of the metal has a mass of D grams. (A.E.B. 1974)

12) The graph of $y = mx + c$ passes through the points $(0, 4)$ and $(-2, 2)$. Find:

(a) c, (b) m. (A.E.B. 1976)

210

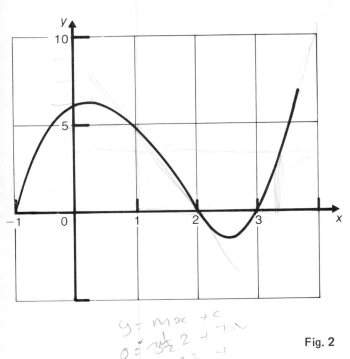

$y = mx + c$
$0 = \frac{1}{3}2 + 2x$
$4 = m2 +$

Fig. 2

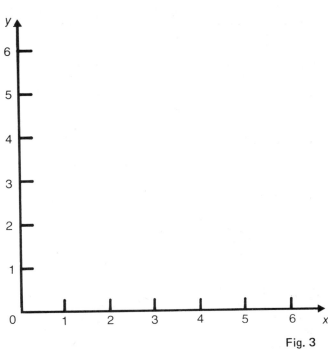

Fig. 3

13) Given that the graph in Fig. 2 has no other turning points,

(a) for what values of x is $y > 4$?
(b) what is the gradient of the curve when $x = 1$? (A.E.B. 1974)

14) The model of a lorry is made on a scale of 1 to 10.

(a) The windscreen of the model has an area of 100 cm^2. Calculate the area, in square centimetres, of the windscreen of the lorry.
(b) The fuel tank of the lorry, when full, holds 100 litres. Calculate the capacity, in cubic centimetres, of the fuel tank of the model. (A.E.B. 1976)

15) Draw the graph of $y = 4 - 2x$ on the axes shown in Fig. 3. (A.E.B. 1976)

16) The quarter circle shown in Fig. 4 is folded to form a circular cone so that AB becomes the circumference of the base. Find the radius of the base circle of the cone.
(A.E.B. 1975)

17) Calculate the rate of change of $4r^3 + 3r^2$ with respect to r when $r = 2$. (J.M.B.)

18) A model aircraft, similar to the full size aircraft, is made to a scale of 1 in 20. The model has a tail 0.15 m high, a wing area of 0.28 m^2 and a cabin volume of 0.016 m^3.

Calculate the corresponding figures for the full size aircraft. (J.M.B.)

19) The triangular region enclosed by the three straight lines $y = 2x$, $y = 0$ and $x = 6$ is rotated completely about the x-axis. Calculate the volume so obtained, giving your answer as a multiple of π. (J.M.B.)

20) A is the area of a circle radius r. Write down the formula connecting A with r. Also write down the formula representing the rate of increase of A with respect to r. (J.M.B.)

21) Given that $\dfrac{dy}{dx} = 3x + 4$ and that $y = 0$ when $x = 1$, express y in terms of x. (J.M.B.)

22) The volume of a cube is 1200 cm^3. Calculate the length of one side. (J.M.B.)

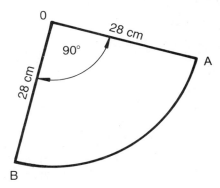

Fig. 4

211

23) Evaluate $\int_1^2 \frac{1}{x^2}\,dx$. (J.M.B.)

24) A prism has a cross-sectional area of 12 cm² and is made of material which has a density of 3.52 g/cm³. Calculate the mass of 1 metre length of such a prism. (J.M.B.)

25) Differentiate $7x^2 + \frac{7}{x^5}$ with respect to x. (L)

26) Evaluate $\int_0^2 (x^3 + x^4)\,dx$. (L)

27) Given that $y = \frac{x^2}{3} + \frac{x^3}{4}$, calculate the value of $\frac{dy}{dx}$ when $x = 6$. (L)

28) Two similar polygons have areas of 160 cm² and 360 cm² respectively. The shortest side of the larger polygon is 18 cm. Calculate the length of the shortest side of the smaller polygon. (L)

29) The vertical height of a stone t seconds after being thrown upwards is 5 metres, where $s = 40t - 5t^2$. Obtain a formula for the upward velocity of the stone after t seconds and hence find the speed with which it was thrown. (L)

30) Given that y is inversely proportional to x^2 and $y = 9$ when $x = 2$, calculate the value of y when $x = 3$.

SECTION B

31) The curve $y = ax^2 + bx - 6$ cuts the x-axis at the points A (1, 0) and B (3, 0).
(a) Calculate the values of a and b.
(b) Find the gradients of the tangents to the curve at the points A and B.
(c) Calculate the co-ordinates of the point at which $\frac{dy}{dx}$ is zero.
(d) Sketch the given curve for $0 \leqslant x \leqslant 4$ and calculate the area bounded by the curve and the x-axis. (A.E.B. 1975)

32) A machine was tested in a laboratory to find the effort, P newtons, required to lift a mass of M kilograms. The following results were obtained:

M	1	3	4	5	7	8
P	7.0	12.7	15.5	18.2	23.5	26.5

Plot these points on a graph and show that M and P could be connected by an equation of the form

$$P = aM + b$$

where a and b are constants. Use your graph to estimate values of a and b. [Scales: take 2 cm to represent 1 kg on the M-axis and 2 cm to represent 2 newtons on the P-axis.]

In a second machine P and M are connected by the formula

$$P = 0.6M + 12$$

Choose any 3 suitable values of M and calculate corresponding values of P in this case. Use the axes and scale of your first graph to draw a further graph which shows the relationship between P and M for the second machine. Use your graph to find which machine requires the greater effort to lift 6 kg and by how much. (A.E.B. 1975)

33) The figure shown in Fig. 5 is obtained by removing the triangle QRT from the rectangle PQRS. The angle QTR = 90° and QT = TR. Given that PQ = 18 cm and PS = $3x$ cm, verify that the area A, in cm², of the figure PQTRS is given by the formula:

$$A = 54x - \frac{9x^2}{4}$$

(a) Calculate A when $x = 7$.
(b) Find the maximum value of A. (J.M.B.)

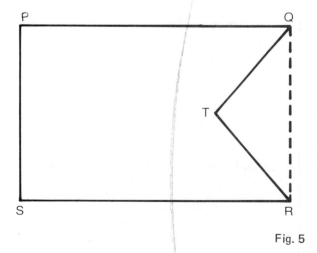

Fig. 5

34) The total cost (P pence) of operating a machine on a workbench was compared with the time (T hours) for which the machine

212

operated, and the following results were obtained:

T	4	10	20	40	60	80
P	65	85	115	145	175	195

Construct another table that shows values of $\sqrt{T}$ against P, and by plotting these results on a graph, show that T and P are approximately connected by a law of the form

$$P = a\sqrt{T} + b$$

where a and b are constants. [Scales: take 2 cm to represent 1 unit on the $\sqrt{T}$-axis and 20 units on the P-axis.]

Use your graph to estimate:

(a) probable values of a and b,
(b) the time for which the total cost of operating the machine is 125 p,
(c) the percentage decrease in the total cost of operating the machine if the time for which it operates is reduced from 64 hours to 32 hours. (A.E.B. 1975)

35) Figure 6 shows a rectangle PMON of perimeter 31 cm inscribed in a quadrant of a circle of radius 12.5 cm. If PN = x cm, PM = y cm, write down two equations in x and y. Solve these equations to find the lengths of the sides of the rectangle. (L)

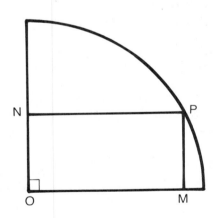

Fig. 6

36) During the first stage of the vertical ascent of a rocket, its velocity, v metres per second, t seconds after the start is given by the formula $v = At + Bt^2$ where A and B are constants. It is known that when $t = 10$, $v = 1000$ and when $t = 20$, $v = 3600$. Calculate the values of A and B. Hence calculate:

(a) the acceleration of the rocket after 2 seconds,
(b) the distance travelled by the rocket in the first 3 seconds of its motion. (L)

37) The length, breadth and height of a rectangular block are 60 cm, 30 cm and 20 cm respectively.
Calculate the exact value of:

(a) the volume of the block,
(b) the total surface area of the block.

The length, breadth and height of the block are increased by 35%. Calculate the resulting percentage increase in:

(c) the volume of the block,
(d) the total surface area of the block.

(J.M.B.)

38)

x	0.5	1	1.5	2	2.5	3	4	5
y	2.5			-0.5	-0.3		0.75	

The table above shows part of a table of values for the graph of $y = x - 4 + \dfrac{3}{x}$. Calculate the four missing values and plot the graph of $y = x - 4 + \dfrac{3}{x}$ for values of x from 0.5 to 5 using a scale of 2 cm to 1 unit on the x-axis and 4 cm to 1 unit on the y-axis. Use your graph to solve the equation $x - 4 + \dfrac{3}{x} = 1$.

(J.M.B.)

39) The pressures at the two ends, A and B, of a straight steam pipe, are maintained at 100 units and 180 units respectively. The pressure in the pipe at distance x, in metres from A is p units where $p = x^2 - 16x + 100$. Calculate:

(a) the difference in pressure between two points in the pipe at distances 3 m and 5 m from A,
(b) the minimum pressure in the pipe, proving that your value is a minimum,
(c) the length of the pipe. (J.M.B.)

40) A swimming bath has vertical sides and the floor slopes uniformly so that, when the bath is full, the water is 1 m deep at the shallow end and 4 m deep at the deep end. If the bath is 25 m long and 12 m wide, calculate the volume of water in the bath when it is full.

The bath is partly drained until the greatest depth of water is 2 m. Calculate:

(a) the area of the surface of the water,
(b) the fraction of the floor of the bath which is not covered by water. (L)

41) A sheet of flat metal is in the shape of a square of side 30 cm. The largest possible circular disc is cut from the sheet and the remainder is thrown away as waste. Find:

(a) the area of the circular disc,
(b) the percentage of the original sheet which is wasted,
(c) the ratio of the perimeter of the circular disc to the perimeter of the original sheet, expressing your answer in the form $n : 1$. (Take $\pi = 3.142$.) (L)

42) A solid rectangular block has a square base of side x cm and a vertical height h cm.

(a) Find expressions for the volume, V cm^3, and the total surface area, A cm^2, of the block in terms of x and h.
(b) Use your results in (a) to show that if the volume of the block is 8 litres, then
$$A = \frac{3.2 \times 10^4}{x} + 2x^2.$$
(c) Find $\dfrac{\mathrm{d}A}{\mathrm{d}x}$ and the value of x which makes A a minimum.
(d) Show that when A is a minimum the box is a cube. (A.E.B. 1975)

43) Draw the graph of $y = 6 + x - x^2$ for values of x from -3 to 4. [Scales: take 2 cm to represent 1 unit on the x-axis and 2 cm to represent 1 unit on the y-axis.]

(a) Use your graph to estimate the positive root of the equation $8 + x - x^2 = 0$.
(b) Find the equation of the straight line joining the points A $(-1, 4)$ and B $(1, 6)$ on the curve and calculate the co-ordinates of the point where the line meets the x-axis.
(c) Calculate the area bounded by the curve, the x-axis and the lines $x = -1$ and $x = 1$. (A.E.B. 1975)

44) Find the co-ordinates of the points on the curve $y = x^3 - 3x^2 + 2$ at which y has a maximum or a minimum value and distinguish clearly between these points. Show that the curve passes through the point A $(3, 2)$. Find:

(a) the gradient of the tangent to the curve at A,

(b) the co-ordinates of the point at which this tangent cuts the y-axis. (L)

45) Find the co-ordinates of the points of intersection, A and B, of the curve $y^2 = 9 - x$ with the y-axis. Show that the area of the region bounded by the arc AB of the curve and the portion AB of the y-axis is 36 square units. The region generates a volume V_1 when rotated through π radians about the x-axis and generates a volume V_2 when rotated through 2π radians about the y-axis. Show that:
$$\frac{V_1}{V_2} = \frac{5}{32} \qquad \text{(J.M.B.)}$$

46) (a) Use logarithms to evaluate
$$\frac{(11.31)^4}{5432 \times 0.978\,5}.$$
(b) Two variable quantities x and y are connected by the relation $y = a + bx^2$, where a and b are constants. Given that $y = 16\frac{1}{2}$ when $x = 2$ and that $y = 9\frac{1}{2}$ when $x = 1\frac{1}{2}$, calculate the values of a and b. Find the value of y when $x = 5$ and the values of x when $y = 1\frac{1}{4}$. (A.E.B. 1976)

47) An isosceles triangle ABC has a perimeter of 24 cm. The sides AB, AC have the same length and the length of BC is $2x$ cm. Show that the area of the triangle is $2x\sqrt{36 - 6x}$ cm^2. Draw the Cartesian graph of the function $f : x \to 2x\sqrt{36 - 6x}$ for values of x from 0 to 6. [Use a scale of 2 cm to 1 unit on the x-axis and 2 cm to 5 units on the other axis.] Use your graph to estimate the greatest possible area for an isosceles triangle with a perimeter 24 cm. (L)

48) Indicate on graph paper, using Cartesian axes, the set of points (x, y) whose co-ordinates satisfy the following inequations: $x \geqslant 0$, $y \geqslant 3 - x$, $y \geqslant 2x - 2$, $2y \leqslant 10 - x$, $3y \leqslant 12 + x$. Find the greatest and least values of $x + 3y$ subject to these inequations. (L)

49) Draw a graph of the curve $y = x^2 - 3$ for values of x in the range $-3 \leqslant x < 3$, including the points for which $x = -2.5$ and $x = 2.5$.

(a) Use your graph to estimate the range of values for which $x^2 - 3 \leqslant 4$, indicating clearly on your graph the limits of the range.

(b) By drawing a certain straight line on the same axes and with the same scales as your graph of $y = x^2 - 3$, estimate those values of x for which $x^2 - x - 3 = 0$.

(c) Use your results in (a) and (b) to estimate the range of values of x for which the inequalities

$$x^2 - 7 \leqslant 0$$

$$x^2 - x - 3 \leqslant 0$$

hold simultaneously. (A.E.B. 1976)

50) (a) Write down the factors of $x^2 - 9y^2$. Hence, or otherwise, solve the equations

$$x^2 - 9y^2 = 15 \qquad [1]$$

$$x - 3y = 5 \qquad [2]$$

(b) When a current passes through a wire, the rate at which heat is produced W watts, is directly proportional to the square of the voltage V volts and inversely proportional to the length of the wire l cm. Express W in terms of V, l and a constant of variation k. Hence calculate:

(i) the value of k given that $W = 800$ when $V = 200$ and $l = 40$,

(ii) the value of l given that $W = 800$ when $V = 240$,

(iii) the value of V given that $W = 800$ when $l = 48.4$. (A.E.B. 1975)

Chapter 33 Angles and Straight Lines

ANGLES

When two lines meet at a point they form an angle. The size of the angle depends only upon the amount of opening between the lines. It does not depend upon the lengths of the lines forming the angle. In Fig. 33.1 the angle A is larger than the angle B despite the fact that the lengths of the arms are shorter.

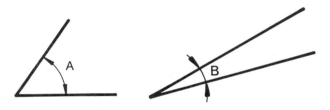

Fig. 33.1

ANGULAR MEASUREMENT

An angle may be looked upon as the amount of rotation or turning. In Fig. 33.2 the line OA has been turned about O until it takes up the position OB. The angle through which the line has turned is the amount of opening between the lines OA and OB.

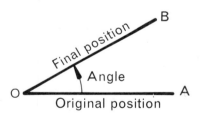

Fig. 33.2

When writing angles we write seventy degrees 70°. The small ° at the right hand corner of the figure replaces the word degrees. Thus 87° reads 87 degrees.

If the line OA is rotated until it returns to its original position it will have described one revolution. Hence we can measure an angle as a fraction of a revolution. Fig. 33.3 shows a circle divided up into 36 equal parts. The first division is split up into 10 equal parts so that each small division is $\frac{1}{360}$ of a complete revolution. We call this division a *degree*.

$$1 \text{ degree} = \frac{1}{360} \text{ of a revolution}$$

$$360 \text{ degrees} = 1 \text{ revolution}$$

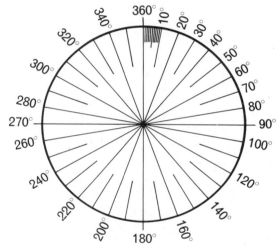

Fig. 33.3

The right-angle is $\frac{1}{4}$ of a revolution and hence it contains $\frac{1}{4}$ of 360° = 90°. Two right-angles contain 180° and three right-angles contain 270°.

EXAMPLE 1
Find the angle in degrees corresponding to $\frac{1}{8}$ of a revolution.

$$1 \text{ revolution} = 360°$$
$$\tfrac{1}{8} \text{ revolution} = \tfrac{1}{8} \times 360° = 45°$$

EXAMPLE 2
Find the angle in degrees corresponding to 0.6 of a revolution.

$$1 \text{ revolution} = 360°$$
$$0.6 \text{ revolution} = 0.6 \times 360° = 216°$$

216

For some purposes the degree is too large a unit and it is sub-divided into minutes and seconds so that:

$$60 \text{ seconds} = 1 \text{ minute}$$

$$60 \text{ minutes} = 1 \text{ degree}$$

$$360 \text{ degrees} = 1 \text{ revolution}$$

An angle of 25 degrees 7 minutes 30 seconds is written $25°7'30''$.

EXAMPLE 3

(1) Add together $22°35'$ and $49°42'$.

$$\begin{array}{r} 22°35' \\ 49°42' \\ \hline 72°17' \end{array}$$

The minutes 35 and 42 add up to 77 minutes which is $1°17'$. The 17 is written in the minutes column and $1°$ carried over to the degrees column. The degrees 22, 49 and 1 add up to 72 degrees.

(2) Subtract $17°49'$ from $39°27'$.

$$\begin{array}{r} 39°27' \\ 17°49' \\ \hline 21°38' \end{array}$$

We cannot subtract $49'$ from $27'$ so we borrow 1 from the $39°$ making it $38°$. The $27'$ now becomes $27' + 60' = 87'$. Subtracting $49'$ from $87'$ gives $38'$ which is written in the minutes column. The degree column is now $30° - 17° = 21°$.

Exercise 149 — *All type A*

1) How many degrees are there in $1\frac{1}{2}$ right-angles?

2) How many degrees are there in $\frac{3}{5}$ of a right-angle?

3) How many degrees are there in $\frac{2}{3}$ of a right-angle?

4) How many degrees are there in 0.7 of a right-angle?

Find the angle in degrees corresponding to the following:

5) $\frac{1}{20}$ revolution.

6) $\frac{3}{8}$ revolution.

7) $\frac{4}{5}$ revolution.

8) 0.8 revolution.

9) 0.3 revolution.

10) 0.25 revolution.

Add together the following angles:

11) $11°8'$ and $17°29'$.

12) $25°38'$ and $43°45'$.

13) $8°38'49''$ and $5°43'45''$.

14) $27°4'52''$ and $35°43'19''$.

15) $72°15'4''$, $89°27'38''$ and $17°28'43''$.

Subtract the following angles:

16) $8°2'$ from $29°5'$.

17) $17°28'$ from $40°16'$.

18) $36°18'39''$ from $44°2'35''$.

19) $0°7'15''$ from $6°2'5''$.

20) $48°19'21''$ from $85°17'32''$.

RADIAN MEASURE

We have seen that an angle is measured in degrees. There is however a second way of measuring an angle. In this second system the unit is known as the *radian*. Referring to Fig. 33.4

$$\text{angle in radians} = \frac{\text{length of arc}}{\text{radius of circle}}$$

$$\theta \text{ radians} = \frac{l}{r}$$

$$l = r\theta$$

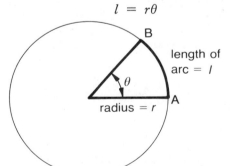

Fig. 33.4

RELATION BETWEEN RADIANS AND DEGREES

If we make the arc AB (Fig. 33.4) equal to a semi-circle then,

$$\text{length of arc} = \pi r$$

$$\text{angle in radians} = \frac{\pi r}{r} = \pi$$

But the angle at the centre subtended by a semi-circle is $180°$ and hence

$$\pi \text{ radians} = 180°$$

$$1 \text{ radian} = \frac{180°}{\pi} = 57.3°$$

It is worth remembering that

$$\theta° = \frac{\pi\theta}{180} \text{ radians}$$

$$60° = \frac{\pi}{3} \text{ radians}$$

$$45° = \frac{\pi}{4} \text{ radians}$$

$$90° = \frac{\pi}{2} \text{ radians}$$

$$30° = \frac{\pi}{6} \text{ radians}$$

EXAMPLE 4

(1) Find the angle in radians subtended by an arc 12.9 cm long whose radius is 4.6 cm.

$$\text{Angle in radians} = \frac{\text{length of arc}}{\text{radius of circle}}$$

$$= \frac{12.9}{4.6}$$

$$= 2.804 \text{ radians}$$

(2) Express an angle of 1.26 radians in degrees and minutes.

Angle in degrees

$$= \frac{180 \times \text{angle in radians}}{\pi}$$

$$= \frac{180 \times 1.26}{\pi} = 72.18°$$

Now

$$0.18° = 0.18 \times 60 \text{ minutes} = 11 \text{ minutes}$$

$$\text{Angle} = 72°11'$$

(3) Express an angle of $104°$ in radians.

Angle in radians

$$= \frac{\pi \times \text{angle in degrees}}{180}$$

$$= \frac{\pi \times 104}{180}$$

$$= 1.815 \text{ radians}$$

218

1) Find the angle in radians subtended by the following arcs:

(a) arc = 10.9 cm, radius = 3.4 cm
(b) arc = 7.2 m, radius = 2.3 m

2) Express the following angles in degrees and minutes:

(a) 5 radians
(b) 1.73 radians
(c) 0.159 radians

3) Express the following angles in radians:

(a) $83°$
(b) $189°$
(c) $295°$
(d) $5.21°$.

TYPES OF ANGLES

An *acute angle* (Fig. 33.5) is less than $90°$.

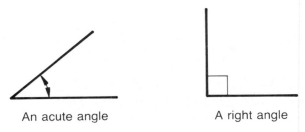

An acute angle

Fig. 33.5

A right angle

Fig. 33.6

A *right angle* (Fig. 33.6) is equal to $90°$.

A *reflex angle* (Fig. 33.7) is greater than $180°$.

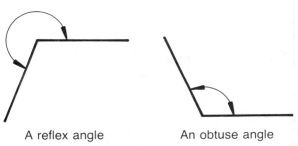

A reflex angle

Fig. 33.7

An obtuse angle

Fig. 33.8

An *obtuse angle* (Fig. 33.8) lies between $90°$ and $180°$.

Complementary angles are angles whose sum is $90°$.

Supplementary angles are angles whose sum is $180°$.

PROPERTIES OF ANGLES AND STRAIGHT LINES

(1) *The total angle on a straight line is* 180° (Fig. 33.9). The angles A and B are called adjacent angles. They are also supplementary.

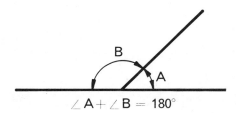

$$\angle A + \angle B = 180°$$

Fig. 33.9

(2) *When two straight lines intersect the opposite angles are equal* (Fig. 33.10). The angles A and C are called vertically opposite angles. Similarly the angles B and D are also vertically opposite angles.

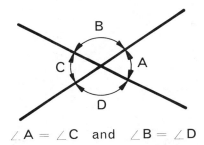

$$\angle A = \angle C \quad \text{and} \quad \angle B = \angle D$$

Fig. 33.10

(3) *When two parallel lines are cut by a transversal* (Fig. 33.11).

(a) *The corresponding angles are equal* $a = l$; $b = m$; $c = p$; $d = q$.

(b) *The alternate angles are equal* $d = m$; $c = l$.

(c) The interior angles are supplementary $d + l = 180°$; $c + m = 180°$.

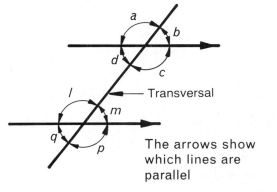

Transversal

The arrows show which lines are parallel

Fig. 33.11

Conversely if two straight lines are cut by a transversal the lines are parallel if any *one* of the following is true:

(a) Two corresponding angles are equal.
(b) Two alternate angles are equal.
(c) Two interior angles are supplementary.

EXAMPLE 5

(1) Find the angle A shown in Fig. 33.12.

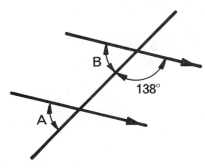

Fig. 33.12

$$\angle B = 180° - 138° = 42°$$

$$\angle B = \angle A \text{ (corresponding angles)}$$

$$\angle A = 42°$$

(2) In Fig. 33.13 the line BF bisects $\angle ABC$. Find the value of the angle α.

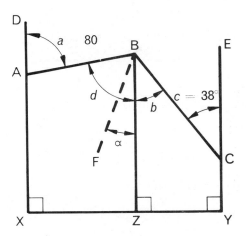

Fig. 33.13

The lines AX, BZ and EY are all parallel because they lie at right-angles to the line XY.

219

$c = b$ (alternate angles: BZ‖EY)

$b = 38°$ (since $c = 38°$)

$a = d$ (alternate angles: XD‖BZ)

$d = 80°$ (since $a = 80°$)

$\angle ABC = b + d = 80° + 38° = 118°$

$\angle FBC = 118° ÷ 2 = 59°$ (since BF bisects $\angle ABC$)

$b + \alpha = 59°$

$38° + \alpha = 59°$

$\alpha = 59° - 38° = 21°$

Exercise 151 — *All type A*

1) Find x in Fig. 33.14.

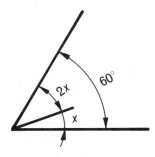

Fig. 33.14

2) Find A in Fig. 33.15.

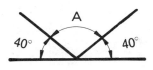

Fig. 33.15

3) Find x in Fig. 33.16.

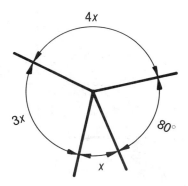

Fig. 33.16

4) In Fig. 33.17 find a, b, c and d.

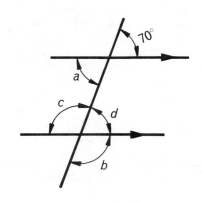

Fig. 33.17

5) Find the angle x in Fig. 33.18.

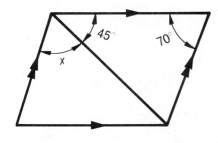

Fig. 33.18

6) Find x in Fig. 33.19.

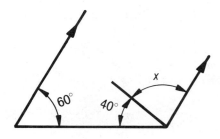

Fig. 33.19

7) A reflex angle is:

a less than 90°   b greater than 90°

c greater than 180°   d equal to 180°

8) Angles whose sum is 180° are called:

a complementary angles

b alternate angles

c supplementary angles

d corresponding angles

9) In Fig. 33.20 find A.

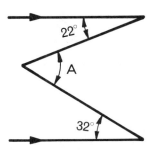

Fig. 33.20

10) In Fig. 33.21, AB is parallel to ED. Find the angle x.

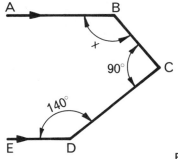

Fig. 33.21

11) Find A in Fig. 33.22.

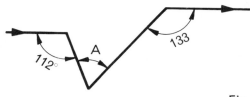

Fig. 33.22

12) In Fig. 33.23 the lines AB, CD and EF are parallel. Find the values of x and y.

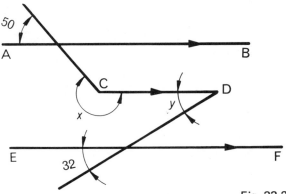

Fig. 33.23

13) In Fig. 33.24:

a $q = p + r$ b $p + q + r = 360°$
c $q = r - p$ d $q = 360 - p - r$

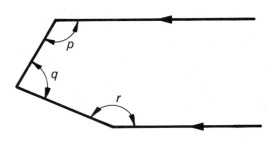

Fig. 33.24

SELF-TEST 33

In the following state the letter (or letters) corresponding to the correct answer (or answers).

1) The angle shown in Fig. 33.25 is

a acute   b right   c reflex   d obtuse

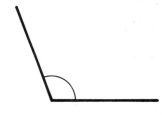

Fig. 33.25

2) The angle a shown in Fig. 33.26 is equal to:
a 120°   b 60°   c neither of these

3) The angle b shown in Fig. 33.26 is equal to:
a 120°   b 60°   c neither of these

4) The angle c shown in Fig. 33.26 is equal to:
a 120°   b 60°   c neither of these

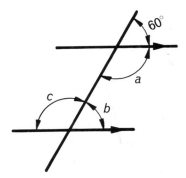

Fig. 33.26

221

5) In Fig. 33.27:

a $a = d$ **b** $a = e$

c $e = b$ **d** $a = c$

6) In Fig. 33.28:

a $x = y$ **b** $x = 180° - y$

c $x = y - 180°$ **d** $x + y = 180°$

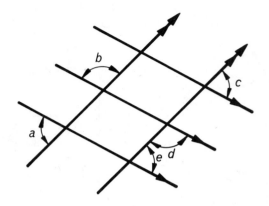

Fig. 33.27

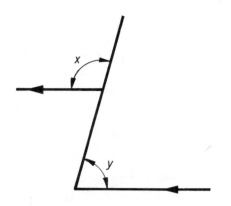

Fig. 33.28

Chapter 34 **Triangles**

TYPES OF TRIANGLE

(1) An *acute-angled* triangle has all its angles less than 90° (Fig. 34.1).

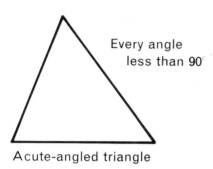

Every angle
less than 90

Acute-angled triangle

Fig. 34.1

(2) A *right-angled* triangle has one of its angles equal to 90°. The side opposite to the right-angle is the longest side and it is called the hypotenuse (Fig. 34.2).

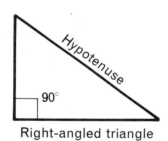

Hypotenuse

90°

Right-angled triangle

Fig. 34.2

(3) An *obtuse-angled* triangle has one angle greater than 90° (Fig. 34.3).

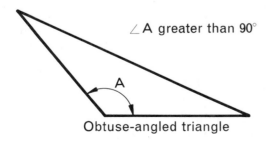

∠A greater than 90°

A

Obtuse-angled triangle

Fig. 34.3

(4) A *scalene* triangle has all three sides of different length.

(5) An *isosceles* triangle has two sides and two angles equal. The equal angles lie opposite to the equal sides (Fig. 34.4).

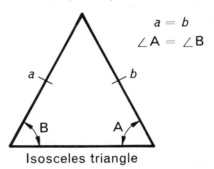

$a = b$
$\angle A = \angle B$

a b

B   A

Isosceles triangle

Fig. 34.4

(6) An *equilateral* triangle has all its sides and angles equal. Each angle of the triangle is 60° (Fig. 34.5).

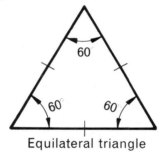

60

60   60

Equilateral triangle

Fig. 34.5

ANGLE PROPERTIES OF TRIANGLES

(1) The sum of the angles of a triangle are equal to 180° (Fig. 34.6).

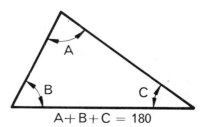

A

B   C

A + B + C = 180

Fig. 34.6

(2) *In every triangle the greatest angle is opposite to the longest side. The smallest angle is opposite to the shortest side.* In every triangle the sum of the lengths of any two sides is always greater than the length of the third side (Fig. 34.7).

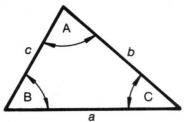

Fig. 34.7. a is the longest side since it lies opposite to the greatest angle A. c is the shortest side since it lies opposite to the smallest angle C. $a + b$ is greater than c, $a + c$ is greater than b and $b + c$ is greater than a.

(3) *When the side of a triangle is produced the exterior angle so formed is equal to the sum of the opposite interior angles* (Fig. 34.8).

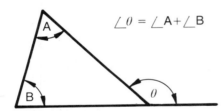

Fig. 34.8

EXAMPLE 1

In Fig. 34.9, find the angles x and y.

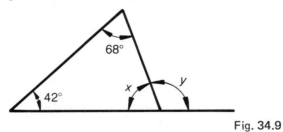

Fig. 34.9

Since the three angles of a triangle add up to 180°,

$$x + 42 + 68 = 180$$
$$x = 180 - 42 - 68 = 70$$

Hence the angle x is 70°.

224

The exterior angle of a triangle is equal to the sum of the opposite interior angles. Hence:

$$y = 42 + 68 = 110$$

Therefore the angle y is 110°.

Exercise 152 — *All type A*

Find the angles x and y shown in Figs. 34.10.

1)

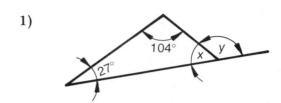

2)

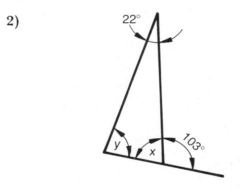

3)

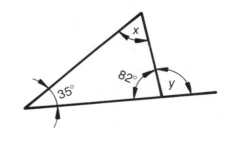

4)

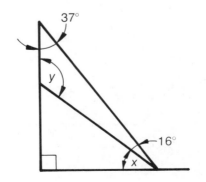

5)

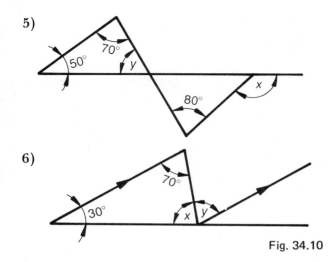

6)

Fig. 34.10

STANDARD NOTATION FOR A TRIANGLE

Fig. 34.11 shows the *standard notation for a triangle*. The three vertices are marked A, B and C. The angles are called by the same letter as the vertices (see diagram). The side a lies opposite the angle A, b lies opposite the angle B and c lies opposite the angle C.

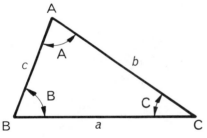

Fig. 34.11

PYTHAGORAS' THEOREM

In any right-angled triangle the square on the hypotenuse is equal to the sum of the squares on the other two sides. In the diagram (Fig. 34.12),

$$AC^2 = AB^2 + BC^2$$

or

$$b^2 = a^2 + c^2$$

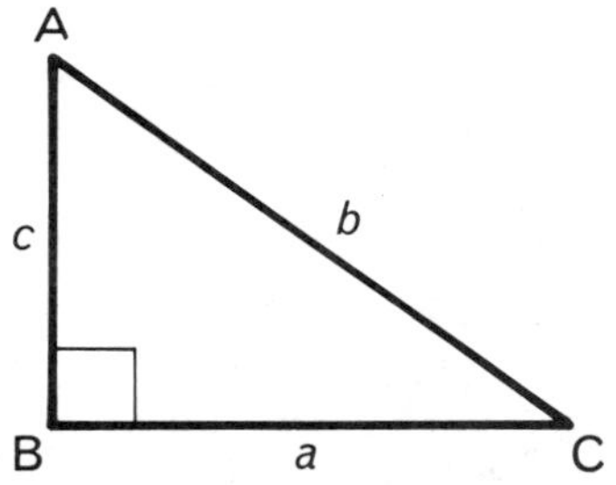

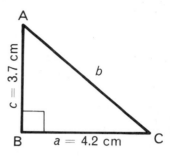

Fig. 34.12

The hypotenuse is the longest side and it always lies opposite to the right-angle. Thus in Fig. 34.12 the side b is the hypotenuse since it lies opposite to the right-angle at B. It is worth remembering that triangles with sides of $3:4:5$; $5:12:13$; $7:24:25$ are right-angled triangles.

EXAMPLE 2
(1) In $\triangle$ ABC, $\angle$ B = 90°, a = 4.2 cm and c = 3.7 cm. Find b (Fig. 34.13).

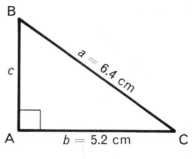

Fig. 34.13

By Pythagoras' theorem,

$$b^2 = a^2 + c^2$$
$$b^2 = 4.2^2 + 3.7^2$$
$$= 17.64 + 13.69$$
$$= 31.33$$
$$b = \sqrt{31.33} = 5.598 \text{ cm}$$

(2) In $\triangle$ ABC, $\angle$ A = 90°, a = 6.4 cm and b = 5.2 cm. Find c (Fig. 34.14).

Fig. 34.14

$$a^2 = b^2 + c^2$$

or

$$c^2 = a^2 - b^2 = 6.4^2 - 5.2^2$$
$$= 40.96 - 27.04 = 13.92$$
$$c = \sqrt{13.92} = 3.731 \text{ cm}$$

225

PROPERTIES OF THE ISOSCELES TRIANGLE

The most important properties of an isosceles triangle is that the perpendicular dropped from the apex to the unequal side:

(1) Bisects the unequal side. Thus in Fig. 34.15, BD = CD.

(2) Bisects the apex angle. Thus in Fig. 34.15, angle BAD = angle CAD.

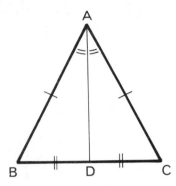

Fig. 34.15

EXAMPLE 3

An isosceles triangle has equal sides 6 cm long and a base 4 cm long.

(a) Find the altitude of the triangle.

(b) Calculate the area of the triangle.

(a) The triangle is shown in Fig. 34.16. The altitude AD is perpendicular to the base and hence it bisects the base.

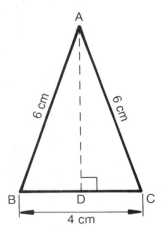

Fig. 34.16

In triangle ABD, by Pythagoras' theorem,

$$AD^2 = AB^2 - BD^2 = 6^2 - 2^2 = 32$$
$$AD = \sqrt{32} = 5.66$$

226

Hence the altitude of the triangle is 5.66 cm.

(b) Area of triangle

$$= \tfrac{1}{2} \times \text{base} \times \text{altitude}$$
$$= \tfrac{1}{2} \times 4 \times 5.66 = 11.32 \text{ cm}^2$$

Exercise 153 — *All type B*

1) Find the side *a* in Fig. 34.17.

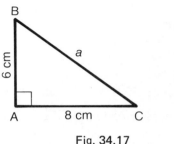

Fig. 34.17

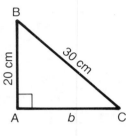

Fig. 34.18

2) Find the side *b* in Fig. 34.18.

3) Find the side *c* in Fig. 34.19.

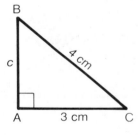

Fig. 34.19

4) Find the sides marked *x* in Fig. 34.20.

(a)

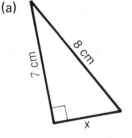

(b)

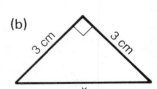

(c)

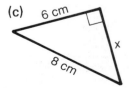

Fig. 34.20

5) Find the altitudes of the triangles shown in Fig. 34.21. All the triangles are isosceles.

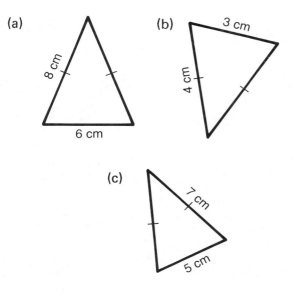

Fig. 34.21

6) Find the angles marked θ for each of the isosceles triangles in Fig. 34.23.

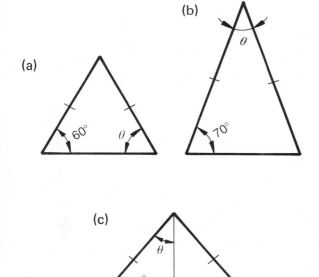

Fig. 34.22

7) Find the angles marked x, y and z in Fig. 34.23.

(a)

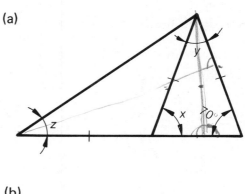

(b)

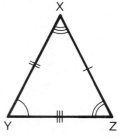

Fig. 34.23

CONGRUENT TRIANGLES

Two triangles are said to be congruent if they are equal in every respect. Thus in Fig. 34.24 the triangles ABC and XYZ are congruent because:

$$AC = XZ \qquad \angle B = \angle Y$$
$$AB = XY \quad \text{and} \quad \angle C = \angle Z$$
$$BC = YZ \qquad \angle A = \angle X$$

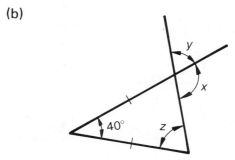

Fig. 34.24

Note that the angles which are equal lie opposite to the corresponding sides.

If two triangles are congruent they will also be equal in area. The notation used to express the fact that △ABC is congruent to △XYZ is △ABC ≡ △XYZ.

For two triangles to be congruent the six elements of one triangle (three sides and three angles) must be equal to the six elements of the second triangle. However to prove that two triangles are congruent it is not necessary to prove all six equalities. Any of the following are sufficient to prove that two triangles are congruent:

(1) *One side and two angles in one triangle equal to one side and two similarly located angles in the second triangle (Fig. 34.25).*

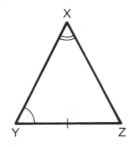

Fig. 34.25

(2) *Two sides and the angle between them in one triangle equal to two sides and the angle between them in the second triangle (Fig. 34.26).*

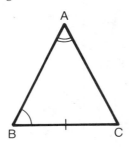

Fig. 34.26

(3) *Three sides of one triangle equal to three sides of the other triangle (Fig. 34.27).*

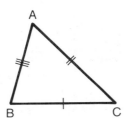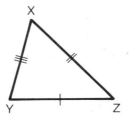

Fig. 34.27

(4) *In right-angled triangles if the hypotenuses are equal and one other side in each triangle are also equal (Fig. 34.28).*

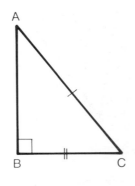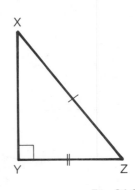

Fig. 34.28

Note that three equal angles are not sufficient to prove congruency and neither are two sides and a non-included angle. An included angle is an angle between the two equal sides of the triangles (e.g., ∠ABC and ∠XYZ in Fig. 34.27 and ∠ACB and ∠XZY in Fig. 34.28).

EXAMPLE 4
(1) The mid-points of the sides MP and ST of △LMP and △RST are X and Y respectively. If LM = RS, MP = ST and LX = RY show that △LMP ≡ △RST.

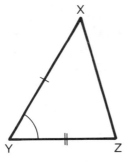

Fig. 34.29

Referring to Fig. 34.29:

△LMX ≡ △RSY (condition (3) above)

therefore ∠M = ∠S

In △s LMP and RST

LM = RS; MP = ST; ∠M = ∠S.

That is, two sides and the included angle in △LMP equal the two sides and the included angle in △RST. Hence △LMP ≡ △RST.

228

(2) The diagonals of the quadrilateral XYZW intersect at O. Given that OX = OW and OY = OZ show that XY = WZ.

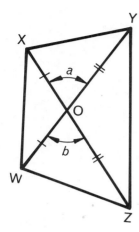

Fig. 34.30

Referring to Fig. 34.30:

In △s XOY and WOZ

OX = OW and OY = OZ (given)

a = b (vertically opposite angles)

Hence the two sides and the included angle in △ XOY equal two sides and the included angle in △ WOZ. Hence △ XOY ≡ △ WOZ.

Therefore XY = WZ

Exercise 154 — *All type B*

1) In Fig. 34.31 state the letter which corresponds to those triangles which are definitely congruent.

(a)

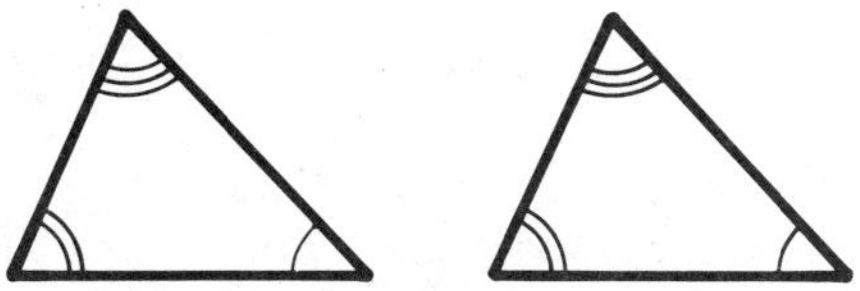

(b)

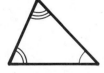

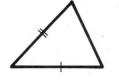

(c)

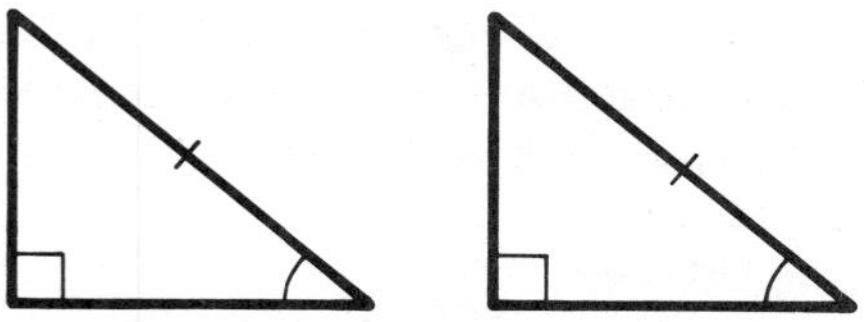

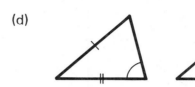

(d)

Fig. 34.31

2) In Fig. 34.32 state the letter which corresponds to those triangles which are definitely congruent.

(a)

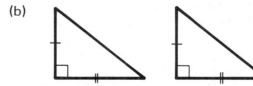

(b)

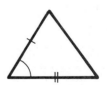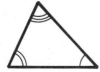

(c)

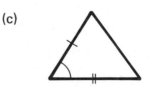

(d)

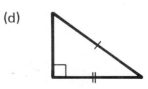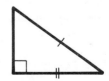

Fig. 34.32

229

3) In Fig. 34.33 find the lengths of RQ and SX. The diagram is not drawn to scale. What is the magnitude of ∠SXP?

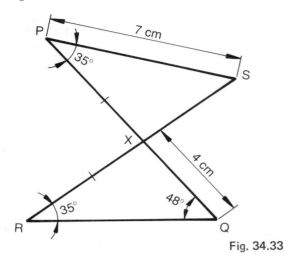

Fig. 34.33

4) In Fig. 34.34 find the length of PY.

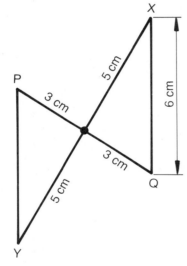

Fig. 34.34

5) In Fig. 34.35 AB is parallel to DC and each is 4 cm long. If AD = 5 cm, find the length of BC. If ∠DAC = 42°, find ∠BCA.

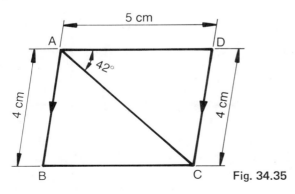

Fig. 34.35

6) In Fig. 34.36 name all the triangles which are congruent. G is the mid-point of DE, H is the mid-point of DF and J is the mid-point of EF.

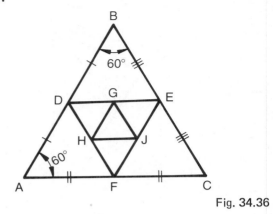

Fig. 34.36

SIMILAR TRIANGLES

Triangles which are equi-angular are called *similar triangles*. Thus in Fig. 34.37 if:

$$\angle A = \angle X, \quad \angle B = \angle Y \quad \text{and} \quad \angle C = \angle Z$$

the triangles ABC and XYZ are similar. In similar triangles the ratios of corresponding sides are equal. Thus for the triangles shown in Fig. 34.37.

$$\frac{a}{x} = \frac{b}{y} = \frac{c}{z} = \frac{H}{h}$$

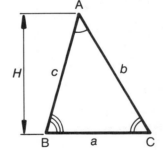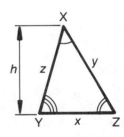

Fig. 34.37

Note that by corresponding sides we mean the sides opposite to the equal angles. It helps in solving problems on similar triangles if we write the two triangles with the equal angles under each other. Thus in △s ABC and XYZ if
∠A = ∠X, ∠B = ∠Y and ∠C = ∠Z

we write $\dfrac{\text{ABC}}{\text{XYZ}}$

The equations connecting the sides of the triangles are then easily obtained by writing any two letters in the first triangle over any two corresponding letters in the second triangle. Thus,

$$\frac{AB}{XY} = \frac{AC}{XZ} = \frac{BC}{YZ}$$

In Fig. 34.38 to prove $\triangle ABC$ is similar to $\triangle XYZ$ it is sufficient to prove any one of the following:

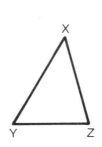

Fig. 34.38

(1) *Two angles in* $\triangle ABC$ *equal to two angles in* $\triangle XYZ$. For instance, the triangles are similar if $\angle A = \angle X$ and $\angle B = \angle Y$, since it follows that $\angle C = \angle Z$.

(2) *The three sides of* $\triangle ABC$ *are proportional to the corresponding sides of* $\triangle XYZ$. Thus $\triangle ABC$ is similar to $\triangle XYZ$ if,

$$\frac{AB}{XY} = \frac{AC}{XZ} = \frac{BC}{YZ}$$

(3) *Two sides in* $\triangle ABC$ *are proportional to two sides in* $\triangle XYZ$ *and the angles included between these sides in each triangle are equal.* Thus $\triangle ABC$ is similar to $\triangle XYZ$ if,

$$\frac{AB}{XY} = \frac{AC}{XZ} \quad \text{and} \quad \angle A = \angle X$$

EXAMPLE 5

(1) In Fig. 34.39 find the dimension marked x.

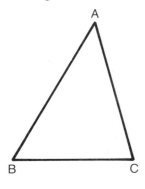

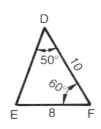

Fig. 34.39

In $\triangle ABC$, angle

$$C = 180° - 50° - 70° = 60°$$

In $\triangle DEF$, angle

$$E = 180° - 50° - 60° = 70°$$

therefore $\triangle ABC$ and $\triangle DEF$ are similar.

$$\frac{40}{10} = \frac{x}{8} \quad \text{or} \quad 320 = 10x$$

$$x = \frac{320}{10} = 32$$

(2) In Fig. 34.40 prove that $\triangle$s PTS and PQR are similar and calculate the length of TS.

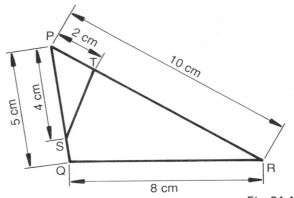

Fig. 34.40

In $\triangle$s PTS and PQR

$$\frac{PS}{PR} = \frac{4}{10} = 0.4$$

$$\frac{PT}{PQ} = \frac{2}{5} = 0.4$$

therefore $\quad \dfrac{PS}{PR} = \dfrac{PT}{PQ}$

Also $\angle P$ is common to both triangles and it is the included angle between PS and PT in $\triangle PTS$ and PR and PQ in $\triangle PQR$. Hence $\triangle$s PTS and PQR are similar.

Writing $\dfrac{\triangle PTS}{\triangle PQR}$ we see that

$$\frac{TS}{QR} = \frac{PT}{PQ}$$

$$\frac{TS}{8} = \frac{2}{5}$$

$$TS = \frac{2 \times 8}{5} = 3.2 \text{ cm}$$

Exercise 155 — *Questions 1–4 type B, remainder C*

1) Fig. 34.41 shows a large number of triangles. Write down the letters representing triangles which are similar. You should be able to find five sets of similar triangles.

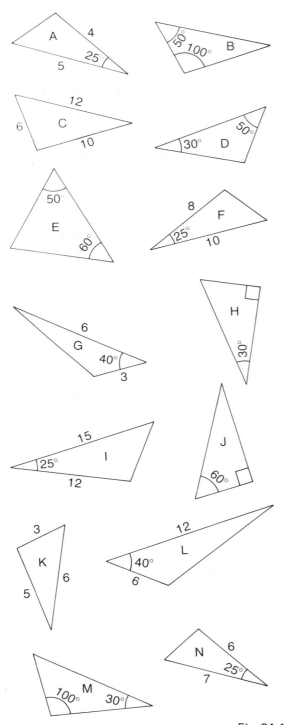

Fig. 34.41

2) The triangles shown in Fig. 34.42 are:

a congruent   **b** similar   **c** neither of these

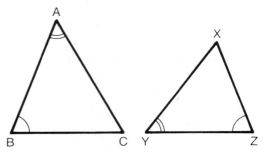

Fig. 34.42

3) If the triangles ABC and XYZ shown in Fig. 34.42 are similar then:

a $\dfrac{AC}{XY} = \dfrac{XZ}{BC}$ **b** $\dfrac{AC}{XY} = \dfrac{BC}{XZ}$

c $\dfrac{BC}{AB} = \dfrac{YZ}{XZ}$ **d** $\dfrac{BC}{AB} = \dfrac{XZ}{YZ}$

4) In Fig. 34.43 if $\dfrac{AB}{XY} = \dfrac{AC}{XZ}$ and $\angle B = \angle Y$ then:

a $\dfrac{AB}{XY} = \dfrac{BC}{YZ}$ **b** $\angle A = \angle X$ **c** $\angle C = \angle Z$

d none of the foregoing are necessarily true.

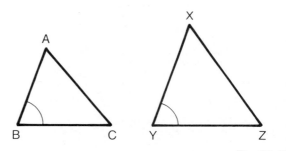

Fig. 34.43

5) In Fig. 34.44, $\angle A = \angle X$ and $\angle B = \angle Y$. Hence:

a $XY = 6\frac{7}{8}$ cm   **b** $XY = 17\frac{3}{5}$ cm

c $YZ = 19\frac{1}{5}$ cm   **d** $YZ = 7\frac{1}{2}$ cm

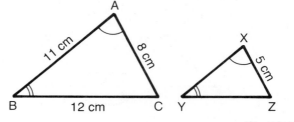

Fig. 34.44

232

6) In Fig. 34.45, PS = 8 cm   and QS = 2 cm.   Hence $\dfrac{ST}{QR}$ is equal to:

a $\dfrac{1}{4}$ b $\dfrac{4}{1}$ c $\dfrac{4}{5}$ d $\dfrac{5}{4}$

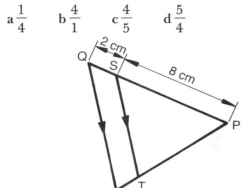

Fig. 34.45

7) In Fig. 34.46, XY is parallel to BC and AB is parallel to YZ. Hence:

a $\angle$ B = $\angle$ Z

b $\triangle$s ABC and YZC are similar

c $\dfrac{YZ}{ZC} = \dfrac{AC}{BC}$ d $\dfrac{ZC}{AC} = \dfrac{YZ}{AB}$

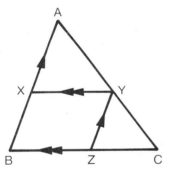

Fig. 34.46

8) In Fig. 34.47, AB is parallel to DC and AB = 3 cm   and   DC = 5 cm.   Hence $\dfrac{XD}{XB}$ is equal to:

a $\dfrac{3}{5}$ b $\dfrac{5}{3}$ c $\dfrac{5}{8}$ d none of these

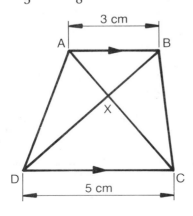

Fig. 34.47

9) In Fig. 34.48 find BC, AB and DE if possible.

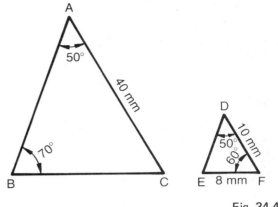

Fig. 34.48

10) In Fig. 34.49, find EC and AB.

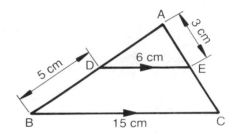

Fig. 34.49

AREAS OF SIMILAR TRIANGLES

The ratio of the areas of similar triangles is equal to the ratio of the squares on corresponding sides.

If in Fig. 34.50 $\triangle$s ABC and XYZ are similar then,

$$\frac{\text{area of } \triangle \text{ ABC}}{\text{area of } \triangle \text{ XYZ}} = \frac{AB^2}{XY^2} = \frac{AC^2}{XZ^2}$$

$$= \frac{BC^2}{YZ^2} = \frac{AD^2}{WX^2}$$

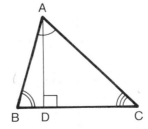
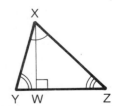

Fig. 34.50

233

EXAMPLE 6

Find the area of triangle XYZ given that the area of triangle ABC is 12 cm² (see Fig. 34.51).

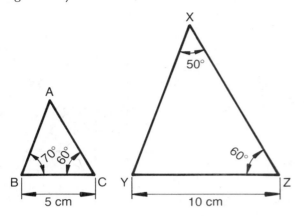

Fig. 34.51

In triangle XYZ, ∠Y = 70° and in triangle ABC, ∠A = 50°. Hence the two triangles are similar because they are equi-angular. BC and YZ correspond, hence:

$$\frac{\text{area of } \triangle XYZ}{\text{area of } \triangle ABC} = \frac{YZ^2}{BC^2}$$

$$\frac{\text{area of } \triangle XYZ}{12} = \frac{10^2}{5^2} = \frac{100}{25} = 4$$

$$\text{area of } \triangle XYZ = 4 \times 12 = 48 \text{ cm}^2$$

Exercise 156 — *All type C*

1) In Fig. 34.52, the triangles ABC and EFG are similar. If the area of △ABC is 8 cm², calculate the area of △EFG.

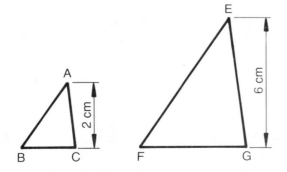

Fig. 34.52

2) In Fig. 34.53, the area of triangle XYZ is 9 cm². What is the area of △ABC?

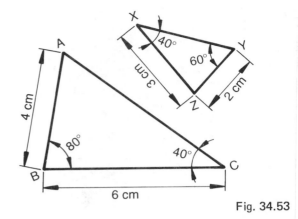

Fig. 34.53

3) In Fig. 34.53 if the area of △XYZ is 10 cm² then the area of △ABC is:

a impossible to find from the given information

b 40 cm²   c 80 cm²   d 160 cm²

4) In Fig. 34.54, △s ABC and DEF are similar triangles. If the area of △ABC is 20 cm² then the area of △DEF is:

a 10 cm²   b 5 cm²   c 8 cm²

d none of these

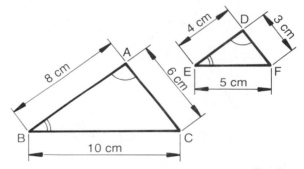

Fig. 34.54

5) In Fig. 34.55, ∠A = ∠X and ∠B = ∠Y. △ABC has an area of 36 cm² and △XYZ has an area of 4 cm². If AB = 4 cm then XY is equal to:

a $\frac{3}{4}$ cm   b $\frac{4}{3}$ cm   c $\frac{4}{9}$ cm   d $\frac{9}{4}$ cm

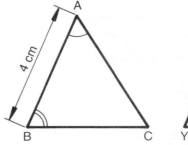

Fig. 34.55

234

6) In Fig. 34.56, $\dfrac{AX}{XB} = \dfrac{2}{1}$. The area of $\triangle ABC$ is 36 cm². Hence the area of XYCB is:

a 12 cm²   b 18 cm²   c 20 cm²

d 16 cm²

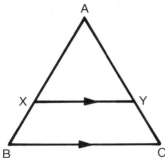

Fig. 34.56

ANGLE BISECTOR THEOREMS

(1) *The internal bisector of an angle of a triangle divides the opposite side in the ratio of the sides containing the angle.* Thus in Fig. 34.57, if AD bisects the angle A then:

$$\frac{AB}{AC} = \frac{BD}{DC} \text{ (see Theorem 9, page 282)}$$

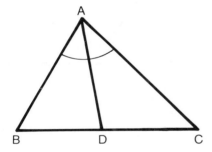

Fig. 34.57

(2) *The external bisector of an angle of a triangle divides the opposite side externally in the ratio of the sides containing the angle.* Thus in Fig. 34.58, if AD bisects the angle $\angle$ CAX then:

$$\frac{AB}{AC} = \frac{BD}{DC}$$

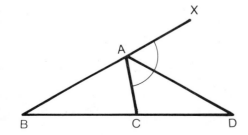

Fig. 34.58

(3) *The converse of the above theorems is also true.* Thus if in Fig. 34.59

$$\frac{BD}{DC} = \frac{AB}{AC} \quad \text{then} \quad \angle BAD = \angle DAC$$

(that is the angle A is bisected).

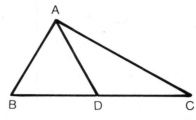

Fig. 34.59

EXAMPLE 7

The area of a triangle ABC is 15 square centimetres and $\dfrac{AB}{AC} = \dfrac{3}{2}$. The line AD bisects angle A and meets BC internally at D. State the value of the ratio $\dfrac{BD}{BC}$ and calculate the area of the triangle ABD.

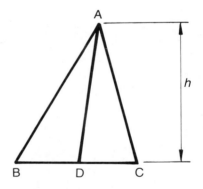

Fig. 34.60

Referring to Fig. 34.60, since $\angle$ A is bisected by AD, then

$$\frac{AB}{AC} = \frac{BD}{DC} = \frac{3}{2}$$

∴ $2BD = 3DC$

But $DC = BC - BD$

∴ $2BD = 3(BC - BD)$

$$2BD = 3BC - 3BD$$

$$5BD = 3BC$$

or $\dfrac{BD}{BC} = \dfrac{3}{5}$

235

$$\text{Area} \triangle ABC = \frac{1}{2} \cdot BC \cdot h$$

$$15 = \frac{1}{2} \cdot BC \cdot h$$

$$h = \frac{30}{BC}$$

$$\text{Area} \triangle ABD = \frac{1}{2} \cdot BD \cdot h$$

$$= \frac{1}{2} \cdot BD \cdot \frac{30}{BC}$$

$$= 15 \cdot \frac{BD}{BC}$$

but
$$\frac{BD}{BC} = \frac{3}{5}$$

$$\therefore \quad \text{Area} \triangle ABD = 15 \times \frac{3}{5} = 9 \text{ cm}^2$$

Exercise 157 — *Questions 1–3, type B,*
4–7 type C, remainder D

1) In $\triangle ABC$, $\angle A$ is bisected by the line AD which meets BC at D. If AB = 8 cm and AC = 10 cm find the ratio $\frac{BD}{DC}$.

2) In $\triangle ABC$, $\angle A$ is bisected by the line AD which meets BC at D. If AB = 5 cm, AC = 4 cm and BC = 6 cm, find BD.

3) In $\triangle XYZ$ the exterior angle at X is bisected by the line XW which meets YZ produced at W. If $\frac{XY}{XZ} = \frac{3}{2}$, find $\frac{WY}{YZ}$.

4) In $\triangle ABC$, AB = 8 cm, AC = 12 cm and BC = 10 cm. D is a point on BC such that BD = 4 cm. Prove that AD bisects $\angle BAC$.

5) The area of a triangle ABC is 20 cm² and $\frac{AB}{AC} = \frac{3}{5}$. Calculate the area of triangle ABD if the line AD bisects $\angle A$ and meets BC at D.

6) ABC is a triangle in which AB = 8 cm, AC = 6 cm and BC = 7 cm. The internal bisector of $\angle BAC$ meets BC at X and the external bisector meets BC produced at Y.

(a) Calculate CX

(b) Calculate XY.

7) The area of a triangle HKL is 16 cm² and HK : HL = 5 : 3. The line HX bisects $\angle KHL$ and meets KL internally at X. State the value of the ratio KX : KL and calculate the area of $\triangle HKX$.

8) The internal and external bisectors of $\angle BAC$ of a triangle ABC meet BC and BC produced at P and Q respectively. If AB = 5 cm, AC = 3 cm and BC = 4 cm, calculate the lengths of BP and PQ.

Exercise 158 (Miscellaneous) — *Questions 1, 2, 4, 6, 7 type B, 3, 5, 8 type C, remainder D*

All the questions in this exercise are of the type found in examination papers at O level.

1) In Fig. 34.61, AB = AC and BCF is a straight line. $\angle BAC = 70°$, $\angle CED = 68°$ and $\angle ECF = 81°$. Prove that two of the sides of $\triangle CDE$ are equal.

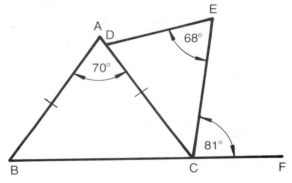

Fig. 34.61

2) In $\triangle ABC$, $\angle A$ is obtuse and $\angle C = 45°$. Name the shortest side of the triangle.

3) In Fig. 34.62, UWR is a straight line. RS = RW, ST = SW, and $\angle R = \angle TSW = x°$. Prove that WS bisects $\angle RWT$ and $\angle TWU = x°$.

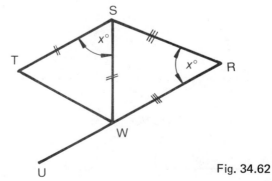

Fig. 34.62

236

4) In △ ABC, the sides AB and AC are equal. The side CA is produced to D and ∠ BAD = 148°. Calculate ∠ ABC.

5) The mid-points of the sides MP and ST of △ LMP and △ RST are X and Y respectively. If LM = RS, MP = ST and LX = RY prove that △ LMP ≡ △ RST.

6) Two similar triangles have areas of 27 cm² and 48 cm². Find the ratio of the lengths of a pair of corresponding sides of the two triangles.

7) In △ ABC, AN is the perpendicular from A to BC. If BN = 9 cm, CN = 16 cm and AN = 12 cm, prove ∠ BAC = 90°.

8) In Fig. 34.63, ABCD is a quadrilateral in which $\dfrac{AB}{AD} = \dfrac{5}{3}$. AX bisects ∠ BAD and XY is parallel to BC. Calculate the ratios $\dfrac{BX}{XD}$ and $\dfrac{XY}{BC}$. Also find

$$\frac{\text{area} \triangle AXD}{\text{area} \triangle ABD} \quad \text{and} \quad \frac{\text{area} \triangle DXY}{\text{area} \triangle DBC}.$$

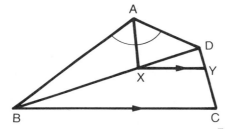

Fig. 34.63

9) In Fig. 34.64, F is the mid-point of the side AB of △ ABC and FE is parallel to BC. If AC = 12 cm, BD = 8 cm and DC = 2 cm, calculate:

(a) the lengths FE and CX;

(b) the ratio of the areas of △s XCD and XEF.

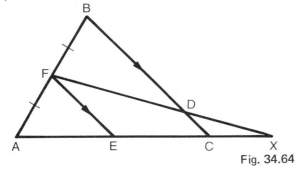

Fig. 34.64

10) BM and CN are altitudes of △ ABC and BN = CM. Prove that:

(a) △ BCN ≡ △ BCM;

(b) AB = AC.

11) PQR is a triangle in which PQ = 5 cm, QR = 8 cm and RP = 10 cm. S and T are points on PQ and PR respectively such that PS = 4 cm and PT = 2 cm. Prove that △s PTS and PQR are similar and calculate the length of ST.

12) PQR is a triangle in which ∠ PRQ = 62°. S is a point on QR between Q and R such that SP = SR and ∠ QPS = 27°. Calculate ∠ PQR and hence prove that SR is greater than QS.

13) In △ ABC, the perpendicular from A to BC meets BC at D and the perpendicular from D to AB meets AB at E. Given that BD = 4 cm, DC = 6 cm and the area of △ ABC is 15 cm², prove that AD = 3 cm and calculate AE.

14) In △ ABC, D is the mid-point of BC and E is the mid-point of CA. The lines AD and BE meet at G. Prove that:

(a) △s ABG and DEG are similar;

(b) △s AGE and BGD are equal in area.

15) In △ PQR, the line ST is drawn parallel to QR meeting PQ at S and PR at T such that PS = 3SQ. Calculate $\dfrac{ST}{QR}$. Given that the area of △ TQS is 3 cm², calculate:

(a) the area of △ PST;

(b) the area of △ TQR.

16) A line cuts three parallel lines at A, B and C such that AB = BC. Another line cuts the parallel lines at P, Q and R. Draw lines through P and Q parallel to AC and use congruent triangles to prove that PQ = QR.

SELF-TEST 34

State the letter (or letters) corresponding to the correct answer (or answers).

1) The triangle shown in Fig. 34.65 is:

a acute-angled   b obtuse-angled

c scalene   d isosceles

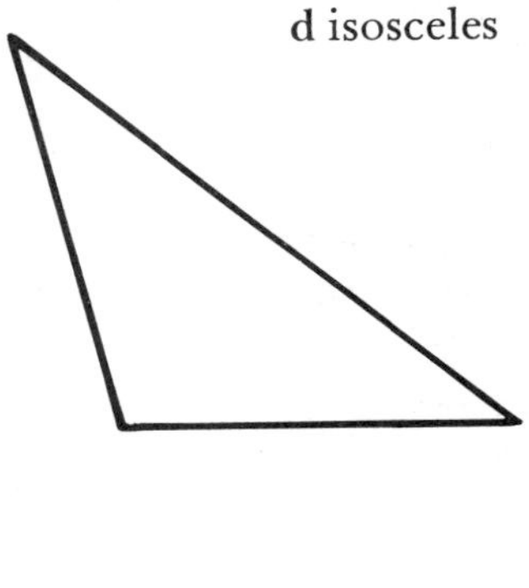

Fig. 34.65

237

2) In Fig. 34.66, ∠ B is equal to:
a 80°   **b** 40°   **c** 50°   **d** 90°

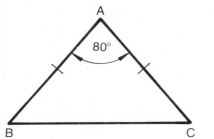

Fig. 34.66

3) In Fig. 34.67, ∠ A is equal to:
a 20°   **b** 40°   **c** 60°   **d** 80°

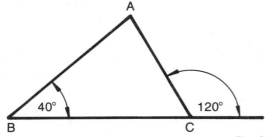

Fig. 34.67

4) In Fig. 34.68, *x* is equal to:
a 140°   **b** 70°   **c** 80°   **d** 60°

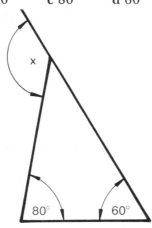

Fig. 34.68

5) In Fig. 34.69 the largest angle of the triangle is:

a ∠ A   **b** ∠ B   **c** ∠ C

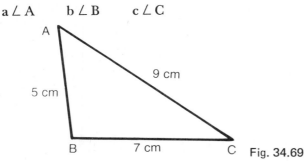

Fig. 34.69

6) A triangle is stated to have sides whose lengths are 5 cm, 8 cm and 14 cm.
a It is possible to draw the triangle.
b It is impossible to draw the triangle.

7) In Fig. 34.70: :
a ∠ BAD = ∠ DAC   **b** ∠ ABD = ∠ ACD
c BD = DC   **d** AD = BD

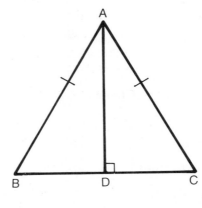

Fig. 34.70

8) In Fig. 34.71, *x* is equal to:
a 17°   **b** 48°   **c** 8°30′   **d** 25°

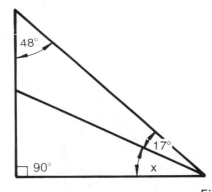

Fig. 34.71

9) In Fig. 34.72, *q* is equal to:
a 80°   **b** 60°   **c** 40°   **d** 100°

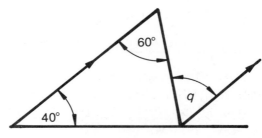

Fig. 34.72

238

10) Two angles of a triangle are $(2x - 40)°$ and $(3x + 10)°$. The third angle is therefore:

a $(210 - 5x)°$ **b** $(230 + x)°$

c $(220 - 5x)°$

11) The three angles of a triangle are $(2x + 20)°$, $(3x + 20)°$ and $(x + 20)°$. The value of x is:

a $60°$ **b** $40°$ **c** $20°$ **d** $10°$

12) In Fig. 34.73, $AD = BC$ and $AC = DB$. Hence:

a $\angle DAC = \angle DBC$ **b** $\angle ADB = \angle DBC$

c $\angle ADC = \angle BCD$ **d** $\angle ADC = \angle BDC$

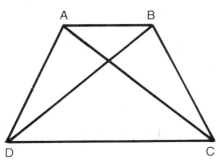

Fig. 34.73

13) In Fig. 34.74 $\triangle DEC$ is equilateral and $ABCD$ is a square. $\angle DEA$ is therefore:

a $30°$ **b** $15°$ **c** $45°$ **d** $20°$

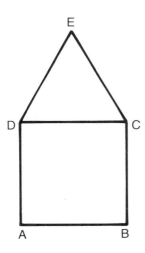

Fig. 34.74

14) In Fig. 34.75 two straight lines bisect each other at X. Therefore:

a $\triangle AXC \equiv \triangle DXB$ **b** $\triangle ABD \equiv \triangle ABC$

c $\triangle ADX \equiv \triangle CXB$ **d** $\angle CAX = \angle XDB$

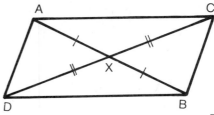

Fig. 34.75

15) The triangles shown in Fig. 34.76 are:

a congruent   **b** similar

c isosceles   **d** none of these

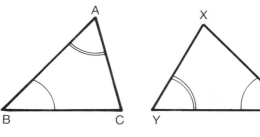

Fig. 34.76

16) If the triangles ABC and XYZ shown in Fig. 34.76 are similar then

a $\dfrac{AC}{XY} = \dfrac{XZ}{BC}$ **b** $\dfrac{AC}{XY} = \dfrac{BC}{XZ}$

c $\dfrac{BC}{AB} = \dfrac{YZ}{XZ}$ **d** $\dfrac{BC}{AB} = \dfrac{XZ}{YZ}$

17) In Fig. 34.77 if $\dfrac{AB}{XY} = \dfrac{AC}{XZ}$ and $\angle B = \angle Y$ then:

a $\dfrac{AB}{XY} = \dfrac{BC}{YZ}$ **b** $\angle A = \angle X$

c $\angle C = \angle Z$

d none of the foregoing are necessarily true.

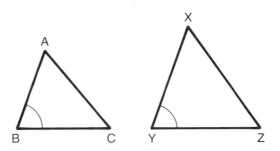

Fig. 34.77

18) In Fig. 34.78, $\angle A = \angle X$ and $\angle B = \angle Y$. Hence:

239

a XY = $6\frac{7}{8}$ cm   **b** XY = $17\frac{3}{5}$ cm

c YZ = $19\frac{1}{5}$ cm   **d** YZ = $7\frac{1}{2}$ cm

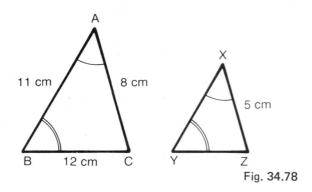

Fig. 34.78

19) In Fig. 34.79,   PS = 4SQ.   Hence $\frac{ST}{QR}$ is equal to:

a $\frac{1}{4}$ **b** $\frac{4}{1}$ **c** $\frac{4}{5}$ **d** $\frac{5}{4}$

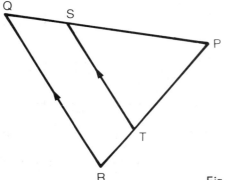

Fig. 34.79

20) In Fig. 34.80, XY is parallel to BC and AB is parallel to YZ. Hence:

a $\angle$ B = $\angle$ Z

b $\triangle$s ABC and YZC are similar

c $\frac{YZ}{ZC} = \frac{AC}{BC}$ **d** $\frac{ZC}{AC} = \frac{YZ}{AB}$

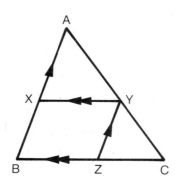

Fig. 34.80

21) In Fig. 34.81, AB is parallel to DC and AB = 3 cm   and   DC = 5 cm.   Hence $\frac{XD}{XB}$ is equal to:

a $\frac{3}{5}$ **b** $\frac{5}{3}$ **c** neither of these   **d** $\frac{5}{8}$

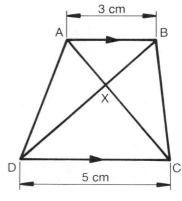

Fig. 34.81

22) In Fig. 34.82,   AD = DE = EB.   Hence:

a $\triangle$s ADC and CEB are equal in area.

b $\triangle$ BCD has twice the area of $\triangle$ ADC.

c $\triangle$ ABC has three times the area of $\triangle$ ACD.

d none of the foregoing is correct.

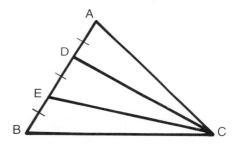

Fig. 34.82

23) In Fig. 34.83, $\triangle$s ABC and DEF are similar triangles. If the area of $\triangle$ ABC is 20 cm² then the area of $\triangle$ DEF is:

a 10 cm²   **b** 5 cm²   **c** 8 cm²

d none of these

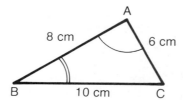

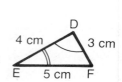

Fig. 34.83

240

24) In Fig. 34.84, if the area of $\triangle$ XYZ is 10 cm² then the area of $\triangle$ ABC is:

a impossible to find from the given information

b 40 cm² **c** 80 cm² **d** 160 cm²

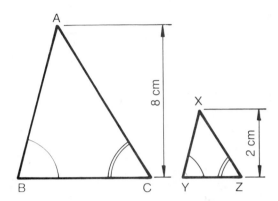

Fig. 34.84

25) In Fig. 34.85, $\angle$ A $= \angle$ X and $\angle$ B $= \angle$ Y. $\triangle$ ABC has an area of 36 cm² and $\triangle$ XYZ has an area of 4 cm². If AB = 4 cm then XY is equal to:

a $\frac{3}{4}$ cm **b** $\frac{4}{3}$ cm **c** $\frac{4}{9}$ cm **d** $\frac{9}{4}$ cm

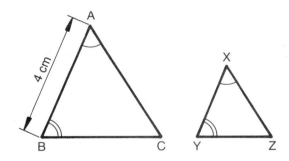

Fig. 34.85

26) In Fig. 34.86, $\frac{AX}{XB} = \frac{2}{1}$. The area of $\triangle$ ABC is 36 cm². Hence the area of XYCB is:

a 12 cm² **b** 18 cm² **c** 20 cm²

d 16 cm²

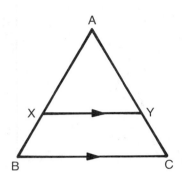

Fig. 34.86

27) In Fig. 34.87 the line AD bisects $\angle$ A. Therefore:

a $\frac{AB}{AC} = \frac{BD}{DC}$ **b** $\frac{AB}{AC} = \frac{DC}{BD}$

c neither of the foregoing is true.

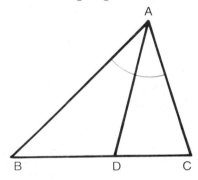

Fig. 34.87

28) In Fig. 34.88, the line AD bisects $\angle$ CAX. Hence:

a $\frac{BD}{DC} = \frac{AC}{AB}$ **b** $\frac{CD}{BC} = \frac{AC}{AB}$

c $\frac{BD}{DC} = \frac{AB}{AC}$ **d** $\frac{CD}{BC} = \frac{AB}{AC}$

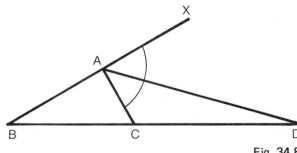

Fig. 34.88

29) In Fig. 34.89, the area of $\triangle$ ABC is 30 cm². The line AD bisects $\angle$ A. If $\frac{AB}{AC} = \frac{3}{2}$ then the area of $\triangle$ ABD is:

241

a impossible to find from the given data
b 9 cm²   **c** 18 cm²   **d** 60 cm²

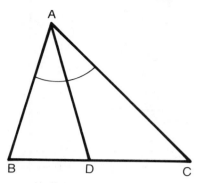

Fig. 34.89

30) In △ ABC (Fig. 34.89), ∠ A is bisected by the line AD and AB = 4 cm and AC = 5 cm. The ratio $\dfrac{BD}{DC}$ is equal to:

a $\dfrac{4}{5}$ **b** $\dfrac{5}{4}$ **c** neither of these

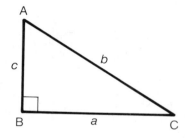

Fig. 34.90

31) In △ ABC (Fig. 34.90):
a $a^2 = b^2 + c^2$ **b** $b^2 = a^2 + c^2$
c $c^2 = a^2 + b^2$
d none of the foregoing is true

32) In a triangle ABC, AB = 3 cm, BC = 4 cm and AC = 5 cm. Hence:
a ∠ A = 90°   **b** ∠ B = 90°   **c** ∠ C = 90°
d none of the angles is 90°.

33) In △ ABC, ∠ B = 90°, BC = 5 cm, AB = 12 cm. Hence AC is equal to:
a 10.91 cm   **b** 34.50 cm
c 41.11 cm   **d** 13.00 cm

34) In △ ABC, ∠ A = 90°, BC = 7.8 cm, AC = 6.3 cm. Hence AB is equal to:
a 14.53 cm   **b** 4.60 cm
c 10.26 cm   **d** 3.25 cm

35) If P is a point inside a rectangle ABCD then:
a $AP^2 + BP^2 = CP^2 + DP^2$
b $AP^2 + DP^2 = BP^2 + CP^2$
c $AP^2 + CP^2 = CB^2 + CD^2$
d None of these is correct.

Chapter 35 **Quadrilaterals and Polygons**

QUADRILATERALS

A quadrilateral is any four sided figure (Fig. 35.1). Since it can be split up into two triangles the sum of its angles is 360°.

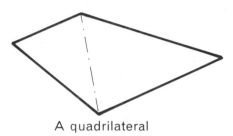

A quadrilateral

Fig. 35.1

PARALLELOGRAM

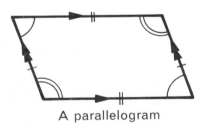

A parallelogram

Fig. 35.2

A parallelogram (Fig. 35.2) has both pairs of opposite sides parallel. It has the following properties:

(1) The sides which are opposite to each other are equal in length.

(2) The angles which are opposite to each other are equal.

(3) The diagonals bisect each other.

(4) The diagonals bisect the parallelogram so that two congruent triangles are formed.

RECTANGLE

A rectangle (Fig. 35.3) is a parallelogram with each of its angles equal to 90°. A rectangle has all the properties of a parallelogram but, in addition, the diagonals are equal in length.

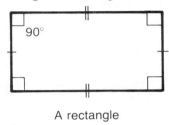

A rectangle

Fig. 35.3

RHOMBUS

A rhombus is a parallelogram with all its sides equal in length (Fig. 35.4). It has all the properties of a parallelogram but, in addition, it has the following properties:

(1) The diagonals bisect at right-angles.

(2) The diagonal bisects the angle through which it passes.

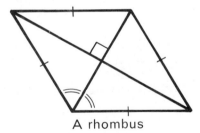

A rhombus

Fig. 35.4

SQUARE

A square (Fig. 35.5) is a rectangle with all its sides equal in length. It has all the properties of a parallelogram, rectangle and rhombus.

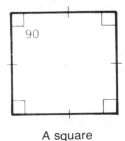

A square

Fig. 35.5

243

TRAPEZIUM

A trapezium (Fig. 35.6) is a quadrilateral with one pair of sides parallel.

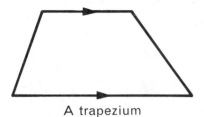

A trapezium

Fig. 35.6

EXAMPLE 1

(1) X, P, Q, Y are points in order on a straight line and XP = QY. The parallelogram PQRS is drawn such that ∠ PQR = 130° and QR = QY. The lines XS and YR are produced to meet at Z. Calculate ∠ XZY.

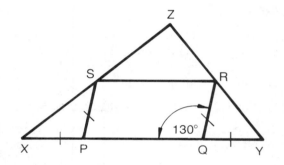

Fig. 35.7

Referring to Fig. 35.7:

Since ∠ PQR = 130°

then ∠ PSR = 130° (PQRS is a parallelogram)

and ∠ SPQ = ∠ SRQ = 50°.

Hence ∠ XPS = 130° and ∠ RQY = 50°.

△ RQY is isosceles (since QR = QY)

∴ ∠ QRY = ∠ RYQ = 65°

△ SXP is isosceles (since XP = SP)

∴ ∠ SXP = ∠ PSX = 25°

In △ ZXY

$$\angle XZY = 180° - \angle SXP - \angle RYQ$$
$$= 180° - 65° - 25° = 90°$$

(2) A rhombus ABCD and an equilateral triangle ABX lie on opposite sides of AB. If ∠ BCD = 82°, calculate ∠ ADX and ∠ BDX.

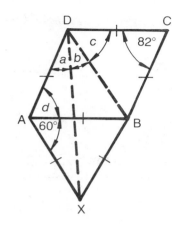

Fig. 35.8

Referring to Fig. 35.8:

$d = 82°$ (opp. angles of a rhombus are equal)

∠ XAB = 60° (angle of an equilateral triangle ABX)

△ DAX is isosceles since AD = AX

$$\angle DAX = 82° + 60° = 142°$$

∴ $a = \frac{1}{2}(180° - 142°) = 19°$

△ CDB is isosceles since CD = CB

∴ $c = \frac{1}{2}(180° - 82°) = 49°$

In the rhombus ABCD

$$\angle D = 180° - 82° = 98°$$
$$a + b + c = 98°$$

$b = 98° - a - c = 98° - 19° - 49° = 30°$

∴

$a = \angle ADX = 19°$ and $b = \angle XDB = 30°$

Exercise 159 — *Questions 1–11 type B, remainder C*

1) Calculate the angle x in Fig. 35.9.

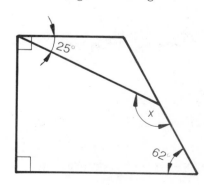

Fig. 35.9

2) Find the angle x in Fig. 35.10.

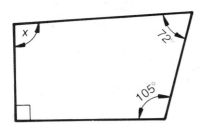

Fig. 35.10

3) In Fig. 35.11, ABCD is a parallelogram. Calculate the angles x and y.

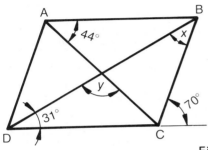

Fig. 35.11

4) A quadrilateral has one pair of sides parallel. It is therefore a:

a rhombus   b parallelogram

c rectangle   d trapezium

5) A quadrilateral has diagonals which bisect at right-angles. It is therefore a:

a rhombus   b square

c rectangle   d parallelogram

6) In Fig. 35.12, x is equal to:

a $a + b + c$ b $360° - (a + b + c)$

c $a + b + c + 180°$ d $360° - a + b + c$

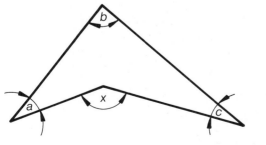

Fig. 35.12

7) In Fig. 35.13, y is equal to:

a 80°   b 70°   c 40°   d 100°

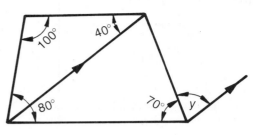

Fig. 35.13

8) In Fig. 35.14, find p.

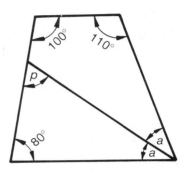

Fig. 35.14

9) In a quadrilateral one angle is equal to 60°. The other three angles are equal. What is the size of the equal angles?

10) Fig. 35.15 shows a rhombus. Are △s ABE and DEC congruent? Does ∠DAC equal ∠DCA? Is the angle DAB bisected by AC?

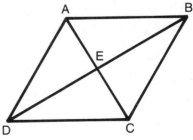

Fig. 35.15

11) ABCD is a quadrilateral in which ∠A = 86°, ∠C = 110° and ∠D = 40°. The angle ABC is bisected to cut the side AD at E. Find ∠AEB.

245

12) In the quadrilateral ABCD, ∠DAB = 60° and the other three angles are equal. The line CE is drawn parallel to BA to meet AD at E. Calculate the angles ABC and ECD.

13) PQRS is a square. T is a point on the diagonal PR such that PT = PQ. The line through T, perpendicular to PR, cuts QR at X. Prove that QX = XT = TR.

14) The diagonals of a rhombus are 12 cm and 9 cm long. Calculate the length of the sides of the rhombus.

15) The diagonals of a quadrilateral XYZW intersect at O. Given that OX = OW and OY = OZ prove that:

(a) XY = ZW;
(b) YZ is parallel to XW.

16) ABCD is a parallelogram. Parallel lines BE and DF meet the diagonal AC at E and F respectively. Prove that:

(a) AE = FC;
(b) BEDF is a parallelogram.

POLYGONS

Any plane closed figure bounded by straight lines is called a polygon.

(1) A *convex* polygon (Fig. 35.16) has no interior angle greater than 180°.

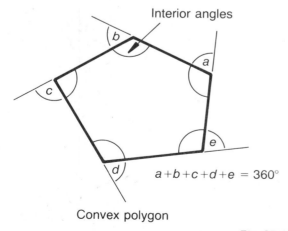

$a+b+c+d+e = 360°$

Convex polygon

Fig. 35.16

(2) A *re-entrant* polygon (Fig. 35.17) has at least one interior angle greater than 180°.

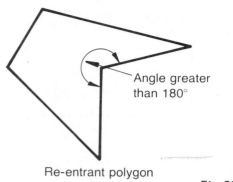

Angle greater than 180°

Re-entrant polygon

Fig. 35.17

(3) A *regular* polygon has all of its sides and all of its angles equal.

(4) A *pentagon* is a polygon with 5 sides.

(5) A *hexagon* is a polygon with 6 sides.

(6) An *octagon* is a polygon with 8 sides.

In a convex polygon having n *sides the sum of the interior angles is* (2n − 4) *right-angles. The sum of the exterior angles is* 360°, *no matter how many sides the polygon has.* Note that these statements apply to all polygons not just regular polygons.

EXAMPLE 2

(1) Each interior angle of a regular polygon is 140°. How many sides has it?

Let the polygon have n sides.

The sum of the interior angles is then $140n$ degrees. But the sum of the interior angles is also $(2n − 4)$ right-angles or $90(2n − 4)$ degrees.

$$\therefore \qquad 90(2n − 4) = 140n$$
$$180n − 360 = 140n$$
$$40n = 360$$
$$n = 9$$

Hence the polygon has 9 sides.

(2) In a regular polygon, each interior angle is greater by 140° than each exterior angle. How many sides has the polygon?

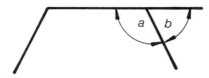

Fig. 35.18

In Fig. 35.18 let a be the interior angle and b the exterior angle of a polygon having n sides. Then

$$a - b = 140° \qquad [1]$$

Also since the sum of the exterior angles is $360°$

$$nb = 360 \qquad [2]$$

and since the sum of the interior angles is $90(2n - 4)°$

$$na = 90(2n - 4) \qquad [3]$$

From equation [2]

$$b = \frac{360}{n}$$

From equation [3]

$$a = \frac{90(2n - 4)}{n}$$

From equation [1]

$$\frac{90(2n - 4)}{n} - \frac{360}{n} = 140$$

$$180n - 360 - 360 = 140n$$

$$40n = 720$$

$$n = 18$$

Hence the polygon has 18 sides.

Exercise 160 — *Questions 1–4 type B, remainder C*

1) Find the sum of the interior angles of a convex polygon with:

(a) 5   (b) 8   (c) 10   (d) 12 sides

2) If the polygons in question 1 are all regular find the size of the interior angle of each.

3) A hexagon has interior angles of $100°$, $110°$, $120°$ and $128°$. If the remaining two angles are equal, what is their size?

4) Each interior angle of a regular polygon is $150°$. How many sides has it?

5) ABCDE is a regular pentagon and ABX is an equilateral triangle drawn outside the pentagon. Calculate $\angle$ AEX.

6) In a regular polygon each interior angle is greater by $150°$ than each exterior angle. Calculate the number of sides of the polygon.

7) A polygon has n sides. Two of its angles are right-angles and each of the remaining angles is $144°$. Calculate n.

8) In a pentagon ABCDE, $\angle$ A = $120°$, $\angle$ B = $138°$ and $\angle$ D = $\angle$ E. The sides AB, DC when produced meet at right-angles. Calculate $\angle$ BCD and $\angle$ E.

9) In a regular pentagon ABCDE, the lines AD and BE intersect at P. Calculate the angles $\angle$ BAD and $\angle$ APE.

10) Calculate the exterior angle of a regular polygon in which the interior angle is four times the exterior angle. Hence find the number of sides in the polygon.

11) Each exterior angle of a regular polygon of n sides exceeds by $6°$ each exterior angle of a regular polygon of $2n$ sides. Find an equation for n and solve it.

12) Calculate the number of sides of a regular polygon in which the exterior angle is one-fifth of the interior angle.

AREA OF A PARALLELOGRAM

(1) *The area of a parallelogram is the product of the base and altitude.* Thus in Fig. 35.19:

Area of parallelogram ABCD = CD x EF

= BC x GH

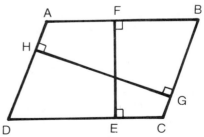

Fig. 35.19

(2) *Parallelograms having equal bases and equal altitudes are equal in area.* Thus in Fig. 35.20:

Area parallelogram ABCD

= area parallelogram CDEF

(see Theorem 3, page 279.)

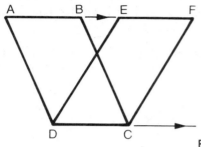

Fig. 35.20

(3) It follows that:

(a) Parallelograms which have equal areas and equal bases must have equal altitudes.

(b) Parallelograms which have equal areas and equal altitudes must have equal bases.

(4) *The area of a triangle is half the area of a parallelogram drawn on the same base and between the same parallels.* Thus in Fig. 35.21:

Area △ ABC = ½ area of parallelogram ABED

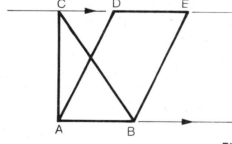

Fig. 35.21

AREA OF A TRAPEZIUM

A *trapezium* is a quadrilateral which has one pair of sides parallel (Fig. 35.22). Its area is easily found by dividing it up into two triangles as shown in the diagram.

Area △ ABC = ½*ah*

Area △ ACD = ½*bh*

Area of trapezium ABCD = ½*ah* + ½*bh*

= ½*h*(*a* + *b*)

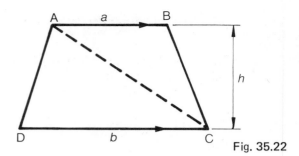

Fig. 35.22

Hence the area of a trapezium is half the product of the sum of the parallel sides and the distance between them.

EXAMPLE 3

(1) Find the area of the parallelogram ABCD (Fig. 35.23).

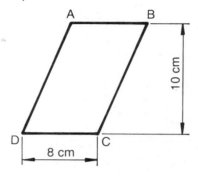

Fig. 35.23

Area of parallelogram ABCD

= base × altitude

= 8 × 10 = 80 cm²

(2) In the trapezium PQRS (Fig. 35.24) the parallel sides PQ and SR are both perpendicular to QR. If PQ = 16 cm, PS = 17 cm and RS = 8 cm, calculate the area of the trapezium.

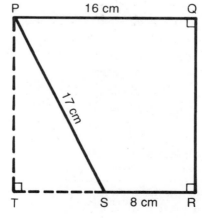

Fig. 35.24

248

In Fig. 35.24 draw the lines PT and TS as shown.

In $\triangle$ PST, TS = 8 cm and PS = 17 cm. Using Pythagoras,

$$PT^2 = PS^2 - TS^2 = 17^2 - 8^2 = 225$$

$$PT = \sqrt{225} = 15 \text{ cm}$$

Area of trapezium

$$PQRS = \frac{1}{2} \times 15 \times (16 + 8)$$

$$= \frac{1}{2} \times 15 \times 24$$

$$= 180 \text{ cm}^2$$

(3) Two parallelograms ABCD and ABEF are as shown in Fig. 35.25. Prove that:

(a) DCEF is a parallelogram;
(b) area ABCD = area ABEF − area DCEF

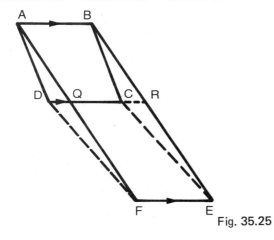

Fig. 35.25

(a) Since ABCD and ABEF are both parallelograms

$$AB = CD = EF$$

and AB, CD and EF are all parallel to each other. Hence DCEF is a parallelogram because the two opposite sides CD and EF are equal and parallel.

(b) Draw CR as shown in Fig. 35.25. Parallelograms ABCD and ABRQ are equal in area since they have the same base AB and the same altitude. Similarly DCEF and QRFE are equal in area.

Area ABEF = area ABRQ + area QREF

$$= \text{area ABCD} + \text{area DCEF}$$

Area ABCD = area ABEF − area DCEF

1) What is the area of a parallelogram whose base is 7 cm long and whose vertical height is 4 cm?

2) A parallelogram ABCD has AB = 12 cm and BC = 10 cm. $\angle$ ABC = 45°. Calculate the area of ABCD.

3) The area of a parallelogram is 80 cm². If the base is 12 cm long what is its altitude?

4) Fig. 35.26 shows a trapezium. Find x.

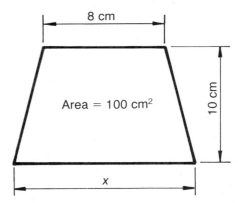

Fig. 35.26

5) E is the mid-point of the side AB of the parallelogram ABCD whose area is 80 cm². Find the area of $\triangle$ DEC.

6) In the rhombus PQRS the side PQ = 17 cm and the diagonal PR = 16 cm. Calculate the area of the rhombus.

7) WXYZ is a parallelogram. A line through W meets ZY at T and XY produced at U. Prove that $\triangle$s WZT and UYT are similar. If $\frac{ZT}{TY} = \frac{3}{2}$ and the area of WXYZ is 20 cm², calculate:

(a) the area of the trapezium WXYT;
(b) the area of $\triangle$ UYT.

8) The area of a rhombus is 16 cm² and the length of one of its diagonals is 6 cm. Calculate the length of the other diagonal.

9) A point P is taken on the side CD of the parallelogram ABCD and CD is produced to Q making DQ = CP. A line through Q parallel to AD meets BP produced at S. AD is produced to meet BS at R. Prove that ARSQ is a parallelogram and that its area is equal to the area of ABCD.

10) In the parallelogram ABCD the side AB is produced to X so that BX = AB. The line DX cuts BC at E. Prove that:

(a) DBXC is a parallelogram;

(b) Area AED = twice area CEX.

SELF-TEST 35

State the letter (or letters) corresponding to the correct answer (or answers).

1) A quadrilateral has one pair of sides parallel. It is therefore a:

a rhombus   b parallelogram

c rectangle   d trapezium

2) A quadrilateral has diagonals which bisect at right-angles. It is therefore a:

a rhombus   b trapezium

c rectangle   d parallelogram

3) In Fig. 35.27, x is equal to:

a 190°   b 110°   c 70°   d 60°

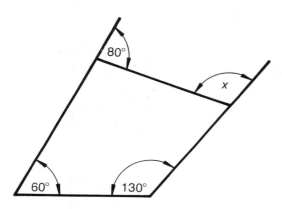

Fig. 35.27

4) A polygon has all its interior angles less than 180°. Hence it is definitely a:

a convex polygon   b regular polygon

c re-entrant polygon   d quadrilateral

5) A regular polygon has each interior angle equal to 108°. It therefore has:

a 4 sides   b 5 sides

c 6 sides   d 7 sides

6) A regular polygon has each exterior angle equal to 40°. It therefore has:

a 7 sides   b 8 sides

c 9 sides   d 10 sides

7) A regular polygon has each interior angle greater by 60° than each exterior angle. It therefore has:

a 4 sides   b 6 sides

c 7 sides   d 8 sides

8) Fig. 35.28 shows a trapezium. The side marked x is equal to:

a 10 cm   b 15 cm   c 5 cm   d 0.75 cm

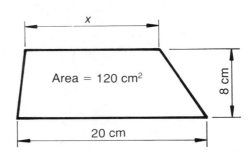

Fig. 35.28

9) In Fig. 35.29, ABCD and ABEF are parallelograms which have equal areas. It *must* be true that:

a AF = AD   b ∠D = ∠F

c AG = AH   d ∠C = ∠E

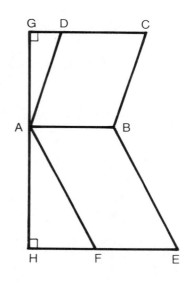

Fig. 35.29

10) In Fig. 35.30, ABCD is a parallelogram and CF = EF. Hence:

a BC = BE   b AD = AE

c Area ABCD = area AFE

d Area ABCD = 2 × area ABE

250

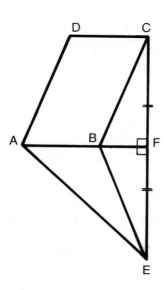

Fig. 35.30

11) In Fig. 35.31, ABCD is a trapezium. Hence:

a ∠ ADB = 40°   **b** ∠ ADB = 70°

c ∠ ADC = 90°   **d** ∠ ADC = 120°

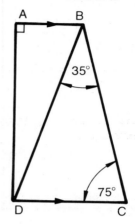

Fig. 35.31

251

Chapter 36 **The Circle**

Fig. 36.1 shows the main components of a circle.

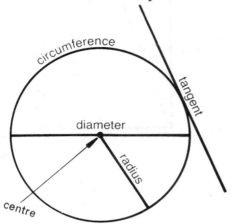

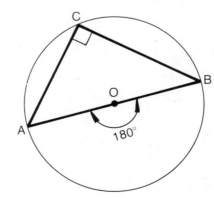

Fig. 36.2

If a triangle is inscribed in a semicircle the angle opposite the diameter is a right-angle (Fig. 36.3).

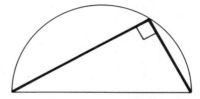

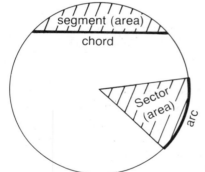

Fig. 36.1

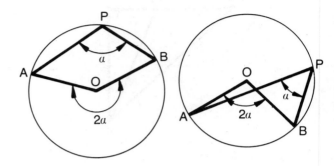

Fig. 36.3

This theorem follows from the fact that *the angle subtended by an arc at the centre is twice the angle subtended by the arc at the circumference.*

Thus in Fig. 36.4:

Angle subtended at the centre by the arc AB = 180°.

Hence the angle subtended at the circumference = 90°.

ANGLES IN CIRCLES

The angle which an arc of a circle subtends at the centre is twice the angle which the arc subtends at the circumference.

Thus in Fig. 36.2,

$$\angle\, AOB \;=\; 2 \times \angle\, APB$$

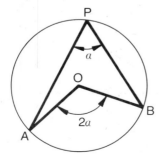

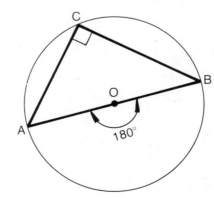

Fig. 36.4

EXAMPLE 1

In Fig. 36.5, O is the centre of the circle. If
∠ AOB = 60°,   find ∠ ACB.

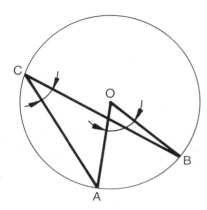

Fig. 36.5

Since ∠ AOB is the angle subtended by the arc
AB at the centre O and ∠ ACB is the angle
subtended by AB at the circumference:

$$\angle AOB = 2 \times \angle ACB$$

Since   ∠ AOB = 60°

             ∠ ACB = 30°

EXAMPLE 2

In Fig. 36.6, find the length of the diameter BC.

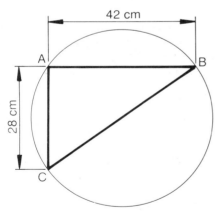

Fig. 36.6

Since BC is a diameter, the angle A is the angle
in a semi-circle and hence it is a right-angle.

In △ ABC, by Pythagoras,

$$BC^2 = 28^2 + 42^2 = 784 + 1764 = 2548$$

$$BC = \sqrt{2548} = 50.48$$

Hence the length of the diameter BC is
50.48 cm.

The chord AB (Fig. 36.7) divides the circle into
two arcs. ABP is called the *major* arc and ABQ
the *minor* arc. The areas ABP and ABQ
are called *segments*.

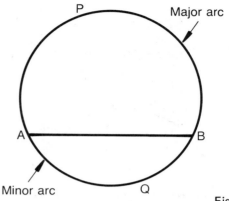

Fig. 36.7

The angles ARB and ASB (Fig. 36.8) are called
angles in the segment APB. The angle ATB is
called an angle in the segment ABQ.

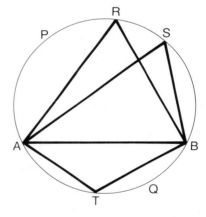

Fig. 36.8

Angles in the same segment of a circle are equal.
Thus in Fig. 36.9,   ∠ APB = ∠ AQB   since
they are angles in the same segment ABQP.

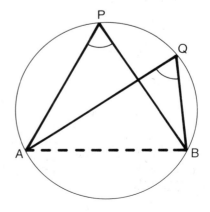

Fig. 36.9

The converse is useful when proving that 4 points are concyclic. Thus in Fig. 36.10, if $\angle Z = \angle Y$, then the points W, X, Y and Z are concyclic (i.e., on the circumference of a circle).

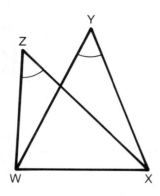

Fig. 36.10

EXAMPLE 3

Find the angles x and y shown in Fig. 36.11.

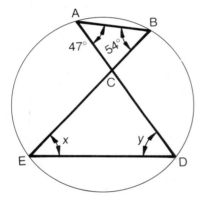

Fig. 36.11

The angles DEC and BAC are in the same segment. Hence

$$\angle DEC = \angle BAC$$

$$\therefore \qquad x = 47°$$

The angles ABC and EDC are in the same segment. Hence

$$\angle EDC = \angle ABC$$

$$y = 54°$$

The opposite angles of any quadrilateral inscribed in a circle are supplementary (i.e., equal to 180°). It follows that *the exterior angle is equal to the interior opposite angle.* A quadrilateral inscribed in a circle is called a

cyclic quadrilateral. Thus the cyclic quadrilateral ABCD (Fig. 36.12) has $\angle A + \angle C = 180°$ and $\angle D + \angle B = 180°$. Also $\angle CDX = \angle B$, $\angle BCY = \angle A$, etc. The converse is also true, i.e., a quadrilateral with two opposite angles that are supplementary is a cyclic quadrilateral.

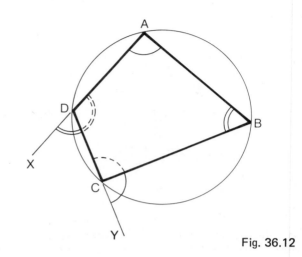

Fig. 36.12

EXAMPLE 4

ABCD is a cyclic quadrilateral with angle A = 100° and angles B and D equal. Find the angles C and D (Fig. 36.13).

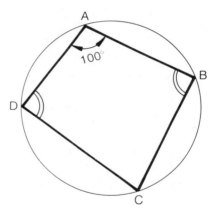

Fig. 36.13

Since ABCD is a cyclic quadrilateral,

$$\angle A + \angle C = 180°$$

$$\therefore \qquad \angle C = 80°$$

Also $\qquad \angle B + \angle D = 180°$

Since $\qquad \angle B = \angle D,$

$$\angle D = 90°$$

254

Exercise 162 — *All type B*

1) In Fig. 36.14, if ∠ AOB = 76°, find ∠ ACB.

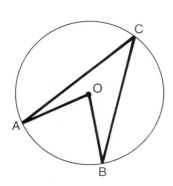

Fig. 36.14

2) In Fig. 36.15, ABC is an equilateral triangle inscribed in a circle whose centre is O. Find ∠ BOC.

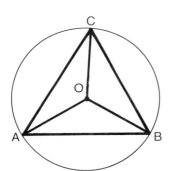

Fig. 36.15

3) ABC is an isosceles triangle inscribed in a circle whose centre is O (Fig. 36.16). If ∠ AOB = 116°, find ∠ ABC.

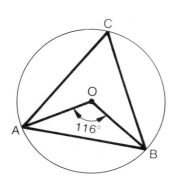

Fig. 36.16

4) In Fig. 36.17, determine the angle x.

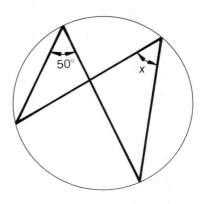

Fig. 36.17

5) Find the angles C and D of the cyclic quadrilateral ABCD shown in Fig. 36.18.

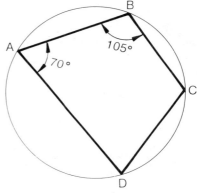

Fig. 36.18

6) In Fig. 36.19, find the angles x and y.

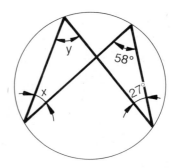

Fig. 36.19

255

7) Figure 36.20 shows a cyclic quadrilateral. Find the angles marked x and y.

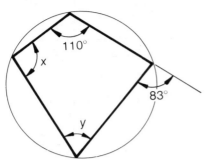

Fig. 36.20

8) In Fig. 36.21, AB is a diameter. Find AC.

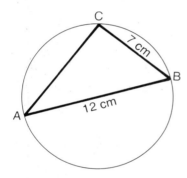

Fig. 36.21

9) In Fig. 36.22, find each of the angles marked a and b.

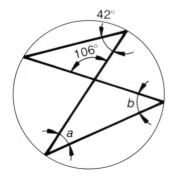

Fig. 36.22

10) In Fig. 36.23, determine the angles x and y, AB being a diameter.

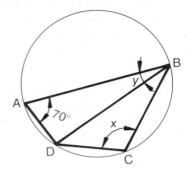

Fig. 36.23

11) In Fig. 36.24, calculate the diameter of the circle.

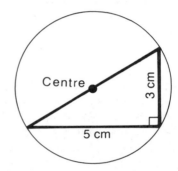

Fig. 36.24

CHORDS

A *chord* is a straight line which joins two points on the circumference of a circle. A *diameter* is a chord drawn through the centre of the circle (Fig. 36.1).

If a diameter of a circle is at right-angles to a chord then it divides the chord into two equal parts (Fig. 36.25). The converse is also true.

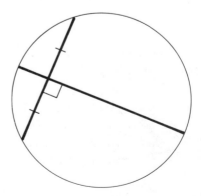

Fig. 36.25

Chords which are equal in length are equidistant from the centre of the circle. Thus, in Fig. 36.26 if the chords AB and CD are equal in length, then the distances OX and OY are also equal. The converse is also true, i.e., chords which are equidistant from the centre of the circle are equal in length.

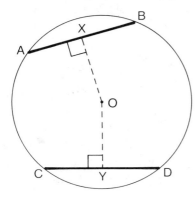

Fig. 36.26

If two chords intersect inside or outside a circle the product of the segments of one chord is equal to the product of the segments of the other chord. Thus in Fig. 36.27, AE x EB = CE x ED. The converse is also true, i.e., if AE x EB = CE x ED then the points ABCD are concyclic (i.e., lie on the circumference of a circle).

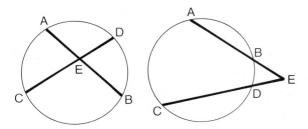

Fig. 36.27

EXAMPLE 5

Figure 36.28 shows a segment of a circle. Find the diameter of the circle.

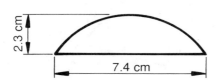

Fig. 36.28

In Fig. 36.29 draw the diameter CD at right-angles to the chord. The chord AB is bisected and AE = EB = 3.7 cm.

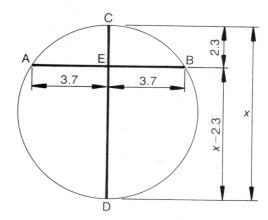

Fig. 36.29

By the theorem of intersecting chords,

$$AE \times EB = CE \times ED$$

Since CE = 2.3 cm, ED = $x - 2.3$, where x is the length of the diameter CD.

$$3.7 \times 3.7 = 2.3 \times (x - 2.3)$$
$$13.69 = 2.3x - 2.3 \times 2.3$$
$$13.69 = 2.3x - 5.29$$
$$2.3x = 13.69 + 5.29 = 18.98$$
$$x = \frac{18.98}{2.3} = 8.25$$

Hence the diameter of the circle is 8.25 cm.

EXAMPLE 6

A chord AB (Fig. 36.30) is drawn in a circle 5 cm radius. If it is 4 cm from the centre of the circle, find its length.

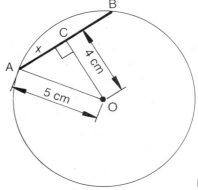

Fig. 36.30

257

In △OAC, by Pythagoras,

$$x^2 = 5^2 - 4^2 = 25 - 16 = 9$$

$$x = \sqrt{9} = 3$$

Hence the chord is   2 × 3 cm = 6 cm.

Exercise 163 — *All type B*

1) In Fig. 36.31 find the distance x.

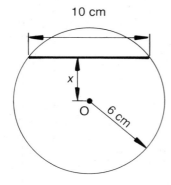

Fig. 36.31

2) In Fig. 36.32, find the length of the chord AB.

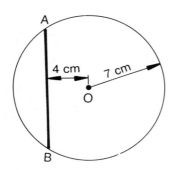

Fig. 36.32

3) Figure 36.33 shows an equilateral triangle inscribed in a circle. Calculate the diameter of the circle.

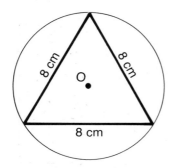

Fig. 36.33

4) In Fig. 36.34, calculate the diameter of the circle.

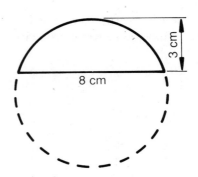

Fig. 36.34

5) Find the length y in Fig. 36.35.

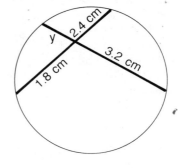

Fig. 36.35

6) Find the length x in Fig. 36.36.

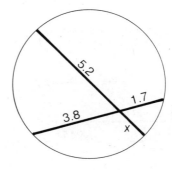

Fig. 36.36

258

7) In Fig. 36.37, calculate the length of the chord *x*.

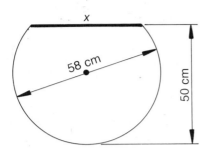

Fig. 36.37

8) In Fig. 36.38, calculate the height of the segment marked *y*.

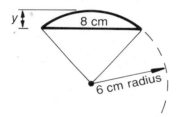

Fig. 36.38

TANGENT PROPERTIES OF A CIRCLE

A tangent is a line which just touches a circle at one point only (Fig. 36.39). This point is called the point of tangency.

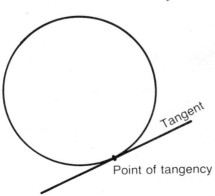

Fig. 36.39

A tangent to a circle is at right-angles to a radius drawn from the point of tangency (Fig. 36.40).

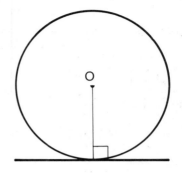

Fig. 36.40

If from a point outside a circle, tangents are drawn to the circle, then the two tangents are equal in length. They also make equal angles with the chord joining the points of tangency (Fig. 36.41 — angle A). It follows that the line drawn from the point where the tangents meet to the centre of the circle bisects the angle between the two tangents (angle B).

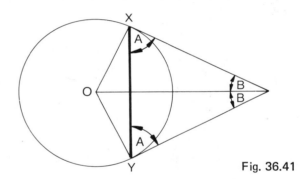

Fig. 36.41

The angle between a tangent and a chord drawn from the point of tangency equals one-half of the angle at the centre subtended by the chord.

Thus in Fig. 36.42, $\angle B = \frac{1}{2} \angle A$.

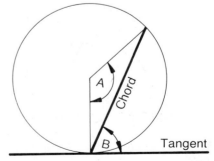

Fig. 36.42

The angle between a tangent and a chord drawn from the point of tangency equals the angle at the circumference subtended by the chord. The angle at the circumference must be in the alternate segment (see Figs. 36.43 (a) and (b)). Thus in Fig. 36.43 (c), $\angle$ B, the angle between the chord XY and the tangent YT equals, $\angle$ A, the angle subtended by the chord at the circumference. Note that $\angle$ A is in the alternate segment to $\angle$ B. In Fig. 36.43 (d), $\angle$ C = $\angle$ D.

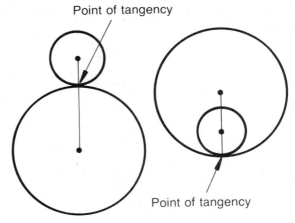

Point of tangency

Point of tangency

Fig. 36.44

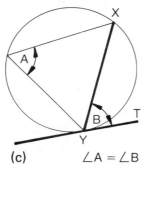

Alternate segment to angle *a*

Tangent

(a)

Alternate segment to angle *b*

b

(b)

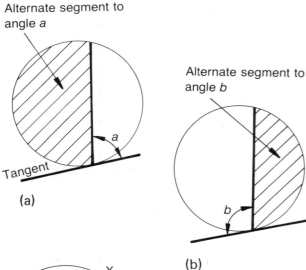

X

A

B

T

Y

(c) $\angle$A = $\angle$B

X

D

T

C

Y

(d) $\angle$C = $\angle$D

Fig. 36.43

If two circles touch internally or externally then the line which passes through their centres, also passes through the point of tangency (Fig. 36.44).

A line (Fig. 36.45) which cuts a circle at two points is called a *secant*.

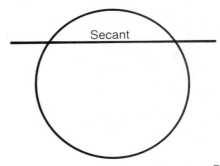

Secant

Fig. 36.45

If from a point outside a circle two lines are drawn, one a secant and the other a tangent to the circle, then the square on the tangent is equal to the rectangle contained by the whole secant and that part of it which lies outside the circle.

Thus in Fig. 36.46, $CT^2 = AC \cdot BC$.

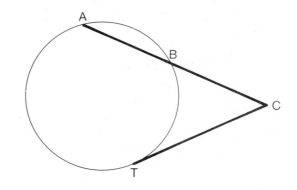

A

B

C

T

Fig. 36.46

260

EXAMPLE 7

In Fig. 36.47, calculate the distance x.

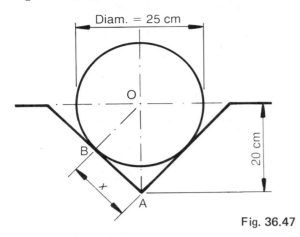

Fig. **36.47**

In triangle OAB,

$$\angle OBA = 90°$$

(angle between a radius and a tangent)

$$OB = 12.5 \text{ cm}$$

(OB is a radius and equals $\frac{1}{2}$ of 25 = 12.5 cm)

Hence, by Pythagoras,

$$AB^2 = OA^2 - OB^2$$
$$x^2 = 20^2 - 12.5^2$$
$$= 400 - 156.25 = 243.75$$
$$x = \sqrt{243.75} = 15.61 \text{ cm}$$

EXAMPLE 8

Three circles are arranged as shown in Fig. 36.48. Find the distance h.

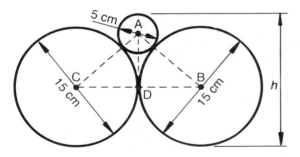

Fig. **36.48**

Because the circles are tangential to each other,

$$AC = 7.5 + 2.5 = 10 \text{ cm}$$
$$AB = 7.5 + 2.5 = 10 \text{ cm}$$
$$BC = 7.5 + 7.5 = 15 \text{ cm}$$

Triangle ABC is therefore isosceles. Therefore

$$CD = \tfrac{1}{2} \times 15 = 7.5 \text{ cm}$$

In ACD, by Pythagoras,

$$AD^2 = AC^2 - CD^2$$
$$= 10^2 - 7.5^2$$
$$= 100 - 56.25 = 43.75$$
$$AD = \sqrt{43.75} = 6.61 \text{ cm}$$
$$h = 7.5 + 6.61 + 2.5 = 16.61 \text{ cm}$$

EXAMPLE 9

Find the angle a in Fig. 36.49. What is the size of angle b?

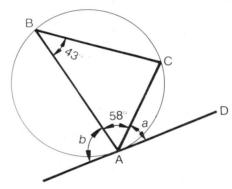

Fig. **36.49**

$$\angle ABC = \angle CAD$$

(angle in the alternate segment to $\angle CAD$)

$$a = 43°$$
$$b = 180° - 58° - 43° = 79°$$

Note that the angle $b = \angle ACB$, because this angle is in the alternate segment to b.

EXAMPLE 10

In Fig. 36.50, find the angles a and b.

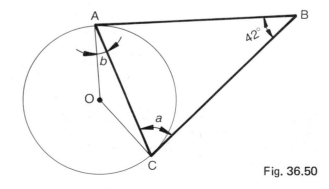

Fig. **36.50**

261

The two tangents AB and BC meet at B and hence

$$AB = BC$$

Therefore △ ABC is isosceles and

$$\angle BAC = \angle BCA$$

$$\angle BCA = \tfrac{1}{2} \times (180° - 42°) = 69°$$

$$a = 69°$$

Since OA is a radius and AB is a tangent

$$\angle OAB = 90°$$

$$b = 90° - a = 90° - 69° = 21°$$

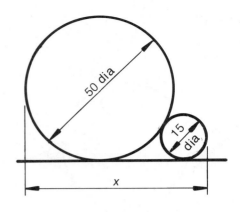

Fig. 36.52

EXAMPLE 11

In Fig. 36.51, the length of the tangent is 8 cm and the length BC is 6 cm. Find the length of the secant AC.

2) In Fig. 36.53 apply Pythagoras' theorem and hence find h.

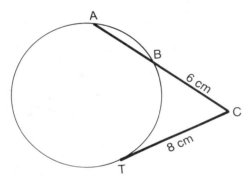

Fig. 36.51

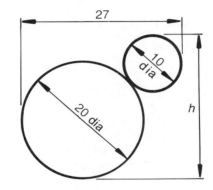

Fig. 36.53

Since the secant AC and the tangent CT meet at C,

$$AC \times BC = CT^2$$

$$AC \times 6 = 8^2$$

$$AC = \frac{64}{6} = 10\tfrac{2}{3} \text{ cm}$$

3) In Fig. 36.54, find h.

Exercise 164 — *All type C*

1) Figure 36.52 shows two circles which are just touching. Find x by using Pythagoras' theorem.

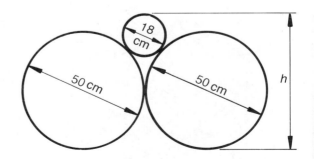

Fig. 36.54

262

4) In Fig. 36.55, find the dimension x.

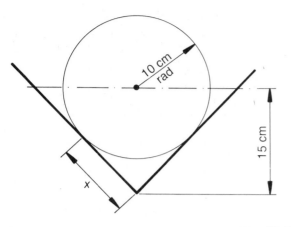

Fig. 36.55

5) In Fig. 36.56, find the angles x and y.

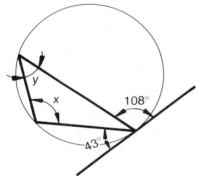

Fig. 36.56

6) In Fig. 36.57, find the angle a.

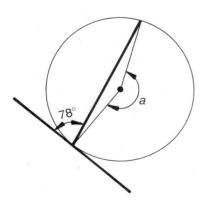

Fig. 36.57

7) In Fig. 36.58, find the angles a and b.

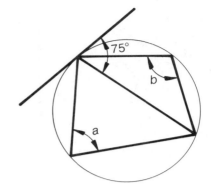

Fig. 36.58

8) In Fig. 36.59 find the angles a and b.

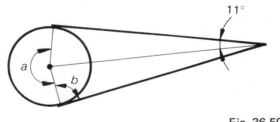

Fig. 36.59

9) In Fig. 36.60 find the angles x and y.

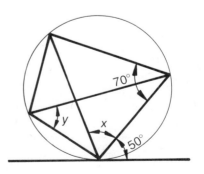

Fig. 36.60

10) In Fig. 36.61, find the angles *a*, *b* and *c*.

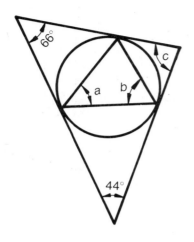

Fig. 36.61

11) In Fig. 36.62 find the length of the secant AC.

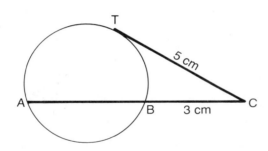

Fig. 36.62

12) In Fig. 36.63 find the length of the chord AB.

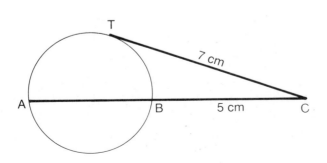

Fig. 36.63

Exercise 165 (Miscellaneous) — *Questions 1–3 type B, remainder C*

All the questions in this exercise are of the type found in examination papers at O level.

1) Two chords PQ and RS are parallel to each other and they lie on opposite sides of the centre of the circle. If PQ = 10 cm and RS = 8 cm and the circle is 12 cm radius, find the distance between the chords.

2) Three points X, Y and Z are marked on the circumference of a circle, so that YZ is a diameter. If YZ = 62 mm and XZ = 41 mm find XY.

3) Two chords AB and CD intersect at E. If CE = 3 cm, ED = 2 cm and AE = 4 cm find BE.

4) In Fig. 36.64, prove that AE . CD = CE . AB.

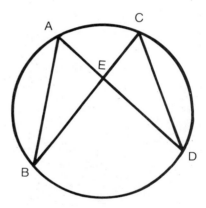

Fig. 36.64

5) In Fig. 36.65 show that WY = WX, WXYZ being a cyclic quadrilateral.

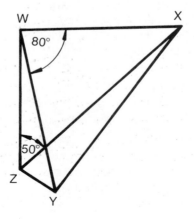

Fig. 36.65

264

6) In Fig. 36.66, O is the centre of the circle and AB is a diameter. BC = CD and ∠AOD = 70°. Calculate the angles of the quadrilateral ABCD if BC = CD.

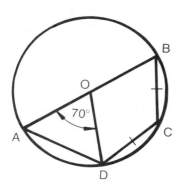

Fig. 36.66

7) In Fig. 36.67, XC is a tangent and Y is the mid-point of the arc BC. If ∠X = 28° and ∠BCA = 2∠ACX, calculate ∠CBA and ∠CBY.

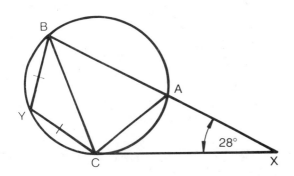

Fig. 36.67

8) Two unequal circles intersect at P and Q with their centres on opposite sides of the common chord PQ. Through P the diameters PA and PB are drawn. The tangents at A and B meet at C. Prove that:

(a) AQB is a straight line;
(b) a circle can be drawn through the points A, P, B and C;
(c) ∠APQ = ∠BPC.

9) Two circles of radii 16 cm and 9 cm touch each other externally. A common tangent to the two circles touches them at R and S. Calculate the length of RS.

10) In Fig. 36.68, BP = 8 cm, DC = 7 cm and CP = 9 cm. Calculate the lengths of the chord AB and the tangent PT.

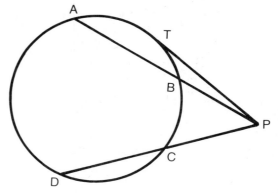

Fig. 36.68

11) In Fig. 36.69, if AB = x, BC = y and CT = t show that $x = \dfrac{t^2 - y^2}{y}$.

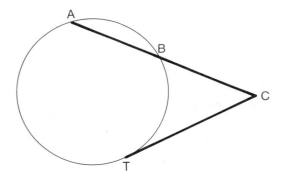

Fig. 36.69

12) The diameter of a circle, XY, is produced to T. From T a tangent is drawn which touches the circle at W. If the radius of the circle is r and XT = x find WT in terms of r and x.

SELF-TEST 36

In the following questions state the letter (or letters) corresponding to the correct answer (or answers).

1) In Fig. 36.70 the line AB is called a:

a secant   b chord

c diameter   d tangent

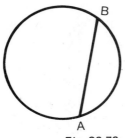

Fig. 36.70

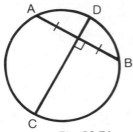

Fig. 36.71

2) In Fig. 36.71 the line AB is bisected at right-angles by the line CD. Hence CD is a:

a secant   b chord

c tangent   d diameter

3) In Fig. 36.72, O is the centre of the circle and AB = CD. It is necessarily true that:

a ABCD is a parallelogram

b ABCD is a rhombus

c ABCD is a rectangle

d ABCD is a square

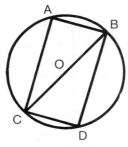

Fig. 36.72

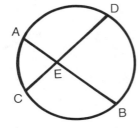

Fig. 36.73

4) In Fig. 36.73, AB and CD are two chords intersecting at E.

a AE.EB = CE.ED

b AE.ED = CE.ED

c AE.CE = ED.EB

d AE² = CE²

5) In Fig. 36.74 it is true that:

a ∠A = ∠D   b ∠A = ∠B

c ∠B = ∠D   d ∠D = ∠F

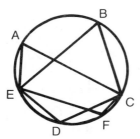

Fig. 36.74

6) A regular five sided figure is inscribed in a circle. The angle subtended at the circumference by the figure is:

a 72°   b 36°   c 54°   d 108°

7) In Fig. 36.75 it is true that:

a AB = BC   b AB = CD

c AB = AD   d BC = AD

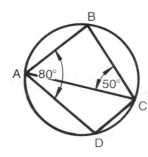

Fig. 36.75

8) In Fig. 36.76, it is true that:

a AC.OD = AO.DB   b AC.OD = DB.OC

c OB.BD = OC.AC   d AO.AC = OB.DB

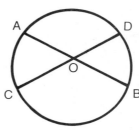

Fig. 36.76

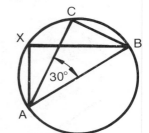

Fig. 36.77

9) In Fig. 36.77, AB is a diameter of the circle and ∠CBX = ∠ABX. Hence ∠CAX is equal to:

a 15°   b 45°   c 60°   d 30°

10) In Fig. 36.78, X is the centre of the circle. The angle B is equal to:

a 120°   b 60°   c 90°   d 80°

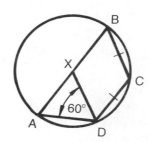

Fig. 36.78

11) In Fig. 36.79, OB = OC. Hence it is necessarily true that:

a ABCD is a parallelogram

b ABCD is a rectangle

c ABCD is a trapezium

d ABCD is a rhombus

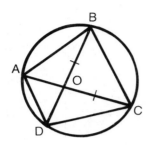

Fig. 36.79

12) In Fig. 36.80, AD and BD are tangents to the circle whose centre is O. If ∠ADB = 40° then ∠ACB is:

a 140°　　　**b** 70°　　　**c** 35°

d 55°

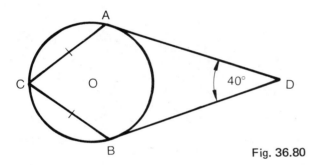

Fig. 36.80

13) In Fig. 36.81, ∠AEB = ∠BED. Hence ∠BCA is equal to:

a 94°　　　**b** 61°　　　**c** 53°

d 47°

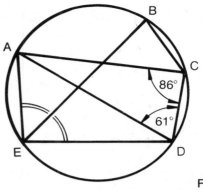

Fig. 36.81

14) In Fig. 36.82, the length of BC is:

a 18 cm　　**b** 4½ cm　　**c** 5⅓ cm　　**d** 14 cm

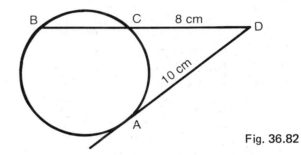

Fig. 36.82

15) In Fig. 36.83, AP is a tangent to the circle. ∠ADC is equal to:

a 102°　　**b** 78°　　**c** 70°　　**d** 110°

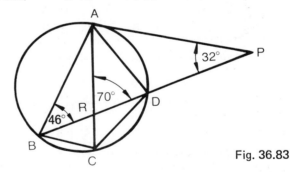

Fig. 36.83

267

Chapter 37 **Symmetry**

LINE SYMMETRY

If the rectangle ABCD (Fig. 37.1) is folded along the line GH, the rectangle ABHG will fit exactly over the rectangle GHCD. The rectangle ABCD is said to be symmetrical about the line GH which is called an *axis of symmetry*. An alternative is to say that the rectangle has line symmetry.

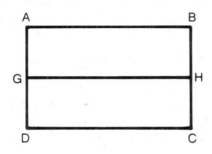

Fig. 37.1

GH is only one of the axes of symmetry of the rectangle ABCD. The line EF is another axis of symmetry (Fig. 37.2). The rectangle, therefore, has two axes of symmetry.

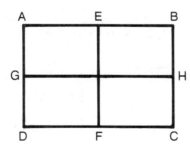

Fig. 37.2

PLANES OF SYMMETRY

If a solid figure, such as a sphere, is cut into two equal parts as shown in Fig. 37.3, the plane of the cut is called a *plane of symmetry*. The cuboid (Fig. 37.4) has been cut into two equal parts by the plane ABDC. Hence the plane ABDC is a plane of symmetry for the cuboid.

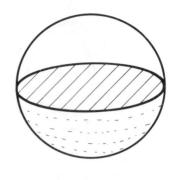

Fig. 37.3

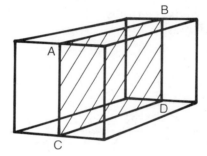

Fig. 37.4

POINT SYMMETRY

A parallelogram has no axes of symmetry. If we draw the diagonals AC and BD to intersect at O (Fig. 37.5) this point is called a *point of symmetry*. This is because if we draw the lines $V_1 V_2$, $W_1 W_2$, $X_1 X_2$ and $Y_1 Y_2$, $OV_1 = OV_2$, $OW_1 = OW_2$, $OX_1 = OX_2$ and $OY_1 = OY_2$. That is, for any line passing through O, there are two points, one on each side of O which are equidistant from O. The parallelogram is said to have *point symmetry*.

Many shapes have both line and point symmetry. Some examples are the square, rectangle and circle.

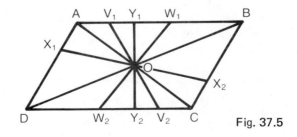

Fig. 37.5

ROTATIONAL SYMMETRY

Consider the square shown in Fig. 37.6. O is the point where the diagonals intersect. Let us draw this square on a piece of cardboard, cut it out and place it exactly over a congruent square drawn on a piece of paper. If we stick a pin

Fig. 37.6

through O and rotate the cardboard square we see that it will fit exactly over the paper square when the angle of rotation is 90°. We say that the square has *rotational symmetry of order* 4 because the angle of rotation when the shape is exactly repeated is $\frac{1}{4}$ of a revolution or $\frac{360°}{4}$.

Fig. 37.7

The shape shown in Fig. 37.7 has rotational symmetry of order 2, because the shape is exactly repeated when the shape is rotated, about O, through $180° = \frac{360°}{2}$. The shape shown in Fig. 37.8 has rotational symmetry of order 5.

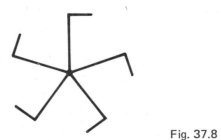

Fig. 37.8

Rotational symmetry is sometimes said to be *radial symmetry*.

Exercise 166 — *All type B*

1) Fig. 37.9 shows a square, a rhombus, an isosceles trapezium, an isosceles triangle, an equilateral triangle and a hexagon. Copy the diagrams and on each draw all the axes of symmetry. Hence write down the number of axes of symmetry that each shape possesses.

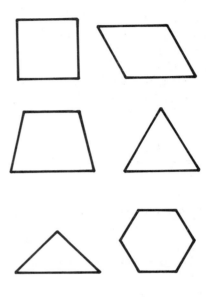

Fig. 37.9

2) Plot the points given below on graph paper and then join them up in alphabetical order. State which of the shapes has (i) line symmetry, (ii) point symmetry.
(a) A(2, 5), B(4, 12), and C(6, 10).
(b) A(4, 5), B(6, 5), C(6, 10) and D(4, 10).
(c) A(3, 5), B(7, 4), C(6, 2) and D(4, 3).
(d) A(4, 10), B(8, 10), C(10, 15) and D(6, 15).
(e) A(4, 3), B(6, 10) and D(8, 3).
(f) A(2, 2), B(6, 5), C(6, 15) and D(2, 15).
(g) A(0, 10), B(5, 5), C(10, 5), D(15, 10), E(15, 15), F(10, 20), G(5, 20) and E(0, 15).
(h) A(0, 5), B(5, 0), C(0, -5) and D(-5, 0).
(i) A(0, 2), B(2, 3), C(6, 3), D(6, 1) and E(2, 1).

3) Write down the order of the rotational symmetry for each of the shapes in question 2. If the shape does not have rotational symmetry then write 'none'.

4) How many axes of symmetry has (a) a regular hexagon, (b) a regular pentagon and (c) a regular octagon.

5) How many planes of symmetry has
(a) a cube, (b) a sphere, (c) a cone,
(d) a pyramid with a square base.

6) Fig. 37.10 shows some letters. For each
(a) write down the number of axes of symmetry,
(b) show the point of symmetry if any, (c) state
the order of rotational symmetry.

Fig. 37.10

Chapter 38 Geometrical Constructions

(1) *To divide a line AB into two equal parts.*

Construction: With A and B as centres and a radius greater than $\frac{1}{2}$AB, draw circular arcs which intersect at X and Y (Fig. 38.1). Join XY. The line XY divides AB into two equal parts and it is also perpendicular to AB.

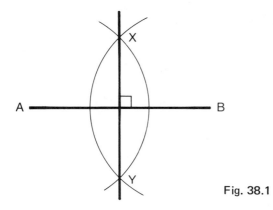

Fig. 38.1

(2) *To draw a perpendicular from a given point A on a straight line.*

Construction: With centre A and any radius draw a circle to cut the straight line at points P and Q (Fig. 38.2). With centres P and Q and a radius greater than AP (or AQ) draw circular arcs to intersect at X and Y. Join XY. This line will pass through A and it is perpendicular to the given line.

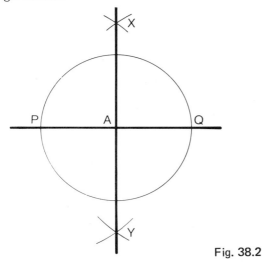

Fig. 38.2

(3) *To draw a perpendicular from a point A at the end of a line* (Fig. 38.3).

Construction: From any point O outside the line and radius OA draw a circle to cut the line at B. Draw the diameter BC and join AC. AC is perpendicular to the straight line (because the angle in a semi-circle is 90°).

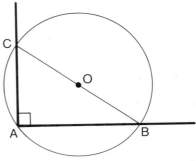

Fig. 38.3

(4) *To draw the perpendicular to a line AB from a given point P which is not on the line.*

Construction: With P as centre draw a circular arc to cut AB at points C and D. With C and D as centres and a radius greater than $\frac{1}{2}$CD, draw circular arcs to intersect at E. Join PE. The line PE is the required perpendicular (Fig. 38.4).

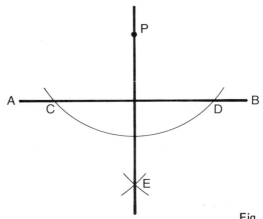

Fig. 38.4

(5) *To construct an angle of 60°.*

Construction: Draw a line AB. With A as centre and any radius draw a circular arc to cut AB at D. With D as centre and the *same* radius draw a second arc to cut the first arc at C. Join AC. The angle CAD is then 60° (Fig. 38.5).

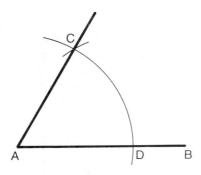

Fig. 38.5

(6) *To bisect a given angle ∠BAC.*

Construction: With centre A and any radius draw an arc to cut AB at D and AC at E. With centres D and E and a radius greater than ½DE draw arcs to intersect at F. Join AF, then AF bisects ∠BAC (Fig. 38.6). Note that by bisecting an angle of 60°, an angle of 30° is obtained. An angle of 45° is obtained by bisecting a right-angle.

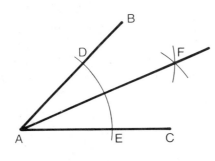

Fig. 38.6

(7) *To construct an angle equal to a given angle BAC.*

Construction: With centre A and any radius draw an arc to cut AB at D and AC at E. Draw the line XY. With centre X and the same radius draw an arc to cut XY at W. With

centre W and radius equal to DE draw an arc to cut the first arc at V. Join VX, then ∠VXW = ∠BAC (Fig. 38.7).

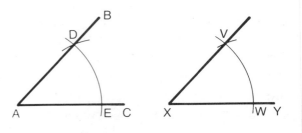

Fig. 38.7

(8) *Through a point P to draw a line parallel to a given line AB.*

Construction: Mark off any two points X and Y on AB. With centre P and radius XY draw an arc. With centre Y and radius XP draw a second arc to cut the first arc at Q. Join PQ, then PQ is parallel to AB (Fig. 38.8).

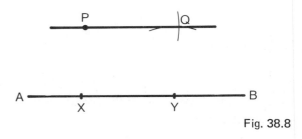

Fig. 38.8

(9) *To divide a straight line AB into a number of equal parts.*

Construction: Suppose that AB has to be divided into four equal parts. Draw AC at any angle to AB. Set off on AC, four equal parts AP, PQ, QR, RS of any convenient length. Join SB. Draw RV, QW and PX each parallel to SB. Then AX = XW = WV = VB (Fig. 38.9).

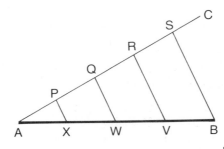

Fig. 38.9

(10) *To draw the circumscribed circle of a given triangle ABC.*

Construction: Construct the perpendicular bisectors of the sides AB and AC (using construction 1) so that they intersect at O. With centre O and radius AO draw a circle which is the required circumscribed circle (Fig. 38.10).

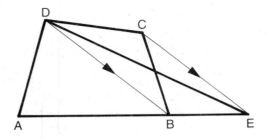

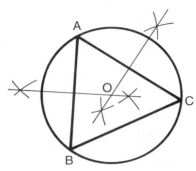

Fig. 38.10

(11) *To draw the inscribed circle of a given triangle ABC.*

Construction: Construct the internal bisectors of ∠B and ∠C (using construction 6) to intersect at O. With centre O draw the inscribed circle of the triangle ABC (Fig. 38.11).

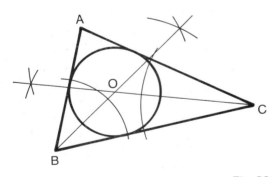

Fig. 38.11

(12) *To draw a triangle whose area is equal to that of a given quadrilateral ABCD.*

Construction: Join BD and draw CE parallel to BD to meet AB produced at E. Then ADE is a triangle whose area is equal to that of the quadrilateral ABCD (Fig. 38.12).

Fig. 38.12

Proof: As DBE and CDB are equal in area. Add to each of these triangles the area ADB.

(13) *To draw a square whose area is equal to that of a given rectangle ABCD.*

Construction: Produce AB to E so that BC is equal to BE. Draw a circle with AE as diameter to meet BC (or BC produced) at F. Then BF is a side of the required square (Fig. 38.13).

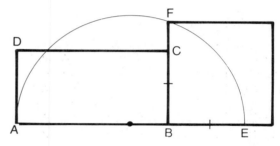

Fig. 38.13

(14) *To draw a tangent to a circle at a given point P on the circumference of the circle.*

Construction: O is the centre of the given circle. Join OP. Using construction 3 draw the line PT which is perpendicular to OP. PT is the required tangent, since at the point of tangency, a tangent is perpendicular to a radius (Fig. 38.14).

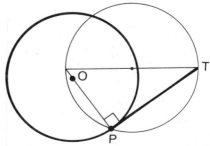

Fig. 38.14

(15) *To draw the segment of a circle so that it contains a given angle* θ.

Construction: Draw the lines AB and AX so that ∠BAX = θ. From A draw AM perpendicular to AX. Draw the perpendicular bisector of AB to meet AM at O. With centre O and radius OA draw the circular arc which terminates at A and B. This is the required segment (Fig. 38.15).

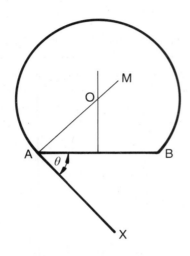

Fig. 38.15

(16) *To construct a triangle given the lengths of each of the three sides.*

Construction: Suppose $a = 6$ cm, $b = 3$ cm and $c = 4$ cm. Draw BC = 6 cm. With centre B and radius 4 cm draw a circular arc. With centre C and radius 3 cm draw a circular arc to cut the first arc at A. Join AB and AC. Then ABC is the required triangle (Fig. 38.16).

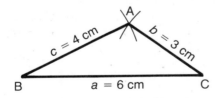

Fig. 38.16

(17) *To construct a triangle given two sides and the included angle between the two sides.*

Construction: Suppose $b = 5$ cm and $c = 6$ cm and ∠A = 60°. Draw AB = 6 cm and draw AX such that ∠BAX = 60°. Along AX mark off

AC = 5 cm. Then ABC is the required triangle (Fig. 38.17).

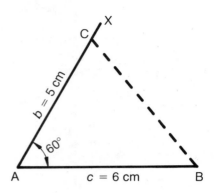

Fig. 38.17

(18) *To construct a triangle (or triangles) given the lengths of two of the sides and an angle which is not the included angle between the two given sides.*

(a) *Construction:* Suppose $a = 5$ cm, $b = 6$ cm and ∠B = 60°. Draw BC = 5 cm and draw BX such that ∠CBX = 60°. With centre C and radius of 6 cm describe a circular arc to cut BX at A. Join CA then ABC is the required triangle ABC (Fig. 38.18).

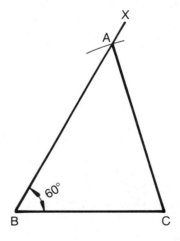

Fig. 38.18

(b) Suppose that $a = 5$ cm, $b = 4.5$ cm and ∠B = 60°. The construction is the same as before but the circular arc drawn with C as centre now cuts BX at two points A and A₁. This means that there are two triangles which meet the given conditions, i.e., △s ABC and

274

A_1 BC (Fig. 38.19). For this reason this case is often called the *ambiguous case*.

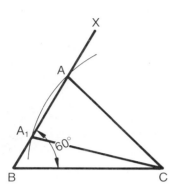

Fig. 38.19

(19) *To construct a common tangent to two given circles.*

Construction: The two given circles have centres X and Y and radii x and y respectively (Fig. 38.20). With centre X draw a circle whose radius is $(x - y)$. With diameter XY draw an arc to cut the previously drawn circle at M. Join XM and produce to P at the circumference of the circle. Draw YQ parallel to XP, Q being at the circumference of the circle. Join PQ which is the required tangent.

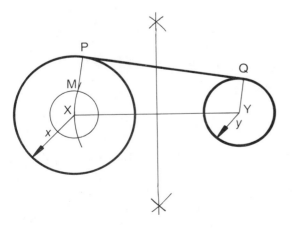

Fig. 38.20

(20) *To construct a pair of tangents from an external point to a given circle* (Fig. 38.21).

Construction: It is required to draw a pair of tangents from the point P to the circle centre O. Join OP. With OP as diameter draw a circle to cut the given circle at points A and B. Join PA and PB which are the required pair of tangents.

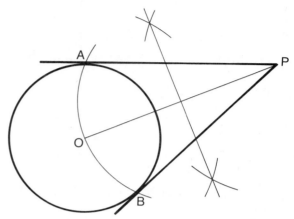

Fig. 38.21

Exercise 167 — *All type B*

1) Construct a triangle ABC with AB = 5 cm, AC = 4 cm and ∠CAB = 45°.

2) Construct the point P inside the triangle ABC in question 1, so that it is equi-distant from the three sides of the triangle.

3) Draw the line AB 4.6 cm long and construct the isosceles triangle ABC with AC = 7.2 cm. Hence construct the rhombus ABCD.

4) Draw the line AB = 8 cm. At A construct an angle of 60° and at B an angle of 45°. Hence complete the triangle ABC.

5) Construct an angle of 60°. Bisect this angle and so obtain an angle of 30°.

6) Draw a line AB = 8 cm. Construct the perpendicular bisector of AB to cut AB at E. Mark off EC = 3 cm and ED = 3 cm. Join A and C, C and B, B and D and D and A to form the quadrilateral ABCD.

(a) Name the quadrilateral ABCD.

(b) State the number of axes of symmetry that ABCD possesses.

7) Construct an angle of 60° and hence construct a regular hexagon.

8) Draw a line AB = 10 cm. At A construct a right-angle and hence construct a rectangle having dimensions 10 cm by 5 cm.

9) Draw WX = 5 cm. At W construct an angle of 60°. Along the inclined arm of this angle mark off WZ = 4 cm. Hence complete a drawing of the parallelogram WXYZ.

10) Construct a rectangle ABCD in which AB = 5.8 cm and the diagonal AC = 7.4 cm.

11) Construct a trapezium AXBC in which BX is parallel to AC and ∠CAX = 60°. Measure the distance AX.

12) Construct an equilateral triangle having sides 5 cm long.

13) Construct △ ABC with AB = 8 cm, BC = 6 cm and AC = 11.2 cm.

14) Construct the inscribed circle of △ ABC (in question 13).

15) Construct △ ABC in which AB = 8 cm, AC = 7 cm and ∠CAB = 45°. Construct the circumcircle of this triangle.

16) Draw a line AB = 9 cm and divide it into 7 equal parts.

17) Draw the line XY = 7 cm. Mark off PX = 3 cm. Erect a perpendicular through P. Mark off PZ = 5 cm, Z being above XY. Hence complete the triangle XYZ.

18) Draw the rectangle ABCD with AB = 6 cm and AD = 4 cm. Construct a square whose area is equal to that of the rectangle ABCD. Measure the side of your square.

19) Draw two circles whose centres are 8 cm apart and whose diameters are 6 cm and 8 cm. Draw the common tangent to these circles.

20) Draw a circle, centre O, whose radius is 4 cm. Mark off any point P so that OP = 8 cm. Construct a pair of tangents from P to the circle.

Chapter 39 Loci

A *locus* is a set of positions traced out by a point which moves according to some law. For instance the locus of a point which moves so that it is always 3 cm from a given fixed point is a circle whose radius is 3 cm. It often helps if we mark off a few points according to the given law. By doing this we may gain some idea of what the locus will be. Sometimes three or four points will be sufficient but sometimes ten or more points may be required before the locus can be recognised.

EXAMPLE 1

Given a straight line AB of length 6 cm, find the locus of a point P so that ∠ APB is always a right angle.

By drawing a number of points $P_1, P_2, \ldots$, etc. so that $\angle AP_1B, \angle AP_2B \ldots$ etc. (Fig. 39.1) are all right angles it appears that the locus is a circle with AB as a diameter. We now try to prove that this is so.

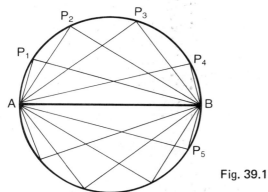

Fig. 39.1

Since the angle in a semi-circle is a right-angle, all angles subtended by the diameter AB at the circumference of the circle will be right-angles. Hence the locus of P is a circle with AB as diameter.

Exercise 168 — *All type B*

1) Find the locus of a point P which is always 5 cm from a fixed straight line of infinite length.

2) Find the locus of a point P which moves so that it is always 3 cm from a given straight line AB which is 8 cm long.

3) XYZ is a triangle whose base XY is fixed. If XY = 5 cm and the area of △ XYZ = 10 cm² find the locus of Z.

4) Given a square of 10 cm side, find all the points which are 8 cm from two of the vertices. How many points are there?

5) Find all the points which are 5 cm from each of two intersecting straight lines inclined at an angle of 45°. How many points are there?

STANDARD LOCI

The following standard loci should be remembered.

(1) The locus of a point equi-distant from two given points A and B is the perpendicular bisector of AB (Fig. 39.2).

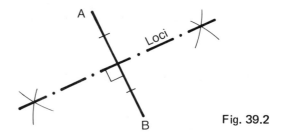

Fig. 39.2

(2) The locus of a point equi-distant from the arms of an angle is the bisector of the angle (Fig. 39.3).

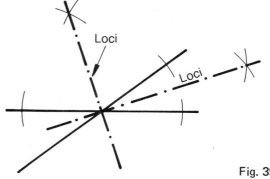

Fig. 39.3

INTERSECTING LOCI

Frequently two pieces of information are given about the position of a point. Each piece of information should then be dealt with separately, since any attempt to comply with the two conditions at the same time will lead to a trial and error method which is not acceptable. Each piece of information will partially locate the point and the intersection of the two loci will determine the required position of the point.

EXAMPLE 2

A point P lies 3 cm from a given straight line and it is also equi-distant from two fixed points not on the line and not perpendicular to it. Find the two possible positions of P.

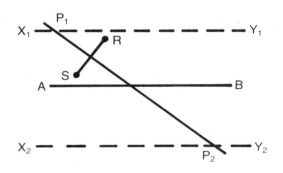

Fig. 39.4

Condition 1. The point P lies 3 cm from the given straight line (AB in Fig. 39.4). To meet this condition draw two straight lines $X_2 Y_2$ and $X_1 Y_1$ parallel to AB and on either side of it.

Condition 2. P is equi-distant from the two fixed points (R and S in Fig. 39.4). To meet this condition we draw the perpendicular bisector of RS (since $\triangle$ RSP must be isosceles).

The intersections of the two loci give the required position of the point P. These are the points P_1 and P_2 in Fig. 39.4.

Exercise 169

1) Find the locus of the centre P of a circle of constant radius 3 cm which passes through a fixed point A.

2) Find the locus of the centre, Q, of a circle of constant radius 2 cm which touches externally a fixed circle, centre B and radius 4 cm.

3) Find the locus of the centre of a variable circle which passes through two fixed points A and B.

4) AB is a fixed line of length 8 cm and P is a variable point. The distance of P from the middle point of AB is 5 cm and the distance of P from AB is 4 cm. Construct a point P so that both of these conditions are satisfied. State the number of possible positions of P.

5) X is a point inside a circle, centre C, and Q is the mid-point of a chord which passes through X. Determine the locus of Q as the chord varies. If CX is 5 cm and the radius of the circle is 8 cm construct the locus of Q accurately and hence construct a chord which passes through X and has its mid-point 3 cm from C.

6) XY is a fixed line of given length. State the locus of a point P which moves so that the size of $\angle$ XPY is constant and sketch the locus.

7) AB is a fixed line of 4 cm and R is a point such that the area of $\triangle$ ABR is 5 cm². S is the mid-point of AR. State the locus of R and the locus of S.

8) T is a fixed point outside a fixed circle whose centre is O. A variable line through T meets the circle at X and Y. Show that the locus of the mid-point of XY is an arc of the circle on OT as diameter.

9) Chords of a circle, centre C, are drawn through a fixed point A within the circle. Show that the mid-points of all these chords lie on a circle and state the position of the centre of the circle.

10) Draw a circle centre O and radius 4 cm. Construct the locus of the mid-points of all chords of this circle which are 6.5 cm long.

Proofs of Theorems

Any of the following proofs may be required. If the diagrams and constructions are remembered the proof can usually be reproduced.

THEOREM 1

When the side of a triangle is produced the exterior angle so formed is equal to the sum of the opposite interior angles.

Given: $\triangle$ ABC with the side BC produced to D.

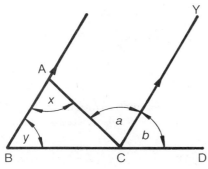

Fig. 1

To prove: $\angle$ ACD = $\angle$ CBA + $\angle$ BAC.

Construction: Draw CY parallel to AB.

Proof: In Fig. 1,

   $x = a$ (alternate angles, AB $\parallel$ CY)

   $y = b$ (corresponding angles, AB $\parallel$ CY)

By addition, $x + y = a + b$

i.e. $\angle$ BAC + $\angle$ CBA = $\angle$ ACD

THEOREM 2

The straight line joining the mid-points of two sides of a triangle is parallel to the third side and equal to half the length of the third side.

Given: AD = BD   and   AE = EC.

To prove: DE is parallel to BC and DE = $\frac{1}{2}$BC.

Construction: From B draw a line parallel to EC to meet ED produced at X (Fig. 2).

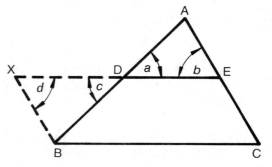

Fig. 2

Proof: In $\triangle$s ADE and XDB

   AD = BD   (given)

   $a = c$ (vertically opp. angles)

   $b = d$ (alternate angles: AE $\parallel$ BX)

$\therefore$ $\triangle$ ADE $\equiv$ $\triangle$ XDB

Hence   DX = DE   and   BX = AE.

But   AE = EC   (given).

$\therefore$ BX = EC

That is, BX is equal and parallel to EC. Hence XECB is a parallelogram.

$\therefore$ XE = BC

$\therefore$ DE = $\frac{1}{2}$BC

Also since XE is parallel to BC, DE is parallel to BC.

THEOREM 3

Parallelograms on the same base and between the same parallels are equal in area.

Given: DCEF is a straight line and ABCD and ABFE are parallelograms (Fig. 3).

279

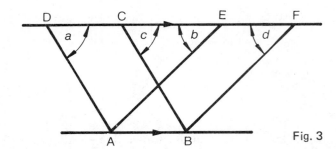

Fig. 3

To prove: ABCD and ABFE are equal in area.

Proof: In △s ADE and BCF.

AD = BC   (opp. sides of a parallelogram)

  a = c   (corresponding angles: AD ∥ BC)

  b = d   (corresponding angles: AE ∥ BF)

∴   △ ADE ≡ △ BCF

Congruent triangles are equal in every respect.
Hence △s ADE and BCF are equal in area.

  Area ABCD = area ABFD — area BCF

  Area ABFE = area ABFD — area ADE

∴   area ABCD = area ABFE

THEOREM 4

Theorem of Pythagoras.

Given: △ABC with ∠ B a right-angle (Fig. 4).

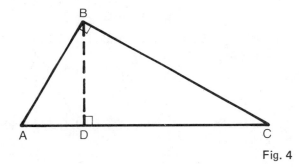

Fig. 4

To prove: $AC^2 = AB^2 + BC^2$.

Construction: Draw BD perpendicular to AC.

Proof: In △s DBA and BCA,

  ∠ ADB = ∠ ABC = 90°

  ∠ BAC is common

Hence △s DBA and BCA are similar.

In △s BCA and DCB,

  ∠ ABC = ∠ BDC

  ∠ BCD is common

Hence △s BCA and DCB are similar.

Therefore △s DBA, BCA and DCB are all similar.

In △s DBA and BCA,

$$\frac{AB}{AC} = \frac{AD}{AB} \quad \text{or} \quad AB^2 = AC \cdot AD$$

In △s DCB and BCA,

$$\frac{BC}{CD} = \frac{AC}{BC} \quad \text{or} \quad BC^2 = AC \cdot CD$$

$$AB^2 + BC^2 = AC \cdot AD + AC \cdot CD$$
$$= AC(AD + CD)$$
$$= AC \cdot AC$$
$$\therefore \quad AB^2 + BC^2 = AC^2$$

THEOREM 5

The angle at the centre of a circle is twice any angle at the circumference, standing on the same arc.

Given: AOB, an arc of a circle centre O. P is any point on the remaining arc (Fig. 5).

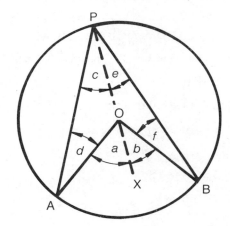

Fig. 5

To prove: ∠ AOB = 2 ∠ APB.

Construction: Join PO and produce it to X.

Proof: Since

OA = OP   (radii)

  c = d

  a = c + d = 2c   (exterior angle of △ APO).

280

Similarly

$b = e + f = 2e$ (exterior angle of $\triangle$ BPO).

Hence $a + b = 2c + 2e = 2(c + e)$

i.e. $\angle$ AOB $= 2 \angle$ APB.

THEOREM 6

If two chords of a circle intersect inside or outside a circle the product of the segments of one chord is equal to the product of the segments of the other chord.

Given: AB and CD are two chords of a circle intersecting at E (Fig. 6).

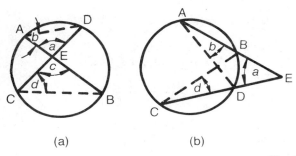

(a)   (b)

Fig. 6

To prove: AE . EB = CE . ED.

Construction: Join AD and BC.

Proof: In $\triangle$s AED and CEB,

$b = d$ (angles on arc BD)

$a = c$ (vertically opp. angles in Fig. (6a))

(or a is common in Fig. (6b)).

$\therefore$ in both diagrams AED and CEB are similar triangles.

Hence $\dfrac{AE}{CE} = \dfrac{ED}{EB}$

or   AE . EB = CE . ED.

THEOREM 7

If from a point outside a circle two lines are drawn, one a secant and the other a tangent to the circle, then the square on the tangent is equal to the rectangle contained by the whole secant and that part of it outside the circle.

Given: Secant ABC and tangent CT (Fig. 7).

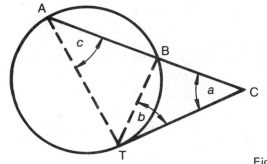

Fig. 7

To prove: $CT^2 = AC . CB$.

Construction: Join AT and BT.

Proof: In $\triangle$s CBT and CTA,

a is common

$b = c$ (alternate segment)

$\therefore$ $\triangle$s CBT and CTA are similar.

Hence $\dfrac{CB}{CT} = \dfrac{CT}{AC}$

or $AC . CB = CT^2$.

THEOREM 8

The ratio of the areas of similar triangles is equal to the ratio of the squares on corresponding sides.

Given: Two similar triangles ABC and XYZ.

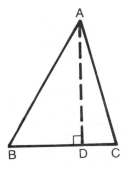 

Fig. 8

To prove: $\dfrac{\text{area of } \triangle \text{ ABC}}{\text{area of } \triangle \text{ XYZ}} = \dfrac{BC^2}{YZ^2}.$

Construction: Draw the altitudes AD and XN of the two triangles.

Proof: area of $\triangle$ ABC $= \frac{1}{2}$BC . AD

area of $\triangle$ XYZ $= \frac{1}{2}$YZ . XN.

281

In $\triangle$s ABD and XYN,

$$\angle B = \angle Y \quad \text{(given)}$$

$$\angle D = \angle N = 90°$$

$\therefore$ $\triangle$s ABD and XYN are similar.

Hence $\dfrac{AD}{XN} = \dfrac{AB}{XY} = \dfrac{BC}{YZ}$

$$\dfrac{\text{area } \triangle ABC}{\text{area } \triangle XYZ} = \dfrac{\frac{1}{2}BC \cdot AD}{\frac{1}{2}YZ \cdot XN} = \dfrac{BC \cdot AD}{YZ \cdot XN}$$

$$= \dfrac{BC \cdot BC}{YZ \cdot YZ} = \dfrac{BC^2}{YZ^2}$$

$\left(\text{since} \quad \dfrac{AD}{XN} = \dfrac{BC}{YZ}\right).$

THEOREM 9

The bisector of any angle of a triangle divides the opposite side in the ratio of the sides containing the angle.

Given: $\triangle$ ABC with AD bisecting $\angle$ CAB (Fig. 9).

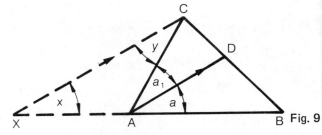

Fig. 9

To prove: $\dfrac{BD}{DC} = \dfrac{BA}{AC}.$

Construction: From C draw a line parallel to AD to meet BA produced at X.

Proof:

$a = x$ (corresponding angles: AD $\parallel$ CX)

$a_1 = y$ (alternate angles: AD $\parallel$ CX)

but $a = a_1$ (given)

$\therefore \qquad\qquad x = y.$

Hence $\triangle$ CXA is isosceles and AC = AX also, since AD is parallel to CX.

$$\dfrac{BD}{DC} = \dfrac{BA}{AX}$$

$\therefore \qquad \dfrac{BD}{DC} = \dfrac{BA}{AC}$

Miscellaneous Exercise

Exercise 170

This exercise is divided into two sections A and B. The questions in Section A are intended to be done very quickly, but those in Section B should take about 20 minutes each to complete. All the questions are of the type found in O Level examination papers.

SECTION A

1) Draw (a) a rectangle and (b) a parallelogram and show all the lines of symmetry (if any). If there are none then write 'none' against your diagram. (A.E.B. 1975)

2) The diagram (Fig. 1) shows two sides of a quadrilateral ABCD which is symmetrical about the point O. Complete the quadrilateral. (A.E.B. 1975)

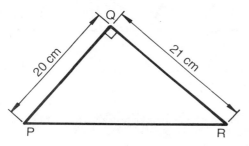

Fig. 1

3) In the triangle PQR (Fig. 2), the lengths of PQ and QR are 20 cm and 21 cm respectively and angle Q is a right angle.

Calculate:
(a) the area of the triangle,
(b) the length of PR. (J.M.B.)

4) AB and BC are two adjacent sides of a regular 12 sided figure. The perpendicular from C meets AB produced at D. Calculate ∠ BCD. (L)

5) ABCDEF is a regular six-sided figure and ABXY is a square in the same plane. Calculate the size of the obtuse angle CXY (Fig. 3). (A.E.B. 1976)

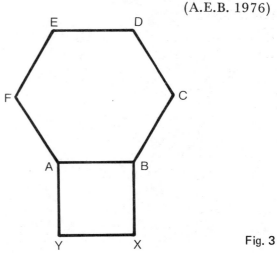

Fig. 3

6) In Fig. 4, O is the centre of the circle, angle POQ = 64°, angle TQR = 72° and PQT is a straight line. Calculate the value of y. (A.E.B. 1976)

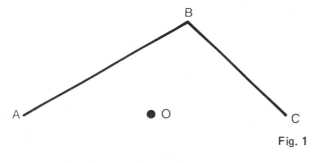

Fig. 2

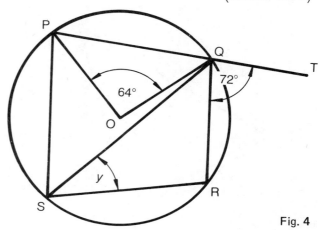

Fig. 4

7) In this question use ruler and compasses only and show all construction lines clearly. Construct △XYZ with YZ = 6 cm, XY = 5 cm and ∠XYZ = 60°. Construct the perpendicular from X to ZY to meet ZY at W. Find, by measurement, the length of XW. Construct the point T such that XYTW is a parallelogram and find, by measurement, the length of XT. (L)

8) Chords AB and CD of a circle intersect inside the circle at point X. Given that AX = 4 cm, XB = 8 cm and CX = 5 cm, calculate the length of CD. (J.M.B.)

9) Calculate the size of each interior angle of a regular 15 sided polygon. (A.E.B. 1975)

10) In Fig. 5, O is the centre of the circle. Find x. (A.E.B. 1975)

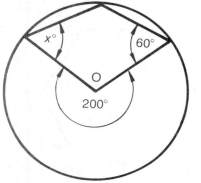

Fig. 5

11) In Fig. 6, ABC is an equilateral triangle and AE, EC and CD are equal in length. Angle ACE is 50° and BCD is a straight line. Calculate angle AED. (A.E.B. 1975)

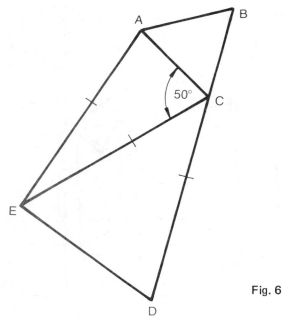

Fig. 6

12) In Fig. 7, ABC is a triangle and CD is one trisector of angle ACB. Given that ∠DBC = 51°, ∠BAC = 75°, ∠ACD = x and ∠DCB = 2x, calculate:

(a) the value of x,

(b) the size of angle BDC. (J.M.B.)

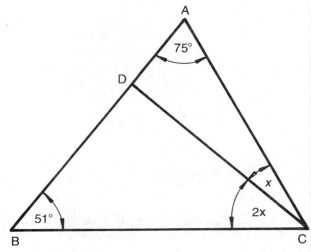

Fig. 7

13) In Fig. 8, PT is the tangent at T to the circle, A and B are points on the circumference of the circle and AB = AT. Given that ∠BTP = 34°, calculate the size of ∠ABT. (J.M.B.)

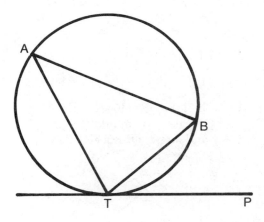

Fig. 8

14) The angles of a triangle are in the ratio 2 : 3 : 4. Calculate the size, in degrees, of the largest angle. (A.E.B. 1976)

15) The figure ABCD is a rhombus (Fig. 9). Find y if $x = 29°$.   (A.E.B. 1976)

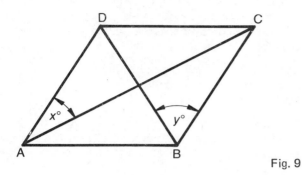

Fig. 9

16) The centre of the circle in Fig. 10 is O. Calculate the value of x.   (A.E.B. 1976)

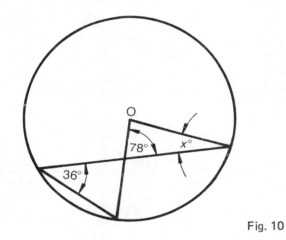

Fig. 10

17) Draw a triangle ABC with AB = 12.0 cm, BC = 11.5 cm and $\angle$ B = 45°. *Without using a protractor*, construct a circle of radius 4 cm which touches AB and AC.   (J.M.B.)

18) Copy Fig. 11 and draw all the lines of symmetry.   (A.E.B. 1976)

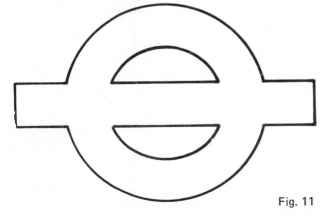

Fig. 11

19) The straight lines AB, CD and EF are parallel (Fig. 12). Given that angle EKG = 47° and that the straight line LHG is at right angles to GK, calculate angle LHB (marked as $x°$).   (A.E.B. 1976)

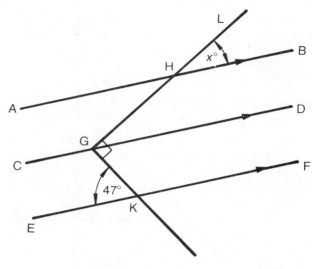

Fig. 12

20) In $\triangle$ ABC the internal bisector of $\angle$ ABC meets AC at P. Given that AB = 16 cm, BC = 8 cm and AC = 15 cm, calculate the length of PC.   (L)

21) Using ruler and compasses only construct a quadrilateral ABCD in which AB = 6 cm, BC = 12 cm, $\angle$ B = 60°, $\angle$ D = 90° and AD = DC. Measure and write down the length of the diagonal BD.   (L)

22) In Fig. 13, AP and BP are diameters of two equal circles which intersect at P and Q. Prove that the triangles APQ and BPQ are congruent.   (L)

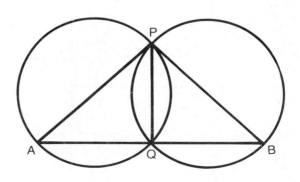

Fig. 13

23) In Fig. 14, $\angle DBC = \angle BAD$ and ADC is a straight line. State which two triangles are similar. If AB = 7 cm, BC = 6 cm and DC = 4 cm, calculate the lengths of AC and BD. (L)

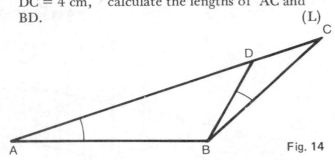

Fig. 14

24) In Fig. 15, AB is parallel to DC, AB = AD and $\angle C = 90°$. Prove that $\angle DAB = 2\angle DBC$. (L)

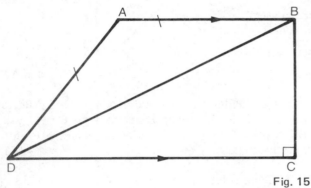

Fig. 15

25) The diagrams (Fig. 16) show (a) an equilateral triangle, (b) a regular pentagon, (c) a rhombus. Sketch the diagrams and show, by dotted lines, all the lines of symmetry in each case.

(a) (b)

(c)

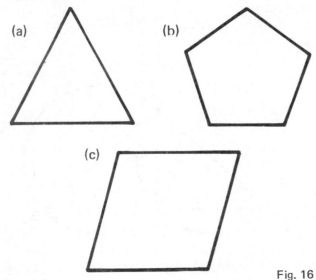

Fig. 16

26) Construct a $\triangle ABC$ in which AB = 12 cm, AC = 8 cm and BC = 10 cm. On the same diagram construct a $\triangle ABD$, equal in area to $\triangle ABC$, such that $\angle ABD = 98°$. Measure the length of BD, giving your answer correct to the nearest mm. (L)

27) PQR is a triangle right-angled at P. If PN is the perpendicular from P to QR, prove that $PN^2 = PR.PQ$. (L)

28) The diameter AOB of the circle ABC is produced to meet the tangent CD at the point D. Given that $\angle ADC = 36°$, calculate $\angle DAC$ (see Fig. 17). (L)

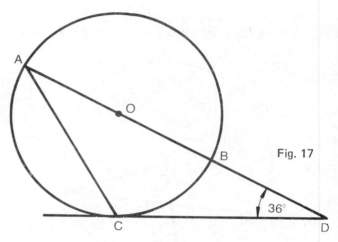

Fig. 17

29) ABCD is a cyclic quadrilateral, AD is a diameter of the circle (Fig. 18), AB = BC and $\angle BCA = 27°$. Calculate $\angle CDA$ and $\angle CAD$. (L)

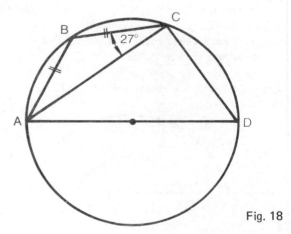

Fig. 18

30) Construct the rectangle ABCD in which AB = 6.2 cm and BC = 4.6 cm. Without calculation and using ruler and compasses only, construct a square equal in area to the rectangle ABCD. Measure the diagonal of the square. (L)

286

SECTION B

31) Prove that the internal bisector of an angle of a triangle divides the opposite side in the ratio of the sides containing the angle.

In Fig. 19, the internal and external bisectors of the angle A of △ ABC meet BC and BC produced at X and Y respectively. Given that AB = 8 cm, AC = 4 cm, and BC = 6 cm, calculate the lengths of BX and BY.

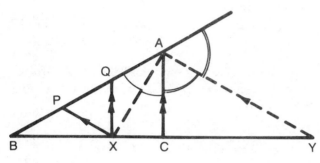

Fig. 19

If, also, XP is drawn parallel to YA, and XQ is drawn parallel to CA, meeting AB at P and Q respectively, prove that BP = PQ = QA.
(L)

32) Fig. 20 shows two unequal circles, with centres X and Y, which touch externally at P. An exterior common tangent touches the circles at A and B respectively and the common tangent at P cuts AB at C. Prove that:

(a) AC = BC,
(b) C is the centre of the circumcircle of △ APB,
(c) ∠ APB is a right angle,
(d) XP is a tangent to the circumcircle of △ APB,
(e) If PXZ is a diameter, then ZA is parallel to PB.
(L)

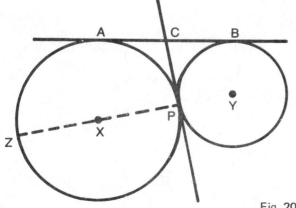

Fig. 20

33) A circle is drawn through the vertices B and C of △ ABC and cuts the sides AB, AC at M, N respectively. Prove that △ ANM and △ ABC are similar.

Given that M is the mid-point of AB, BC = 5 cm, ∠ ABC = 81° and ∠ ACB = 69°, calculate the lengths of (a) AM, (b) AC, (c) MN. (L)

34) Fig. 21 shows a circle, centre C, drawn through the vertices B and D of the rhombus ABCD. The side AD is produced to meet the circle again at E and the lines EB and CD intersect at H. Given the angle DAB = $x°$, calculate, in terms of x, the angles BCD, CDE, BED and DHB.

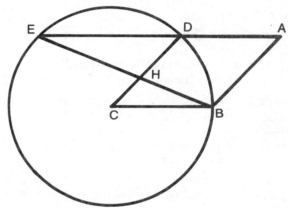

Fig. 21

Given the length AD = 15 cm, the length DE = 25 cm and the bisector of the angle EDC meets EC at Y, calculate:

(a) the ratio of the areas of the triangles CHB and DHE,
(b) the ratio of the areas of the triangles ADB and EDB,
(c) the length EY. (A.E.B. 1977)

35) (a) In a circle two chords AXB and CXD meet at a point X. Given that AX = 5 cm, CX = 9 cm, AC = 7 cm and BX = 7.2 cm, calculate:

(i) the length of DX,
(ii) the ratio of the area of the triangle AXC to the area of the triangle BXD.

Given that the bisector of the angle AXC meets AC at E, calculate the length of AE.

287

(b) *Use ruler and compasses only:*

(i) to construct a rectangle XYZW in which
XW = 6 cm and the diagonal
YW = 13 cm,

(ii) to find the length of the side of a square
which has an area equal to that of the
rectangle XYZW. Measure and state this
length. (A.E.B. 1976)

36) In a triangle ABC, the side AB is 21 cm.
Points D and E are taken on AB and AC
respectively such that AD is 7 cm, AE is
6 cm and DE is 8 cm and parallel to BC.
Calculate:

(a) the length BC,
(b) the ratio of the area of the triangle AED to
the area of the trapezium BDEC.

A point P is taken on AE such that DP
bisects the angle ADE, and DP produced
meets the line through A, parallel to BC, at
Q. Calculate:

(c) the length EP,
(d) the length AQ,
(e) the ratio of the area of triangle DPE to the
area of the triangle PAD. (A.E.B. 1977)

37) Fig. 22 shows a triangle ABC inscribed in
a circle with AB as a diameter. The tangent at
C meets AB produced at D; the point E is
on the line BD such that BE = BC. Given
the angle DCE = $x°$ and angle BCE = $y°$
calculate, in terms of x and y only, the angles
CEB, CBA and CAB. Hence find the value of
y in terms of x.

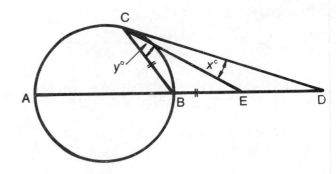

Fig. 22

The length DC = 7 cm and the radius of the
circle is 2 cm. Show that the length DB (l cm)
is given by

$$l^2 + 4l - 49 = 0,$$

and hence find the value of l, correct to two
significant figures. (A.E.B. 1976)

38) (a) Using ruler and protractor, draw a
rectangle ABCD with AB = 9 cm and
BC = 5 cm. *Using ruler and compasses only*,
construct a square BPQR equal in area to the
rectangle. Measure and state the length of the
diagonal BQ.

(b) *Using ruler and compasses only*, construct a
triangle DEF with DE = 12 cm,
EF = 11 cm and DF = 10 cm. Also
construct the inscribed circle of the triangle
DEF. Measure and state the radius of this circle.
(A.E.B. 1976)

Chapter 40 **Trigonometry**

THE NOTATION FOR A RIGHT-ANGLED TRIANGLE

The sides of a right-angled triangle are given special names. In Fig. 40.1 the side AB lies opposite the right-angle and it is called the *hypotenuse*. The side BC lies opposite to the angle A and it is called the side opposite to A. The side AC is called the side adjacent to A.

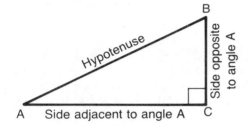

Fig. 40.1

When we consider the angle B (Fig. 40.2) the side AB is still the hypotenuse but AC is now the side opposite to B and BC is the side adjacent to B.

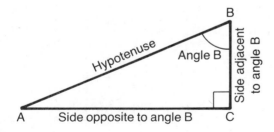

Fig. 40.2

THE TRIGONOMETRICAL RATIOS

Consider any angle θ which is bounded by the lines OA and OB as shown in Fig. 40.3. Take any point P on the boundary line OB. From P draw line PM perpendicular to OA to meet it at the point M. Then,

the ratio $\dfrac{MP}{OP}$ is called the sine of $\angle$ AOB

the ratio $\dfrac{OM}{OP}$ is called the cosine of $\angle$ AOB

and

the ratio $\dfrac{MP}{OM}$ is called the tangent of $\angle$ AOB

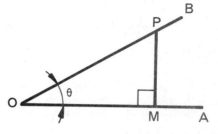

Fig. 40.3

THE SINE OF AN ANGLE

The abbreviation 'sin' is usually used for sine. In any right-angled triangle (Fig. 40.4), the sine of angle

$$= \frac{\text{side opposite the angle}}{\text{hypotenuse}}$$

$$\sin A = \frac{BC}{AC}$$

$$\sin C = \frac{AB}{AC}$$

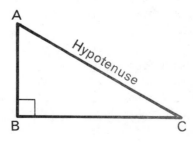

Fig. 40.4

289

EXAMPLE 1

Find by drawing a suitable triangle the value of sin 30°.

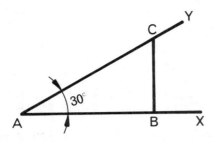

Fig. 40.5

Draw the lines AX and AY which intersect at A so that the angle ∠YAX = 30° as shown in Fig. 40.5. Along AY measure off AC equal to 1 unit (say 10 cm) and from C draw CB perpendicular to AX. Measure CB which will be found to be 0.5 units (5 cm in this case).

Therefore $\sin 30° = \dfrac{5}{10} = 0.5$.

Although it is possible to find the sines of angles by drawing, this is inconvenient and not very accurate. Tables of sines have been calculated which allow us to find the sine of any angle. Part of this table is reproduced below and in full, with the other trigonometrical tables, at the end of the book.

READING THE TABLE OF SINES OF ANGLES

(1) *To find* sin 12°. The sine of an angle with an exact number of degrees is shown in the column headed 0. Thus sin 12° = 0.2079.

(2) *To find* sin 12° 36′. The value will be found under the column headed 36′. Thus sin 12° 36′ = 0.2181.

(3) *To find* sin 12° 40′. If the number of minutes is not an exact multiple of 6 we use the table of mean differences. Now 12° 36′ = 0.2181 and 40′ is 4′ more than 36′. Looking in the mean difference column headed 4 we find the value 11. This is *added* on to the sine of 12° 36′ and we have sin 12° 40′ = 0.2181 + 0.0011 = 0.2192.

(4) *To find the angle whose sine is* 0.1711. Look in the table of sines to find the nearest number *lower* than 0.1711. This is found to be 0.1702 which corresponds to an angle of 9° 48′. Now 0.1702 is 0.0009 less than 0.1711 so we look in the mean difference table in the row marked 9° and find 9 in the column headed 3′. The angle whose sine is 0.1711 is then 9° 48′ + 3′ = 9°51′ or sin 9° 51′ = 0.1711.

NATURAL SINES

Mean Differences

	0′	6′	12′	18′	24′	30′	36′	42′	48′	54′	1′	2′	3′	4′	5′
0°	.0000	0017	0035	0052	0070	0087	0105	0122	0140	0157	3	6	9	12	15
1	.0175	0192	0209	0227	0244	0262	0279	0297	0314	0332	3	6	9	12	15
2	.0349	0366	0384	0401	0419	0436	0454	0471	0488	0506	3	6	9	12	15
3	.0523	0541	0558	0576	0593	0610	0628	0645	0663	0680	3	6	9	12	15
4	.0698	0715	0732	0750	0767	0785	0802	0819	0837	0854	3	6	9	12	14
5	.0872	0889	0906	0924	0941	0958	0976	0993	1011	1028	3	6	9	12	14
6	.1045	1063	1080	1097	1115	1132	1149	1167	1184	1201	3	6	9	12	14
7	.1219	1236	1253	1271	1288	1305	1323	1340	1357	1374	3	6	9	12	14
8	.1392	1409	1426	1444	1461	1478	1495	1513	1530	1547	3	6	9	12	14
9	.1564	1582	1599	1616	1633	1650	1668	1685	1702	1719	3	6	9	11	14
10	.1736	1754	1771	1788	1805	1822	1840	1857	1874	1891	3	6	9	11	14
11	.1908	1925	1942	1959	1977	1994	2011	2028	2045	2062	3	6	9	11	14
12	.2079	2096	2113	2130	2147	2164	2181	2198	2215	2233	3	6	9	11	14
13	.2250	2267	2284	2300	2317	2334	2351	2368	2385	2402	3	6	8	11	14
14	.2419	2436	2453	2470	2487	2504	2521	2538	2554	2571	3	6	8	11	14
15	.2588	2605	2622	2639	2656	2672	2689	2706	2723	2740	3	6	8	11	14
16	.2756	2773	2790	2807	2823	2840	2857	2874	2890	2907	3	6	8	11	14
17	.2924	2940	2957	2974	2990	3007	3024	3040	3057	3074	3	6	8	11	14
18	.3090	3107	3123	3140	3156	3173	3190	3206	3223	3239	3	6	8	11	14

EXAMPLE 2

(1) Find the length of AB in Fig. 40.6.

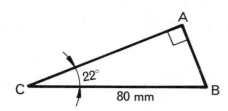

Fig. 40.6

AB is the side opposite ∠ ACB. BC is the hypotenuse since it is opposite to the right-angle.

Therefore

$$\frac{AB}{BC} = \sin 22°$$

$$AB = BC \times \sin 22° = 80 \times 0.3746$$

$$= 29.97 \text{ mm}$$

(2) Find the length of AB in Fig. 40.7.

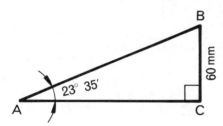

Fig. 40.7

BC is the side opposite to ∠ BAC and AB is the hypotenuse.

Therefore

$$\frac{BC}{AB} = \sin 23° 35'$$

$$AB = \frac{BC}{\sin 23° 35'} = \frac{60}{0.4000}$$

$$= 150 \text{ mm}$$

(3) Find the angles CAB and ABC in △ ABC which is shown in Fig. 40.8.

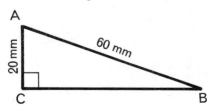

Fig. 40.8

$$\sin B = \frac{AC}{AB} = \frac{20}{60} = 0.3333$$

From the sine tables

$$\angle B = 19° 28'$$

$$\angle A = 90° - 19° 28' = 70° 32'$$

Exercise 171 — *All type A*

1) Find, by drawing, the sines of the following angles:

(a) 30°   (b) 45°   (c) 68°

2) Find, by drawing, the angles whose sines are:

(a) $\frac{1}{3}$ (b) $\frac{3}{4}$ (c) 0.72

3) Use the tables to write down the values of:

(a) sin 12°   (b) sin 18° 12'
(c) sin 74° 42'   (d) sin 7° 23'
(e) sin 87° 35'   (f) sin 0° 11'

4) Use the tables to write down the angles whose sines are:

(a) 0.1564   (b) 0.9135   (c) 0.9880
(d) 0.0802   (e) 0.9814   (f) 0.7395
(g) 0.0500   (h) 0.2700

5) Find the lengths of the sides marked x in Fig. 40.9 the triangles being right-angled.

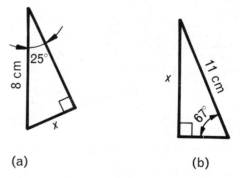

(a)   (b)

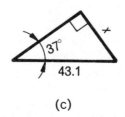

(c)

Fig. 40.9

291

6) Find the angles marked θ in Fig. 40.10, the triangles being right-angled.

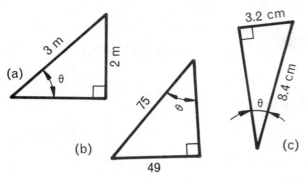

Fig. 40.10

7) In $\triangle ABC$, $\angle C = 90°$, $\angle B = 23° 17'$ and $AC = 11.2$ cm. Find AB.

8) In $\triangle ABC$, $\angle B = 90°$, $\angle A = 67° 28'$ and $AC = 0.86$ m. Find BC.

9) An equilateral triangle has an altitude of 18.7 cm. Find the length of the equal sides.

10) Find the altitude of an isosceles triangle whose vertex angle is $38°$ and whose equal sides are 7.9 m long.

11) The equal sides of an isosceles triangle are each 27 cm long and the altitude is 19 cm. Find the angles of the triangle.

THE COSINE OF AN ANGLE

In any right-angled triangle (Fig. 40.11):

the cosine of an angle

$$= \frac{\text{side adjacent to the angle}}{\text{hypotenuse}}$$

$$\cos A = \frac{AB}{AC}$$

$$\cos C = \frac{BC}{AC}$$

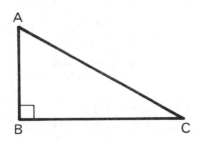

Fig. 40.11

The abbreviation 'cos' is usually used for cosine.

The cosine of an angle may be found by drawing, the construction being similar to that used for the sine of an angle. However, tables of cosines are available and these are used in a similar way to the table of sines except that the mean differences are now *subtracted*.

EXAMPLE 3

(1) Find the length of the side BC in Fig. 40.12.

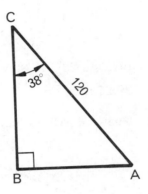

Fig. 40.12

BC is the side adjacent to $\angle BCA$ and AC is the hypotenuse.

Therefore

$$\frac{BC}{AC} = \cos 38°$$

$$BC = AC \times \cos 38° = 120 \times 0.788\,0$$

$$= 94.56 \text{ mm}$$

(2) Find the length of the side AC in Fig. 40.13.

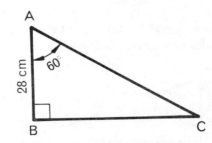

Fig. 40.13

AB is the side adjacent to ∠ BAC and AC is the hypotenuse.

Therefore

$$\frac{AB}{AC} = \cos 60°$$

$$AC = \frac{AB}{\cos 60°} = \frac{28}{0.5000} = 56 \text{ cm}$$

(3) Find the angle θ shown in Fig. 40.14.

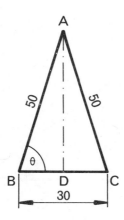

Fig. 40.14

Since △ ABC is isosceles the perpendicular AD bisects the base BC and hence BD = 15 mm.

$$\cos \theta = \frac{BD}{AB} = \frac{15}{50} = 0.3$$

$$\theta = 72° 32'$$

Exercise 172 — All type A

1) Use the tables to write down the values of:

(a) cos 15° (b) cos 24° 18′
(c) cos 78° 24′ (d) cos 0° 11′
(e) cos 73° 22′ (f) cos 39° 59′

2) Use the tables to write down the angles whose cosine are:

(a) 0.9135 (b) 0.3420 (c) 0.9673
(d) 0.4289 (e) 0.9586 (f) 0.0084
(g) 0.2611 (h) 0.4700

3) Find the lengths of the sides marked x in Fig. 40.15, the triangles being right-angled.

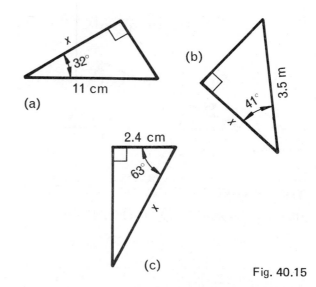

Fig. 40.15

4) Find the angles marked θ in Fig. 40.16, the triangles being right-angled.

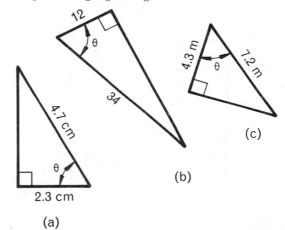

Fig. 40.16

5) An isosceles triangle has a base of 3.4 cm and the equal sides are each 4.2 cm long. Find the angles of the triangle and also its altitude.

6) In △ ABC, ∠ C = 90°, ∠ B = 33° 27′ and BC = 2.4 cm. Find AB.

7) In △ ABC, ∠ B = 90°, ∠ A = 62° 45′ and AC = 4.3 cm. Find AB.

8) In Fig. 40.17, calculate ∠ BAC and the length BC.

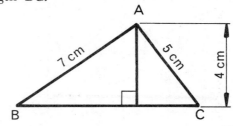

Fig. 40.17

9) In Fig. 40.18 calculate BD, AD, AC and BC.

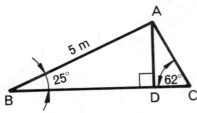

Fig. 40.18

THE TANGENT OF AN ANGLE

In any right-angled triangle (Fig. 40.19),

the tangent of an angle

$$= \frac{\text{side opposite to the angle}}{\text{side adjacent to the angle}}$$

$$\tan A = \frac{BC}{AB}$$

$$\tan C = \frac{AB}{BC}$$

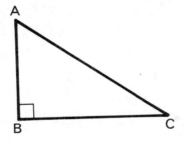

Fig. 40.19

The abbreviation 'tan' is usually used for tangent. From the table of tangents the tangents of angles from 0° to 90° can be read directly. For example:

$$\tan 37° = 0.7536$$

and $$\tan 62° 29' = 1.9196$$

EXAMPLE 4

(1) Find the length of the side AB in Fig. 40.20.

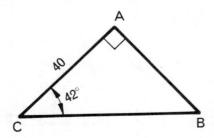

Fig. 40.20

AB is the side opposite ∠C and AC is the side adjacent to ∠C. Hence,

$$\frac{AB}{AC} = \tan \angle C$$

$$\frac{AB}{AC} = \tan 42°$$

$$AB = AC \times \tan 42° = 40 \times 0.9004$$

$$= 36.02 \text{ mm}$$

(2) Find the length of the side BC in Fig. 40.21.

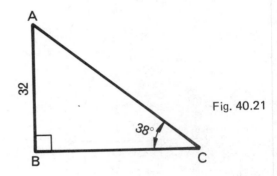

Fig. 40.21

There are two ways of doing this problem.

(a) $\frac{AB}{BC} = \tan 38°$ or $BC = \frac{AB}{\tan 38°}$

Therefore $BC = \frac{32}{0.7813} = 40.96 \text{ mm}$

(b) Since ∠C = 38°

$$\angle A = 90° - 38° = 52°$$

now

$$\frac{BC}{AB} = \tan A \quad \text{or} \quad BC = AB \times \tan A$$

$$BC = 32 \times 1.280 = 40.96 \text{ mm}$$

Both methods produce the same answer but method (b) is better because it is quicker and more convenient to multiply than divide. Whenever possible the ratio should be arranged so that the quantity to be found is the numerator of the ratio.

Exercise 173 — All type A

1) Use tables to write down the values of:

(a) tan 18°   (b) tan 32° 24'

(c) tan 53° 42'   (d) tan 39° 27'

(e) tan 11° 20'   (f) tan 69° 23'

2) Use tables to write down the angles whose tangents are:

(a) 0.4452 (b) 3.2709 (c) 0.0769
(d) 0.3977 (e) 0.3568 (f) 0.8263
(g) 1.9251 (h) 0.0163

3) Find the lengths of the sides marked y in Fig. 40.22, the triangles being right-angled.

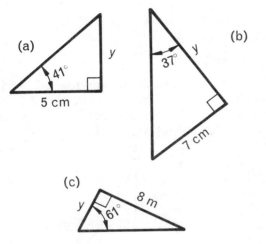

Fig. 40.22

4) Find the angles marked α in Fig. 40.23, the triangles being right-angled.

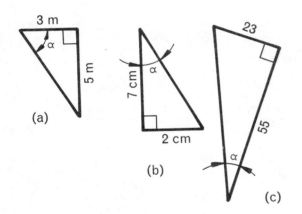

Fig. 40.23

5) An isosceles triangle has a base 10 cm long and the two equal angles are each 57°. Calculate the altitude of the triangle.

6) In $\triangle ABC$, $\angle B = 90°$, $\angle C = 49°$ and $AB = 3.2$ cm. Find BC.

7) In $\triangle ABC$, $\angle A = 12°\ 23'$, $\angle B = 90°$ and $BC = 7.31$ cm. Find AB.

8) Calculate the distance x in Fig. 40.24.

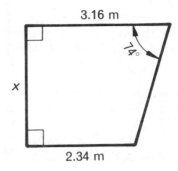

Fig. 40.24

9) Calculate the distance d in Fig. 40.25.

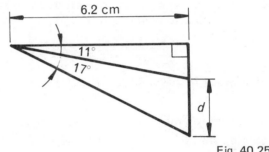

Fig. 40.25

LOGARITHMS OF THE TRIGONOMETRICAL RATIOS

Tables are used to find the log of a trig ratio in the same way as to find the ratio itself.

EXAMPLE 5

(1) Find the value of $28.25 \times \sin 39°17'$.

	number	log
	28.25	1.4510
	sin 39° 17'	$\bar{1}.8015$
Answer $=$	17.88	1.2525

(2) Find the angle A given that
$$\cos \angle A = \frac{20.23}{29.86}$$

number	log
20.23	1.3060
29.86	1.4751
cos A	$\bar{1}.8309$

The angle A is found directly from the log cos table:

$$\angle A = 47° 21'$$

(3) If $b = \dfrac{c \sin \angle B}{\sin \angle C}$ find b when
$c = 19.28$, $\angle B = 61°$ and $\angle C = 22° 7'$.

	number	log
	19.28	1.2851
	sin 61°	$\overline{1}.9418$
		1.2269
	sin 22° 7'	$\overline{1}.5757$
Answer =	44.79	1.6512

(A scientific type calculator will perform the above calculations much more quickly and accurately.)

Exercise 174 — *Questions 1 and 2 type A, remainder B*

1) From the tables find the following:
(a) log sin 28° 33'   (b) log sin 74° 24'
(c) log cos 8° 2'   (d) log cos 24° 15'
(e) log tan 44° 31'   (f) log tan 7° 5'

2) From the tables find the following:
(a) If   log cos $\angle A = \overline{1}.7357$ find $\angle A$.
(b) If   log sin $\angle A = \overline{1}.5813$ find $\angle A$.
(c) If   log tan $\angle B = 0.5755$ find $\angle B$.
(d) If   log sin $\phi = \overline{1}.3069$ find ϕ.
(e) If   log cos $\theta = \overline{1}.2381$ find θ.
(f) If   log tan $a = 1.5569$ find a.

3) By using logs find the following:

(a) If $\cos \angle A = \dfrac{19.26}{27.58}$ find $\angle A$.

(b) If $\sin \angle B = \dfrac{11.23}{35.35}$ find $\angle B$.

(c) If $\tan \theta = \dfrac{28.13}{17.57}$ find θ.

4) If $a = \dfrac{b \sin \angle A}{\sin \angle B}$,   find, by using logs, the value of a when $b = 8.16$ cm,
$\angle A = 43° 27'$ and $\angle B = 37° 11'$.

5) If $\cos A = \dfrac{b^2 + c^2 - a^2}{2bc}$,   find, by using logs, the value of $\angle A$ when $b = 11.23$ cm, $c = 9.16$ cm   and $a = 8.23$ cm.

6) If $\sin \angle C = \dfrac{c \sin \angle B}{b}$ find, by using logs, the value of C when $c = 0.323$, $\angle B = 29° 8'$ and $b = 0.517$.

7) If $b^2 = a^2 + c^2 - 2ac \cos \angle B$ find the value of b when $a = 11.36$ cm, $c = 8.26$ cm and   B = 29° 25'.

TRIGONOMETRICAL RATIOS FOR 30°, 60° AND 45°

Ratios for 30° and 60°

Fig. 40.26 shows an equilateral triangle ABC with each of the sides equal to 2 units. From C draw the perpendicular CD which bisects the base AB and also bisects $\angle$ C.

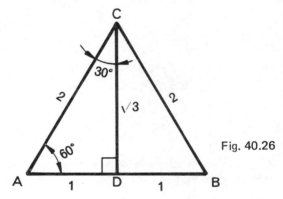

Fig. 40.26

In $\triangle$ ACD,

$$CD^2 = AC^2 - AD^2 = 2^2 - 1^2 = 3$$

therefore

$$CD = \sqrt{3}$$

Since all the angles of $\triangle$ ABC are 60° and $\angle$ ACD = 30°,

$$\sin 60° = \frac{\sqrt{3}}{2}$$

$$\tan 60° = \frac{\sqrt{3}}{1} = \sqrt{3}$$

$$\cos 60° = \frac{1}{2}$$

$$\sin 30° = \frac{1}{2}$$

$$\tan 30° = \frac{1}{\sqrt{3}} = \frac{\sqrt{3}}{3}$$

$$\cos 30° = \frac{\sqrt{3}}{2}$$

296

Ratios for 45°

Fig. 40.27 shows a right-angled isosceles triangle ABC with the equal sides each 1 unit in length. The equal angles are each 45°. Now,

$$AC^2 = AB^2 + BC^2 = 1^2 + 1^2 = 2$$

therefore

$$AC = \sqrt{2}$$

$$\sin 45° = \frac{1}{\sqrt{2}} = \frac{\sqrt{2}}{2}$$

$$\cos 45° = \frac{1}{\sqrt{2}} = \frac{\sqrt{2}}{2}$$

$$\tan 45° = \frac{1}{1} = 1$$

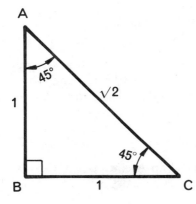

Fig. **40.27**

GIVEN ONE RATIO TO FIND THE OTHERS

The method is shown in the following example.

EXAMPLE 6

If $\cos \angle A = 0.7$, find, without using tables, the values of $\sin \angle A$ and $\tan \angle A$.

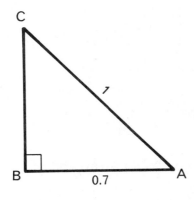

Fig. **40.28**

In Fig. 40.28 if we make AB = 0.7 units and AC = 1 unit, then

$$\cos \angle A = \frac{0.7}{1} = 0.7$$

By Pythagoras' theorem,

$$BC^2 = AC^2 - AB^2 = 1^2 - 0.7^2 = 0.51$$

$$BC = \sqrt{0.51} = 0.7141$$

$$\sin \angle A = \frac{BC}{AC} = \frac{0.7141}{1} = 0.7141$$

$$\tan \angle A = \frac{BC}{AB} = \frac{0.7141}{0.7} = 1.020$$

COMPLEMENTARY ANGLES

Complementary angles are angles whose sum is 90°.

Consider the triangle ABC shown in Fig. 40.29.

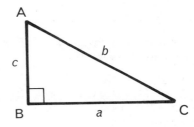

Fig. **40.29**

$$\sin A = \frac{a}{b} \qquad \cos C = \frac{a}{b}$$

Hence,

$$\sin A = \cos C = \cos (90° - A)$$

Similarly,

$$\cos A = \sin (90° - A)$$

Therefore, *the sine of an angle is equal to the cosine of its complementary angle and vice versa.*

$$\sin 26° = \cos 64° = 0.4384$$

$$\cos 70° = \sin 20° = 0.3420$$

THE SQUARES OF THE TRIGONOMETRICAL RATIOS

The square of $\sin A$ is usually written as $\sin^2 A$. Thus,

$$\sin^2 A = (\sin A)^2$$

297

and similarly for the remaining trigonometrical ratios. That is,

$$\cos^2 A = (\cos A)^2$$

and

$$\tan^2 A = (\tan A)^2$$

EXAMPLE 7

(1) Find the value of $\cos^2 37°$.

$$\cos 37° = 0.7986$$
$$\cos^2 37° = (0.7986)^2 = 0.6378$$

(2) Find the value of $\tan^2 60° + \sin^2 60°$.

$$\tan 60° = \sqrt{3} \qquad \therefore \tan^2 60° = 3$$
$$\sin 60° = \frac{\sqrt{3}}{2} \qquad \therefore \sin^2 60° = \frac{3}{4}$$
$$\tan^2 60° + \sin^2 60° = 3 + \frac{3}{4} = 3\frac{3}{4}$$

It is sometimes useful to remember that

$$\sin^2 A + \cos^2 A = 1$$

which may easily be proved by considering a right-angled triangle (Fig. 40.30).

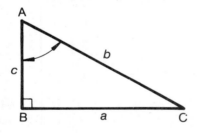

Fig. 40.30

$$\sin A = \frac{a}{b} \qquad \sin^2 A = \frac{a^2}{b^2}$$

$$\cos A = \frac{c}{b} \qquad \cos^2 A = \frac{c^2}{b^2}$$

$$\sin^2 A + \cos^2 A = \frac{a^2}{b^2} + \frac{c^2}{b^2} = \frac{a^2 + c^2}{b^2}$$

But, by Pythagoras

$$a^2 + c^2 = b^2$$

$$\therefore \qquad \sin^2 A + \cos^2 A = \frac{b^2}{b^2} = 1$$

EXAMPLE 8

The angle A is acute and $5 \sin^2 A - 2 = \cos^2 A$. Find the angle A.

Since $\sin^2 A + \cos^2 A = 1$

$$\cos^2 A = 1 - \sin^2 A$$

$$\therefore \quad 5 \sin^2 A - 2 = 1 - \sin^2 A$$

$$6 \sin^2 A - 3 = 0$$

$$6 \sin^2 A = 3$$

$$\sin^2 A = 0.5$$

$$\sin A = \pm\sqrt{0.5} = \pm 0.7071$$

Since A is acute $\sin A$ must be positive.

Hence, $\sin A = 0.7071$

$$A = 45°$$

Exercise 175 — *Questions 1—10 type B, remainder C*

1) If $\sin A = 0.3171$ find the values of $\cos A$ and $\tan A$ without using tables.

2) If $\tan A = \frac{3}{4}$, find the values of $\sin A$ and $\cos A$ without using tables.

3) If $\cos A = \frac{12}{13}$, find without using tables the values of $\sin A$ and $\tan A$.

4) Show that $\cos 60° + \cos 30° = \dfrac{1 + \sqrt{3}}{2}$.

5) Show that $\sin 60° + \cos 30° = \sqrt{3}$.

6) Show that
$$\cos 45° + \sin 60° + \sin 30° = \frac{\sqrt{2} + \sqrt{3} + 1}{2}.$$

7) Given that $\sin 48° = 0.7431$ find the values of $\cos 42°$, without using tables.

8) If $\cos 63° = 0.4540$, what is the value of $\sin 27°$?

9) (a) Find the value of $\cos^2 30°$.
   (b) Find the value of $\tan^2 30°$.
   (c) Find the value of $\sin^2 60°$.

10) Evaluate
(a) $\cos^2 41°$ (b) $\sin^2 27°$ (c) $\tan^2 58°$

11) If the angle A is acute and $2 \sin^2 A - \dfrac{1}{3} = \cos^2 A$ find A.

12) If the angle θ is acute and $\cos^2 \theta + \dfrac{1}{8} = \sin^2 \theta$ find θ.

ANGLE OF ELEVATION

If you look upwards at an object, say the top of a tree, the angle formed between the horizontal and your line of sight is called the *angle of elevation* (Fig. 40.31). It is the angle through which the line of your sight has been elevated.

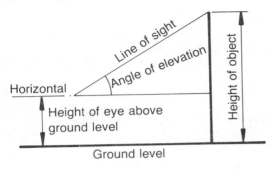

Fig. 40.31

EXAMPLE 9

To find the height of a tower a surveyor sets up his theodolite 100 m from the base of the tower. He finds that the angle of elevation to the top of the tower is 30°. If the instrument is 1.5 m from the ground, what is the height of the tower?

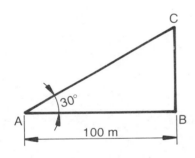

Fig. 40.32

In Fig. 40.32,

$$\frac{BC}{AB} = \tan 30°$$

$$BC = AB \times \tan 30°$$

$$= 100 \times 0.5774 = 57.74$$

Hence, height of tower

$$= 57.74 + 1.5 = 59.24 \text{ m}$$

EXAMPLE 10

To find the height of a pylon, a surveyor sets up his theodolite some distance from the pylon and finds the angle of elevation to the top of the pylon to be 30°. He then moves 60 m nearer to the pylon and finds the angle of elevation to be 42°. Find the height of the pylon assuming the ground to be horizontal and that the instrument is 1.5 m above ground level.

This problem is much more difficult than Example 9 because we have to use two triangles and some algebra.

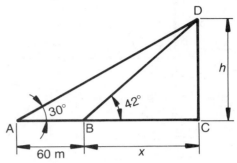

Fig. 40.33

Looking at Fig. 40.33 let BC = x and DC = h. Our problem is to find h.

In $\triangle$ ACD,

$$\frac{DC}{AC} = \tan 30°$$

$$DC = AC \times \tan 30°$$

$$h = 0.5774(x + 60) \qquad [1]$$

In $\triangle$ BDC

$$\frac{DC}{BC} = \tan 42°$$

$$DC = BC \times \tan 42°$$

$$h = 0.9004x \qquad [2]$$

$$x = \frac{h}{0.9004} = 1.1106h$$

Substituting for x in equation [1] we have,

$$h = 0.5774(1.1106h + 60)$$

$$h = 0.6413h + 34.64$$

$$h - 0.6413h = 34.64$$

$$0.3587h = 34.64$$

$$h = \frac{34.64}{0.3587} = 96.57 \text{ m}$$

Hence   height of the pylon

$$= 96.57 + 1.5 = 98.07 \text{ m}$$

ALTITUDE OF THE SUN

The altitude of the Sun is simply the angle of elevation of the Sun (Fig. 40.34).

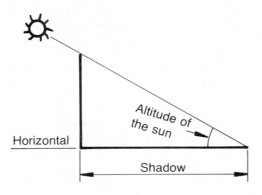

Fig. 40.34

EXAMPLE 11

A flagpole is 15 m high. What length of shadow will it cast when the altitude of the Sun is 57°?

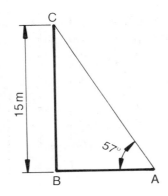

Fig. 40.35

Looking at Fig. 40.35 we have

$$\angle ACB = 90° - 57° = 33°$$

$$\frac{AB}{BC} = \tan \angle ACB$$

$$AB = BC \times \tan \angle ACB$$

$$= 15 \times \tan 33° = 9.741$$

Hence the flagpole will cast a shadow 9.741 m long.

ANGLE OF DEPRESSION

If you look downwards at an object, the angle formed between the horizontal and your line of sight is called the angle of depression

(Fig. 40.36). It is therefore the angle through which the line of sight is depressed from the horizontal. Note carefully that both the angle of elevation and the angle of depression are measured from the horizontal.

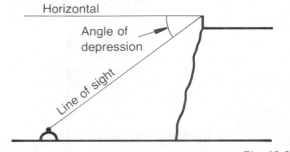

Fig. 40.36

EXAMPLE 12

A person standing on top of a cliff 50 m high is in line with two buoys whose angles of depression are 18° and 20°. Calculate the distance between the buoys.

The problem is illustrated in Fig. 40.37 where the buoys are C and D and the observer is A

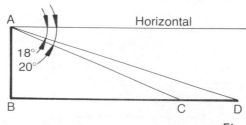

Fig. 40.37

In $\triangle$ BAC, BAC = 90° - 20° = 70°

$$\frac{BC}{AB} = \tan \angle BAC$$

$$BC = AB \times \tan \angle BAC$$

$$= 50 \times \tan 70° = 137.4 \text{ m}$$

In $\triangle$ ABD, $\angle$ BAD = 90° - 18° = 72°

$$\frac{BD}{AB} = \tan \angle BAD$$

$$BD = AB \times \tan \angle BAD$$

$$= 50 \times \tan 72° = 153.9 \text{ m}$$

The distance between the buoys

$$= BD - BC = 153.9 - 137.4 = 16.5 \text{ m}$$

Exercise 176 — *Questions 1–8 type B, remainder C*

1) From a point, the angle of elevation of a tower is 30°. If the tower is 20 m distant from the point, what is the height of the tower?

2) A man 1.8 m tall observes the angle of elevation of a tree to be 26°. If he is standing 16 m from the tree, find the height of the tree.

3) A man 1.5 m tall is 15 m away from a tower 20 m high. What is the angle of elevation of the top of the tower from his eyes?

4) A man, lying down on top of a cliff 40 m high observes the angle of depression of a buoy to be 20°. If he is in line with the buoy, calculate the distance between the buoy and the foot of the cliff (which may be assumed to be vertical).

5) A tree is 20 m tall. When the altitude of the Sun is 62°, what length of shadow will it cast?

6) A flagpole casts a shadow 18 m long when the altitude of the Sun is 54°. What is the height of the flagpole?

7) A man standing on top of a mountain 1200 m high observes the angle of depression of a steeple to be 43°. How far is the steeple from the mountain?

8) In Fig. 40.38, a vertical cliff is 40 m high and is observed from a boat which is 50 m from the foot of the cliff. Calculate the angle of elevation of the top of the cliff from the boat.

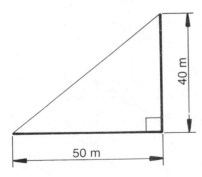

Fig. 40.38

9) To find the height of a tower a surveyor stands some distance away from its base and he observes the angle of elevation to the top of the tower to be 45°. He then moves 80 m nearer to the tower and he then finds the angle of

elevation to be 60°. Find the height of the tower.

10) A tower is known to be 60 m high. A man using a theodolite stands some distance away from the tower and measures its angle of elevation as 38°. How far away from the tower is he if the theodolite stands 1.5 m above the ground. If the man now moves 80 m further away from the tower what is now the angle of elevation of the tower?

11) A man standing 20 m away from a tower observes the angles of elevation to the top and bottom of a flagstaff standing on the tower as 62° and 60° respectively. Calculate the height of the flagstaff.

12) A surveyor stands 100 m from the base of a tower on which an aerial stands. He measures the angles of elevation to the top and bottom of the aerial as 58° and 56°. Find the height of the aerial.

13) Figure 40.39 shows a tower TR and an observer at O. From O which is 100 m from the base R of tower TR the angle of elevation of the top of the tower is found to be 35°.

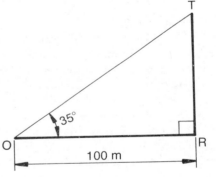

Fig. 40.39

(a) Calculate the height of the tower TR, to 3 significant figures.

(b) The observer walks forward towards the tower until the angle of elevation of the top T is 45°. How far does he walk forward?

(c) Find the distance of the observer from the base of the tower when the angle of elevation of the top is 65°. Give your answer to 3 significant figures.

14) A man standing on top of a cliff 80 m high is in line with two buoys whose angles of depression are 17° and 21°. Calculate the distance between the buoys.

301

15) Figure 40.40 represents two plotting stations, A and B, 4000 m apart. T is a stationary target in the same vertical plane as A and B. It is recorded that, when the distance of the target from station A is 10 000 m, the angle of elevation is 29°. Calculate:

(a) the vertical height of the target, TX;
(b) the distance AX;
(c) the distance BX;
(d) the angle of elevation of the target, T, from B;
(e) the distance TB.

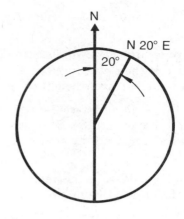

Fig. 40.42

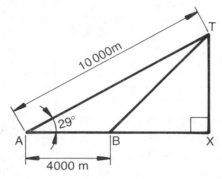

Fig. 40.40

BEARINGS

The four cardinal directions are North, South, East and West (Fig. 40.41). The directions NE, NW, SE and SW are frequently used and are as shown in Fig. 40.41. A bearing of N20°E means an angle of 20° measured from the N towards E as shown in Fig. 40.42. Similarly a bearing of S40°E means an angle 40° measured from the S towards E (Fig. 40.43). A bearing of N50°W means an angle of 50° measured from N towards W (Fig. 40.44). *Bearings quoted in this way are always measured from N and S and never from E and W.*

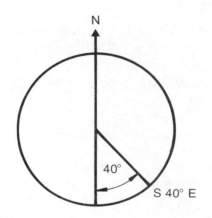

Fig. 40.43

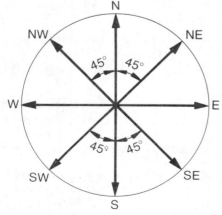

Fig. 40.41

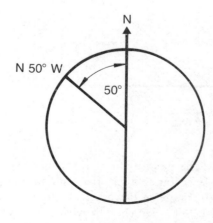

Fig. 40.44

However, bearings are usually measured from North in a clockwise direction, N being taken as 0°. Three figures are always stated. For example 005° is written instead of 5° and 035° instead of 35° and so on. East will be 090°, South 180° and West 270°. Some typical bearings are shown in Fig. 40.45.

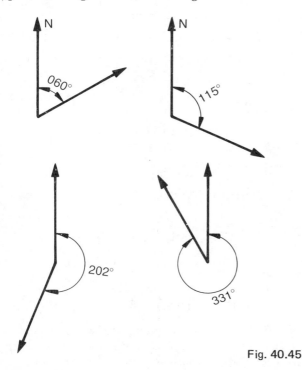

Fig. 40.45

EXAMPLE 13

(1) B is a point due east of a point A on the coast. C is another point on the coast and is 6 km due south of A. The distance BC is 7 km. Calculate the bearing of C from B.

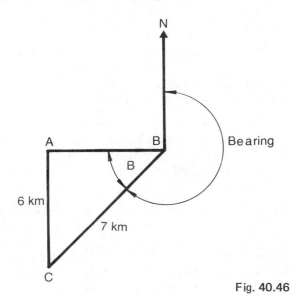

Fig. 40.46

Referring to Fig. 40.46,

$$\sin \angle B = \frac{AC}{BC} = \frac{6}{7} = 0.8572$$

$$\angle B = 59°$$

The bearing of C from B

$$= 270° - 59° = 211°.$$

(2) B is 5 km due north of P and C is 2 km due east of P. A ship started from C and steamed in a direction N30°E. Calculate the distance the ship had to go before it was due east of B. Find also the distance it is then from B.

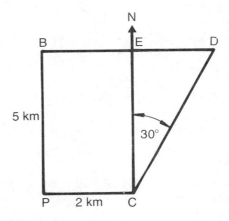

Fig. 40.47

Referring to Fig. 40.47, the ship will be due east of B when it has sailed the distance CD. The bearing N30°E makes the angle $\angle$ ECD equal to 30°. In $\triangle$ CED, EC = 5 km and $\angle$ ECD = 30°. Hence,

$$\frac{EC}{CD} = \cos 30°$$

$$CD = \frac{EC}{\cos 30°} = \frac{5}{\cos 30°} = 5.77 \text{ km}$$

Hence the ship had to sail 5.77 km to become due east of B.

$$\frac{ED}{CD} = \sin 30°$$

$$ED = CD \times \sin 30° = 5.77 \times 0.5000$$
$$= 2.885 \text{ km}$$

$$BD = BE + ED = 2 + 2.885 = 4.885 \text{ km}$$

Hence the ship will be 4.885 km due east of B.

303

(3) A boat sails 8 km from a port P on a bearing of 070°. It then sails 5 km on a bearing of 040°. Calculate the distance that the boat is from P and also its bearing from P.

The details of the journey are shown in Fig. 40.48. The problem is to find the distance PB and the angle BPN.

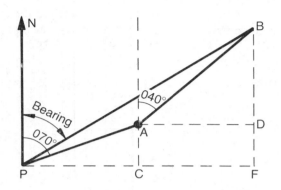

Fig. 40.48

Draw the triangles PAC and ABD as shown in the diagram.

In △ PAC, AP = 8 km and ∠ APC = 20°.

$$\frac{PC}{AP} = \cos \angle APC$$

$$PC = AP \times \cos \angle APC = 8 \times \cos 20°$$

$$= 7.518 \text{ km}$$

$$\frac{AC}{AP} = \sin \angle APC$$

$$AC = AP \times \sin \angle APC = 8 \times \sin 20°$$

$$= 2.736 \text{ km}$$

In △ ABD, AB = 5 km and ∠BAD = 50°

$$\frac{AD}{AB} = \cos \angle BAD$$

$$AD = AB \times \cos \angle BAD = 5 \times \cos 50°$$

$$= 3.214 \text{ km}$$

$$\frac{BD}{AB} = \sin \angle BAD$$

$$BD = AB \times \sin \angle BAD = 5 \times \sin 50°$$

$$= 3.830 \text{ km}$$

In △ PBF,

$$PF = PC + AD = 7.518 + 3.214$$

$$= 10.732 \text{ km}$$

$$BF = AC + BD = 2.736 + 3.830$$

$$= 6.566 \text{ km}$$

Using Pythagoras' theorem,

$$PB^2 = PF^2 + BF^2 = 10.732^2 + 6.566^2$$

$$= 115.2 + 43.1 = 158.3$$

$$PB = \sqrt{158.3} = 12.58 \text{ km}$$

$$\tan \angle BPF$$

$$= \frac{BF}{PF} = \frac{6.566}{10.732}$$

$$\angle BPF = 31° \ 28'$$

The bearing from P is

$$90° - 31° \ 28' = 58° \ 32'$$

Exercise 177 — *All type B*

1) A ship sets out from a point A and sails due north to a point B, a distance of 120 km. It then sails due east to a point C. If the bearing of C from A is 037° 40′ calculate:

(a) the distance BC;
(b) the distance AC.

2) A boat leaves a harbour A on a course of S60°E and it sails 50 km in this direction until it reaches a point B. How far is B east of A? What distance south of A is B?

3) X is a point due west of a point P. Y is a point due south of P. If the distances PX and PY are 10 km and 15 km respectively, calculate the bearing of X from Y.

4) B is 10 km north of P and C is 5 km due west of P. A ship starts from C and sails in a direction of 330°. Calculate the distance the ship has to sail before it is due west of B and find also the distance it is then from B.

5) A fishing boat places a float on the sea at A, 50 metres due north of a buoy B. A second boat places a float at C, whose bearing from A is S30°E. A taut net connecting the floats at A and C is 80 metres long. Calculate the distance BC and the bearing of C from B.

304

6) An aircraft starts to fly from A to B a distance of 140 km, B being due north of A. The aircraft flies on course 18°E of N for a distance of 80 km. Calculate how far the aircraft is then from the line AB and in what direction it should then fly to reach B.

7) X and Y are two lighthouses, Y being 20 km due east of X. From a ship due south of X, the bearing of Y was 055°. Find:

(a) the distance of the ship from Y;
(b) the distance of the ship from X.

8) An aircraft flies 50 km from an aerodrome A on a bearing of 065° and then flies 80 km on a bearing of 040°. Find the distance of the aircraft from A and also its bearing from A.

9) A boat sails 10 km from a harbour H on a bearing of S30°E. It then sails 15 km on a bearing of N20°E. How far is the boat from H? What is its bearing from H?

10) Three towns A, B and C lie on a straight road running east from A. B is 6 km from A and C is 22 km from A. Another town D lies to the north of this road and it lies 10 km from both B and C. Calculate the distance of D from A and the bearing of D from A.

TRIGONOMETRY AND THE CIRCLE

Many problems involving the circle can be solved by trigonometry. The geometrical theorems needed are as follows:

(1) The angle between a tangent and a radius drawn to the point of tangency is 90°.

(2) The angle in a semi-circle is 90°.

(3) The straight line joining the centres of two circles in contact passes through the point of contact.

EXAMPLE 14

(1) Fig. 40.49 shows an end view of two cylinders (of radius 5 cm and 3 cm respectively) in a V shaped slot. The cylinders touch each other and the sides of the slot. Calculate ∠XYZ and the depth TY of the slot.

A and B are the centres of the circle.

∴ $\qquad$ AB = 5 + 3 = 8 cm

C and D are the points of tangency. Join AC and BD and draw BE parallel to XY.

∴ $\qquad$ EA = 5 − 3 = 2 cm

$\qquad$ ∠AEB = 90°

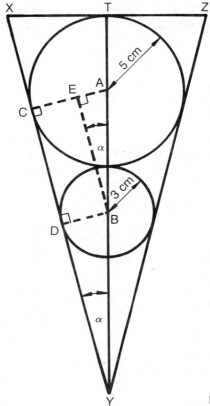

Fig. 40.49

In △EAB, $\quad \dfrac{EA}{AB} = \sin \alpha$

∴ $\qquad \sin \alpha = \dfrac{2}{8} = 0.25$

$\qquad \alpha = 14° \, 29'$

$\quad$ ∠XYZ = 2α = 2 × 14° 29′ = 28° 58′

In △DBY,

$\dfrac{DB}{BY} = \sin \alpha$

$BY = \dfrac{DB}{\sin \alpha} = \dfrac{3}{0.25} = 12 \text{ cm}$

$TY = TA + AB + BY = 5 + 8 + 12 = 25 \text{ cm}$

(2) Fig. 40.50 shows a dovetail. Two cylinders each 4 cm diameter are held against the dovetail as shown in the diagram. Find the distance M.

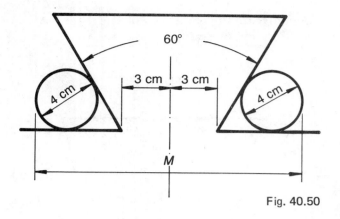

Fig. 40.50

Referring to Fig. 40.51 we need to find WY. The circle touches XY at V and ZY at W.

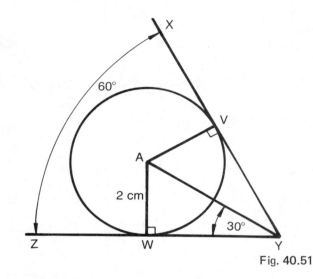

Fig. 40.51

Since

$$VY = WY \quad \text{(both tangents)}$$

and

$$\angle AWY = \angle AVY = 90° \quad \text{(angle between a radius and a tangent)}$$

$\angle WYV$ is bisected

$\therefore \angle AYW = 30°$

$$\frac{AW}{WY} = \tan 30°$$

$$WY = \frac{AW}{\tan 30°} = \frac{2}{0.5774} = 3.464 \text{ cm}$$

$$\therefore \quad M = 3 + 3 + 3.464 + 3.464 + 2 + 2$$

$$= 16.928 \text{ cm}$$

306

Exercise 178 — *All type B*

1) In Fig. 40.52 find the distance x.

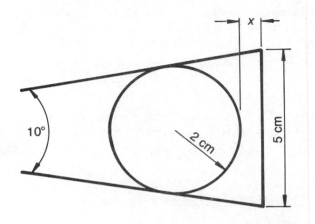

Fig. 40.52

2) In Fig. 40.53 find the distance M.

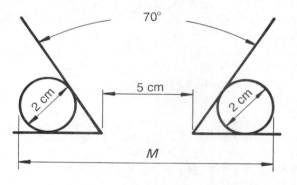

Fig. 40.53

3) In Fig. 40.54 find the distances x and H.

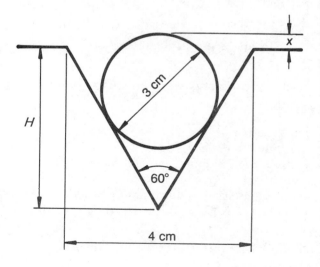

Fig. 40.54

4) In Fig. 40.55 find the distance L.

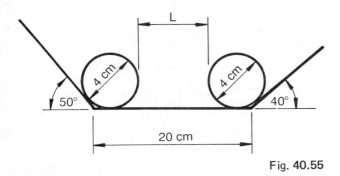

Fig. 40.55

5) In Fig. 40.56 find the angle α and the distance x.

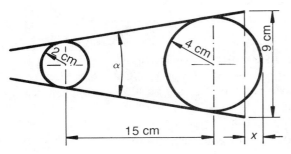

Fig. 40.56

6) Fig. 40.57 consists of two circular arcs joined by straight lines. Find the perimeter of the figure.

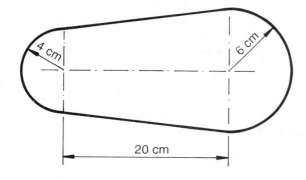

Fig. 40.57

POLAR CO-ORDINATES

It was shown on page 164 that a point on a graph may be positioned by using rectangular co-ordinates (sometimes called Cartesian co-ordinates.) Hence if P is the point (3, 4) its position is as shown in Fig. 40.58.

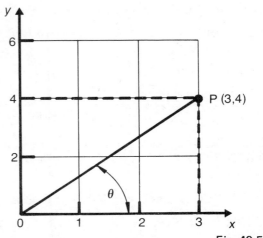

Fig. 40.58

However, the position of P may also be indicated by stating the length OP and the angle θ. Thus in Fig. 40.58,

$$OP = \sqrt{3^2 + 4^2} = \sqrt{25} = 5$$

(by using Pythagoras' theorem)

and $\quad \tan \theta = \dfrac{4}{3} = 1.333$

$$\theta = 53° 7'$$

P is then said to have the polar co-ordinates (5, 53° 7'). The angle θ may be expressed in degrees or in radians. If Q is the point $\left(7, \dfrac{\pi}{3}\right)$ the angle θ is $\dfrac{\pi}{3}$ radians or 60°.

EXAMPLE 15

(1) A point P has Cartesian co-ordinates $(5, -7)$. State the polar co-ordinates of P.

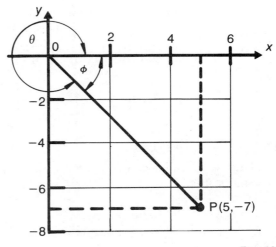

Fig. 40.59

From Fig. 40.59,

$$OP = \sqrt{5^2 + 7^2} = \sqrt{74} = 8.602$$

$$\tan \phi = \frac{7}{5} = 1.4$$

$$\phi = 54° \, 28'$$

$$\theta = 360° - 54° \, 28' = 305° \, 32'$$

Hence the polar co-ordinates of P are (8.602, 305° 32').

(2) A point A has the polar co-ordinates $\left(8, \frac{5\pi}{6}\right)$. Determine the Cartesian co-ordinates of A.

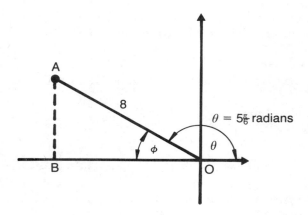

Fig. 40.60

In Fig. 40.60,

$$\theta = \frac{5\pi}{6} \text{ radians} = \frac{5 \times 180}{6} = 150°$$

$$\phi = 180° - 150° = 30°$$

$$OB = OA \cos 30° = 8 \times 0.8660 = 6.928$$

$$AB = OA \sin 30° = 8 \times 0.5000 = 4$$

Hence the Cartesian co-ordinates of A are (− 6.928, 4).

Exercise 179 − *All type B*

1) Calculate the polar co-ordinates for the following points:

(a) (3, 2)   (b) (5, 8)
(c) (− 4, 8)   (d) (− 3, − 5)
(e) (6, − 4)   (f) (− 4, − 6)
(g) (8, − 7)   (h) (− 1, 3)

308

2) Calculate the Cartesian co-ordinates of the following points:

(a) (5, 30°)   (b) (7, 65°)
(c) (2, 112°)   (d) (4, 148°)
(e) (7, 198°)   (f) (3, 265°)
(g) (5, 297°)   (h) (3, 330°)

3) Calculate the Cartesian co-ordinates for the following points:

(a) $\left(5, \frac{\pi}{3}\right)$ (b) $\left(4, \frac{\pi}{2}\right)$

(c) $\left(6, \frac{3\pi}{4}\right)$ (d) $\left(10, \frac{5\pi}{3}\right)$

4) Calculate the polar co-ordinates for the following points, stating the angle in radian measure:

(a) (2, 1)   (b) (− 3, 5)
(c) (− 2, − 4)   (d) (4, − 2)

5) In Fig. 40.61, with origin O, the polar co-ordinates of the point X are (5, 40°). YPX is a straight line parallel to the x-axis. Find:

(a) the polar co-ordinates of Y,
(b) the polar co-ordinates of P.

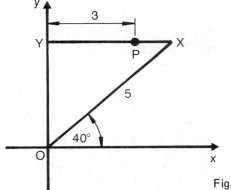

Fig. 40.61

SELF-TEST 40

1) In Fig. 40.62, $\sin x$ is equal to:

a $\dfrac{h}{p}$ b $\dfrac{h}{m}$ c $\dfrac{m}{p}$ d $\dfrac{p}{h}$

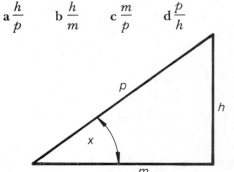

Fig. 40.62

2) In Fig. 40.62, $\cos x$ is equal to:

a $\dfrac{h}{p}$ b $\dfrac{h}{m}$ c $\dfrac{m}{p}$ d $\dfrac{p}{h}$

3) In Fig. 40.62, $\tan x$ is equal to:

a $\dfrac{h}{p}$ b $\dfrac{h}{m}$ c $\dfrac{m}{p}$ d $\dfrac{p}{h}$

4) In Fig. 40.63, $\sin A$ is equal to:

a $\dfrac{a}{b}$ b $\dfrac{a}{c}$ c $\dfrac{b}{c}$ d $\dfrac{c}{a}$

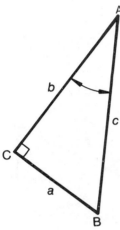

Fig. 40.63

5) In Fig. 40.64, $\tan x$ is equal to:

a $\dfrac{q}{p}$ b $\dfrac{q}{r}$ c $\dfrac{p}{q}$ d $\dfrac{r}{q}$

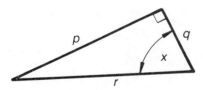

Fig. 40.64

6) In Fig. 40.65, $\cos y$ is equal to:

a $\dfrac{s}{t}$ b $\dfrac{r}{s}$ c $\dfrac{s}{r}$ d $\dfrac{t}{s}$

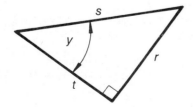

Fig. 40.65

7) The expression for the length AB (Fig. 40.66) is:

a $40 \tan 50°$ b $40 \sin 50°$

c $\dfrac{40}{\tan 50°}$ d $\dfrac{40}{\sin 50°}$

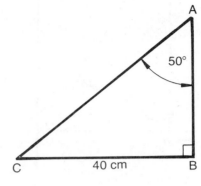

Fig. 40.66

8) The expression for the length AC (Fig. 40.66) is:

a $40 \sin 50°$ b $40 \cos 50°$

c $\dfrac{40}{\sin 50°}$ d $\dfrac{40}{\cos 50°}$

9) In Fig. 40.67, the expression for the side RN is:

a $(2 \sin 30° + 3 \sin 60°)$ cm

b $(2 \sin 30° + 3 \cos 60°)$ cm

c $(2 \cos 30° + 3 \cos 60°)$ cm

d $(2 \cos 30° + 3 \sin 60°)$ cm

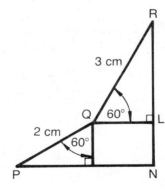

Fig. 40.67

10) In Fig. 40.68, an expression for the length AD is:

a $\dfrac{16\sqrt{3}}{3}$ b $\dfrac{16}{\sqrt{3}}$

c $8\sqrt{3}$ d $\dfrac{40\sqrt{3}}{3}$

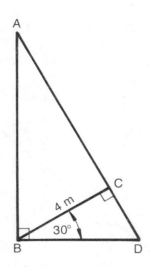

Fig. 40.68

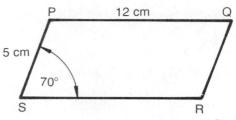

Fig. 40.70

13) In Fig. 40.71, PT and PQ are tangents to the circle whose radius is 2 cm. Hence $\angle$ TPQ is:

a 30°   b 45°   c 60°   d 90°

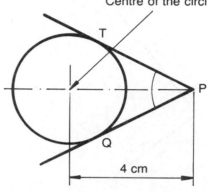

Centre of the circle

Fig. 40.71

11) In Fig. 40.69, an expression for the angle θ is:

a $\tan \theta = \dfrac{30 - 10\sqrt{3}}{40}$

b $\tan \theta = \dfrac{40}{30 - 10\sqrt{3}}$

c $\tan \theta = \dfrac{20}{50 - 10\sqrt{3}}$

d $\tan \theta = \dfrac{50 - 10\sqrt{3}}{20}$

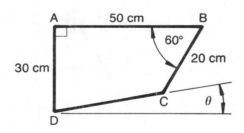

Fig. 40.69

12) The area of the parallelogram PQRS (Fig. 40.70) is:

a 30 sin 70° cm²   b 30 cos 70° cm²
c 60 sin 70° cm²   d 60 cos 70° cm²

14) log cos 51° 34′ is:

a 0.7935   b 0.7947   c $\overline{1}$.7935
d $\overline{1}$.7947

15) A bearing of S40°E can be expressed as a bearing of:

a 050°   b 040°   c 140°   d 130°

16) A man standing on top of a cliff 80 m high is in line with two buoys whose angles of depression are 15° and 20°. The distance between the buoys is given by the expression:

a 80(tan 20° − tan 15°)

b 80(tan 75° − tan 70°)

c 80 tan 5°

d $\dfrac{80}{\tan 20° - \tan 15°}$

17) The polar co-ordinates of the point P(− 4, 3) are:

a (5, 36° 52′)   b (5, 53° 8′)
c (5, 143° 8′)   d (5, 216° 52′)

Chapter 41 **The Sine and Cosine Rules**

TRIGONOMETRICAL RATIOS BETWEEN 0° AND 360°

In Chapter 40 the definitions for the sine, cosine and tangent of an angle between 0° and 90° were given. In this chapter we show how to deal with angles between 0° and 360°.

In Fig. 41.1, the axes XOX' and YOY', have been drawn at right-angles to each other to form the four quadrants. In each of these four quadrants we make use of the sign convention used when drawing graphs.

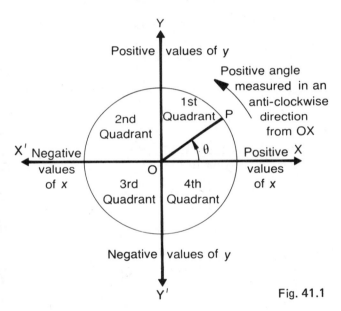

Fig. 41.1

Now an angle, if positive, is always measured in an anti-clockwise direction from OX and an angle is formed by rotating a line (such as OP) in an anti-clockwise direction. It is convenient to make the length of OP equal to 1 unit. Referring to Fig. 41.2, we see:

In the first quadrant,

$$\sin \theta_1 = \frac{P_1 M_1}{OP_1} = P_1 M_1$$

$$= y \text{ co-ordinate of } P_1$$

$$\cos \theta_1 = \frac{OM_1}{OP_1} = OM_1$$

$$= x \text{ co-ordinate of } P_1$$

$$\tan \theta_1 = \frac{P_1 M_1}{OM_1} = \frac{y \text{ co-ordinate of P}}{x \text{ co-ordinate of P}}$$

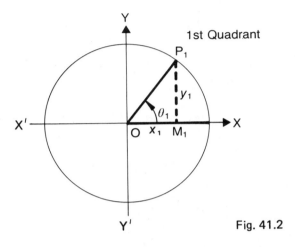

Fig. 41.2

Hence in the *first quadrant* all the trigonometrical ratios are *positive*.

In the second quadrant

$$\sin \theta_2 = \frac{P_2 M_2}{OP_2} = P_2 M_2$$

$$= y \text{ co-ordinate of } P_2$$

The y co-ordinate of P_2 is positive and hence in the second quadrant the sine of an angle is positive.

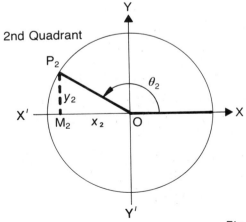

Fig. 41.2

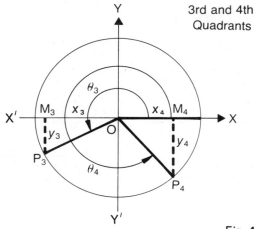

3rd and 4th Quadrants

Fig. 41.2

In the third quadrant by similar considerations

$$\sin \theta_3 = -\sin (\theta_3 - 180°)$$
$$\cos \theta_3 = -\cos (\theta_3 - 180°)$$
$$\tan \theta_3 = \tan (\theta_3 - 180°)$$

In the fourth quadrant,

$$\sin \theta_4 = -\sin (360° - \theta_4)$$
$$\cos \theta_4 = \cos (360° - \theta_4)$$
$$\tan \theta_4 = -\tan (360° - \theta_4)$$

$$\cos \theta_2 = \frac{OM_2}{OP_2} = OM_2$$

$$= x \text{ co-ordinate of } P_2$$

The x co-ordinate of P_2 is negative and hence in the second quadrant the cosine of an angle is negative.

$$\tan \theta_2 = \frac{P_2 M_2}{OM_2} = \frac{y \text{ co-ordinate of } P_2}{x \text{ co-ordinate of } P_2}$$

But the y co-ordinate of P_2 is positive and the x co-ordinate of P_2 is negative, hence the tangent of an angle in the second quadrant is negative.

The trigonometrical tables usually give values of the trigonometrical ratios for angles between $0°$ and $90°$. In order to use these tables for angles greater than $90°$ we make use of the triangle $OP_2 M_2$, where we see that

$$P_2 M_2 = OP_2 \sin (180 - \theta_2)$$
$$= \sin (180 - \theta_2)$$

But

$$P_2 M_2 = \sin \theta_2$$
$$\therefore \quad \sin \theta_2 = \sin (180 - \theta_2)$$

Also

$$OM_2 = -OP_2 \cos (180 - \theta_2)$$
$$= -\cos (180 - \theta_2)$$
$$\therefore \quad \cos \theta_2 = -\cos (180 - \theta_2)$$

Similarly

$$\tan \theta_2 = -\tan (180 - \theta_2)$$

The results are summarised in Fig. 41.3.

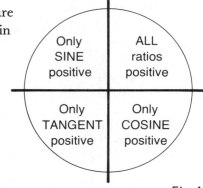

Fig. 41.3

EXAMPLE 1

Find the values of $\sin 158°$, $\cos 158°$ and $\tan 158°$. Referring to Fig. 41.4,

$$\sin 158° = \frac{MP}{OP} = \sin \angle POM$$
$$= \sin (180° - 158°)$$
$$= \sin 22° = 0.3746$$

$$\cos 158° = \frac{OM}{OP} = -\cos \angle POM$$
$$= -\cos (180° - 158°)$$
$$= -\cos 22° = -0.9272$$

$$\tan 158° = \frac{MP}{OM} = -\tan \angle POM$$
$$= -\tan (180° - 158°)$$
$$= -\tan 22° = -0.4040$$

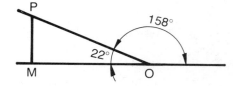

Fig. 41.4

The table below may be used for angles in any quadrant.

Quadrant	Angle	$\sin\theta =$	$\cos\theta =$	$\tan\theta =$
First	$0°-90°$	$\sin\theta$	$\cos\theta$	$\tan\theta$
Second	$90°-180°$	$\sin(180°-\theta)$	$-\cos(180°-\theta)$	$-\tan(180°-\theta)$
Third	$180°-270°$	$-\sin(\theta-180°)$	$-\cos(\theta-180°)$	$\tan(\theta-180°)$
Fourth	$270°-360°$	$-\sin(360°-\theta)$	$\cos(360°-\theta)$	$-\tan(360°-\theta)$

EXAMPLE 2

(1) Find the sine and cosine of the following angles:

(a) $171°$ (b) $216°$ (c) $289°$.

(a) $\sin 171° = \sin(180° - 171°) = \sin 9°$

$\qquad = 0.1564$

$\cos 171° = -\cos(180° - 171°)$

$\qquad = -\cos 9° = -0.9877$

(b) $\sin 216° = -\sin(216° - 180°)$

$\qquad = -\sin 36° = -0.5878$

$\cos 216° = -\cos(216° - 180°)$

$\qquad = -\cos 36° = -0.8090$

(c) $\sin 289° = -\sin(360° - 289°)$

$\qquad = -\sin 71° = -0.9455$

$\cos 289° = \cos(360° - 289°)$

$\qquad = \cos 71° = 0.3256$.

(2) Find all the angles between $0°$ and $180°$:

(a) whose sine is 0.4676;

(b) whose cosine is -0.3572.

(a) The angles whose sines are 0.4676 occur in the first and second quadrants.

In the first quadrant:

$\qquad \sin\theta = 0.4676$

$\qquad \theta = 27° 53'$

In the second quadrant:

$\qquad \theta = 180° - 27° 53'$

$\qquad = 152° 7'$ (see Fig. 41.5)

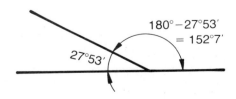

$$180° - 27°53'$$
$$= 152°7'$$
$$27°53'$$

Fig. 41.5

(b) The angle whose cosine is -0.3572 occurs in the second quadrant (i.e., the angle is between $90°$ and $180°$).

If $\cos\theta = 0.3572$

$\qquad \theta = 69° 4'$

In the second quadrant:

$\qquad \theta = 180° - 69° 4'$

$\qquad \theta = 110° 56'$ (see Fig. 41.6)

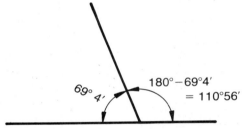

$$69° 4'$$
$$180° - 69°4'$$
$$= 110°56'$$

Fig. 41.6

(3) If $\sin A = \dfrac{3}{5}$ find the values of $\cos A$.

As shown in Fig. 41.7, the angle A may be in the first or second quadrants. In the first quadrant, by Pythagoras,

$$OM_1{}^2 = OP_1{}^2 - P_1M_1{}^2 = 5^2 - 3^2 = 16$$

$\therefore \qquad\qquad OM_1 = 4$

$$\cos A = \frac{OM_1}{OP_1} = \frac{4}{5}$$

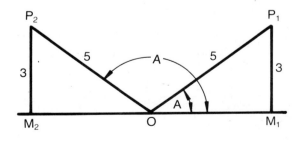

Fig. 41.7

313

In the second quadrant:

$$OM_2 = -4$$

$$\cos A = \frac{OM_2}{M_2 P_2} = -\frac{4}{5}$$

Exercise 180 — *All type C*

1) Copy and complete the following table.

θ	$\sin \theta$	$\cos \theta$	$\tan \theta$
108°			
163°			
207°			
320°			
134°			
168°			
225°			
286°			
300°			
95°			

2) If $\sin A = \dfrac{a \sin B}{b}$, find the values of A between 0° and 180° when $a = 7.26$ cm, $b = 9.15$ cm and $B = 18° 29'$.

3) If $\cos C = \dfrac{a^2 + b^2 - c^2}{2ab}$, find the values of C between 0° and 180° when $a = 1.26$ m, $b = 1.41$ m and $c = 2.13$ m.

4) Copy and complete the following table.

Trigonometrical ratio	Angle in			
	1st quadrant	2nd quadrant	3rd quadrant	4th quadrant
$\sin \theta = 0.5163$				
$\sin \theta = 0.2167$				
$\sin \theta = -0.4069$				
$\cos \theta = 0.8817$				
$\cos \theta = -0.7613$				
$\cos \theta = -0.0812$				
$\tan \theta = 1.6042$				
$\tan \theta = 0.8142$				
$\tan \theta = -0.2316$				

5) Use tables to find the angles x and y between 0° and 360° where $\sin x = 0.5688$ and $\cos y = 0.8774$.

6) If $\sin A = \dfrac{12}{13}$ find, without using tables, the values of $\tan A$ and $\cos A$, A being acute.

7) Evaluate $\sin A \cos B - \sin B \cos A$ given that $\sin A = \dfrac{3}{5}$ and $\tan B = \dfrac{4}{3}$. A and B are both acute angles.

8) The angle A is acute and $\tan A = \dfrac{15}{8}$. Without using tables find the value of $\sin(180° - A)$. If $B = 90° - A$ find the value of $\tan B$.

9) The angle A is acute and $\cos A = \dfrac{60}{61}$. Without using trigonometry tables, find the value of $\tan A$.

THE STANDARD NOTATION FOR A TRIANGLE

In $\triangle ABC$ (Fig. 41.8) the angles are denoted by the capital letters as shown in the diagram. The side a lies opposite the angle A, the side b opposite the angle B and the side c opposite the angle C. This is the standard notation for a triangle.

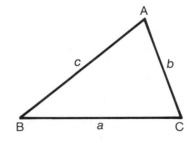

Fig. 41.8

THE SOLUTION OF TRIANGLES

We now deal with triangles which are not right-angled. Every triangle consists of six elements — three sides and three angles. If we are given any three of these elements we can find the other three elements by using either the sine rule or the cosine rule. When we have found the values of the three missing elements we are said to have solved the triangle.

THE SINE RULE

The sine rule may be used when we are given:

(1) One side and any two angles.

(2) Two sides and an angle opposite to one of the sides.

Using the notation of Fig. 41.8

$$\frac{a}{\sin A} = \frac{b}{\sin B} = \frac{c}{\sin C}$$

This formula is proved as follows for both acute-angled and obtuse-angled triangles.

(1) When $\triangle$ ABC is acute angled (Fig. 41.9).

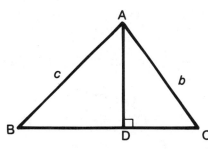

Fig. 41.9

In $\triangle$ ABD,

$$AD = c \sin B$$

In $\triangle$ ADC,

$$AD = b \sin C$$

$\therefore$ $b \sin C = c \sin B$

or

$$\frac{b}{\sin B} = \frac{c}{\sin C}$$

Similarly, by drawing the perpendicular from B to AC,

$$\frac{a}{\sin A} = \frac{c}{\sin C}$$

$\therefore$

$$\frac{a}{\sin A} = \frac{b}{\sin B} = \frac{c}{\sin C}$$

(2) When $\triangle$ ABC is obtuse-angled (Fig. 41.10).

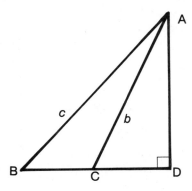

Fig. 41.10

In $\triangle$ ACD,

$$AD = b \sin (180° - C) = b \sin C$$

In $\triangle$ ABD,

$$AD = c \sin B$$

$\therefore$ $b \sin C = c \sin B$

$$\frac{b}{\sin B} = \frac{c}{\sin C}$$

As before,

$$\frac{a}{\sin A} = \frac{b}{\sin B} = \frac{c}{\sin C}$$

EXAMPLE 3

Solve $\triangle$ ABC given that   A = 42°,   C = 72° and   b = 61.8 mm.

The triangle should be drawn for reference as shown in Fig. 41.11 but there is no need to draw it to scale.

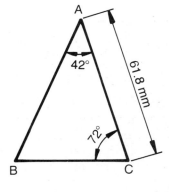

Fig. 41.11

Since

$$A + B + C = 180°$$

$$B = 180° - 42° - 72° = 66°$$

315

The sine rule states:

$$\frac{a}{\sin A} = \frac{b}{\sin B}$$

$$a = \frac{b \sin A}{\sin B}$$

$$= \frac{61.8 \times \sin 42°}{\sin 66°}$$

$$= 45.27 \text{ mm}$$

number	log
61.8	1.7910
sin 42°	$\bar{1}.8255$
	1.6165
sin 66°	$\bar{1}.9607$
45.27	1.6558

also,

$$\frac{c}{\sin C} = \frac{b}{\sin B}$$

$$c = \frac{b \sin C}{\sin B}$$

$$= \frac{61.8 \times \sin 72°}{\sin 66°}$$

$$= 64.34 \text{ mm}$$

number	log
61.8	1.7910
sin 72°	$\bar{1}.9782$
	1.7692
sin 66°	$\bar{1}.9607$
64.34	1.8085

The complete solution is:

$$\angle B = 66°, \quad a = 45.27 \text{ mm}$$

$$c = 64.34 \text{ mm}$$

A rough check on sine rule calculations may be made by remembering that in any triangle the longest side lies opposite to the largest angle and the shortest side lies opposite to the smallest angle. Thus in the previous example:

smallest angle $= 42° = A$;

shortest side $= a = 45.27$ mm

largest angle $= 72° = C$;

longest side $= c = 64.34$ mm

USE OF THE SINE RULE TO FIND THE DIAMETER OF THE CIRCUMSCRIBING CIRCLE OF A TRIANGLE

Using the notation of Fig. 41.12

$$\frac{a}{\sin A} = \frac{b}{\sin B} = \frac{c}{\sin C} = D$$

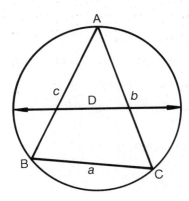

Fig. 41.12

EXAMPLE 4

In $\triangle$ ABC, B $= 41°$, $b = 112.5$ mm and $a = 87.63$ mm. Find the diameter of the circumscribing circle. Referring to Fig. 41.13

$$D = \frac{b}{\sin B} = \frac{112.5}{\sin 41°} = 171.5 \text{ mm}$$

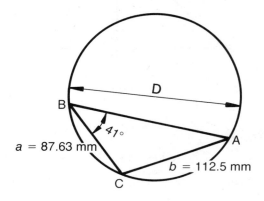

Fig. 41.13

Exercise 181 — *Questions 1–13 type C, remainder B*

Solve the following triangles ABC by using the sine rule, given:

1) A $= 75°$ B $= 34°$ $a = 10.2$ cm

2) C $= 61°$ B $= 71°$ $b = 91$ mm

3) A $= 19°$ C $= 105°$ $c = 11.1$ m

4) A = 116°   C = 18° a = 17 cm

5) A = 36°   B = 77° b = 2.5 m

6) A = 49° 11'   B = 67° 17' c = 11.22 mm

7) A = 17° 15'   C = 27° 7' b = 22.15 m

8) A = 77° 3'   C = 21° 3' a = 9.793 m

9) B = 115° 4'   C = 11° 17' c = 516.2 mm

10) a = 7 m c = 11 m   C = 22° 7'

11) b = 15.13 cm

c = 11.62 cm   B = 85° 17'

12) a = 23 cm c = 18.2 cm   A = 49° 19'

13) a = 9.217 cm

b = 7.152 cm   A = 105° 4'

Find the diameter of the circumscribing circle of the following triangles ABC given:

14) A = 75°   B = 48° a = 21 cm

15) C = 100°   B = 50° b = 90 mm

16) A = 20°   C = 102° c = 11 m

17) A = 70°   C = 35° a = 8.5 cm

18) a = 16 cm b = 14 cm   B = 40°

THE COSINE RULE

This rule is used when we are given:

either (1) two sides of a triangle and the angle between them

or   (2) three sides of a triangle.

In all other cases the sine rule is used. The cosine rule states:

either $a^2 = b^2 + c^2 - 2bc \cos A$

or $b^2 = a^2 + c^2 - 2ac \cos B$

or $c^2 = a^2 + b^2 - 2ab \cos C$

When using the cosine rule remember that if an angle is greater than 90° its cosine is negative.

EXAMPLE 5

(1) Solve △ ABC if a = 70 mm, b = 40 mm and C = 64°.

Referring to Fig. 41.14, to find the side c we use:

$$c^2 = a^2 + b^2 - 2ab \cos C$$
$$= 70^2 + 40^2 - 2 \times 70 \times 40 \times \cos 64°$$
$$= 4044$$
$$c = \sqrt{4044} = 63.59 \text{ mm}$$

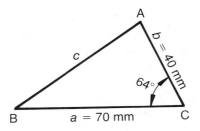

Fig. 41.14

We now use the sine rule to find the angle A:

$$\frac{a}{\sin A} = \frac{c}{\sin C}$$

$$\sin A = \frac{a \sin C}{c} = \frac{70 \times \sin 64°}{63.59}$$

$$A = 81° 42'$$

$$B = 180° - 81° 42' - 64° = 34° 18'$$

The complete solution is

$$A = 81° 42', \quad B = 34° 18'$$

and c = 63.59 mm

(2) Find the side b in △ ABC if a = 160 mm, c = 200 mm and B = 124° 15'.

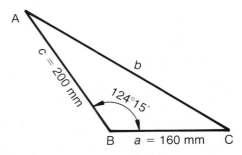

Fig. 41.15

Referring to Fig. 41.15, to find the side b we use:

$$b^2 = a^2 + c^2 - 2ac \cos B$$
$$= 160^2 + 200^2 - 2 \times 160$$
$$\times 200 \times \cos 124° 15'$$

Now $\cos 124° 15'$

$$= -\cos (180° - 124° 15')$$

$$= -\cos 55° 45' = -0.5628$$

$\therefore$

$$b^2 = 160^2 + 200^2 - 2 \times 160$$

$$\times 200 \times (-0.5628)$$

$$= 160^2 + 200^2 + 2 \times 160 \times 200 \times 0.5628$$

$$b = 318.7 \text{ mm}$$

Exercise 182 — *All type C*

Solve the following triangles ABC using the cosine rule, given:

1) $a = 9$ cm $b = 11$ cm $C = 60°$

2) $b = 10$ cm $c = 14$ cm $A = 56°$

3) $a = 8.16$ m $c = 7.14$ m $B = 37° 18'$

4) $a = 5$ m $b = 8$ m $c = 7$ m

5) $a = 312$ mm $b = 527.3$ mm $c = 700$ mm

6) $a = 7.912$ cm $b = 4.318$ cm $c = 11.08$ cm

7) $a = 12$ cm $b = 9$ cm $C = 118°$

8) $b = 8$ cm $c = 12$ cm $A = 132°$

AREA OF A TRIANGLE

In Chapter 26, two formulae for the area of a triangle were used. They are:

(1) Given the base and altitude of the triangle (Fig. 41.16)

$$\text{Area} = \tfrac{1}{2} \times \text{base} \times \text{altitude}$$

or $A = \tfrac{1}{2}bh$

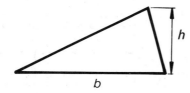

Fig. 41.16

(2) Given the three sides of the triangle (Fig. 41.17)

$$A = \sqrt{s(s-a)(s-b)(s-c)}$$

318

where

$$s = \tfrac{1}{2}(a + b + c)$$

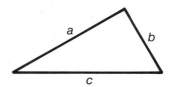

Fig. 41.17

However a third formula can be used to find the area of a triangle when we are given two sides of the triangle and the angle included between these sides. Referring to Fig. 41.18,

$$\text{Area} = \tfrac{1}{2}ab \sin C$$

$$\text{Area} = \tfrac{1}{2}ac \sin B$$

$$\text{Area} = \tfrac{1}{2}bc \sin A$$

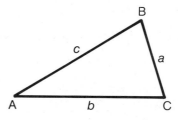

Fig. 41.18

EXAMPLE 6

Find the area of the triangle shown in (Fig. 41.19)

$$\text{Area} = \tfrac{1}{2}ac \sin B$$

$$= \tfrac{1}{2} \times 4 \times 3 \times \sin 30° = 3 \text{ cm}^2$$

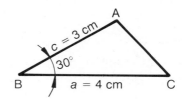

Fig. 41.19

EXAMPLE 7

Find the area of the obtuse angled triangle shown in Fig. 41.20.

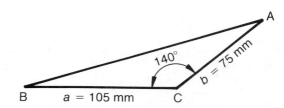

Fig. 41.20

Area $= \frac{1}{2}ab \sin C$

$\qquad = \frac{1}{2} \times 105 \times 75 \times \sin 140°$

We find the value of $\sin 140°$ by the method used earlier in this chapter.

$\sin 140° = \sin (180° - 140°)$

$\qquad = \sin 40° = 0.6428$

Area $= \frac{1}{2} \times 105 \times 75 \times 0.6428$

$\qquad = 2531 \text{ mm}^2$

Exercise 183 — *All type C*

In this exercise any of the three formulae given above may be needed.

1) Obtain the area of a triangle whose sides are 39.3 cm and 41.5 cm if the angle between them is $41° 30'$.

2) Find the area of the template shown in Fig. 41.21.

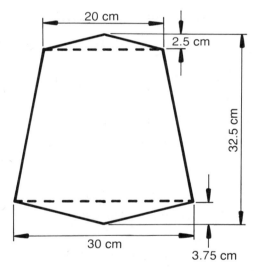

Fig. 41.21

3) Calculate the area of a triangle ABC if:

(a) $a = 4$ cm, $b = 5$ cm and $C = 49°$.

(b) $a = 3$ m, $c = 6$ m and $B = 63° 44'$.

4) Find the areas of the quadrilaterals shown in Fig. 41.22.

5) Find the areas of the following triangles:

(a) $a = 5$ cm, $b = 7$ cm and $\angle C = 105°$.

(a)

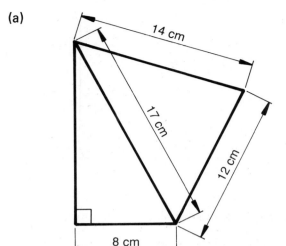

(b)

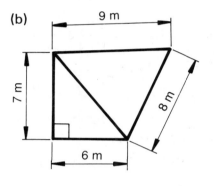

(c)

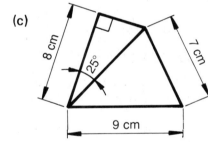

Fig. 41.22

(b) $b = 7.3$ cm, $c = 12.2$ cm and $\angle A = 135°$.

(c) $a = 9.6$ cm, $c = 11.2$ cm and $\angle B = 163°$.

6) Find the area of the parallelogram shown in Fig. 41.23.

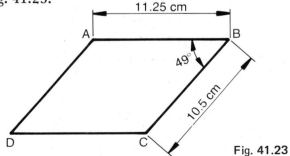

Fig. 41.23

319

7) Find the area of the trapezium shown in Fig. 41.24.

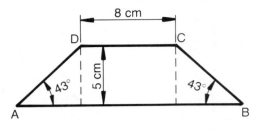

Fig. 41.24

8) Find the area of a regular octagon which has sides 2 cm long.

SELF-TEST 41

1) $\cos 120°$ is equal to:

a $-\dfrac{1}{2}$ b $+\dfrac{1}{2}$ c $+\dfrac{\sqrt{3}}{2}$ d $-\dfrac{\sqrt{3}}{2}$

2) $\sin 150°$ is equal to:

a $-\dfrac{1}{2}$ b $+\dfrac{1}{2}$ c $-\dfrac{\sqrt{3}}{2}$ d $+\dfrac{\sqrt{3}}{2}$

3) $\tan 120°$ is equal to:

a $+\sqrt{3}$ b $+\dfrac{\sqrt{3}}{3}$ c $-\sqrt{3}$ d $-\dfrac{\sqrt{3}}{3}$

4) $\sin 240°$ is equal to:

a $-\dfrac{1}{2}$ b $+\dfrac{1}{2}$ c $-\dfrac{\sqrt{3}}{2}$ d $+\dfrac{\sqrt{3}}{2}$

5) $\cos 210°$ is equal to:

a $-\dfrac{1}{2}$ b $+\dfrac{1}{2}$ c $-\dfrac{\sqrt{3}}{2}$ d $+\dfrac{\sqrt{3}}{3}$

6) $\tan 240°$ is equal to:

a $+\sqrt{3}$ b $-\sqrt{3}$ c $+\dfrac{\sqrt{3}}{3}$ d $-\dfrac{\sqrt{3}}{3}$

7) $\sin 300°$ is equal to:

a $-\dfrac{1}{2}$ b $+\dfrac{1}{2}$ c $-\dfrac{\sqrt{3}}{2}$ d $+\dfrac{\sqrt{3}}{2}$

8) $\cos 300°$ is equal to:

a $-\dfrac{1}{2}$ b $+\dfrac{1}{2}$ c $-\dfrac{\sqrt{3}}{2}$ d $+\dfrac{\sqrt{3}}{2}$

9) $\tan 330°$ is equal to:

a $+\sqrt{3}$ b $-\sqrt{3}$ c $+\dfrac{\sqrt{3}}{3}$ d $-\dfrac{\sqrt{3}}{3}$

10) In Fig. 41.25, given $\angle A$ and sides a and b. The angle B is given by the expression:

a $b^2 = a^2 + c^2 - 2ac \cos B$

b $\cos B = \dfrac{a^2 + c^2 - b^2}{-2ac}$

c $\dfrac{a}{\sin A} = \dfrac{b}{\sin B}$ d $\dfrac{a}{b \sin A}$

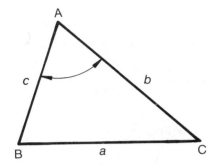

Fig. 41.25

11) In Fig. 41.26, given $\angle B$ and sides a and c. The side b is given by the expression:

a $b^2 = a^2 + c^2 - 2ac \cos B$

b $b^2 = a^2 + c^2 + 2ac \cos B$

c $b = \dfrac{a \sin B}{\sin A}$ d $b = \dfrac{\sin A}{a \sin B}$

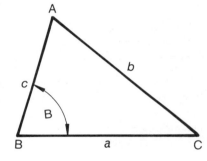

Fig. 41.26

12) If $\sin A = \dfrac{5}{13}$ then $\cos A$ is equal to:

a $\dfrac{12}{13}$ b $\dfrac{5}{12}$ c $\dfrac{-12}{13}$ d $\dfrac{-5}{12}$

13) If $\tan A = \dfrac{3}{4}$ then $\cos A$ is equal to:

a $\dfrac{3}{5}$ b $\dfrac{4}{5}$ c $\dfrac{-3}{5}$ d $\dfrac{-4}{5}$

14) If $\cos A = -\dfrac{11}{61}$ then $\sin A$ is equal to:

a $\dfrac{11}{60}$ b $\dfrac{-11}{60}$ c $\dfrac{60}{61}$ d $\dfrac{-60}{61}$

15) If $\tan A = -\dfrac{12}{5}$ then $\cos A$ is equal to:

a $\dfrac{5}{13}$ b $\dfrac{12}{13}$ c $\dfrac{-5}{13}$ d $\dfrac{-12}{13}$

Chapter 42 Solid Trigonometry

THE PLANE

A plane is a surface such as the top of a table or the cover of a book.

THE ANGLE BETWEEN A LINE AND A PLANE

In Fig. 42.1 the line PA intersects the plane WXYZ at A. To find the angle between PA and the plane draw PL which is perpendicular to the plane and join AL. The angle between PA and the plane is ∠ PAL.

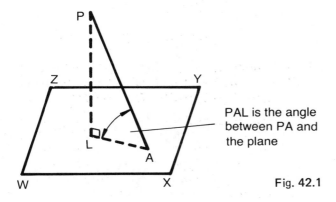

PAL is the angle between PA and the plane

Fig. 42.1

THE ANGLE BETWEEN TWO PLANES

Two planes which are not parallel intersect in a straight line. Examples of this are the floor and a wall of a room and two walls of a room. To find the angle between two planes draw a line in each plane which is perpendicular to the common line of intersection. The angle between the two lines is the same as the angle between the two planes.

Three planes usually intersect at a point as, for instance, two walls and the floor of a room.

Problems with solid figures are solved by choosing suitable right-angled triangles in different planes. It is essential to make a clear three-dimensional drawing in order to find these triangles. The examples which follow show the methods that should be adopted.

EXAMPLE 1

Figure 42.2 shows a cuboid. Calculate the length of the diagonal AG.

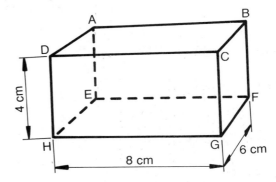

Fig. 42.2

Figure 42.3 shows that in order to find AG we must use the right-angled triangle AGE. GE is the diagonal of the base rectangle.

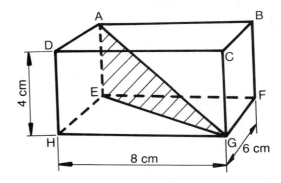

Fig. 42.3

In △ EFG,   EF = 8 cm,   GF = 6 cm   and ∠ EFG = 90°.

Using Pythagoras' theorem,

$$EG^2 = EF^2 + GF^2 = 8^2 + 6^2$$
$$= 64 + 36 = 100$$
$$EG = \sqrt{100} = 10 \text{ cm}$$

In △ AGE,   AE = 4 cm,   EG = 10 cm   and ∠ AEG = 90°.

321

Using Pythagoras' theorem,

$$AG^2 = AE^2 + EG^2 = 4^2 + 10^2$$
$$= 16 + 100 = 116$$
$$AG = \sqrt{116} = 10.77 \text{ cm}$$

EXAMPLE 2

Figure 42.4 shows a triangular prism with the face YDC inclined as shown. Find the angle that this sloping face YDC makes with the base.

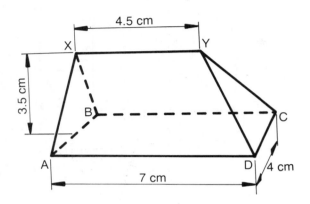

Fig. 42.4

As shown in Fig. 42.5, if we use △ YEF then the required angle is YFE. In △ YEF,

$$EF = 7 - 4.5 = 2.5 \text{ cm}$$
$$YE = 3.5 \text{ cm}$$
$$\tan \angle YFE = \frac{YE}{EF} = \frac{3.5}{2.5}$$
$$\therefore \qquad \angle YFE = 54° \ 28'$$

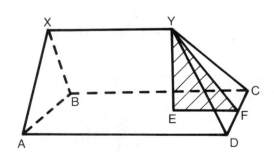

Fig. 42.5

Hence the angle that the sloping face YDC makes with the base is 54° 28'.

EXAMPLE 3

Figure 42.6 shows a pyramid with a square base. The base has sides 6 cm long and the edges of the pyramid, VA, VB, VC and VD are each 10 cm long. Find the altitude of the pyramid.

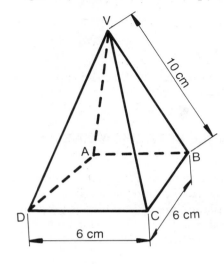

Fig. 42.6

The right-angled triangle VBE (Fig. 42.7) allows the altitude VE to be found, but first we must find BE from the right-angled triangle BEF.

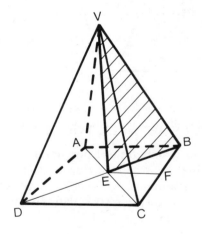

Fig. 42.7

In △ BEF, BF = EF = 3 cm and ∠ BFE = 90°.

Using Pythagoras' theorem,

$$BE^2 = BF^2 + EF^2 = 3^2 + 3^2 = 9 + 9 = 18$$
$$BE = \sqrt{18} = 4.243 \text{ cm}$$

In △ VBE, BE = 4.243 cm, VB = 10 cm and ∠ VEB = 90°.

Using Pythagoras' theorem,

$$VE^2 = VB^2 - BE^2 = 10^2 - 18$$
$$= 100 - 18 = 82$$
$$VE = \sqrt{82} = 9.055 \text{ cm}$$

Hence the altitude of the pyramid is 9.055 cm.

Exercise 184 — *All type C*

1) Figure 42.8 shows a cuboid.

(a) Sketch the rectangle EFGH.
(b) Calculate the diagonal FH of rectangle EFGH.
(c) Sketch the rectangle FHDB adding known dimensions.
(d) Calculate the diagonal BH of rectangle FHDB.

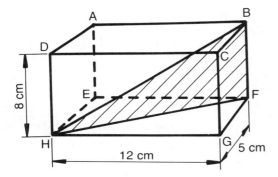

Fig. 42.8

2) Figure 42.9 shows a pyramid on a square base of side 8 cm. The altitude of the pyramid is 12 cm.

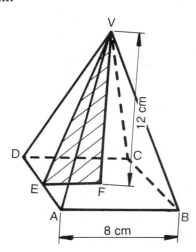

Fig. 42.9

(a) Calculate EF.
(b) Draw the triangle VEF adding known dimensions.
(c) Find the angle VEF.
(d) Calculate the slant height VE.
(e) Calculate the area of △VAD.
(f) Calculate the complete surface area of the pyramid.

3) Figure 42.10 shows a pyramid on a rectangular base. Calculate the length VA.

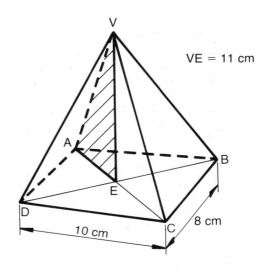

VE = 11 cm

Fig. 42.10

4) Figure 42.11 shows a pyramid on a square base with VA = VB = VC = VD = 5 cm. Calculate the altitude of the pyramid.

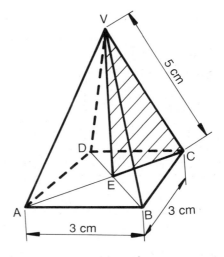

Fig. 42.11

323

5) Figure 42.12 shows a wooden wedge. Find the length EA and the angle q. The end faces ADF and EBC are isosceles triangles.

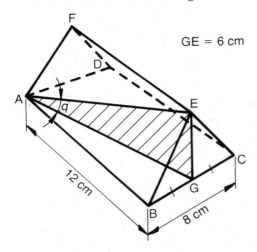

GE = 6 cm

12 cm

8 cm

Fig. 42.12

6) The base of the triangular wedge shown in Fig. 42.13 is a rectangle 8 cm long and 6 cm wide. The vertical faces ABC and PQR are equilateral triangles of side 6 cm. Calculate:

(a) the angle between the diagonals PB and PC;

(b) the angle between the plane PBC and the base;

(c) the angle between the diagonal PC and the base.

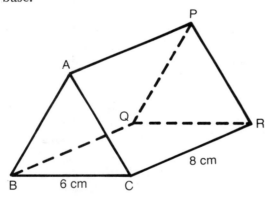

8 cm

6 cm

Fig. 42.13

7) Figure 42.14 represents a wooden block in the shape of a triangular prism in which the edges AD, BE and CF are equal and vertical and the base DEF is horizontal.
AB = BC = DE = EF = 14 cm and
∠ ABC = ∠ DEF = 40°. The points G and H are on the edges AB and BC respectively.
BG = BH = 4 cm and DG = FH = 20 cm.

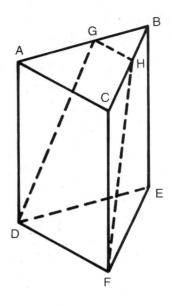

Fig. 42.14

Calculate:

(a) the length of BE;

(b) the angle between FH and the base DEF;

(c) the angle between the plane GHFD and the base DEF;

(d) the distance between the mid-points of GH and DF.

8) Figure 42.15 shows a shed with a slanting roof ABCD. The rectangular base ABEF rests on level ground and the shed has three vertical sides. Calculate:

(a) the angle of inclination of the roof to the ground;

(b) the volume of the shed in cubic metres.

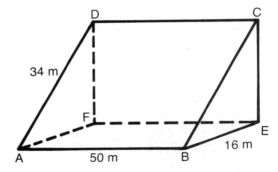

34 m

50 m

16 m

Fig. 42.15

9) The base of a pyramid consists of a regular hexagon ABCDEF of side 4 cm. The vertex of the pyramid is V and
VA = VB = VC = VD = VE = VF = 7 cm. Sketch a general view of the solid. Indicate on your diagram the angles p and q described below and calculate the size of these angles:

(a) the angle p between VA and the base;
(b) the angle q between the face VCD and the base.

10) In Fig. 42.16, ABCD represents part of a hillside. A line of greatest slope AB is inclined at 36° to the horizontal AE and runs due North from A. The line AC bears 050° (N 50° E) and C is 2500 m East of B. The lines BE and CF are vertical. Calculate:

(a) the height of C above A;
(b) the angle between AB and AC.

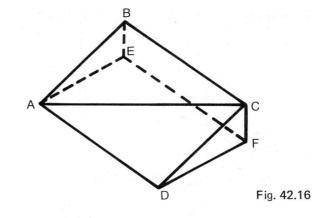

Fig. 42.16

325

Chapter 43 Maps and Contours

MAP SCALES

Map scales may be expressed as:

(1) *a ratio*, for example $1 : 25\,000$ or $\dfrac{1}{25\,000}$.

No units are involved when a scale is expressed in this way. Any distance measured off the map represents $25\,000$ times this distance on the ground.

(2) *A scale*, for example $1\text{ cm} = 1\text{ km}$.   This means that 1 cm on the map represents an actual horizontal distance of 1 kilometre.

EXAMPLE 1

(1) The scale of a map is $1 : 50\,000$. What distance does 3 cm on the map represent?

1 cm on the map represents $50\,000$ cm on the ground

or $\dfrac{50\,000}{100} = 500\text{ m}$

3 cm on the map represents $3 \times 500 = 1500$ m on the ground.

(2) The scale of a map is $1 : 25\,000$. What distance in kilometres does 1 cm represent?

1 cm on the map represents $25\,000$ cm on the ground

or $\dfrac{25\,000}{100 \times 1000} = 0.25\text{ km}$

(3) The scale of a map is $1\text{ cm} = 2\text{ km}$.

(a) What distance does 3.5 cm on the map represent?
(b) What is the scale expressed as a ratio?

(a) 3.5 cm on the map represents $3.5 \times 2 = 7$ km   on the ground.

(b) map scale $= \dfrac{1\text{ cm}}{2\text{ km}}$

$= \dfrac{1\text{ cm}}{2 \times 1000 \times 100\text{ cm}}$

$= \dfrac{1}{200\,000}$

The map scale is $1 : 200\,000$.

326

1) The scale of a map is $1 : 20\,000$. What distance does 5 cm on the map represent?

2) The scale of a map is $1 : 100\,000$. What distance does 28 cm on the map represent?

3) The scale of a map is $1 : 50\,000$. What distance does 1 cm on the map represent?

4) The scale of a map is $1\text{ cm} = 5\text{ km}$. Express this scale as a ratio.

5) The scale of a map is $1\text{ cm} = 100\text{ km}$. Express this scale as a ratio.

6) The scale of a map is $1\text{ cm} = 10\text{ km}$. What distance does 8 cm on the map represent?

7) The scale of a map is $1 : 200\,000$. What distance on the map represents 150 km?

8) The scale of a map is $1\text{ cm} = 50\text{ km}$. What distance on the map represents 80 km?

9) The distance, measured on a map, between two towns is 8.3 cm. If the map scale is $1 : 25\,000$ how far are the two towns apart?

10) The scale of a map is $2\text{ cm} = 1\text{ km}$. The distance, measured on the map, between two points is 11.2 cm. How far apart are the two points?

AREAS ON MAPS

When areas are to be compared it is necessary to use the square of the map scale.

EXAMPLE 2

(1) If a map scale is $1 : 25\,000$ what area does 5 cm^2 represent?

5 cm^2 on the map represents

$5 \times (25\,000)^2$ on the ground

or $\dfrac{5 \times (25\,000)^2}{100^2}\text{ m}^2$ on the ground

$= 312\,500\text{ m}^2$ on the ground

(2) The scale of a map is 1 cm = 5 km. What area does 8 cm² represent? How many cm² represents 1 km².

8 cm² on the map represents 8×5^2 km² or 200 km².

Since   5 km = 1 cm

$$1 \text{ km} = \frac{1}{5} \text{ cm}$$

and $1 \text{ km}^2 = \left(\frac{1}{5}\right)^2 \text{ cm}^2 = \frac{1}{25} \text{ cm}^2$

Hence 0.04 cm² represents 1 km².

Exercise 186 — *All type B*

1) The scale of a map is 1 : 20 000. What area does 3 cm² represent?

2) The scale of a map is 1 : 10 000. What area does 8 cm² represent?

3) The scale of a map is 1 cm = 2 km. How many cm² represents 1 km²?

4) The scale of a map is 1 cm = 10 km. What area does 7 cm² represent?

5) A, B and C are three positions on a map whose scale is 10 cm to 1 km. AB = 7 cm, AC = 5 cm and ∠ BAC = 50°. Calculate:
(a) the area of the triangle ABC on the map;
(b) the length of BC on the ground in metres;
(c) the actual area represented by the triangle ABC.

6) The scale of a map is 5 cm to 1 km. A field is represented by a trapezium (Fig. 43.1). What is the actual area of the field?

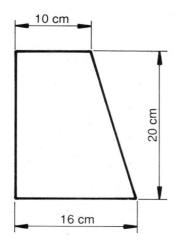

10 cm
20 cm
16 cm

Fig. 43.1

7) A triangular plot of land when measured on a map has sides of 8 cm, 9 cm and 11 cm. If the scale of the map is 1 : 10 000 what is the actual area of the plot in hectares.
(1 hectare = 10 000 m²).

GRADIENT

When used in connection with roads and railways the gradient is used to denote the ratio of the vertical distance to the corresponding distance measured along the slope. Thus in Fig. 43.2:

$$\text{gradient} = \frac{BC}{AB}$$

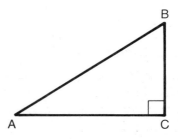

Fig. 43.2

The gradient is usually expressed as a ratio or a percentage. If a road has a gradient of 1 in 20, we mean that for every 20 m along the slope the road rises 1 m vertically. This gradient is often stated as being 5%, i.e. $\frac{1}{20} \times 100 = 5\%$.

EXAMPLE 3
(1) Two points P and Q are linked by a straight road with a uniform gradient. If Q is 50 m higher than P and the distance PQ measured along the road is 800 m, what is the gradient of the road?

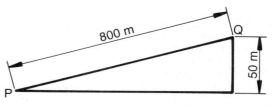

800 m
Q
50 m
P

Fig. 43.3

Referring to Fig. 43.3 we see that:

$$\text{gradient} = \frac{50}{800} = \frac{1}{16} = \frac{1}{16} \times 100 = 6\tfrac{1}{4}\%$$

The gradient of the road is 1 in 16 or $6\tfrac{1}{4}\%$.

(2) A man walks 3 km up a road whose gradient is 1 in 15. How much higher is he than when he started?

From Fig. 43.4

$$\text{gradient of road} = \frac{x}{3000}$$

$$\therefore \qquad \frac{x}{3000} = \frac{1}{15}$$

$$x = \frac{3000}{15} = 200 \text{ m}$$

The man is 200 m higher than when he started.

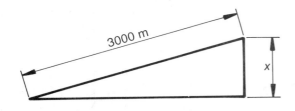

Fig. 43.4

Exercise 187 — *All type B*

1) Two points A and B are connected by a straight road with a uniform gradient. If A is 40 m higher than B and the distance AB (measured along the road) is 1 km, what is the gradient of the road?

2) Two points P and Q whose heights differ by 50 m are connected by a straight road 2 km long. What is the gradient of the road?

3) A road has a gradient of 1 in 15. A man walks $1\frac{1}{2}$ km up the road. How much higher is he than when he first started?

4) A man walks up a road whose gradient is 1 in 30. If he walks a distance of 900 m how much higher is he than when he first started?

5) A road has a gradient of $12\frac{1}{2}\%$. What angle does the road make with the horizontal?

6) A mountain track is inclined at $12°$ to the horizontal. Express the gradient of the track as $1 : n$.

7) A man walks 100 m up a slope whose gradient is 5% and then a further 80 m up a slope whose gradient is $12\frac{1}{2}\%$. How much higher is he than when he first started?

8) Two points P and Q have heights which differ by 100 m. If the gradient of the line joining P and Q is 1 in 12 what is the distance PQ?

CONTOURS

The contour lines on a map join places which have the same height. Figure 43.5 shows a small hill. The bottom view (the plan view) is the one which would be shown on a map.

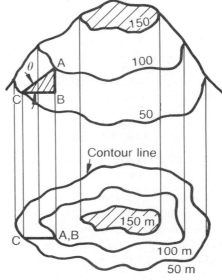

Fig. 43.5

Suppose A and C are two positions on a path up the hill, the path being taken as a straight line. It will be seen that C is on the 50 m contour and A is on the 100 m contour. B is directly below A (within the hill) and on the same contour as C. A and B appear as the same point on the map but the height AB is 50 m. The distance AC measured on the map corresponds to the length BC on the elevation.

The angle of elevation is θ and $\tan\theta = \dfrac{AB}{BC}$.

The gradient is $\dfrac{AB}{AC}$.

EXAMPLE 4

(1) Two points P and Q whose heights differ by 50 m are shown 0.60 cm apart on a map whose scale is 1 : 25 000. Calculate the angle of elevation of the line PQ.

328

0.60 cm on the map represents 0.6 × 25 000 cm on the ground.

or $\dfrac{0.6 \times 25\,000}{100}$ m on the ground

$= 150$ m

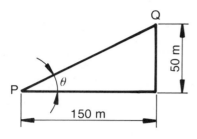

Fig. 43.6

From Fig. 43.6,

$$\tan \theta = \frac{50}{150} = 0.333\,3$$

$$\theta = 18° \, 26'$$

∴ angle of elevation $= 18° \, 26'$.

(2) Two points A and B are linked by a straight road with a uniform gradient. A is on the 100 m contour and B is on the 125 m contour. If the scale of the map is 10 cm to 1 km and the distance AB on the map is 4 cm find the gradient of the road giving the answer in the form '1 in n'.

The map is shown in Fig. 43.7.

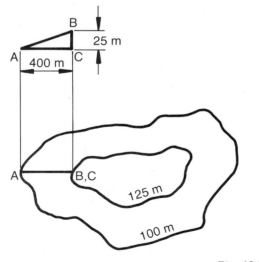

Fig. 43.7

Since the map scale is 10 cm to 1 km, 4 cm represents

$$\frac{4}{10} \times 1 = 0.4 \text{ km}$$

$= 400$ m on the ground

Referring to the triangle ABC,

$$\text{Gradient} = \frac{\text{vertical height}}{\text{distance along slope}} = \frac{\text{BC}}{\text{AB}}$$

$$\text{AB} = \sqrt{\text{AC}^2 + \text{BC}^2} = \sqrt{400^2 + 25^2}$$

$$= 400.6 \text{ m}$$

$$\text{Gradient} = \frac{25}{400.6}$$

$$= 25 : 400.6$$

$$= 1 : 16.024$$

Exercise 188 — *All type B*

1) Two points A and B whose heights differ by 100 m are shown 1.2 cm apart on a map whose scale is 1 : 10 000. Calculate the angle of elevation of the line AB.

2) Two points P and Q whose heights differ by 150 m are shown 0.8 cm apart on a map whose scale is 1 cm = 500 m. Calculate the gradient of the line PQ, giving the answer in the form '1 in n'.

3) A and B are two positions on a map whose scale is 10 cm to 1 km. A is on the 500 m contour and B is on the 250 m contour. The distance AB measured on the map is 8 cm. Find the angle of elevation from B to A.

4) Fig. 43.8 is a scale drawing of a contour map.

Heights in metres

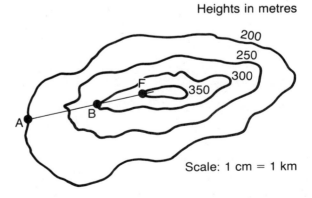

Scale: 1 cm = 1 km

Fig. 43.8

From the map:

(a) Find the difference in levels between A and and B.

(b) The horizontal distance between A and B.

(c) The average gradient between A and B.

(d) Draw a section from A to F using a vertical scale of 1 cm = 50 m and for horizontal distances 2 cm = 1 km.

5) Figure 43.9 is a scale drawing (scale 2 cm to 1 km) of part of a contour map of a given area.

(a) What is the difference in levels between:
  (i) B and G;
  (ii) the highest and lowest points on the drawing?

(b) What is the horizontal distance between:
  (i) A and C;
  (ii) D and J?

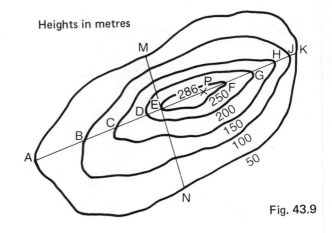

Heights in metres

Fig. 43.9

(c) What is the average angle of slope of the roadway ME?

(d) On graph paper, draw a section from A to K, using a vertical scale of 1 cm to 50 cm.

Chapter 44 The Sphere, Latitude and Longitude

THE EARTH AS A SPHERE

The earth is usually assumed to be a sphere whose radius is 6370 km.

A circle on the surface of the earth whose centre is at the centre of the earth is called a *great circle*. The shortest distance between any two places on the earth's surface is the minor arc of the great circle passing through them. The semi-circles whose end points are N and S are called *meridians*.

LATITUDE AND LONGITUDE

Any point on the earth's surface can be fixed by using two angles, but we must fix two reference planes at right-angles to each other. The two reference planes which are used are:

(1) The equatorial plane, which is a plane through the earth's centre at right-angles to the polar axis NS. The intersection of this plane with the earth's surface is called the *equator*.

(2) A plane at right-angles to the equatorial plane containing the polar axis NS and also Greenwich. This plane is a meridian plane and its intersection with the earth's surface is called the *Greenwich meridian*.

The *latitude* of the point P (Fig. 44.1) is the angle POQ marked θ in the diagram. It is measured from $0°$ to $90°$N or S of the equator. A circle on the surface of the earth whose centre is not the centre of the earth is called a *small circle*. Small circles whose centres lie on the polar axis NS are *circles of latitude*.

The *longitude* of the point P is the angle POP$_1$ or QOQ$_1$ marked ϕ in Fig. 44.1. It is measured east or west of the Greenwich meridian from $0°$ to $180°$ each way. The angle ϕ which denotes the longitude is rather like the angle of a slice of an orange. It should be noted that all meridian circles are great circles but all great circles are not meridian circles. For instance, the equator is a great circle but it is not a meridian circle

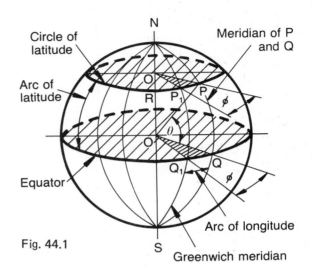

Fig. 44.1

because it does not contain the poles N and S. All points with the *same* longitude lie on the same meridian circle. All points with the same latitude lie on the same circle of latitude. Thus in Fig. 44.1 the points P and R have the same latitude.

EXAMPLE 1

(1) Two places A and B have the same longitude. A has latitude $30°$N and B has latitude $15°$S. Find the distance between them along their meridian.

This problem boils down to finding the length of the arc AB (Fig. 44.2).

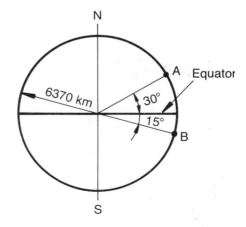

Fig. 44.2

331

$$\text{Length of arc AB} = 2\pi \times 6370 \times \frac{45°}{360°}$$

$$= 5005 \text{ km}$$

Therefore distance between the places A and B is 5005 km.

(2) Two places P and Q are on the equator. P has longitude 20°W and Q has longitude 40°E. What is the distance between them?

This problem boils down to finding the length of the arc PQ (Fig. 44.3).

$$\text{Length of arc PQ} = 2\pi \times 6370 \times \frac{60°}{360°}$$

$$= 6673 \text{ km}$$

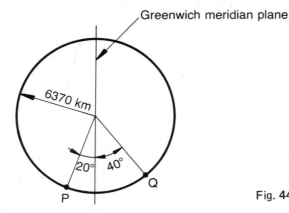

Fig. 44.3

CIRCLES OF LATITUDE

When two places have the same latitude but different longitudes, to find the distance between them we must first find the radius of the circle of latitude.

Referring to Fig. 44.4, O is the centre of the

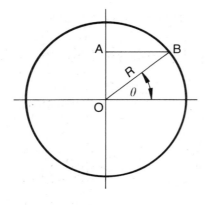

Fig. 44.4

earth and θ is the latitude. The radius of this circle of latitude is AB and

$$AB = R \cos \theta$$

where R is the radius of the earth.

EXAMPLE 2

(1) Find the distance along the parallel of latitude between two places which have the latitude 30°N and which differ in longitude by 60°.

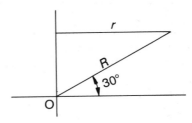

Fig. 44.5

If r (Fig. 44.5) is the radius of the circle of latitude then

$$r = R \cos \theta = 6370 \times \cos 30° = 5516 \text{ km}$$

If, in Fig. 44.6, A and B represent the two places then the problem boils down to finding the length of the arc AB.

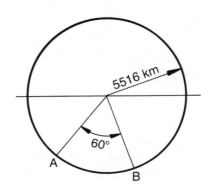

Fig. 44.6

$$\text{Length of arc AB} = 2\pi \times 5516 \times \frac{60°}{360°}$$

$$= 5777 \text{ km}$$

Therefore distance along the parallel of latitude between the two places is 5777 km.

(2) P and Q are both in latitude 50°N and the distance between them, measured along the parallel of latitude, is 2000 km. The longitude of P is 16° 46′ W and Q is situated west of P. Calculate the longitude of Q.

The first step is to find the radius of the circle of latitude. Thus,

$$r = R \cos \theta = 6370 \times \cos 50° = 4095 \text{ km}$$

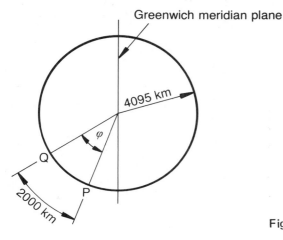

Fig. 44.7

The problem now boils down to finding the angle ϕ (Fig. 44.7).

$$2000 = 2\pi \times 4095 \times \frac{\phi}{360}$$

$$\phi = \frac{2000 \times 360}{2\pi \times 4095} = 28°$$

The longitude of Q is

$$28° + 16° \ 46′ = 44° \ 46′ \text{ W}$$

Exercise 189 — *All type B*

(Take the radius of the earth as 6370 km)

1) The latitudes of two places A and B are 43°N and 12°S and they both lie on the same meridian. Find the distance between them measured along the meridian.

2) The latitudes of two places P and Q are 17°S and 35°S and they both lie on the same meridian. Find the distance between them measured along the meridian.

3) The latitudes of two places are 30° 52′ N and 9° 8′ S and they both lie on the same meridian. Find the distance between them measured along the meridian.

4) Find the radius of the circle of latitude 30°S.

5) Find the distance along the parallel of latitude between two places both having a latitude of 60°N which differ in longitude by 40°.

6) The position of Leningrad is Lat. 60°N, Long. 34°E.

(a) Calculate the distance from Leningrad to the North Pole.

(b) Calculate the longitude of the point P that you will reach if you travel this distance due east from Leningrad.

7) A classroom globe has a radius of 22.5 cm. Calculate, in centimetres, the distance, measured along their line of latitude, between two cities both in latitude 50° 30′ N and in longitudes 5°E and 13° 30′ E.

8) A ship steamed 500 km due E from A (Latitude 20°N, Longitude 40°W) to B and then 300 km due N from B to C. Calculate the latitude and longitude of C to the nearest minute.

9) A ship sails due south from a port in latitude 24°S, longitude 46° 20′ W to a point in latitude 38°S. Find the distance that the ship has travelled. The ship now turns and travels the same distance due east along the line of latitude 38°S. Calculate the new longitude.

10) (a) The distance measured along a parallel of latitude, between two points of longitude 24°W and 28°W respectively is 300 km. Calculate the latitude of either point.

(b) Calculate the great circle distance of Vladivostock (43° 10′ N, 132°E) from the equator.

LONGITUDE AND TIME

The earth rotates from west to east. The earth rotates once in 24 hours. We may use this fact to calculate the difference in time between two places provided we know the longitudes of the two places.

EXAMPLE 3

(1) Two places A and B have longitudes 40°E and 84°E respectively. Find the time at B when it is noon at A.

333

Difference in longitude
$$= 84° - 40° = 44°$$

Difference in time
$$44 \times \frac{24}{360} = 2.93 \text{ hours}$$
$$= 2 \text{ hours } 56 \text{ min}$$

Since B is further east than A, the time at B when it is noon at A is 2.56 p.m. or 14.56 hours, provided the clocks were set to agree with the sun.

(2) Aberdeen has a longitude of $2° 5'$ W and Stockholm's longitude is $18° 3'$ E. How much earlier does the sun set in Stockholm?

Difference in longitude
$$= 2° 5' + 18° 3' = 20° 8' = 20\tfrac{8}{60}°$$

Difference in time
$$= 20\tfrac{8}{60} \times \tfrac{24}{360} = 1.33 \text{ hours}$$
$$= 1 \text{ hour } 20 \text{ minutes}$$

The sun sets 1 hour 20 minutes earlier in Stockholm than it does in Aberdeen.

Clock times are arranged to be the same in specified areas. For instance in Great Britain all clock times are the same as those at Greenwich, that is, they are based on Greenwich Mean Time (often abbreviated to G.M.T.). Central European Time is one hour ahead of G.M.T. and Eastern European Time is two hours ahead of G.M.T.

Exercise 190 — *All type B*

1) Two places X and Y have longitudes of 30°E and 50°E respectively. Find the time at Y when it is noon at X.

2) Town A has longitude $4° 6'$ W and town B has longitude $9° 7'$ E. How much earlier does the sun set in B?

3) Two places have longitudes $112° 46'$ E and $48° 44'$ E respectively. What is the difference in local time?

4) K is a town on the equator whose longitude is 120°W and F is on the Greenwich meridian. Find the difference in time between the two places.

5) P has latitude 47°N and longitude 18°E. R has latitude 47°N and longitude 54°W. What time is it at R when it is 11 a.m. at P?

6) Two places A and B have longitudes 10°E and 90°E respectively.

(a) When local time at A is 11.00 hours, what is the local time at B?

(b) When local time at B is 12.00 hours, what is the local time at A?

(c) When the local time at A is 16.00 hours the local time at a third place C is 11.00 hours on the same day. What is the longitude of C?

Chapter 45 Vectors

VECTOR QUANTITIES

A *vector* is a quantity which possesses both magnitude (or size) and direction. Some examples of vector quantities are:

(1) A displacement from one point to another, e.g. 15 m due east.

(2) A velocity in a given direction, e.g. 8 m/s due north.

(3) A force acting in a given direction, e.g. 20 newtons acting downwards.

REPRESENTING VECTOR QUANTITIES

If Susan walks 8 metres due east, how can we represent this vector quantity in a diagram? We first choose a suitable scale to represent the information. In Fig. 45.1 a scale of   1 cm = 1 m has been chosen. We then draw a line 8 cm long to represent 8 m in an easterly direction. An arrow is placed on the line to make it clear that Susan walked to the east (and not to the west).

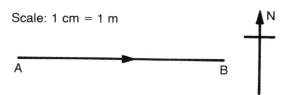

Scale: 1 cm = 1 m

Fig. 45.1

When we want to refer to a vector several times we need a shorthand way of doing this. The usual way is to name the end points of the vector. The vector described by Susan would have started at A and ended at B. If we now want to refer to the vector we write $\overrightarrow{AB}$ which means 'the vector from A to B'.

Exercise 191 — *All type A*

Draw the following vectors using a convenient scale for each. Label each vector correctly.

1) $\overrightarrow{AB}$ 5 m due North

2) $\overrightarrow{XY}$ 8 km due South

3) $\overrightarrow{PQ}$ 7 km due West

4) $\overrightarrow{MN}$ 10 m due East

5) $\overrightarrow{RS}$ 6 m South-East

RESULTANT VECTORS

In Fig. 45.2, A, B and C are three points marked out in a field. A man walks from A to B (i.e. he describes $\overrightarrow{AB}$) and then walks from B to C (i.e. he describes $\overrightarrow{BC}$). Instead, the man could have walked from A to C, thus describing the vector $\overrightarrow{AC}$.

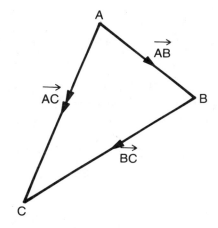

Fig. 45.2

Now going from A to C direct has the same result as going from A to C via B. We therefore call $\overrightarrow{AC}$ the *resultant* of the vectors $\overrightarrow{AB}$ and $\overrightarrow{BC}$. Note carefully that the arrows on the vectors $\overrightarrow{AB}$ and $\overrightarrow{BC}$ follow nose to tail. The resultant $\overrightarrow{AC}$ is marked with a double arrow which opposes the arrows on AB and BC.

TRIANGLE LAW

The resultant of any two vectors is equal to the length and direction of the line needed to complete the triangle. This is called the triangle law.

335

EXAMPLE 1

Two vectors act as shown in Fig. 45.3. Find the resultant of these two vectors.

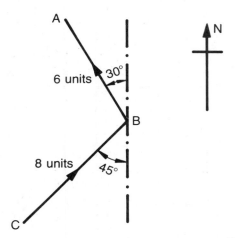

Fig. 45.3

The vector triangle is drawn to scale in Fig. 45.4. The resultant is $\overrightarrow{CA}$. The length of $\overrightarrow{CA}$, written $|\overrightarrow{CA}|$, is 11.2 units. To state its direction we measure the angle ACX which is found to be 31°.

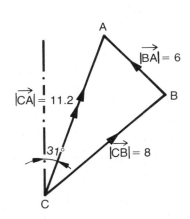

Fig. 45.4

Exercise 192 — *All type B*

Find the resultant (in magnitude and direction) of the pairs of vectors shown in Fig. 45.5.

1)

2)

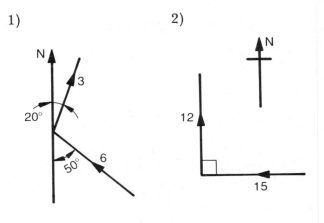

3)

4)

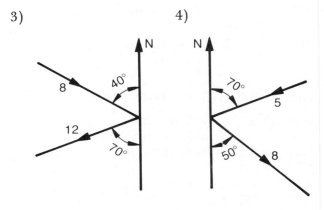

5)

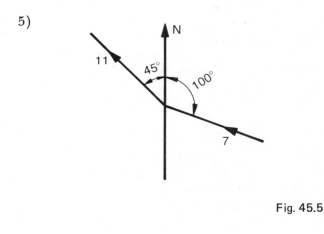

Fig. 45.5

EQUAL VECTORS

Two vectors are equal if they have the *same magnitude* and the same direction. Hence in Fig. 45.6, the vector AB is equal to the vector CD, because the length of AB is equal to that of CD and AB is parallel to CD.

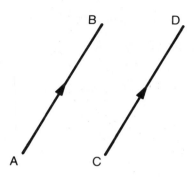

Fig. 45.6

INVERSE VECTORS

In Fig. 45.7, the vector $\overrightarrow{BA}$ has the same magnitude as $\overrightarrow{AB}$ but its direction is reversed. Hence $\overrightarrow{BA} = -\overrightarrow{AB}$. $\overleftarrow{BA}$ is said to be the inverse of $\overleftarrow{AB}$.

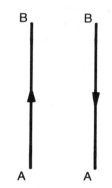

Fig. 45.7

THE SUM OF TWO VECTORS

In Fig. 45.8 the arrows on the vectors $\overrightarrow{AB}$ and $\overrightarrow{BC}$ follow nose to tail. Hence we say that $\overrightarrow{AC}$ is the resultant of these two vectors and we write:

$$\overrightarrow{AB} + \overrightarrow{BC} = \overrightarrow{AC}$$

The resultant vector $\overrightarrow{AC}$ is the sum of the two vectors $\overrightarrow{AB}$ and $\overrightarrow{BC}$.

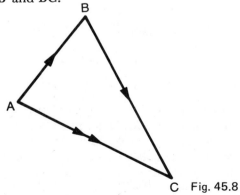

Fig. 45.8

EXAMPLE 2

ABCD is a parallelogram (Fig. 45.9). $\overrightarrow{AB} = x$ and $\overrightarrow{BC} = y$.

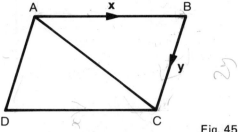

Fig. 45.9

(a) Express $\overrightarrow{DC}$ in terms of x.

(b) Express $\overrightarrow{AD}$ in terms of y.

(c) Express $\overrightarrow{AC}$ in terms of x and y.

(a) $\overrightarrow{DC}$ is equal to $\overrightarrow{AB}$ because they have the same magnitude and AB and DC are parallel. Hence $\overrightarrow{DC} = x$.

(b) For the same reasons, $\overrightarrow{AD} = \overrightarrow{BC}$ and hence $\overrightarrow{AD} = y$.

(c) AC is the resultant of AB and BC because the arrows on AB and AC follow nose to tail. Hence:

$$\overrightarrow{AC} = \overrightarrow{AB} + \overrightarrow{BC} = x + y$$

More than two vectors may be added together. The resultant of the four vectors shown in Fig. 45.10 is found by drawing the vector diagram as shown. Thus:

$$a + b + c + d = r$$

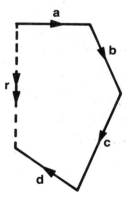

Fig. 45.10

The addition of vectors is commutative. That is, it does not matter in which order the vectors are added. In Fig. 45.11 in (a) a has been added to b whilst in (b) b has been added to a. In each case the resultant is the same.

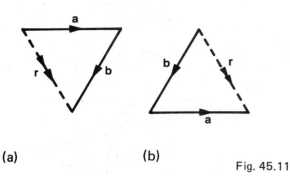

(a)   (b)

Fig. 45.11

SUBTRACTION OF VECTORS

To subtract a vector we add its inverse. Hence

$$\overrightarrow{AC} - \overrightarrow{BC} = \overrightarrow{AC} + \overrightarrow{CB} = \overrightarrow{AB}$$

as shown in Fig. 45.12.

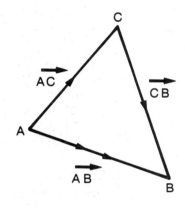

Fig. 45.12

MULTIPLYING BY A SCALAR

If a vector $\overrightarrow{AB}$ is 5 m due North, then the vector $3\overrightarrow{AB}$ is 15 m due North. In general, if k is any number, the vector $k\overrightarrow{AB}$ is a vector in the same direction as $\overrightarrow{AB}$ whose length is k times the length of $\overrightarrow{AB}$.

EXAMPLE 3
C is the mid-point of AD (Fig. 45.13) and $AC = \mathbf{a}$. Express $\overrightarrow{DA}$ in terms of $\mathbf{a}$.

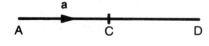

Fig. 45.13

$$\overrightarrow{AD} = \overrightarrow{AC} + \overrightarrow{CD} = \mathbf{a} + \mathbf{a} = 2\mathbf{a}$$

Since $\overrightarrow{DA}$ is the inverse of $\overrightarrow{AD}$,

$$\overrightarrow{DA} = -2\mathbf{a}$$

DISTRIBUTIVE LAW FOR VECTORS

From our previous work

$$3\mathbf{a} = \mathbf{a} + \mathbf{a} + \mathbf{a}$$

$$\therefore \quad 3(\mathbf{a} + \mathbf{b}) = (\mathbf{a} + \mathbf{b}) + (\mathbf{a} + \mathbf{b}) + (\mathbf{a} + \mathbf{b})$$

$$= \mathbf{a} + \mathbf{b} + \mathbf{a} + \mathbf{b} + \mathbf{a} + \mathbf{b}$$

$$= (\mathbf{a} + \mathbf{a} + \mathbf{a}) + (\mathbf{b} + \mathbf{b} + \mathbf{b})$$

$$= 3\mathbf{a} + 3\mathbf{b}$$

Similarly it can be shown that, if k is a scalar,

$$k(\mathbf{a} + \mathbf{b}) = k\mathbf{a} + k\mathbf{b}$$

This is the distributive law for vectors.

EXAMPLE 4
In Fig. 45.14, $\overrightarrow{PX} = \mathbf{a}$ and $\overrightarrow{XQ} = \mathbf{b}$. $\overrightarrow{YP} = 2\mathbf{a}$ and $\overrightarrow{QZ} = 2\mathbf{b}$. Find $\overrightarrow{YZ}$ in terms of $\mathbf{a}$ and $\mathbf{b}$ and show that PQ and YZ are parallel.

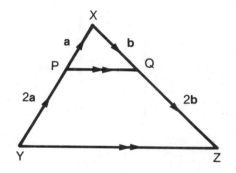

Fig. 45.14

Referring to Fig. 45.14, we see that

$$\overrightarrow{PQ} = \mathbf{a} + \mathbf{b}$$

$$\overrightarrow{YZ} = \overrightarrow{YX} + \overrightarrow{XZ} = (2\mathbf{a} + \mathbf{a}) + (2\mathbf{b} + \mathbf{b})$$

$$= 3\mathbf{a} + 3\mathbf{b} = 3(\mathbf{a} + \mathbf{b})$$

Hence $\overrightarrow{YZ}$ is 3 times the magnitude of $\overrightarrow{PQ}$. Since $\overrightarrow{PQ} = (\mathbf{a} + \mathbf{b})$ and $\overrightarrow{YZ} = 3(\mathbf{a} + \mathbf{b})$, $\overrightarrow{PQ}$ and $\overrightarrow{YZ}$ must be in the same direction; i.e. they are parallel to each other.

EXAMPLE 5
In Fig. 45.15, M is the mid-point of RS. $PQ = \mathbf{a}$, $QR = \mathbf{b}$ and $MR = \mathbf{c}$. Express each of the following in terms of $\mathbf{a}$, $\mathbf{b}$ and $\mathbf{c}$.

(a) $\overrightarrow{SR}$ (b) $\overrightarrow{PR}$ (c) $\overrightarrow{QM}$ (d) $\overrightarrow{PM}$

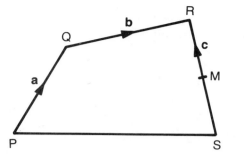

(a)

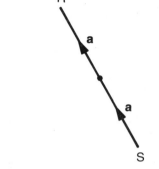

(b)

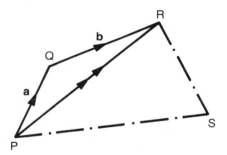

(c)

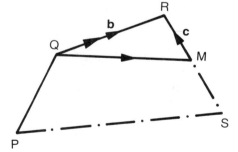

(d)

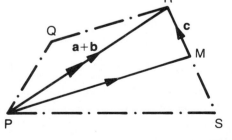

Fig. 45.15

Fig. 45.16

(a) In Fig. 45.16(a),

$$\overrightarrow{SR} = 2\overrightarrow{MR} = 2c$$

(b) In △PQR (Fig. 45.16(b)), PR is the resultant of PQ and QR. Hence:

$$\overrightarrow{PR} = \overrightarrow{PQ} + \overrightarrow{QR} = a + b$$

(c) In △QRM (Fig. 45.16(c)), QR is the resultant of QM and RM. Hence:

$$\overrightarrow{QR} = \overrightarrow{QM} + \overrightarrow{MR}$$

$$\overrightarrow{QM} = \overrightarrow{QR} - \overrightarrow{MR} = b - c$$

(d) In △PRM (Fig. 45.16(d)), PR is the resultant of PM and MR. Hence:

$$\overrightarrow{PR} = \overrightarrow{PM} + \overrightarrow{MR}$$

$$\overrightarrow{PM} = \overrightarrow{PR} - \overrightarrow{MR} = a + b - c$$

Exercise 193 — *All type C*

1) In Fig. 45.17, ABCD is a parallelogram. AB = **a** and BC = **b**. Express in terms of **a** and **b**:

(a) $\overrightarrow{AD}$ (b) $\overrightarrow{CD}$ (c) $\overrightarrow{AC}$.

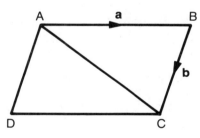

Fig. 45.17

2) In Fig. 45.18, NP = 2MN. If MN = **a**, express in terms of **a**:

(a) $\overrightarrow{NP}$ (b) $\overrightarrow{PM}$.

Fig. 45.18

3) In Fig. 45.19, XYZ is an isosceles triangle. W is the mid-point of XZ. If $\overrightarrow{XY} = $ **a** and $\overrightarrow{YZ} = $ **b**, express in terms of **a** and **b**:

(a) $\overrightarrow{XZ}$ (b) $\overrightarrow{ZW}$ (c) $\overrightarrow{YW}$.

339

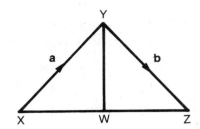

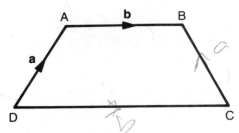

Fig. 45.19

Fig. 45.22

4) In Fig. 45.20, ABC is a triangle in which AC = **a**, BC = **b** and AD = **c**. D is the mid-point of AB. Express in terms of **a, b** and **c**:

(a) $\overrightarrow{DB}$ (b) $\overrightarrow{BA}$ (c) $\overrightarrow{CD}$.

7) In Fig. 45.23, ST = 2TP. If $\overrightarrow{TP}$ = **a**, $\overrightarrow{PQ}$ = **b** and $\overrightarrow{QR}$ = **c**, express in terms of **a, b** and **c**:

(a) $\overrightarrow{RT}$ (b) $\overrightarrow{ST}$ (c) $\overrightarrow{SR}$.

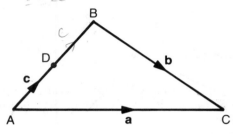

Fig. 45.20

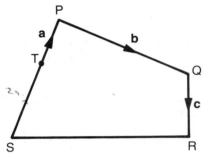

Fig. 45.23

5) In Fig. 45.21, D and E are the mid-points of AB and AC respectively. AD = **a** and AE = **b**. Express in terms of **a** and **b**:

(a) $\overrightarrow{ED}$ (b) $\overrightarrow{DE}$ (c) $\overrightarrow{BD}$
(d) $\overrightarrow{AB}$ (e) $\overrightarrow{CE}$ (f) $\overrightarrow{AC}$.

8) In Fig. 45.24, ABCDEF is a regular hexagon. If AF = **a**, AB = **b** and BC = **c**, express each of the following in terms of **a, b** and **c**:

(a) $\overrightarrow{DC}$ (b) $\overrightarrow{DE}$ (c) $\overrightarrow{FE}$
(d) $\overrightarrow{FC}$ (e) $\overrightarrow{AE}$ (f) $\overrightarrow{AD}$.

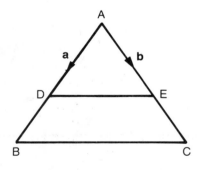

Fig. 45.21

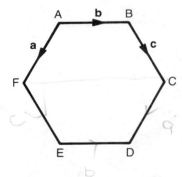

Fig. 45.24

THE PARALLELOGRAM OF VECTORS

Two vectors may be added by drawing a parallelogram of vectors. This is an alternative method to the triangle of vectors so far used. The method is shown in Example 6.

6) In Fig. 45.22, AB is parallel to DC and DC = 2AB. If $\overrightarrow{DA}$ = **a** and $\overrightarrow{AB}$ = **b**, express in terms of **a** and **b**:

(a) $\overrightarrow{DB}$ (b) $\overrightarrow{DC}$ (c) $\overrightarrow{BC}$.

EXAMPLE 6

Draw the parallelogram of vectors for the two vectors shown in Fig. 45.25(a) and hence find their resultant in magnitude and direction.

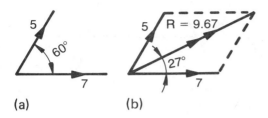

Scale: 1 cm = 1 unit

Fig. 45.25

The two vectors are drawn to scale with the angle between them accurately made by using a protractor. The parallelogram is then completed as shown by the dotted lines in diagram (b). The diagonal drawn from the point where the two original vectors meet gives the resultant vector, in magnitude and direction. On scaling, it is found to be 9.6 units acting in a direction of 27° to the 7 unit vector.

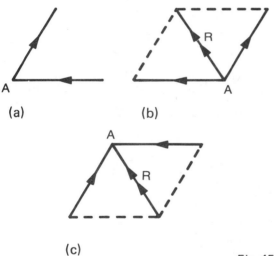

Fig. 45.26

Note that when using a parallelogram of vectors both the arrows on the original vectors must either point away from the point of intersection of the two vectors or they must point towards it. In Fig. 45.26(a) the arrows on the two vectors do not conform to the rule. One arrow points towards A whilst the other points away from A. However, the horizontal vector remains unchanged if we draw it as shown in diagram (b), i.e. with its arrow pointing away from A. Alternatively, the parallelogram may be drawn as shown in diagram (c) with both arrows

pointing towards A. Note that if both arrows point away from A (diagram (b)) then the arrows on the resultant also point away from A. If both arrows point towards A, then the resultant vector also points towards A.

Exercise 194 — *All type B*

By drawing a parallelogram of vectors find the resultant vector in each of the cases shown in Fig. 45.27.

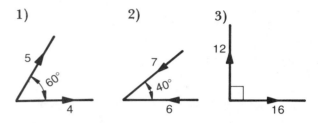

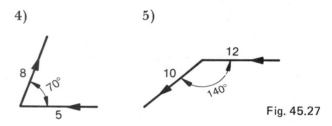

Fig. 45.27

APPLICATION OF VECTORS TO GEOMETRY

It will be recalled that the vectors **a** and k**a**, where k is a scalar, are parallel, and also that $k(\mathbf{a} + \mathbf{b}) = k\mathbf{a} + k\mathbf{b}$.

These two facts are useful in solving certain geometric problems.

EXAMPLE 7

(1) ABCD is a parallelogram. DN and BM are perpendicular to the diagonal AC. Show that BM = DN.

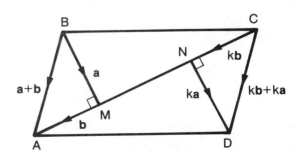

Fig. 45.28

341

BM and DN are parallel since they both lie at 90° to AC. Let $\overrightarrow{BM} = \mathbf{a}$ and $\overrightarrow{ND} = k\mathbf{a}$ (Fig. 45.28).

Also, AM and NC lie in the same straight line. Let $\overrightarrow{MA} = \mathbf{b}$ and $\overrightarrow{CN} = k\mathbf{b}$.

$$\overrightarrow{BA} = \overrightarrow{BM} + \overrightarrow{MA} = \mathbf{a} + \mathbf{b}$$

$$\overrightarrow{CD} = \overrightarrow{CN} + \overrightarrow{ND} = k\mathbf{b} + k\mathbf{a} = k(\mathbf{a} + \mathbf{b})$$

Since $\overrightarrow{BA} = \overrightarrow{CD}$

$$\mathbf{a} + \mathbf{b} = k(\mathbf{a} + \mathbf{b})$$

$\therefore \qquad\qquad k = 1$

$\therefore \qquad\qquad \mathbf{a} = k\mathbf{a}$

Hence $\qquad\qquad BM = DN$

(2) In $\triangle ABC$, D is a point on AB such that BD = 2AD and E is a point in AC such that CE = 2AE. Show that DE is parallel to BC and that BC = 3DE.

The conditions are shown in Fig. 45.29.

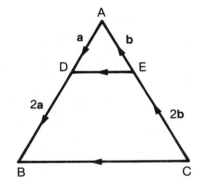

Fig. 45.29

Let $\overrightarrow{AD} = \mathbf{a}$, then $\overrightarrow{DB} = 2\mathbf{a}$.

Let $\overrightarrow{EA} = \mathbf{b}$, then $\overrightarrow{CE} = 2\mathbf{b}$.

Referring to Fig. 42.29, we see that

$$\overrightarrow{ED} = \mathbf{b} + \mathbf{a}$$

$$\overrightarrow{CB} = (\mathbf{b} + 2\mathbf{b}) + (\mathbf{a} + 2\mathbf{a})$$

$$= 3\mathbf{b} + 3\mathbf{a} = 3(\mathbf{b} + \mathbf{a})$$

Hence DE is parallel to BC and BC = 3DE.

Exercise 195 — *All type C*

The following questions should be solved by using vectors.

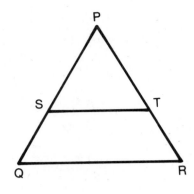

Fig. 45.30

1) In $\triangle PQR$ (Fig. 45.30), the line ST is drawn parallel to QR so that PS = 3SQ. Prove that PT = 3TR.

2) In the parallelogram ABCD, the point P is taken on the side AB such that AP = 2PB. The lines BD and PC intersect at O. Show that OC = 3PO.

3) In $\triangle ABC$, the point P is the mid-point of AB. A line through P parallel to BC meets AC at Q. Prove that PQ = ½BC.

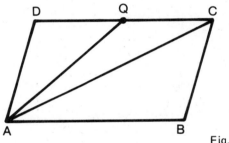

Fig. 45.31

4) In Fig. 45.31, ABCD is a parallelogram. Q is the mid-point of CD. Show that 2AQ = AD + AC = 2AD + AB.

5) AB is parallel to DC and AB = DC. Prove that BC is parallel to AD and that BC = AD.

6) In Fig. 45.32, D is the mid-point of BC and AG = ⅔AD. Prove that 2BD + AB = 3BG.

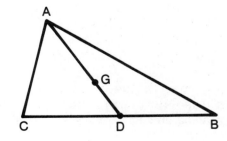

Fig. 45.32

7) In △ABC, P is the mid-point of AB and Q is the mid-point of AC. Show that BC is parallel to PQ and that BC = 2PQ.

8) Two parallelograms ABCD and ABEF are shown in Fig. 45.33. Prove that DCEF is a parallelogram.

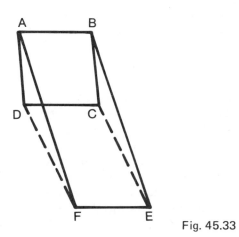

Fig. 45.33

VELOCITY VECTORS

Velocity is speed in a given direction. Hence velocity is a vector quantity. Common examples of velocity vectors is the flight of aeroplanes and the motion of a boat through water.

COURSE AND AIRSPEED

The direction in which an aircraft is heading (i.e. pointing) is called its *course*. It is the angle between the longitudinal axis of the aircraft and the direction of north (Fig. 45.34).

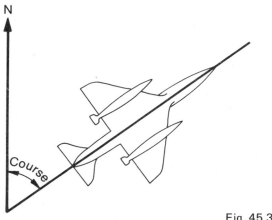

Fig. 45.34

The course is usually given in the three digit notation, e.g. 036° or 205°. The airspeed is the speed of the aircraft in still air and the airspeed at which an aircraft is flying may be read directly from the airspeed indicator which is an instrument mounted in the cockpit. The course is measured by means of the aircraft's compass and hence airspeed and course form a vector quantity.

TRACK AND GROUNDSPEED

The track is the direction which the aircraft follows relative to the ground. If the sun is immediately overhead the track is the path of the aircraft's shadow over the ground. When a pilot wishes to fly from aerodrome A to aerodrome B, his track would be the straight line joining A and B. The groundspeed is the speed of the aircraft relative to the ground and it is affected by the direction and speed of the wind. It is the groundspeed which determines the time that a flight will take. Groundspeed and track form a vector quantity just as did airspeed and course.

WIND DIRECTION AND SPEED

The direction of the wind is always given as the direction from which the wind is blowing. The arrow on the wind vector always points in the direction to which the wind blows. Thus a wind of 40 km/h blowing from 060° will be represented as shown in Fig. 45.35.

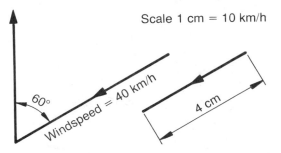

Scale 1 cm = 10 km/h

Fig. 45.35

DRIFT

The wind always tries to blow an aircraft off course, that is, it causes *drift*. The drift is the angle between the course and the track (Fig. 45.36). If there is no wind there is no drift and the airspeed and groundspeed are identical as are the course and the track.

343

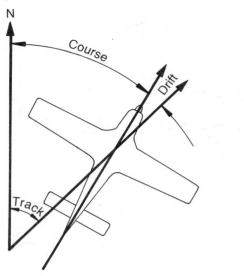

Fig. 45.36

THE TRIANGLE OF VELOCITIES

When an aeroplane is flying it has two velocities as follows:

(1) its velocity through the air due to the engine,

(2) the velocity due to the wind.

These two velocities combine to give a resultant velocity which is the groundspeed.

In order to determine this resultant velocity we draw a triangle of velocities similar to the one shown in Fig. 45.37. In drawing this triangle note carefully that *the arrows on the airspeed and windspeed vectors follow nose to tail.*

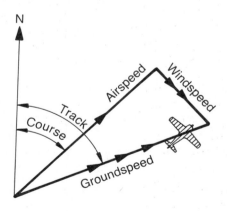

Fig. 45.37

Case 1: Given airspeed and course, windspeed and direction and to find groundspeed and track.

344

EXAMPLE 7

An aircraft whose airspeed is 400 km/h flies on a course of 050°. If the wind blows at 50 km/h from 310° find the track and groundspeed.

(a) Draw diagram (a) in Fig. 45.38 which shows the directions of the airspeed (A/S) and the windspeed (W/S). On this diagram only the angles are drawn accurately.

(b) To draw the velocity triangle first choose a suitable scale to represent the velocities. In Fig. 45.38 (b) a scale of 1 cm = 50 km/h has been chosen. Using set-squares draw AB parallel to the A/S and 8 cm long to represent 400 km/h. From B draw a line parallel to the W/S 1 cm long to give the point C. Join AC. AC represents the groundspeed (G/S) in magnitude and direction. Scale off AC which is found to be 8.24 cm representing 412 km/h. To find the direction of AC (i.e. the track) draw a line parallel to AC onto diagram (a) as shown. Using a protractor the track is found to be 57°.

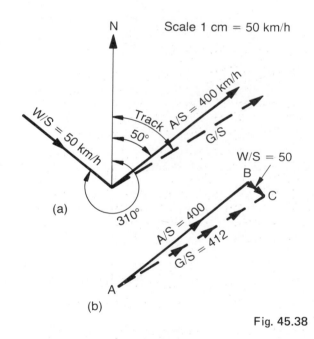

Fig. 45.38

Case 2: Given airspeed and course, groundspeed and track to find windspeed and direction.

EXAMPLE 8

The course and airspeed of an aircraft are 060° and 500 km/h whilst its track and groundspeed are 070° and 520 km/h. Find the speed and direction of the wind.

(a)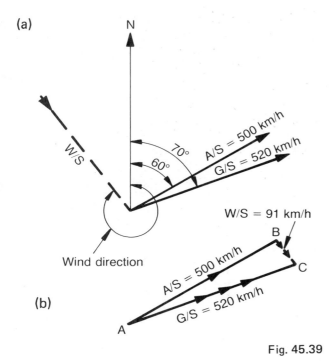

(b)

Fig. 45.39

(a)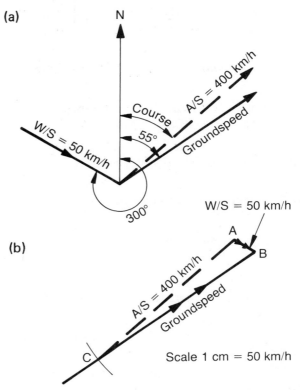

(b)

Scale 1 cm = 50 km/h

Fig. 45.40

(a) Draw diagram (a) in Fig. 45.39 which shows the directions of the airspeed (A/S) and the groundspeed (G/S). On this diagram only the angles are drawn accurately.

(b) To draw the velocity triangle shown in diagram (b) a scale of 1 cm = 50 km/h has been chosen. Using set squares draw AB, 10 cm long, parallel to A/S and then draw AC, 10.4 cm long, parallel to G/S. Join BC. BC represents the windspeed and scaling BC the windspeed is found to be 91 km/h. To find the wind direction draw a line parallel to BC on diagram (a) as shown. By using a protractor the wind direction is found to be 322° (that is, the wind blows from 322°).

Case 3: Given airspeed, track, windspeed and wind direction to find the course and groundspeed.

Since a navigator knows his airspeed and the track required and also the windspeed and direction this is the case usually met with in practice.

EXAMPLE 9
An aircraft has an airspeed of 400 km/h and its track is 055°. The speed of the wind is 50 km/h blowing from 300°. Find the course and groundspeed.

On diagram (a) in Fig. 45.40 we can draw the wind direction and also the track of the aircraft.

(a) Choosing a scale of 1 cm = 50 km/h we draw AB = 1 cm to represent to windspeed (diagram (b)). From B draw a line parallel to G/S. The length of this line is not known as yet. With compasses set at 8 cm (to represent the A/S of 400 km/h) and centre A draw an arc to cut the G/S line at C. BC represents the G/S and by scaling, the G/S = 419. Drawing a line parallel to AC on diagram (a) the course is found to be 048° 30′.

Exercise 196 — *All type C*

Find the track and groundspeed in each of the following:

1) Course 270°, airspeed 300 km/h; wind 135°, 60 km/h.

2) Course 090°, airspeed 500 km/h; wind 010°, 50 km/h.

3) Course 150°, airspeed 400 km/h; wind 070°, 50 km/h.

4) Course 310°, airspeed 350 km/h; wind 110°, 40 km/h.

345

5) Course 020°, airspeed 300 km/h; wind 320°, 80 km/h.

Find the wind velocity for each of the following:

6) Course 050°, airspeed 280 km/h; track 060°, groundspeed 300 km/h.

7) Course 160°, airspeed 350 km/h; track 180°, groundspeed 330 km/h.

8) Course 210°, airspeed 420 km/h; track 190°, groundspeed 410 km/h.

9) Course 300°, airspeed 450 km/h; track 320°, groundspeed 435 km/h.

10) Course 060°, airspeed 250 km/h; track 040°, groundspeed 260 km/h.

Find the course and groundspeed for each of the following:

11) Track 090°, airspeed 300 km/h; wind 060°, 50 km/h.

12) Track 150°, airspeed 400 km/h; wind 040°, 30 km/h.

13) Track 210°, airspeed 350 km/h; wind 100°, 50 km/h.

14) Track 300°, airspeed 250 km/h; wind 120°, 45 km/h.

15) Track 010°, airspeed 300 km/h; wind 330°, 60 km/h.

THE TRIANGLE OF VELOCITIES APPLIED TO BOATS

The motion of a boat through water is very similar to the flight of an aeroplane through air. The corresponding terms are: for wind velocity read current velocity; for airspeed read the speed of the boat through the water (i.e., waterspeed); for groundspeed and track read resultant speed and the direction of motion of the boat.

EXAMPLE 10

P is the point on the bank of a river 240 m wide flowing at 2 m/s. R is directly opposite P. A boat travels through the water at 8 m/s.

(a) If the boat starts from P and heads directly across the stream how far downstream from R will it reach the bank.

(b) Calculate the speed relative to the banks with which a direct crossing from P to R will be made.

(a) The triangle of velocities is shown in Fig. 45.41 from which $\theta = 14°$.

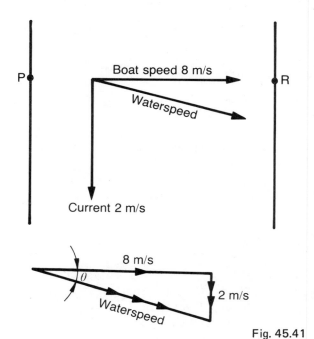

Fig. 45.41

Referring to Fig. 45.42, it will be seen that distance downstream from
R = 240 tan 14° = 60 m.

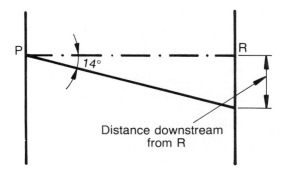

Fig. 45.42

(b) The problem here is to find the waterspeed. From the triangle of velocities (Fig. 45.43)

$$\text{Waterspeed} = \sqrt{8^2 - 2^2} = \sqrt{60} = 7.75 \text{ m/s}.$$

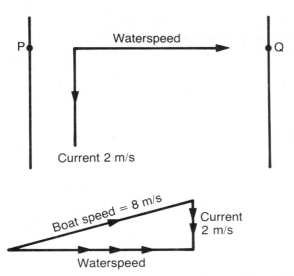

Fig. 45.43

Exercise 197 — *All type C*

1) A boat which has a speed of 10 km/h is to be steered across a river in which there is a steady current of 5 km/h flowing parallel to the banks. If the river is 800 m wide and the boat is to cross at right-angles to the bank find the direction in which it should be steered (relative to the bank).

2) A stream flows at 8 km/h. A motor boat can travel at 20 km/h in still water. What angle must the boat make with the direction of the flow of the stream to reach a point directly across the stream?

3) The speed of a boat in still water is 12 km/h. The navigator wishes to travel due east from A to B (Fig. 45.44) in a current which he estimates to be of velocity 5 km/h in a direction 140°. Unknown to the navigator when he sails the actual velocity of the current is 4 km/h in a direction 140°. By drawing show the actual path of the boat and find the speed of the boat and the bearing of its path.

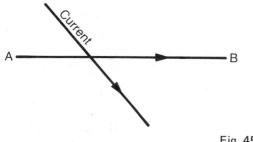

Fig. 45.44

4) A man crosses a river, flowing at 2 m/s by means of a rowing boat which he can propel through still water at 5 m/s. Q is the point on the far bank directly opposite his starting point P. By accurate drawing find:

(a) at what angle to PQ he must head the boat in order to land at Q;

(b) how far downstream from Q he will land if the river is 240 m wide and he heads the boat slightly upstream at 15° to PQ.

5) A river flows at 6 km/h due south between parallel banks.

(a) A motor boat whose speed in still water is 9 km/h leaves a point on one bank and steers a course due east. Find by scale drawing the actual path of the boat and state the bearing.

(b) A second motor boat, whose speed in still water is also 9 km/h, leaves a point on one bank and sets a course so as to travel due east. Find by a second scale drawing, the course set by the boat.

SELF-TEST 45 (Miscellaneous)

1) In Fig. 45.45, $\cos \theta$ is equal to:

a $\dfrac{p}{r}$ b $\dfrac{r}{p}$ c $\dfrac{q}{r}$ d $\dfrac{r}{q}$

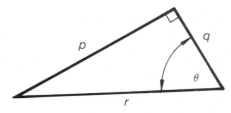

Fig. 45.45

2) In Fig. 45.46, the expression for the length BC is:

a $30 \tan 50°$ b $\dfrac{30}{\tan 50°}$

c $30 \sin 50°$ d $\dfrac{30}{\sin 50°}$

347

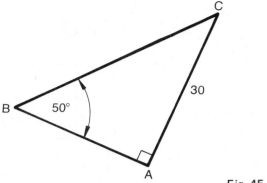

Fig. 45.46

3) In Fig. 45.47, the expression for the length DC is:

a $30 \sin 70° + 42 \cos 44°$

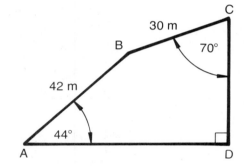

Fig. 45.47

b $30 \cos 70° + 42 \sin 44°$

c $\dfrac{30}{\sin 70°} + \dfrac{42}{\cos 44°}$

d $\dfrac{30}{\cos 70°} + \dfrac{42}{\sin 44°}$

4) In Fig. 45.48, AC is equal to:

a $10(\sqrt{3} + 1)$ **b** $\dfrac{40}{\sqrt{3}} + 10$

c $\dfrac{80\sqrt{3}}{3}$ **d** $\dfrac{80}{\sqrt{3}}$

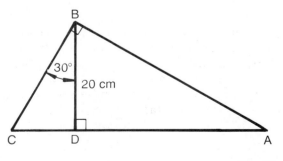

Fig. 45.48

5) In Fig. 45.49, the expression that may be used to find the angle x is:

a $\tan x = \dfrac{8 - 3\sqrt{3}}{7}$ **b** $\sin x = \dfrac{8 - 3\sqrt{3}}{7}$

c $\tan x = \dfrac{10 - 3\sqrt{3}}{5}$ **d** $\sin x = \dfrac{10 - 3\sqrt{3}}{5}$

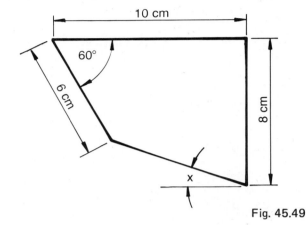

Fig. 45.49

6) The area of the parallelogram in Fig. 45.50 is:

a 30 cm² **b** 15 cm²

c $15\sqrt{3}$ cm² **d** $30\sqrt{3}$ cm²

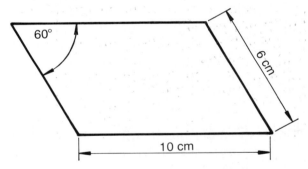

Fig. 45.50

7) In Fig. 45.51, PT and PQ are tangents to the circle. The radius of the circle is:

a $8 \sin 25°$ **b** $8 \sin 50°$

c $8 \tan 25°$ **d** $8 \tan 50°$

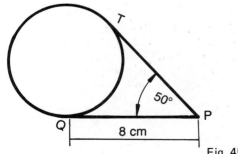

Fig. 45.51

8) In Fig. 45.52, PQ is a common tangent to two circles that touch externally. Hence:

a $\sin x = \dfrac{1}{5}$ **b** $\tan x = \dfrac{1}{5}$

c $\cos x = \dfrac{1}{5}$ **d** none of these is correct

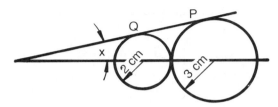

Fig. 45.52

9) The angle A is acute and $\tan A = \dfrac{12}{5}$.
Hence, sin A is equal to:

a $\dfrac{13}{12}$ **b** $\dfrac{13}{5}$ **c** $\dfrac{12}{13}$ **d** $\dfrac{5}{13}$

10) The angle A is obtuse and $\sin A = \dfrac{4}{5}$.
The value of cos A is:

a $\dfrac{3}{5}$ **b** $\dfrac{3}{4}$ **c** $-\dfrac{3}{4}$ **d** $-\dfrac{3}{5}$

11) If $\tan A = \sqrt{3}$ then $\cos(180 - A)$ is equal to:

a $\dfrac{1}{2}$ **b** $-\dfrac{1}{2}$ **c** $\dfrac{\sqrt{3}}{2}$ **d** $-\dfrac{\sqrt{3}}{2}$

12) A pyramid has a square base of side 6 cm and it is 4 cm high, the vertex being above the centre of the base. The angle of inclination of one of the faces to the base is equal to:

a 36° 52′   **b** 53° 7′

c 33° 42′   **d** 56° 19′

13) cos 150° is equal to:

a $-\dfrac{1}{2}$ **b** $\dfrac{1}{2}$ **c** $\dfrac{\sqrt{3}}{2}$ **d** $-\dfrac{\sqrt{3}}{2}$

14) In Fig. 45.53 given $\angle A = 140°$ and the length of the sides b and c. The side a is given by the expression:

a $\sqrt{b^2 + c^2 + 2bc \cos 140°}$

b $\sqrt{b^2 + c^2 + 2bc \cos 40°}$

c $\dfrac{b \sin 40°}{\sin B}$ **d** $\dfrac{c \sin 140°}{\sin C}$

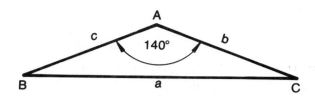

Fig. 45.53

15) If the angle A is obtuse and $\sin A = \dfrac{60}{61}$
then cos A is equal to:

a $\dfrac{11}{61}$ **b** $\dfrac{11}{60}$ **c** $-\dfrac{11}{61}$ **d** $-\dfrac{11}{60}$

16) The pyramid in Fig. 45.54 has a square base of side 8 cm and it is 3 cm high. If the vertex is directly above the centre of the base then the length of the edge AB is:

a 5   **b** $\sqrt{89}$ **c** $\sqrt{41}$ **d** $\sqrt{39}$

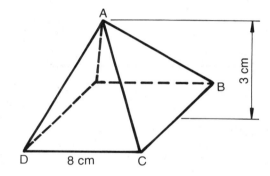

Fig. 45.54

17) If $\log \cos C = \overline{1}.812\,9$ then C is equal to:

a 49° 30′   **b** 49° 33′

c 49° 24′   **d** 49° 27′

18) A bearing of N 50° W can be expressed as:

a 050°   **b** 040°   **c** 310°   **d** 220°

19) To find the height of a tower a surveyor stands some distance from its base and finds the angle of elevation to the top of the tower is 30°. He moves 150 m nearer to the base and finds the angle of elevation is now 60°. If the ground is horizontal, the height of the tower is:

a $75\sqrt{3}$ metres   **b** $50\sqrt{3}$ metres

c 75 metres   **d** 50 metres

20) A man on top of a cliff 20 m high observes the angle of depression of a buoy at sea as 15°. The distance of the buoy from the foot of the cliff is:

a 20 tan 15°   **b** $\dfrac{20}{\tan 15°}$

c 20 sin 15°   **d** $\dfrac{20}{\sin 15°}$

21) An aeroplane has an airspeed of 300 km/h and a course of 030°. The windspeed is 50 km/h from 330°. The vector diagram to find the ground speed and track is one of the diagrams in Fig. 45.55. It is:

a diagram (1)   **b** diagram (2)
c diagram (3)   **d** diagram (4)

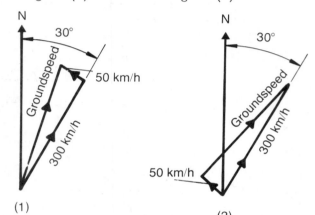

Fig. 45.55

22) A motor boat has a speed of 20 km/h through still water. The current of the stream is 6 km/h in a direction parallel to the banks. In order to cross the river at right-angles to the banks the boat will steer in a direction shown in one of the diagrams in Fig. 45.56. It is:

a diagram (1)   **b** diagram (2)
c diagram (3)   **d** diagram (4)

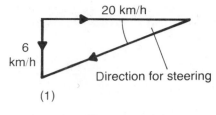

(1)

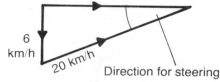

(2)

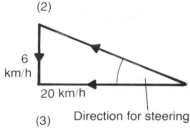

(3)

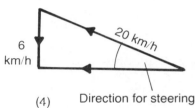

(4)

Fig. 45.56

23) A point A is in latitude 65° N and longitude 35° E. The distance between A and the North Pole along a meridian is given by the expression:

a $2\pi \times 6370 \times \dfrac{35}{360}$ **b** $2\pi \times 6370 \times \dfrac{55}{360}$

c $2\pi \times 6370 \times \dfrac{65}{360}$ **d** $2\pi \times 6370 \times \dfrac{25}{360}$

(The radius of the earth is 6370 km.)

24) Two points A and B are in lat. 50° N long. 30° E and lat. 50° N and long. 50° W. The distance between the points A and B measured along a circle of latitude is given by the expression:

a $2\pi \times 6370 \cos 50° \times \dfrac{80}{360}$

b $2\pi \times 6370 \cos 40° \times \dfrac{70}{360}$

c $2\pi \times 6370 \cos 50° \times \dfrac{20}{360}$

d $2\pi \times 6370 \cos 40° \times \dfrac{20}{360}$

Miscellaneous Exercise

Exercise 198

This exercise is divided into two sections A and B. The questions in Section A are intended to be done very quickly, but those in Section B should take about 20 minutes each to complete. All the questions are of the type found in O Level examination papers.

SECTION A

1) Calculate from

Fig. 1:

(a) the length of CD,

(b) the value of the ratio

$$\frac{\text{area of triangle ACB}}{\text{area of triangle BCD}}$$

(A.E.B. 1976)

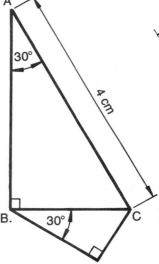

Fig. 1

2) In Fig. 2 the lengths of the line segments AB and BC are 10 cm and 5 cm respectively and angle ABC is a right-angle. Calculate:

(a) the perpendicular distance from B to the line q,

(b) the perpendicular distance from C to q.

(Give your answers correct to one decimal place.) (L)

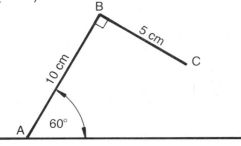

Fig. 2

3) In Fig. 3 DB is perpendicular to the line ABC. Calculate the length of DE. (A.E.B. 1976)

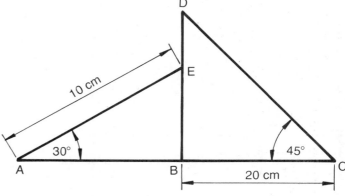

Fig. 3

4) In Fig. 4, angle ABC = 50°, angle AED = 20°, BC = AE = 10 cm. Angle ACB = angle ADE = 90°. Calculate:

(a) the length of AC,

(b) the length of AD. (A.E.B. 1976)

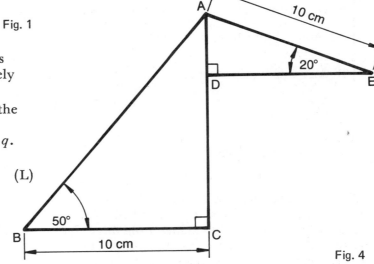

Fig. 4

5) In a triangle ABC, AB = 25 m, $\angle$B = 50° and $\angle$C = 30°. Calculate the length of AC. (J.M.B.)

351

6) Calculate the length of AC in Fig. 5.
(A.E.B. 1976)

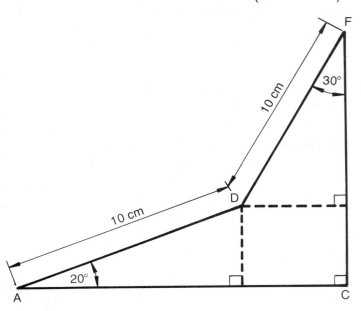

Fig. 5

7) In the acute angled △ PQR,   PQ = 6 cm, QR = 4 cm   and the area of the triangle is 10.8 cm². Calculate ∠ PQR.   (L)

8) In a trapezium ABCD, the sides BC and AD are parallel,   angle A = angle D = 60° and   AB = BC = CD = 8 cm.   Calculate the area of the trapezium ABCD.   (L)

9) If $\sin A = \dfrac{8}{17}$ and   A   is an acute angle, calculate, without using tables the value of tan A.   (L)

10) An isosceles triangle ABC has AB = AC = 8 cm   and   ∠ BAC = 28°. Calculate the length of BC.   (L)

11) Given that $\sin^2 x = 0.2652$,   find the value of the acute angle   x,   correct to the nearest degree.   (L)

12) In Fig. 6, with origin O, the polar co-ordinates of the point B are (6, 30°), APB is a straight line parallel to the central direction OX and OA is perpendicular to OX. (All distances are measured in centimetres.)

(a) What are the polar co-ordinates of A?
(b) If   AP = 4 cm,   what are the values of r and θ?   (A.E.B. 1977)

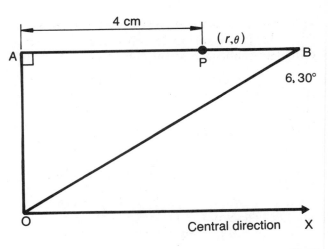

Fig. 6

13) In the triangle ABC (Fig. 7), calculate:
(a) the length of AC,
(b) the area of triangle ABC.   (A.E.B. 1977)

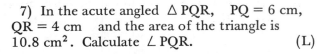

Fig. 7

14) A man climbs from A to C up two straight slopes AB and BC. Fig. 8 represents his path made up of two straight sections AB and BC which are inclined to the horizontal at angles   x and y   respectively, where tan x = 1/50   and   tan y = 1/30.   The horizontal distance between A and B is 530 m and between B and C is 630 m. Calculate the height of C above A.   (J.M.B.)

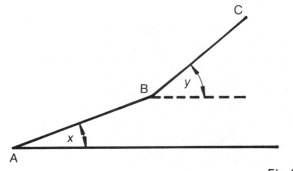

Fig. 8

15) The equal sides of an isosceles triangle are 25 cm long and the angle between them is 10°. Calculate the length of the third side. (J.M.B.)

16) In the right-angled triangle ABC (Fig. 9), angle BAC = 30°. AB = x cm and AC = 10 cm. Calculate the value of x correct to 3 significant figures. (J.M.B.)

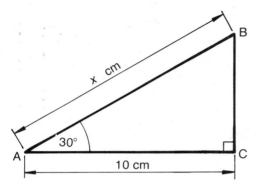

Fig. 9

17) In triangle ABC, AB = 7 cm, BC = 8 cm and ∠ACB = 53° 13'. Calculate ∠BAC, given that it is acute. (J.M.B.)

18) Calculate the angle between the longer side and diagonal of a rectangle with sides of 4 cm and 5 cm. (L)

19) A ladder rests with its foot on horizontal ground and its top resting against a vertical wall. If the foot of the ladder is 8 m from the wall and the ladder makes an angle of 59° 18' with the ground, calculate the height of the top of the ladder above the ground. (L)

20) ABC is a triangle with AB = 10 cm, BC = 12 cm and angle ABC = 35°. Calculate:

(a) the length of the perpendicular from A to BC,

(b) the area of the triangle ABC. (L)

SECTION B

21) A and B are points on a coast, B being 2000 m due east of A. A man sails from A on a bearing of 060° (N 60° E) for 800 m to a buoy P, where he changes course to 070° (N 70° E) and sails for 1000 m to another buoy Q. Calculate:

(a) the distances of P and Q from the line AB,

(b) the distance QB,

(c) the course he must set to sail directly from Q to B. (L)

22) C, B, D are three points on level ground not in a straight line. B is the foot of a vertical mast, BT. The angle of elevation of the top of the mast, T, from C is 15° 18'. Given that BC = 200 m, BD = 150 m, and the angle CBD = 40° calculate

(a) the height of the mast BT,

(b) the angle of elevation of T from D,

(c) the shortest distance of C from BD,

(d) the angle CDB. (L)

23) ABCD is a trapezium with AB parallel to DC. Given that AB = 50 cm, AD = 25 cm, DC = 20 cm and angle DAB = 60°, calculate:

(a) the distance between the parallel sides correct to the nearest mm,

(b) the angle ABC,

(c) the length of DB correct to the nearest mm,

(d) the area of ABCD correct to the nearest cm². (L)

24) Fig. 10 (a) represents the roof of a house, the plan of which is shown in Fig. 10 (b). The horizontal ridge XY is 6 m long and it is placed symmetrically 3 m above the horizontal rectangle ABCD formed by the walls. Given that AD = BC = 10 m and that AB = DC = 7.5 m, calculate:

(a) the angle of inclination of the triangular "end" XBA to the horizontal,

(b) the angle of inclination of the trapezium XADY to the horizontal,

(c) the angle AX makes with the horizontal. (J.M.B.)

(a)

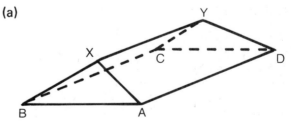

(b)

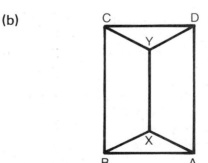

Fig. 10

25) In a triangle ABC, AB = 13 cm, AC = 15 cm and BC = 7 cm. Prove that ∠ C = 60° and calculate the radius of the circumcircle of the triangle.

The centre of this circle is O and the feet of the perpendiculars from O to AC and BC are P and Q respectively. Prove that $OQ^2 - OP^2 = 44$.

Calculate the length, in cm, of the side of the square which is equal in area to a rectangle whose adjacent sides are equal in length to OQ + OP and OQ − OP. (J.M.B.)

26) In a quadrilateral ABCD, AB = 5 cm, AD = 3 cm and BCD is an equilateral triangle of side 7 cm.

Calculate ∠ A and hence prove that the quadrilateral is cyclic.

The diagonals of the quadrilateral intersect at P. Prove that AC bisects ∠ BAD and hence calculate the length of BP. Prove that the area of the quadrilateral is $16\sqrt{3}$ cm². (J.M.B.)

27) C is the foot of a vertical tower 30 m high. A is a point due south of the tower from which the angle of elevation of the top of the tower is 17°. B is a point due west of the tower from which the angle of elevation of the top of the tower is 32°. Given that A, B and C are all in the same horizontal plane, calculate:

(a) the length of AC,
(b) the length of BC,
(c) the bearing of B from A.

P is the point on AB which is nearest to C. Calculate the angle of elevation of the top of the tower from P. (A.E.B. 1976)

28) Three village centres, P, Q and R, are joined by straight roads with PQ = 8 km, PR = 5.5 km and the angle RPQ = 108°. Calculate:

(a) the area, in km², bounded by the three roads,
(b) the length of the road RQ,
(c) the time it would take to walk from R to Q at an average speed of 1.5 m/s, giving your answer correct to the nearest minute. (A.E.B. 1976)

29) A point B is 10 km due north of a point A, and at mid-day a man sets out to walk from A to B. After covering 5 km, he changes the direction of his walk to 036° (N 36° E) and covers another 14 km to reach a point C.

Calculate:
(a) his distance from B, when he was nearest to B,
(b) the time at which he was due east of B, assuming that he walked at an average speed of 4 km/h,
(c) the shortest distance from A to C. (A.E.B. 1976)

30) In triangle ABC, AB = 35 cm, AC = 12 cm and the angle BAC = 72° 32′. Calculate:

(a) the area of the triangle ABC,
(b) the length BC.

The point D is on the side AB such that CD = 12 cm. Calculate the length of the perpendicular from D to AC. Hence calculate the area of the triangle ACD.

31) (a) Two points A and B in the same latitude are in longitudes 30° E and 24° W respectively, and the distance AB, measured along the parallel of latitude, is 2400 km. Taking the earth to be a sphere of radius 6370 km, calculate the latitude of A and B.

(b) A ship travels due south from a point P (12° 10′ N, 60° 20′ E) to a point Q at an average speed of 22 knots* for 95 hours.

Calculate the latitude and longitude of Q. (L)

32) A man in a boat at A (Fig. 11) sees three landmarks B, C and D on a straight road inclined at 20° to the horizontal. A, B, C and D are all in the same vertical plane. B is at sea level, the angles of elevation of C and D observed from A are 12° and 17° respectively and CD = 124 m. Calculate:

(a) the angle ADB
(b) the distance AD,
(c) the height of D above sea level,
(d) the distance AB. (L)

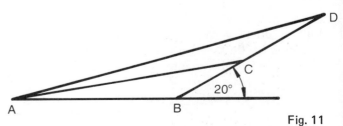
Fig. 11

*1 sea mile is the length of arc on the surface of the earth corresponding to an angle of 1 minute. 1 knot = 1 sea mile per hour.

33) Fig. 12 represents a roof-truss in which
AB = AC = 8 m,   BC = 11 m,   BD = DC
and   ∠ DBC = 20°.   Calculate:

(a) the length of BD,
(b) the angle ABC,
(c) the length of AD.   (L)

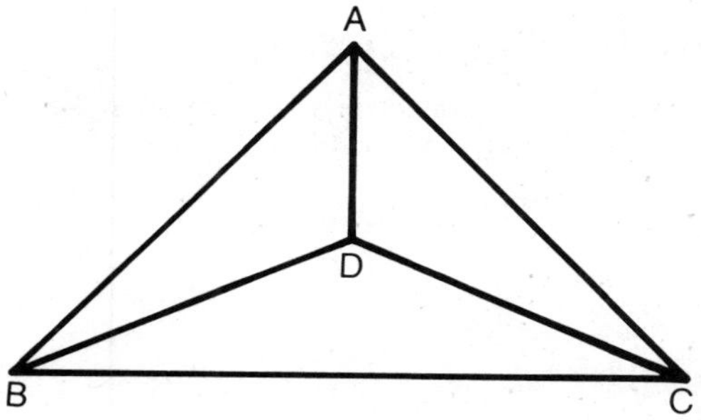

Fig. 12

Chapter 46 Sets

COLLECTIONS

A set is a word for a collection of objects, numbers, ideas, etc. Some sets have special names such as a *pack* of cards, a *fleet* of ships, a *pride* of lions and so on. However many sets do not have special names because the objects in the set are seldom considered collectively, for example, the objects in a girl's handbag.

ELEMENTS

The different objects, numbers, etc. which form a set are called the *members* or elements of the set, just as the people who belong to a club are called members of the club.

The elements of a set may be specified in two ways:

(a) by listing the elements,
(b) by description.

Some examples are:

Listing	Description
{2, 4, 6, 8, 10}	the set of even numbers between 1 and 11,
{a, e, i, o, u}	the set of vowels in the alphabet.

The elements making up the set are enclosed in curly brackets or braces { }. The braces stand for the words 'the set of' or 'the set'. Braces can also be used with descriptions. Thus the second set above could be written

{vowels in the alphabet}

NAMING SETS

When a set is to be used more than once a capital letter is used to denote it. Thus we might write

$$A = \{1, 3, 5, 7, 9, 11\}$$

Now consider

$$B = \{\text{all the even numbers}\}$$

It is not possible to list all of the elements of B and so we write

$$B = \{2, 4, 6, 8, \ldots\}$$

where the dots mean and so on.

Exercise 199 — *All type A*

Write down the members of the following sets:

1) $A = \{\text{odd numbers from 5 to 15 inclusive}\}$

2) $X = \{\text{days of the week beginning with T}\}$

3) $B = \{\text{even numbers less than } 12\}$

4) $P = \{\text{prime numbers less than } 25\}$

5) $Q = \{\text{multiples of 3 up to } 33\}$

Name each of the following sets:

6) $A = \{5, 10, 15, 20, 25\}$

7) $B = \{\text{brothers, sisters, mother, father}\}$

8) $C = \{3, 5, 7, 11, 13, 17\}$

TYPES OF SETS

A set in which all of the elements can be listed is called a *finite* set. Thus the set of coins which a collector possesses is a finite set and so is the set of even numbers between 0 and 50.

In some cases it is impossible to list all the members of a set. Such sets are called *infinite* sets. Thus the set of natural numbers is an infinite set. If $A = \{1, 2, 3, 4, \ldots\}$ then A is an infinite set because no matter which is the last number we write, we can always go one larger.

The number of elements in a set A is denoted by $n(A)$. Thus if $A = \{2, 4, 6, 8, 10\}$, $n(A) = 5$ because there are 5 elements in the set A.

A set containing no elements is called a *null* set. It is represented by { } or by Ø (the Danish

356

letter oe). The set of whole numbers between 0.5 and 0.9 is null and so is the set of prime numbers between 8 and 11.

Exercise 200 — *All type A*

Say which of the following sets are finite, infinite or null:

1) $A = \{1, 3, 5, 7, 9, \dots\}$

2) $B = \{2, 4, 6, 8, 10, 12\}$

3) The set of points on the circumference of a circle.

4) The set of letters in the alphabet.

5) The set of even numbers which can be divided exactly by 3.

6) The set of odd numbers which can be exactly divided by 2.

7) The set of planets in the solar system.

8) The number of people that have swam the Atlantic Ocean.

9) If $A = \{a, b, c, d\}$ what is $n(A)$?

10) $B = \{2, 4, 6, 8, 10, 12, 14, 16, 18, 20\}$. Write down the value of $n(B)$.

MEMBERSHIP OF A SET

The symbol $\in$ means 'is a member of'. Thus if

$$A = \{3, 5, 7, 9\}$$

the fact that 5 is a member of A is written $5 \in A$.

The symbol $\notin$ means 'is not a member of'. Because 4 is not a member of A we write $4 \notin A$.

EXAMPLE 1
In the following set, one of the elements is incorrect. Rewrite the set correctly and, using set notation, state which element is not a member of the corrected set.

$$P = \{1, 6, 11, 17, 21, 26\}$$

The sequence of numbers in the set should all differ by 5. Hence the corrected set is:

$$P = \{1, 6, 11, 16, 21, 26\}$$

In the corrected set 17, which appeared in the original set, is not a member and we write

$$17 \notin P$$

Exercise 201 — *All type A*

In the following sets one of the elements is incorrect. Rewrite the set correctly and state, using set notation, the element which is not a member of the corrected set.

1) $P = \{2, 4, 7, 8, 10\}$

2) $Q = \{1, 4, 9, 18, 25, 36\}$

3) $R = \{17, 14, 11, 9, 5, 2\}$

4) $S = \{a, b, c, \phi, e, f\}$

5) $T = \{5, 9, 11, 13, 17, 19, 23, 29\}$

State which of the following statements are true:

6) $7 \in \{\text{prime factors of } 63\}$

7) $\text{Cod} \in \{\text{fish}\}$

8) $24 \notin \{\text{multiples of } 5\}$

9) $\text{hexagon} \in \{\text{quadrilaterals}\}$

10) $\text{octagon} \notin \{\text{polygons}\}$

SUBSETS

Four groups of people belonging to a youth club are taking part in different activities. The first group is listening to records, the second is playing table tennis, the third is preparing for a concert and the fourth group is listening to a talk.

All the people in the four groups are contained in the set of members of the youth club but each of the groups form a set in their own right. Each of the groups forms a subset of the set of members of the youth club. A subset can be the set of all the members of the club because the leader of the club might want to talk to all the members of the club as well as to each individual group. The leader may choose not talk to any of the groups and hence the null set is also a subset of the set of members of the club.

$\{1, 3, 5\}$ is a subset of $\{1, 3, 5, 7, 9\}$ because each of the three elements of $\{1, 3, 5\}$ is also an element of $\{1, 3, 5, 7, 9\}$. To indicate that one set is a subset of another we use the symbol $\subset$, which means 'is contained in'. Thus $\{3\} \subset \{1, 3, 5\}$ and $\{1, 3, 5\} \subset \{1, 3, 5, 7, 9\}$. These two statements could be written

$$\{3\} \subset \{1, 3, 5\} \subset \{1, 3, 5, 7, 9\}$$

Out of the set $\{7, 8, 9\}$ we can select either 0 elements, 1 element, 2 elements or 3 elements as follows:

(a) $\{\ \}$ (b) $\{7\}$ (c) $\{8\}$
(d) $\{9\}$ (e) $\{7, 8\}$ (f) $\{7, 9\}$
(g) $\{8, 9\}$ (h) $\{7, 8, 9\}$

The two extremes, the null set and the original set are regarded as subsets of the original set as pointed out above. Thus every set is a subset of itself and the null set is a subset of every set. The sets numbered (b) to (g) inclusive are called *proper* subsets.

The symbol $\subset$ can be used the other way round. Thus if $C = \{2, 4, 6, 8\}$ and $D = \{4, 6\}$ we can write $C \supset D$, i.e. C contains D.

THE NUMBER OF SUBSETS

If there are n members in a set then the number of subsets that can be formed is given by the formula

$$N = 2^n$$

Hence, if there are 4 members in a set, the number of subsets that can be formed is

$$N = 2^4 = 16$$

Exercise 202 — *All type B*

1) $A = \{3, 5, 6, 8, 9, 11, 12, 13, 15\}$.
List the subsets whose members are:

(a) all the odd numbers of A;
(b) all the even numbers of A;
(c) all the prime numbers in A;
(d) all the numbers in A divisible by 2.

2) $B = \{5, 10, 15, 20\}$. Form *all* the subsets of B. How many are there?

3) If $A = \{3, 6, 9, 12, 15\}$, $B = \{3, 6, 7, 12\}$ and $C = \{3, 12\}$, state which of the following statements are correct:

a $A \subset B$ b $B \subset A$ c $C \subset A$
d $C \subset B$ e $C \subset B \subset A$

4) If $A = \{1, 3\}$, $B = \{1, 3, 5, 7\}$ and $C = \{1, 3, 5\}$ is the statement $A \subset B \subset C$ correct? If not write down the correct statement.

5) Write down all the proper subsets of $\{a, b, c, d\}$.

6) Below are given eight sets. Connect appropriate sets by the symbol $\subset$.

(a) {natural numbers between 1 and 24}
(b) {all cutlery}
(c) {all footwear}
(d) {letters of the alphabet}
(e) {boot, shoe}
(f) {a, e, i, o, u}
(g) {2, 4, 6, 8}
(h) {knife, fork, spoon}.

7) $A = \{\text{all sports}\}$. List:

(a) a subset of A containing three sports played with a ball
(b) a subset of A containing three sports generally played by girls
(c) four sports not played with a ball.

8) If $A = \{2, 4, 6, 8, 10\}$ say which of the following statements are correct:

a $2 \in A$ b $8 \notin A$
c $7 \in A$ d $\{6, 8\} \subset A$
e $\{3, 4\} \subset A$ f $\{2, 6, 8\} \supset A$
g $A \supset \{4, 6\}$ h $A \subset \{3, 8\}$

9) A set has 5 members. How many subsets can be formed from it?

10) If $P = \{2, 4, 6, 8, 10, 12, 14, 16\}$, how many subsets can be formed from P?

EQUALITY

The order in which the elements of a set are written does not matter. Thus $\{1, 3, 5, 7\}$ is the same as $\{5, 3, 7, 1\}$ and $\{3, 1, 7, 5\}$.

Two sets are said to be equal if their elements are identical. Thus if $A = \{2, 4, 6, 8\}$ and $B = \{8, 6, 2, 4\}$ then, because the elements in A are the same as those in B, $A = B$.

If two sets are not equal we use the symbol $\neq$ (meaning not equal to). Thus if $A = \{3, 5, 7, 9\}$ and $B = \{2, 4, 6, 8\}$ then $A \neq B$.

THE UNIVERSAL SET

Frequently we use sets which are subsets of much larger sets. Thus suppose that in a class in a school we are asked to form sets (a) of those who like playing hockey, (b) of those who wear spectacles and (c) of those who cycle to school. Each of these sets are subsets of {class}. The class in this case is the universal set.

The universal set is represented by the symbol &, an abbreviation for ensemble, which is the French word for set.

If   & = {natural numbers}   then if
A = {even numbers}   and B = {odd numbers} then $A \subset$ &   and $B \subset$ &.

Exercise 203 — *All type B*

1) & = {letters of the alphabet}.   Give the subsets:

(a) of vowels,
(b) of letters after t,
(c) of consonants.

2) & = {all polygons}.   Write down the subsets of polygons with less than nine sides.

3) & = {natural numbers}.   Give the subsets of:

(a) prime numbers less than 20,
(b) numbers less than 20 which are multiples of 3,
(c) all the prime factors of 210.

4) & = {months of the year}.   Write down the subsets of:

(a) the winter months,
(b) the autumn months.

5) & = {squares of natural numbers}.   Write down the subset of the squares of the first five natural numbers (i.e. 1, 2, 3, 4, 5).

SET BUILDER NOTATION

Another way of describing a set is to state a condition which is satisfied by the elements of the set and by no other elements. For example, the equation $x^2 - x = 2$ is only satisfied by certain real numbers. It is satisfied when $x = 2$,   since $2^2 - 2 = 2$ and when $x = -1$ since $(-1)^2 - (-1) = 2$.   It is *not* satisfied by any other real numbers. Hence the set which satisfies the equation $x^2 - x = 2$ is $\{-1, 2\}$.

This set may be described as $\{x : x^2 - x = 2\}$ which is read as 'the set x such that $x^2 - x = 2$'.   When a set is described in this way we are using set builder notation. Set builder notation is very useful when we cannot possibly or cannot conveniently list all the members of a set. Thus suppose we are discussing the set P of all the fifth formers in the United Kingdom. Then the set of all fifth formers who live in Wales is defined by the condition living in Wales. We can denote this set as:

$$\{x \in P : x \text{ lives in Wales}\}$$

Similarly the set of all fifth formers in the U.K. who are over 16 years of age may be denoted by:

$$\{x \in P: x \text{ is over 16 years old}\}$$

EXAMPLE 2
Show that

$$\{x: 2 \leqslant x \leqslant 4\} \subset \{x: 1 \leqslant x \leqslant 7\},$$
$$\{x: 1 \leqslant x \leqslant 7\} = \{1, 2, 3, 4, 5, 6, 7\}$$

and

$$\{x: 2 \leqslant x \leqslant 4\} = \{2, 3, 4\}$$

Hence

$$\{x: 2 \leqslant x \leqslant 4\} \subset \{x: 1 \leqslant x \leqslant 7\}$$

VENN DIAGRAMS

Sets and set problems may be represented by diagrams called Venn diagrams, after mathematician Joseph Venn who lived in the nineteenth century and who first represented sets diagrammatically.

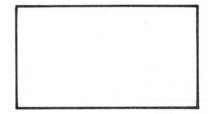
Fig. 46.1

A universal set is represented by a rectangle (Fig. 46.1). If the universal set is   & = {class} then all the children in the class would be represented by all the points inside the rectangle or on its perimeter. All the children in the class who cycled to school would be a subset to the universal set. If we use the letter C to represent this subset, then a circle drawn within the rectangle shows that C is a subset of & or $C \subset$ &   (Fig. 46.2).

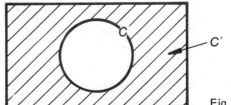
Fig. 46.2

COMPLEMENT

The shaded part of the rectangle in Fig. 46.2, is called the *complement* of the set C and is written C'. It represents all the children in the class who do not cycle to school.

EXAMPLE 3
The universal set is $\mathcal{E} = \{1, 2, 3, 4, 5, 6\}$. If $A = \{1, 3, 5\}$ find the complement of A.

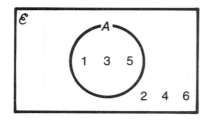

Fig. 46.3

The Venn diagram is shown in Fig. 46.3. The subset A is represented by the circle which contains the numbers 1, 3 and 5 which are the elements of A. The numbers outside the circle, 2, 4 and 6 form the complement of A and hence $A' = \{2, 4, 6\}$.

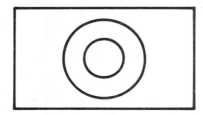

Fig. 46.4

Subsets of a given set are represented by a circle within a circle as shown in Fig. 46.4. If $\mathcal{E} = \{1, 2, 3, 4, 5, 6, 7, 8\}$ and $A = \{2, 3, 4, 5, 6\}$ then $A \subset \mathcal{E}$. If $B = \{3, 4\}$ then $B \subset A \subset \mathcal{E}$. This is represented as shown in Fig. 46.5.

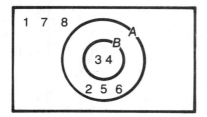

Fig. 46.5

INTERSECTION

The intersection of two sets A and B is the set of elements which are members of both A and B. The shaded portion of Fig. 46.6 represents the intersection of A and B.

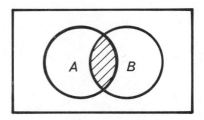

Fig. 46.6

The intersection of A and B is written, in set notation, as $A \cap B$, which is read as 'A intersection B'.

EXAMPLE 4
If $A = \{1, 3, 5, 7, 9\}$ and $B = \{7, 9, 11\}$ find $A \cap B$.

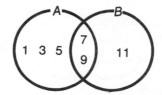

Fig. 46.7

As shown in Fig. 46.7, $A \cap B = \{7, 9\}$. Note that the intersection of A and B is the set which contains all the elements which are common to both A and B. If there are no common elements in two sets the Venn diagram would look like Fig. 46.8. Thus if $A = \{1, 3, 5, 7\}$ and $B = \{2, 4, 6, 8\}$ then $A \cap B = \emptyset$, $\emptyset$ being the null set. When there is no intersection between two or more sets the sets are said to be *disjoint*. Thus in Fig. 46.8, the sets A and B are disjoint.

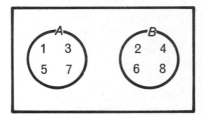

Fig. 46.8

UNION

The union of sets A and B is all of the elements contained in A or B. Thus if $A = \{3, 4, 5\}$ and $B = \{6, 7, 8\}$ then the union of A and B is $\{3, 4, 5, 6, 7, 8\}$.

If this set is called C then we write $C = A \cup B$, which is read as 'A union B', the symbol $\cup$ standing for 'union'. The Venn diagram (Fig. 46.9) shows $C = A \cup B$, the shaded portion representing C.

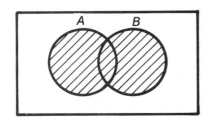

Fig. 46.9

EXAMPLE 5

If $S = \{1, 3, 5, 7\}$ and $R = \{7, 9, 11\}$, write down $S \cup R$.

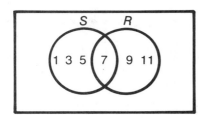

Fig. 46.10

As shown in Fig. 46.10,

$$S \cup R = \{1, 3, 5, 7, 9, 11\}$$

Note that the element 7, which is contained in both S and R, appears only once in the union of S and R.

Exercise 204 — *All type B*

Fig. 46.11 shows the universal set $\mathscr{E}$ and the two subsets A and B. For each of the following write down the answer in the way suggested.

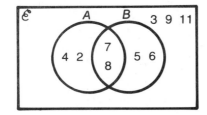

Fig. 46.11

1) Write down all the elements of the universal set. $\mathscr{E} = \{\qquad\}$.

2) Write down all the elements of set A. $A = \{\qquad\}$.

3) Write down all the elements of set B. $B = \{\qquad\}$.

4) Write down the complement of A. $A' = \{\qquad\}$.

5) Write down the complement of B. $B' = \{\qquad\}$.

6) Write down $A \cap B$. $A \cap B = \{\qquad\}$.

7) Write down $A \cup B$. $A \cup B = \{\qquad\}$.

8) Write down the complement of $(A \cup B)$. $(A \cup B)' = \{\qquad\}$.

Link each of the following with one of the symbols: $\in, \notin, =, \neq, \subset, \supset, \cup$ or $\cap$.

9) 7 $\{2, 4, 6, 8\}$.

10) $\{1, 3, 5, 7\}$ $\{2, 3, 5, 6\}$ $\{3, 5\}$.

11) 8 $\{4, 8, 16, 32\}$.

12) $\{3, 4, 6\}$ $\{6, 3, 4\}$.

13) $\{\text{rectangles, triangles}\}$ $\{\text{all plane figures}\}$.

14) $\{1, 3, 5, 7, 9\}$ $\{5, 7\}$.

15) $\{2, 4, 6, 8\}$ $\{3, 5, 7, 9, 11\}$.

16) $\{2, 4\}$ $\{2, 4, 8, 9\}$ $\{1, 2, 4, 8, 9\}$.

17) $\{\text{John}\}$ $\{\text{all girls' names}\}$.

18) $\{7, 14, 21, 28\}$ $\{\text{multiples of } 7\}$.

19) $\{x : 1 \leqslant x \leqslant 7\}$ $\{2, 3, 4, 5, 6, 7\}$.

20) $\{x : 3 \leqslant x \leqslant 5\}$ $\{x : 1 \leqslant x \leqslant 10\}$.

The Venn diagram (Fig. 46.12), shows two sets A and B. Copy and complete:

21) $A = \{\qquad\}$.

22) $B = \{\qquad\}$.

23) $A \cup B = \{\qquad\}$.

24) $A \cap B = \{\qquad\}$.

25) A B.

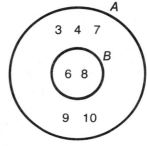

Fig. 46.12

361

The Venn diagram (Fig. 46.13) shows two sets *A* and *B* which are subsets of the universal set &. Copy and complete the following:

26) & = { }.

27) *A* = { }.

28) *B* = { }.

29) *A* ∩ *B* = { }.

30) *A* ∪ *B* = { }.

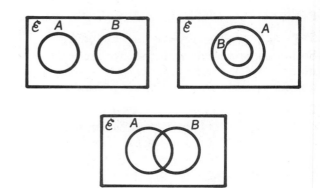

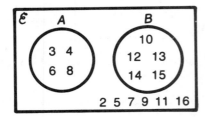

Fig. 46.13

Fig. 46.14 shows a Venn diagram representing the universal set and two subsets. Draw a similar diagram, inserting the elements, to represent each of the following:

31) & = {1, 2, 3, 4, 5, 6, 7, 8, 9, 10}, *A* = {1, 2, 3, 4}, *B* = {4, 5, 6, 7, 8}.

32) & = {a, b, c, d, e, f, g, h}, *A* = {a, b, c, d}, *A* ∩ *B* = {c, d}, *A* ∪ *B* = {a, b, c, d, g, h}.

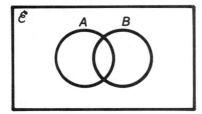

Fig. 46.14

Fig. 46.15 shows three Venn diagrams. Using diagrams similar to these, represent the following:

33) & = {*x*: 5 ⩽ *x* ⩽ 12}, *X* = {6, 7, 9, 10, 11}, *Y* = {6, 7}.

34) & = {*x*: 3 ⩽ *x* ⩽ 10}, *A* = {4, 5}, *B* = {6, 7}.

35) & = {natural numbers between 1 and 9}, *P* = {3, 4, 5, 6}, *Q* = {5, 6, 7, 8, 9}.

Fig. 46.15

36) Use set notation to describe the shaded portions of the Venn diagrams shown in Fig. 46.16.

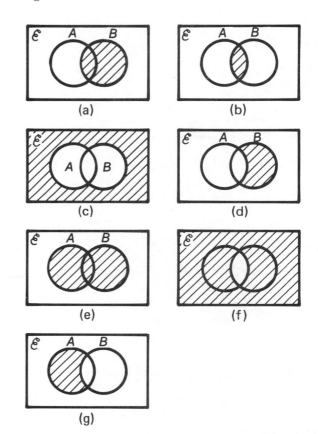

Fig. 46.16

37) Draw a Venn diagram to represent the following information.

    & = {A, B, C, D, E, F, G, H}

    X = {A, B, C, D}

    Y = {C, D, E, F, G}

362

PROBLEMS WITH INTERSECTIONS AND UNIONS

So far we have dealt with the intersection and union of only two sets. It is quite usual for there to be intersections between three or more sets.

In the Venn diagram (Fig. 46.17) the three sets A, B and C intersect. The shaded portion represents $A \cap B \cap C$.

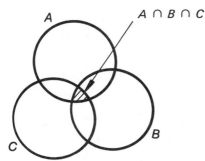

Fig. 46.17

EXAMPLE 6
If $A = \{1, 2, 3, 4, 5\}$, $B = \{2, 3, 5, 6\}$ and $C = \{2, 5, 6, 7\}$, determine:

(a) $A \cap (B \cap C)$,
(b) $(A \cap B) \cap C$.

(a) In problems of this kind always work out the brackets first. Thus:

$$B \cap C = \{2, 5, 6\}$$

Then,

$$A \cap (B \cap C)$$
$$= \{1, 2, 3, 4, 5\} \cap \{2, 5, 6\} = \{2, 5\}$$

(b) Working out the bracket we have,

$$A \cap B = \{2, 3, 5\}$$

Then

$$(A \cap B) \cap C$$
$$= \{2, 3, 5\} \cap \{2, 5, 6, 7\} = \{2, 5\}$$

It will be noticed that the way in which we group A, B and C makes no difference to the final result. That is, $A \cap (B \cap C)$ produces the same result as $(A \cap B) \cap C$. This is known as the *associative law* for sets.

EXAMPLE 7
If $A = \{3, 4\}$, $B = \{2, 4, 6, 8\}$ and $C = \{3, 6, 8, 10\}$ find:

(a) $A \cup (B \cup C)$,
(b) $(A \cup B) \cup C$.

(a) Again, working out the brackets first we have,

$$B \cup C = \{2, 3, 4, 6, 8, 10\}$$

Then

$$A \cup (B \cup C) = \{3, 4\} \cup \{2, 3, 4, 6, 8, 10\}$$
$$= \{2, 3, 4, 6, 8, 10\}$$

(b) $A \cup B = \{2, 3, 4, 6, 8\}$

$$(A \cup B) \cup C = \{2, 3, 4, 6, 8\} \cup \{3, 6, 8, 10\}$$
$$= \{2, 3, 4, 6, 8, 10\}$$

We see that the associative law is again applicable because we have shown that

$$A \cup (B \cup C) = (A \cup B) \cup C$$

Exercise 205 — *All type B*

If $A = \{2, 3, 5, 7\}$, $B = \{2, 3, 4, 6\}$ and $C = \{2, 5, 6, 7\}$, list the following sets:

1) $A \cap (B \cap C)$

2) $(A \cap B) \cap C$

3) $B \cup (A \cup C)$

4) $A \cup (B \cup C)$

5) $(A \cap B) \cup (B \cap C)$

Given that $\& = \{1, 2, 3, 4, 5, 6, 7, 8, 9\}$, $A = \{2, 3, 4, 5\}$ and $B = \{4, 5, 7, 8\}$ list the following sets:

6) $A \cup (A' \cap B)$ 9) $B' \cup (A \cap B')$

7) $B \cup (A' \cap B)$ 10) $A \cup (A' \cap B')$

8) $A' \cap (A \cap B')$

THE NUMBER OF ELEMENTS IN A SET

The number of elements in a set A is denoted by $n(A)$. Thus if $A = \{1, 3, 5, 7, 9\}$ then $n(A) = 5$ because there are 5 elements in the set A. We can, if we wish, write $n\{1, 3, 5, 7, 9\} = 5$.

Consider the two sets $A = \{1, 2, 3, 4, 5\}$ and $B = \{3, 5, 7, 9\}$ (see Fig. 46.18).

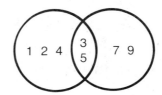

Fig. 46.18

$$A \cup B = \{1, 2, 3, 4, 5, 7, 9\}$$

$$A \cap B = \{3, 5\}$$

$$n(A) = n\{1, 2, 3, 4, 5\} = 5$$

$$n(B) = n\{3, 5, 7, 9\} = 4$$

$$n(A \cap B) = n\{3, 5\} = 2$$

$$n(A \cup B) = n\{1, 2, 3, 4, 5, 7, 9\} = 7$$

The equation connecting the four sets can be seen to be

$$n(A \cup B) = n(A) + n(B) - n(A \cap B)$$

It can be shown that this equation applies to any two sets which intersect.

EXAMPLE 8

If $n(A) = 20$, $n(B) = 30$ and $n(A \cup B) = 40$, find $n(A \cap B)$.

Using the equation:

$$n(A \cup B) = n(A) + n(B) - n(A \cap B)$$

we have

$$40 = 20 + 30 - n(A \cap B)$$

$$n(A \cap B) = 20 + 30 - 40 = 10$$

EXAMPLE 9

In a school of 150 pupils, 85 take physics and 115 take mathematics. Each pupil takes at least one of these subjects. How many take both?

Let P = set of physics pupils

and M = set of mathematics pupils

Then $n(P) = 85$ = number taking physics

$n(M) = 115$ = number taking mathematics

$n(P \cup M) = 150$ = total number of pupils

$n(P \cap M)$ = number taking both mathematics and physics

Using the equation:

$$n(P \cup M) = n(P) + n(M) - n(P \cap M)$$

$$150 = 85 + 115 - n(P \cap M)$$

$$n(P \cap M) = 85 + 115 - 150 = 50$$

Hence 50 pupils take both mathematics and physics.

364

EXAMPLE 10

The entries on the diagram (Fig. 46.19) show the number of elements in sets A and B. The number of elements in A is equal to the number of elements in B. Find:

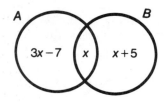

Fig. 46.19

(a) x (b) $n(A)$ (c) $n(B)$
(d) $n(A \cup B)$.

(a) The number of elements in

$$A = n(A) = 3x - 7 + x = 4x - 7$$

The number of elements in

$$B = n(B) = x + 5 + x = 2x + 5$$

We are given that $n(A) = n(B)$. Hence

$$4x - 7 = 2x + 5$$

$$2x = 12$$

$$x = 6$$

(b) $n(A) = 4x - 7 = 4 \times 6 - 7 = 24 - 7 = 17$

(c) $n(B) = 2x + 5 = 2 \times 6 + 5 = 12 + 5 = 17$

(d) $n(A \cup B) = n(A) + n(B) - n(A \cap B)$

$$= 17 + 17 - 6 = 28$$

INTERSECTION OF THREE SETS

If three sets A, B and C intersect then it can be shown that

$$n(A \cup B \cup C) = n(A) + n(B) + n(C)$$
$$- n(A \cap B) - n(A \cap C)$$
$$- n(B \cap C) + n(A \cap B \cap C)$$

In Fig. 46.20,

region I + region IV represents $n(A \cap B)$

region II + region IV represents $n(B \cap C)$

region III + region IV represents $n(A \cap C)$

region IV represents $n(A \cap B \cap C)$

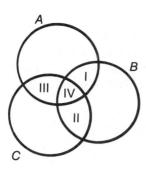

Fig. 46.20

EXAMPLE 11

The entries in Fig. 46.21 show the number of elements in the various regions. Find:

(a) $n(A)$ (b) $n(B)$
(c) $n(C)$ (d) $n(A \cap B)$
(e) $n(A \cap C)$ (f) $n(B \cap C)$
(g) $n(A \cap B \cap C)$ (h) $n(A \cup B \cup C)$

(a) $n(A) = 12 + 8 + 6 + 2 = 28$

(b) $n(B) = 8 + 2 + 13 + 5 = 28$

(c) $n(C) = 18 + 6 + 2 + 5 = 31$

(d) $n(A \cap B) = 8 + 2 = 10$

(e) $n(A \cap C) = 6 + 2 = 8$

(f) $n(B \cap C) = 5 + 2 = 7$

(g) $n(A \cap B \cap C) = 2$

(h) To find $n(A \cup B \cup C)$ we use:

$$n(A \cup B \cup C) = n(A) + n(B) + n(C)$$
$$- n(A \cap B) - n(A \cap C)$$
$$- n(B \cap C) + n(A \cap B \cap C)$$
$$= 28 + 28 + 31 - 10 - 8 - 7 + 2$$
$$= 89 - 25 = 64$$

Alternatively:

$$n(A \cup B \cup C) = 12 + 6 + 2 + 8$$
$$+ 18 + 5 + 13$$
$$= 64$$

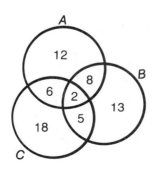

Fig. 46.21

EXAMPLE 12

Out of three recreations, gardening, reading and playing sport, 120 people were invited to state in which they were interested. 60 were interested in gardening, 86 were interested in reading and 64 were interested in playing sport. 32 gardened and read, 38 gardened and played sport and 34 read and played sport. How many were interested in all three activities?

We are given,

$$n(G \cup R \cup S) = 120 \quad n(G) = 60$$
$$n(R) = 86 \quad n(S) = 64$$
$$n(G \cap R) = 32 \quad n(G \cap S) = 38$$

and $\qquad\qquad n(R \cap S) = 34.$

The problem is to find $n(G \cap R \cap S)$. Using the equation,

$$n(G \cup R \cup S) = n(G) + n(R) + n(S)$$
$$- n(G \cap R) - n(G \cap S)$$
$$- n(R \cap S) + n(G \cap R \cap S)$$
$$120 = 60 + 86 + 64 - 32 - 38$$
$$- 34 + n(G \cap R \cap S)$$
$$120 = 106 + n(G \cap R \cap S)$$
$$n(G \cap R \cap S) = 120 - 106 = 14$$

Hence 14 people are interested in all three activities.

Exercise 206 — *All type C*

1) Figure 46.22 shows two intersecting sets A and B. The entries give the number of elements in each region. Find:

(a) $n(A)$ (b) $n(B)$
(c) $n(A \cap B)$ (d) $n(A \cup B)$

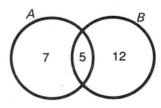

Fig. 46.22

2) The number of elements in sets A and B are shown in Fig. 46.23. Find:

(a) x (b) $n(A)$ (c) $n(B)$
(d) $n(A \cup B)$ if $n(A) = n(B)$

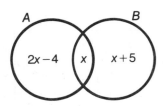

Fig. 46.23

3) 60 candidates in an examination offered history and geography. Every student takes at least one of these subjects and some take two. 55 take history and 45 take geography. How many take both?

4) In a class of 30 pupils, 18 take French and 17 take German. 3 take neither. How many take both French and German?

5) In a group of 25 boys, 18 like Association Football whilst 14 like Rugby Football. How many like both kinds of football?

6) The entries in the diagram (Fig. 46.24) show the number of elements in the various regions. Find:

(a) $n(X)$ (b) $n(Y)$
(c) $n(Z)$ (d) $n(X \cap Y)$
(e) $n(X \cap Z)$ (f) $n(Y \cap Z)$
(g) $n(X \cap Y \cap Z)$ (h) $n(X \cup Y \cup Z)$

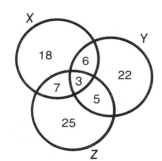

Fig. 46.24

7) Figure 46.25 shows the number of elements in the various regions of a Venn diagram. If $n(A \cup B \cup C) = 150$, find

(a) x (b) $n(A)$ (c) $n(B)$
(d) $n(C)$ (e) $n(A \cap B)$
(f) $n(B \cap C)$ (g) $n(A \cap C)$

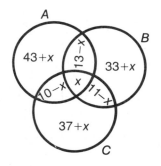

Fig. 46.25

8) Out of 136 students in a school, 60 take French, 100 take chemistry and 48 take physics. If 28 take French and chemistry, 44 take chemistry and physics and 20 take French and physics, how many take all three subjects?

9) In an examination, 60 candidates offered mathematics, 80 offered English and 50 offered physics. If 20 offered maths and English, 15 English and physics, 25 maths and physics and 10 offered all three, how many candidates sat the examination?

10) Of 100 students, 42 take physics, 35 take chemistry and 30 take botany. 20 take none of these subjects. 9 take botany and physics, 10 take botany and chemistry and 11 take physics and chemistry. Find:

(a) the number of students that take all three subjects;
(b) the number that take physics only;
(c) the number that take botany and chemistry only.

CORRESPONDENCE AND EQUIVALENCE

It has been said, earlier in this chapter, that two sets are equal if the elements in each of them are identical. Thus if $A = \{a, e, i, o, u\}$ and $B = \{e, o, u, a, i\}$ then $A = B$.

When two sets have the same number of elements we say that a *one to one correspondence* exists. Thus if $A = \{1, 3, 5, 7, 9\}$ and $B = \{a, e, i, o, u\}$ then $n(A) = n(B) = 5$ and A and B have one to one correspondence. This is often indicated by using a two way arrow thus $A \leftrightarrows B$, meaning that the members of A can be paired off with the members of B or that the members of B can be paired off with the members of A.

If two sets possess one to one correspondence they are said to be *equivalent*. Thus if $X = \{1, 2, 3, 4, 5, 6\}$ and $Y = \{3, 5, 6, 7, 8, 9\}$ the sets X and Y are equivalent, that is, $X \leftrightarrows Y$, because $n(X) = n(Y) = 6$. Note that two sets which are equivalent need not be equal.

There are very many examples of equivalent sets. For instance if we have six knives and six forks we can pair each knife with each fork. We have matched up all the members of the set of knives with all the members of the set of forks.

366

Again, when we count articles we have one to one correspondence, because in every case a number is matched with an article.

Now suppose we have articles packaged so that there are ten articles to a packet. Thus, for every packet there are 10 articles and we say that we have *one to many correspondence*. If we buy oranges at a cost of 12 pence for five oranges we get 5 oranges for 12 pence and we say that we have *many to many correspondence*.

One to many and many to many correspondence is just another way of stating a ratio. Thus 1 to 10 correspondence means the same as the ratio 1 : 10 and 5 to 12 correspondence means the same as 5 : 12 (see Chapter 6).

Exercise 207 — *All type B*

1) Below are two lots of five sets. Using the two way arrow, write down the sets which are equivalent.

Lot 1. $A = \{$rectangle, square, rhombus, parallelogram$\}$

$B = \{$a, b, c, d, e, f, g$\}$

$C = \{$mother, father, sister$\}$

$D = \{1, 3, 5, 7, 9\}$

$E = \{$hammer, chisel, saw, nail, screw, rule$\}$

Lot 2. $V = \{1, 2, 3, 4, 5, 6, 7\}$

$W = \{$a, e, u, o, i$\}$

$X = \{$knife, fork, spoon$\}$

$Y = \{$trowel, hoe, fork, spade, stake, mower$\}$

$Z = \{$cylinder, sphere, cuboid, pyramid$\}$

2) State which of the following statements are true and which are false:

(a) $\{$m, n, o, p$\} \leftrightarrow \{2, 4, 6, 9\}$
(b) $\{1, 3, 5\} = \{3, 1, 6\}$
(c) $\{$coal, peat, wood, gas$\}$
        $\leftrightarrow \{$boy, girl, man, woman$\}$
(d) $\{$screw, nail, nut, bolt, rivet$\}$
        $\leftrightarrow \{1, 2, 3, 4, 5\}$
(e) $\{$lion, tiger, cat, mouse$\}$
        $= \{$chair, table, bed, settee$\}$

If the statement is false, replace the symbol connecting the sets with the correct symbol.

3) In the following statements write down the type of correspondence which has been used.

(a)   12 eggs for 50 pence.
(b)   25 pins to a packet.
(c)   50 kilograms for £2.
(d)   20 students to a class.
(e)   6 gas rings to a cooker.
(f)   12 months to a year.
(g)   5 items of cutlery to a table place.
(h)   11 players to a team.
(i)   3 pears for 20 pence.
(j)   7 chairs used by 7 people.

Chapter 47 Number Scales

THE BINARY SYSTEM

In the ordinary decimal system (sometimes known as the denary system) the digits 0 to 9 are used.

Consider the number 5623. It means

$$5 \times 1000 + 6 \times 100 + 2 \times 10 + 3 \times 1$$

Remembering that $10^0 = 1$, we may write

$$5623 = 5 \times 10^3 + 6 \times 10^2 + 2 \times 10^1 + 3 \times 10^0$$

Thus

$$80\,321 = 8 \times 10^4 + 0 \times 10^3 + 3 \times 10^2 + 2 \times 10^1 + 1 \times 10^0$$

Now consider the decimal fraction 0.381 3. It means

$$\frac{3}{10} + \frac{8}{100} + \frac{1}{1000} + \frac{3}{10\,000}$$

Therefore,

$$0.381\,3 = 3 \times 10^{-1} + 8 \times 10^{-2} + 1 \times 10^{-3} + 3 \times 10^{-4}$$

Now consider the number 736.58.

$$736.58 = 7 \times 10^2 + 3 \times 10^1 + 6 \times 10^0 + 5 \times 10^{-1} + 8 \times 10^{-2}$$

Note that the decimal point indicates the change from positive powers of 10 to negative powers of 10.

It is perfectly possible to have a number system which works on the powers of any number. The most popular of these systems is the binary (bi meaning two) which operates with powers of 2.

It will be noticed in the decimal system that the greatest digit used is 9 which is one less than 10. Thus, in the binary system the greatest digit that can be used is 1 which is one less than 2.

A number written in binary consists only of the digits 0 and 1 and a typical binary number is 1 0 1 0 1 1 1.

The number 1 0 1 0 1 1 1 means:

$$1 \times 2^6 + 0 \times 2^5 + 1 \times 2^4 + 0 \times 2^3 + 1 \times 2^2 + 1 \times 2^1 + 1 \times 2^0$$

The number .1 1 0 1 1 means:

$$1 \times 2^{-1} + 1 \times 2^{-2} + 0 \times 2^{-3} + 1 \times 2^{-4} + 1 \times 2^{-5}$$

The number 1 0 1.1 1 means:

$$1 \times 2^2 + 0 \times 2^1 + 1 \times 2^0 + 1 \times 2^{-1} + 1 \times 2^{-2}$$

The *binary point* separates the positive powers of 2 from the negative powers of 2. Numbers containing a binary point are sometimes called *bicimals*.

CONVERSION FROM BINARY TO DECIMAL AND VICE VERSA

There are several ways of converting decimal numbers to binary numbers. A simple method is shown in the Example 1.

EXAMPLE 1

(1) Convert 59 to a binary number.

	Remainder	Power of 2	Explanation
59	1	0	$59 \div 2 = 29$ remainder 1
29	1	1	$29 \div 2 = 14$ remainder 1
14	0	2	$14 \div 2 = 7$ remainder 0
7	1	3	$7 \div 2 = 3$ remainder 1
3	1	4	$3 \div 2 = 1$ remainder 1
1	1	5	$1 \div 2 = 0$ remainder 1

Therefore,

$$59 \text{ (decimal)} = 1\ 1\ 1\ 0\ 1\ 1 \text{ (binary)}$$

(2) Convert 0.378 to binary.

0.378	Whole Number	Power of 2	Explanation
0.756	0	2^{-1}	$2 \times 0.378 = 0.756$. Whole number = 0
1.512	1	2^{-2}	$2 \times 0.756 = 1.512$. Whole number = 1 Remove the whole number 1. Then,
1.024	1	2^{-3}	$2 \times 0.512 = 1.024$. Whole number = 1 Remove the whole number 1. Then,
0.048	0	2^{-4}	$2 \times 0.024 = 0.048$. Whole number = 0
0.096	0	2^{-5}	$2 \times 0.048 = 0.096$. Whole number = 0
0.192	0	2^{-6}	$2 \times 0.096 = 0.192$. Whole number = 0
0.384	0	2^{-7}	$2 \times 0.192 = 0.384$. Whole number = 0
0.768	0	2^{-8}	$2 \times 0.384 = 0.768$. Whole number = 0
1.536	1	2^{-9}	$2 \times 0.768 = 1.536$. Whole number = 1 Remove the whole number 1. Then,
1.072	1 etc.	2^{-10}	$2 \times 0.536 = 1.072$. Whole number = 1

Therefore,   0.378 = .0 1 1 0 0 0 0 0 1 1
(correct to 10 binary places).

Most decimal fractions do not have an exact equivalent in binary. When converting these all we can do is to work to a specified number of binary places as in the example above. When converting numbers which have a whole number and a decimal part we convert the whole number part as shown in the first example and the decimal part as shown in the second example. Thus,

59.378 = 1 1 1 0 1 1.0 1 1 0 0 0 0 0 1 1
(correct to 10 binary places).

To convert a binary number into its decimal equivalent we make use of a table similar to the one shown below. The table may be extended in either direction as required.

2^6	2^5	2^4	2^3	2^2
64	32	16	8	4

2^1	2^0	2^{-1}	2^{-2}	2^{-3}
2	1	0.5	0.25	0.125

EXAMPLE 2
Convert 1 1 0 1.1 0 1 to decimal.

$$1\,1\,0\,1.1\,0\,1 \text{ (binary)}$$
$$= 1 \times 2^3 + 1 \times 2^2 + 0 \times 2^1 + 1 \times 2^0$$
$$+ 1 \times 2^{-1} + 0 \times 2^{-2} + 1 \times 2^{-3}$$
$$= 8 + 4 + 0 + 1 + 0.5 + 0 + 0.125$$
$$= 13.625 \text{ (decimal)}$$

The binary system is used in computers and other calculating machines. Since only the digits 0 and 1 are used in the system this is equivalent to a two-state system. For instance if a device is *off* it represents a 0 — if it is *on* a 1 is represented. Fig. 47.1 shows how the number 1 0 1 1 0 can be represented by 5 electric light bulbs.

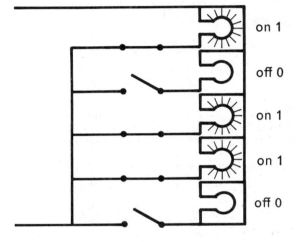

on 1

off 0

on 1

on 1

off 0

Fig. 47.1

ADDITION OF BINARY NUMBERS

When adding binary numbers the following rules apply:

$$1 + 0 = 1$$
$$0 + 1 = 1$$
$$1 + 1 = 1\,0$$

Note that   1 + 1 = 2   in the decimal system but it is 1 0 in binary, i.e. one two and no units.

EXAMPLE 3
(1)
```
      1 1
        1
              numbers
    1 1       carried
    ------
    1 0 0
```

(2)
```
        1 0 1 1 1
          1 0 1 1
          1 1 0 1  ← numbers
        1 1 1 1 1      carried
        ─────────
      1 0 1 1 1 1
```

(3)
```
        1 1 0 1 0 1
          1 1 1 1 1  ← numbers
        1 1 1 1 1 1      carried
        ───────────
      1 0 1 0 1 0 0
```

SUBTRACTION OF BINARY NUMBERS

In decimal subtraction we 'borrow' and 'pay back' in tens. Similarly, in binary subtraction we 'borrow' and 'pay back' in twos. In Example 4, decimal numbers are used to show the result of 'borrowing' and 'paying back'.

EXAMPLE 4

(1)
```
      2
    1 Ø
    1
  1
  ───
    1
```

(2)
```
      3 2
    1 Ⅹ Ø 1 1
      Ⅹ 1 0 1
      1 2
    ─────────
      1 1 1 0
```

MULTIPLICATION OF BINARY NUMBERS

The multiplication table in binary is as follows:

$$0 \times 0 = 0 \qquad 0 \times 1 = 0$$
$$1 \times 0 = 0 \qquad 1 \times 1 = 1$$

When multiplying, remember the importance of starting each line of the multiplication under the number we are multiplying by.

EXAMPLE 5

Multiply 1 1 0 1 by 1 0 1.

```
            1 1 0 1
              1 0 1
          ─────────
            1 1 0 1
          0 0 0 0
        1 1 0 1
        1 1 1 1 ←──── numbers carried
      ───────────
      1 0 0 0 0 0 1
```

A check may be made by converting into decimal.

```
    1 1 0 1 (binary)   = 13 (decimal)
      1 0 1 (binary)   =  5 (decimal)
  13 x 5 (decimal)     = 65 (decimal)
                       = 1 0 0 0 0 0 1 (binary)
```

Hence the binary product 1 0 0 0 0 0 1 is correct and

$$1 1 0 1 \times 1 0 1 = 1 0 0 0 0 0 1$$

DIVISION OF BINARY NUMBERS

Division is really repeated subtraction as shown in Example 6.

EXAMPLE 6

Divide 1 0 0 0 0 1 by 1 1 0 1

```
      1 1 0 1 ) 1 0 0 0 0 0 1 ( 1 0 1
                1 1 0 1
                ───────
                  1 1 0 1
                  1 1 0 1
                  ───────
                  · · · ·
```

1 1 0 1 x 1 = 1 1 0 1. Place 1 in the answer. 1 0 0 0 0 − 1 1 0 1 = 1 1. Bring down next figure which is 0. 1 1 0 1 will not go into 1 1 0 so place 0 in answer and bring down the next figure, which is 1. 1 1 0 1 goes into 1 1 0 1 exactly 1. Hence the answer is 1 0 1.

A check can be made by converting the binary numbers into decimal. Thus 1 1 0 1 (binary) = 13 (decimal) and 1 0 0 0 0 0 1 (binary) = 65 (decimal). 65 ÷ 13 = 5 (decimal) = 1 0 1 (binary). Hence

$$1 0 0 0 0 0 1 \div 1 1 0 1 = 1 0 1$$

OPERATIONS WITH BICIMALS

EXAMPLE 7

Multiply 1 0 1.1 by 1 1.1.

First disregard the binary point and multiply 1 0 1 1 by 1 1 1.

```
              1 0 1 1
                1 1 1
            ─────────
              1 0 1 1
            1 0 1 1
          1 0 1 1
        ───────────
        1 0 0 1 1 0 1
```

Now count up the number of digits following the binary point in each number, i.e. 1 + 1 = 2. In the answer to the multiplication (the product), count this total number of digits from the right and insert the binary point. The product then becomes 1 0 0 1 1.0 1.

370

To check the product, convert each of the original numbers to decimal. Thus

$$1\,0\,1.1 = 5\tfrac{1}{2} \quad \text{and} \quad 1\,1.1 = 3\tfrac{1}{2}$$

$$5\tfrac{1}{2} \times 3\tfrac{1}{2} = 19\tfrac{1}{4} = 1\,0\,0\,1\,1.0\,1$$

Hence

$$1\,0\,1.1 \times 1\,1.1 = 1\,0\,0\,1\,1.0\,1$$

EXAMPLE 8

Divide 1 0 1.1 by 1 1 giving the answer to 4 places after the binary point.

```
11)1 0 1.1(1.1 1 0 1
   1 1
   ───
   1 0 1
     1 1
   ─────
     1 0 0
       1 1
   ───────
       1 0 0
         1 1
   ─────────
           1
```

The first line 1 1 × 1 = 1 1.
1 0 1 − 1 1 = 1 0. Bring down 1. Since this figure lies behind the binary point insert a point in the answer.

1 0 1 − 1 1 = 1 0. Since all the figures in the dividend have been used up bring down a zero. 1 1 will not go into 1 0 so place a zero in the answer and bring down a second zero. Now divide 1 1 into 1 0 0. It goes 1 remainder 1. We now have the answer to 4 places after the binary point.

1 0 1 ÷ 1 1 = 1.1 1 0 1 correct to 4 figures after the binary point.

Exercise 208 — *Questions 1–5 type A,*
6–8 type B, remainder C

1) Convert to binary:

(a) 23   (b) 42   (c) 61   (d) 57

2) Convert to denary:

(a) 1 0 1 1 0   (b) 1 1 1 0 0 1
(c) 1 0 1 1 0 1 0   (d) 1 1 0 1 1 1

3) Convert to denary:

(a) 0.1 1 0 1   (b) 0.0 1 1 1   (c) 0.0 0 1 1

4) Convert to binary:

(a) $\dfrac{3}{8}$ (b) $\dfrac{5}{16}$ (c) $\dfrac{7}{8}$

5) Convert to binary and correct to 7 places of binary:

(a) 0.169   (b) 18.467   (c) 108.710

6) Add the following binary numbers:

(a) 1 0 1 1 + 1 1
(b) 1 1 0 1 1 + 1 0 1 1
(c) 1 0 1 1 1 + 1 1 0 1 0 + 1 1 1
(d) 1 0 1 1 0 1 + 1 0 1 0 + 1 0 1 1 0 1
(e) 0.1 1 0 1 + 0.0 1 1 0
(f) 0.1 1 0 0 1 + 0.1 1 0 1 1
(g) 1 1.1 1 0 1 + 1 1 1.1 0 0 1 + 1.1 1 0 0
(h) 1 0 1.1 1 + 1 1 1.1 0 + 1 0 0.1 1

7) Subtract the following binary numbers:

(a) 1 1 1 − 1 0
(b) 1 0 1 1 − 1 1 1
(c) 1 1 0 1 1 − 1 1 0 1
(d) 1 1.0 1 1 − 1.1 0 1
(e) 1 0 1.1 1 0 − 1 1.1 0 1

8) Multiply together the following binary numbers:

(a) 1 1 × 1 0
(b) 1 0 1 × 1 1 1
(c) 1 0 1 1 × 1 0 1 0
(d) 1 1 0 1 1 × 1 1 0 1
(e) 1 1 0 1 0 × 1 0 1 1

9) Divide the following binary numbers:

(a) 1 0 0 1 ÷ 1 1
(b) 1 1 0 0 ÷ 1 1
(c) 1 0 0 1 0 1 1 ÷ 1 1 1 1
(d) 1 1 0 0 1 0 0 ÷ 1 0 1 0
(e) 1 0 1 0 1 1 1 1 1 ÷ 1 1 0 1 1

10) Find the values of the following giving your answer in binary:

(a) 1 1 0 1.1 × 1.1 1
(b) 1 0 1.0 1 × 1 1.1 0 1
(c) 1 0 1 0.1 ÷ 1 0 1 giving the answer to 4 figures after the binary point.
(d) 1 1 1 1.0 1 ÷ 1 1 0 1 giving the answer to 5 figures after the binary point.

OTHER NUMBER SCALES

In the scale of 5, powers of 5 are used. Only the digits 0, 1, 2, 3 and 4 are available because the greatest digit used must be one less than 5. If you are told that the number 3 4 1 2 is in the scale of 5 it means that the number is *based* upon powers of 5. To show that this is so we write 3412_5. The suffix 5 indicates that the number scale of 5 is being used. The number scale is usually called the *base*. We say that the number 3412_5 is to the base 5. Similarly 463_8 is a number to the base 8.

$$3412_5 = 3 \times 5^3 + 4 \times 5^2 + 1 \times 5^1 + 2 \times 5^0$$
$$= 3 \times 125 + 4 \times 25 + 1 \times 5 + 2 \times 1$$
$$= 482_{10}$$
$$463_8 = 4 \times 8^2 + 6 \times 8^1 + 3 \times 8^0$$
$$= 4 \times 64 + 6 \times 8 + 3 \times 1 = 307_{10}$$

In a number system in base 3 we have

$$1 + 0 = 1 \quad 1 + 1 = 2 \quad 1 + 2 = 0 \text{ carry } 1$$

EXAMPLE 9
(1) Find $212_3 + 121_3$.

$$\begin{array}{r} 212 \\ 121 \\ \hline 1110 \end{array} \qquad 212_3 + 121_3 = 1110_3$$

(2) Find $1220_3 + 2212_3 + 111_3$.

$$\begin{array}{r} 1220 \\ 2212 \\ 111 \\ \hline 12\,020 \end{array} \qquad 1220_3 + 2212_3 + 111_3 = 12\,020_3$$

Similar considerations apply to any other number system.

The addition table for the base 6 is shown below.

+	0	1	2	3	4	5
0	0	1	2	3	4	5
1	1	2	3	4	5	10
2	2	3	4	5	10	11
3	3	4	5	10	11	12
4	4	5	10	11	12	13
5	5	10	11	12	13	14

Note that $1 + 5 = 6$ in the decimal system but it is 10 in the base 6, i.e., one six and no units. Similarly, $4 + 5 = 13$ in the base 6, i.e., one six and three units.

EXAMPLE 10
Find $52_6 + 35_6$.

$$\begin{array}{r} 52 \\ 35 \\ \hline 131 \end{array}$$

$$\therefore \qquad 52_6 + 35_6 = 131_6$$

EXAMPLE 11
Find $637_8 + 56_8$.

$$\begin{array}{r} 637 \\ 56 \\ \hline 715 \end{array} \qquad 637_8 + 56_8 = 715_8$$

Subtraction is done similarly.

EXAMPLE 12
Find $62_8 - 37_8$.

$$\begin{array}{r} 62 \\ 37 \\ \hline 23 \end{array} \qquad 62_8 - 37_8 = 23_8$$

CONVERSION FROM ONE BASE TO ANOTHER

It is difficult to change directly from one base to another without going through 10 first because the calculation would have to be done in a strange system. A simple method of converting a number in base 10 to a number in any other base is shown in Example 13.

EXAMPLE 13
(1) Convert 413_{10} into its equivalent in base 8.

	Remainder	Power of 8	Explanation
413			
51	5	8^0	$413 \div 8 = 51$ remainder 5
6	3	8^1	$51 \div 8 = 6$ remainder 3
0	6	8^2	$6 \div 8 = 0$ remainder 6

Hence $413_{10} = 635_8$.

(2) Express $(101_8 - 101_2)$ as a number in base eight.

$$101_2 = (1 \times 2^2 + 0 \times 2^1 + 1 \times 2^0)_{10} = 5_{10}$$
$$5_{10} = 5_8$$
$$\therefore \quad (101_8 - 101_2) = 101_8 - 5_8 = 74_8$$

Exercise 209 — *Questions 1–3 type B, remainder C*

1) Perform the following additions:
(a) $12_3 + 22_3$ (b) $201_3 + 212_3$
(c) $2222_3 + 1212_3$ (d) $413_5 + 324_5$
(e) $315_6 + 24_6 + 52_6$
(f) $31_4 + 303_4 + 213_4$ (g) $36_8 + 44_8 + 57_8$
(h) $514_6 + 325_6 + 14_6 + 3_6$

2) Perform the following subtractions:
(a) $212_3 - 112_3$
(b) $32_4 - 23_4$
(c) $2122_3 - 1022_3$
(d) $311_4 - 232_4$
(e) $5321_8 - 677_8$
(f) $403_5 - 214_5$

3) Convert the following numbers to base 10:
(a) 325_6 (b) 2120_3 (c) 342_6
(d) 625_7 (e) 2323_4

4) (a) Express $325_{10} + 325_8$ as a number in base 8.
    (b) Express $212_3 - 110_2$ as a number in base 3.
    (c) Express $222_8 - 222_3$ as a number in base 3.
    (d) Express $111_8 + 111_2$ as a number in base 8.

MODULAR ARITHMETIC

If we start with 0 and count in units, in base 5, we get 0, 1, 2, 3, 4, 10, 11, 12, 13, 14, 20, 21, 22, 23, 24, 30, etc. If we retain only the units we get the set $\{0, 1, 2, 3, 4\}$. We are said to be working in *modulo 5*, which is usually abbreviated to mod 5.

It is worth while noting that the same set would be obtained if we divided the set of natural numbers by 5 and kept only the remainder.

Thus $\dfrac{27}{5} = 5$ remainder 2

$\dfrac{631}{5} = 126$ remainder 1

Hence 27 is equivalent to 2 in the modulo 5 system and 631 is equivalent to 1 in the same system.

Now consider the clock face shown in Fig. 47.2.

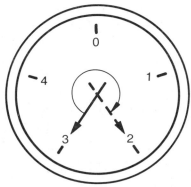

Fig. 47.2

It is numbered 0 to 4, the same digits as those used in the modulo 5 system. If the pointer is on 3 and we add 4 more spaces clockwise, where will the pointer finish? As shown in the diagram it will end up on 2. We say

$$3 + 4 \equiv 2 \ (\text{mod } 5)$$

which is read as 'three plus four is congruent to 2 modulo 5'. Using the clock face we can make an addition table as shown below·

+	0	1	2	3	4
0	0	1	2	3	4
1	1	2	3	4	0
2	2	3	4	0	1
3	3	4	0	1	2
4	4	0	1	2	3

You will notice that although

$$3_5 + 4_5 = 12_5$$
$$3 + 4 \equiv 2 \ (\text{mod } 5)$$

that is, we retain only the units digit.

We can also use our clockface for subtraction. When we added the pointer was moved clockwise so when we subtract we must move it anticlockwise.

What is $1 - 3$ in the modulo 5 system? Starting with the pointer on 1 we move 3 spaces anticlockwise and find that the pointer finishes on 3 (Fig. 47.3). Hence

$$1 - 3 \equiv 3 \ (\text{mod } 5)$$

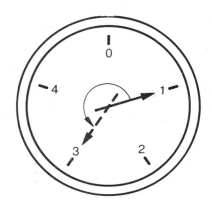

Fig. 47.3

A multiplication table in modulo 5 is as follows:

x	0	1	2	3	4
0	0	0	0	0	0
1	0	1	2	3	4
2	0	2	4	1	3
3	0	3	1	4	2
4	0	4	3	2	1

Thus by finding where row 3 and column 2 meet we have $3 \times 2 \equiv 1 \pmod 5$. Note that $4_5 \times 4_5 = 31_5$. Hence $4 \times 4 \equiv 1 \pmod 5$ because we retain only the units digit.

EXAMPLE 14

What is $32 \times 18 \pmod 5$?

$32 \equiv 2 \bmod 5$ (because
     $32 \div 5 = 6$ remainder 2)

$18 \equiv 3 \bmod 5$ (because
     $18 \div 5 = 3$ remainder 3)

$32 \times 18 \equiv 2 \times 3 \equiv 1 \pmod 5$

Alternatively $32 \times 18 = 576$ and $576 \div 5 = 115$ remainder 1. Hence

$$32 \times 18 \equiv 1 \pmod 5$$

There is nothing special about the modulo 5 system — any number can be used as the modulus.

EXAMPLE 15

$5 + 4 \equiv 3 \pmod 6$ because $5_6 + 4_6 = 13_6$. The units digit is 3.

$8 + 7 \equiv 6 \pmod 9$ because $8_9 + 7_9 = 16_9$. The units digit is 6.

$5 \times 7 \equiv 3 \pmod 8$ because $5_8 \times 7_8 = 43_8$. The units digit is 3.

$6 \times 5 \equiv 2 \pmod 7$ because $6_7 \times 5_7 = 42_7$. The units digit is 2.

EXAMPLE 16

(1) If $x + 3 \equiv 2 \pmod 5$ find x.

This problem boils down to 'in the modulo 5 system what number added to 3 makes 2?'

The answer is clearly 4 and hence $x = 4$.

Check: $4 + 3 \equiv 2 \pmod 5$.

An alternative way of solving the congruence is to find a number such that $3 + ? \equiv 0 \pmod 5$. The number is 2 and hence

$$x + 3 + 2 \equiv 2 + 2 \pmod 5$$
$$x + 0 \equiv 4 \pmod 5$$
or $x = 4$

(2) If $2x + 3 \equiv 6 \pmod 7$ find x.

Adding 4 to each side we get

$$2x + 3 + 4 \equiv 6 + 4 \pmod 7$$
$$2x + 0 \equiv 3 \pmod 7$$
$$2x \equiv 3 \pmod 7$$

The problem now boils down to 'what do we multiply 2 by in order to make $1x$?' The answer is 4 because

$$2 \times 4 \equiv 1 \pmod 7$$
$$(2 \times 4)x \equiv 3 \times 4$$
$$x \equiv 5$$

Check: $(2 \times 5) + 3 \equiv 3 + 3 \equiv 6 \pmod 7$.

(3) If $2x \equiv 4 \pmod 6$ find x.

The solutions are $x = 2$ and $x = 5$ because

$$2 \times 2 \equiv 4 \pmod 6$$
and $2 \times 5 \equiv 4 \pmod 6$

(Whenever the modulus is not a prime number it is possible to have more than 1 solution although sometimes no solution is possible, see next example.)

(4) Solve $4x \equiv 3 \pmod 6$.

It is impossible to find a solution because 4 times any number will not give 3 in the modulo 6 system. Try them

$4 \times 0 \equiv 0 \pmod 6$ $4 \times 1 \equiv 4 \pmod 6$

$4 \times 2 \equiv 2 \pmod 6$ $4 \times 3 \equiv 0 \pmod 6$

$4 \times 4 \equiv 4 \pmod 6$ $4 \times 5 \equiv 2 \pmod 6$

Similarly $4x \equiv 1$ and $4x \equiv 5$ have no solutions.

(5) In arithmetic modulo 5 evaluate the square root of 9.

Now $\sqrt{9} = \pm 3$
$$+ 3 \equiv 3 \pmod 5$$
$$- 3 \equiv 2 \pmod 5$$

Exercise 210 – *Questions 1–3 type B,*
remainder C

1) In the modulo 5 system find:

(a) $2 + 4$ (b) $3 + 4$ (c) $2 - 4$
(d) $1 - 2$ (e) 3×3 (f) 4×2
(g) 27×16 (h) 11×9

2) In the modulo 8 system find:

(a) $3 + 7$ (b) $2 + 6$ (c) $5 - 7$
(d) $3 - 5$ (e) 7×7 (f) 2×5
(g) 15×18 (h) 16×19

3) Perform the following computations in the modulo 7 system:

(a) $3 + 4 + 6$ (b) $2 + 3 + 4 + 5 + 6$
(c) $(3 \times 5) + (2 \times 6)$ (d) $(6 \times 5) + (3 \times 4)$

4) If $65 \equiv 5 \pmod{n}$ find all the possible values of n.

5) Solve the following congruences for x:

(a) $x + 4 \equiv 3 \pmod 5$
(b) $x + 6 \equiv 3 \pmod 7$
(c) $x + 6 \equiv 2 \pmod 8$

6) Solve the following congruences for x:

(a) $2x \equiv 4 \pmod 5$
(b) $2x + 3 \equiv 6 \pmod 7$
(c) $5x + 3 \equiv 1 \pmod 6$
(d) $2x \equiv 4 \pmod 8$

7) In arithmetic modulo 7 find the square root of 16.

COMMUTATIVITY

If an operation $a * b = b * a$ then the operation is said to be *commutative*. This means that if we can interchange the two numbers a and b without altering the result the operation is commutative. Thus, in the decimal system:

$$5 + 4 = 9 \quad \text{and} \quad 4 + 5 = 9$$

and similarly for any other two numbers. The operation of addition in the decimal system is commutative.

Also, in the decimal system,

$$12 \div 6 = 2 \quad \text{but} \quad 6 \div 12 = \tfrac{1}{2}$$

In the decimal system the operation of division is *not* commutative.

EXAMPLE 17
The operation $a * b$ means $2a + 3b$. Is this operation commutative?

Let us try two numbers, for example, $a = 3$ and $b = 5$.

$$a * b = 2a + 3b$$
$$= 2 \times 3 + 3 \times 5 = 6 + 15 = 21$$

Now let us interchange the numbers so that $a = 5$ and $b = 3$. We get

$$a * b = 2a + 3b$$
$$= 2 \times 5 + 3 \times 3 = 10 + 9 = 19$$

Hence this operation is not commutative.

ASSOCIATIVITY

If an operation $(a * b) * c = a * (b * c)$ the operation is said to be *associative*. In the decimal system,

$$(2 \times 3) \times 4 = 6 \times 4 = 24$$

and $\qquad 2 \times (3 \times 4) = 2 \times 12 = 24$

Hence, in the decimal system, the operation of multiplication is associative. Now look at

$$(24 \div 6) \div 2 = 4 \div 2 = 2$$
$$24 \div (6 \div 2) = 24 \div 3 = 8$$

The operation of division is not associative.

EXAMPLE 18
In the modulo 5 system, is the operation $a - (b + c)$ associative?

If the operation $a - b + c$ is associative then

$$a - (b + c) = (a - b) + c$$

Let $a = 2$, $b = 3$ and $c = 4$. Then

$$a - (b + c) = 2 - (3 + 4)$$
$$= 2 - 2 = 0 \pmod 5$$
$$(a - b) + c = (2 - 3) + 4$$
$$= 4 + 4 = 3 \pmod 5$$

The operation $a - (b + c)$ is not commutative in the modulo 5 system.

Exercise 211 – *All type C*

1) State which of the following are commutative:

(a) Addition in the modulo 3 system.
(b) Subtraction in the modulo 3 system.
(c) Multiplication in the modulo 5 system.
(d) Division in the decimal system.

2) The operation $a * b$ means $2a - b$. Is this operation commutative?

3) The table below represents the result of an operation $*$ on the set $\{0, 1, 2, 3\}$. Is the operation commutative?

$*$	0	1	2	3
0	0	0	0	0
1	0	2	4	6
2	0	4	8	12
3	0	6	12	18

4) State which of the following are associative:

(a) $a + (b + c)$ in the modulo 6 system.
(b) $a - (b - c)$ in the modulo 5 system.
(c) $a \times (b + c)$ in the modulo 3 system.
(d) $a \times (b \times c)$ in the modulo 4 system.
(e) $a \div (b \div c)$ in the decimal system.

5) An operation $a * b$ means $2a - 3b$. Is $a * (b * c)$ associative?

CLOSED SETS

The modulo 6 system uses only the set of numbers $N = \{0, 1, 2, 3, 4, 5\}$. The addition table for the modulo 6 system is given below.

$+$	0	1	2	3	4	5
0	0	1	2	3	4	5
1	1	2	3	4	5	0
2	2	3	4	5	0	1
3	3	4	5	0	1	2
4	4	5	0	1	2	3
5	5	0	1	2	3	4

The table shows that when any two numbers which are members of the set N are added the result is always a member of N. The set N is said to be *closed* under the operation of addition.

EXAMPLE 19

The table below represents the result of an operation $*$ on the set $\{0, 1, 2, 3\}$. Is the set closed under the operation $*$?

$*$	0	1	2	3
0	0	2	4	6
1	1	3	5	7
2	2	4	6	8
3	3	5	7	9

The numbers in the body of the table are not all members of the set $\{0, 1, 2, 3\}$ and hence the set is not closed under the operation $*$.

THE IDENTITY ELEMENT

Look at the table of addition for modulo 6. Is there a number in the set which, when added to the other numbers in the set, leaves the original set unchanged? We see that, on looking at the first row of the table, 0 has this property. 0 is said to be the *identity element* for the operation of addition in modulo 6.

Now look at the table below.

$*$	0	1	2	3
0	0	0	0	0
1	0	2	4	6
2	0	4	8	12
3	0	6	12	18

We see that there is no number which, under the operation $*$, leaves the set $\{0, 1, 2, 3\}$ unchanged. Hence there is no identity element for this operation.

EXAMPLE 20

The table below gives the result of applying the operation $\bullet$ to the elements of the set $\{1, 2, 3\}$. Which is the identity element?

$\bullet$	1	2	3
1	2	1	2
2	1	2	3
3	2	3	1

The identity element is 2 because the other members of the set are not changed when combined with 2 by the operation $\bullet$.

INVERSE PAIRS

Look again at the addition table for modulo 6. We see that the identity element, which is 0, appears in every row and every column of the table. Thus

$$1 + 5 = 0 \quad \text{and} \quad 5 + 1 = 0$$

also, $\quad 2 + 4 = 0 \quad \text{and} \quad 4 + 2 = 0$

We call each of these pairs of numbers *inverse pairs*.

Consider the number 3. The addition table shows that

$$3 + 3 = 0$$

The number 3 is said to be its own inverse.

EXAMPLE 21

The table below gives the result of applying the operation $*$ to the elements of the set $\{0, 1, 2, 3\}$. Has every element of the set an inverse under this operation?

$*$	1	2	3
1	2	3	1
2	3	1	2
3	1	2	3

The identity element is 3.

$$1 * 2 = 3 \quad \text{and} \quad 2 * 1 = 3$$

Hence 1 and 2 are inverse pairs.

$$3 + 3 = 3$$

Hence 3 is its own inverse.

DEFINING A GROUP

For a set to form a group it must possess each of the following properties:

(1) It must be closed.

(2) The operation must be associative.

(3) There must be an identity element.

(4) Every element in the set must have an inverse.

EXAMPLE 22

The table shows the effect of combining the elements $\{a, b, c, d\}$ under the operation $\circ$.

$\circ$	a	b	c	d
a	c	d	a	b
b	d	c	b	a
c	a	b	c	d
d	b	a	d	c

Is the table a group table?

(a) The set is closed under the operation $\circ$ because every symbol in the table is a member of the set $\{a, b, c, d\}$.

(b) The operation is commutative because the table is symmetrical about the leading diagonal, i.e., about the line shown in the table.

(c) The operation is not associative because, for instance,

$$b \circ (d \circ a) = b \circ b = b$$

$$(b \circ d) \circ a = a \circ a = c$$

(d) The identity element is c because:

$$c \circ a = a; \quad c \circ b = b;$$

$$c \circ c = c; \quad c \circ d = d$$

(e) The identity element does not appear in every row and every column. Hence every element of the set $\{a, b, c, d\}$ does not have an inverse under the operation $\circ$.

The table, therefore is not a group table because conditions (2) and (4) are not met.

ISOMORPHIC GROUPS

The addition table for arithmetic (mod 3) is

+	0	1	2
0	0	1	2
1	1	2	0
2	2	0	1

The set $\{0, 1, 2\}$ forms a group under the operation of addition arithmetic (mod 3).

Now consider the table

$\otimes$	A	B	C
A	A	B	C
B	B	C	A
C	C	A	B

If we put the two sets into a one-to-one correspondence then

$$
\begin{array}{ccc}
0 & 1 & 2 \\
\updownarrow & \updownarrow & \updownarrow \\
A & B & C
\end{array}
$$

By looking at the two tables we see that

$$1 + 2 = 0$$

$$B \otimes C = A$$

and so on for all pairs. The operations $+$ and $\otimes$ also correspond. We say that the two groups are identical in structure, that is, they are *isomorphic*.

Another way of saying this is two groups are isomorphic if their combination tables have the same pattern.

EXAMPLE 23

Let A be the operation which rotates OP (Fig. 47.4) through $90°$ anticlockwise to OP$'$, B the operation which rotates OP through $180°$; C the operation which rotates OP through $270°$. Let I be the identity operation which rotates OP through $0°$. Draw up a composition table for $x \circ y$ which means first perform one operation y followed by a second operation x.

Also draw up a composition table for the set $\{0, 1, 2, 3,\}$ (mod 4) under the operation of addition.

Hence show that the two groups are isomorphic.

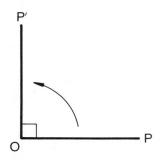

Fig. 47.4

$I \circ I = I$ (rotation of $0°$ followed by a rotation of $0°$)

$I \circ A = A$ (rotation of $90°$ followed by a rotation of $0°$)

$I \circ B = B$ (rotation of $180°$ followed by a rotation of $0°$)

$I \circ C = C$ (rotation of $270°$ followed by a rotation of $0°$)

$A \circ I = A$ (rotation of $0°$ followed by a rotation of $90°$)

$A \circ A = B$ (rotation of $90°$ followed by a rotation of $90°$ giving a rotation of $180°$)

$A \cup B = C$ (rotation of $180°$ followed by a rotation of $90°$ giving a rotation of $270°$)

$A \circ C = I$ (rotation of $270°$ followed by a rotation of $90°$ giving a rotation of $360°$. OP has returned to its starting place which is equivalent to a rotation of $0°$)

The remaining elements in the composition table are obtained in a similar way.

$\circ$	I	A	B	C
I	I	A	B	C
A	A	B	C	I
B	B	C	I	A
C	C	I	A	B

The second composition table is as follows:

+	0	1	2	3
0	0	1	2	3
1	1	2	3	0
2	2	3	0	1
3	3	0	1	2

If I, A, B and C are replaced by 0, 1, 2 and 3 respectively then the two composition tables are the same. Each table has the same pattern and hence the two groups are isomorphic.

Exercise 212 — *All type C*

1) $M = \{d, e, f, g\}$. The table shows the members of M combined under the operation $*$.

$*$	d	e	f	g
d	g	f	e	d
e	f	g	d	e
f	e	d	g	f
g	d	e	f	g

(a) Which is the identity element?
(b) Is the operation $*$ commutative?
(c) Which element is the inverse of (i) d, (ii) f?
(d) Give an example to show that the operation $*$ is associative.
(e) Is the table a group table?

2) The table shows the effect of the operation $\bullet$ on the elements of the set $\{1, 2, 3\}$.

$\bullet$	1	2	3
1	1	2	3
2	2	0	2
3	3	2	1

(a) Is the set closed under the operation $\bullet$?
(b) If there is an identity element, write it down.
(c) Which element is its own inverse?
(d) Does the set $\{1, 2, 3\}$ form a group under the operation $\bullet$.

378

3) Copy and complete the table below for subtraction in modulo 5.

−	0	1	2	3	4
0					
1		0			
2				4	
3					
4					

(a) Find the value of x if $3 - x = 4 \pmod 5$.
(b) Give an example to show that the operation of subtraction in this arithmetic is not commutative.

4) $a * b$ means $a + ab + b$.

(a) What is $2 * 3$?   (b) What is $1 * 0$?
(c) What is the identity element for the operation $*$.
(d) What is the inverse of 2 for this operation?
(e) Is the operation $*$ commutative? Give an example.
(f) Is the operation $*$ associative? Give an example.

5) For each of the following tables give one reason why it is not a group table.

(a) (Base 2)

+	0	1
0	0	1
0	1	10

(b)

×	0	1
0	0	0
1	0	1

(c)

~	0	2	4
0	0	2	4
2	2	0	2
4	4	2	0

(d)

R	x	y	z
x	x	y	z
y	x	y	z
z	x	y	z

6) Copy and complete the following table for the numbers 1, 5, 7, 11 under multiplication in arithmetic modulo 12.

×	1	5	7	11
1	1			11
5	5		11	
7	7	11		
11			5	1

(a) Is there an identity element? If so what is it?
(b) Is the operation of multiplication modulo 12, commutative?
(c) Is the table a group table?

7) The operation $*$ is defined on the set $\{2, 4, 6, 8\}$ by $a * b =$ the units digit in the product ab. For example $2 * 8 = 6$, since $2 \times 8 = 16$ and the units digit of 16 is 6.

(a) Copy and complete the table below:

*	2	4	6	8
2				6
4				
6				
8				

(b) Use your table to find solution sets for each of the following equations:
(i) $c * 8 = 6$ (ii) $d * d = 4$
(iii) $e * e = e$ (iv) $(4 * f) * 4 = f$

(c) (i) Explain why the set is closed under the operation $*$.
(ii) State which element of the set is the identity element.
(iii) State the inverse of 8.
(iv) Show, by means of a clearly worked example, that the operation $*$ is associative.

8) Copy and complete the following table for the set $S = \{1, 2, 3, 4, 5, 6\} \pmod 7$ under the operation of multiplication.

×	1	2	3	4	5	6
1						
2		4			3	
3	3					4
4		1				
5				6		2
6			4			

Use your table to answer the following questions:

(a) What is the inverse of 4 and what is the inverse of 6?
(b) Show that in the system, $(2 \times 4) \times 5 = 2 \times (4 \times 5)$.
(c) If $x \in S$, find the value of x in each of the following:
(i) $5x \equiv 6 \pmod 7$
(ii) $\dfrac{x}{3} \equiv 6 \pmod 7$

9) The following information refers to the operation $*$ on the set $\{A, B, C, D, E\}$:

  (i) The operation is commutative.

 (ii) D is the identity element.

(iii) $A * C = F, \quad A * E = B, \quad B * A = E,$
     $B * C = E, \quad B * E = E.$

 (iv) For all the elements in the set $\quad x * x = x$
     (for instance $\quad A * A = A$).

  (v) The inverse of E is C.

(a) Copy and complete the following table, using the given information:

$*$	A	B	C	D	E
A					
B					
C					
D					
E					

(b) Is the set closed under the operation $*$?

(c) Find $(B * C) * C$ and $B * (C * C)$. Is the operation associative?

(d) Find the solution set of the equation $x * E = E$.

10) The table for multiplication (mod 8) on the set $\{1, 3, 5, 7\}$ is:

$\times$	1	3	5	7
1	1	3	5	7
3	3	1	7	5
5	5	7	1	3
7	7	5	3	1

Find:

(a) the identity element for this operation,

(b) the solution set for $\quad 3 \times x = 7 \text{ (mod 8)}$, $x \in \{1, 3, 5, 7\}$,

(c) the solution set for $\quad x \times x = 1 \text{ (mod 8)}$, $x \in \{1, 3, 5, 7\}$,

(d) the solution set for $\quad x \times x = 3 \text{ (mod 8)}$.

11) The line OA (Fig. 47.5) is rotated about the point O in an anticlockwise direction. The operation which rotates OA through $120°$ is P, the operation which rotates OA through $240°$ is Q. The operation which rotates OA through $0°$ (the identity operation) is I. The rule of combination is $x \circ y$ which means perform one operation y and then follow it by a second operation x.

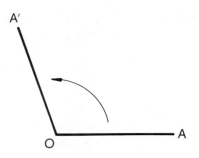

Fig. 47.5

(a) Complete the combination table shown below.

$\circ$	I	P	Q
I			Q
P	P		
Q		I	

(b) Copy and complete the following table for the set $S = \{0, 1, 2\}$ (mod 3) under the operation of addition.

+	0	1	2
0		1	
1			0
2	2		

(c) Show that the two groups are isomorphic.

12) (a) Let the operation of reflecting a point P in the x-axis be X, the operation of reflecting P in the y-axis be Y and the operation of reflecting P in the origin be Z. If leaving P unchanged is I complete the composition table below given that the rule of combination is $x \bullet y$ which means do an operation y followed by a second operation x.

$\bullet$	I	X	Y	Z
I				Z
X			I	
Y	Y			
Z			X	

(b) Copy and complete the following table for the set $\{1, 3, 5, 7\}$ (mod 8) under the operation of multiplication.

$\times$	1	3	5	7
1				7
3		1		
5	5			
7			5	

(c) Show that the two groups are isomorphic.

13) (a) The rhombus shown in Fig. 47.6 can be mapped on to itself by the identity transformation I (do nothing), the reflection Y in the y-diagonal, the reflection X in the x-diagonal and the half turn H about the centre. If, for instance, $X \circ H$ means a half turn followed by a reflection in the x-diagonal, complete the composition table shown below.

$\circ$	I	Y	X	H
I				
Y				
X				Y
H				

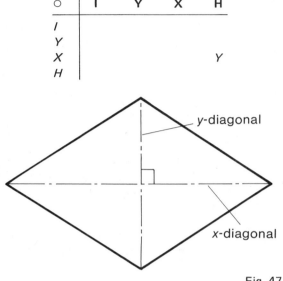

y-diagonal

x-diagonal

Fig. 47.6

(b) Show that this group of operations is isomorphic to a group formed by the set $\{1, 2, 3, 4\}$ (mod 5) under the operation of multiplcation.

14) (a) Fig. 47.7 shows an equilateral triangle in a frame ABC. The altidutes of the triangle are AD, BE and CF.

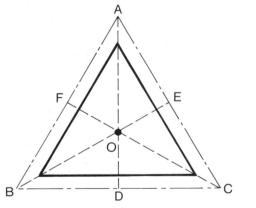

Fig. 47.7

The six symmetries of the triangle are:

P: the identity (do nothing)

Q: a rotation of $120°$ anticlockwise about O

R: a rotation of $240°$ anticlockwise about O

S: a reflection in AD

T: a reflection in BE

U: a reflection in CF

Copy and complete the table shown below. The entry U in row R and column T means that performing R upon the result of performing T gives the same position as would U.

	P	Q	R	S	T	U
P						
Q						
R						U
S						
T						
U						

(b) Write down the inverse of the six symmetries.

15) The composition table below shows the effects of combining the elements $\{a, b, c, d\}$ under the operation $\circ$.

$\circ$	a	b	c	d
a	a	b	c	d
b	b	a	d	c
c	c	d	a	b
d	d	c	b	a

Show that this is isomorphic to the group formed under the operation of multiplication on the set $\{1, 3, 5, 7\}$ (mod 8).

16) The following is part of a multiplication table of arithmetic mod 4.

$\times$	1	3
1	1	3
3	3	1

Find groups having multiplication as the operation in mod 8 arithmetic, isomorphic with the above group.

17)

$*$	A	B	C	D
A	A	B	C	D
B	B	D	A	C
C	C	A	D	B
D	D	C	B	A

$\bullet$	P	Q	R	S
P	P	Q	R	S
Q	Q	S	P	R
R	R	P	S	Q
S	S	R	Q	P

(a) Does $\{A, B, C, D\}$ form a group under the operation of *?

(b) Show that the two groups are isomorphic.

Chapter 48 **Functions and Relations**

RELATIONS

A relation is a set of ordered pairs. Thus the set

$$\{(0, 0), (4, 2), (8, 4), (10, 5), (16, 8)\}$$

is a relation.

The *domain* of the relation is the set of first elements of the ordered pairs whilst the *range* is the second elements of the ordered pairs. Thus for the above set of ordered pairs the domain is $\{0, 4, 8, 10, 16\}$. The range is $\{0, 2, 4, 5, 8\}$.

The relation may be shown in the form of a diagram (Fig. 48.1). The values of the domain and range connected by the arrowed lines constitute ordered pairs. The relation may also be shown in the form of a graph (Fig. 48.2). Note that the range is taken on the vertical axis whilst the domain is taken on the horizontal axis.

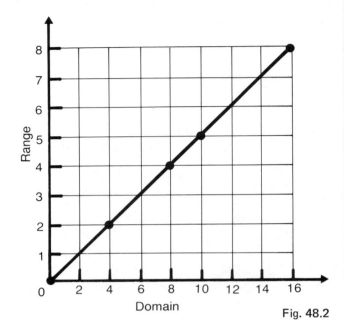

Fig. 48.2

$$x = 0: \quad 3x + 2 = 3 \times 0 + 2 = 2$$
$$x = 1: \quad 3x + 2 = 3 \times 1 + 2 = 5$$
$$x = 2: \quad 3x + 2 = 3 \times 2 + 2 = 8$$

and so on.

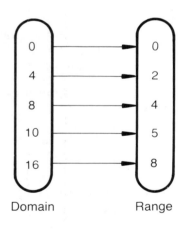

Domain   Range

Fig. 48.1

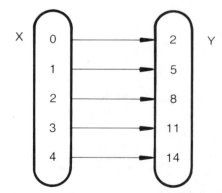

Fig. 48.3

Fig. 48.3 shows a relationship between the domain X and the range Y. X and Y are related by the relationship $x \rightarrow 3x + 2$ which reads 'x is mapped onto $3x + 2$'. The elements in Y are obtained by substituting the values in X into the expression $3x + 2$. Thus, when

Exercise 213 — *All type A*

1) Copy and complete Fig. 48.4 if the relation is:

(a) $x \rightarrow 2x + 4$ (b) $x \rightarrow 6x$

382

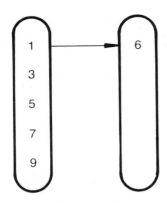

Fig. 48.4

2) For the relation $x \to x^2$:

(a) what is 3 mapped onto?
(b) what is 6 mapped onto?

3) The diagram (Fig. 48.5) shows a relationship between A and B.

(a) What number should be in the position marked *?
(b) Give the relationship between an element, x, in A and the corresponding element in B.

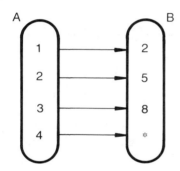

Fig. 48.5

4) With 2, 3, 4 and 5 as domain draw a mapping diagram for:

(a) $x \to 4 - 2x$ (b) $x \to 2^x$

5) The diagram (Fig. 48.6) shows a relationship between the domain X and the range Y. Find:

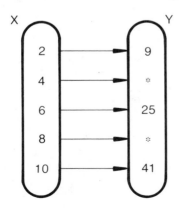

Fig. 48.6

(a) The relationship between an element x in X and the corresponding element in Y.
(b) The numbers marked *.

6) If a relation from X to Y is defined by $y = x^2 - 3x + 2$ (i.e. $x \to x^2 - 3x + 2$) complete the mapping diagram shown in Fig. 48.7.

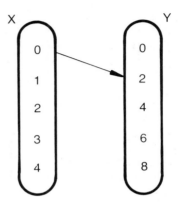

Fig. 48.7

7) State the relationship that gives the mapping shown in Fig. 48.8.

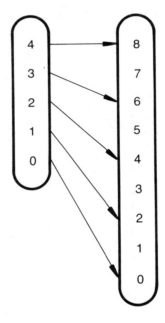

Fig. 48.8

FUNCTIONS

A function is a relation in which each first element of an ordered pair has only one second element. Thus the relations depicted in Figs. 48.1 and 48.3 are functions. However, the relation

383

'is a factor of' shown in Fig. 48.9 is not a function because the element 2 is mapped onto more than one element in the range.

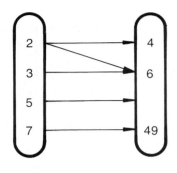

Fig. 48.9

If a relation is not a function a vertical line will pass through the graph of two ordered pairs (Fig. 48.10).

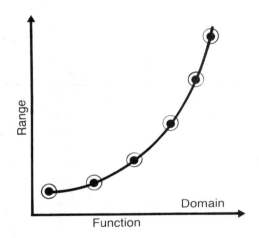

Function

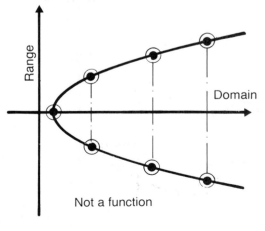

Not a function

Fig. 48.10

384

FUNCTION NOTATION

Consider the relation $x \to 2x + 5$ with domain $\{0, 1, 2, 3\}$. The range is found by substituting each element of the domain into $2x + 5$. Thus when:

$$x = 0 \quad 2x + 5 = (2 \times 0) + 5 = 5$$
$$x = 1 \quad 2x + 5 = (2 \times 1) + 5 = 7$$
$$x = 2 \quad 2x + 5 = (2 \times 2) + 5 = 9$$
$$x = 3 \quad 2x + 5 = (2 \times 3) + 5 = 11$$

Hence the range is the set $\{5, 7, 9, 11\}$.

The relation $x \to 2x + 5$ is a function and we therefore write $f: x \to 2x + 5$ which is read as 'the function of x is $2x + 5$'.

Instead of writing a function $f: x \to 2x + 5$ we often write $y = f(x)$ meaning that y is a function of x. Thus if $y = 3x^2 - 2x + 5$ we may write $f(x) = 3x^2 - 2x + 5$ or $f: x \to 3x^2 - 2x + 5$. The symbols F, g, h and ϕ are also used to represent functions and we may have

$$n = F(m)$$

n being the range and m the domain.

$$p = g(r)$$

p being the range and r the domain.

$$s = h(t)$$

s being the range and t the domain.

$$X = \phi(u)$$

X being the range and u the domain.

Note carefully that $f(x)$ does not mean f multiplied by x but is simply shorthand for the statement 'is a function of x'.

EXAMPLE 1

If $f(x) = x^2 + 7x - 5$ find the values of $f(2)$ and $f(-1)$.

To find $f(2)$ substitute $x = 2$ into the expression $x^2 + 7x - 5$. Thus:

$$f(2) = 2^2 + 7 \times 2 - 5$$
$$= 4 + 14 - 5 = 13$$
$$f(-1) = (-1)^2 + 7 \times (-1) - 5$$
$$= 1 - 7 - 5 = -11$$

EXAMPLE 2

If $g: x \to 4x - 1$, find the values of $g(3)$ and $g(-2)$.

$$g(3) = 4 \times 3 - 1 = 12 - 1 = 11$$

$$g(-2) = 4 \times (-2) - 1 = -8 - 1 = -9$$

GRAPHS AND FUNCTIONS

Functions may be represented as graphs.

EXAMPLE 3

Plot the graph of $f(x) = 3x^2 + 10x - 8$ between $x = -6$ and $x = 4$.

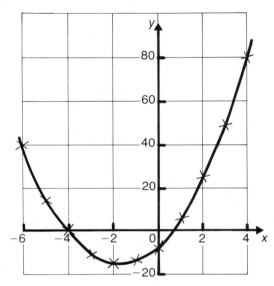

Fig. 48.11

A table may be drawn up as follows giving corresponding values of $f(x)$ for chosen values of x.

x	-6	-5	-4	-3	-2	-1
$3x^2$	108	75	48	27	12	3
$10x$	-60	-50	-40	-30	-20	-10
-8	-8	-8	-8	-8	-8	-8
$f(x)$	40	17	0	-11	-16	-15

x	0	1	2	3	4
$3x^2$	0	3	12	27	48
$10x$	0	10	20	30	40
-8	-8	-8	-8	-8	-8
$f(x)$	-8	5	24	49	80

The graph is shown in Fig. 48.11 and it is a smooth curve. Equations which are non-linear always give a graph which is a smooth curve.

Exercise 214 — *All type B*

1) If $f(x) = 3x^2 - 5x + 2$ find:
(a) $f(2)$ (b) $f(0)$
(c) $f(-3)$ (d) $f(\frac{1}{2})$.

2) If $f(v) = 8v - 7$ find:
(a) $f(3)$ (b) $f(-2)$ (c) $f(0)$.

3) If $M = \phi(p) = 3p^2 - 2p$ find:
(a) $\phi(1)$ (b) $\phi(3)$ (c) $\phi(0)$
(d) $\phi(-1)$ (e) $\phi(-3)$.

4) $F(h) = h^3 - 3h + 1$. Find $F(1)$, $F(4)$ and $F(-2)$.

5) If $f: x \to \frac{1}{2}(4x + 1)$ find the values of $f(3)$ and $f(-2)$.

6) $g: t \to \frac{1}{4}(1 - 5t)$. Find the values of $g(-1)$, $g(0)$ and $g(3)$.

7) State which of the graphs in Fig. 48.12 represents a function.

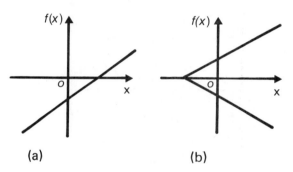

(a)   (b)

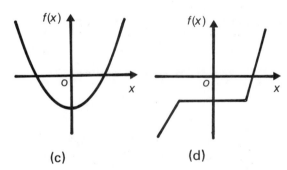

(c)   (d)

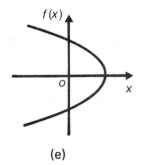

(e)

Fig. 48.12

385

8) Draw graphs of the following functions:

(a) $f(x) = 5 - 4x$ taking values of x between -2 and 4.

(b) $f(x) = 2x^2 - 7x - 5$ between $x = -4$ and $x = 12$.

(c) $f(x) = x^2 - 4x + 4$ between $x = -3$ and $x = 3$.

FLOW CHARTS

There are many times when a series of operations of instructions has to be carried out. If these are written down in sequence then this list is called a *programme*.

A simple and clear way of giving a programme is by using a *flow chart*. An example of a flow chart is shown in Fig. 48.13.

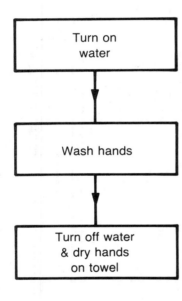

Fig. 48.13

The instructions are given in rectangles which are connected by arrows showing the order in which to proceed.

The flow chart for mathematical calculations may be drawn in a similar way to Fig. 48.13.

EXAMPLE 4
Draw a flow chart for the calculation of $5 \times 4 \div 2$.

The flow chart is shown in Fig. 48.14.

Frequently, algebraic expressions are represented on flow charts.

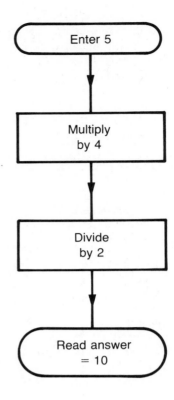

Fig. 48.14

EXAMPLE 5
Draw a flow chart to represent the equation $y = 3(2x + 5)$.

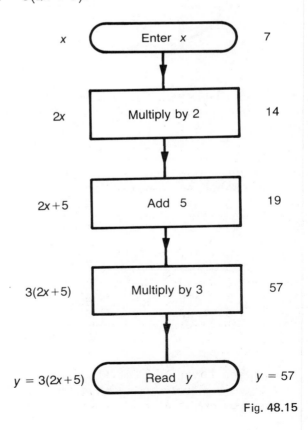

Fig. 48.15

386

The flow chart is shown in Fig. 48.15. This flow chart allows the value of y to be calculated for any value of x. Thus if $x = 7$, the flow chart gives the results shown alongside Fig. 48.15.

EXAMPLE 6

Use the flow chart shown in Fig. 48.16 to find the relationship between x and y.

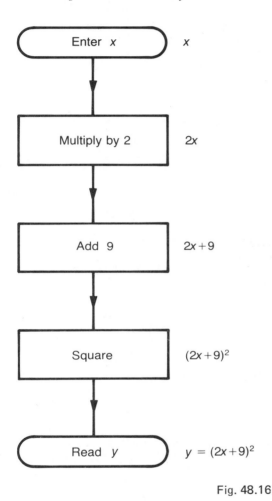

Fig. 48.16

The symbols shown alongside the chart show the operations performed and we see that the relationship between x and y is $y = (2x + 9)^2$.

Exercise 215 — *All type C*

1) Draw a flow chart for the calculation $7 + 8 \times 3$.

2) Draw a flow chart for the arithmetic operations $5 \times (3 + 4) - 7$.

3) Draw a flow chart to represent the equation $y = 2(3x - 5)$ and use it to find the value of y when $x = 4$.

4) Use the flow diagram shown in Fig. 48.17 to express y in terms of x.

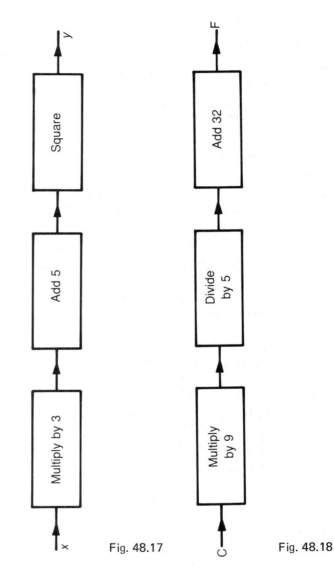

Fig. 48.17   Fig. 48.18

5) The flow diagram shown in Fig. 48.18 is used to convert degrees Celsius into degrees Fahrenheit.

(a) Draw a flow diagram for converting degrees Fahrenheit into degrees Celsius.
(b) By using the two flow diagrams:
   (i) Convert $30°F$ into degrees Celsius.
   (ii) Convert $20°C$ into degrees Fahrenheit.

INVERSE FUNCTIONS

Consider the relation

$$F = \{(1, 3), (2, 6), (3, 4), (4, 12)\}$$

Interchanging the domain and the range, we have

$$G = \{(3, 1), (6, 2), (4, 3), (12, 4)\}$$

F and G are said to be *inverse relations*. G is the inverse of F which is denoted by F^{-1}. Thus

$$G = F^{-1}$$

We see that the inverse of a relation F is obtained by interchanging the elements of each ordered pair in F.

EXAMPLE 7

If f is a function defined by $f(x) = \dfrac{3x - 5}{x + 2}$, write down an expression for $f^{-1}(x)$ and find the value of $f^{-1}(2)$.

Writing the equation as

$$y = \frac{3x - 5}{x + 2}$$

the defining equation for $f^{-1}(x)$ is

$$x = \frac{3y - 5}{y + 2}$$

since the inverse of a function is obtained by interchanging corresponding values of x and y.

We now transpose this equation to make y the subject. Thus

$$y = \frac{2x + 5}{3 - x}$$

$$\therefore \quad f^{-1}(x) = \frac{2x + 5}{3 - x}$$

$$f^{-1}(2) = \frac{2 \times 2 + 5}{3 - 2} = \frac{9}{1} = 9$$

For some kinds of functions an inverse flow diagram is useful when finding the inverse of a function.

Figure 48.19 is a flow diagram for the function $f: x \to \dfrac{x + 4}{5}$.

The inverse function is obtained from the reverse flow diagram (Fig. 48.20).

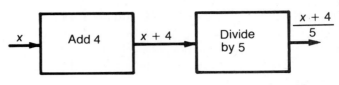

Fig. 48.19

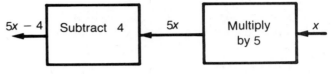

Fig. 48.20

Note that in reversing the flow diagram add becomes subtract, subtract becomes add, multiply becomes divide and divide becomes multiply.

The inverse function is denoted by either f^{-1} or $\tilde{f}$ (f twiddle).

Thus if $f: x \to \dfrac{x + 4}{5}$ then $f^{-1}: x \to 5x - 4$.

The inverse of a function may be used to solve equations.

EXAMPLE 8

By finding the inverse of $f(x) = \dfrac{4x + 5}{x + 2}$, solve the equation $\dfrac{4x + 5}{x + 2} = 3$.

Writing the defining equation for $f(x)$ as

$$y = \frac{4x + 5}{x + 2}$$

the defining equation for $f^{-1}(x)$ is

$$x = \frac{4y + 5}{y + 2}$$

Transposing this equation to make y the subject gives

$$y = \frac{5 - 2x}{x - 4}$$

$$\therefore \quad f^{-1}(x) = \frac{5 - 2x}{x - 4}$$

The solution of the given equation is found by finding the value of $f^{-1}(3)$. Thus

$$f^{-1}(3) = \frac{5 - 2 \times 3}{3 - 4} = 1$$

Hence the solution of the given equation is $x = 1$.

COMPOSITE FUNCTIONS

Suppose $f: x \to 2x - 1$ and $g: x \to 3x + 2$

then $\qquad gf: x \to 3(2x - 1) + 2$

or $\qquad gf: x \to 6x - 1$

Note that gf means do f first and then g.

Composite functions are seldom commutative, that is,

$$gf \neq fg$$

For the above,

$$fg: x \to 2(3x + 2) - 1$$

or $\qquad fg: x \to 6x + 3 = 3(2x + 1)$

Hence $\qquad gf \neq fg$

EXAMPLE 9

If $f: x \to 2x + 5$, $g: x \to \frac{1}{2}x$ and $h: x \to 3x - 1$ find:

(a) $fg(2)$ (b) $gf(-1)$ (c) $fgh(3)$
(d) $ghf(-2)$.

(a) $fg: x \to 2(\frac{1}{2}x) + 5 = x + 5$

$$fg(2) = 2 + 5 = 7$$

(b) $gf: x \to \frac{1}{2}(2x + 5) = x + \frac{5}{2}$

$$gf(-1) = -1 + \frac{5}{2} = \frac{3}{2}$$

(c) $fgh: x \to 2[\frac{1}{2}(3x - 1)] + 5 = 3x + 4$

$$fgh(3) = 3 \times 3 + 4 = 13$$

(d) $ghf: x \to \frac{1}{2}[3(2x + 5) - 1] = 3x + 7$

$$ghf(-2) = 3 \times (-2) + 7 = 1$$

THE INVERSE OF A COMPOSITE FUNCTION

If $f: x \to 3x - 5$ and $g: x \to 2x + 1$

then $\quad gf: x \to 2(3x - 5) + 1 = 6x - 9$

$$(gf)^{-1}: x \to \tfrac{1}{6}(x + 9)$$

Now $f^{-1}: x \to \frac{1}{3}(x + 5)$ and
$g^{-1}: x \to \frac{1}{2}(x - 1)$

$f^{-1}g^{-1}: x \to \frac{1}{3}[\frac{1}{2}(x - 1)] + \frac{5}{3} = \frac{1}{6}(x - 1) + \frac{5}{3}$

$\qquad = \frac{1}{6}x - \frac{1}{6} + \frac{5}{3} = \frac{1}{6}x + \frac{9}{6} = \frac{1}{6}(x + 9)$

Hence $(gf)^{-1} = f^{-1}g^{-1}$.

Using this relationship often simplifies the work in finding the inverse of a composite function.

EXAMPLE 10

If $f: x \to 7x + 2$ and $g: x \to 2x - 1$ find $(gf)^{-1}$.

Now $f^{-1}: x \to \frac{1}{7}(x - 2)$ and
$g^{-1}: x \to \frac{1}{2}(x + 1)$

$(gf)^{-1} = f^{-1}g^{-1}: x \to \frac{1}{7}[\frac{1}{2}(x + 1)] - \frac{2}{7}$

$\qquad = \frac{1}{14}(x + 1) - \frac{2}{7}$

$\qquad = \frac{1}{14}x + \frac{1}{14} - \frac{2}{7}$

$\qquad = \frac{1}{14}(x - 3)$

Exercise 216 — *All type C*

Find the inverse functions for the following:

1) $f: x \to 3x$

2) $f: x \to 2x - 3$

3) $f: x \to \dfrac{x - 3}{2}$

4) $f: x \to 3(2x - 5)$

5) $f: x \to \dfrac{2x - 5}{x + 2}$

6) If $f: x \to 2(3x - 1)$ find:
(a) $f^{-1}(-2)$ (b) $f^{-1}(3)$.

7) If $f: x \to \dfrac{x - 4}{3 - x}$ find:

(a) $f^{-1}(2)$ (b) $f^{-1}(-2)$

8) If $f: x \to 4x - 7$ find $f^{-1}(3)$ and $f^{-1}(-2)$.

9) If $f: x \to 2x - 5$, $g: x \to 3x + 1$ and $h: x \to 4x$, find:
(a) $fg(2)$ (b) $gf(2)$ (c) $fgh(-1)$
(d) $ghf(-3)$ (e) $hgf(2)$.

10) If $f: x \to 5x - 1$ and $g: x \to 3x + 2$, find $(fg)^{-1}$ and $(gf)^{-1}$.

11) By finding the inverse of $f(x) = \dfrac{x + 3}{x - 5}$,

solve the equation $\dfrac{x + 3}{x - 5} = 2$.

12) By finding the inverse of $f(x) = \dfrac{3x + 1}{4x - 3}$,

solve the equation $\dfrac{3x + 1}{4x - 3} = 5$.

Chapter 49 **Matrices**

When a large amount of numerical data has to be used it is often convenient to arrange the numbers in the form of a matrix.

Suppose that a nurseryman offers collections of fruit trees in three separate collections. The table below shows the name of each collection and the number of each type of tree included in it.

	Apple	Pear	Plum	Cherry
Collection				
A	6	2	1	1
B	3	2	2	1
C	3	1	1	0

After a time the headings and titles could be removed because those concerned with the packing of the collections would know what the various numbers meant. The table could then look like this

$$\begin{pmatrix} 6 & 2 & 1 & 1 \\ 3 & 2 & 2 & 1 \\ 3 & 1 & 1 & 0 \end{pmatrix}$$

The information has now been arranged in the form of a *matrix*, that is, in the form of an array of numbers.

A matrix is always enclosed in curved brackets. The above matrix has 3 rows and 4 columns. It is called a matrix of order 3 x 4. In defining the order of a matrix the number of rows is always stated first and then the number of columns. The matrix shown below is of order 2 x 5 because it has 2 rows and 5 columns.

$$\begin{pmatrix} 1 & 2 & 5 & 2 & 4 \\ 3 & 0 & 3 & 1 & 2 \end{pmatrix}$$

TYPES OF MATRICES

(1) *Row matrix*. This is a matrix having only one row. Thus $(3 \quad 5)$ is a row matrix.

(2) *Column matrix*. This is a matrix having only one column. Thus $\begin{pmatrix} 1 \\ 6 \end{pmatrix}$ is a column matrix.

(3) *Null matrix*. This is a matrix with all its elements zero. Thus $\begin{pmatrix} 0 & 0 \\ 0 & 0 \end{pmatrix}$ is a null matrix.

(4) *Square matrix*. This is a matrix having the same number of rows and columns. Thus

$\begin{pmatrix} 2 & 1 \\ 6 & 3 \end{pmatrix}$ is a square matrix.

(5) *Diagonal matrix*. This is a square matrix in which all the elements are zero except the diagonal elements. Thus $\begin{pmatrix} 2 & 0 \\ 0 & 3 \end{pmatrix}$ is a diagonal matrix. Note that the diagonal in a matrix always runs from upper left to lower right.

(6) *Unit matrix*. This is a diagonal matrix in which the diagonal elements equal 1. A unit matrix is usually denoted by the symbol I. Thus

$$I = \begin{pmatrix} 1 & 0 \\ 0 & 1 \end{pmatrix}$$

ADDITION AND SUBTRACTION OF MATRICES

Two matrices may be added or subtracted provided they are of the *same order*. Addition is done by adding together the corresponding elements of each of the two matrices. Thus

$$\begin{pmatrix} 3 & 5 \\ 6 & 2 \end{pmatrix} + \begin{pmatrix} 4 & 7 \\ 8 & 1 \end{pmatrix} = \begin{pmatrix} 3+4 & 5+7 \\ 6+8 & 2+1 \end{pmatrix}$$

$$= \begin{pmatrix} 7 & 12 \\ 14 & 3 \end{pmatrix}$$

Subtraction is done in a similar fashion except the corresponding elements are subtracted.

Thus $\begin{pmatrix} 6 & 2 \\ 1 & 8 \end{pmatrix} - \begin{pmatrix} 4 & 3 \\ 7 & 5 \end{pmatrix} = \begin{pmatrix} 6-4 & 2-3 \\ 1-7 & 8-5 \end{pmatrix}$

$$= \begin{pmatrix} 2 & -1 \\ -6 & 3 \end{pmatrix}$$

MULTIPLICATION OF MATRICES

(1) *Scalar multiplication.* A matrix may be multiplied by a number as follows:

$$3\begin{pmatrix} 2 & 1 \\ 6 & 4 \end{pmatrix} = \begin{pmatrix} 3 \times 2 & 3 \times 1 \\ 3 \times 6 & 3 \times 4 \end{pmatrix} = \begin{pmatrix} 6 & 3 \\ 18 & 12 \end{pmatrix}$$

(2) *General matrix multiplication.* Two matrices can only be multiplied together if the number of columns in the one is equal to the number of rows in the other. The multiplication is done by multiplying a row by a column as shown below.

$$\begin{pmatrix} 2 & 3 \\ 4 & 5 \end{pmatrix} \times \begin{pmatrix} 5 & 2 \\ 3 & 6 \end{pmatrix}$$

$$= \begin{pmatrix} 2 \times 5 + 3 \times 3 & 2 \times 2 + 3 \times 6 \\ 4 \times 5 + 5 \times 3 & 4 \times 2 + 5 \times 6 \end{pmatrix}$$

$$= \begin{pmatrix} 19 & 22 \\ 35 & 38 \end{pmatrix}$$

$$\begin{pmatrix} 3 & 4 \\ 2 & 5 \end{pmatrix} \times \begin{pmatrix} 6 \\ 7 \end{pmatrix}$$

$$= \begin{pmatrix} 3 \times 6 + 4 \times 7 \\ 2 \times 6 + 5 \times 7 \end{pmatrix} = \begin{pmatrix} 46 \\ 47 \end{pmatrix}$$

MATRIX NOTATION

It is usual to denote matrices by capital letters. Thus

$$A = \begin{pmatrix} 3 & 1 \\ 7 & 4 \end{pmatrix} \quad \text{and} \quad B = \begin{pmatrix} 2 \\ 3 \end{pmatrix}$$

Generally speaking matrix products are *non-commutative*, that is

$$A \times B \text{ does not equal } B \times A$$

If A is of order 4×3 and B is of order 3×2, then AB is of order 4×2.

EXAMPLE 1

(1) Form $C = A + B$ if:

$$A = \begin{pmatrix} 3 & 4 \\ 2 & 1 \end{pmatrix} \quad \text{and} \quad B = \begin{pmatrix} 2 & 3 \\ 4 & 2 \end{pmatrix}$$

$$C = \begin{pmatrix} 3 & 4 \\ 2 & 1 \end{pmatrix} + \begin{pmatrix} 2 & 3 \\ 4 & 2 \end{pmatrix} = \begin{pmatrix} 5 & 7 \\ 6 & 3 \end{pmatrix}$$

(2) Form $Q = RS$ if:

$$R = \begin{pmatrix} 1 & 2 \\ 3 & 4 \end{pmatrix} \quad \text{and} \quad S = \begin{pmatrix} 3 & 1 \\ 5 & 6 \end{pmatrix}$$

$$Q = \begin{pmatrix} 1 & 2 \\ 3 & 4 \end{pmatrix}\begin{pmatrix} 3 & 1 \\ 5 & 6 \end{pmatrix} = \begin{pmatrix} 13 & 13 \\ 29 & 27 \end{pmatrix}$$

Note that just as in ordinary algebra the multiplication sign is omitted so we omit it in matrix algebra.

(3) Form $M = PQR$ if:

$$P = \begin{pmatrix} 2 & 0 \\ 1 & 0 \end{pmatrix}, \quad Q = \begin{pmatrix} -1 & 0 \\ 0 & 1 \end{pmatrix}$$

and

$$R = \begin{pmatrix} 2 & 1 \\ 3 & 0 \end{pmatrix}$$

$$PQ = \begin{pmatrix} 2 & 0 \\ 1 & 0 \end{pmatrix}\begin{pmatrix} -1 & 0 \\ 0 & 1 \end{pmatrix} = \begin{pmatrix} -2 & 0 \\ -1 & 0 \end{pmatrix}$$

$$M = (PQ)R = \begin{pmatrix} -2 & 0 \\ -1 & 0 \end{pmatrix}\begin{pmatrix} 2 & 1 \\ 3 & 0 \end{pmatrix}$$

$$= \begin{pmatrix} -4 & -2 \\ -2 & -1 \end{pmatrix}$$

TRANSPOSITION OF MATRICES

When the rows of a matrix are interchanged with its column the matrix is said to be *transposed*. If the original matrix is A, the transpose is denoted by A^T. Thus

$$A = \begin{pmatrix} 3 & 4 \\ 5 & 6 \end{pmatrix} \qquad A^T = \begin{pmatrix} 3 & 5 \\ 4 & 6 \end{pmatrix}$$

INVERTING A MATRIX

If $AB = I$ (I is the unit matrix) then B is called the *inverse or reciprocal* of A. The inverse of A is usually written A^{-1} and hence

$$AA^{-1} = I$$

If

$$A = \begin{pmatrix} a & b \\ c & d \end{pmatrix}$$

$$A^{-1} = \frac{1}{ad - bc}\begin{pmatrix} d & -b \\ -c & a \end{pmatrix}$$

EXAMPLE 2

If $A = \begin{pmatrix} 4 & 1 \\ 2 & 3 \end{pmatrix}$ form A^{-1}

$$A^{-1} = \frac{1}{4 \times 3 - 1 \times 2} \begin{pmatrix} 3 & -1 \\ -2 & 4 \end{pmatrix}$$

$$= \frac{1}{10} \begin{pmatrix} 3 & -1 \\ -2 & 4 \end{pmatrix}$$

$$= \begin{pmatrix} 0.3 & -0.1 \\ -0.2 & 0.4 \end{pmatrix}$$

To check

$$AA^{-1} = \begin{pmatrix} 4 & 1 \\ 2 & 3 \end{pmatrix} \begin{pmatrix} 0.3 & -0.1 \\ -0.2 & 0.4 \end{pmatrix}$$

$$= \begin{pmatrix} 1 & 0 \\ 0 & 1 \end{pmatrix}$$

EQUALITY OF MATRICES

If two matrices are equal then their corresponding elements are equal. Thus if

$$\begin{pmatrix} a & b \\ c & d \end{pmatrix} = \begin{pmatrix} e & f \\ g & h \end{pmatrix}$$

then $a = e$, $b = f$, $c = g$ and $d = h$.

EXAMPLE 3

Find the values of x and y if

$$\begin{pmatrix} 2 & 1 \\ 3 & 4 \end{pmatrix} \begin{pmatrix} x & 2 \\ 5 & y \end{pmatrix} = \begin{pmatrix} 7 & 10 \\ 23 & 30 \end{pmatrix}$$

$$\begin{pmatrix} 2x + 5 & 4 + y \\ 3x + 20 & 6 + 4y \end{pmatrix} = \begin{pmatrix} 7 & 10 \\ 23 & 30 \end{pmatrix}$$

$\therefore \qquad 2x + 5 = 7$ and $x = 1$

$\qquad\qquad 4 + y = 10$ and $y = 6$

(We could have used $3x + 20 = 23$ and $6 + 4y = 30$ if we had desired.)

SOLUTION OF SIMULTANEOUS EQUATIONS

Consider the two simultaneous equations

$$3x + 2y = 12 \qquad [1]$$

$$4x + 5y = 23 \qquad [2]$$

We may write these equations in matrix form as follows:

$$\begin{pmatrix} 3 & 2 \\ 4 & 5 \end{pmatrix} \begin{pmatrix} x \\ y \end{pmatrix} = \begin{pmatrix} 12 \\ 23 \end{pmatrix}$$

392

If we let

$$A = \begin{pmatrix} 3 & 2 \\ 4 & 5 \end{pmatrix}, \quad X = \begin{pmatrix} x \\ y \end{pmatrix}, \quad K = \begin{pmatrix} 12 \\ 23 \end{pmatrix}$$

Then $AX = K$

and $X = A^{-1} K$

$$A^{-1} = \frac{1}{3 \times 5 - 2 \times 4} \begin{pmatrix} 5 & -2 \\ -4 & 3 \end{pmatrix}$$

$$= \begin{pmatrix} \dfrac{5}{7} & -\dfrac{2}{7} \\ -\dfrac{4}{7} & \dfrac{3}{7} \end{pmatrix}$$

$$\begin{pmatrix} x \\ y \end{pmatrix} = \begin{pmatrix} \dfrac{5}{7} & -\dfrac{2}{7} \\ -\dfrac{4}{7} & \dfrac{3}{7} \end{pmatrix} \begin{pmatrix} 12 \\ 23 \end{pmatrix} = \begin{pmatrix} 2 \\ 3 \end{pmatrix}$$

$\therefore$ The solutions are $x = 2$ and $y = 3$.

Exercise 217 — *Questions 1–3, 6 and 7 type B, remainder C*

1) Find the values of L and M in the following matrix addition:

$$\begin{pmatrix} L & 4 \\ -3 & 1 \end{pmatrix} + \begin{pmatrix} 1 & 2 \\ -2 & 4 \end{pmatrix} + \begin{pmatrix} -1 & 2 \\ M & 4 \end{pmatrix} = \begin{pmatrix} 3 & 8 \\ -6 & 9 \end{pmatrix}$$

2) If $A = \begin{pmatrix} 4 & 5 \\ 2 & 3 \end{pmatrix}$ find A^2.

3) If $A = \begin{pmatrix} 3 & 1 \\ 2 & 0 \end{pmatrix}$ and $B = \begin{pmatrix} 4 & -1 \\ 2 & 3 \end{pmatrix}$ calculate the following matrices:
(a) $A + B$ (b) $3A - 2B$
(c) AB (d) BA

4) $P = \begin{pmatrix} 2 & 1 \\ 3 & 1 \end{pmatrix}$ $Q = \begin{pmatrix} 1 & 0 \\ 0 & 1 \end{pmatrix}$

$R = \begin{pmatrix} 0 & 1 \\ 1 & 0 \end{pmatrix}$ $S = \begin{pmatrix} 1 & -2 \\ -6 & 3 \end{pmatrix}$

(a) Find each of the following as a single matrix: PQ, RS, $PQRS$, $P^2 - Q^2$.
(b) Find the values of a and b if $aP + bQ = S$.

5) A and B are two matrices.
If $A = \begin{pmatrix} -2 & 3 \\ 4 & -1 \end{pmatrix}$ find A^2 and then use your answer to find B, given that $A^2 = A - B$.

6) Find the value of

$$\begin{pmatrix} 2 & 3 & 1 \\ 0 & 1 & 2 \end{pmatrix}\begin{pmatrix} 1 \\ 3 \\ -2 \end{pmatrix}$$

7) If $\begin{pmatrix} 2 & 3 \\ 4 & 5 \end{pmatrix}\begin{pmatrix} p & 2 \\ 7 & q \end{pmatrix} = \begin{pmatrix} 31 & 1 \\ 55 & 3 \end{pmatrix}$

find p and q.

8) If $A = \begin{pmatrix} 2 & -1 \\ 1 & 1 \end{pmatrix}$ and $B = \begin{pmatrix} 1 & 2 \\ 1 & 1 \end{pmatrix}$,

write as a single:

(a) $A + B$ (b) $A \times B$
(c) the multiplicative inverse of B.

9) If   matrix $A = \begin{pmatrix} 3 & 1 \\ 2 & 4 \end{pmatrix}$ and

matrix $B = \begin{pmatrix} 4 & 2 \\ 1 & 0 \end{pmatrix}$.

(a) Calculate:
   (i) $A + B$ (ii) $3A - 2B$
   (iii) AB
(b) (i) Eastern Airlines have 6 Tridents,
      4 VC10's and 2 Jumbo Jets. Western
      Airlines have 3 Tridents, 6 VC10's
      and 1 Jumbo Jet. Write this
      information as a 2 by 3 matrix.
   (ii) Tridents carry 150 passengers, VC10's
      carry 120 passengers and Jumbo Jets
      carry 375 passengers. Write this
      information as a 3 by 1 matrix.
   (iii) Multiply these matrices to find a
      2 by 1 matrix.
   (iv) What does the 2 by 1 matrix
      represent?

10)
(a) The scores of five soccer clubs in the first
    12 matches of the 1975−6 season are given
    by the matrix:

	Won	Drawn	Lost
Aston Villa	4	4	4
Birmingham	3	2	7
Derby	6	3	3
Stoke	5	2	5
Wolverhampton	2	4	6

The points awarded for a win, a draw or a
lost match are given by the matrix

$$\begin{matrix} \text{Won} \\ \text{Drawn} \\ \text{Lost} \end{matrix} \begin{pmatrix} 2 \\ 1 \\ 0 \end{pmatrix}$$

Calculate a matrix which shows the total
number of points scored by each of these
clubs, showing clearly the method used.

(b) If $A = \begin{pmatrix} 3 & 1 \\ -2 & 0 \end{pmatrix}$ and $B = \begin{pmatrix} -1 & 3 \\ -4 & 2 \end{pmatrix}$
   calculate AB and BA.

(c) Solve the equation $\begin{pmatrix} 2 & 5 \\ 1 & 3 \end{pmatrix}\begin{pmatrix} x \\ y \end{pmatrix} = \begin{pmatrix} 3 \\ 1 \end{pmatrix}$.

11) Solve the following simultaneous equations:

a) $x + 3y = 7$ [1]
     $2x + 5y = 12$ [2]

b) $4x + 3y = 24$ [1]
     $2x + 5y = 26$ [2]

c) $2x + 7y = 11$ [1]
     $5x + 3y = 13$ [2]

Chapter 50 Vectors and Transformations

VECTORS

A vector is a quantity which has both magnitude and direction. For instance a velocity of 20 km/h due east is a vector quantity and so is a force of 50 newtons acting downwards.

The point P (Fig. 50.1) has the rectangular co-ordinates $x = 4$ and $y = 3$ usually written $(4, 3)$ for brevity. If OP is a vector the length OP represents the magnitude and the arrow the direction and it may be denoted by $\overrightarrow{OP}$.

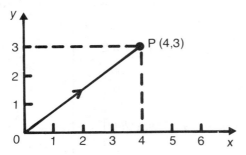

Fig. 50.1

The column matrix $\begin{pmatrix} 4 \\ 3 \end{pmatrix}$ can be thought of as a position vector representing the carriage from the origin to the point P where the co-ordinates are $(4, 3)$.

In general if the co-ordinates of P are (x, y) the position vector corresponding to $\overrightarrow{OP}$ is $\begin{pmatrix} x \\ y \end{pmatrix}$. The magnitude (or modulus) of $\overrightarrow{OP}$ is the distance from O to P and is found by using Pythagoras. In the example of Fig. 50.1 the magnitude of $\overrightarrow{OP}$ is $\sqrt{4^2 + 3^2} = 5$.

ADDITION OF VECTORS

Two vectors may be added by drawing a parallelogram of vectors (Fig. 50.2). If $\overrightarrow{OA}$ represents the vector P and $\overrightarrow{OB}$ the vector Q then P + Q is represented by the vector $\overrightarrow{OC}$. We may write $\overrightarrow{OA} + \overrightarrow{OB} = \overrightarrow{OC}$ or P + Q = R.

In Fig. 50.2, $P = \begin{pmatrix} r \\ s \end{pmatrix}$, $Q = \begin{pmatrix} p \\ q \end{pmatrix}$ and hence

$$R = P + Q = \begin{pmatrix} r \\ s \end{pmatrix} + \begin{pmatrix} p \\ q \end{pmatrix} = \begin{pmatrix} r + p \\ s + q \end{pmatrix}$$

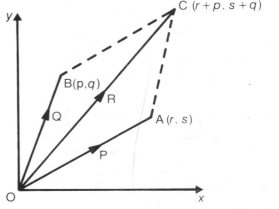

Fig. 50.2

EXAMPLE 1

If $U = \begin{pmatrix} 2 \\ 1 \end{pmatrix}$ and $V = \begin{pmatrix} 1 \\ 3 \end{pmatrix}$ find $R = U + V$ and determine the magnitude of R. What is the direction of R?

$$R = \begin{pmatrix} 2 \\ 1 \end{pmatrix} + \begin{pmatrix} 1 \\ 3 \end{pmatrix} = \begin{pmatrix} 3 \\ 4 \end{pmatrix}$$

Since the co-ordinates of point P (Fig. 50.3) are $(3, 4)$ the length from O to P is

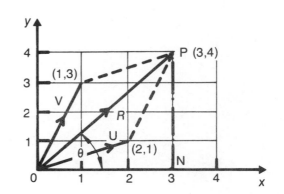

Fig. 50.3

$\sqrt{3^2 + 4^2} = 5.$ Hence the magnitude of R is 5.

$$\tan \theta = \frac{PN}{ON} = \frac{4}{3}$$

$$\therefore \qquad \theta = 53° 8'$$

SCALAR PRODUCT

If $\quad \mathbf{a} = \begin{pmatrix} a_1 \\ a_2 \end{pmatrix} \quad$ and $\quad \mathbf{b} = \begin{pmatrix} b_1 \\ b_2 \end{pmatrix} \quad$ the scalar product (or dot product) is denoted by $\mathbf{a.b}$ (read as $\mathbf{a}$ dot $\mathbf{b}$) where

$$\mathbf{a.b} = ab \cos \theta = a_1 b_1 + a_2 b_2$$

a and b being the magnitudes or moduli of the vectors $\mathbf{a}$ and $\mathbf{b}$ and θ the angle between them.

EXAMPLE 2

(1) Find the dot product of the following pairs of vectors:

(a) $a = 3, \quad b = 5 \quad$ and $\quad \theta = 20°$ (b) $a = 3,$ $b = 7 \quad$ and $\quad \theta = 120°$ (c) $\mathbf{a} = \begin{pmatrix} 4 \\ 3 \end{pmatrix}, \quad b = \begin{pmatrix} 5 \\ 2 \end{pmatrix}.$

(a) $\mathbf{a.b} = ab \cos \theta = 3 \times 5 \times \cos 20°$
$$= 15 \times 0.9397 = 14.1$$

(b) $\mathbf{a.b} = 3 \times 7 \times \cos 120°$
$$= 21 \times (-0.5000) = -10.5$$

(c) We are given $a_1 = 4, \ a_2 = 3, \ b_1 = 5,$ $b_2 = 2.$ Hence

$$\mathbf{a.b} = 4 \times 5 + 3 \times 2 = 26$$

(2) If $\quad \mathbf{a} = \begin{pmatrix} 6 \\ 3 \end{pmatrix} \quad$ and $\quad \mathbf{b} = \begin{pmatrix} 2 \\ 7 \end{pmatrix} \quad$ find the angle between the vectors $\mathbf{a}$ and $\mathbf{b}$.

$$a = \sqrt{6^2 + 3^2} = 6.71$$
$$b = \sqrt{2^2 + 7^2} = 7.28$$

Since

$$ab \cos \theta = a_1 b_1 + a_2 b_2$$

$$\cos \theta = \frac{a_1 b_1 + a_2 b_2}{ab}$$

$$= \frac{6 \times 2 + 3 \times 7}{6.71 \times 7.28} = 0.6756$$

$$\theta = 47° 30'$$

If the angle between two non-zero vectors $\mathbf{a}$ and $\mathbf{b}$ is $90°$ then $\mathbf{a.b} = ab \cos 90° = 0.$

This property provides an easy way of telling whether two vectors are perpendicular.

EXAMPLE 3

Given that $\quad \mathbf{p} = \begin{pmatrix} 3 \\ 4 \end{pmatrix}, \ \mathbf{q} = \begin{pmatrix} 5 \\ 0 \end{pmatrix}, \ r = \frac{1}{4}(\mathbf{p} + \mathbf{q})$ and $\quad s = \frac{1}{2}(\mathbf{p} - \mathbf{q}) \quad$ show that $\mathbf{r}$ is perpendicular to s.

$$\mathbf{p} + \mathbf{q} = \begin{pmatrix} 3 \\ 4 \end{pmatrix} + \begin{pmatrix} 5 \\ 0 \end{pmatrix} = \begin{pmatrix} 8 \\ 4 \end{pmatrix}$$

$$\mathbf{r} = \begin{pmatrix} 2 \\ 1 \end{pmatrix}$$

$$\mathbf{p} - \mathbf{q} = \begin{pmatrix} 3 \\ 4 \end{pmatrix} - \begin{pmatrix} 5 \\ 0 \end{pmatrix} = \begin{pmatrix} -2 \\ 4 \end{pmatrix}$$

$$\mathbf{s} = \begin{pmatrix} -1 \\ 2 \end{pmatrix}$$

$$\mathbf{a.b} = 2 \times (-1) + 1 \times 2 = -2 + 2 = 0$$

Hence $\theta = 90°$ and the vector $\mathbf{r}$ is perpendicular to the vector $\mathbf{s}$.

Exercise 218 — *All type B*

1) Find the modulus of each of the following vectors and state its direction:

(a) $\begin{pmatrix} 3 \\ 1 \end{pmatrix}$ (b) $\begin{pmatrix} 5 \\ 7 \end{pmatrix}$ (c) $\begin{pmatrix} 3 \\ 8 \end{pmatrix}$

2) If $\quad U = \begin{pmatrix} 1 \\ 4 \end{pmatrix} \quad$ and $\quad V = \begin{pmatrix} 3 \\ 2 \end{pmatrix} \quad$ find $R = U + V.$ State the magnitude of R and its direction.

3) If $\quad P = \begin{pmatrix} 2 \\ 6 \end{pmatrix} \quad$ and $\quad Q = \begin{pmatrix} 4 \\ 2 \end{pmatrix} \quad$ find $R = P + Q.$ State the modulus of R and give its direction.

4) $R = M + N.$ If $\quad R = \begin{pmatrix} 7 \\ 6 \end{pmatrix} \quad$ and $\quad N = \begin{pmatrix} 2 \\ 4 \end{pmatrix}$ find $M.$ Calculate the magnitude of M and determine its direction.

5) Find the dot product of the following pairs of vectors:

(a) $5, 7, \quad \theta = 25°$ (b) $3, 8, \quad \theta = 38°$
(c) $-5, 6, \quad \theta = 80°$ (d) $-3, -2, \quad \theta = 75°$
(e) $4, 6, \quad \theta = 90°$ (f) $2, 5, \quad \theta = 120°$
(g) $-5, -3, \quad \theta = 170°$ (h) $-2, 5, \quad \theta = 140°$

6) Find the dot product for each of the following pairs of vectors and also find the angle between them:

(a) $\mathbf{a} = \begin{pmatrix} 2 \\ 3 \end{pmatrix}$, $\mathbf{b} = \begin{pmatrix} 4 \\ 7 \end{pmatrix}$

(b) $\mathbf{p} = \begin{pmatrix} 5 \\ 2 \end{pmatrix}$, $\mathbf{q} = \begin{pmatrix} -4 \\ 3 \end{pmatrix}$

(c) $\mathbf{m} = \begin{pmatrix} -2 \\ -5 \end{pmatrix}$, $\mathbf{n} = \begin{pmatrix} 5 \\ 3 \end{pmatrix}$

(d) $\mathbf{x} = \begin{pmatrix} -3 \\ -4 \end{pmatrix}$, $\mathbf{y} = \begin{pmatrix} -1 \\ 3 \end{pmatrix}$

7) If $\mathbf{r} = \begin{pmatrix} 8 \\ 2 \end{pmatrix}$ and $\mathbf{s} = \begin{pmatrix} -1 \\ 4 \end{pmatrix}$ show that $\mathbf{r}$ is perpendicular to $\mathbf{s}$ and hence find their resultant in magnitude and direction.

8) Given that $\mathbf{a} = \begin{pmatrix} 6 \\ 2 \end{pmatrix}$, $\mathbf{b} = \begin{pmatrix} 7 \\ -1 \end{pmatrix}$,

$\mathbf{p} = \frac{1}{2}(\mathbf{a} + \mathbf{b})$ and $\mathbf{q} = \mathbf{a} - \mathbf{b}$ find (a) $p - q$, (b) the angle between $\mathbf{a}$ and $\mathbf{b}$, (c) show that $\mathbf{p}$ is perpendicular to $\mathbf{q}$.

TRANSFORMATIONS

When a point P is given a new position, the point P is said to have undergone a transformation. Thus in Fig. 50.4, the point P(2, 3) has been transformed into the point P'(4, 5).

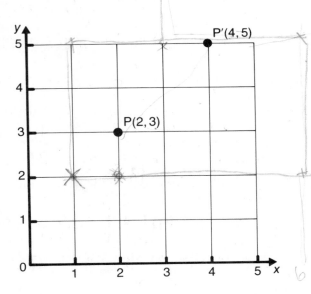

Fig. 50.4

TRANSLATION

If every point in a line or a plane figure moves the same distance in the same direction, the transformation is called a *translation*.
In Fig. 50.5 the point P(4, 6) has been translated to P'(9, 8). That is, it has been moved 5 units to the right and 2 units upwards. The displacement may be described by the displacement vector $\begin{pmatrix} 5 \\ 2 \end{pmatrix}$.

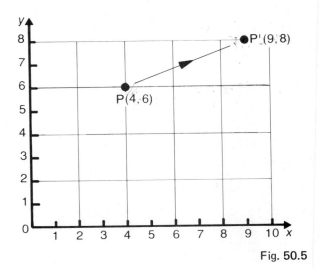

Fig. 50.5

It can be seen that to find the position vector of P' we add the position vector of P and the displacement vector. Thus

$$\text{position vector of P'} = \begin{pmatrix} 4 \\ 6 \end{pmatrix} + \begin{pmatrix} 5 \\ 2 \end{pmatrix}$$
$$= \begin{pmatrix} 9 \\ 8 \end{pmatrix}$$

The co-ordinates of P' are (9, 8).

EXAMPLE 4

A rectangle ABCD has vertices A(1, 2), B(6, 2), C(6, 5) and D(1, 5). It is translated by the displacement vector $\begin{pmatrix} 2 \\ 3 \end{pmatrix}$. Write down the co-ordinate matrix for the transformation.

The co-ordinate matrix for ABCD is
A B C D
$\begin{pmatrix} 1 & 6 & 6 & 1 \\ 2 & 2 & 5 & 5 \end{pmatrix}$. The matrix describing the

translation is $\begin{pmatrix} 2 & 2 & 2 & 2 \\ 3 & 3 & 3 & 3 \end{pmatrix}$ since each of the

396

points A, B, C and D must be displaced by the same amount. If A'B'C'D' is the translated rectangle then the co-ordinate matrix of A'B'C'D' is

$$\begin{array}{cccc} A & B & C & D \end{array}$$
$$\begin{pmatrix} 1 & 6 & 6 & 1 \\ 2 & 2 & 5 & 5 \end{pmatrix} + \begin{pmatrix} 2 & 2 & 2 & 2 \\ 3 & 3 & 3 & 3 \end{pmatrix} = \begin{pmatrix} 3 & 8 & 8 & 3 \\ 5 & 5 & 8 & 8 \end{pmatrix}$$
$$\begin{array}{cccc} & A' & B' & C' & D' \end{array}$$

REFLECTION

If a point P (Fig. 50.6) is reflected in a mirror so that its image is P', the mirror (or line of reflection) is the perpendicular bisector of PP'.

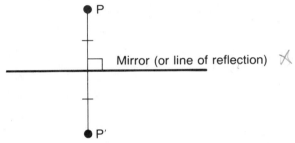

Mirror (or line of reflection)

Fig. 50.6

REFLECTION IN THE x-AXIS

In Fig. 50.7, the point P is reflected in the x-axis so that its image is P'. The line PP' is bisected by the x-axis.

If the position vector of a point P(x, y) is

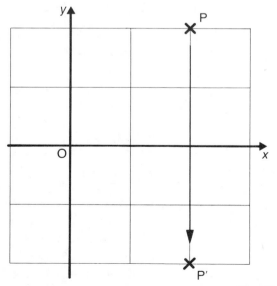

Fig. 50.7

pre-multiplied by the matrix $\begin{pmatrix} 1 & 0 \\ 0 & -1 \end{pmatrix}$ the position vector of the image of P in the x-axis is obtained.

EXAMPLE 5

A(2, 3) is reflected in the x-axis. Find the position vector of the image of A.

$$\begin{pmatrix} 1 & 0 \\ 0 & -1 \end{pmatrix} \begin{pmatrix} 2 \\ 3 \end{pmatrix} = \begin{pmatrix} 2 \\ -3 \end{pmatrix}$$

Hence the position vector of the image of A is $\begin{pmatrix} 2 \\ -3 \end{pmatrix}$ as shown in Fig. 50.8.

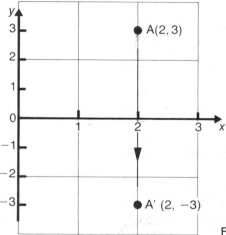

Fig. 50.8

EXAMPLE 6

ABCD is a rectangle with vertices A(1, 1), B(4, 1), C(4, 4) and D(1, 4). Find the co-ordinates of A'B'C'D', the image of ABCD in the x-axis.

The rectangle ABCD can be described by the co-ordinate matrix:

$$\begin{array}{cccc} & A & B & C & D \end{array}$$
$$M = \begin{pmatrix} 1 & 4 & 4 & 1 \\ 1 & 1 & 4 & 4 \end{pmatrix}$$

To find the co-ordinate matrix for A'B'C'D' we pre-multiply M by $\begin{pmatrix} 1 & 0 \\ 0 & -1 \end{pmatrix}$.

$$\begin{array}{cccc} & & A & B & C & D \end{array}$$
$$\begin{pmatrix} 1 & 0 \\ 0 & -1 \end{pmatrix} \begin{pmatrix} 1 & 4 & 4 & 1 \\ 1 & 1 & 4 & 4 \end{pmatrix}$$
$$\begin{array}{cccc} & A' & B' & C' & D' \end{array}$$
$$= \begin{pmatrix} 1 & 4 & 4 & 1 \\ -1 & -1 & -4 & -4 \end{pmatrix}$$

397

REFLECTION IN THE *y*-AXIS

In Fig. 50.9, the point P is reflected in the *y*-axis so that its image is P'. The line PP' is bisected by the *y*-axis.

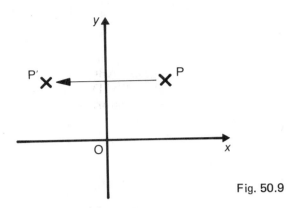

Fig. 50.9

If the position vector of the point to be reflected in the *y*-axis is pre-multiplied by $\begin{pmatrix} -1 & 0 \\ 0 & 1 \end{pmatrix}$ the position vector of its image will be obtained.

REFLECTION IN THE LINE *y* = *x*

If the scales on the *x* and *y* axes are the same, the line $y = x$ will be inclined at $45°$ to the *x*-axis. The reflection of the point P(4, 2) in the line $y = x$ is P'(2, 4). Note that the line $y = x$ is the perpendicular bisector of PP' and that the effect of this transformation is to reverse the co-ordinates of P (Fig. 50.10).

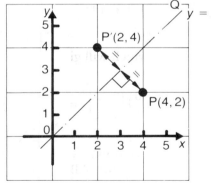

Fig. 50.10

The matrix $\begin{pmatrix} 0 & 1 \\ 1 & 0 \end{pmatrix}$ will transform the point P into its reflection in the line $y = x$.

REFLECTION IN THE LINE *y* = −*x*

In Fig. 50.11 the point P has been reflected so that its image is P'. The line $y = -x$ is the perpendicular bisector of PP'.

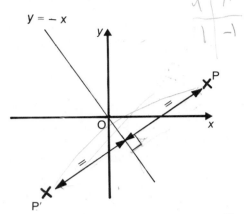

Fig. 50.11

The matrix $\begin{pmatrix} 0 & -1 \\ -1 & 0 \end{pmatrix}$ will transform the point P into its reflection in the line $y = -x$.

EXAMPLE 7

If a point P has the co-ordinates (3, 2) find its reflection (a) in the *x*-axis, (b) in the *y*-axis, (c) in the line $y = -x$, (d) in the line $y = x$.

(a) To find the co-ordinates of the image of P, the position vector $\begin{pmatrix} 3 \\ 2 \end{pmatrix}$ is pre-multiplied by the matrix $\begin{pmatrix} 1 & 0 \\ 0 & -1 \end{pmatrix}$. Thus:

$$\begin{pmatrix} 1 & 0 \\ 0 & -1 \end{pmatrix}\begin{pmatrix} 3 \\ 2 \end{pmatrix} = \begin{pmatrix} 3 \\ -2 \end{pmatrix}$$

Hence the point P is transformed to the point $(3, -2)$.

(b) The co-ordinates of the image of P are found by the matrix multiplication:

$$\begin{pmatrix} -1 & 0 \\ 0 & 1 \end{pmatrix}\begin{pmatrix} 3 \\ 2 \end{pmatrix} = \begin{pmatrix} -3 \\ 2 \end{pmatrix}$$

Hence the point P has the image P'$(-3, 2)$.

(c) The following matrix product gives the co-ordinates of the image of P:

$$\begin{pmatrix} 0 & -1 \\ -1 & 0 \end{pmatrix}\begin{pmatrix} 3 \\ 2 \end{pmatrix} = \begin{pmatrix} -2 \\ -3 \end{pmatrix}$$

Hence the co-ordinates of the image of P in the origin are $(-2, -3)$.

(d) The co-ordinates of the image of P are found by obtaining the following matrix product:

$$\begin{pmatrix} 0 & 1 \\ 1 & 0 \end{pmatrix}\begin{pmatrix} 3 \\ 2 \end{pmatrix} = \begin{pmatrix} 2 \\ 3 \end{pmatrix}$$

Hence the point P has the image P'(2, 3).

ISOMETRICS

These are transformations which preserve all lengths. Hence in an *isometric* transformation shape, size, area and angles are unaltered. Translation and reflection are examples of isometric transformations.

OTHER TRANSFORMATIONS

If a position vector is pre-multiplied by a 2 x 2 matrix it is transformed into another column matrix.

EXAMPLE 8

A parallelogram has the coordinate matrix

$$\begin{matrix} A & B & C & D \\ \end{matrix}$$
$$\begin{pmatrix} 1 & 3 & 4 & 2 \\ 1 & 2 & 5 & 4 \end{pmatrix}$$

It is transformed into A'B'C'D' by the matrix $\begin{pmatrix} 2 & 0 \\ 1 & 1 \end{pmatrix}$. Find the co-ordinate matrix for A'B'C'D'.

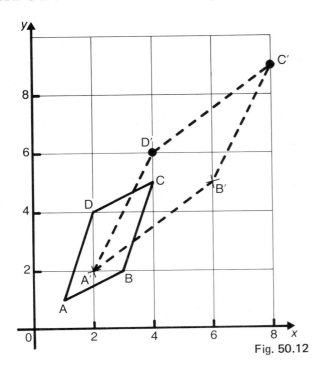

Fig. 50.12

$$\begin{matrix} & A & B & C & D \\ \begin{pmatrix} 2 & 0 \\ 1 & 1 \end{pmatrix} & \begin{pmatrix} 1 & 3 & 4 & 2 \\ 1 & 2 & 5 & 4 \end{pmatrix} \end{matrix}$$
$$\begin{matrix} & A' & B' & C' & D' \\ = & \begin{pmatrix} 2 & 6 & 8 & 4 \\ 2 & 5 & 9 & 6 \end{pmatrix} \end{matrix}$$

The transformed parallelogram A'B'C'D' and the original parallelogram ABCD are shown in Fig. 50.12. Note that A'B'C'D' is larger than ABCD and hence the transformation is not isometric.

DOUBLE TRANSFORMATIONS

A double transformation is one transformation (e.g. a reflection) followed by a second transformation (e.g. a translation). A double transformation may be made into a single operation by multiplying the two matrices, which describe the transformations, together. We pre-multiply the matrix describing the first transformation by the matrix describing the second transformation.

EXAMPLE 9

A rectangle ABCD has the co-ordinate matrix

$$\begin{matrix} A & B & C & D \\ \end{matrix}$$
$$\begin{pmatrix} 2 & 6 & 6 & 2 \\ 1 & 1 & 3 & 3 \end{pmatrix}$$

It is given a double transformation under $\begin{pmatrix} 1 & 3 \\ 0 & 1 \end{pmatrix}$ followed by $\begin{pmatrix} 1 & 0 \\ 4 & 1 \end{pmatrix}$. Find the co-ordinate matrix for the image of ABCD.

The single matrix which will give the double transformation is:

$$M = \begin{pmatrix} 1 & 0 \\ 4 & 1 \end{pmatrix}\begin{pmatrix} 1 & 3 \\ 0 & 1 \end{pmatrix} = \begin{pmatrix} 1 & 3 \\ 4 & 13 \end{pmatrix}$$

If A'B'C'D' is the image of ABCD, its co-ordinate matrix is found by pre-multiplying the co-ordinate matrix for ABCD by M. Thus:

$$\begin{matrix} & A & B & C & D \\ \begin{pmatrix} 1 & 3 \\ 4 & 13 \end{pmatrix} & \begin{pmatrix} 2 & 6 & 6 & 2 \\ 1 & 1 & 3 & 3 \end{pmatrix} \end{matrix}$$
$$\begin{matrix} & A' & B' & C' & D' \\ = & \begin{pmatrix} 5 & 9 & 15 & 11 \\ 21 & 37 & 63 & 47 \end{pmatrix} \end{matrix}$$

GLIDE REFLECTION

This transformation is produced by a translation followed by a reflection.

EXAMPLE 10

The point $P(2, 4)$ is given a glide reflection.

After translation under $\begin{pmatrix} 4 \\ 0 \end{pmatrix}$ it is reflected in the x-axis. Determine the co-ordinates of the image of P. The translation is:

$$\begin{pmatrix} 2 \\ 4 \end{pmatrix} + \begin{pmatrix} 4 \\ 0 \end{pmatrix} = \begin{pmatrix} 6 \\ 4 \end{pmatrix}$$

The reflection is:

$$\begin{pmatrix} 1 & 0 \\ 0 & -1 \end{pmatrix}\begin{pmatrix} 6 \\ 4 \end{pmatrix} = \begin{pmatrix} 6 \\ -4 \end{pmatrix}$$

As shown in Fig. 50.13, the co-ordinates of the image of P are $(6, -4)$.

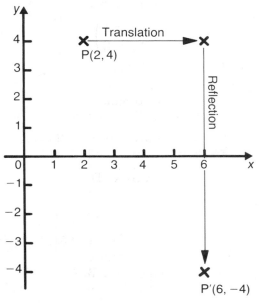

Fig. 50.13

ROTATION

In Fig. 50.14 the point P has been given an anticlockwise rotation of $30°$ about the origin.

The matrix $\begin{pmatrix} \cos \alpha & -\sin \alpha \\ \sin \alpha & \cos \alpha \end{pmatrix}$ will rotate the point $\begin{pmatrix} x \\ y \end{pmatrix}$ through the angle α counterclockwise about the origin.

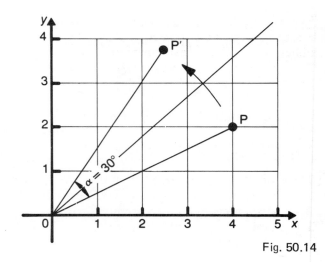

Fig. 50.14

EXAMPLE 11

A point P has the co-ordinates $(3, 4)$. Find its new co-ordinates if it is rotated through $30°$ counterclockwise about the origin.

The new co-ordinates are found by pre-multiplying the position vector $\begin{pmatrix} 3 \\ 4 \end{pmatrix}$ by the matrix

$$\begin{pmatrix} \cos 30° & -\sin 30° \\ \sin 30° & \cos 30° \end{pmatrix} = \begin{pmatrix} 0.866 & -0.5 \\ 0.5 & 0.866 \end{pmatrix}.$$

Thus

$$\begin{pmatrix} 0.866 & -0.5 \\ 0.5 & 0.866 \end{pmatrix}\begin{pmatrix} 3 \\ 4 \end{pmatrix} = \begin{pmatrix} 0.598 \\ 4.964 \end{pmatrix}$$

EXAMPLE 12

The point $P(2, 4)$ is rotated $\frac{1}{4}$ of a turn about the origin. Find the co-ordinates of P', the image of P.

Since $\frac{1}{4}$ turn $= 90°$, the co-ordinates of P' are found by pre-multiplying the position vector $\begin{pmatrix} 2 \\ 4 \end{pmatrix}$ by the matrix

$$\begin{pmatrix} \cos 90° & -\sin 90° \\ \sin 90° & \cos 90° \end{pmatrix} = \begin{pmatrix} 0 & -1 \\ 1 & 0 \end{pmatrix}$$

$$\begin{pmatrix} 0 & -1 \\ 1 & 0 \end{pmatrix}\begin{pmatrix} 2 \\ 4 \end{pmatrix} = \begin{pmatrix} -4 \\ 2 \end{pmatrix}$$

Hence the image is $P'(-4, 2)$.

INVERSE TRANSFORMATIONS

The inverse of a transformation puts a point (or a figure) back to its original position.

Suppose that a point P is given a transformation described by a matrix A so that its image is P′. The transformation of P′ back to P is described by the matrix A^{-1}, i.e., the inverse of the matrix A.

EXAMPLE 13

The image of a rectangle is A′(8, 12), B′(12, 16), C′(21, 31), D′(17, 27). The matrix $\begin{pmatrix} 2 & 3 \\ 2 & 5 \end{pmatrix}$ effects the transformation of ABCD onto A′B′C′D′. Find the co-ordinate matrix of ABCD.

$$\begin{pmatrix} 2 & 3 \\ 2 & 5 \end{pmatrix}^{-1} = \frac{1}{4}\begin{pmatrix} 5 & -3 \\ -2 & 2 \end{pmatrix}$$

$$= \begin{pmatrix} 1.25 & -0.75 \\ -0.5 & 0.5 \end{pmatrix}$$

Hence,

$$\begin{matrix} & A' & B' & C' & D' \\ \begin{pmatrix} 1.25 & -0.75 \\ -0.5 & 0.5 \end{pmatrix} & \begin{pmatrix} 8 & 12 & 21 & 17 \\ 12 & 16 & 31 & 27 \end{pmatrix} \end{matrix}$$

$$= \begin{matrix} A & B & C & D \\ \begin{pmatrix} 1 & 3 & 3 & 1 \\ 2 & 2 & 5 & 5 \end{pmatrix} \end{matrix}$$

Exercise 219 — *All type C*

1) The vertices of the square ABCD are respectively (0, 1), (2, 1), (2, 3) and (0, 3). Obtain the co-ordinate matrix for the image of ABCD after each of the following reflections:

(a) Reflection in the x-axis.
(b) Reflection in the y-axis.
(c) Reflection in the line $y = -x$.
(d) Reflection in the line $y = x$.
(e) If the square ABCD is translated by the vector $\begin{pmatrix} 1 \\ 3 \end{pmatrix}$ write down the co-ordinate matrix for the image of ABCD after the transformation.

2) Triangle A′B′C′ is the image of triangle ABC after translation by the vector $\begin{pmatrix} -3 \\ 2 \end{pmatrix}$. A′, B′ and C′ have the co-ordinates (5, 3), (3, 1) and (4, 2) respectively. Give the co-ordinates of A, B and C before translation.

3) Write down the co-ordinates of the following points under the translation $\begin{pmatrix} -2 \\ 4 \end{pmatrix}$.

(a) $\begin{pmatrix} 1 \\ 3 \end{pmatrix}$ (b) $\begin{pmatrix} 2 \\ 1 \end{pmatrix}$ (c) $\begin{pmatrix} -4 \\ -3 \end{pmatrix}$

(d) $\begin{pmatrix} -2 \\ 5 \end{pmatrix}$ (e) $\begin{pmatrix} 7 \\ 0 \end{pmatrix}$

4) The vertices of a triangle ABC have the following co-ordinates: (2, 1), (5, 1) and (5, 4). Find the co-ordinates of A, B and C under the translation $\begin{pmatrix} -3 \\ -7 \end{pmatrix}$. On graph paper show the original triangle ABC and its transformation.

5) A plane figure has the co-ordinate matrix:

$$\begin{matrix} A & B & C & D & E \\ \begin{pmatrix} 1 & 3 & 4 & 2 & 0 \\ -2 & 0 & 2 & 4 & 5 \end{pmatrix} \end{matrix}$$

Obtain the co-ordinate matrix of the figure after the following transformations:

(a) Translation under $\begin{pmatrix} -1 \\ -2 \end{pmatrix}$

(b) Reflection in the x-axis.
(c) Reflection in the y-axis.
(d) Reflection in the origin.
(e) Reflection in the line $y = x$.

6) Map the points shown in the following co-ordinate matrix:

$$\begin{matrix} A & B & C & D \\ \begin{pmatrix} 1 & 3 & 6 & 4 \\ 2 & 3 & 5 & 0 \end{pmatrix} \end{matrix}$$

Join them up to give the figure ABCD. Rotate ABCD through 50° anticlockwise about the origin to give the image of ABCD. Mark the image A′B′C′D′ and write down the co-ordinate matrix for this image.

7) The vertices of the square WXYZ are respectively (1, 2), (3, 2), (3, 4) and (1, 4). It is given a rotation of 40° about the origin. Find the co-ordinates of the vertices of the transposed figure.

8) The triangle ABC whose vertices are the points (1, 3), (3, 5) and (2, 7) respectively is given a glide reflection. After translation under $\begin{pmatrix} 0 \\ 3 \end{pmatrix}$ it is reflected in the y-axis. Determine the co-ordinate matrix for the image of ABC.

401

9) The point $P(-3, -1)$ is given a transformation under $\begin{pmatrix} 3 & 1 \\ 3 & 2 \end{pmatrix}$ followed by a second transformation under $\begin{pmatrix} 2 & 1 \\ 4 & 2 \end{pmatrix}$.

(a) Find the single matrix which will accomplish the double transformation.

(b) Determine the co-ordinates of the image of P under these transformations.

10) The triangle ABC with vertices (10, 10), (20, 15) and (15, 20) respectively is given a transformation under $\begin{pmatrix} 1 & 4 \\ 0 & 1 \end{pmatrix}$ followed by a reflection in the x-axis.

(a) Determine the single matrix which will give the double transformation.

(b) Find the co-ordinate matrix for the image of ABC under these transformations.

11) The point $P(2, 6)$ is given an anticlockwise rotation of $45°$ about the origin followed by a translation under $\begin{pmatrix} -4 \\ -5 \end{pmatrix}$. Find by an accurate drawing the co-ordinates of the image of P.

12) The square $A(2, 1)$, $B(4, 1)$, $C(4, 3)$, $D(2, 3)$ is given a rotation (anticlockwise) of $\frac{1}{4}$ turn followed by a translation under $\begin{pmatrix} -1 \\ 5 \end{pmatrix}$. Draw the transformed figure and state the co-ordinates of its vertices.

13) If A denotes the translation $\begin{pmatrix} 3 \\ 2 \end{pmatrix}$ and B denotes the translation $\begin{pmatrix} 1 \\ -1 \end{pmatrix}$, write down the co-ordinates of the points onto which $(2, 1)$ is mapped under the following transformations:

(a) AB (b) BA (c) B^2
(d) A^{-1} (e) B^{-1} (f) ABA
(g) BAB

14) Let T be the transformation described by the matrix $\begin{pmatrix} 2 & 1 \\ 1 & 1 \end{pmatrix}$. After transformation under this matrix the image of $\triangle ABC$ is $A'(8, 5)$, $B'(12, 7)$, $C'(11, 7)$. Find the co-ordinates of the points A, B and C.

SIMILARITIES

Similarities are transformations which multiply all lengths by a scale factor. If the scale factor is greater than 1, the transformation is called an *enlargement*. If the scale factor is less than 1, the transformation is said to be a *reduction*. With both reductions and enlargements, angles are preserved and hence the transformed figures are similar to the original figures (see Chapter 34).

In Fig. 50.15, the points A(3, 2), B(8, 2), C(8, 3) and D(3, 3) have been plotted. The points have been joined to give the rectangle ABCD. In order to form the rectangle A'B'C'D', each of the points (x, y) have been mapped onto (x', y') by the mapping:

$$(x, y) \rightarrow (2x, 2y)$$

Thus, $A(3, 2) \rightarrow A'(6, 4)$
and $B(8, 2) \rightarrow B'(16, 4)$ etc.

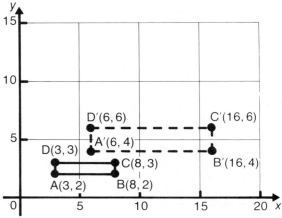

Fig. 50.15

As can be seen from the diagram, the image A'B'C'D' is twice the size of ABCD. That is, ABCD has been enlarged by a factor of 2. The same result could have been obtained by multiplying the co-ordinate matrix of ABCD by the scalar 2. Thus,

$$2 \begin{matrix} \text{A} & \text{B} & \text{C} & \text{D} \\ \begin{pmatrix} 3 & 8 & 8 & 3 \\ 2 & 2 & 3 & 3 \end{pmatrix} \end{matrix} = \begin{matrix} \text{A}' & \text{B}' & \text{C}' & \text{D}' \\ \begin{pmatrix} 6 & 16 & 16 & 6 \\ 4 & 4 & 6 & 6 \end{pmatrix} \end{matrix}$$

The same enlargement would be produced by pre-multiplying the co-ordinate matrix of ABCD by the 2×2 matrix $\begin{pmatrix} 2 & 0 \\ 0 & 2 \end{pmatrix}$. Thus,

$$\begin{pmatrix} 2 & 0 \\ 0 & 2 \end{pmatrix} \begin{matrix} \text{A} & \text{B} & \text{C} & \text{D} \\ \begin{pmatrix} 3 & 8 & 8 & 3 \\ 2 & 2 & 3 & 3 \end{pmatrix} \end{matrix}$$

$$= \begin{matrix} \text{A}' & \text{B}' & \text{C}' & \text{D}' \\ \begin{pmatrix} 6 & 16 & 16 & 6 \\ 4 & 4 & 6 & 6 \end{pmatrix} \end{matrix}$$

If an enlargement or reduction of $n:1$ is required then the co-ordinate matrix of the figure is pre-multiplied by the 2×2 matrix $\begin{pmatrix} n & 0 \\ 0 & n \end{pmatrix}$.

An enlargement with a scale factor n and centre O can be constructed by drawing lines from O (the origin) through the points A, B and C (Fig. 50.16) and marking off $OA' = n \times OA$, $OB' = n \times OB$ and $OC' = n \times OC$. When a figure is enlarged in this way the enlarged figure (A'B'C' in the diagram) is similar to the original figure ABC and corresponding lines are parallel.

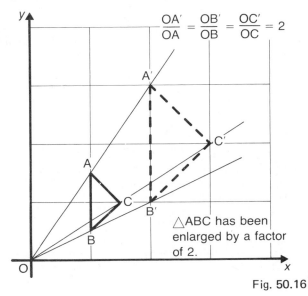

$$\frac{OA'}{OA} = \frac{OB'}{OB} = \frac{OC'}{OC} = 2$$

△ABC has been enlarged by a factor of 2.

Fig. 50.16

The centre of an enlargement or reduction need not be at the origin. Consider the triangle A(2, 1), B(4, 2), C(3, 3) shown in Fig. 50.17. It is transformed onto A'(7, 6), B'(11, 8), C'(9, 10) by means of an enlargement, centre the origin, and a translation. The centre of enlargement, C, is found by joining AA', BB' and CC' and producing them to intersect at a single point. This point is the centre of enlargement.

From the diagram we see that the centre of enlargement is C(−3, −4).

The centre of enlargement can be found by solving a matrix equation of the type:

$$\begin{pmatrix} n & 0 \\ 0 & n \end{pmatrix}\begin{pmatrix} x \\ y \end{pmatrix} + \begin{pmatrix} h \\ k \end{pmatrix} = \begin{pmatrix} x \\ y \end{pmatrix}$$

Where n is the enlargement factor, x and y are the co-ordinates of the centre of rotation and $\begin{pmatrix} h \\ k \end{pmatrix}$ is a vector describing a translation.

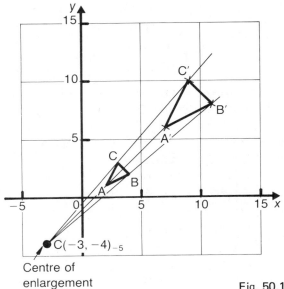

Centre of enlargement

Fig. 50.17

EXAMPLE 14

The rectangle A(2, 1), B(4, 1), C(4, 4), D(2, 4) is mapped onto A"B"C"D" by the enlargement

$$\begin{pmatrix} x \\ y \end{pmatrix} \rightarrow \begin{pmatrix} 4 & 0 \\ 0 & 4 \end{pmatrix}\begin{pmatrix} x \\ y \end{pmatrix} + \begin{pmatrix} 6 \\ 9 \end{pmatrix}$$

(a) Find the co-ordinates of the centre of the enlargement.
(b) On a diagram show the transformation and the centre of enlargement. To find the co-ordinates of the centre of enlargement we solve the matrix equation:

$$\begin{pmatrix} 4 & 0 \\ 0 & 4 \end{pmatrix}\begin{pmatrix} x \\ y \end{pmatrix} + \begin{pmatrix} 6 \\ 9 \end{pmatrix} = \begin{pmatrix} x \\ y \end{pmatrix}$$

$$\begin{pmatrix} 4x \\ 4y \end{pmatrix} + \begin{pmatrix} 6 \\ 9 \end{pmatrix} = \begin{pmatrix} x \\ y \end{pmatrix}$$

$$\begin{pmatrix} 4x + 6 \\ 4y + 9 \end{pmatrix} = \begin{pmatrix} x \\ y \end{pmatrix}$$

$4x + 6 = x \quad 3x = -6 \quad$ and $\quad x = -2$

$4y + 9 = y \quad 3y = -9 \quad$ and $\quad y = -3$

The co-ordinates of the centre of enlargement are therefore $(-2, -3)$.

The enlargement gives the image:

$$\begin{array}{cccc} & A & B & C & D \\ \begin{pmatrix} 4 & 0 \\ 0 & 4 \end{pmatrix} & \begin{pmatrix} 2 & 4 & 4 & 2 \\ 1 & 1 & 4 & 4 \end{pmatrix} \end{array}$$

$$\begin{array}{cccc} & A' & B' & C' & D' \\ = & \begin{pmatrix} 8 & 16 & 16 & 8 \\ 4 & 4 & 16 & 16 \end{pmatrix} \end{array}$$

403

The translation gives the image:

$$\begin{array}{cccc} A'' & B'' & C'' & D'' \\ \end{array}$$
$$\begin{pmatrix} 14 & 22 & 22 & 14 \\ 13 & 13 & 25 & 25 \end{pmatrix}$$

The transformation and the centre of enlargement are shown in Fig. 50.18.

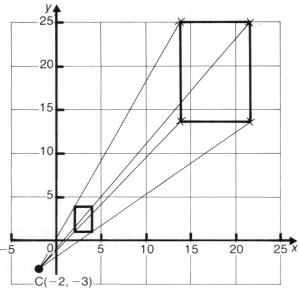

C(−2, −3)

Fig. 50.18

SHEARING

Shear is a transformation which maps parallel lines onto parallel lines. Thus in Fig. 50.19 a shear transforms the rectangle ABCD into the parallelogram ABC'D'. Note that the line AB is invariant (i.e., it does not alter) and that all other points have to move parallel to this invariant line. One of the important features of this transformation is that area is preserved although shape is not.

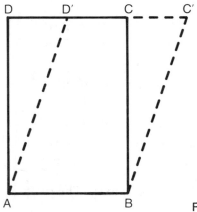

Fig. 50.19

In Fig. 50.19, the invariant line AB coincided with one side of the rectangle ABCD. However this need not be the case. Thus in Fig. 50.20, MN is the invariant line which maps ABCD onto A'B'C'D'.

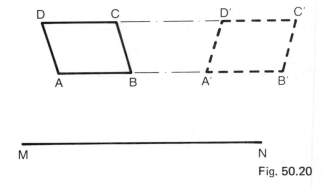

M   N

Fig. 50.20

A matrix that describes a shear, keeping each point of $y = 0$ fixed is of the type:

$$\begin{pmatrix} 1 & K \\ 0 & 1 \end{pmatrix}$$

The element K in the matrix gives the amount of translation of the points C and D in Fig. 50.21. The transformation of ABCD into ABC'D' is obtained as follows:

$$\begin{array}{cccc} & A & B & C & D \\ \end{array}$$
$$\begin{pmatrix} 1 & 2 \\ 0 & 1 \end{pmatrix}\begin{pmatrix} 1 & 2 & 2 & 1 \\ 0 & 0 & 1 & 1 \end{pmatrix}$$
$$\begin{array}{cccc} & A & B & C' & D' \\ \end{array}$$
$$= \begin{pmatrix} 1 & 2 & 4 & 3 \\ 0 & 0 & 1 & 1 \end{pmatrix}$$

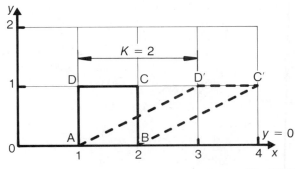

Fig. 50.21

Similarly, the matrix

$$\begin{pmatrix} 1 & 0 \\ K & 1 \end{pmatrix}$$

describes the shear which keeps each point of $x = 0$ fixed.

STRETCH

A *one way stretch* is an enlargement in one direction only. Thus in Fig. 50.22 ABCD has been mapped onto AB'C'D by a one way stretch of scale factor 2. The scale factor gives the ratio

$$\frac{\text{area AB'C'D}}{\text{area ABCD}}$$

Thus in the diagram area AB'C'D is twice area ABCD.

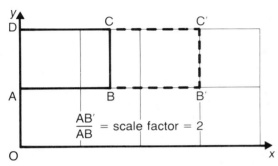

Fig. 50.22

A one way stretch is described by the matrix

$$\begin{pmatrix} K & 0 \\ 0 & 1 \end{pmatrix}$$

where K is the scale factor and the y-axis is the invariant line.

If the x-axis is the invariant line then a one way stretch is described by

$$\begin{pmatrix} 1 & 0 \\ 0 & K \end{pmatrix}$$

EXAMPLE 15

Find the image of the rectangle A(2, 3), B(2, 0), C(3, 0), D(3, 3) under the transformation given by the matrix $\begin{pmatrix} 1 & 0 \\ 0 & 2 \end{pmatrix}$.

$$\begin{array}{cccc} & A & B & C & D \\ \begin{pmatrix} 1 & 0 \\ 0 & 2 \end{pmatrix} & \begin{pmatrix} 2 & 2 & 3 & 3 \\ 3 & 0 & 0 & 3 \end{pmatrix} \end{array}$$

$$\begin{array}{cccc} & A' & B & C & D' \\ = & \begin{pmatrix} 2 & 2 & 3 & 3 \\ 6 & 0 & 0 & 6 \end{pmatrix} \end{array}$$

As shown in Fig. 50.23, the transformation is a one way stretch with a scale factor of 2, the x-axis being the invariant line.

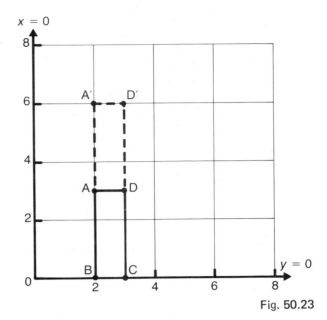

Fig. 50.23

When two one way stretches are combined at right-angles the result is a *two way stretch*. There are two scale factors, one in each direction, and the origin is the invariant point. A two way stretch is described by the matrix

$$\begin{pmatrix} H & 0 \\ 0 & K \end{pmatrix}$$

where H and K are the two scale factors. Note that if H or K is equal to 1 the stretch is one way. If $H = K$ the stretch is an enlargement with a scale factor of K and centre $(0, 0)$.

EXAMPLE 16

Find the image of the rectangle 0(0, 0), A(2, 0), B(2, 1) and C(0, 1) under the transformation given by the matrix $\begin{pmatrix} 2 & 0 \\ 0 & 3 \end{pmatrix}$.

$$\begin{array}{cccc} & 0 & A & B & C \\ \begin{pmatrix} 2 & 0 \\ 0 & 3 \end{pmatrix} & \begin{pmatrix} 0 & 2 & 2 & 0 \\ 0 & 0 & 1 & 1 \end{pmatrix} \end{array}$$

$$\begin{array}{cccc} & 0 & A' & B' & C' \\ = & \begin{pmatrix} 0 & 4 & 4 & 0 \\ 0 & 0 & 3 & 3 \end{pmatrix} \end{array}$$

As can be seen from Fig. 50.24, the transformation is a two way stretch with a scale factor of 3 parallel to the y-axis and a scale factor of 2 parallel to the x-axis. The origin is the invariant point.

405

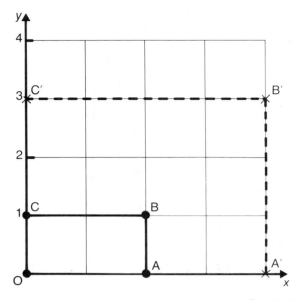

Fig. 50.24

Exercise 220 — *All type C*

1) Draw on graph paper the triangle A(2, 3), B(4, 1), C(4, 4). Draw the image of △ ABC if it is enlarged by a scale factor of 3, centre at the origin.

2) Draw on graph paper the triangle A(1, 1), B(3, 1), C(3, 2). Then draw its image under the transformations whose matrices are:

(a) $\begin{pmatrix} 2 & 0 \\ 0 & 2 \end{pmatrix}$ (b) $\begin{pmatrix} \frac{1}{2} & 0 \\ 0 & \frac{1}{2} \end{pmatrix} + \begin{pmatrix} 2 \\ 1 \end{pmatrix}$

(c) $\begin{pmatrix} -2 & 0 \\ 0 & -2 \end{pmatrix}$ (d) $\begin{pmatrix} 4 & 0 \\ 0 & 4 \end{pmatrix}$

For each transformation find the centre of enlargement.

3) The rectangle A(2, 2), B(4, 2), C(4, 3), D(2, 3) is mapped onto A′B′C′D′ by the enlargement

$$\begin{pmatrix} x \\ y \end{pmatrix} \rightarrow \begin{pmatrix} 3 & 0 \\ 0 & 3 \end{pmatrix}\begin{pmatrix} x \\ y \end{pmatrix} + \begin{pmatrix} 3 \\ 5 \end{pmatrix}$$

Find the co-ordinates of the centre of enlargement.

4) Apply the shear described by the matrix $\begin{pmatrix} 1 & 3 \\ 0 & 1 \end{pmatrix}$ to the following figures. Illustrate the transformations on separate diagrams.

(a) The square with vertices (0, 0), (2, 0), (2, 2) and (0, 2).

(b) The rectangle with vertices (− 2, 0), (1, 0), (1, 2) and (− 2, 2).

(c) The parallelogram with vertices (5, 2), (8, 2), (7, 4) and (4, 4).

(d) The trapezium with vertices (2, 1), (6, 1), (6, 3) and (3, 3).

5) Find the image of the rectangle W(2, 4), X(2, 0), Y(4, 0), Z(4, 4) under the transformations given by the following matrices:

(a) $\begin{pmatrix} 2 & 0 \\ 0 & 1 \end{pmatrix}$ (b) $\begin{pmatrix} -3 & 0 \\ 0 & 1 \end{pmatrix}$

(c) $\begin{pmatrix} 1 & 0 \\ 0 & 1\frac{1}{2} \end{pmatrix}$ (d) $\begin{pmatrix} 1 & 0 \\ 0 & -\frac{1}{2} \end{pmatrix}$

6) Find the image of the rectangle A(0, 0), B(2, 0), C(2, 1), D(0, 1) under the transformations given by the following matrices:

(a) $\begin{pmatrix} 2 & 0 \\ 0 & 3 \end{pmatrix}$ (b) $\begin{pmatrix} -\frac{1}{2} & 0 \\ 0 & 2 \end{pmatrix}$

(c) $\begin{pmatrix} \frac{1}{2} & 0 \\ 0 & 4 \end{pmatrix}$ (d) $\begin{pmatrix} 1\frac{1}{2} & 0 \\ 0 & -1\frac{1}{2} \end{pmatrix}$

Chapter 51 **Statistics**

INTRODUCTION

Statistics is the name given to the science of collecting and analysing facts. In almost all scientific and business publications, in newspapers and in Government reports these facts are presented by means of tables and diagrams. The most commonly used diagrams and charts are discussed below.

THE PROPORTIONATE BAR CHART

The proportionate bar chart (Fig. 51.1) relies on heights (or areas) to convey the proportions of a whole. The bar should be of the same width throughout its length or height. This diagram is accurate, quick and easy to construct and it can show quite a large number of components without confusion. Although Fig. 51.1 shows the bar drawn vertically it may also be drawn horizontally if desired.

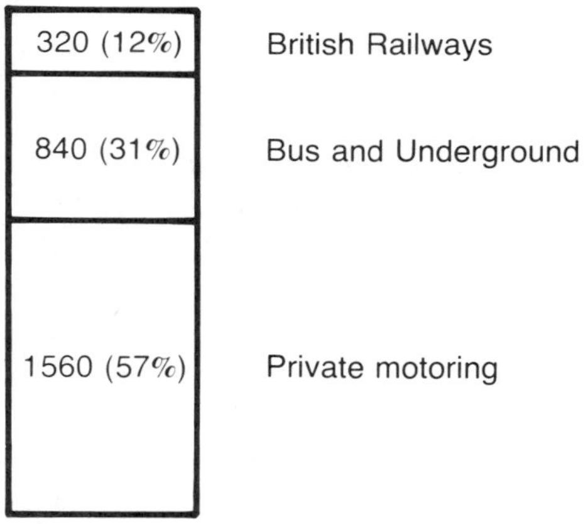

320 (12%)	British Railways
840 (31%)	Bus and Underground
1560 (57%)	Private motoring

A proportionate bar chart

Fig. 51.1

EXAMPLE 1

Draw a proportionate bar chart for the figures below which show the way commuters in the South-east region travelled to the London area.

Type of transport	Numbers using
Private motoring	1560
Bus and underground	840
British Railways	320

The easiest way is to draw the chart on graph paper. However, if plain paper is used, the lengths of the component parts must be calculated and then drawn accurately using a rule (Fig. 51.1).

Total number $= 1560 + 840 + 320 = 2720$

Suppose that the total height of the diagram is to be 6 cm. Then

1560 commuters are represented by

$$\frac{1560}{2720} \times 6 = 3.44 \text{ cm}$$

840 commuters are represented by

$$\frac{840}{2720} \times 6 = 1.85 \text{ cm}$$

320 commuters are represented by

$$\frac{320}{2720} \times 6 = 0.71 \text{ cm}$$

Alternatively, the proportions can be expressed as percentages which are calculated as shown below.

Type of transport	Percentage of commuters using
Private motoring	$\dfrac{1560}{2720} \times 100 = 57\%$
Bus and underground	$\dfrac{840}{2720} \times 100 = 31\%$
British Railways	$\dfrac{320}{2720} \times 100 = 12\%$

SIMPLE BAR CHARTS

In these charts the information is represented by a series of bars all of the same width. The height or the length of each bar represents the magnitude of the figures. The bars may be drawn vertically or horizontally as shown in Figs. 51.2 and 51.3 which present the information given in Example 1.

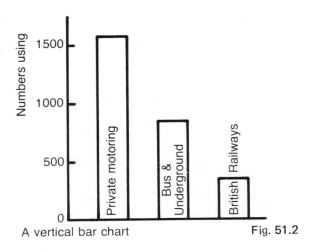

A vertical bar chart   Fig. 51.2

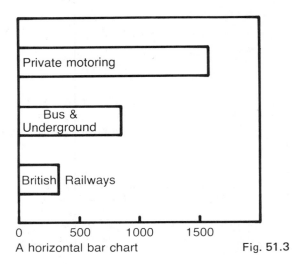

A horizontal bar chart   Fig. 51.3

CHRONOLOGICAL BAR CHARTS

This type of chart compares quantities over periods of time. It is very similar to the vertical bar chart and its construction is basically the same as a graph.

EXAMPLE 2

The information below gives the number of television colour sets sold in Southern England during the period 1970—75.

Year	Number of sets sold (thousands)
1970	77.2
1971	84.0
1972	91.3
1973	114.6
1974	130.9
1975	142.5

Draw a chronological bar chart to represent this information.

When drawing a chronological bar chart, time is always marked off along the horizontal axis. The chart is drawn in Fig. 51.4 and it clearly shows how the sales of TV sets has increased over the period illustrated.

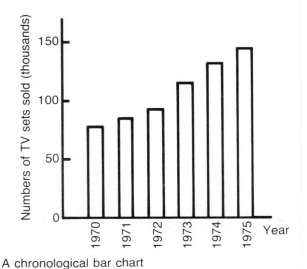

A chronological bar chart

Fig. 51.4

PIE CHART

A pie chart displays the proportions of a whole as sector angles or sector areas. The circle as a whole representing the component parts.

EXAMPLE 3

Represent the information given in Example 1 in the form of a pie chart.

The first step is to calculate the sector angles. Remembering that a circle contains 360° the sector angles are calculated as shown below:

Type of transport	Sector angle (degrees)
Private motoring	$\frac{1560}{2720} \times 360 = 206°$
Bus and underground	$\frac{840}{2720} \times 360 = 111°$
British Railways	$\frac{320}{2720} \times 360 = 43°$

Using a protractor the pie chart (Fig. 51.5) can now be drawn. If desired percentages can be displayed on the diagram.

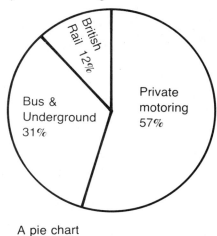

A pie chart   Fig. 51.5

Pie charts are very useful when component parts of a whole are to be represented. Up to eight component parts can be accommodated but above this number the chart loses its effectiveness.

Exercise 221 — *All type A*

1) In Fig. 51.6, find the values of x and y.

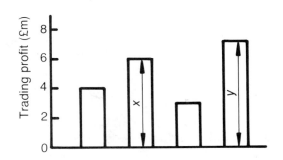

Fig. 51.6

2) Draw a proportionate bar chart for the information below which relates to expenditure per head on transport. In each case find the percentage expenditure and show it on your diagram.

Type of transport	Expenditure (£)
Private motoring	£1.10
Rail	£2.75
Other public transport	£3.15
Total	£7.00

3) The table below shows the number of people employed on various kinds of work in a factory.

Type of personnel	Number employed
Unskilled workers	45
Craftsmen	25
Draughtsmen	5
Clerical staff	10
Total	85

(a) Draw a vertical bar chart to represent this information.
(b) Draw a simple horizontal bar chart to show this data.
(c) Draw a pie chart, showing percentages, for this information.

4) The information below gives details of the temperature range used when forging various metals. Draw a horizontal bar chart to represent this data.

Metal	Temperature °C
Carbon steel	770—1300
Wrought iron	860—1340
Brass	600— 800
Copper	500—1000

5) The figures below give the World population (in millions of people) from 1750 to 1950. Draw a chronological bar chart to represent this information.

Year	Population
1750	728
1800	906
1850	1171
1900	1608
1950	2504

6) The information in the following table gives the production of grain on a certain farm during the period from 1968—1973. Draw a chronological bar chart to represent this information.

409

Year	Grain production (tonnes)
1968	395
1969	410
1970	495
1971	560
1972	420
1973	515

7) The data below gives the area of the various continents of the world.

Continent	Area (millions of square miles)
Africa	30.3
Asia	26.9
Europe	4.9
N. America	24.3
S. America	17.9
Oceania	22.8
U.S.S.R.	20.5

Draw a pie chart to depict this information.

8) Figure 51.7 is a pie chart which shows the total sales of a Departmental Store for one week. Find the correct size of each sector angle. (The diagram is NOT drawn to scale.)

Fig. 51.7

PICTOGRAMS AND IDEOGRAPHS

These are diagrams in the form of pictures which are used to present information to those who are unskilled in dealing with figures or to those who have only a limited interest in the topic depicted.

410

EXAMPLE 4

The table below shows the output of bicycles for the years 1970 to 1974.

Year	Output
1970	2000
1971	4000
1972	7000
1973	8500
1974	9000

Represent this data in the form of a pictogram.

The pictogram is shown in Fig. 51.8. It will be seen that each bicycle in the diagram represents an output of 2000 bicycles. Part of a symbol is shown in 1972, 1973 and 1974 to represent a fraction of 2000 but clearly this is not a very precise way of representing the output.

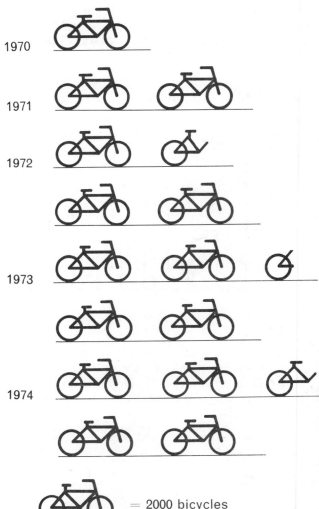

 = 2000 bicycles

A pictogram

Fig. 51.8

It is essential that the diagram is labelled correctly and that the source of the information is stated.

A method not recommended is shown in Fig. 51.9. Comparison is difficult because the reader is not sure whether to compare heights, areas or volumes. However, if this method is used the ways shown in Examples 5 and 6 should be used.

Sales of milk in 1950 and 1970

(millions of litres)   Fig. 51.9

EXAMPLE 5

If a square of 3 cm side represents a population of 18 000, what population is represented by a square of 4 cm side?

Here the quantities are represented by the areas of squares.

The area of the square is
3 cm x 3 cm = 9 square centimetres.

Hence   9 square centimetres represents a population of 18 000

and   1 square centimetre represents a population of $\frac{18\,000}{9} = 2000$.

The area of a square of side 4 cm is
4 cm x 4 cm = 16 square centimetres.

Hence a square of 4 cm side represents a population of 2000 x 16 = 32 000.

EXAMPLE 6

A production of 1000 tonnes of steel is represented by a cube of side 2 cm. Calculate the production of steel represented by a cube of side 3 cm.

Here, the quantities are represented by the volumes of cubes. Since the volume of a cube is side x side x side = side³ :

Volume of a cube of 2cm
side = 2 cm x 2 cm x 2 cm = 8 cubic centimetres.

Therefore 8 cubic centimetres represents 1000 tonnes and 1 cubic centimetre represents

$$\frac{1000}{8} = 125 \text{ tonnes}$$

Volume of a cube of 3 cm
side = 3 cm x 3 cm x 3 cm = 27 cubic centimetres. Hence a cube of 3 cm side represents

125 tonnes x 27 = 3375 tonnes

Exercise 222 — *All type B*

1) Figure 51.10 is a pictogram showing the method by which first year boys come to school.

(a) How many come by bus?
(b) How many come by car?
(c) Estimate the number of boys who live within 1 kilometre of the school (i.e. those who walk).

WALKING

BUS

BICYCLE

CAR

Represents 5 boys

(Head 1, Arms and Legs 1 each)

Fig. 51.10

2) The sales of motor cars by Mortimer & Co. Ltd. were as follows:

Year	Sales
1972	2000
1973	2500
1974	3200
1975	2700
1976	3000

Represent this information in a pictogram.

3) The table below gives the number of houses completed in the S.W. of England.

Year	Number (thousands)
1965	81
1967	69
1969	73
1971	84
1973	80

Draw a pictogram to represent this information.

4) The information below gives the production of tyres (in thousands) produced by Treadwell & Co. for the first six months of 1977.

Month	Production
January	40
February	43
March	39
April	38
May	37
June	45

Draw a pictogram to represent this information.

5) The pictogram (Fig. 51.11) is an attempt to show the sales of a company in the years 1972, 1974 and 1976. Why does the pictogram not give a true indication of the company's sales?

1972
1 000 000 cornets of ice cream

1974
1 500 000 cornets of ice cream

1976
2 000 000 cornets of ice cream

Fig. 51.11

6) A firm of carriers indicated their increase in parcel traffic as shown in Fig. 51.12. This indicated that they had increased eightfold. In 1970 the firm carried 1500 parcels.

(a) How many did they carry in 1972?
(b) Draw a figure in the same pattern to indicate the volume of parcel traffic in 1976 if it was 40 500 parcels.

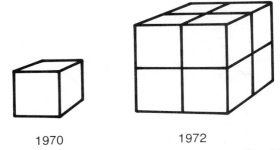

1970   1972

Fig. 51.12

7) A circle of 2 cm radius represents sales of 200 items. If sales are depicted by area what does a circle of 4 cm radius represent?

8) The volume of a sphere of diameter 3 cm represents a production of 54 000 articles. What production will a sphere of 2 cm diameter represent?

RAW DATA

Raw data is collected information which is not organised numerically, that is, it is not arranged in any sort of order.

Consider the marks of 50 students obtained in a test:

4 3 5 4 3 5 5 4 3 6 5 4 5 3 4 4 5 5 7
4 3 4 3 4 5 4 3 6 1 3 6 3 2 6 6 3 5 2
7 5 7 1 7 6 5 8 6 4 3 5

This is an example of raw data and we see that it is not organised into any sort of order.

FREQUENCY DISTRIBUTIONS

One way of organising raw data into order is to arrange it in the form of a frequency distribution. The number of students obtaining 3 marks is found, the number obtaining 4 marks is found, and so on. A tally chart is the best way of doing this.

On examining the raw data we see that the smallest mark is 1 and the greatest is 8. The marks from 1 to 8 inclusive are written in column 1 of the tally chart. We now take each figure in the raw data, just as it comes, and for each figure we place a tally mark opposite the appropriate mark.

The fifth tally mark for each number is usually made in an oblique direction thereby tying the tally marks into bundles of five.

When the tally marks are complete they are counted and the numerical value recorded in the column headed 'frequency'. Hence the frequency is the number of times each mark occurs. From the tally chart below it will be seen that the mark 1 occurs twice (a frequency of 2), the mark 5 occurs twelve times (a frequency of 12) and so on.

Table 1

Mark	Tally	Frequency
1	1 1	2
2	1 1	2
3	11111 11111 1	11
4	11111 11111 1	11
5	11111 11111 11	12
6	11111 11	7
7	1 1 1 1	4
8	1	1
	Total	50

GROUPED DISTRIBUTIONS

When dealing with a large amount of numerical data it is useful to group the numbers into classes or categories. We can then find out the number of items belonging to each class thus obtaining a class frequency. The table below shows a grouped frequency distribution for the heights of 100 male workers in a certain factory.

The first class consists of heights from 150 cm to 154 cm. Eight workers have heights belonging to this class and the class frequency is therefore 8.

Table 2

Height (cm)	Frequency
150—154	8
155—159	16
160—164	43
165—169	29
170—174	4
Total	100

The main advantage of grouping is that it produces a clear overall picture of the distribution. However too many groups destroy the pattern of the distribution whilst too few will destroy much of the detail contained in the raw data. Depending upon the amount of raw data, the number of classes is usually between 5 and 20.

CLASS INTERVALS

In Table 2, the first class is 150—154. These figures give the class interval. For the second class the class interval is 155—159. The end numbers 155 and 159 are called the *class limits* for the second class, 155 being the lower limit and 159 the upper limit.

CLASS BOUNDARIES

In Table 2, the heights have been recorded to the nearest centimetre. The class interval 155—159 theoretically includes all the heights between 154.5 cm and 159.5 cm. These numbers are called the lower and upper class boundaries respectively.

For any frequency distribution the class boundaries may be found by adding the upper limit of one class to the lower limit of the next class and dividing the sum by two.

EXAMPLE 7

The figures below show part of a frequency distribution. State the lower and upper class boundaries for the second class.

Lifetime of electric bulbs

Lifetime (hours)	Frequency
400—449	22
450—499	38
500—549	62

For the second class:

lower class boundary

$$= \frac{449 + 450}{2} = 449.5 \text{ hours}$$

upper class boundary

$$= \frac{499 + 500}{2} = 499.5 \text{ hours}$$

413

WIDTH OF A CLASS INTERVAL

The width of a class interval is the difference between the lower and upper class boundaries. That is

> width of class interval
>
> = upper class boundary
>
> − lower class boundary

For Example 7,

> width of second class interval
>
> = 499.5 − 449.5 = 50 hours

(A common mistake is to take the class width as being the difference between the upper and lower class limits, giving in Example 7, 499−450 = 49 hours, which is incorrect.)

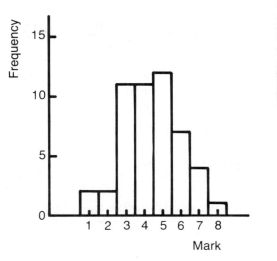

Fig. 51.13

DISCRETE AND CONTINUOUS VARIABLES

A variable which can take any value between two given values is called a *continuous variable*. Thus the height of an individual which can be 158 cm, 164.2 cm or 177.832 cm, depending upon the accuracy of measurement, is a continuous variable.

A variable which can only have certain values is called a *discrete variable*. Thus the number of children in à family can only take whole number values such as 0, 1, 2, 3, etc. It cannot be $2\frac{1}{2}$, $3\frac{1}{4}$, etc., and it is therefore a discrete variable. Note that the values of a discrete variable need not be whole numbers. The sizes of shoes is a discrete variable but these can be $4\frac{1}{2}$, 5, $5\frac{1}{2}$, 6, etc.

THE HISTOGRAM

The *histogram* is a diagram which is used to represent a frequency distribution. It consists of a set of rectangles whose *areas* represent the frequencies of the various classes. If all the classes have the same width then all the rectangles will be the same width and the frequencies are then represented by the heights of the rectangles. Figure 51.13 shows the histogram for the frequency distribution of Table 1.

HISTOGRAM FOR A GROUPED DISTRIBUTION

A histogram for a grouped distribution may be drawn by using the mid-points of the class intervals as the centres of the rectangles. The histogram for the distribution of Table 2 is shown in Fig. 51.14. Note that the extremes of the base of each rectangle represent the lower and upper class boundaries.

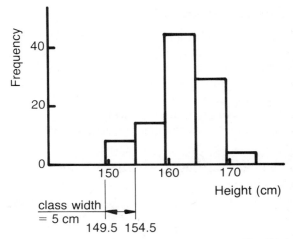

Fig. 51.14

DISCRETE DISTRIBUTIONS

The histogram shown in Fig. 51.14 represents a distribution in which the variable is continuous. The data in Example 8 is discrete and we shall see how a discrete distribution is represented.

414

EXAMPLE 8

Five coins were tossed 100 times and after each toss the number of heads was recorded. The table below gives the number of tosses during which 0, 1, 2, 3, 4 and 5 heads were obtained. Represent this data in a suitable diagram.

Number of heads	Number of tosses (frequency)
0	4
1	15
2	34
3	29
4	16
5	2
Total	100

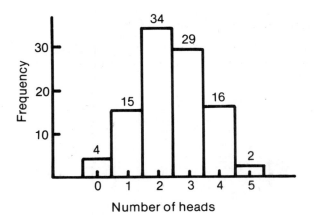

Fig. 51.16

Since the data is discrete (there cannot be 2.3 or 3.6 heads) Fig. 51.15 seems the most natural diagram to use. This diagram is in the form of a vertical bar chart in which the bars have zero width. Figure 51.16 shows the same data represented as a histogram. Note that the area under the diagram gives the total frequency of 100 which is as it should be. Discrete data is often represented as a histogram as was done in Fig. 51.13, despite the fact that in doing this we are treating the data as though it was continuous.

FREQUENCY POLYGONS

The frequency polygon provides a second way of representing a frequency distribution. It is drawn by connecting the mid-points of the tops of the rectangles in the histogram by straight lines.

EXAMPLE 9

Draw a frequency polygon to represent the information given below:

Age of employee	Frequency
15–19	5
20–24	23
25–29	58
30–34	104
35–39	141
40–44	98
45–49	43
50–54	19
55–59	6

The frequency polygon is drawn in Fig. 51.17. It is customary to add the extensions PQ and RS to the next lower and next higher class mid-points as shown in the diagram. When this is done the area of the polygon is equal to the area of the histogram.

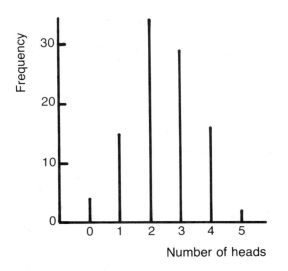

Fig. 51.15

415

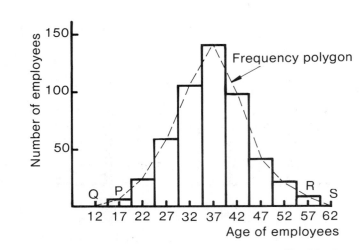

Fig. 51.17

Exercise 223 — *All type B*

1) The following marks were obtained by 50 students during a test:

5 4 6 5 4 6 6 6 5 4 7 6 5 6 4 5 5 6 6 8 5 4 2
8 6 8 3 6 4 7 7 3 4 7 4 1 7 4 5 6 4 5 8 7 6
9 7 5 4 6 2

Draw up a frequency distribution by means of a tally chart.

2) The following is a record of the percentage marks obtained by 100 students in an examination:

45 93 35 56 16 50 63 30 86 65 57 39 44
75 25 45 74 93 84 25 77 28 54 50 12 85
55 34 50 57 55 48 78 15 27 79 68 26 66
80 91 62 67 52 50 75 96 36 83 20 45 71
63 51 40 46 61 62 67 57 53 45 51 40 46
31 54 67 66 52 49 54 55 52 56 59 38 52
43 55 51 47 54 56 56 42 53 40 51 58 52
27 56 42 86 50 31 61 33 36

Draw up a tally chart for the classes 0—9, 10—19, 20—29, . . . , 90—99 and hence form a frequency distribution.

3) Draw a histogram and a frequency polygon of the following data which relates to the earnings of full-time girl employees in 1971.

Wage £	Frequency
12—15	2
16—19	5
17—20	8
21—23	6
24—27	2

4) Draw a histogram and a frequency polygon for the data shown below.

Mass (kg)	Frequency
0—4	50
5—9	64
10—14	43
15—19	26
20—25	17

5) The data below gives the diameter of machined parts:

Diameter (mm)	Frequency
14.96—14.98	3
14.99—15.01	8
15.02—15.04	12

Write down:

(a) The upper and lower class boundaries for the second class.
(b) The class width of the classes shown in the table.
(c) The class interval for the first class.

6) Classify each of the following as continuous or discrete variables:

(a) The diameters of ball bearings.
(b) The number of shirts sold per day.
(c) The mass of packets of chemical.
(d) The number of bunches of daffodils packed by a grower.
(e) The daily temperature.
(f) The lifetime of electric light bulbs.
(g) The number of telephone calls made per day by a person.

7) An industrial organisation gives an aptitude test to all applicants for employment. The results of 150 people taking the test were:

Score (out of 10)	Frequency
1	6
2	12
3	15
4	21
5	35
6	24
7	20
8	10
9	6
10	1

Draw a histogram of this information.

416

8) The lengths of 100 pieces of wood were measured with the following results:

Length (cm)	Frequency
29.5	2
29.6	4
29.7	11
29.8	18
29.9	31
30.0	22
30.1	8
30.2	3
30.3	1

Draw a histogram and a frequency polygon of this information.

STATISTICAL AVERAGES

We have seen that a mass of raw data does not mean very much until it is arranged into a frequency distribution or until it is represented as a histogram.

A second way of making the data more understandable is to try to find a single value which will represent all the values in a distribution. This single representative value is called an average.

In statistics several kinds of average are used. The more important are:

(a) The arithmetic mean, often referred to as the mean.
(b) The median.
(c) The mode.

THE ARITHMETIC MEAN

This is found by adding up all the values in a set and dividing this sum by the number of values making up the set. That is,

arithmetic mean

$$= \frac{\text{sum of all the values}}{\text{the number of values}}$$

EXAMPLE 10

The heights of 5 men were measured as follows: 177.8, 175.3, 174.8, 179.1, 176.5 cm. Calculate the mean height of the 5 men.

$$\text{Mean} = \frac{177.8 + 175.3 + 174.8 + 179.1 + 176.5}{5}$$

$$= \frac{883.5}{5} = 176.7 \text{ cm}$$

Note that the unit of the mean is the same as the unit used for each of the quantities in the set.

THE MEAN OF A FREQUENCY DISTRIBUTION

When finding the mean of a frequency distribution we must take into account the frequencies as well as the measured observations.

EXAMPLE 11

Five packets of chemical have a mass of 20.01 grams, 3 have a mass of 19.98 grams and 2 have a mass of 20.03 grams. What is the mean mass of the packets?

Mass of 5 packets @ 20.01 grams = 100.05
Mass of 3 packets @ 19.98 grams = 59.94
Mass of 2 packets @ 20.03 grams = 40.06

Total mass of 10 packets = 200.05

Mean mass

$$= \frac{\text{total mass}}{10} = \frac{200.05}{10}$$

$$= 20.005 \text{ grams}$$

This example gives the clue whereby we may find the mean of a frequency distribution.

EXAMPLE 12

Each of 200 similar engine components are measured correct to the nearest millimetre and recorded as follows:

Length (mm)	Frequency
198	8
199	30
200	132
201	24
202	6

Calculate the mean length of the 200 components.

Mean length = [(198 × 8) + (199 × 30)
            + (200 × 132) + (201 × 24)
            + (202 × 6)] ÷ 200

= 199.95 mm

The calculation is often set out in tabular form as shown below. This method reduces the risk of making errors when performing the calculation.

Length (mm)	Frequency	Length × frequency
198	8	1584
199	30	5970
200	132	26400
201	24	4824
202	6	1212
Total	200	39990

$$\text{mean} = \frac{\text{total of (length} \times \text{frequency)}}{\text{total frequency}}$$

$$= \frac{39\,990}{200} = 199.95 \text{ mm}$$

THE MEDIAN

If a set of values is arranged in ascending (or descending) order of size the median is the value which lies half-way along the series. Thus the median of 3, 4, 4, 5, 6, 8, 8, 9, 10 is 6 because there are four numbers below this value and four numbers above it.

When there are an even number of values in the set the median is found by taking the mean of the middle two values. Thus the median of 3, 3, 5, 7, 9, 10, 13, 15 is $\frac{7 + 9}{2} = 8$.

The median of a discrete frequency distribution may be found by setting out the scores in numerical order and finding the middle value.

EXAMPLE 13
The table below shows the distribution of numbers obtained when a die is thrown 30 times. Determine the median.

Number obtained	1	2	3	4	5	6
Frequency	2	7	5	7	3	6

The total frequency is 30. Hence the median must lie between the 15th and 16th items in the distribution. We now look at the values of the 15th and 16th items. These are both 4 and hence the median is 4.

It is unnecessary to write down all the values in numerical order to find the median but if we do this we obtain:

1, 1, 2, 2, 2, 2, 2, 2, 2, 3, 3, 3, 3, 3, 4, 4,
4, 4, 4, 4, 4, 5, 5, 5, 6, 6, 6, 6, 6, 6

Looking at this set of values we see that the two middle values are 4 and hence the median is 4.

THE MODE

The mode of a set of values is the value which occurs most frequently. That is, it is the most common value. Thus the mode of 2, 3, 3, 4, 4, 4, 5, 6, 6, 7 is 4 because this number occurs three times, which is more than any of the other numbers in the set.

Sometimes, in a set of numbers, no mode exists, as for the set 2, 4, 7, 8, 9, 11 in which each number occurs once. It is possible for there to be more than one mode. The set 2, 3, 3, 3, 4, 4, 5, 6, 6, 6, 7, 8 has two modes 3 and 6, because each of these numbers occurs three times which is more than any of the other numbers.

A set of values which has two modes is called *bimodal*. If the set has only one mode it is said to be *unimodal* but if there are more than two modes the set is called *multimodal*.

THE MODE OF A FREQUENCY DISTRIBUTION

To find the mode of a frequency distribution we draw a histogram. By drawing the diagonals as shown in Fig. 51.18 the mode is found.

EXAMPLE 14
The heights of a group of boys are measured to the nearest centimetre with the following results:

Height (cm)	157	158	159	160	161	162
Frequency	20	36	44	46	39	30
Height (cm)	163	164	165	166	167	
Frequency	22	17	10	4	2	

Find the mode of distribution.

By constructing the histogram (Fig. 51.18) the mode is found to be 159.7. It is worthwhile noting that the modal class is 159.5 to 160.5 cm.

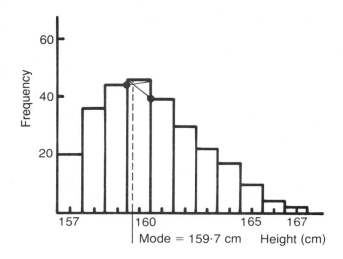

Mode = 159·7 cm   Height (cm)

Fig. 51.18

MEAN DEVIATION

A statistical average gives some idea about the position of a distribution (Fig. 51.19). Hence statistical averages are called measures of location. We now need a measure which will define the spread or dispersion of the data. A measure of dispersion which is often used is the mean deviation. This is the mean of the deviations of the data from a statistical average which may be the mean, median or mode. A deviation is the difference between the value of the average and a value in the distribution. The mean deviation is calculated from the formula

$$\text{mean deviation} = \frac{\Sigma|x - \bar{x}|}{n}$$

where x = a value in the distribution

$\bar{x}$ = the statistical average

n = the number of items in the distribution.

The symbol Σ (Greek letter capital sigma) means 'the sum of'. The lines $||$ indicate that all the differences are to be taken as positive. Thus $\Sigma|x - \bar{x}|$ tells us to find all the differences and add them together.

EXAMPLE 15
Find the mean deviation from the mean of the numbers 3, 5, 7, 9 and 11.

$$\bar{x} = \frac{3 + 5 + 7 + 9 + 11}{5} = \frac{35}{5} = 7$$

x	$x - \bar{x}$
3	4
5	2
7	0
9	2
11	4

$$\Sigma|x - \bar{x}| = 12$$

Since there are five numbers, $n = 5$. Hence

$$\text{mean deviation} = \frac{12}{5} = 2.4$$

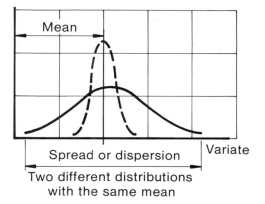

Two different distributions with the same mean

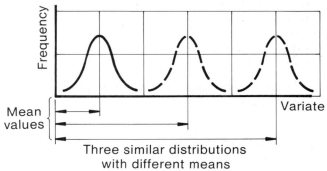

Three similar distributions with different means

Fig. 51.19

MEAN DEVIATION OF A FREQUENCY DISTRIBUTION

The mean deviation of a frequency distribution is found by using the following formula:

$$\text{mean deviation} = \frac{\Sigma f|x - \bar{x}|}{n}$$

where $\bar{x}$ = the value of the statistical average

x = a value in the distribution

f = the corresponding frequency

n = the number of values in the distribution

419

EXAMPLE 16

Calculate the mean deviation from the mean for the following distribution:

Length (cm)	15	16	17	18	19	20
Frequency	1	6	12	15	7	2

x	f	fx	$\lvert x - \bar{x} \rvert$	$f\lvert x - \bar{x} \rvert$
15	1	15	2.6	2.6
16	6	96	1.6	9.6
17	12	204	0.6	7.2
18	15	270	0.4	6.0
19	7	133	1.4	9.8
20	2	40	2.4	4.8
	43	758		40.0

$$\bar{x} = \frac{758}{43} = 17.6$$

Since there are 43 values, $n = 43$

$$\text{Mean deviation} = \frac{40.0}{43} = 0.93$$

Exercise 224 — *Questions 1–3, 6–11 type A, remainder B*

1) Find the mean of £23, £27, £30, £28 and £32.

2) The heights of some men are as follows: 172, 170, 181, 175, 179 and 173 cm. Calculate the mean height of the men.

3) Five people earn £42 per week, 3 earn £38 per week and 2 earn £44 per week. What is the mean wage for the 10 people?

4) Calculate the mean length from the following table:

Length (mm)	Frequency
198	1
199	4
200	17
201	2
202	1

5) Calculate the mean height of 50 people from the table below:

Height (cm)	Frequency
160	1
161	5
162	10
163	16
164	10
165	6
166	2

6) Find the median of the numbers 5, 3, 8, 6, 4, 2, 8.

7) Find the median of the numbers 2, 4, 6, 5, 3, 1, 8, 9.

8) The marks of a student in five examinations were: 54, 63, 49, 78 and 57. What is his median mark?

9) Find the mode of the following set of numbers 3, 5, 2, 7, 5, 8, 5, 2, 7.

10) Find the mode of 38.7, 29.6, 32.1, 35.8, 43.2.

11) Find the modes of 8, 4, 9, 3, 5, 3, 8, 5, 3, 8, 9, 5, 6, 7.

12) The marks of 100 students were as follows:

Mark	Frequency
1	2
2	8
3	20
4	32
5	18
6	9
7	6
8	3
9	2

Obtain the median mark.

13) Find the mode of the distribution of question 4.

14) Find the mode of the distribution of question 5.

15) Find the mean deviation from the mean of the numbers 3, 5, 7 and 9.

16) Calculate the mean deviation from the mean of the numbers 2.3, 3.4, 4.1 and 2.9.

17) Calculate the mean deviation from the mean for the following distribution:

Length (mm)	167	168	169	170	171
Frequency	2	8	15	6	3

18) The table below gives the number of passes in an examination obtained by 30 pupils in a particular class.

Number of passes	3	4	5	6	7	8
Frequency	4	4	6	8	5	3

Calculate the mean deviation from the mean.

19) 32 children in a class were asked to estimate the length of a metal rod. The results were as follows:

Length (cm)	35	36	37	38	39	40	41	42
Frequency	1	3	4	8	6	5	3	2

Calculate the mean deviation from the mean.

20) Calculate the mean deviation from the mean of the numbers 5, 8, 8, 8, 8, and 11.

Chapter 52 Probability

SIMPLE PROBABILITY

The probability of an event occurring in a single trial is

$$P = \frac{\text{number of ways in which the event can happen}}{\text{total number of possibilities}}$$

EXAMPLE 1

(1) The probability of obtaining a head in a single toss of a coin is

$$P(\text{heads}) = \frac{1}{2}$$

(2) The probability of obtaining a two in a single roll of a die is

$$P(\text{two}) = \frac{1}{6}$$

(3) The probability of cutting a king from a deck of 52 playing cards is

$$P(\text{king}) = \frac{4}{52} = \frac{1}{13}$$

(4) 20 discs are marked with the numbers 1 to 20 inclusive. They are placed in a box and one disc is drawn from it. What is the probability that the number on the disc will be a multiple of 5.

Any of the numbers, 5, 10, 15 and 20 is a multiple of 5. Hence the number of ways in which a multiple of 5 can occur is 4. The total possibilities are 20. Hence

$$P(\text{multiple of } 5) = \frac{4}{20} = \frac{1}{5}$$

THE PROBABILITY SCALE

When an event is absolutely certain to happen we say that the probability of it happening is 1. When an event can never happen we say that the probability is 0. Therefore all probabilities lie between 0 and 1 and they may be expressed as a fraction or a decimal. Thus

$$P(\text{head}) = \frac{1}{2} = 0.5$$

Probabilities can be expressed on a probability scale (Fig. 52.1).

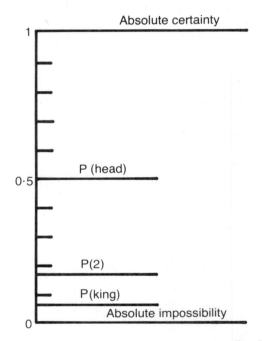

Fig. 52.1

TOTAL PROBABILITY

The total probability covering all possible events is 1. Thus

$$P(\text{success}) + P(\text{failure}) = 1$$

The probability of cutting a king is $\frac{1}{13}$. The probability of not cutting a king is $1 - \frac{1}{13} = \frac{12}{13}$.

EXAMPLE 2

A bag contains 5 red balls, 8 blue balls and 7 yellow balls. What is the probability of:

(a) drawing a red ball,
(b) not drawing a red ball in a single draw from the bag.

(a) $P(\text{red}) = \dfrac{5}{20} = 0.25$

(b) $P(\text{not red}) = 1 - 0.25 = 0.75$.

EMPIRICAL PROBABILITY

Although it is possible to calculate many probabilities in the way shown above, in a great many cases we have to rely on an experiment or an enquiry in order to establish the probability of an event happening.

Suppose that we have 100 ball bearings and on examining them we find that 4 are not round. What is the probability of selecting a not-round ball bearing out of the hundred?

Total possibilities = 100

Possibilities of selecting a not-round ball bearing = 4

$$P(\text{not-round}) = \dfrac{4}{100}$$

In industry probabilities are worked out just like this and these empirical probabilities can usually be relied on. However, some probabilities, met with in every day conversation are not reliable. Suppose on 20 days we checked to see if it snowed in Gloucester and we found that on 3 of these days it did, in fact, snow. Would we be right in saying

$$P(\text{snow}) = \dfrac{3}{20}?$$

For a start in which part of the year were the observations taken? It must have been in the deep winter. So perhaps in December, January and February the probability might be fairly accurate. But what of July and August?

Simple empirical probabilities can only be very crude measures but they are useful in conveying information in a simple direct way.

Exercise 225 — *All type A*

1) A die is rolled. Calculate the probability of:

(a) a four,
(b) a number less than four,
(c) a two or a three,
(d) an odd number.

2) 40 discs marked with the numbers 1 to 40 are placed in a box and one disc is drawn from it. Determine the probability that the number on the disc will be:

(a) a multiple of 5,
(b) odd,
(c) more than 7,
(d) less than 4.

3) A card is drawn from a deck of 52 playing cards. Find the probability that it will be:

(a) the queen of spades,
(b) a king,
(c) a picture card (i.e. an ace, king, queen or jack),
(d) the jack of hearts or the ace of clubs.

4) A letter is chosen from the word FLAGSTAFF. Find the probability that it will be:

(a) L   (b) A   (c) F

5) A bag contains 3 red balls, 4 blue, 6 black and 7 white. One ball is drawn from the bag. Calculate the probability that it will be:

(a) blue,
(b) red or black,
(c) not white.

6) Two dice are thrown together and their scores added. Determine the probability that the sum will be:

(a) 7   (b) less than 6,   (c) more than 8.

7) What is the least likely of (a), (b) or (c) in question 6?

8) In a factory, 200 components are checked and 15 are found to be faulty. If one component is chosen at random from the 200 components, what is the probability that it will be a good component?

THE ADDITION LAW OF PROBABILITY

If two events could not happen at the same time the events are said to be *mutually exclusive*. For instance suppose we want to know the probability of a 3 or a 4 occurring in a single roll of a die. In a single roll a 3 or a 4 can occur; it is not possible for a 3 and a 4 to occur together. Hence the events of throwing a 3 or a 4 in a single roll of a die are mutually exclusive. Similarly it is impossible to cut a jack and a king in a single cut of a deck of cards. Hence these two events are mutually exclusive.

If $p_1, p_2, p_3, \ldots$ are the separate probabilities of a set of mutually exclusive events then the probability of *one* of the events happening is

$$P = p_1 + p_2 + p_3 + \ldots$$

EXAMPLE 3

A die with faces numbered 1 to 6 is rolled once. What is the probability of obtaining either a 3 or a 4?

$$P(3) = p_1 = \frac{1}{6}$$

$$P(4) = p_2 = \frac{1}{6}$$

$$P(3 \text{ or } 4) = \frac{1}{6} + \frac{1}{6} = \frac{1}{3}$$

EXAMPLE 4

A pack of cards is cut once. Find the probability that the card will be the ace of spades, a king or the queen of hearts.

$$P(\text{ace of spades}) = p_1 = \frac{1}{52}$$

$$P(\text{king}) = p_2 = \frac{4}{52}$$

$$P(\text{queen of hearts}) = p_3 = \frac{1}{52}$$

$P(\text{ace of spades, a king or queen of hearts})$

$$= p_1 + p_2 + p_3$$

$$= \frac{1}{52} + \frac{4}{52} + \frac{1}{52}$$

$$= \frac{6}{52} = \frac{3}{26}$$

Sometimes the addition law is called the OR law because we seek the probability that one event OR another event will happen.

THE MULTIPLICATION LAW OF PROBABILITY

An *independent* event is one which has no effect on subsequent events. Thus if the first event to occur has no effect on subsequent events, the events are independent. Thus if a die is rolled twice what happens on the first roll does not affect what happens on the second roll. Hence the two rolls of the die are independent events. The event of cutting an ace and tossing a head are also independent events since what happens during the cut has no effect on the way in which the coin lands.

If $p_1, p_2, p_3, \ldots$ are the separate probabilities of a set of independent events then the probability that *all* the events will occur is

$$P = p_1 \times p_2 \times p_3 \times \ldots$$

EXAMPLE 5

If a coin is tossed and a card is cut from a deck of cards find the probability that the result will be a head and an ace.

$$P(\text{head}) = \frac{1}{2}$$

$$P(\text{ace}) = \frac{1}{13}$$

$$P(\text{head and ace}) = \frac{1}{2} \times \frac{1}{13} = \frac{1}{26}$$

EXAMPLE 6

A coin is tossed 4 times. What is the probability that each toss will result in a head?

The four tosses of the coin are independent events since what happens on the first toss in no way affects the subsequent tosses.

$$P(4 \text{ heads}) = \frac{1}{2} \times \frac{1}{2} \times \frac{1}{2} \times \frac{1}{2} = \frac{1}{16}$$

The multiplication law is sometimes called the AND law because we seek the probability that one event AND another event will happen.

THE PROBABILITY TREE

EXAMPLE 7

A coin is tossed three times. Find the probabilities that:

(a) a head will occur on all three tosses,

(b) only one head will appear.

We can work out these probabilities by using a probability tree (Fig. 52.2). Possible heads are shown in full and possible tails in a dotted line.

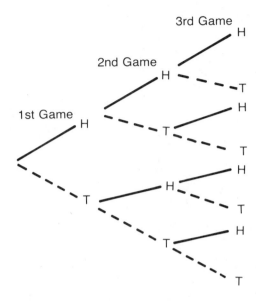

The branches of the tree which give the probabilities needed for example 7 are

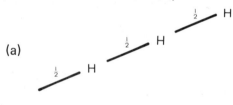

(a)

$$P \text{ (3 heads)} = \tfrac{1}{2} \times \tfrac{1}{2} \times \tfrac{1}{2} = \tfrac{1}{8}$$

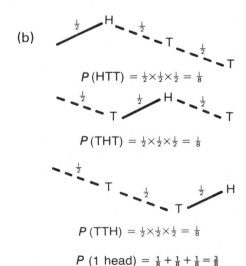

(b)

$$P \text{ (HTT)} = \tfrac{1}{2} \times \tfrac{1}{2} \times \tfrac{1}{2} = \tfrac{1}{8}$$

$$P \text{ (THT)} = \tfrac{1}{2} \times \tfrac{1}{2} \times \tfrac{1}{2} = \tfrac{1}{8}$$

$$P \text{ (TTH)} = \tfrac{1}{2} \times \tfrac{1}{2} \times \tfrac{1}{2} = \tfrac{1}{8}$$

$$P \text{ (1 head)} = \tfrac{1}{8} + \tfrac{1}{8} + \tfrac{1}{8} = \tfrac{3}{8}$$

A probability tree   Fig. 52.2

EXAMPLE 8

A box contains 4 black and 6 red balls. A ball is drawn from the box and is not replaced. A second ball is then drawn. Find the probabilities of:

(a) red and red being drawn,
(b) black then red,
(c) red then black,
(d) black then black.

The probability tree and the probabilities required are shown in Fig. 52.3.

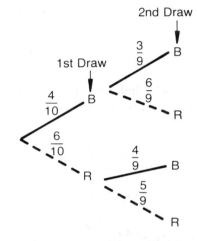

The branches of the tree to give the required probabilities are:

(a) $P \text{ (R and R)}$

$$= \tfrac{6}{10} \times \tfrac{5}{9} = \tfrac{1}{3}$$

(b) $P \text{ (B and R)}$

$$= \tfrac{4}{10} \times \tfrac{6}{9} = \tfrac{4}{15}$$

(c) $P \text{ (R and B)}$

$$= \tfrac{6}{10} \times \tfrac{4}{9} = \tfrac{4}{15}$$

(d) $P \text{ (B and B)}$

$$= \tfrac{4}{10} \times \tfrac{3}{9} = \tfrac{2}{15}$$

Fig. 52.3

Exercise 226 — *All type C*

1) A card is cut from a pack of playing cards. Determine the probability that it will be an ace or the king of hearts.

2) A coin is tossed and a die is rolled. Calculate the probabilities of:

(a) a tail and a 5,

(b) a head and an even number.

3) A box contains 8 red counters and 12 white ones. A counter is drawn from the box and then replaced. A second counter is then drawn. Determine the probabilities that:

(a) both counters will be red,

(b) both counters will be white,

(c) one counter will be white and the other red.

4) Out of 20 components 3 are defective Two components are chosen at random, from a large batch, for testing. What is the probability that they will both be defective?

5) A loaded die shows scores with these probabilities:

Score	1	2	3	4	5	6
Probability	0.14	0.18	0.16	0.15	0.17	0.20

(a) If I throw it once what is the probability of a score less than 3?

(b) If I throw it twice, what is the probability of a 4 followed by a 6?

6) From a shuffled pack of 52 cards I deal two cards. What is the probability of:

(a) the first card being an ace,

(b) the second card being an ace if it was known that the first card was an ace?

7) A, B and C are points on a toy train system. The probability of going straight on at each point is $\frac{2}{3}$ (see Fig. 52.4). Find the probability that:

(a) the train T hits the waiting train,

(b) the train T goes into the shed.

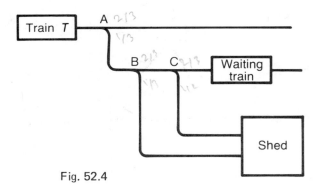

Fig. 52.4

8) EVENT: spin the pointer (Fig. 52.5).

(a) Find the probability that the pointer stops in 'B' section.

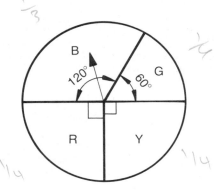

Fig. 52.5

(b) Find the probability that the pointer stops in either the 'R' or the 'G' sections.

(c) The results of two successive spins are noted. Find:

 (i) the probability that the first spin is an 'R' and the second spin is a 'G'.

 (ii) the probability that the pointer stops in either 'R' then 'G' or 'G' then 'R'.

9) (a) If you cast an unbiased die, what is the probability of it being a 6?

(b) If you cast two such dice, what is the probability of throwing:

 (i) two sixes,

 (ii) a six and a five?

(c) Write down all the various ways in which a total of 7 can be thrown with two dice and use this information to calculate the probability of throwing a total of 7 with two dice.

10) Two ordinary dice, one coloured red, the other blue, are thrown at the same time.

(a) What is the probability that the number on the red die will be 4?

(b) What is the probability that the number on the blue die will be an even number?

(c) Copy and complete the table below which shows the total score of the two dice.

Number on red die

	1	2	3	4	5	6
1	2	3	4	5	6	7
2	3					8
3	4					9
4	5					10
5	6					11
6	7	8	9	10	11	12

Number on blue die

(d) What is the probability of getting a total score of (i) 5, (ii) at least 9?

11) The letters of the word TERRIFIC are written one on each of eight cards. The cards are placed face down on a table, shuffled and one of them is turned face upwards. What is the probability that it is

(a) a letter R,

(b) not a vowel (i.e. not I or E)?

The experiment is repeated but now two cards are turned over together. What is the probability that

(c) both are letter R's?

(d) one, at least, is a vowel?

12) Two dice are thrown together. The table below shows some of the possible results.

(a) Copy out this table and complete it to show all the possible results.

1, 1	2, 1	3, 1	4, 1	5, 1	6, 1
1, 2	2, 2	3, 2			
1, 3	2, 3				
1, 4					

(b) Write down the probability of a result:

   (i) 1, 1,

  (ii) containing two numbers which are the same,

 (iii) not containing the figure 1.

(c) If the two numbers in the result are added together (for example 6, 3 adds up to 9), what is the probability that any one result will add up to a total less than 4?

13) A bag contains 14 yellow counters and 10 red counters. Two counters are taken out in succession and not replaced.

(a) Copy and complete the tree diagram (Fig. 52.6) by writing in the correct fractions for boxes A, B, C and D.

(b) What is the probability that two red counters are taken out?

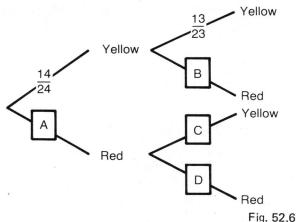

Fig. 52.6

14) Figure 52.7 shows a circle divided into five equal sectors which are numbered from 1 to 5. A pointer attached to the centre of the circle is free to spin. A 'trial' consists of spinning the pointer twice. The result of a trial will be (2, 3) if the pointer stops at 2 on the first spin and on 3 on the second spin. The total for a trial is found by adding the two numbers together. Thus the total for the trial (2, 3) is 5.

(a) Show all the possible different results of 'trials'.

(b) What is the probability of obtaining each of the following totals:

$$1, 2, 3, 6, 10?$$

(c) How many possible different results of 'trials' would there be if the circle was divided into

  (i) 2 equal sectors numbered 1 and 2?

 (ii) 3 equal sectors numbered 1, 2 and 3?

(iii) 4 equal sectors numbered 1, 2, 3 and 4?

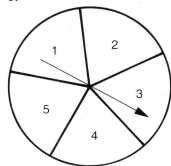

Fig. 52.7

427

Chapter 53 Linear Programming

INTRODUCTION

Linear programming is a useful application of systems of linear inequalities. Similar systems are used in business management in many industries, where there is a need to determine maximum profits or to find minimum costs or overhead expenses.

THE FUNDAMENTAL THEOREM OF LINEAR PROGRAMMING

A system of linear inequalities, such as that given in Example 1, when plotted on graph paper gives a region which is either a triangle, a quadrilateral or a polygon of some sort. When this happens the system of inequalities is called a *polygonal convex set*. The maximum or minimum value occurs at a vertex of the polygon or at all points along one of its sides.

EXAMPLE 1

Draw the graph of the solution set

$$x \geqslant 0$$
$$y \geqslant 0$$
$$x + 2y \leqslant 15$$

Hence find the maximum value of $3x + y$ for the system.

The solution set is given as the shaded area of Fig. 53.1 and the boundaries of $\triangle$ OAB.

The maximum value of $3x + y$ lies at one of the vertices of OAB, i.e. at either O, A or B.

At O, $x = 0$ and $y = 0$. Hence $3x + y = 0$.

At A, $x = 0$ and $y = 7.5$. Hence $3x + y = 7.5$.

At B, $x = 15$ and $y = 0$. Hence $3x + y = 45$.

Therefore the maximum value of $3x + y$ is 45.

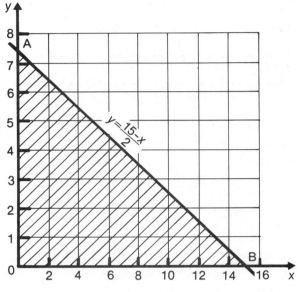

Fig. 53.1

EXAMPLE 2

Draw the graph of the solution set

$$x \geqslant 10$$
$$y \geqslant 5$$
$$4y + 3x \leqslant 120$$
$$y \geqslant 3x - 45$$

Hence find the maximum and minimum values of $3x + 2y - 3$.

The solution set is given by the shaded area shown in Fig. 53.2 and the boundaries of the quadrilateral ABCD.

The maximum and minimum values of $3x + 2y - 3$ occur at one of the vertices of ABCD.

At A $(10, 5)$, $3x + 2y - 3 = 37$.

At B $(10, 25)$, $3x + 2y - 3 = 77$.

At C $(20, 15)$, $3x + 2y - 3 = 87$.

At D $(\frac{50}{3}, 5)$, $3x + 2y - 3 = 57$.

Therefore the maximum value of $3x + 2y - 3$ is 87 and its minimum value is 37.

428

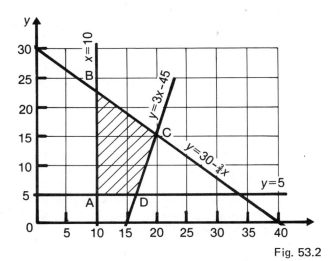
Fig. 53.2

EXAMPLE 3

A shopper wants to buy oranges at 15 p each and grapefruits at 20 p each. She must buy at least one grapefruit and her basket can hold no more than 5 fruits. If the greengrocer makes 4 p profit on each orange and 6 p profit on each grapefruit:

(a) write down three inequalities to represent the conditions given above;
(b) draw graphs on the same axes to show these conditions;
(c) find how many oranges and how many grapefruits the shopper buys if the shopkeeper is to realise the maximum profit;
(d) what is the greatest profit?

Let x = the number of oranges bought
and y = the number of grapefruit bought.

Then, $x \geqslant 1$, $y \geqslant 1$, $x + y \leqslant 5$.

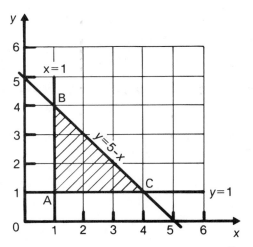
Fig. 53.3

The graphs are shown in Fig. 53.3. To find the greatest profit we have to find the maximum value of $4x + 6y$. This occurs at one of the vertices of $\triangle$ ABC.

At A $(1, 1)$, $4x + 6y = 10$.

At B $(1, 4)$, $4x + 6y = 28$.

At C $(4, 1)$, $4x + 6y = 22$.

Hence, for a maximum profit, the shopper must buy 1 orange and 4 grapefruits.

The maximum profit to the shopkeeper is then 28 p.

Exercise 227 — *All type C*

1) Find the maximum value of $3x - y + 2$ over the polygonal convex set shown in Fig. 53.4.

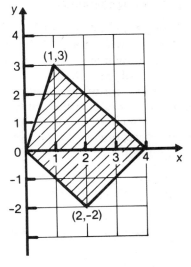
Fig. 53.4

2) Draw the graph of the solution set which satisfies the following inequalities: $x \geqslant 0$, $y \geqslant 0$, $x + y \leqslant 5$ and $y \leqslant -2x + 8$. Find the maximum and minimum values of $4x + y - 5$ for the system.

3) A supermarket sells two kinds of washing powder, Sure-clean and Quick-wash. At least 3 times as much Sure-clean is sold as Quick-wash. The supermarket has, at most, 1800 cm² of shelf space for washing powder. A box of Sure-clean requires 25 cm² of shelf space and a box of Quick-wash requires 15 cm². The profit per box is 8 p per box for Sure-clean and 12 p per box for Quick-wash. How many boxes of each kind of powder should be stocked for the greatest profit to be made? What is the greatest profit?

429

4) A radio shop stocks two types of radio, Type P and Type Q. It can sell at least 3 times as many of Type P as Type Q but there is only room to store 32 radios in all. It costs £1 per month to store Type P and £4 per month to store Type Q and the total cost of storage must not exceed £80 per month. If a profit of £20 is made on Type P and a profit of £50 on Type Q, how many of each type should be stored in order that the greatest profit shall be made? What is the greatest profit?

5) Part of a farm is to be planted with wheat and part with kale, observing the following restrictions:

	Wheat	Kale	Max. total
Labour per hectare (days)	4	3	32
Cost of labour per hectare (£'s)	1	2	18
Cost of fertiliser per hectare (£'s)	4	1	24

On graph paper illustrate the above table and from your graph find:

(a) The greatest numbers of hectares of wheat and kale that can be planted.
(b) The area of each crop that should be planted to give a maximum profit if wheat gives a profit of £8 per hectare and kale £4 per hectare.
(c) The maximum profit.

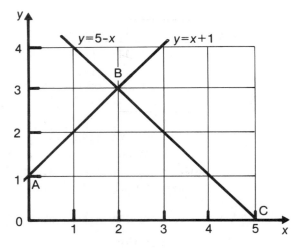

Fig. 53.5

6) Make a sketch of Fig. 53.5 and shade the region which represents the solution set for the following inequalities: $x \geqslant 0$, $y \geqslant 0$, $y \leqslant x + 1$ and $x + y \leqslant 5$. Calculate the coordinates of the points A, B and C and hence find the maximum value of $2x + 3y$.

7) A mail order firm has to transport 900 parcels using a lorry which takes 150 at a time and a van which takes 80 a time. The cost of each journey is £5 for the lorry and £4 for the van. If the total cost must be less than £44 and the van must make more journeys than the lorry, how many trips should each make to keep the cost to a minimum? What is the minimum cost?

8) The two positive numbers x and y are such that $A = \{(x, y): 2y - x \leqslant 14\}$, $B = \{(x, y): y + 2x \geqslant 12\}$ and $C = \{(x, y): y \geqslant 3x - 13\}$.

(a) Draw a graph to illustrate the solution set.
(b) If x and y are further defined as being whole numbers how many possible values are there for x and y?
(c) What is the maximum value of $x + y$?
(d) What is the minimum value of $x + y$?

9) A shop sells tins of ham at £1 each and tins of beef at 80 p each. A customer decides that she will buy at least one tin of each but she cannot carry more than 6 tins altogether and she must not spend more than £5.

(a) Draw graphs on the same axes to represent these conditions.
(b) If the shopkeeper makes a profit of 40 p on a tin of ham and 20 p on a tin of beef find how many tins of each the customer buys so that the shopkeeper obtains the greatest amount of profit.
(c) Calculate this greatest profit.

10) The owner of a business plans to buy two types of machine, Type A and Type B. Type A needs $4 \, m^2$ of floor space and Type B needs $5 \, m^2$. There is $55 \, m^2$ of floor space available. Type A costs £30 and Type B costs £60 and up to £720 can be spent. If at least 5 of Type A and at least 2 of Type B must be bought find the maximum number of machines that can be bought.

Multi-choice Questions

Exercise 228

Write down the letter corresponding to the correct answer.

1) The inverse under multiplication of the matrix $\begin{pmatrix} 5 & 7 \\ 2 & 3 \end{pmatrix}$ is:

a $\begin{pmatrix} -3 & -7 \\ -2 & -5 \end{pmatrix}$ b $\begin{pmatrix} -5 & 2 \\ 7 & -3 \end{pmatrix}$

c $\begin{pmatrix} 3 & -7 \\ -2 & 5 \end{pmatrix}$ d $\begin{pmatrix} 0 & 0 \\ 0 & 0 \end{pmatrix}$

2) The matrix $\begin{pmatrix} 3 & 0 \\ 0 & 1 \end{pmatrix}$ will produce:

a an enlargement   b a reflection
c a rotation   d a one way stretch

3) The tree diagram drawn in Fig. 1 shows that the probability of '2 Reds' is:

a $\frac{3}{7} + \frac{2}{6}$ b $\frac{3}{7} \times \frac{2}{6}$

c $\frac{3}{7} \times \frac{3}{6}$ d $\frac{2}{6} + \frac{3}{6}$

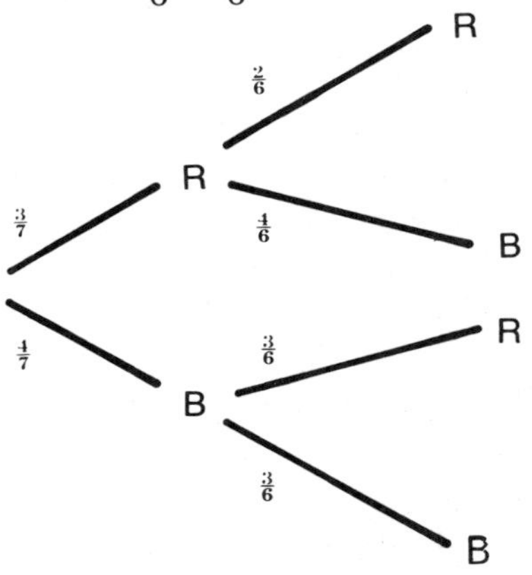

Fig. 1

4) The inverse of the 2×2 matrix $\begin{pmatrix} 6 & 10 \\ 2 & 4 \end{pmatrix}$ is:

a $\begin{pmatrix} 1 & -2\frac{1}{2} \\ -\frac{1}{2} & 1\frac{1}{2} \end{pmatrix}$ b $\begin{pmatrix} 4 & -10 \\ -2 & 6 \end{pmatrix}$

c $\begin{pmatrix} -2 & 6 \\ -10 & 4 \end{pmatrix}$ d $\begin{pmatrix} 1 & 2\frac{1}{2} \\ \frac{1}{2} & 1\frac{1}{2} \end{pmatrix}$

5) 42_5 is equivalent to:
a 21_{10} b 10101_2 c 112_4 d 212_3

6) The denary (base 10) number 37, written in binary (base 2) is:
a 1 0 0 0 1 1   b 1 0 0 1 1 1
c 1 0 0 0 0 1   d 1 1 0 0 0 1
e 1 0 0 1 0 1

7) If both numbers are in binary the average of 1 0 1 1 and 1 1 1 is:
a 1 0 0 0   b 1 0 0 1 0   c 1 0 0 1
d 1 0 0 0 1   e 1 0 0 0 0

8) When the binary numbers 1 0 1 and 1 1 are multiplied together the answer is:
a 1 0 0 1   b 1 0 1 0   c 1 0 1 1
d 1 1 1 0   e 1 1 1 1

9)

BRAZILS	卌
WALNUTS	卌 11
ALMONDS	卌 111
CHESTNUTS	卌 111
COBNUTS	卌 卌 11

The tally marks above show the distribution in a sample of mixed nuts. What fraction of the nuts were almonds?

a $\frac{1}{8}$ b $\frac{7}{40}$ c $\frac{1}{5}$ d $\frac{1}{4}$ e $\frac{3}{10}$

10) In a school's examination 480 candidates were awarded Grade 4 out of a total of 720 results. On a pie-chart showing all the grades what would be the angle at the centre for grade 4?
a 270°   b 240°   c 210°
d 180°   e 120°

11) 24_5 is equivalent to:

a 40_3 **b** 112_3 **c** 11000_2

d 120_{10} **e** 31_4

12) The pie chart (Fig. 2) illustrates how a group of children travel to school. What percentage walk to school?

a 50%   **b** 20%   **c** 25%

d 10%   **e** 30%

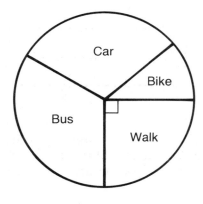

Fig. 2

13) Evaluate $2002_3 - 202_3$.

a 100_3 **b** 101_3 **c** 1100_3

d 1010_3 **e** 1001_3

14) Evaluate $1\,0\,0\,1_2 \times 1\,0\,1_2$.

a $1\,0\,0\,1\,1\,1_2$ **b** $1\,1\,1\,0\,0\,1_2$

c $1\,0\,1\,1\,0\,1_2$ **d** $1\,1\,0\,0\,1_2$

e $1\,1\,1\,0\,1\,0_2$

15) Evaluate $1\,0\,1\,0_2 \div 1\,0\,1_2$.

a $1\,0\,1_2$ **b** $1\,1_2$ **c** $1\,0_2$ **d** $1\,0\,0_2$

e 1_2

16) What is 1204_5 in base ten?

a 179   **b** 895   **c** 1 434

d 2 408   **e** 14 304

17) $R = \{2, 4, 6, 8, 10\}$. How many sub-sets of R have one member only?

a 1   **b** 5   **c** 6   **d** 10   **e** 32

18) All the points on the line PQ (Fig. 3) satisfy a certain relation. What is this relation?

a $y = x$ **b** $y = -3$ **c** $y = x + 3$

d $y = x - 3$ **e** $y = 3$

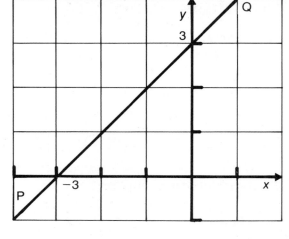

Fig. 3

19) What is the relation illustrated in Fig. 4?

a $x \rightarrow x + 1$ **b** $x \rightarrow x + 4$ **c** $x \rightarrow x + 3$

d $x \rightarrow 3x$ **e** $x \rightarrow 2x + 1$

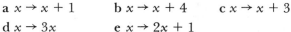
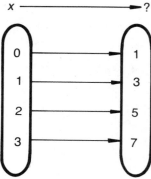

Fig. 4

20) Which one of the following pairs of sets is equal?

a {Positive even numbers < 10}{2, 4, 6, 8, 10}

b {Positive prime numbers > 10 and < 20} {11, 13, 17, 19}

c {Positive odd numbers $\leqslant 9$}{1, 3, 5, 7}

d {Square numbers < 10}{1, 2, 4, 9}

e {Square numbers > 10 and < 20} {1, 2, 4, 9, 12, 16}

21) $\mathscr{E} = \{$Whole numbers $x: x \geqslant 3$ and $< 7\}$. What is the set of values of x?

a {2, 3, 4, 5, 6, 7}   **b** {3, 4, 5, 6, 7}

c {1, 2, 3, 4, 5, 6}   **d** {3, 4, 5, 6}

e {2, 3, 4, 5, 6}

22) ℰ = {A pack of playing cards without Jokers}

R = {Aces}

S = {Picture cards}

H = {All hearts}

What are the members of $(R \cup S \cup H)'$?

a {diamonds, spades, clubs}

b {2, 3, 4, 5, 6, 7, 8, 9, 10 of spades, clubs and diamonds}

c {2, 3, 4, 5, 6, 7, 8, 9, 10, Jack, Queen, King of spades, clubs and diamonds}

d {1, 2, 3, 4, 5, 6, 7, 8, 9, 10, Jack, Queen, King of spades, clubs and diamonds}

e {1, 2, 3, 4, 5, 6, 7, 8, 9, 10 of spades, clubs and diamonds}

23) The point $P(3, 1)$ is reflected in the x-axis $(y = 0)$. What are the co-ordinates of the point P'?

a $(3, -1)$ b $(-3, 1)$ c $(-3, -1)$

d $(-1, -3)$ e $(-1, 3)$

24) What is the column vector of the translation which will map the point $(4, 2)$ on to the image $(6, 1)$?

a $\begin{pmatrix} 2 \\ -1 \end{pmatrix}$ b $\begin{pmatrix} 2 \\ 1 \end{pmatrix}$ c $\begin{pmatrix} -2 \\ 1 \end{pmatrix}$

d $\begin{pmatrix} 1 \\ 2 \end{pmatrix}$ e $\begin{pmatrix} 1 \\ -2 \end{pmatrix}$

25) The point $(0, 0)$ is given a translation of $\begin{pmatrix} 4 \\ -2 \end{pmatrix}$ followed by a reflection in the x-axis.

What are the co-ordinates of the final image?

a $(2, -4)$ b $(-2, 4)$ c $(-4, -2)$

d $(-4, 2)$ e $(4, 2)$

26) 6 x 5 (mod 7) equals

a 1   b 2   c 30   d 4   e 5

27) How many subsets of $\{v, w, x, y\}$ are there which contain just three elements?

a 6   b 2   c 3   d 4   e 5

28) Which of the functions on the set $\{1, 2, 3, 4\}$ does Fig. 5 represent?

a $f(x) = 2x$ b $f(x) = 2x + 2$

c $f(x) = 2x - 2$ d $f(x) = \frac{1}{2}x + 2$

e $f(x) = \frac{1}{2}x - 2$

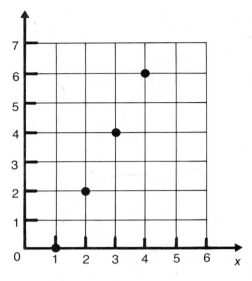

Fig. 5

29) If I pick a ball at random out of a bag containing 5 white, 2 blue and 4 green balls, what is the probability that the ball picked out is NOT white?

a $\frac{5}{11}$ b $\frac{2}{11}$ c $\frac{4}{11}$

d $\frac{8}{121}$ e $\frac{6}{11}$

30) What is the reflection of $(3, -2)$ in the line $y = 1$?

a $(-3, -2)$ b $(3, 2)$ c $(-2, -2)$

d $(3, 4)$ e $(-2, 3)$

31) Which of the binary numbers below represent the denary number 52?

a 1 0 0 1 1 0   b 1 1 1 1 1 0

c 1 1 0 1 1 1   d 1 1 0 1 0 0

e 1 1 0 1 1 0

32) The mode of the histogram (Fig. 6) is:

a 0   b 1   c 2   d 3   e 5

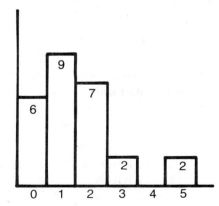

Fig. 6

33) The heights of 5 people are 120 cm, 116 cm, 140 cm, 178 cm, 116 cm. The median height is:

a 120 cm   b 116 cm   c 140 cm

d 178 cm   e 116 cm

34) If $X = \begin{pmatrix} -4 & 3 \\ 2 & -1 \end{pmatrix}$ then X^2 equals:

a $\begin{pmatrix} 22 & -15 \\ -10 & 7 \end{pmatrix}$ b $\begin{pmatrix} 16 & 9 \\ 4 & 1 \end{pmatrix}$

c $\begin{pmatrix} -8 & 6 \\ 4 & -2 \end{pmatrix}$ d $\begin{pmatrix} -16 & 9 \\ 4 & -1 \end{pmatrix}$

e $\begin{pmatrix} 22 & -10 \\ -15 & 7 \end{pmatrix}$

35) Which of the following is the largest number?

a 1111_2 b 21_3 c 13_4 d 12_5

e 11_6

36) What is the base of the following addition sum?

$$\begin{array}{r} 324 \\ 135 \\ \hline 503 \\ \hline \end{array}$$

a 2   b 3   c 4   d 5   e 6

Questions 37 to 40 refer to the composition tables shown below, which give the results of applying operations $\square$, $*$, $\circ$, $\bullet$, and $\triangle$ to the elements of the set $\{1, 2, 3\}$.

$\square$	1	2	3
1	2	3	1
2	3	1	2
3	1	2	3

$*$	1	2	3
1	1	2	3
2	2	0	2
3	3	2	1

$\circ$	1	2	3
1	1	2	3
2	3	1	2
3	2	3	1

$\bullet$	1	2	3
1	2	1	2
2	1	2	3
3	2	3	1

$\triangle$	1	2	3
1	1	2	3
2	2	1	3
3	3	3	1

37) Under which operation is the system not closed?

a $\square$ b $*$ c $\circ$ d $\bullet$ e $\triangle$

38) Under which operation is the system not commutative?

a $\square$ b $*$ c $\circ$ d $\bullet$ e $\triangle$

39) Under which operation has the system no identity element?

a $\square$ b $*$ c $\circ$ d $\bullet$ e $\triangle$

40) Under which operation is each element its own inverse?

a $\square$ b $*$ c $\circ$ d $\bullet$ e $\triangle$

Miscellaneous Exercise

Exercise 229

1) If $p = \begin{pmatrix} 4 \\ 2 \end{pmatrix}$ and $q = \begin{pmatrix} 2 \\ 3 \end{pmatrix}$ calculate
$p - 2q$. (A.E.B. 1975)

2) In arithmetic modulo 5 evaluate:
(a) 4×3 (b) $4 \div 3$ (A.E.B. 1975)

3) Express $1\,0\,1\,1\,1\,1_2$ as a number in base 8. (A.E.B. 1975)

4) Copy Fig. 1 and draw and label a Venn diagram to illustrate the relationship between the sets

$$\mathcal{E} = \{\text{natural numbers}\}$$
$$P = \{\text{even numbers}\}$$
$$Q = \{\text{multiples of 3}\}$$

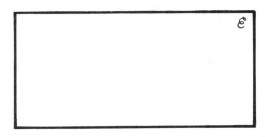

Fig. 1

Write each of the numbers 3, 4, 5 and 6 in the appropriate position on your Venn diagram.
Describe a set R such that $Q \cap P = R$.
(A.E.B. 1975)

5) Transformations A and B are represented by matrices $\begin{pmatrix} 1 & 0 \\ 0 & -1 \end{pmatrix}$ and $\begin{pmatrix} -1 & 0 \\ 0 & 1 \end{pmatrix}$ respectively. A maps the square S onto S_1 and B maps square S onto S_2.

(a) Copy Fig. 2, then draw and label clearly S_1 and S_2.

(b) Write down a matrix which represents the mapping of S_1 directly onto S_2. (A.E.B. 1975)

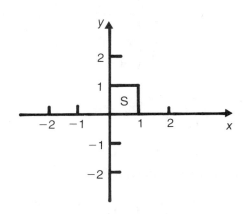

Fig. 2

6) The table shows the number of goals scored in 46 football matches on the same day.

Total number of goals in a match	0	1	2	3	4	5	6
Number of matches with this score	7	11	6	7	7	5	3

(a) State the mode of the distribution.
(b) Find the median.
(c) Calculate the mean number of goals scored per match. (A.E.B. 1975)

7) Fig. 3 represents two sets A and B which are subsets of the universal set $\mathcal{E}$, shade the region which represents $(A \cup B) \cap B'$. (J.M.B.)

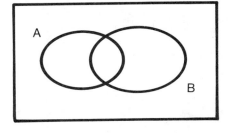

Fig. 3

8) Obtain the median of the five numbers 2, 1, 5, 1, 6. (J.M.B.)

9) Draw a mapping diagram for the function $x \to 3^x$ defined on the domain $\{0, 1, 2\}$. (J.M.B.)

10) In an election for a sixth form representative 72 voted for Brown, 16 for

435

Jones and 8 for Smith. Represent this information on a circular (pie) diagram. (J.M.B.)

11) If $a = \begin{pmatrix} 1 \\ 3 \end{pmatrix}$, $b = \begin{pmatrix} 2 \\ 5 \end{pmatrix}$, $c = \begin{pmatrix} 7 \\ 18 \end{pmatrix}$ find the value of n if $a + nb = c$. (A.E.B. 1975)

12) Express 27_{10} as a number in base 2. (A.E.B. 1975)

13) In arithmetic modulo 5 evaluate
(a) 3×3 (b) the square root of 4. (A.E.B. 1975)

14) $\mathscr{E} = \{5, 6, 7, 8, 9, 10, 11, 12, 13\}$. List the members of the following subsets of $\mathscr{E}$.
(a) $\{x: 54 - 5x = 19\}$;
(b) a set X such that $X \cup \mathscr{E} = \mathscr{E}$. (A.E.B. 1975)

15) $A = \begin{pmatrix} 1 & 2 \\ 0 & 3 \end{pmatrix}$ and $B = \begin{pmatrix} 1 \\ 4 \end{pmatrix}$. Calculate where possible:
(a) $A + B$ (b) AB (c) A^{-1}. (A.E.B. 1975)

16) (a) Express 64_{10} as a number in base eight.
(b) Express 1111_2 as a number in base eight. (A.E.B. 1976)

17) If $a = \begin{pmatrix} -1 \\ 2 \end{pmatrix}$ and $b = \begin{pmatrix} 3 \\ 5 \end{pmatrix}$, calculate:
(a) $a + b$
(b) x, if $a + x = 2b$. (A.E.B. 1976)

18) In arithmetic modulo 5 evaluate:
(a) 3×3 (b) 2^4 (A.E.B. 1976)

19) A transformation which maps L onto L' is represented by the matrix $\begin{pmatrix} 3 & 1 \\ 5 & 2 \end{pmatrix}$. Find the inverse matrix which maps L' onto L. (A.E.B. 1976)

20) $\mathscr{E} = \{x: x \text{ is a positive integer}\}$, $A = \{x: x < 10\}$ and $B = \{x: x \geqslant 3\}$.
(a) List the members of $A \cap B$.
(b) Find $n(B')$. (A.E.B. 1976)

21) (a) What transformation does the matrix $\begin{pmatrix} -1 & 0 \\ 0 & 1 \end{pmatrix}$ represent?
(b) Write down the matrix which represents an anticlockwise rotation of $90°$ about the origin. (A.E.B. 1976)

22) The sets A, B, C are subsets of the universal set $\{x: x \text{ is an integer and } 10 \leqslant x \leqslant 30\}$. $A = \{x: x \text{ is a multiple of } 5\}$, $B = \{x: 12 \leqslant x \leqslant 18\}$, $C = \{x: x \text{ is a prime number}\}$. Find (a) $A' \cap B$ (b) $n(C)$. (J.M.B.)

23) Given that $f: x \to \dfrac{3}{x}$ for the domain $\{x: x \text{ is a real number and } x \neq 0\}$,
(a) calculate $f(-3)$,
(b) calculate x when $f(x) = 5$. (J.M.B.)

24) A transformation is defined by the matrix $\begin{pmatrix} 3 & 2 \\ 1 & 2 \end{pmatrix}$. Find the co-ordinates of the point which is mapped onto $(4, 1)$ by this transformation. (J.M.B.)

25) A translation maps the point $P(6, 3)$ onto the point $P'(3, 5)$. State the co-ordinates of Q', the image of $Q(-1, -2)$ under the same translation. (J.M.B.)

26) Write down (in binary notation) the number which is four times the binary number $1\,0\,1\,1$. (J.M.B.)

27) The function $x \to (x-1)(x-3)$ is defined on the domain $\{0, 1, 2, 3\}$. Complete the mapping diagram for the function, part of which is shown in Fig. 4. (J.M.B.)

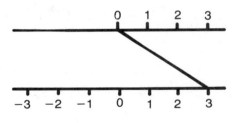

Fig. 4

28) On a particular day, a boy spent 6 hours working, 10 hours playing and 8 hours sleeping. Illustrate this information in a circular diagram, indicating the size of the angle at the centre of the circle for each sector. (J.M.B.)

29) The minimum air temperatures on four consecutive days were $+5°, +2°, -3°, -1°$. Find the minimum air temperature on the fifth day given that the arithmetic mean of the five temperatures was $-1°$. (J.M.B.)

30) Find the matrix A such that
$$A \begin{pmatrix} 3 & 4 \\ 1 & 2 \end{pmatrix} = \begin{pmatrix} 1 & 0 \\ 0 & 1 \end{pmatrix} \qquad \text{(J.M.B.)}$$

Important Data and Formulae

MATHEMATICAL SYMBOLS

$=$ is equal to

$\neq$ is not equal to

$\approx$ is approximately equal to

$<$ is less than

$\leqslant$ is less than or equal to

$>$ is greater than

$\geqslant$ is greater than or equal to

$\Rightarrow$ implies; if . . . then

$\Leftrightarrow$ implies and is implied by; if and only if

Profit % $= \dfrac{\text{selling price} - \text{cost price}}{\text{cost price}} \times 100$

Loss % $= \dfrac{\text{cost price} - \text{selling price}}{\text{cost price}} \times 100$

Simple interest: $\quad I = \dfrac{PRT}{100}$

Compound interest:

$$A = P\left(1 + \frac{r}{100}\right)^n$$

Factors:

$$a^2 + 2ab + b^2 = (a + b)^2$$
$$a^2 - 2ab + b^2 = (a - b)^2$$
$$a^2 - b^2 = (a + b)(a - b)$$

Indices:

$$a^m \times a^n = a^{m+n}$$
$$a^m \div a^n = a^{m-n}$$
$$(a^m)^n = a^{mn}$$
$$a^{m/n} = \sqrt[n]{a^m}$$
$$a^0 = 1$$
$$a^{-m} = \frac{1}{a^m}$$

Logarithms:

$$\log(ab) = \log a + \log b$$
$$\log\left(\frac{a}{b}\right) = \log a - \log b$$
$$\log a^m = m \log a$$
$$\log \sqrt[m]{a} = \frac{1}{m} \log a$$
$$\text{number} = \text{base}^{\text{logarithm}}$$

Quadratic equation:

If $\quad ax^2 + bx + c = 0$

then $\quad x = \dfrac{-b \pm \sqrt{b^2 - 4ac}}{2a}$

MENSURATION

Circumference of circle, $\quad C = \pi D = 2\pi r$

Area of circle, $\quad A = \pi r^2$

Area of a triangle $= \frac{1}{2}$ base $\times$ height, $\quad$ or $\frac{1}{2}ab \sin C$, or $\sqrt{s(s-a)(s-b)(s-c)}$

Area of a trapezium $= \frac{1}{2}(a + b)h$

Area of curved surface of a cylinder $= 2\pi rh$

Area of curved surface of a cone $= \pi rl$, $\quad$ where l is the 'slant height'

Area of surface of a sphere $= 4\pi r^2$

Volume of a prism $=$ area of cross-section $\times$ length

Volume of a cylinder $= \pi r^2 h$

Volume of a pyramid $= \frac{1}{3}$ area of base $\times$ height

Volume of a cone $= \frac{1}{3}\pi r^2 h$

Volume of a sphere $= \frac{4}{3}\pi r^3$

Density $= \dfrac{\text{mass}}{\text{volume}}$

Relative density $= \dfrac{\text{density of substance}}{\text{density of water}}$

Flow of water: Quantity flowing = area of bore of pipe × speed of flow

Similar solids: $\dfrac{A_1}{A_2} = \left(\dfrac{h_1}{h_2}\right)^2$

$\dfrac{V_1}{V_2} = \left(\dfrac{h_1}{h_2}\right)^3$

Equation of straight line:

$$y = mx + c$$

Direct variation:

If $y \propto x$ then $y = kx$

Inverse variation:

If $y \propto \dfrac{1}{x}$ then $y = \dfrac{k}{x}$

Differentiation:

If $y = ax^n$ then $\dfrac{dy}{dx} = nax^{n-1}$

Velocity: $v = \dfrac{ds}{dt}$

Acceleration: $a = \dfrac{dv}{dt}$

For max or min: $\dfrac{dy}{dx} = 0$

Integration: $\displaystyle\int ax^n \; dx = \dfrac{ax^{n+1}}{n+1} + c$

Area under a curve: $\displaystyle\int_a^b y \; dx$

Distance $= \displaystyle\int v \; dt$

Velocity $= \displaystyle\int a \; dt$

Volume of solid of revolution $= \displaystyle\int_a^b \pi y^2 \; dx$

MEASURES

Lengths: 1000 mm = 1 m: 100 cm = 1 m: 1000 m = 1 km

Area: 1 hectare (ha) = 10 000 m²

Cubic Capacity: 1 litre = 1000 cm³

$= \dfrac{1}{1000}$ m³

Speed: 18 km/h = 5 m/s

Mass: 1000 g = 1 kg

Pythagoras' theorem

$$a^2 = b^2 + c^2$$

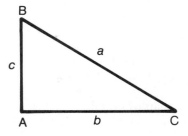

TRIGONOMETRY

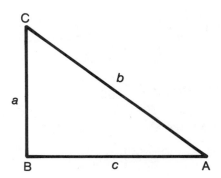

$\sin A = \dfrac{\text{side opposite to A}}{\text{hypotenuse}} = \dfrac{a}{b}$

$\cos A = \dfrac{\text{side adjacent to A}}{\text{hypotenuse}} = \dfrac{c}{b}$

$\tan A = \dfrac{\text{side opposite to A}}{\text{side adjacent to A}} = \dfrac{a}{c}$

$\tan A = \dfrac{\sin A}{\cos A}$

$$\sin^2 A + \cos^2 A = 1$$

Sine rule

$$\frac{a}{\sin A} = \frac{b}{\sin B} = \frac{c}{\sin C}$$

Cosine rule

$$a^2 = b^2 + c^2 - 2bc \cos A$$

Polar co-ordinates

$$x = r \cos \theta$$

$$y = r \sin \theta$$

$$\tan \theta = \frac{y}{x}$$

$$r = \sqrt{x^2 + y^2}$$

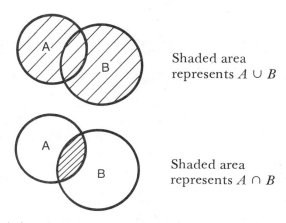

SETS

$\&$ stands for the universal set.

$A = \{1, 3, 5\}$ means that A is the set of the first three odd integers.

$5 \in A$ means that 5 is an element of set A.

$A \subset B$ means that A is a subset of B.

$B \supset A$ means that B includes A (i.e. A is a subset of B).

A' is the complement of A (i.e. the elements of $\& -$ the elements of A).

$A \cap B$ is the intersection of sets A and B.

$A \cup B$ is the union of sets A and B.

Shaded area represents $A \cup B$

Shaded area represents $A \cap B$

$n(A)$ means the number of elements in A.

$$n(A \cup B) = n(A) + n(B) - n(A \cap B)$$

$$n(A \cup B \cup C) = n(A) + n(B) + n(C)$$
$$- n(A \cap B) - n(A \cap C)$$
$$- n(B \cap C) + n(A \cap B \cap C)$$

$A \longleftrightarrow B$ means that A is equivalent to B (i.e. that the two sets A and B have the same number of elements or $n(A) = n(B)$).

MATRICES

$$\begin{pmatrix} a & b \\ c & d \end{pmatrix} + \begin{pmatrix} u & v \\ w & x \end{pmatrix} = \begin{pmatrix} a+u & b+v \\ c+w & d+x \end{pmatrix}$$

$$\begin{pmatrix} a & b \\ c & d \end{pmatrix} \begin{pmatrix} u & v \\ w & x \end{pmatrix} = \begin{pmatrix} au+bw & av+bx \\ cu+dw & cv+dx \end{pmatrix}$$

If $A = \begin{pmatrix} a & b \\ c & d \end{pmatrix}$; $A^{-1} = \dfrac{1}{ad-bc} \begin{pmatrix} d & -b \\ -c & a \end{pmatrix}$

If $AX = K$ then $X = A^{-1}K$

If $U = \begin{pmatrix} a \\ b \end{pmatrix}$ and $V = \begin{pmatrix} x \\ y \end{pmatrix}$ then

$$U + V = \begin{pmatrix} a+x \\ b+y \end{pmatrix}$$

NUMBER SYSTEMS

The number 4325 in base x means
$$5 \times x^0 + 2 \times x^1 + 3 \times x^2 + 4 \times x^3.$$

STATISTICS

$$\text{Arithmetic mean} = \frac{x_1 f_1 + x_2 f_2 + x_3 f_3 + \ldots}{f_1 + f_2 + f_3 + \ldots}$$

Probability

$$\text{probability} = \frac{\text{number of ways in which an event can happen}}{\text{total number of possibilities}}$$

If $p_1, p_2, p_3, \ldots$ are the separate probabilities of $1, 2, 3, \ldots$ mutually exclusive events then the probability of *one* of the events happening is $p = p_1 + p_2 + p_3 + \ldots$

If $p_1, p_2, p_3 \ldots$ are the separate probabilities of $1, 2, 3, \ldots$ independent events then the probability of *all* of the events happening is $p = p_1 \times p_2 \times p_3 \times \ldots$

TABLE OF SQUARES

x	0	1	2	3	4	5	6	7	8	9	1	2	3	4	5	6	7	8	9
1.0	1.000	1.020	1.040	1.061	1.082	1.103	1.124	1.145	1.166	1.188	2	4	6	8	10	13	15	17	19
1.1	1.210	1.232	1.254	1.277	1.300	1.323	1.346	1.369	1.392	1.416	2	5	7	9	11	14	16	18	21
1.2	1.440	1.464	1.488	1.513	1.538	1.563	1.588	1.613	1.638	1.664	2	5	7	10	12	15	17	20	22
1.3	1.690	1.716	1.742	1.769	1.796	1.823	1.850	1.877	1.904	1.932	3	5	8	11	13	16	19	22	24
1.4	1.960	1.988	2.016	2.045	2.074	2.103	2.132	2.161	2.190	2.220	3	6	9	12	14	17	20	23	26
1.5	2.250	2.280	2.310	2.341	2.372	2.403	2.434	2.465	2.496	2.528	3	6	9	12	15	19	22	25	28
1.6	2.560	2.592	2.624	2.657	2.690	2.723	2.756	2.789	2.822	2.856	3	7	10	13	16	20	23	26	30
1.7	2.890	2.924	2.958	2.993	3.028	3.063	3.098	3.133	3.168	3.204	3	7	10	14	17	21	24	28	31
1.8	3.240	3.276	3.312	3.349	3.386	3.423	3.460	3.497	3.534	3.572	4	7	11	15	18	22	26	30	33
1.9	3.610	3.648	3.686	3.725	3.764	3.803	3.842	3.881	3.920	3.960	4	8	12	16	19	23	27	31	35
2.0	4.000	4.040	4.080	4.121	4.162	4.203	4.244	4.285	4.326	4.368	4	8	12	16	20	25	29	33	37
2.1	4.410	4.452	4.494	4.537	4.580	4.623	4.666	4.709	4.752	4.796	4	9	13	17	21	26	30	34	39
2.2	4.840	4.884	4.928	4.973	5.018	5.063	5.108	5.153	5.198	5.244	4	9	13	18	22	27	31	36	40
2.3	5.290	5.336	5.382	5.429	5.476	5.523	5.570	5.617	5.664	5.712	5	9	14	19	23	28	33	38	42
2.4	5.760	5.808	5.856	5.905	5.954	6.003	6.052	6.101	6.150	6.200	5	10	15	20	24	29	34	39	44
2.5	6.250	6.300	6.350	6.401	6.452	6.503	6.554	6.605	6.656	6.708	5	10	15	20	25	31	36	41	46
2.6	6.760	6.812	6.864	6.917	6.970	7.023	7.076	7.129	7.182	7.236	5	11	16	21	26	32	37	42	48
2.7	7.290	7.344	7.398	7.453	7.508	7.563	7.618	7.673	7.728	7.784	5	11	16	22	27	33	38	44	49
2.8	7.840	7.896	7.952	8.009	8.066	8.123	8.180	8.237	8.294	8.352	6	11	17	23	28	34	40	46	51
2.9	8.410	8.468	8.526	8.585	8.644	8.703	8.762	8.821	8.880	8.940	6	12	18	24	29	35	41	47	53
3.0	9.000	9.060	9.120	9.181	9.242	9.303	9.364	9.425	9.486	9.548	6	12	18	24	30	37	43	49	55
3.1	9.610	9.672	9.734	9.797	9.860	9.923	9.986	10.05	10.11	10.18	6	13	19	25	31	38	44	50	57
3.2	10.24	10.30	10.37	10.43	10.50	10.56	10.63	10.69	10.76	10.82	1	1	2	3	3	4	5	5	6
3.3	10.89	10.96	11.02	11.09	11.16	11.22	11.29	11.36	11.42	11.49	1	1	2	3	3	4	5	5	6
3.4	11.56	11.63	11.70	11.76	11.83	11.90	11.97	12.04	12.11	12.18	1	1	2	3	3	4	5	6	6
3.5	12.25	12.32	12.39	12.46	12.53	12.60	12.67	12.74	12.82	12.89	1	1	2	3	4	4	5	6	6
3.6	12.96	13.03	13.10	13.18	13.25	13.32	13.40	13.47	13.54	13.62	1	1	2	3	4	4	5	6	7
3.7	13.69	13.76	13.84	13.91	13.99	14.06	14.14	14.21	14.29	14.36	1	2	2	3	4	5	5	6	7
3.8	14.44	14.52	14.59	14.67	14.75	14.82	14.90	14.98	15.05	15.13	1	2	2	3	4	5	5	6	7
3.9	15.21	15.29	15.37	15.44	15.52	15.60	15.68	15.76	15.84	15.92	1	2	2	3	4	5	6	6	7
4.0	16.00	16.08	16.16	16.24	16.32	16.40	16.48	16.56	16.65	16.73	1	2	2	3	4	5	6	6	7
4.1	16.81	16.89	16.97	17.06	17.14	17.22	17.31	17.39	17.47	17.56	1	2	2	3	4	5	6	7	7
4.2	17.64	17.72	17.81	17.89	17.98	18.06	18.15	18.23	18.32	18.40	1	2	3	3	4	5	6	7	8
4.3	18.49	18.58	18.66	18.75	18.84	18.92	19.01	19.10	19.18	19.27	1	2	3	3	4	5	6	7	8
4.4	19.36	19.45	19.54	19.62	19.71	19.80	19.89	19.98	20.07	20.16	1	2	3	4	4	5	6	7	8
4.5	20.25	20.34	20.43	20.52	20.61	20.70	20.79	20.88	20.98	21.07	1	2	3	4	5	5	6	7	8
4.6	21.16	21.25	21.34	21.44	21.53	21.62	21.72	21.81	21.90	22.00	1	2	3	4	5	6	7	7	8
4.7	22.09	22.18	22.28	22.37	22.47	22.56	22.66	22.75	22.85	22.94	1	2	3	4	5	6	7	8	9
4.8	23.04	23.14	23.23	23.33	23.43	23.52	23.62	23.72	23.81	23.91	1	2	3	4	5	6	7	8	9
4.9	24.01	24.11	24.21	24.30	24.40	24.50	24.60	24.70	24.80	24.90	1	2	3	4	5	6	7	8	9
5.0	25.00	25.10	25.20	25.30	25.40	25.50	25.60	25.70	25.81	25.91	1	2	3	4	5	6	7	8	9
5.1	26.01	26.11	26.21	26.32	26.42	26.52	26.63	26.73	26.83	26.94	1	2	3	4	5	6	7	8	9
5.2	27.04	27.14	27.25	27.35	27.46	27.56	27.67	27.77	27.88	27.98	1	2	3	4	5	6	7	8	9
5.3	28.09	28.20	28.30	28.41	28.52	28.62	28.73	28.84	28.94	29.05	1	2	3	4	5	6	7	9	10
5.4	29.16	29.27	29.38	29.48	29.59	29.70	29.81	29.92	30.03	30.14	1	2	3	4	5	7	8	9	10

x	0	1	2	3	4	5	6	7	8	9	1	2	3	4	5	6	7	8	9
5.5	30.25	30.36	30.47	30.58	30.69	30.80	30.91	31.02	31.14	31.25	1	2	3	4	6	7	8	9	10
5.6	31.36	31.47	31.58	31.70	31.81	31.92	32.04	32.15	32.26	32.38	1	2	3	5	6	7	8	9	10
5.7	32.49	32.60	32.72	32.83	32.95	33.06	33.18	33.29	33.41	33.52	1	2	3	5	6	7	8	9	10
5.8	33.64	33.76	33.87	33.99	34.11	34.22	34.34	34.46	34.57	34.69	1	2	4	5	6	7	8	9	11
5.9	34.81	34.93	35.05	35.16	35.28	35.40	35.52	35.64	35.76	35.88	1	2	4	5	6	7	8	10	11
6.0	36.00	36.12	36.24	36.36	36.48	36.60	36.72	36.84	36.97	37.09	1	2	4	5	6	7	9	10	11
6.1	37.21	37.33	37.45	37.58	37.70	37.82	37.95	38.07	38.19	38.32	1	2	4	5	6	7	9	10	11
6.2	38.44	38.56	38.69	38.81	38.94	39.06	39.19	39.31	39.44	39.56	1	3	4	5	6	8	9	10	11
6.3	39.69	39.82	39.94	40.07	40.20	40.32	40.45	40.58	40.70	40.83	1	3	4	5	6	8	9	10	11
6.4	40.96	41.09	41.22	41.34	41.47	41.60	41.73	41.86	41.99	42.12	1	3	4	5	6	8	9	10	12
6.5	42.25	42.38	42.51	42.64	42.77	42.90	43.03	43.16	43.30	43.43	1	3	4	5	7	8	9	10	12
6.6	43.56	43.69	43.82	43.96	44.09	44.22	44.36	44.49	44.62	44.76	1	3	4	5	7	8	9	11	12
6.7	44.89	45.02	45.16	45.29	45.43	45.56	45.70	45.83	45.97	46.10	1	3	4	5	7	8	9	11	12
6.8	46.24	46.38	46.51	46.65	46.79	46.92	47.06	47.20	47.33	47.47	1	3	4	5	7	8	10	11	12
6.9	47.61	47.75	47.89	48.02	48.16	48.30	48.44	48.58	48.72	48.86	1	3	4	6	7	8	10	11	13
7.0	49.00	49.14	49.28	49.42	49.56	49.70	49.84	49.98	50.13	50.27	1	3	4	6	7	8	10	11	13
7.1	50.41	50.55	50.69	50.84	50.98	51.12	51.27	51.41	51.55	51.70	1	3	4	6	7	9	10	11	13
7.2	51.84	51.98	52.13	52.27	52.42	52.56	52.71	52.85	53.00	53.14	1	3	4	6	7	9	10	12	13
7.3	53.29	53.44	53.58	53.73	53.88	54.02	54.17	54.32	54.46	54.61	1	3	4	6	7	9	10	12	13
7.4	54.76	54.91	55.06	55.20	55.35	55.50	55.65	55.80	55.95	56.10	1	3	4	6	7	9	10	12	13
7.5	56.25	56.40	56.55	56.70	56.85	57.00	57.15	57.30	57.46	57.61	2	3	5	6	8	9	11	12	14
7.6	57.76	57.91	58.06	58.22	58.37	58.52	58.68	58.83	58.98	59.14	2	3	5	6	8	9	11	12	14
7.7	59.29	59.44	59.60	59.75	59.91	60.06	60.22	60.37	60.53	60.68	2	3	5	6	8	9	11	12	14
7.8	60.84	61.00	61.15	61.31	61.47	61.62	61.78	61.94	62.09	62.25	2	3	5	6	8	9	11	13	14
7.9	62.41	62.57	62.73	62.88	63.04	63.20	63.36	63.52	63.68	63.84	2	3	5	6	8	10	11	13	14
8.0	64.00	64.16	64.32	64.48	64.64	64.80	64.96	65.12	65.29	65.45	2	3	5	6	8	10	11	13	14
8.1	65.61	65.77	65.93	66.10	66.26	66.42	66.59	66.75	66.91	67.08	2	3	5	7	8	10	11	13	15
8.2	67.24	67.40	67.57	67.73	67.90	68.06	68.23	68.39	68.56	68.72	2	3	5	7	8	10	12	13	15
8.3	68.89	69.06	69.22	69.39	69.56	69.72	69.89	70.06	70.22	70.39	2	3	5	7	8	10	12	13	15
8.4	70.56	70.73	70.90	71.06	71.23	71.40	71.57	71.74	71.91	72.08	2	3	5	7	8	10	12	14	15
8.5	72.25	72.42	72.59	72.76	72.93	73.10	73.27	73.44	73.62	73.79	2	3	5	7	9	10	12	14	15
8.6	73.96	74.13	74.30	74.48	74.65	74.82	75.00	75.17	75.34	75.52	2	3	5	7	9	10	12	14	16
8.7	75.69	75.86	76.04	76.21	76.39	76.56	76.74	76.91	77.09	77.26	2	4	5	7	9	11	12	14	16
8.8	77.44	77.62	77.79	77.97	78.15	78.32	78.50	78.68	78.85	79.03	2	4	5	7	9	11	12	14	16
8.9	79.21	79.39	79.57	79.74	79.92	80.10	80.28	80.46	80.64	80.82	2	4	5	7	9	11	13	14	16
9.0	81.00	81.18	81.36	81.54	81.72	81.90	82.08	82.26	82.45	82.63	2	4	5	7	9	11	13	14	16
9.1	82.81	82.99	83.17	83.36	83.54	83.72	83.91	84.09	84.27	84.46	2	4	5	7	9	11	13	15	16
9.2	84.64	84.82	85.01	85.19	85.38	85.56	85.75	85.93	86.12	86.30	2	4	6	7	9	11	13	15	17
9.3	86.49	86.68	86.86	87.05	87.24	87.42	87.61	87.80	87.98	88.17	2	4	6	7	9	11	13	15	17
9.4	88.36	88.55	88.74	88.92	89.11	89.30	89.49	89.68	89.87	90.06	2	4	6	7	9	11	13	15	17
9.5	90.25	90.44	90.63	90.82	91.01	91.20	91.39	91.58	91.78	91.97	2	4	6	8	10	11	13	15	17
9.6	92.16	92.35	92.54	92.74	92.93	93.12	93.32	93.51	93.70	93.90	2	4	6	8	10	12	14	15	17
9.7	94.09	94.28	94.48	94.67	94.87	95.06	95.26	95.45	95.65	95.84	2	4	6	8	10	12	14	16	18
9.8	96.04	96.24	96.43	96.63	96.83	97.02	97.22	97.42	97.61	97.81	2	4	6	8	10	12	14	16	18
9.9	98.01	98.21	98.41	98.60	98.80	99.00	99.20	99.40	99.60	99.80	2	4	6	8	10	12	14	16	18

TABLE OF SQUARE ROOTS 1—10

	0	1	2	3	4	5	6	7	8	9
1.0	1.000	1.005	1.010	1.015	1.020	1.025	1.030	1.034	1.039	1.044
1.1	1.049	1.054	1.058	1.063	1.068	1.072	1.077	1.082	1.086	1.091
1.2	1.095	1.100	1.105	1.109	1.114	1.118	1.122	1.127	1.131	1.136
1.3	1.140	1.145	1.149	1.153	1.158	1.162	1.166	1.170	1.175	1.179
1.4	1.183	1.187	1.192	1.196	1.200	1.204	1.208	1.212	1.217	1.221
1.5	1.225	1.229	1.233	1.237	1.241	1.245	1.249	1.253	1.257	1.261
1.6	1.265	1.269	1.273	1.277	1.281	1.285	1.288	1.292	1.296	1.300
1.7	1.304	1.308	1.311	1.315	1.319	1.323	1.327	1.330	1.334	1.338
1.8	1.342	1.345	1.349	1.353	1.356	1.360	1.364	1.367	1.371	1.375
1.9	1.378	1.382	1.386	1.389	1.393	1.396	1.400	1.404	1.407	1.411
2.0	1.414	1.418	1.421	1.425	1.428	1.432	1.435	1.439	1.442	1.446
2.1	1.449	1.453	1.456	1.459	1.463	1.466	1.470	1.473	1.476	1.480
2.2	1.483	1.487	1.490	1.493	1.497	1.500	1.503	1.507	1.510	1.513
2.3	1.517	1.520	1.523	1.526	1.530	1.533	1.536	1.539	1.543	1.546
2.4	1.549	1.552	1.556	1.559	1.562	1.565	1.568	1.572	1.575	1.578
2.5	1.581	1.584	1.587	1.591	1.594	1.597	1.600	1.603	1.606	1.609
2.6	1.612	1.616	1.619	1.622	1.625	1.628	1.631	1.634	1.637	1.640
2.7	1.643	1.646	1.649	1.652	1.655	1.658	1.661	1.664	1.667	1.670
2.8	1.673	1.676	1.679	1.682	1.685	1.688	1.691	1.694	1.697	1.700
2.9	1.703	1.706	1.709	1.712	1.715	1.718	1.720	1.723	1.726	1.729
3.0	1.732	1.735	1.738	1.741	1.744	1.746	1.749	1.752	1.755	1.758
3.1	1.761	1.764	1.766	1.769	1.772	1.775	1.778	1.780	1.783	1.786
3.2	1.789	1.792	1.794	1.797	1.800	1.803	1.806	1.808	1.811	1.814
3.3	1.817	1.819	1.822	1.825	1.828	1.830	1.833	1.836	1.838	1.841
3.4	1.844	1.847	1.849	1.852	1.855	1.857	1.860	1.863	1.865	1.868
3.5	1.871	1.873	1.876	1.879	1.881	1.884	1.887	1.889	1.892	1.895
3.6	1.897	1.900	1.903	1.905	1.908	1.910	1.913	1.916	1.918	1.921
3.7	1.924	1.926	1.929	1.931	1.934	1.936	1.939	1.942	1.944	1.947
3.8	1.949	1.952	1.954	1.957	1.960	1.962	1.965	1.967	1.970	1.972
3.9	1.975	1.977	1.980	1.982	1.985	1.987	1.990	1.992	1.995	1.997
4.0	2.000	2.002	2.005	2.007	2.010	2.012	2.015	2.017	2.020	2.022
4.1	2.025	2.027	2.030	2.032	2.035	2.037	2.040	2.042	2.045	2.047
4.2	2.049	2.052	2.054	2.057	2.059	2.062	2.064	2.066	2.069	2.071
4.3	2.074	2.076	2.078	2.081	2.083	2.086	2.088	2.090	2.093	2.095
4.4	2.098	2.100	2.102	2.105	2.107	2.110	2.112	2.114	2.117	2.119
4.5	2.121	2.124	2.126	2.128	2.131	2.133	2.135	2.138	2.140	2.142
4.6	2.145	2.147	2.149	2.152	2.154	2.156	2.159	2.161	2.163	2.166
4.7	2.168	2.170	2.173	2.175	2.177	2.179	2.182	2.184	2.186	2.189
4.8	2.191	2.193	2.195	2.198	2.200	2.202	2.205	2.207	2.209	2.211
4.9	2.214	2.216	2.218	2.220	2.223	2.225	2.227	2.229	2.232	2.234
5.0	2.236	2.238	2.241	2.243	2.245	2.247	2.249	2.252	2.254	2.256
5.1	2.258	2.261	2.263	2.265	2.267	2.269	2.272	2.274	2.276	2.278
5.2	2.280	2.283	2.285	2.287	2.289	2.291	2.293	2.296	2.298	2.300
5.3	2.302	2.304	2.307	2.309	2.311	2.313	2.315	2.317	2.319	2.322
5.4	2.324	2.326	2.328	2.330	2.332	2.335	2.337	2.339	2.341	2.343

TABLE OF SQUARE ROOTS 1—10 (continued)

	0	1	2	3	4	5	6	7	8	9
5.5	2.345	2.347	2.349	2.352	2.354	2.356	2.358	2.360	2.362	2.364
5.6	2.366	2.369	2.371	2.373	2.375	2.377	2.379	2.381	2.383	2.385
5.7	2.387	2.390	2.392	2.394	2.396	2.398	2.400	2.402	2.404	2.406
5.8	2.408	2.410	2.412	2.415	2.417	2.419	2.421	2.423	2.425	2.427
5.9	2.429	2.431	2.433	2.435	2.437	2.439	2.441	2.443	2.445	2.447
6.0	2.449	2.452	2.454	2.456	2.458	2.460	2.462	2.464	2.466	2.468
6.1	2.470	2.472	2.474	2.476	2.478	2.480	2.482	2.484	2.486	2.488
6.2	2.490	2.492	2.494	2.496	2.498	2.500	2.502	2.504	2.506	2.508
6.3	2.510	2.512	2.514	2.516	2.518	2.520	2.522	2.524	2.526	2.528
6.4	2.530	2.532	2.534	2.536	2.538	2.540	2.542	2.544	2.546	2.548
6.5	2.550	2.551	2.553	2.555	2.557	2.559	2.561	2.563	2.565	2.567
6.6	2.569	2.571	2.573	2.575	2.577	2.579	2.581	2.583	2.585	2.587
6.7	2.588	2.590	2.592	2.594	2.596	2.598	2.600	2.602	2.604	2.606
6.8	2.608	2.610	2.612	2.613	2.615	2.617	2.619	2.621	2.623	2.625
6.9	2.627	2.629	2.631	2.632	2.634	2.636	2.638	2.640	2.642	2.644
7.0	2.646	2.648	2.650	2.651	2.653	2.655	2.657	2.659	2.661	2.663
7.1	2.665	2.666	2.668	2.670	2.672	2.674	2.676	2.678	2.680	2.681
7.2	2.683	2.685	2.687	2.689	2.691	2.693	2.694	2.696	2.698	2.700
7.3	2.702	2.704	2.706	2.707	2.709	2.711	2.713	2.715	2.717	2.718
7.4	2.720	2.722	2.724	2.726	2.728	2.729	2.731	2.733	2.735	2.737
7.5	2.739	2.740	2.742	2.744	2.746	2.748	2.750	2.751	2.753	2.755
7.6	2.757	2.759	2.760	2.762	2.764	2.766	2.768	2.769	2.771	2.773
7.7	2.775	2.777	2.778	2.780	2.782	2.784	2.786	2.787	2.789	2.791
7.8	2.793	2.795	2.796	2.798	2.800	2.802	2.804	2.805	2.807	2.809
7.9	2.811	2.812	2.814	2.816	2.818	2.820	2.821	2.823	2.825	2.827
8.0	2.828	2.830	2.832	2.834	2.835	2.837	2.839	2.841	2.843	2.844
8.1	2.846	2.848	2.850	2.851	2.853	2.855	2.857	2.858	2.860	2.862
8.2	2.864	2.865	2.867	2.869	2.871	2.872	2.874	2.876	2.877	2.879
8.3	2.881	2.883	2.884	2.886	2.888	2.890	2.891	2.893	2.895	2.897
8.4	2.898	2.900	2.902	2.903	2.905	2.907	2.909	2.910	2.912	2.914
8.5	2.915	2.917	2.919	2.921	2.922	2.924	2.926	2.927	2.929	2.931
8.6	2.933	2.934	2.936	2.938	2.939	2.941	2.943	2.944	2.946	2.948
8.7	2.950	2.951	2.953	2.955	2.956	2.958	2.960	2.961	2.963	2.965
8.8	2.966	2.968	2.970	2.972	2.973	2.975	2.977	2.978	2.980	2.982
8.9	2.983	2.985	2.987	2.988	2.990	2.992	2.993	2.995	2.997	2.998
9.0	3.000	3.002	3.003	3.005	3.007	3.008	3.010	3.012	3.013	3.015
9.1	3.017	3.018	3.020	3.022	3.023	3.025	3.027	3.028	3.030	3.032
9.2	3.033	3.035	3.036	3.038	3.040	3.041	3.043	3.045	3.046	3.048
9.3	3.050	3.051	3.053	3.055	3.056	3.058	3.059	3.061	3.063	3.064
9.4	3.066	3.068	3.069	3.071	3.072	3.074	3.076	3.077	3.079	3.081
9.5	3.082	3.084	3.085	3.087	3.089	3.090	3.092	3.094	3.095	3.097
9.6	3.098	3.100	3.102	3.103	3.105	3.106	3.108	3.110	3.111	3.113
9.7	3.114	3.116	3.118	3.119	3.121	3.122	3.124	3.126	3.127	3.129
9.8	3.130	3.132	3.134	3.135	3.137	3.138	3.140	3.142	3.143	3.145
9.9	3.146	3.148	3.150	3.151	3.153	3.154	3.156	3.158	3.159	3.161

TABLE OF SQUARE ROOTS FROM 10—100

x	0	1	2	3	4	5	6	7	8	9	1	2	3	4	5	6	7	8	9
10	3.162	3.178	3.194	3.209	3.225	3.240	3.256	3.271	3.286	3.302	2	3	5	6	8	10	11	13	14
11	3.317	3.332	3.347	3.362	3.376	3.391	3.406	3.421	3.435	3.450	1	3	4	6	7	9	10	12	13
12	3.464	3.479	3.493	3.507	3.521	3.536	3.550	3.564	3.578	3.592	1	3	4	6	7	8	10	11	13
13	3.606	3.619	3.633	3.647	3.661	3.674	3.688	3.701	3.715	3.728	1	3	4	5	7	8	10	11	12
14	3.742	3.755	3.768	3.782	3.795	3.808	3.821	3.834	3.847	3.860	1	3	4	5	7	8	9	10	12
15	3.873	3.886	3.899	3.912	3.924	3.937	3.950	3.962	3.975	3.987	1	3	4	5	6	8	9	10	11
16	4.000	4.012	4.025	4.037	4.050	4.062	4.074	4.087	4.099	4.111	1	2	4	5	6	7	9	10	11
17	4.123	4.135	4.147	4.159	4.171	4.183	4.195	4.207	4.219	4.231	1	2	4	5	6	7	8	10	11
18	4.243	4.254	4.266	4.278	4.290	4.301	4.313	4.324	4.336	4.347	1	2	3	5	6	7	8	9	10
19	4.359	4.370	4.382	4.393	4.405	4.416	4.427	4.438	4.450	4.461	1	2	3	5	6	7	8	9	10
20	4.472	4.483	4.494	4.506	4.517	4.528	4.539	4.550	4.561	4.572	1	2	3	4	5	7	8	9	10
21	4.583	4.593	4.604	4.615	4.626	4.637	4.648	4.658	4.669	4.680	1	2	3	4	5	6	8	9	10
22	4.690	4.701	4.712	4.722	4.733	4.743	4.754	4.764	4.775	4.785	1	2	3	4	5	6	7	8	10
23	4.796	4.806	4.817	4.827	4.837	4.848	4.858	4.868	4.879	4.889	1	2	3	4	5	6	7	8	9
24	4.899	4.909	4.919	4.930	4.940	4.950	4.960	4.970	4.980	4.990	1	2	3	4	5	6	7	8	9
25	5.000	5.010	5.020	5.030	5.040	5.050	5.060	5.070	5.079	5.089	1	2	3	4	5	6	7	8	9
26	5.099	5.109	5.119	5.128	5.138	5.148	5.158	5.167	5.177	5.187	1	2	3	4	5	6	7	8	9
27	5.196	5.206	5.215	5.225	5.235	5.244	5.254	5.263	5.273	5.282	1	2	3	4	5	6	7	8	9
28	5.292	5.301	5.310	5.320	5.329	5.339	5.348	5.357	5.367	5.376	1	2	3	4	5	6	7	7	8
29	5.385	5.394	5.404	5.413	5.422	5.431	5.441	5.450	5.459	5.468	1	2	3	4	5	5	6	7	8
30	5.477	5.486	5.495	5.505	5.514	5.523	5.532	5.541	5.550	5.559	1	2	3	4	5	5	6	7	8
31	5.568	5.577	5.586	5.595	5.604	5.612	5.621	5.630	5.639	5.648	1	2	3	4	4	5	6	7	8
32	5.657	5.666	5.675	5.683	5.692	5.701	5.710	5.718	5.727	5.736	1	2	3	3	4	5	6	7	8
33	5.745	5.753	5.762	5.771	5.779	5.788	5.797	5.805	5.814	5.822	1	2	3	3	4	5	6	7	8
34	5.831	5.840	5.848	5.857	5.865	5.874	5.882	5.891	5.899	5.908	1	2	3	3	4	5	6	7	8
35	5.916	5.925	5.933	5.941	5.950	5.958	5.967	5.975	5.983	5.992	1	2	2	3	4	5	6	7	7
36	6.000	6.008	6.017	6.025	6.033	6.042	6.050	6.058	6.066	6.075	1	2	2	3	4	5	6	7	7
37	6.083	6.091	6.099	6.107	6.116	6.124	6.132	6.140	6.148	6.156	1	2	2	3	4	5	6	6	7
38	6.164	6.173	6.181	6.189	6.197	6.205	6.213	6.221	6.229	6.237	1	2	2	3	4	5	6	6	7
39	6.245	6.253	6.261	6.269	6.277	6.285	6.293	6.301	6.309	6.317	1	2	2	3	4	5	6	6	7
40	6.325	6.332	6.340	6.348	6.356	6.364	6.372	6.380	6.387	6.395	1	2	2	3	4	5	5	6	7
41	6.403	6.411	6.419	6.427	6.434	6.442	6.450	6.458	6.465	6.473	1	2	2	3	4	5	5	6	7
42	6.481	6.488	6.496	6.504	6.512	6.519	6.527	6.535	6.542	6.550	1	2	2	3	4	5	5	6	7
43	6.557	6.565	6.573	6.580	6.588	6.595	6.603	6.611	6.618	6.626	1	2	2	3	4	5	5	6	7
44	6.633	6.641	6.648	6.656	6.663	6.671	6.678	6.686	6.693	6.701	1	1	2	3	4	4	5	6	7
45	6.708	6.716	6.723	6.731	6.738	6.745	6.753	6.760	6.768	6.775	1	1	2	3	4	4	5	6	7
46	6.782	6.790	6.797	6.804	6.812	6.819	6.826	6.834	6.841	6.848	1	1	2	3	4	4	5	6	7
47	6.856	6.863	6.870	6.877	6.885	6.892	6.899	6.907	6.914	6.921	1	1	2	3	4	4	5	6	6
48	6.928	6.935	6.943	6.950	6.957	6.964	6.971	6.979	6.986	6.993	1	1	2	3	4	4	5	6	6
49	7.000	7.007	7.014	7.021	7.029	7.036	7.043	7.050	7.057	7.064	1	1	2	3	4	4	5	6	6
50	7.071	7.078	7.085	7.092	7.099	7.106	7.113	7.120	7.127	7.134	1	1	2	3	4	4	5	6	6
51	7.141	7.148	7.155	7.162	7.169	7.176	7.183	7.190	7.197	7.204	1	1	2	3	4	4	5	6	6
52	7.211	7.218	7.225	7.232	7.239	7.246	7.253	7.259	7.266	7.273	1	1	2	3	3	4	5	5	6
53	7.280	7.287	7.294	7.301	7.308	7.314	7.321	7.328	7.335	7.342	1	1	2	3	3	4	5	5	6
54	7.348	7.355	7.362	7.369	7.376	7.382	7.389	7.396	7.403	7.409	1	1	2	3	3	4	5	5	6

TABLE OF SQUARE ROOTS FROM 10—100 (continued)

x	0	1	2	3	4	5	6	7	8	9	1	2	3	4	5	6	7	8	9
55	7.416	7.423	7.430	7.436	7.443	7.450	7.457	7.463	7.470	7.477	1	1	2	3	3	4	5	5	6
56	7.483	7.490	7.497	7.503	7.510	7.517	7.523	7.530	7.537	7.543	1	1	2	3	3	4	5	5	6
57	7.550	7.556	7.563	7.570	7.576	7.583	7.589	7.596	7.603	7.609	1	1	2	3	3	4	4	5	6
58	7.616	7.622	7.629	7.635	7.642	7.649	7.655	7.662	7.668	7.675	1	1	2	3	3	4	4	5	6
59	7.681	7.688	7.694	7.701	7.707	7.714	7.720	7.727	7.733	7.740	1	1	2	3	3	4	4	5	6
60	7.746	7.752	7.759	7.765	7.772	7.778	7.785	7.791	7.797	7.804	1	1	2	3	3	4	4	5	6
61	7.810	7.817	7.823	7.829	7.836	7.842	7.849	7.855	7.861	7.868	1	1	2	2	3	4	4	5	6
62	7.874	7.880	7.887	7.893	7.899	7.906	7.912	7.918	7.925	7.931	1	1	2	2	3	4	4	5	6
63	7.937	7.944	7.950	7.956	7.962	7.969	7.975	7.981	7.987	7.994	1	1	2	2	3	4	4	5	5
64	8.000	8.006	8.012	8.019	8.025	8.031	8.037	8.044	8.050	8.056	1	1	2	2	3	4	4	5	5
65	8.062	8.068	8.075	8.081	8.087	8.093	8.099	8.106	8.112	8.118	1	1	2	2	3	4	4	5	5
66	8.124	8.130	8.136	8.142	8.149	8.155	8.161	8.167	8.173	8.179	1	1	2	2	3	4	4	5	5
67	8.185	8.191	8.198	8.204	8.210	8.216	8.222	8.228	8.234	8.240	1	1	2	2	3	4	4	5	5
68	8.246	8.252	8.258	8.264	8.270	8.276	8.283	8.289	8.295	8.301	1	1	2	2	3	4	4	5	5
69	8.307	8.313	8.319	8.325	8.331	8.337	8.343	8.349	8.355	8.361	1	1	2	2	3	4	4	5	5
70	8.367	8.373	8.379	8.385	8.390	8.396	8.402	8.408	8.414	8.420	1	1	2	2	3	4	4	5	5
71	8.426	8.432	8.438	8.444	8.450	8.456	8.462	8.468	8.473	8.479	1	1	2	2	3	4	4	5	5
72	8.485	8.491	8.497	8.503	8.509	8.515	8.521	8.526	8.532	8.538	1	1	2	2	3	4	4	5	5
73	8.544	8.550	8.556	8.562	8.567	8.573	8.579	8.585	8.591	8.597	1	1	2	2	3	4	4	5	5
74	8.602	8.608	8.614	8.620	8.626	8.631	8.637	8.643	8.649	8.654	1	1	2	2	3	3	4	5	5
75	8.660	8.666	8.672	8.678	8.683	8.689	8.695	8.701	8.706	8.712	1	1	2	2	3	3	4	5	5
76	8.718	8.724	8.729	8.735	8.741	8.746	8.752	8.758	8.764	8.769	1	1	2	2	3	3	4	4	5
77	8.775	8.781	8.786	8.792	8.798	8.803	8.809	8.815	8.820	8.826	1	1	2	2	3	3	4	4	5
78	8.832	8.837	8.843	8.849	8.854	8.860	8.866	8.871	8.877	8.883	1	1	2	2	3	3	4	4	5
79	8.888	8.894	8.899	8.905	8.911	8.916	8.922	8.927	8.933	8.939	1	1	2	2	3	3	4	4	5
80	8.944	8.950	8.955	8.961	8.967	8.972	8.978	8.983	8.989	8.994	1	1	2	2	3	3	4	4	5
81	9.000	9.006	9.011	9.017	9.022	9.028	9.033	9.039	9.044	9.050	1	1	2	2	3	3	4	4	5
82	9.055	9.061	9.066	9.072	9.077	9.083	9.088	9.094	9.099	9.105	1	1	2	2	3	3	4	4	5
83	9.110	9.116	9.121	9.127	9.132	9.138	9.143	9.149	9.154	9.160	1	1	2	2	3	3	4	4	5
84	9.165	9.171	9.176	9.182	9.187	9.192	9.198	9.203	9.209	9.214	1	1	2	2	3	3	4	4	5
85	9.220	9.225	9.230	9.236	9.241	9.247	9.252	9.257	9.263	9.268	1	1	2	2	3	3	4	4	5
86	9.274	9.279	9.284	9.290	9.295	9.301	9.306	9.311	9.317	9.322	1	1	2	2	3	3	4	4	5
87	9.327	9.333	9.338	9.343	9.349	9.354	9.359	9.365	9.370	9.375	1	1	2	2	3	3	4	4	5
88	9.381	9.386	9.391	9.397	9.402	9.407	9.413	9.418	9.423	9.429	1	1	2	2	3	3	4	4	5
89	9.434	9.439	9.445	9.450	9.455	9.460	9.466	9.471	9.476	9.482	1	1	2	2	3	3	4	4	5
90	9.487	9.492	9.497	9.503	9.508	9.513	9.518	9.524	9.529	9.534	1	1	2	2	3	3	4	4	5
91	9.539	9.545	9.550	9.555	9.560	9.566	9.571	9.576	9.581	9.586	1	1	2	2	3	3	4	4	5
92	9.592	9.597	9.602	9.607	9.612	9.618	9.623	9.628	9.633	9.638	1	1	2	2	3	3	4	4	5
93	9.644	9.649	9.654	9.659	9.664	9.670	9.675	9.680	9.685	9.690	1	1	2	2	3	3	4	4	5
94	9.695	9.701	9.706	9.711	9.716	9.721	9.726	9.731	9.737	9.742	1	1	2	2	3	3	4	4	5
95	9.747	9.752	9.757	9.762	9.767	9.772	9.778	9.783	9.788	9.793	1	1	2	2	3	3	4	4	5
96	9.798	9.803	9.808	9.813	9.818	9.823	9.829	9.834	9.839	9.844	1	1	2	2	3	3	4	4	5
97	9.849	9.854	9.859	9.864	9.869	9.874	9.879	9.884	9.889	9.894	1	1	2	2	2	3	3	4	4
98	9.899	9.905	9.910	9.915	9.920	9.925	9.930	9.935	9.940	9.945	1	1	2	2	2	3	3	4	4
99	9.950	9.955	9.960	9.965	9.970	9.975	9.980	9.985	9.990	9.995	0	1	1	2	2	3	3	4	4

TABLE OF RECIPROCALS OF NUMBERS FROM 1–10

Subtract

	0	1	2	3	4	5	6	7	8	9	1	2	3	4	5	6	7	8	9
1.0	1.0000	0.9901	0.9804	0.9709	0.9615	0.9524	0.9434	0.9346	0.9259	0.9174									
1.1	0.9091	0.9009	0.8929	0.8850	0.8772	0.8696	0.8621	0.8547	0.8475	0.8403.									
1.2	0.8333	0.8264	0.8197	0.8130	0.8065	0.8000	0.7937	0.7874	0.7813	0.7752									
1.3	0.7692	0.7634	0.7576	0.7519	0.7463	0.7407	0.7353	0.7299	0.7246	0.7194									
1.4	0.7143	0.7092	0.7042	0.6993	0.6944	0.6897	0.6849	0.6803	0.6757	0.6711									
1.5	0.6667	0.6623	0.6579	0.6536	0.6494	0.6452	0.6410	0.6369	0.6329	0.6289	4	8	12	17	21	25	29	33	37
1.6	0.6250	0.6211	0.6173	0.6135	0.6098	0.6061	0.6024	0.5988	0.5952	0.5917	4	7	11	15	18	22	26	29	33
1.7	0.5882	0.5848	0.5814	0.5780	0.5747	0.5714	0.5682	0.5650	0.5618	0.5587	3	7	10	13	16	20	23	26	29
1.8	0.5556	0.5525	0.5495	0.5464	0.5435	0.5405	0.5376	0.5348	0.5319	0.5291	3	6	9	12	15	18	20	23	26
1.9	0.5263	0.5236	0.5208	0.5181	0.5155	0.5128	0.5102	0.5076	0.5051	0.5025	3	5	8	11	13	16	18	21	24
2.0	0.5000	0.4975	0.4950	0.4926	0.4902	0.4878	0.4854	0.4831	0.4808	0.4785	2	5	7	10	12	14	17	19	21
2.1	0.4762	0.4739	0.4717	0.4695	0.4673	0.4651	0.4630	0.4608	0.4587	0.4566	2	4	6	9	11	13	15	17	19
2.2	0.4545	0.4525	0.4505	0.4484	0.4464	0.4444	0.4425	0.4405	0.4386	0.4367	2	4	6	8	10	12	14	16	18
2.3	0.4348	0.4329	0.4310	0.4292	0.4274	0.4255	0.4237	0.4219	0.4202	0.4184	2	4	5	7	9	11	13	14	16
2.4	0.4167	0.4149	0.4132	0.4115	0.4098	0.4082	0.4065	0.4049	0.4032	0.4016	2	3	5	7	8	10	12	13	15
2.5	0.4000	0.3984	0.3968	0.3953	0.3937	0.3922	0.3906	0.3891	0.3876	0.3861	2	3	5	6	8	9	11	12	14
2.6	0.3846	0.3831	0.3817	0.3802	0.3788	0.3774	0.3759	0.3745	0.3731	0.3717	1	3	4	6	7	9	10	11	13
2.7	0.3704	0.3690	0.3676	0.3663	0.3650	0.3636	0.3623	0.3610	0.3597	0.3584	1	3	4	5	7	8	9	11	12
2.8	0.3571	0.3559	0.3546	0.3534	0.3521	0.3509	0.3497	0.3484	0.3472	0.3460	1	2	4	5	6	7	9	10	11
2.9	0.3448	0.3436	0.3425	0.3413	0.3401	0.3390	0.3378	0.3367	0.3356	0.3344	1	2	3	5	6	7	8	9	10
3.0	0.3333	0.3322	0.3311	0.3300	0.3289	0.3279	0.3268	0.3257	0.3247	0.3236	1	2	3	4	5	6	8	9	10
3.1	0.3226	0.3215	0.3205	0.3195	0.3185	0.3175	0.3165	0.3155	0.3145	0.3135	1	2	3	4	5	6	7	8	9
3.2	0.3125	0.3115	0.3106	0.3096	0.3086	0.3077	0.3067	0.3058	0.3049	0.3040	1	2	3	4	5	6	7	8	9
3.3	0.3030	0.3021	0.3012	0.3003	0.2994	0.2985	0.2976	0.2967	0.2959	0.2950	1	2	3	4	4	5	6	7	8
3.4	0.2941	0.2933	0.2924	0.2915	0.2907	0.2899	0.2890	0.2882	0.2874	0.2865	1	2	3	3	4	5	6	7	8
3.5	0.2857	0.2849	0.2841	0.2833	0.2825	0.2817	0.2809	0.2801	0.2793	0.2786	1	2	2	3	4	5	6	6	7
3.6	0.2778	0.2770	0.2762	0.2755	0.2747	0.2740	0.2732	0.2725	0.2717	0.2710	1	2	2	3	4	5	5	6	7
3.7	0.2703	0.2695	0.2688	0.2681	0.2674	0.2667	0.2660	0.2653	0.2646	0.2639	1	1	2	3	4	4	5	6	6
3.8	0.2632	0.2625	0.2618	0.2611	0.2604	0.2597	0.2591	0.2584	0.2577	0.2571	1	1	2	3	3	4	5	5	6
3.9	0.2564	0.2558	0.2551	0.2545	0.2538	0.2532	0.2525	0.2519	0.2513	0.2506	1	1	2	3	3	4	4	5	6
4.0	0.2500	0.2494	0.2488	0.2481	0.2475	0.2469	0.2463	0.2457	0.2451	0.2445	1	1	2	2	3	4	4	5	5
4.1	0.2439	0.2433	0.2427	0.2421	0.2415	0.2410	0.2404	0.2398	0.2392	0.2387	1	1	2	2	3	3	4	5	5
4.2	0.2381	0.2375	0.2370	0.2364	0.2358	0.2353	0.2347	0.2342	0.2336	0.2331	1	1	2	2	3	3	4	4	5
4.3	0.2326	0.2320	0.2315	0.2309	0.2304	0.2299	0.2294	0.2288	0.2283	0.2278	1	1	2	2	3	3	4	4	5
4.4	0.2273	0.2268	0.2262	0.2257	0.2252	0.2247	0.2242	0.2237	0.2232	0.2227	1	1	2	2	3	3	4	4	5
4.5	0.2222	0.2217	0.2212	0.2208	0.2203	0.2198	0.2193	0.2188	0.2183	0.2179	0	1	1	2	2	3	3	4	4
4.6	0.2174	0.2169	0.2165	0.2160	0.2155	0.2151	0.2146	0.2141	0.2137	0.2132	0	1	1	2	2	3	3	4	4
4.7	0.2128	0.2123	0.2119	0.2114	0.2110	0.2105	0.2101	0.2096	0.2092	0.2088	0	1	1	2	2	3	3	4	4
4.8	0.2083	0.2079	0.2075	0.2070	0.2066	0.2062	0.2058	0.2053	0.2049	0.2045	0	1	1	2	2	3	3	3	4
4.9	0.2041	0.2037	0.2033	0.2028	0.2024	0.2020	0.2016	0.2012	0.2008	0.2004	0	1	1	2	2	2	3	3	4
5.0	0.2000	0.1996	0.1992	0.1988	0.1984	0.1980	0.1976	0.1972	0.1969	0.1965	0	1	1	2	2	2	3	3	4
5.1	0.1961	0.1957	0.1953	0.1949	0.1946	0.1942	0.1938	0.1934	0.1931	0.1927	0	1	1	2	2	2	3	3	3
5.2	0.1923	0.1919	0.1916	0.1912	0.1908	0.1905	0.1901	0.1898	0.1894	0.1890	0	1	1	1	2	2	3	3	3
5.3	0.1887	0.1883	0.1880	0.1876	0.1873	0.1869	0.1866	0.1862	0.1859	0.1855	0	1	1	1	2	2	2	3	3
5.4	0.1852	0.1848	0.1845	0.1842	0.1838	0.1835	0.1832	0.1828	0.1825	0.1821	0	1	1	1	2	2	2	3	3

TABLE OF RECIPROCALS OF NUMBERS FROM 1–10 (continued)

Subtract

	0	1	2	3	4	5	6	7	8	9	1	2	3	4	5	6	7	8	9
5.5	0.1818	0.1815	0.1812	0.1808	0.1805	0.1802	0.1799	0.1795	0.1792	0.1789	0	1	1	1	2	2	2	3	3
5.6	0.1786	0.1783	0.1779	0.1776	0.1773	0.1770	0.1767	0.1764	0.1761	0.1757	0	1	1	1	2	2	2	3	3
5.7	0.1754	0.1751	0.1748	0.1745	0.1742	0.1739	0.1736	0.1733	0.1730	0.1727	0	1	1	1	2	2	2	2	3
5.8	0.1724	0.1721	0.1718	0.1715	0.1712	0.1709	0.1706	0.1704	0.1701	0.1698	0	1	1	1	1	2	2	2	3
5.9	0.1695	0.1692	0.1689	0.1686	0.1684	0.1681	0.1678	0.1675	0.1672	0.1669	0	1	1	1	1	2	2	2	3
6.0	0.1667	0.1664	0.1661	0.1658	0.1656	0.1653	0.1650	0.1647	0.1645	0.1642	0	1	1	1	1	2	2	2	2
6.1	0.1639	0.1637	0.1634	0.1631	0.1629	0.1626	0.1623	0.1621	0.1618	0.1616	0	1	1	1	1	2	2	2	2
6.2	0.1613	0.1610	0.1608	0.1605	0.1603	0.1600	0.1597	0.1595	0.1592	0.1590	0	1	1	1	1	2	2	2	2
6.3	0.1587	0.1585	0.1582	0.1580	0.1577	0.1575	0.1572	0.1570	0.1567	0.1565	0	0	1	1	1	1	2	2	2
6.4	0.1563	0.1560	0.1558	0.1555	0.1553	0.1550	0.1548	0.1546	0.1543	0.1541	0	0	1	1	1	1	2	2	2
6.5	0.1538	0.1536	0.1534	0.1531	0.1529	0.1527	0.1524	0.1522	0.1520	0.1517	0	0	1	1	1	1	2	2	2
6.6	0.1515	0.1513	0.1511	0.1508	0.1506	0.1504	0.1502	0.1499	0.1497	0.1495	0	0	1	1	1	1	2	2	2
6.7	0.1493	0.1490	0.1488	0.1486	0.1484	0.1481	0.1479	0.1477	0.1475	0.1473	0	0	1	1	1	1	2	2	2
6.8	0.1471	0.1468	0.1466	0.1464	0.1462	0.1460	0.1458	0.1456	0.1453	0.1451	0	0	1	1	1	1	1	2	2
6.9	0.1449	0.1447	0.1445	0.1443	0.1441	0.1439	0.1437	0.1435	0.1433	0.1431	0	0	1	1	1	1	1	2	2
7.0	0.1429	0.1427	0.1425	0.1422	0.1420	0.1418	0.1416	0.1414	0.1412	0.1410	0	0	1	1	1	1	1	2	2
7.1	0.1408	0.1406	0.1404	0.1403	0.1401	0.1399	0.1397	0.1395	0.1393	0.1391	0	0	1	1	1	1	1	2	2
7.2	0.1389	0.1387	0.1385	0.1383	0.1381	0.1379	0.1377	0.1376	0.1374	0.1372	0	0	1	1	1	1	1	2	2
7.3	0.1370	0.1368	0.1366	0.1364	0.1362	0.1361	0.1359	0.1357	0.1355	0.1353	0	0	1	1	1	1	1	1	2
7.4	0.1351	0.1350	0.1348	0.1346	0.1344	0.1342	0.1340	0.1339	0.1337	0.1335	0	0	1	1	1	1	1	1	2
7.5	0.1333	0.1332	0.1330	0.1328	0.1326	0.1325	0.1323	0.1321	0.1319	0.1318	0	0	1	1	1	1	1	1	2
7.6	0.1316	0.1314	0.1312	0.1311	0.1309	0.1307	0.1305	0.1304	0.1302	0.1300	0	0	1	1	1	1	1	1	2
7.7	0.1299	0.1297	0.1295	0.1294	0.1292	0.1290	0.1289	0.1287	0.1285	0.1284	0	0	0	1	1	1	1	1	1
7.8	0.1282	0.1280	0.1279	0.1277	0.1276	0.1274	0.1272	0.1271	0.1269	0.1267	0	0	0	1	1	1	1	1	1
7.9	0.1266	0.1264	0.1263	0.1261	0.1259	0.1258	0.1256	0.1255	0.1253	0.1252	0	0	0	1	1	1	1	1	1
8.0	0.1250	0.1248	0.1247	0.1245	0.1244	0.1242	0.1241	0.1239	0.1238	0.1236	0	0	0	1	1	1	1	1	1
8.1	0.1235	0.1233	0.1232	0.1230	0.1229	0.1227	0.1225	0.1224	0.1222	0.1221	0	0	0	1	1	1	1	1	1
8.2	0.1220	0.1218	0.1217	0.1215	0.1214	0.1212	0.1211	0.1209	0.1208	0.1206	0	0	0	1	1	1	1	1	1
8.3	0.1205	0.1203	0.1202	0.1200	0.1199	0.1198	0.1196	0.1195	0.1193	0.1192	0	0	0	1	1	1	1	1	1
8.4	0.1190	0.1189	0.1188	0.1186	0.1185	0.1183	0.1182	0.1181	0.1179	0.1178	0	0	0	1	1	1	1	1	1
8.5	0.1176	0.1175	0.1174	0.1172	0.1171	0.1170	0.1168	0.1167	0.1166	0.1164	0	0	0	1	1	1	1	1	1
8.6	0.1163	0.1161	0.1160	0.1159	0.1157	0.1156	0.1155	0.1153	0.1152	0.1151	0	0	0	1	1	1	1	1	1
8.7	0.1149	0.1148	0.1147	0.1145	0.1144	0.1143	0.1142	0.1140	0.1139	0.1138	0	0	0	1	1	1	1	1	1
8.8	0.1136	0.1135	0.1134	0.1133	0.1131	0.1130	0.1129	0.1127	0.1126	0.1125	0	0	0	1	1	1	1	1	1
8.9	0.1124	0.1122	0.1121	0.1120	0.1119	0.1117	0.1116	0.1115	0.1114	0.1112	0	0	0	0	1	1	1	1	1
9.0	0.1111	0.1110	0.1109	0.1107	0.1106	0.1105	0.1104	0.1103	0.1101	0.1100	0	0	0	0	1	1	1	1	1
9.1	0.1099	0.1098	0.1096	0.1095	0.1094	0.1093	0.1092	0.1091	0.1089	0.1088	0	0	0	0	1	1	1	1	1
9.2	0.1087	0.1086	0.1085	0.1083	0.1082	0.1081	0.1080	0.1079	0.1078	0.1076	0	0	0	0	1	1	1	1	1
9.3	0.1075	0.1074	0.1073	0.1072	0.1071	0.1070	0.1068	0.1067	0.1066	0.1065	0	0	0	0	1	1	1	1	1
9.4	0.1064	0.1063	0.1062	0.1060	0.1059	0.1058	0.1057	0.1056	0.1055	0.1054	0	0	0	0	1	1	1	1	1
9.5	0.1053	0.1052	0.1050	0.1049	0.1048	0.1047	0.1046	0.1045	0.1044	0.1043	0	0	0	0	1	1	1	1	1
9.6	0.1042	0.1041	0.1040	0.1038	0.1037	0.1036	0.1035	0.1034	0.1033	0.1032	0	0	0	0	1	1	1	1	1
9.7	0.1031	0.1030	0.1029	0.1028	0.1027	0.1026	0.1025	0.1024	0.1022	0.1021	0	0	0	0	1	1	1	1	1
9.8	0.1020	0.1019	0.1018	0.1017	0.1016	0.1015	0.1014	0.1013	0.1012	0.1011	0	0	0	0	1	1	1	1	1
9.9	0.1010	0.1009	0.1008	0.1007	0.1006	0.1005	0.1004	0.1003	0.1002	0.1001	0	0	0	0	1	1	1	1	1

	0	1	2	3	4	5	6	7	8	9	1	2	3	4	5	6	7	8	9
10	0000	0043	0086	0128	0170	0212	0253	0294	0334	0374	4	8	13	17	21	25	30	34	38
11	0414	0453	0492	0531	0569	0607	0645	0682	0719	0755	4	8	12	16	20	24	28	32	36
12	0792	0828	0864	0899	0934	0969	1004	1038	1072	1106	4	7	11	15	19	23	27	31	35
13	1139	1173	1206	1239	1271	1303	1335	1367	1399	1430	3	7	10	14	17	21	24	28	31
14	1461	1492	1523	1553	1584	1614	1644	1673	1703	1732	3	6	9	12	15	18	21	24	27
15	1761	1790	1818	1847	1875	1903	1931	1959	1987	2014	3	6	8	11	14	17	20	22	25
16	2041	2068	2095	2122	2148	2175	2201	2227	2253	2279	3	5	8	11	13	16	18	21	24
17	2304	2330	2355	2380	2405	2430	2455	2480	2504	2529	2	5	7	10	12	15	17	20	22
18	2553	2577	2601	2625	2648	2672	2695	2718	2742	2765	2	5	7	9	12	14	16	19	21
19	2788	2810	2833	2856	2878	2900	2923	2945	2967	2989	2	4	7	9	11	13	16	18	20
20	3010	3032	3054	3075	3096	3118	3139	3160	3181	3201	2	4	6	8	11	13	15	17	19
21	3222	3243	3263	3284	3304	3324	3345	3365	3385	3404	2	4	6	8	10	12	14	16	18
22	3424	3444	3464	3483	3502	3522	3541	3560	3579	3598	2	4	6	8	10	12	14	15	17
23	3617	3636	3655	3674	3692	3711	3729	3747	3766	3784	2	4	6	7	9	11	13	15	17
24	3802	3820	3838	3856	3874	3892	3909	3927	3945	3962	2	4	5	7	9	11	12	14	16
25	3979	3997	4014	4031	4048	4065	4082	4099	4116	4133	2	3	5	7	9	10	12	14	15
26	4150	4166	4183	4200	4216	4232	4249	4265	4281	4298	2	3	5	7	8	10	11	13	15
27	4314	4330	4346	4362	4378	4393	4409	4425	4440	4456	2	3	5	6	8	9	11	13	14
28	4472	4487	4502	4518	4533	4548	4564	4579	4594	4609	2	3	5	6	8	9	11	12	14
29	4624	4639	4654	4669	4683	4698	4713	4728	4742	4757	1	3	4	6	7	9	10	12	13
30	4771	4786	4800	4814	4829	4843	4857	4871	4886	4900	1	3	4	6	7	9	10	11	13
31	4914	4928	4942	4955	4969	4983	4997	5011	5024	5038	1	3	4	6	7	8	10	11	12
32	5051	5065	5079	5092	5105	5119	5132	5145	5159	5172	1	3	4	5	7	8	9	11	12
33	5185	5198	5211	5224	5237	5250	5263	5276	5289	5302	1	3	4	5	6	8	9	10	12
34	5315	5328	5340	5353	5366	5378	5391	5403	5416	5428	1	3	4	5	6	8	9	10	11
35	5441	5453	5465	5478	5490	5502	5514	5527	5539	5551	1	2	4	5	6	7	9	10	11
36	5563	5575	5587	5599	5611	5623	5635	5647	5658	5670	1	2	4	5	6	7	8	10	11
37	5682	5694	5705	5717	5729	5740	5752	5763	5775	5786	1	2	3	5	6	7	8	9	10
38	5798	5809	5821	5832	5843	5855	5866	5877	5888	5899	1	2	3	5	6	7	8	9	10
39	5911	5922	5933	5944	5955	5966	5977	5988	5999	6010	1	2	3	4	5	7	8	9	10
40	6021	6031	6042	6053	6064	6075	6085	6096	6107	6117	1	2	3	4	5	6	8	9	10
41	6128	6138	6149	6160	6170	6180	6191	6201	6212	6222	1	2	3	4	5	6	7	8	9
42	6232	6243	6253	6263	6274	6284	6294	6304	6314	6325	1	2	3	4	5	6	7	8	9
43	6335	6345	6355	6365	6375	6385	6395	6405	6415	6425	1	2	3	4	5	6	7	8	9
44	6435	6444	6454	6464	6474	6484	6493	6503	6513	6522	1	2	3	4	5	6	7	8	9
45	6532	6542	6551	6561	6571	6580	6590	6599	6609	6618	1	2	3	4	5	6	7	8	9
46	6628	6637	6646	6656	6665	6675	6684	6693	6702	6712	1	2	3	4	5	6	7	7	8
47	6721	6730	6739	6749	6758	6767	6776	6785	6794	6803	1	2	3	4	5	5	6	7	8
48	6812	6821	6830	6839	6848	6857	6866	6875	6884	6893	1	2	3	4	4	5	6	7	8
49	6902	6911	6920	6928	6937	6946	6955	6964	6972	6981	1	2	3	4	4	5	6	7	8

	0	1	2	3	4	5	6	7	8	9	1	2	3	4	5	6	7	8	9
50	6990	6998	7007	7016	7024	7033	7042	7050	7059	7067	1	2	3	3	4	5	6	7	8
51	7076	7084	7093	7101	7110	7118	7126	7135	7143	7152	1	2	2	3	4	5	6	7	8
52	7160	7168	7177	7185	7193	7202	7210	7218	7226	7235	1	2	2	3	4	5	6	7	7
53	7243	7251	7259	7267	7275	7284	7292	7300	7308	7316	1	2	2	3	4	5	6	6	7
54	7324	7332	7340	7348	7356	7364	7372	7380	7388	7396	1	2	2	3	4	5	5	6	7
55	7404	7412	7419	7427	7435	7443	7451	7459	7466	7474	1	2	2	3	4	5	5	6	7
56	7482	7490	7497	7505	7513	7520	7528	7536	7543	7551	1	2	2	3	4	5	5	6	7
57	7559	7566	7574	7582	7589	7597	7604	7612	7619	7627	1	2	2	3	4	5	5	6	7
58	7634	7642	7649	7657	7664	7672	7679	7686	7694	7701	1	1	2	3	4	4	5	6	7
59	7709	7716	7723	7731	7738	7745	7752	7760	7767	7774	1	1	2	3	4	4	5	6	7
60	7782	7789	7796	7803	7810	7818	7825	7832	7839	7846	1	1	2	3	4	4	5	6	6
61	7853	7860	7868	7875	7882	7889	7896	7903	7910	7917	1	1	2	3	4	4	5	6	6
62	7924	7931	7938	7945	7952	7959	7966	7973	7980	7987	1	1	2	3	3	4	5	6	6
63	7993	8000	8007	8014	8021	8028	8035	8041	8048	8055	1	1	2	3	3	4	5	5	6
64	8062	8069	8075	8082	8089	8096	8102	8109	8116	8122	1	1	2	3	3	4	5	5	6
65	8129	8136	8142	8149	8156	8162	8169	8176	8182	8189	1	1	2	3	3	4	5	5	6
66	8195	8202	8209	8215	8222	8228	8235	8241	8248	8254	1	1	2	3	3	4	5	5	6
67	8261	8267	8274	8280	8287	8293	8299	8306	8312	8319	1	1	2	2	3	4	4	5	6
68	8325	8331	8338	8344	8351	8357	8363	8370	8376	8382	1	1	2	2	3	4	4	5	6
69	8388	8395	8401	8407	8414	8420	8426	8432	8439	8445	1	1	2	2	3	4	4	5	6
70	8451	8457	8463	8470	8476	8482	8488	8494	8500	8506	1	1	2	2	3	4	4	5	5
71	8513	8519	8525	8531	8537	8543	8549	8555	8561	8567	1	1	2	2	3	4	4	5	5
72	8573	8579	8585	8591	8597	8603	8609	8615	8621	8627	1	1	2	2	3	4	4	5	5
73	8633	8639	8645	8651	8657	8663	8669	8675	8681	8686	1	1	2	2	3	4	4	5	5
74	8692	8698	8704	8710	8716	8722	8727	8733	8739	8745	1	1	2	2	3	4	4	5	5
75	8751	8756	8762	8768	8774	8779	8785	8791	8797	8802	1	1	2	2	3	3	4	5	5
76	8808	8814	8820	8825	8831	8837	8842	8848	8854	8859	1	1	2	2	3	3	4	5	5
77	8865	8871	8876	8882	8887	8893	8899	8904	8910	8915	1	1	2	2	3	3	4	4	5
78	8921	8927	8932	8938	8943	8949	8954	8960	8965	8971	1	1	2	2	3	3	4	4	5
79	8976	8982	8987	8993	8998	9004	9009	9015	9020	9025	1	1	2	2	3	3	4	4	5
80	9031	9036	9042	9047	9053	9058	9063	9069	9074	9079	1	1	2	2	3	3	4	4	5
81	9085	9090	9096	9101	9106	9112	9117	9122	9128	9133	1	1	2	2	3	3	4	4	5
82	9138	9143	9149	9154	9159	9165	9170	9175	9180	9186	1	1	2	2	3	3	4	4	5
83	9191	9196	9201	9206	9212	9217	9222	9227	9232	9238	1	1	2	2	3	3	4	4	5
84	9243	9248	9253	9258	9263	9269	9274	9279	9284	9289	1	1	2	2	3	3	4	4	5
85	9294	9299	9304	9309	9315	9320	9325	9330	9335	9340	1	1	2	2	3	3	4	4	5
86	9345	9350	9355	9360	9365	9370	9375	9380	9385	9390	1	1	2	2	3	3	4	4	5
87	9395	9400	9405	9410	9415	9420	9425	9430	9435	9440	0	1	1	2	2	3	3	4	4
88	9445	9450	9455	9460	9465	9469	9474	9479	9484	9489	0	1	1	2	2	3	3	4	4
89	9494	9499	9504	9509	9513	9518	9523	9528	9533	9538	0	1	1	2	2	3	3	4	4
90	9542	9547	9552	9557	9562	9566	9571	9576	9581	9586	0	1	1	2	2	3	3	4	4
91	9590	9595	9600	9605	9609	9614	9619	9624	9628	9633	0	1	1	2	2	3	3	4	4
92	9638	9643	9647	9652	9657	9661	9666	9671	9675	9680	0	1	1	2	2	3	3	4	4
93	9685	9689	9694	9699	9703	9708	9713	9717	9722	9727	0	1	1	2	2	3	3	4	4
94	9731	9736	9741	9745	9750	9754	9759	9763	9768	9773	0	1	1	2	2	3	3	4	4
95	9777	9782	9786	9791	9795	9800	9805	9809	9814	9818	0	1	1	2	2	3	3	4	4
96	9823	9827	9832	9836	9841	9845	9850	9854	9859	9863	0	1	1	2	2	3	3	4	4
97	9868	9872	9877	9881	9886	9890	9894	9899	9903	9908	0	1	1	2	2	3	3	3	4
98	9912	9917	9921	9926	9930	9934	9939	9943	9948	9952	0	1	1	2	2	3	3	3	4
99	9956	9961	9965	9969	9974	9978	9983	9987	9991	9996	0	1	1	2	2	3	3	3	4

ANTILOGARITHMS

	0	1	2	3	4	5	6	7	8	9	1	2	3	4	5	6	7	8	9
0.00	1000	1002	1005	1007	1009	1012	1014	1016	1019	1021	0	0	1	1	1	1	2	2	2
0.01	1023	1026	1028	1030	1033	1035	1038	1040	1042	1045	0	0	1	1	1	1	2	2	2
0.02	1047	1050	1052	1054	1057	1059	1062	1064	1067	1069	0	0	1	1	1	1	2	2	2
0.03	1072	1074	1076	1079	1081	1084	1086	1089	1091	1094	0	0	1	1	1	1	2	2	2
0.04	1096	1099	1102	1104	1107	1109	1112	1114	1117	1119	0	1	1	1	1	2	2	2	2
0.05	1122	1125	1127	1130	1132	1135	1138	1140	1143	1146	0	1	1	1	1	2	2	2	2
0.06	1148	1151	1153	1156	1159	1161	1164	1167	1169	1172	0	1	1	1	1	2	2	2	2
0.07	1175	1178	1180	1183	1186	1189	1191	1194	1197	1199	0	1	1	1	1	2	2	2	2
0.08	1202	1205	1208	1211	1213	1216	1219	1222	1225	1227	1	1	1	1	1	2	2	2	3
0.09	1230	1233	1236	1239	1242	1245	1247	1250	1253	1256	1	1	1	1	1	2	2	2	3
0.10	1259	1262	1265	1268	1271	1274	1276	1279	1282	1285	1	1	1	1	1	2	2	2	3
0.11	1288	1291	1294	1297	1300	1303	1306	1309	1312	1315	1	1	1	1	2	2	2	2	3
0.12	1318	1321	1324	1327	1330	1334	1337	1340	1343	1346	1	1	1	1	2	2	2	3	3
0.13	1349	1352	1355	1358	1361	1365	1368	1371	1374	1377	1	1	1	1	2	2	2	3	3
0.14	1380	1384	1387	1390	1393	1396	1400	1403	1406	1409	1	1	1	1	2	2	2	3	3
0.15	1413	1416	1419	1422	1426	1429	1432	1435	1439	1442	1	1	1	1	2	2	2	3	3
0.16	1445	1449	1452	1455	1459	1462	1466	1469	1472	1476	1	1	1	1	2	2	2	3	3
0.17	1479	1483	1486	1489	1493	1496	1500	1503	1507	1510	1	1	1	1	2	2	2	3	3
0.18	1514	1517	1521	1524	1528	1531	1535	1538	1542	1545	1	1	1	1	2	2	2	3	3
0.19	1549	1552	1556	1560	1563	1567	1570	1574	1578	1581	1	1	1	2	2	2	3	3	3
0.20	1585	1589	1592	1596	1600	1603	1607	1611	1614	1618	0	1	1	2	2	2	3	3	3
0.21	1622	1626	1629	1633	1637	1641	1644	1648	1652	1656	0	1	1	2	2	2	3	3	3
0.22	1660	1663	1667	1671	1675	1679	1683	1687	1690	1694	0	1	1	2	2	2	3	3	3
0.23	1698	1702	1706	1710	1714	1718	1722	1726	1730	1734	0	1	1	2	2	2	3	3	4
0.24	1738	1742	1746	1750	1754	1758	1762	1766	1770	1774	0	1	1	2	2	2	3	3	4
0.25	1778	1782	1786	1791	1795	1799	1803	1807	1811	1816	0	1	1	2	2	2	3	3	4
0.26	1820	1824	1828	1832	1837	1841	1845	1849	1854	1858	0	1	1	2	2	3	3	3	4
0.27	1862	1866	1871	1875	1879	1884	1888	1892	1897	1901	0	1	1	2	2	3	3	4	4
0.28	1905	1910	1914	1919	1923	1928	1932	1936	1941	1945	0	1	1	2	2	3	3	4	4
0.29	1950	1954	1959	1963	1968	1972	1977	1982	1986	1991	0	1	1	2	2	3	3	4	4
0.30	1995	2000	2004	2009	2014	2018	2023	2028	2032	2037	0	1	1	2	2	3	3	4	4
0.31	2042	2046	2051	2056	2061	2065	2070	2075	2080	2084	0	1	1	2	2	3	3	4	4
0.32	2089	2094	2099	2104	2109	2113	2118	2123	2128	2133	0	1	1	2	2	3	3	4	4
0.33	2138	2143	2148	2153	2158	2163	2168	2173	2178	2183	1	1	2	2	3	3	4	4	5
0.34	2188	2193	2198	2203	2208	2213	2218	2223	2228	2234	1	1	2	2	3	3	4	4	5
0.35	2239	2244	2249	2254	2259	2265	2270	2275	2280	2286	1	1	2	2	3	3	4	4	5
0.36	2291	2296	2301	2307	2312	2317	2323	2328	2333	2339	1	1	2	2	3	3	4	4	5
0.37	2344	2350	2355	2360	2366	2371	2377	2382	2388	2393	1	1	2	2	3	3	4	5	5
0.38	2399	2404	2410	2415	2421	2427	2432	2438	2443	2449	1	1	2	2	3	4	4	5	5
0.39	2455	2460	2466	2472	2477	2483	2489	2495	2500	2506	1	1	2	2	3	4	4	5	5
0.40	2512	2518	2523	2529	2535	2541	2547	2553	2559	2564	1	1	2	2	3	4	4	5	5
0.41	2570	2576	2582	2588	2594	2600	2606	2612	2618	2624	1	1	2	2	3	4	4	5	6
0.42	2630	2636	2642	2649	2655	2661	2667	2673	2679	2685	1	1	2	3	3	4	4	5	6
0.43	2692	2698	2704	2710	2716	2723	2729	2735	2742	2748	1	1	2	3	3	4	5	5	6
0.44	2754	2761	2767	2773	2780	2786	2793	2799	2805	2812	1	1	2	3	3	4	5	5	6
0.45	2818	2825	2831	2838	2844	2851	2858	2864	2871	2877	1	1	2	3	3	4	5	5	6
0.46	2884	2891	2897	2904	2911	2917	2924	2931	2938	2944	1	1	2	3	3	4	5	5	6
0.47	2951	2958	2965	2972	2979	2985	2992	2999	3006	3013	1	1	2	3	4	4	5	6	6
0.48	3020	3027	3034	3041	3048	3055	3062	3069	3076	3083	1	1	2	3	4	4	5	6	6
0.49	3090	3097	3105	3112	3119	3126	3133	3141	3148	3155	1	2	2	3	4	5	5	6	6

ANTILOGARITHMS (continued)

	0	1	2	3	4	5	6	7	8	9	1	2	3	4	5	6	7	8	9
0.50	3162	3170	3177	3184	3192	3199	3206	3214	3221	3228	1	1	2	3	4	4	5	6	7
0.51	3236	3243	3251	3258	3266	3273	3281	3289	3296	3304	1	2	2	3	4	5	5	6	7
0.52	3311	3319	3327	3334	3342	3350	3357	3365	3373	3381	1	2	2	3	4	5	5	6	7
0.53	3388	3396	3404	3412	3420	3428	3436	3443	3451	3459	1	2	2	3	4	5	6	6	7
0.54	3467	3475	3483	3491	3499	3508	3516	3524	3532	3540	1	2	2	3	4	5	6	6	7
0.55	3548	3556	3565	3573	3581	3589	3597	3606	3614	3622	1	2	2	3	4	5	6	6	7
0.56	3631	3639	3648	3656	3664	3673	3681	3690	3698	3707	1	2	3	3	4	5	6	7	8
0.57	3715	3724	3733	3741	3750	3758	3767	3776	3784	3793	1	2	3	3	4	5	6	7	8
0.58	3802	3811	3819	3828	3837	3846	3855	3864	3873	3882	1	2	3	4	4	5	6	7	8
0.59	3890	3899	3908	3917	3926	3936	3945	3954	3963	3972	1	2	3	4	5	5	6	7	8
0.60	3981	3990	3999	4009	4018	4027	4036	4046	4055	4064	1	2	3	4	5	5	6	7	8
0.61	4074	4083	4093	4102	4111	4121	4130	4140	4150	4159	1	2	3	4	5	6	6	7	8
0.62	4169	4178	4188	4198	4207	4217	4227	4236	4246	4256	1	2	3	4	5	6	7	8	9
0.63	4266	4276	4285	4295	4305	4315	4325	4335	4345	4355	1	2	3	4	5	6	7	8	9
0.64	4365	4375	4385	4395	4406	4416	4426	4436	4446	4457	1	2	3	4	5	6	7	8	9
0.65	4467	4477	4487	4498	4508	4519	4529	4539	4550	4560	1	2	3	4	5	6	7	8	9
0.66	4571	4581	4592	4603	4613	4624	4634	4645	4656	4667	1	2	3	4	5	6	8	9	10
0.67	4677	4688	4699	4710	4721	4732	4742	4753	4764	4775	1	2	3	4	5	7	8	9	10
0.68	4786	4797	4808	4819	4831	4842	4853	4864	4875	4887	1	2	3	4	6	7	8	9	10
0.69	4898	4909	4920	4932	4943	4955	4966	4977	4989	5000	1	2	3	5	6	7	8	9	10
0.70	5012	5023	5035	5047	5058	5070	5082	5093	5105	5117	1	2	4	5	6	7	8	10	11
0.71	5129	5140	5152	5164	5176	5188	5200	5212	5224	5236	1	2	4	5	6	7	8	10	11
0.72	5248	5260	5272	5284	5297	5309	5321	5333	5346	5358	1	2	4	5	6	7	8	10	11
0.73	5370	5383	5395	5408	5420	5433	5445	5458	5470	5483	1	3	4	5	6	8	9	10	11
0.74	5495	5508	5521	5534	5546	5559	5572	5585	5598	5610	1	3	4	5	6	8	9	10	12
0.75	5623	5636	5649	5662	5675	5689	5702	5715	5728	5741	1	3	4	5	7	8	9	10	12
0.76	5754	5768	5781	5794	5808	5821	5834	5848	5861	5875	1	3	4	5	7	8	9	11	12
0.77	5888	5902	5916	5929	5943	5957	5970	5984	5998	6012	1	3	4	6	7	8	10	11	12
0.78	6026	6039	6053	6067	6081	6095	6109	6124	6138	6152	1	3	4	6	7	8	10	11	13
0.79	6166	6180	6194	6209	6223	6237	6252	6266	6281	6295	1	3	4	6	7	9	10	11	13
0.80	6310	6324	6339	6353	6368	6383	6397	6412	6427	6442	1	3	4	6	7	9	10	12	13
0.81	6457	6471	6486	6501	6516	6531	6546	6561	6577	6592	2	3	5	6	8	9	11	12	14
0.82	6607	6622	6637	6653	6668	6683	6699	6714	6730	6745	2	3	5	6	8	9	11	12	14
0.83	6761	6776	6792	6808	6823	6839	6855	6871	6887	6902	2	3	5	6	8	9	11	13	14
0.84	6918	6934	6950	6966	6982	6998	7015	7031	7047	7063	2	3	5	6	8	10	11	13	15
0.85	7079	7096	7112	7129	7145	7161	7178	7194	7211	7228	2	3	5	7	8	10	11	13	15
0.86	7244	7261	7278	7295	7311	7328	7345	7362	7379	7396	2	3	5	7	8	10	12	13	15
0.87	7413	7430	7447	7464	7482	7499	7516	7534	7551	7568	2	3	5	7	9	10	12	14	15
0.88	7586	7603	7621	7638	7656	7674	7691	7709	7727	7745	2	4	5	7	9	11	12	14	16
0.89	7762	7780	7798	7816	7834	7852	7870	7889	7907	7925	2	4	5	7	9	11	13	14	16
0.90	7943	7962	7980	7998	8017	8035	8054	8072	8091	8110	2	4	6	7	9	11	13	15	17
0.91	8128	8147	8166	8185	8204	8222	8241	8260	8279	8299	2	4	6	7	9	11	13	15	17
0.92	8318	8337	8356	8375	8395	8414	8433	8453	8472	8492	2	4	6	8	10	11	13	15	17
0.93	8511	8531	8551	8570	8590	8610	8630	8650	8670	8690	2	4	6	8	10	12	14	16	18
0.94	8710	8730	8750	8770	8790	8810	8831	8851	8872	8892	2	4	6	8	10	12	14	16	18
0.95	8913	8933	8954	8974	8995	9016	9036	9057	9078	9099	2	4	6	8	10	12	15	17	19
0.96	9120	9141	9162	9183	9204	9226	9247	9268	9290	9311	2	4	6	9	11	13	15	17	19
0.97	9333	9354	9376	9397	9419	9441	9462	9484	9506	9528	2	4	7	9	11	13	15	18	20
0.98	9550	9572	9594	9616	9638	9661	9683	9705	9727	9750	2	4	7	9	11	14	16	18	20
0.99	9772	9795	9817	9840	9863	9886	9908	9931	9954	9977	2	5	7	9	11	14	16	18	20

NATURAL SINES

°	0' 0.0°	6' 0.1°	12' 0.2°	18' 0.3°	24' 0.4°	30' 0.5°	36' 0.6°	42' 0.7°	48' 0.8°	54' 0.9°	1'	2'	3'	4'	5'
0	0.0000	0.0017	0.0035	0.0052	0.0070	0.0087	0.0105	0.0122	0.0140	0.0157	3	6	9	12	15
1	0.0175	0.0192	0.0209	0.0227	0.0244	0.0262	0.0279	0.0297	0.0314	0.0332	3	6	9	12	15
2	0.0349	0.0366	0.0384	0.0401	0.0419	0.0436	0.0454	0.0471	0.0488	0.0506	3	6	9	12	15
3	0.0523	0.0541	0.0558	0.0576	0.0593	0.0610	0.0628	0.0645	0.0663	0.0680	3	6	9	12	15
4	0.0698	0.0715	0.0732	0.0750	0.0767	0.0785	0.0802	0.0819	0.0837	0.0854	3	6	9	12	14
5	0.0872	0.0889	0.0906	0.0924	0.0941	0.0958	0.0976	0.0993	0.1011	0.1028	3	6	9	12	14
6	0.1045	0.1063	0.1080	0.1097	0.1115	0.1132	0.1149	0.1167	0.1184	0.1201	3	6	9	12	14
7	0.1219	0.1236	0.1253	0.1271	0.1288	0.1305	0.1323	0.1340	0.1357	0.1374	3	6	9	12	14
8	0.1392	0.1409	0.1426	0.1444	0.1461	0.1478	0.1495	0.1513	0.1530	0.1547	3	6	9	12	14
9	0.1564	0.1582	0.1599	0.1616	0.1633	0.1650	0.1668	0.1685	0.1702	0.1719	3	6	9	12	14
10	0.1736	0.1754	0.1771	0.1788	0.1805	0.1822	0.1840	0.1857	0.1874	0.1891	3	6	9	12	14
11	0.1908	0.1925	0.1942	0.1959	0.1977	0.1994	0.2011	0.2028	0.2045	0.2062	3	6	9	11	14
12	0.2079	0.2096	0.2113	0.2130	0.2147	0.2164	0.2181	0.2198	0.2215	0.2232	3	6	9	11	14
13	0.2250	0.2267	0.2284	0.2300	0.2317	0.2334	0.2351	0.2368	0.2385	0.2402	3	6	8	11	14
14	0.2419	0.2436	0.2453	0.2470	0.2487	0.2504	0.2521	0.2538	0.2554	0.2571	3	6	8	11	14
15	0.2588	0.2605	0.2622	0.2639	0.2656	0.2672	0.2689	0.2706	0.2723	0.2740	3	6	8	11	14
16	0.2756	0.2773	0.2790	0.2807	0.2823	0.2840	0.2857	0.2874	0.2890	0.2907	3	6	8	11	14
17	0.2924	0.2940	0.2957	0.2974	0.2990	0.3007	0.3024	0.3040	0.3057	0.3074	3	6	8	11	14
18	0.3090	0.3107	0.3123	0.3140	0.3156	0.3173	0.3190	0.3206	0.3223	0.3239	3	6	8	11	14
19	0.3256	0.3272	0.3289	0.3305	0.3322	0.3338	0.3355	0.3371	0.3387	0.3404	3	5	8	11	14
20	0.3420	0.3437	0.3453	0.3469	0.3486	0.3502	0.3518	0.3535	0.3551	0.3567	3	5	8	11	14
21	0.3584	0.3600	0.3616	0.3633	0.3649	0.3665	0.3681	0.3697	0.3714	0.3730	3	5	8	11	14
22	0.3746	0.3762	0.3778	0.3795	0.3811	0.3827	0.3843	0.3859	0.3875	0.3891	3	5	8	11	13
23	0.3907	0.3923	0.3939	0.3955	0.3971	0.3987	0.4003	0.4019	0.4035	0.4051	3	5	8	11	13
24	0.4067	0.4083	0.4099	0.4115	0.4131	0.4147	0.4163	0.4179	0.4195	0.4210	3	5	8	11	13
25	0.4226	0.4242	0.4258	0.4274	0.4289	0.4305	0.4321	0.4337	0.4352	0.4368	3	5	8	11	13
26	0.4384	0.4399	0.4415	0.4431	0.4446	0.4462	0.4478	0.4493	0.4509	0.4524	3	5	8	10	13
27	0.4540	0.4555	0.4571	0.4586	0.4602	0.4617	0.4633	0.4648	0.4664	0.4679	3	5	8	10	13
28	0.4695	0.4710	0.4726	0.4741	0.4756	0.4772	0.4787	0.4802	0.4818	0.4833	3	5	8	10	13
29	0.4848	0.4863	0.4879	0.4894	0.4909	0.4924	0.4939	0.4955	0.4970	0.4985	3	5	8	10	13
30	0.5000	0.5015	0.5030	0.5045	0.5060	0.5075	0.5090	0.5105	0.5120	0.5135	3	5	8	10	13
31	0.5150	0.5165	0.5180	0.5195	0.5210	0.5225	0.5240	0.5255	0.5270	0.5284	3	5	8	10	12
32	0.5299	0.5314	0.5329	0.5344	0.5358	0.5373	0.5388	0.5402	0.5417	0.5432	2	5	7	10	12
33	0.5446	0.5461	0.5476	0.5490	0.5505	0.5519	0.5534	0.5548	0.5563	0.5577	2	5	7	10	12
34	0.5592	0.5606	0.5621	0.5635	0.5650	0.5664	0.5678	0.5693	0.5707	0.5721	2	5	7	10	12
35	0.5736	0.5750	0.5764	0.5779	0.5793	0.5807	0.5821	0.5835	0.5850	0.5864	2	5	7	9	12
36	0.5878	0.5892	0.5906	0.5920	0.5934	0.5948	0.5962	0.5976	0.5990	0.6004	2	5	7	9	12
37	0.6018	0.6032	0.6046	0.6060	0.6074	0.6088	0.6101	0.6115	0.6129	0.6143	2	5	7	9	12
38	0.6157	0.6170	0.6184	0.6198	0.6211	0.6225	0.6239	0.6252	0.6266	0.6280	2	5	7	9	11
39	0.6293	0.6307	0.6320	0.6334	0.6347	0.6361	0.6374	0.6388	0.6401	0.6414	2	4	7	9	11
40	0.6428	0.6441	0.6455	0.6468	0.6481	0.6494	0.6508	0.6521	0.6534	0.6547	2	4	7	9	11
41	0.6561	0.6574	0.6587	0.6600	0.6613	0.6626	0.6639	0.6652	0.6665	0.6678	2	4	7	9	11
42	0.6691	0.6704	0.6717	0.6730	0.6743	0.6756	0.6769	0.6782	0.6794	0.6807	2	4	6	9	11
43	0.6820	0.6833	0.6845	0.6858	0.6871	0.6884	0.6896	0.6909	0.6921	0.6934	2	4	6	8	11
44	0.6947	0.6959	0.6972	0.6984	0.6997	0.7009	0.7022	0.7034	0.7046	0.7059	2	4	6	8	10

NATURAL SINES (continued)

°	0' 0.0°	6' 0.1°	12' 0.2°	18' 0.3°	24' 0.4°	30' 0.5°	36' 0.6°	42' 0.7°	48' 0.8°	54' 0.9°	1'	2'	3'	4'	5'
45	0.7071	0.7083	0.7096	0.7108	0.7120	0.7133	0.7145	0.7157	0.7169	0.7181	2	4	6	8	10
46	0.7193	0.7206	0.7218	0.7230	0.7242	0.7254	0.7266	0.7278	0.7290	0.7302	2	4	6	8	10
47	0.7314	0.7325	0.7337	0.7349	0.7361	0.7373	0.7385	0.7396	0.7408	0.7420	2	4	6	8	10
48	0.7431	0.7443	0.7455	0.7466	0.7478	0.7490	0.7501	0.7513	0.7524	0.7536	2	4	6	8	10
49	0.7547	0.7558	0.7570	0.7581	0.7593	0.7604	0.7615	0.7627	0.7638	0.7649	2	4	6	8	9
50	0.7660	0.7672	0.7683	0.7694	0.7705	0.7716	0.7727	0.7738	0.7749	0.7760	2	4	6	7	9
51	0.7771	0.7782	0.7793	0.7804	0.7815	0.7826	0.7837	0.7848	0.7859	0.7869	2	4	5	7	9
52	0.7880	0.7891	0.7902	0.7912	0.7923	0.7934	0.7944	0.7955	0.7965	0.7976	2	4	5	7	9
53	0.7986	0.7997	0.8007	0.8018	0.8028	0.8039	0.8049	0.8059	0.8070	0.8080	2	3	5	7	9
54	0.8090	0.8100	0.8111	0.8121	0.8131	0.8141	0.8151	0.8161	0.8171	0.8181	2	3	5	7	8
55	0.8192	0.8202	0.8211	0.8221	0.8231	0.8241	0.8251	0.8261	0.8271	0.8281	2	3	5	7	8
56	0.8290	0.8300	0.8310	0.8320	0.8329	0.8339	0.8348	0.8358	0.8368	0.8377	2	3	5	6	8
57	0.8387	0.8396	0.8406	0.8415	0.8425	0.8434	0.8443	0.8453	0.8462	0.8471	2	3	5	6	8
58	0.8480	0.8490	0.8499	0.8508	0.8517	0.8526	0.8536	0.8545	0.8554	0.8563	2	3	5	6	8
59	0.8572	0.8581	0.8590	0.8599	0.8607	0.8616	0.8625	0.8634	0.8643	0.8652	1	3	4	6	7
60	0.8660	0.8669	0.8678	0.8686	0.8695	0.8704	0.8712	0.8721	0.8729	0.8738	1	3	4	6	7
61	0.8746	0.8755	0.8763	0.8771	0.8780	0.8788	0.8796	0.8805	0.8813	0.8821	1	3	4	6	7
62	0.8829	0.8838	0.8846	0.8854	0.8862	0.8870	0.8878	0.8886	0.8894	0.8902	1	3	4	5	7
63	0.8910	0.8918	0.8926	0.8934	0.8942	0.8949	0.8957	0.8965	0.8973	0.8980	1	3	4	5	6
64	0.8988	0.8996	0.9003	0.9011	0.9018	0.9026	0.9033	0.9041	0.9048	0.9056	1	3	4	5	6
65	0.9063	0.9070	0.9078	0.9085	0.9092	0.9100	0.9107	0.9114	0.9121	0.9128	1	2	4	5	6
66	0.9135	0.9143	0.9150	0.9157	0.9164	0.9171	0.9178	0.9184	0.9191	0.9198	1	2	3	5	6
67	0.9205	0.9212	0.9219	0.9225	0.9232	0.9239	0.9245	0.9252	0.9259	0.9265	1	2	3	4	6
68	0.9272	0.9278	0.9285	0.9291	0.9298	0.9304	0.9311	0.9317	0.9323	0.9330	1	2	3	4	5
69	0.9336	0.9342	0.9348	0.9354	0.9361	0.9367	0.9373	0.9379	0.9385	0.9391	1	2	3	4	5
70	0.9397	0.9403	0.9409	0.9415	0.9421	0.9426	0.9432	0.9438	0.9444	0.9449	1	2	3	4	5
71	0.9455	0.9461	0.9466	0.9472	0.9478	0.9483	0.9489	0.9494	0.9500	0.9505	1	2	3	4	5
72	0.9511	0.9516	0.9521	0.9527	0.9532	0.9537	0.9542	0.9548	0.9553	0.9558	1	2	3	4	4
73	0.9563	0.9568	0.9573	0.9578	0.9583	0.9588	0.9593	0.9598	0.9603	0.9608	1	2	2	3	4
74	0.9613	0.9617	0.9622	0.9627	0.9632	0.9636	0.9641	0.9646	0.9650	0.9655	1	2	2	3	4
75	0.9659	0.9664	0.9668	0.9673	0.9677	0.9681	0.9686	0.9690	0.9694	0.9699	1	1	2	3	4
76	0.9703	0.9707	0.9711	0.9715	0.9720	0.9724	0.9728	0.9732	0.9736	0.9740	1	1	2	3	3
77	0.9744	0.9748	0.9751	0.9755	0.9759	0.9763	0.9767	0.9770	0.9774	0.9778	1	1	2	3	3
78	0.9781	0.9785	0.9789	0.9792	0.9796	0.9799	0.9803	0.9806	0.9810	0.9813	1	1	2	2	3
79	0.9816	0.9820	0.9823	0.9826	0.9829	0.9833	0.9836	0.9839	0.9842	0.9845	1	1	2	2	3
80	0.9848	0.9851	0.9854	0.9857	0.9860	0.9863	0.9866	0.9869	0.9871	0.9874	0	1	1	2	2
81	0.9877	0.9880	0.9882	0.9885	0.9888	0.9890	0.9893	0.9895	0.9898	0.9900	0	1	1	2	2
82	0.9903	0.9905	0.9907	0.9910	0.9912	0.9914	0.9917	0.9919	0.9921	0.9923	0	1	1	2	2
83	0.9925	0.9928	0.9930	0.9932	0.9934	0.9936	0.9938	0.9940	0.9942	0.9943	0	1	1	1	2
84	0.9945	0.9947	0.9949	0.9951	0.9952	0.9954	0.9956	0.9957	0.9959	0.9960	0	1	1	1	2
85	0.9962	0.9963	0.9965	0.9966	0.9968	0.9969	0.9971	0.9972	0.9973	0.9974	0	0	1	1	1
86	0.9976	0.9977	0.9978	0.9979	0.9980	0.9981	0.9982	0.9983	0.9984	0.9985	0	0	1	1	1
87	0.9986	0.9987	0.9988	0.9989	0.9990	0.9990	0.9991	0.9992	0.9993	0.9993	0	0	0	1	1
88	0.9994	0.9995	0.9995	0.9996	0.9996	0.9997	0.9997	0.9997	0.9998	0.9998	0	0	0	0	1
89	0.9998	0.9999	0.9999	0.9999	0.9999	1.0000	1.0000	1.0000	1.0000	1.0000	0	0	0	0	0
90	1.0000														

NATURAL COSINES

°	0' 0.0°	6' 0.1°	12' 0.2°	18' 0.3°	24' 0.4°	30' 0.5°	36' 0.6°	42' 0.7°	48' 0.8°	54' 0.9°	Subtract 1'	2'	3'	4'	5'
0	1.0000	1.0000	1.0000	1.0000	1.0000	1.0000	0.9999	0.9999	0.9999	0.9999	0	0	0	0	0
1	0.9998	0.9998	0.9998	0.9997	0.9997	0.9997	0.9996	0.9996	0.9995	0.9995	0	0	0	0	0
2	0.9994	0.9993	0.9993	0.9992	0.9991	0.9990	0.9990	0.9989	0.9988	0.9987	0	0	0	0	1
3	0.9986	0.9985	0.9984	0.9983	0.9982	0.9981	0.9980	0.9979	0.9978	0.9977	0	0	0	1	1
4	0.9976	0.9974	0.9973	0.9972	0.9971	0.9969	0.9968	0.9966	0.9965	0.9963	0	0	1	1	1
5	0.9962	0.9960	0.9959	0.9957	0.9956	0.9954	0.9952	0.9951	0.9949	0.9947	0	1	1	1	1
6	0.9945	0.9943	0.9942	0.9940	0.9938	0.9936	0.9934	0.9932	0.9930	0.9928	0	1	1	1	2
7	0.9925	0.9923	0.9921	0.9919	0.9917	0.9914	0.9912	0.9910	0.9907	0.9905	1	1	1	2	2
8	0.9903	0.9900	0.9898	0.9895	0.9893	0.9890	0.9888	0.9885	0.9882	0.9880	1	1	1	2	2
9	0.9877	0.9874	0.9871	0.9869	0.9866	0.9863	0.9860	0.9857	0.9854	0.9851	1	1	1	2	2
10	0.9848	0.9845	0.9842	0.9839	0.9836	0.9833	0.9829	0.9826	0.9823	0.9820	1	1	2	2	3
11	0.9816	0.9813	0.9810	0.9806	0.9803	0.9799	0.9796	0.9792	0.9789	0.9785	1	1	2	2	3
12	0.9781	0.9778	0.9774	0.9770	0.9767	0.9763	0.9759	0.9755	0.9751	0.9748	1	1	2	2	3
13	0.9744	0.9740	0.9736	0.9732	0.9728	0.9724	0.9720	0.9715	0.9711	0.9707	1	1	2	3	3
14	0.9703	0.9699	0.9694	0.9690	0.9686	0.9681	0.9677	0.9673	0.9668	0.9664	1	1	2	3	4
15	0.9659	0.9655	0.9650	0.9646	0.9641	0.9636	0.9632	0.9627	0.9622	0.9617	1	2	2	3	4
16	0.9613	0.9608	0.9603	0.9598	0.9593	0.9588	0.9583	0.9578	0.9573	0.9568	1	2	3	3	4
17	0.9563	0.9558	0.9553	0.9548	0.9542	0.9537	0.9532	0.9527	0.9521	0.9516	1	2	3	3	4
18	0.9511	0.9505	0.9500	0.9494	0.9489	0.9483	0.9478	0.9472	0.9466	0.9461	1	2	3	4	5
19	0.9455	0.9449	0.9444	0.9438	0.9432	0.9426	0.9421	0.9415	0.9409	0.9403	1	2	3	4	5
20	0.9397	0.9391	0.9385	0.9379	0.9373	0.9367	0.9361	0.9354	0.9348	0.9342	1	2	3	4	5
21	0.9336	0.9330	0.9323	0.9317	0.9311	0.9304	0.9298	0.9291	0.9285	0.9278	1	2	3	4	5
22	0.9272	0.9265	0.9259	0.9252	0.9245	0.9239	0.9232	0.9225	0.9219	0.9212	1	2	3	5	6
23	0.9205	0.9198	0.9191	0.9184	0.9178	0.9171	0.9164	0.9157	0.9150	0.9143	1	2	4	5	6
24	0.9135	0.9128	0.9121	0.9114	0.9107	0.9100	0.9092	0.9085	0.9078	0.9070	1	2	4	5	6
25	0.9063	0.9056	0.9048	0.9041	0.9033	0.9026	0.9018	0.9011	0.9003	0.8996	1	3	4	5	6
26	0.8988	0.8980	0.8973	0.8965	0.8957	0.8949	0.8942	0.8934	0.8926	0.8918	1	3	4	5	7
27	0.8910	0.8902	0.8894	0.8886	0.8878	0.8870	0.8862	0.8854	0.8846	0.8838	1	3	4	5	7
28	0.8829	0.8821	0.8813	0.8805	0.8796	0.8788	0.8780	0.8771	0.8763	0.8755	1	3	4	6	7
29	0.8746	0.8738	0.8729	0.8721	0.8712	0.8704	0.8695	0.8686	0.8678	0.8669	1	3	4	6	7
30	0.8660	0.8652	0.8643	0.8634	0.8625	0.8616	0.8607	0.8599	0.8590	0.8581	2	3	4	6	7
31	0.8572	0.8563	0.8554	0.8545	0.8536	0.8526	0.8517	0.8508	0.8499	0.8490	2	3	5	6	8
32	0.8480	0.8471	0.8462	0.8453	0.8443	0.8434	0.8425	0.8415	0.8406	0.8396	2	3	5	6	8
33	0.8387	0.8377	0.8368	0.8358	0.8348	0.8339	0.8329	0.8320	0.8310	0.8300	2	3	5	6	8
34	0.8290	0.8281	0.8271	0.8261	0.8251	0.8241	0.8231	0.8221	0.8211	0.8202	2	3	5	7	8
35	0.8192	0.8181	0.8171	0.8161	0.8151	0.8141	0.8131	0.8121	0.8111	0.8100	2	3	5	7	9
36	0.8090	0.8080	0.8070	0.8059	0.8049	0.8039	0.8028	0.8018	0.8007	0.7997	2	3	5	7	9
37	0.7986	0.7976	0.7965	0.7955	0.7944	0.7934	0.7923	0.7912	0.7902	0.7891	2	4	5	7	9
38	0.7880	0.7869	0.7859	0.7848	0.7837	0.7826	0.7815	0.7804	0.7793	0.7782	2	4	5	7	9
39	0.7771	0.7760	0.7749	0.7738	0.7727	0.7716	0.7705	0.7694	0.7683	0.7672	2	4	5	7	9
40	0.7660	0.7649	0.7638	0.7627	0.7615	0.7604	0.7593	0.7581	0.7570	0.7559	2	4	6	7	9
41	0.7547	0.7536	0.7524	0.7513	0.7501	0.7490	0.7478	0.7466	0.7455	0.7443	2	4	6	8	10
42	0.7431	0.7420	0.7408	0.7396	0.7385	0.7373	0.7361	0.7349	0.7337	0.7325	2	4	6	8	10
43	0.7314	0.7302	0.7290	0.7278	0.7266	0.7254	0.7242	0.7230	0.7218	0.7206	2	4	6	8	10
44	0.7193	0.7181	0.7169	0.7157	0.7145	0.7133	0.7120	0.7108	0.7096	0.7083	2	4	6	8	10

NATURAL COSINES (continued)

°	0' 0.0°	6' 0.1°	12' 0.2°	18' 0.3°	24' 0.4°	30' 0.5°	36' 0.6°	42' 0.7°	48' 0.8°	54' 0.9°	Subtract 1'	2'	3'	4'	5'
45	0.7071	0.7059	0.7046	0.7034	0.7022	0.7009	0.6997	0.6984	0.6972	0.6959	2	4	6	8	10
46	0.6947	0.6934	0.6921	0.6909	0.6896	0.6884	0.6871	0.6858	0.6845	0.6833	2	4	6	8	11
47	0.6820	0.6807	0.6794	0.6782	0.6769	0.6756	0.6743	0.6730	0.6717	0.6704	2	4	6	9	11
48	0.6691	0.6678	0.6665	0.6652	0.6639	0.6626	0.6613	0.6600	0.6587	0.6574	2	4	7	9	11
49	0.6561	0.6547	0.6534	0.6521	0.6508	0.6494	0.6481	0.6468	0.6455	0.6441	2	4	7	9	11
50	0.6428	0.6414	0.6401	0.6388	0.6374	0.6361	0.6347	0.6334	0.6320	0.6307	2	4	7	9	11
51	0.6293	0.6280	0.6266	0.6252	0.6239	0.6225	0.6211	0.6198	0.6184	0.6170	2	5	7	9	11
52	0.6157	0.6143	0.6129	0.6115	0.6101	0.6088	0.6074	0.6060	0.6046	0.6032	2	5	7	9	12
53	0.6018	0.6004	0.5990	0.5976	0.5962	0.5948	0.5934	0.5920	0.5906	0.5892	2	5	7	9	12
54	0.5878	0.5864	0.5850	0.5835	0.5821	0.5807	0.5793	0.5779	0.5764	0.5750	2	5	7	9	12
55	0.5736	0.5721	0.5707	0.5693	0.5678	0.5664	0.5650	0.5635	0.5621	0.5606	2	5	7	10	12
56	0.5592	0.5577	0.5563	0.5548	0.5534	0.5519	0.5505	0.5490	0.5476	0.5461	2	5	7	10	12
57	0.5446	0.5432	0.5417	0.5402	0.5388	0.5373	0.5358	0.5344	0.5329	0.5314	2	5	7	10	12
58	0.5299	0.5284	0.5270	0.5255	0.5240	0.5225	0.5210	0.5195	0.5180	0.5165	2	5	8	10	12
59	0.5150	0.5135	0.5120	0.5105	0.5090	0.5075	0.5060	0.5045	0.5030	0.5015	3	5	8	10	13
60	0.5000	0.4985	0.4970	0.4955	0.4939	0.4924	0.4909	0.4894	0.4879	0.4863	3	5	8	10	13
61	0.4848	0.4833	0.4818	0.4802	0.4787	0.4772	0.4756	0.4741	0.4726	0.4710	3	5	8	10	13
62	0.4695	0.4679	0.4664	0.4648	0.4633	0.4617	0.4602	0.4586	0.4571	0.4555	3	5	8	10	13
63	0.4540	0.4524	0.4509	0.4493	0.4478	0.4462	0.4446	0.4431	0.4415	0.4399	3	5	8	11	13
64	0.4384	0.4368	0.4352	0.4337	0.4321	0.4305	0.4289	0.4274	0.4258	0.4242	3	5	8	11	13
65	0.4226	0.4210	0.4195	0.4179	0.4163	0.4147	0.4131	0.4115	0.4099	0.4083	3	5	8	11	13
66	0.4067	0.4051	0.4035	0.4019	0.4003	0.3987	0.3971	0.3955	0.3939	0.3923	3	5	8	11	14
67	0.3907	0.3891	0.3875	0.3859	0.3843	0.3827	0.3811	0.3795	0.3778	0.3762	3	5	8	11	14
68	0.3746	0.3730	0.3714	0.3697	0.3681	0.3665	0.3649	0.3633	0.3616	0.3600	3	5	8	11	14
69	0.3584	0.3567	0.3551	0.3535	0.3518	0.3502	0.3486	0.3469	0.3453	0.3437	3	5	8	11	14
70	0.3420	0.3404	0.3387	0.3371	0.3355	0.3338	0.3322	0.3305	0.3289	0.3272	3	5	8	11	14
71	0.3256	0.3239	0.3223	0.3206	0.3190	0.3173	0.3156	0.3140	0.3123	0.3107	3	6	8	11	14
72	0.3090	0.3074	0.3057	0.3040	0.3024	0.3007	0.2990	0.2974	0.2957	0.2940	3	6	8	11	14
73	0.2924	0.2907	0.2890	0.2874	0.2857	0.2840	0.2823	0.2807	0.2790	0.2773	3	6	8	11	14
74	0.2756	0.2740	0.2723	0.2706	0.2689	0.2672	0.2656	0.2639	0.2622	0.2605	3	6	8	11	14
75	0.2588	0.2571	0.2554	0.2538	0.2521	0.2504	0.2487	0.2470	0.2453	0.2436	3	6	8	11	14
76	0.2419	0.2402	0.2385	0.2368	0.2351	0.2334	0.2317	0.2300	0.2284	0.2267	3	6	8	11	14
77	0.2250	0.2233	0.2215	0.2198	0.2181	0.2164	0.2147	0.2130	0.2113	0.2096	3	6	9	11	14
78	0.2079	0.2062	0.2045	0.2028	0.2011	0.1994	0.1977	0.1959	0.1942	0.1925	3	6	9	12	14
79	0.1908	0.1891	0.1874	0.1857	0.1840	0.1822	0.1805	0.1788	0.1771	0.1754	3	6	9	12	14
80	0.1736	0.1719	0.1702	0.1685	0.1668	0.1650	0.1633	0.1616	0.1599	0.1582	3	6	9	12	14
81	0.1564	0.1547	0.1530	0.1513	0.1495	0.1478	0.1461	0.1444	0.1426	0.1409	3	6	9	12	14
82	0.1392	0.1374	0.1357	0.1340	0.1323	0.1305	0.1288	0.1271	0.1253	0.1236	3	6	9	12	14
83	0.1219	0.1201	0.1184	0.1167	0.1149	0.1132	0.1115	0.1097	0.1080	0.1063	3	6	9	12	14
84	0.1045	0.1028	0.1011	0.0993	0.0976	0.0958	0.0941	0.0924	0.0906	0.0889	3	6	9	12	14
85	0.0872	0.0854	0.0837	0.0819	0.0802	0.0785	0.0767	0.0750	0.0732	0.0715	3	6	9	12	14
86	0.0698	0.0680	0.0663	0.0645	0.0628	0.0610	0.0593	0.0576	0.0558	0.0541	3	6	9	12	15
87	0.0523	0.0506	0.0488	0.0471	0.0454	0.0436	0.0419	0.0401	0.0384	0.0366	3	6	9	12	15
88	0.0349	0.0332	0.0314	0.0297	0.0279	0.0262	0.0244	0.0227	0.0209	0.0192	3	6	9	12	15
89	0.0175	0.0157	0.0140	0.0122	0.0105	0.0087	0.0070	0.0052	0.0035	0.0017	3	6	9	12	15
90	0.0000														

NATURAL TANGENTS

°	0' 0.0°	6' 0.1°	12' 0.2°	18' 0.3°	24' 0.4°	30' 0.5°	36' 0.6°	42' 0.7°	48' 0.8°	54' 0.9°	1'	2'	3'	4'	5'
0	0.0000	0.0017	0.0035	0.0052	0.0070	0.0087	0.0105	0.0122	0.0140	0.0157	3	6	9	12	15
1	0.0175	0.0192	0.0209	0.0227	0.0244	0.0262	0.0279	0.0297	0.0314	0.0332	3	6	9	12	15
2	0.0349	0.0367	0.0384	0.0402	0.0419	0.0437	0.0454	0.0472	0.0489	0.0507	3	6	9	12	15
3	0.0524	0.0542	0.0559	0.0577	0.0594	0.0612	0.0629	0.0647	0.0664	0.0682	3	6	9	12	15
4	0.0699	0.0717	0.0734	0.0752	0.0769	0.0787	0.0805	0.0822	0.0840	0.0857	3	6	9	12	15
5	0.0875	0.0892	0.0910	0.0928	0.0945	0.0963	0.0981	0.0998	0.1016	0.1033	3	6	9	12	15
6	0.1051	0.1069	0.1086	0.1104	0.1122	0.1139	0.1157	0.1175	0.1192	0.1210	3	6	9	12	15
7	0.1228	0.1246	0.1263	0.1281	0.1299	0.1317	0.1334	0.1352	0.1370	0.1388	3	6	9	12	15
8	0.1405	0.1423	0.1441	0.1459	0.1477	0.1495	0.1512	0.1530	0.1548	0.1566	3	6	9	12	15
9	0.1584	0.1602	0.1620	0.1638	0.1655	0.1673	0.1691	0.1709	0.1727	0.1745	3	6	9	12	15
10	0.1763	0.1781	0.1799	0.1817	0.1835	0.1853	0.1871	0.1890	0.1908	0.1926	3	6	9	12	15
11	0.1944	0.1962	0.1980	0.1998	0.2016	0.2035	0.2053	0.2071	0.2089	0.2107	3	6	9	12	15
12	0.2126	0.2144	0.2162	0.2180	0.2199	0.2217	0.2235	0.2254	0.2272	0.2290	3	6	9	12	15
13	0.2309	0.2327	0.2345	0.2364	0.2382	0.2401	0.2419	0.2438	0.2456	0.2475	3	6	9	12	15
14	0.2493	0.2512	0.2530	0.2549	0.2568	0.2586	0.2605	0.2623	0.2642	0.2661	3	6	9	13	16
15	0.2679	0.2698	0.2717	0.2736	0.2754	0.2773	0.2792	0.2811	0.2830	0.2849	3	6	9	13	16
16	0.2867	0.2886	0.2905	0.2924	0.2943	0.2962	0.2981	0.3000	0.3019	0.3038	3	6	9	13	16
17	0.3057	0.3076	0.3096	0.3115	0.3134	0.3153	0.3172	0.3191	0.3211	0.3230	3	6	10	13	16
18	0.3249	0.3269	0.3288	0.3307	0.3327	0.3346	0.3365	0.3385	0.3404	0.3424	3	6	10	13	16
19	0.3443	0.3463	0.3482	0.3502	0.3522	0.3541	0.3561	0.3581	0.3600	0.3620	3	7	10	13	16
20	0.3640	0.3659	0.3679	0.3699	0.3719	0.3739	0.3759	0.3779	0.3799	0.3819	3	7	10	13	17
21	0.3839	0.3859	0.3879	0.3899	0.3919	0.3939	0.3959	0.3979	0.4000	0.4020	3	7	10	13	17
22	0.4040	0.4061	0.4081	0.4101	0.4122	0.4142	0.4163	0.4183	0.4204	0.4224	3	7	10	14	17
23	0.4245	0.4265	0.4286	0.4307	0.4327	0.4348	0.4369	0.4390	0.4411	0.4431	3	7	10	14	17
24	0.4452	0.4473	0.4494	0.4515	0.4536	0.4557	0.4578	0.4599	0.4621	0.4642	4	7	11	14	18
25	0.4663	0.4684	0.4706	0.4727	0.4748	0.4770	0.4791	0.4813	0.4834	0.4856	4	7	11	14	18
26	0.4877	0.4899	0.4921	0.4942	0.4964	0.4986	0.5008	0.5029	0.5051	0.5073	4	7	11	15	18
27	0.5095	0.5117	0.5139	0.5161	0.5184	0.5206	0.5228	0.5250	0.5272	0.5295	4	7	11	15	18
28	0.5317	0.5340	0.5362	0.5384	0.5407	0.5430	0.5452	0.5475	0.5498	0.5520	4	8	11	15	19
29	0.5543	0.5566	0.5589	0.5612	0.5635	0.5658	0.5681	0.5704	0.5727	0.5750	4	8	12	15	19
30	0.5774	0.5797	0.5820	0.5844	0.5867	0.5890	0.5914	0.5938	0.5961	0.5985	4	8	12	16	20
31	0.6009	0.6032	0.6056	0.6080	0.6104	0.6128	0.6152	0.6176	0.6200	0.6224	4	8	12	16	20
32	0.6249	0.6273	0.6297	0.6322	0.6346	0.6371	0.6395	0.6420	0.6445	0.6469	4	8	12	16	20
33	0.6494	0.6519	0.6544	0.6569	0.6594	0.6619	0.6644	0.6669	0.6694	0.6720	4	8	13	17	21
34	0.6745	0.6771	0.6796	0.6822	0.6847	0.6873	0.6899	0.6924	0.6950	0.6976	4	9	13	17	21
35	0.7002	0.7028	0.7054	0.7080	0.7107	0.7133	0.7159	0.7186	0.7212	0.7239	4	9	13	17	22
36	0.7265	0.7292	0.7319	0.7346	0.7373	0.7400	0.7427	0.7454	0.7481	0.7508	5	9	14	18	23
37	0.7536	0.7563	0.7590	0.7618	0.7646	0.7673	0.7701	0.7729	0.7757	0.7785	5	9	14	18	23
38	0.7813	0.7841	0.7869	0.7898	0.7926	0.7954	0.7983	0.8012	0.8040	0.8069	5	9	14	19	24
39	0.8098	0.8127	0.8156	0.8185	0.8214	0.8243	0.8273	0.8302	0.8332	0.8361	5	10	15	19	24
40	0.8391	0.8421	0.8451	0.8481	0.8511	0.8541	0.8571	0.8601	0.8632	0.8662	5	10	15	20	25
41	0.8693	0.8724	0.8754	0.8785	0.8816	0.8847	0.8878	0.8910	0.8941	0.8972	5	10	16	21	26
42	0.9004	0.9036	0.9067	0.9099	0.9131	0.9163	0.9195	0.9228	0.9260	0.9293	5	11	16	21	27
43	0.9325	0.9358	0.9391	0.9424	0.9457	0.9490	0.9523	0.9556	0.9590	0.9623	6	11	17	22	28
44	0.9657	0.9691	0.9725	0.9759	0.9793	0.9827	0.9861	0.9896	0.9930	0.9965	6	11	17	23	28

NATURAL TANGENTS (continued)

°	0' 0.0°	6' 0.1°	12' 0.2°	18' 0.3°	24' 0.4°	30' 0.5°	36' 0.6°	42' 0.7°	48' 0.8°	54' 0.9°	1'	2'	3'	4'	5'
45	1.0000	1.0035	1.0070	1.0105	1.0141	1.0176	1.0212	1.0247	1.0283	1.0319	6	12	18	24	30
46	1.0355	1.0392	1.0428	1.0464	1.0501	1.0538	1.0575	1.0612	1.0649	1.0686	6	12	18	25	31
47	1.0724	1.0761	1.0799	1.0837	1.0875	1.0913	1.0951	1.0990	1.1028	1.1067	6	13	19	25	32
48	1.1106	1.1145	1.1184	1.1224	1.1263	1.1303	1.1343	1.1383	1.1423	1.1463	7	13	20	27	33
49	1.1504	1.1544	1.1585	1.1626	1.1667	1.1708	1.1750	1.1792	1.1833	1.1875	7	14	21	28	34
50	1.1918	1.1960	1.2002	1.2045	1.2088	1.2131	1.2174	1.2218	1.2261	1.2305	7	14	22	29	36
51	1.2349	1.2393	1.2437	1.2482	1.2527	1.2572	1.2617	1.2662	1.2708	1.2753	8	15	23	30	38
52	1.2799	1.2846	1.2892	1.2938	1.2985	1.3032	1.3079	1.3127	1.3175	1.3222	8	16	24	31	39
53	1.3270	1.3319	1.3367	1.3416	1.3465	1.3514	1.3564	1.3613	1.3663	1.3713	8	16	25	33	41
54	1.3764	1.3814	1.3865	1.3916	1.3968	1.4019	1.4071	1.4124	1.4176	1.4229	9	17	26	34	43
55	1.4281	1.4335	1.4388	1.4442	1.4496	1.4550	1.4605	1.4659	1.4715	1.4770	9	18	27	36	45
56	1.4826	1.4882	1.4938	1.4994	1.5051	1.5108	1.5166	1.5224	1.5282	1.5340	10	19	29	38	48
57	1.5399	1.5458	1.5517	1.5577	1.5637	1.5697	1.5757	1.5818	1.5880	1.5941	10	20	30	40	50
58	1.6003	1.6066	1.6128	1.6191	1.6255	1.6319	1.6383	1.6447	1.6512	1.6577	11	21	32	43	53
59	1.6643	1.6709	1.6775	1.6842	1.6909	1.6977	1.7045	1.7113	1.7182	1.7251	11	23	34	45	56
60	1.7321	1.7391	1.7461	1.7532	1.7603	1.7675	1.7747	1.7820	1.7893	1.7966	12	24	36	48	60
61	1.8040	1.8115	1.8190	1.8265	1.8341	1.8418	1.8495	1.8572	1.8650	1.8728	13	26	38	51	64
62	1.8807	1.8887	1.8967	1.9047	1.9128	1.9210	1.9292	1.9375	1.9458	1.9542	14	27	41	55	68
63	1.9626	1.9711	1.9797	1.9883	1.9970	2.0057	2.0145	2.0233	2.0323	2.0413	14	29	44	58	73
64	2.0503	2.0594	2.0686	2.0778	2.0872	2.0965	2.1060	2.1155	2.1251	2.1348	16	31	47	63	78
65	2.1445	2.1543	2.1642	2.1742	2.1842	2.1943	2.2045	2.2148	2.2251	2.2355	17	34	51	68	85
66	2.2460	2.2566	2.2673	2.2781	2.2889	2.2998	2.3109	2.3220	2.3332	2.3445	18	37	55	73	92
67	2.3559	2.3673	2.3789	2.3906	2.4023	2.4142	2.4262	2.4383	2.4504	2.4627	20	40	60	79	99
68	2.4751	2.4876	2.5002	2.5129	2.5257	2.5386	2.5517	2.5649	2.5782	2.5916	22	43	65	87	108
69	2.6051	2.6187	2.6325	2.6464	2.6605	2.6746	2.6889	2.7034	2.7179	2.7326	24	47	71	95	119
70	2.7475	2.7625	2.7776	2.7929	2.8083	2.8239	2.8397	2.8556	2.8716	2.8878	26	52	78	104	131
71	2.9042	2.9208	2.9375	2.9544	2.9714	2.9887	3.0061	3.0237	3.0415	3.0595	29	58	87	116	145
72	3.0777	3.0961	3.1146	3.1334	3.1524	3.1716	3.1910	3.2106	3.2305	3.2506	32	64	96	129	161
73	3.2709	3.2914	3.3122	3.3332	3.3544	3.3759	3.3977	3.4197	3.4420	3.4646	36	72	108	144	180
74	3.4874	3.5105	3.5339	3.5576	3.5816	3.6059	3.6305	3.6554	3.6806	3.7062	41	81	122	163	204
75	3.7321	3.7583	3.7848	3.8118	3.8391	3.8667	3.8947	3.9232	3.9520	3.9812	46	93	139	186	232
76	4.0108	4.0408	4.0713	4.1022	4.1335	4.1653	4.1976	4.2303	4.2635	4.2972	53	107	160	213	267
77	4.3315	4.3662	4.4015	4.4374	4.4737	4.5107	4.5483	4.5864	4.6252	4.6646					
78	4.7046	4.7453	4.7867	4.8288	4.8716	4.9152	4.9594	5.0045	5.0504	5.0970					
79	5.1446	5.1929	5.2422	5.2924	5.3435	5.3955	5.4486	5.5026	5.5578	5.6140					
80	5.6713	5.7297	5.7894	5.8502	5.9124	5.9758	6.0405	6.1066	6.1742	6.2432					
81	6.3138	6.3859	6.4596	6.5350	6.6122	6.6912	6.7720	6.8548	6.9395	7.0264					
82	7.1154	7.2066	7.3002	7.3962	7.4947	7.5958	7.6996	7.8062	7.9158	8.0285		Differences	untrustworthy	here	
83	8.1443	8.2636	8.3863	8.5126	8.6427	8.7769	8.9152	9.0579	9.2052	9.3572					
84	9.5144	9.677	9.845	10.02	10.20	10.39	10.58	10.78	10.99	11.20					
85	11.43	11.66	11.91	12.16	12.43	12.71	13.00	13.30	13.62	13.95					
86	14.30	14.67	15.06	15.46	15.89	16.35	16.83	17.34	17.89	18.46					
87	19.08	19.74	20.45	21.20	22.02	22.90	23.86	24.90	26.03	27.27					
88	28.64	30.14	31.82	33.69	35.80	38.19	40.92	44.07	47.74	52.08					
89	57.29	63.66	71.62	81.85	95.49	114.6	143.2	191.0	286.5	573.0					
90	∞														

448

LOGARITHMS OF SINES

°	0′ 0.0°	6′ 0.1°	12′ 0.2°	18′ 0.3°	24′ 0.4°	30′ 0.5°	36′ 0.6°	42′ 0.7°	48′ 0.8°	54′ 0.9°	1′	2′	3′	4′	5′
0	−∞	$\bar{3}.2419$	$\bar{3}.5429$	$\bar{3}.7190$	$\bar{3}.8439$	$\bar{3}.9408$	$\bar{2}.0200$	$\bar{2}.0870$	$\bar{2}.1450$	$\bar{2}.1961$	Differences untrustworthy here				
1	$\bar{2}.2419$	$\bar{2}.2832$	$\bar{2}.3210$	$\bar{2}.3558$	$\bar{2}.3880$	$\bar{2}.4179$	$\bar{2}.4459$	$\bar{2}.4723$	$\bar{2}.4971$	$\bar{2}.5206$					
2	$\bar{2}.5428$	$\bar{2}.5640$	$\bar{2}.5842$	$\bar{2}.6035$	$\bar{2}.6220$	$\bar{2}.6397$	$\bar{2}.6567$	$\bar{2}.6731$	$\bar{2}.6889$	$\bar{2}.7041$					
3	$\bar{2}.7188$	$\bar{2}.7330$	$\bar{2}.7468$	$\bar{2}.7602$	$\bar{2}.7731$	$\bar{2}.7857$	$\bar{2}.7979$	$\bar{2}.8098$	$\bar{2}.8213$	$\bar{2}.8326$					
4	$\bar{2}.8436$	$\bar{2}.8543$	$\bar{2}.8647$	$\bar{2}.8749$	$\bar{2}.8849$	$\bar{2}.8946$	$\bar{2}.9042$	$\bar{2}.9135$	$\bar{2}.9226$	$\bar{2}.9315$	16	32	48	64	80
5	$\bar{2}.9403$	$\bar{2}.9489$	$\bar{2}.9573$	$\bar{2}.9655$	$\bar{2}.9736$	$\bar{2}.9816$	$\bar{2}.9894$	$\bar{2}.9970$	$\bar{1}.0046$	$\bar{1}.0120$	13	26	39	52	65
6	$\bar{1}.0192$	$\bar{1}.0264$	$\bar{1}.0334$	$\bar{1}.0403$	$\bar{1}.0472$	$\bar{1}.0539$	$\bar{1}.0605$	$\bar{1}.0670$	$\bar{1}.0734$	$\bar{1}.0797$	11	22	33	44	55
7	$\bar{1}.0859$	$\bar{1}.0920$	$\bar{1}.0981$	$\bar{1}.1040$	$\bar{1}.1099$	$\bar{1}.1157$	$\bar{1}.1214$	$\bar{1}.1271$	$\bar{1}.1326$	$\bar{1}.1381$	10	19	29	38	48
8	$\bar{1}.1436$	$\bar{1}.1489$	$\bar{1}.1542$	$\bar{1}.1594$	$\bar{1}.1646$	$\bar{1}.1697$	$\bar{1}.1747$	$\bar{1}.1797$	$\bar{1}.1847$	$\bar{1}.1895$	8	17	25	34	42
9	$\bar{1}.1943$	$\bar{1}.1991$	$\bar{1}.2038$	$\bar{1}.2085$	$\bar{1}.2131$	$\bar{1}.2176$	$\bar{1}.2221$	$\bar{1}.2266$	$\bar{1}.2310$	$\bar{1}.2353$	8	15	23	30	38
10	$\bar{1}.2397$	$\bar{1}.2439$	$\bar{1}.2482$	$\bar{1}.2524$	$\bar{1}.2565$	$\bar{1}.2606$	$\bar{1}.2647$	$\bar{1}.2687$	$\bar{1}.2727$	$\bar{1}.2767$	7	14	20	27	34
11	$\bar{1}.2806$	$\bar{1}.2845$	$\bar{1}.2883$	$\bar{1}.2921$	$\bar{1}.2959$	$\bar{1}.2997$	$\bar{1}.3034$	$\bar{1}.3070$	$\bar{1}.3107$	$\bar{1}.3143$	6	12	19	25	31
12	$\bar{1}.3179$	$\bar{1}.3214$	$\bar{1}.3250$	$\bar{1}.3284$	$\bar{1}.3319$	$\bar{1}.3353$	$\bar{1}.3387$	$\bar{1}.3421$	$\bar{1}.3455$	$\bar{1}.3488$	6	11	17	23	28
13	$\bar{1}.3521$	$\bar{1}.3554$	$\bar{1}.3586$	$\bar{1}.3618$	$\bar{1}.3650$	$\bar{1}.3682$	$\bar{1}.3713$	$\bar{1}.3745$	$\bar{1}.3775$	$\bar{1}.3806$	5	11	16	21	26
14	$\bar{1}.3837$	$\bar{1}.3867$	$\bar{1}.3897$	$\bar{1}.3927$	$\bar{1}.3957$	$\bar{1}.3986$	$\bar{1}.4015$	$\bar{1}.4044$	$\bar{1}.4073$	$\bar{1}.4102$	5	10	15	20	24
15	$\bar{1}.4130$	$\bar{1}.4158$	$\bar{1}.4186$	$\bar{1}.4214$	$\bar{1}.4242$	$\bar{1}.4269$	$\bar{1}.4296$	$\bar{1}.4323$	$\bar{1}.4350$	$\bar{1}.4377$	5	9	14	18	23
16	$\bar{1}.4403$	$\bar{1}.4430$	$\bar{1}.4456$	$\bar{1}.4482$	$\bar{1}.4508$	$\bar{1}.4533$	$\bar{1}.4559$	$\bar{1}.4584$	$\bar{1}.4609$	$\bar{1}.4634$	4	9	13	17	21
17	$\bar{1}.4659$	$\bar{1}.4684$	$\bar{1}.4709$	$\bar{1}.4733$	$\bar{1}.4757$	$\bar{1}.4781$	$\bar{1}.4805$	$\bar{1}.4829$	$\bar{1}.4853$	$\bar{1}.4876$	4	8	12	16	20
18	$\bar{1}.4900$	$\bar{1}.4923$	$\bar{1}.4946$	$\bar{1}.4969$	$\bar{1}.4992$	$\bar{1}.5015$	$\bar{1}.5037$	$\bar{1}.5060$	$\bar{1}.5082$	$\bar{1}.5104$	4	8	11	15	19
19	$\bar{1}.5126$	$\bar{1}.5148$	$\bar{1}.5170$	$\bar{1}.5192$	$\bar{1}.5213$	$\bar{1}.5235$	$\bar{1}.5256$	$\bar{1}.5278$	$\bar{1}.5299$	$\bar{1}.5320$	4	7	11	14	18
20	$\bar{1}.5341$	$\bar{1}.5361$	$\bar{1}.5382$	$\bar{1}.5402$	$\bar{1}.5423$	$\bar{1}.5443$	$\bar{1}.5463$	$\bar{1}.5484$	$\bar{1}.5504$	$\bar{1}.5523$	3	7	10	13	17
21	$\bar{1}.5543$	$\bar{1}.5563$	$\bar{1}.5583$	$\bar{1}.5602$	$\bar{1}.5621$	$\bar{1}.5641$	$\bar{1}.5660$	$\bar{1}.5679$	$\bar{1}.5698$	$\bar{1}.5717$	3	6	10	13	16
22	$\bar{1}.5736$	$\bar{1}.5754$	$\bar{1}.5773$	$\bar{1}.5792$	$\bar{1}.5810$	$\bar{1}.5828$	$\bar{1}.5847$	$\bar{1}.5865$	$\bar{1}.5883$	$\bar{1}.5901$	3	6	9	12	15
23	$\bar{1}.5919$	$\bar{1}.5937$	$\bar{1}.5954$	$\bar{1}.5972$	$\bar{1}.5990$	$\bar{1}.6007$	$\bar{1}.6024$	$\bar{1}.6042$	$\bar{1}.6059$	$\bar{1}.6076$	3	6	9	12	14
24	$\bar{1}.6093$	$\bar{1}.6110$	$\bar{1}.6127$	$\bar{1}.6144$	$\bar{1}.6161$	$\bar{1}.6177$	$\bar{1}.6194$	$\bar{1}.6210$	$\bar{1}.6227$	$\bar{1}.6243$	3	6	8	11	14
25	$\bar{1}.6259$	$\bar{1}.6276$	$\bar{1}.6292$	$\bar{1}.6308$	$\bar{1}.6324$	$\bar{1}.6340$	$\bar{1}.6356$	$\bar{1}.6371$	$\bar{1}.6387$	$\bar{1}.6403$	3	5	8	11	13
26	$\bar{1}.6418$	$\bar{1}.6434$	$\bar{1}.6449$	$\bar{1}.6465$	$\bar{1}.6480$	$\bar{1}.6495$	$\bar{1}.6510$	$\bar{1}.6526$	$\bar{1}.6541$	$\bar{1}.6556$	3	5	8	10	13
27	$\bar{1}.6570$	$\bar{1}.6585$	$\bar{1}.6600$	$\bar{1}.6615$	$\bar{1}.6629$	$\bar{1}.6644$	$\bar{1}.6659$	$\bar{1}.6673$	$\bar{1}.6687$	$\bar{1}.6702$	2	5	7	10	12
28	$\bar{1}.6716$	$\bar{1}.6730$	$\bar{1}.6744$	$\bar{1}.6759$	$\bar{1}.6773$	$\bar{1}.6787$	$\bar{1}.6801$	$\bar{1}.6814$	$\bar{1}.6828$	$\bar{1}.6842$	2	5	7	9	12
29	$\bar{1}.6856$	$\bar{1}.6869$	$\bar{1}.6883$	$\bar{1}.6896$	$\bar{1}.6910$	$\bar{1}.6923$	$\bar{1}.6937$	$\bar{1}.6950$	$\bar{1}.6963$	$\bar{1}.6977$	2	4	7	9	11
30	$\bar{1}.6990$	$\bar{1}.7003$	$\bar{1}.7016$	$\bar{1}.7029$	$\bar{1}.7042$	$\bar{1}.7055$	$\bar{1}.7068$	$\bar{1}.7080$	$\bar{1}.7093$	$\bar{1}.7106$	2	4	6	9	11
31	$\bar{1}.7118$	$\bar{1}.7131$	$\bar{1}.7144$	$\bar{1}.7156$	$\bar{1}.7168$	$\bar{1}.7181$	$\bar{1}.7193$	$\bar{1}.7205$	$\bar{1}.7218$	$\bar{1}.7230$	2	4	6	8	10
32	$\bar{1}.7242$	$\bar{1}.7254$	$\bar{1}.7266$	$\bar{1}.7278$	$\bar{1}.7290$	$\bar{1}.7302$	$\bar{1}.7314$	$\bar{1}.7326$	$\bar{1}.7338$	$\bar{1}.7349$	2	4	6	8	10
33	$\bar{1}.7361$	$\bar{1}.7373$	$\bar{1}.7384$	$\bar{1}.7396$	$\bar{1}.7407$	$\bar{1}.7419$	$\bar{1}.7430$	$\bar{1}.7442$	$\bar{1}.7453$	$\bar{1}.7464$	2	4	6	8	10
34	$\bar{1}.7476$	$\bar{1}.7487$	$\bar{1}.7498$	$\bar{1}.7509$	$\bar{1}.7520$	$\bar{1}.7531$	$\bar{1}.7542$	$\bar{1}.7553$	$\bar{1}.7564$	$\bar{1}.7575$	2	4	6	7	9
35	$\bar{1}.7586$	$\bar{1}.7597$	$\bar{1}.7607$	$\bar{1}.7618$	$\bar{1}.7629$	$\bar{1}.7640$	$\bar{1}.7650$	$\bar{1}.7661$	$\bar{1}.7671$	$\bar{1}.7682$	2	4	5	7	9
36	$\bar{1}.7692$	$\bar{1}.7703$	$\bar{1}.7713$	$\bar{1}.7723$	$\bar{1}.7734$	$\bar{1}.7744$	$\bar{1}.7754$	$\bar{1}.7764$	$\bar{1}.7774$	$\bar{1}.7785$	2	3	5	7	9
37	$\bar{1}.7795$	$\bar{1}.7805$	$\bar{1}.7815$	$\bar{1}.7825$	$\bar{1}.7835$	$\bar{1}.7844$	$\bar{1}.7854$	$\bar{1}.7864$	$\bar{1}.7874$	$\bar{1}.7884$	2	3	5	7	8
38	$\bar{1}.7893$	$\bar{1}.7903$	$\bar{1}.7913$	$\bar{1}.7922$	$\bar{1}.7932$	$\bar{1}.7941$	$\bar{1}.7951$	$\bar{1}.7960$	$\bar{1}.7970$	$\bar{1}.7979$	2	3	5	6	8
39	$\bar{1}.7989$	$\bar{1}.7998$	$\bar{1}.8007$	$\bar{1}.8017$	$\bar{1}.8026$	$\bar{1}.8035$	$\bar{1}.8044$	$\bar{1}.8053$	$\bar{1}.8063$	$\bar{1}.8072$	2	3	5	6	8
40	$\bar{1}.8081$	$\bar{1}.8090$	$\bar{1}.8099$	$\bar{1}.8108$	$\bar{1}.8117$	$\bar{1}.8125$	$\bar{1}.8134$	$\bar{1}.8143$	$\bar{1}.8152$	$\bar{1}.8161$	1	3	4	6	7
41	$\bar{1}.8169$	$\bar{1}.8178$	$\bar{1}.8187$	$\bar{1}.8195$	$\bar{1}.8204$	$\bar{1}.8213$	$\bar{1}.8221$	$\bar{1}.8230$	$\bar{1}.8238$	$\bar{1}.8247$	1	3	4	6	7
42	$\bar{1}.8255$	$\bar{1}.8264$	$\bar{1}.8272$	$\bar{1}.8280$	$\bar{1}.8289$	$\bar{1}.8297$	$\bar{1}.8305$	$\bar{1}.8313$	$\bar{1}.8322$	$\bar{1}.8330$	1	3	4	6	7
43	$\bar{1}.8338$	$\bar{1}.8346$	$\bar{1}.8354$	$\bar{1}.8362$	$\bar{1}.8370$	$\bar{1}.8378$	$\bar{1}.8386$	$\bar{1}.8394$	$\bar{1}.8402$	$\bar{1}.8410$	1	3	4	5	7
44	$\bar{1}.8418$	$\bar{1}.8426$	$\bar{1}.8433$	$\bar{1}.8441$	$\bar{1}.8449$	$\bar{1}.8457$	$\bar{1}.8464$	$\bar{1}.8472$	$\bar{1}.8480$	$\bar{1}.8487$	1	3	4	5	6

LOGARITHMS OF SINES (continued)

°	0′ 0.0°	6′ 0.1°	12′ 0.2°	18′ 0.3°	24′ 0.4°	30′ 0.5°	36′ 0.6°	42′ 0.7°	48′ 0.8°	54′ 0.9°	1′	2′	3′	4′	5′
45	$\bar{1}.8495$	$\bar{1}.8502$	$\bar{1}.8510$	$\bar{1}.8517$	$\bar{1}.8525$	$\bar{1}.8532$	$\bar{1}.8540$	$\bar{1}.8547$	$\bar{1}.8555$	$\bar{1}.8562$	1	2	4	5	6
46	$\bar{1}.8569$	$\bar{1}.8577$	$\bar{1}.8584$	$\bar{1}.8591$	$\bar{1}.8598$	$\bar{1}.8606$	$\bar{1}.8613$	$\bar{1}.8620$	$\bar{1}.8627$	$\bar{1}.8634$	1	2	4	5	6
47	$\bar{1}.8641$	$\bar{1}.8648$	$\bar{1}.8655$	$\bar{1}.8662$	$\bar{1}.8669$	$\bar{1}.8676$	$\bar{1}.8683$	$\bar{1}.8690$	$\bar{1}.8697$	$\bar{1}.8704$	1	2	3	5	6
48	$\bar{1}.8711$	$\bar{1}.8718$	$\bar{1}.8724$	$\bar{1}.8731$	$\bar{1}.8738$	$\bar{1}.8745$	$\bar{1}.8751$	$\bar{1}.8758$	$\bar{1}.8765$	$\bar{1}.8771$	1	2	3	4	6
49	$\bar{1}.8778$	$\bar{1}.8784$	$\bar{1}.8791$	$\bar{1}.8797$	$\bar{1}.8804$	$\bar{1}.8810$	$\bar{1}.8817$	$\bar{1}.8823$	$\bar{1}.8830$	$\bar{1}.8836$	1	2	3	4	5
50	$\bar{1}.8843$	$\bar{1}.8849$	$\bar{1}.8855$	$\bar{1}.8862$	$\bar{1}.8868$	$\bar{1}.8874$	$\bar{1}.8880$	$\bar{1}.8887$	$\bar{1}.8893$	$\bar{1}.8899$	1	2	3	4	5
51	$\bar{1}.8905$	$\bar{1}.8911$	$\bar{1}.8917$	$\bar{1}.8923$	$\bar{1}.8929$	$\bar{1}.8935$	$\bar{1}.8941$	$\bar{1}.8947$	$\bar{1}.8953$	$\bar{1}.8959$	1	2	3	4	5
52	$\bar{1}.8965$	$\bar{1}.8971$	$\bar{1}.8977$	$\bar{1}.8983$	$\bar{1}.8989$	$\bar{1}.8995$	$\bar{1}.9000$	$\bar{1}.9006$	$\bar{1}.9012$	$\bar{1}.9018$	1	2	3	4	5
53	$\bar{1}.9023$	$\bar{1}.9029$	$\bar{1}.9035$	$\bar{1}.9041$	$\bar{1}.9046$	$\bar{1}.9052$	$\bar{1}.9057$	$\bar{1}.9063$	$\bar{1}.9069$	$\bar{1}.9074$	1	2	3	4	5
54	$\bar{1}.9080$	$\bar{1}.9085$	$\bar{1}.9091$	$\bar{1}.9096$	$\bar{1}.9101$	$\bar{1}.9107$	$\bar{1}.9112$	$\bar{1}.9118$	$\bar{1}.9123$	$\bar{1}.9128$	1	2	3	4	5
55	$\bar{1}.9134$	$\bar{1}.9139$	$\bar{1}.9144$	$\bar{1}.9149$	$\bar{1}.9155$	$\bar{1}.9160$	$\bar{1}.9165$	$\bar{1}.9170$	$\bar{1}.9175$	$\bar{1}.9181$	1	2	3	3	4
56	$\bar{1}.9186$	$\bar{1}.9191$	$\bar{1}.9196$	$\bar{1}.9201$	$\bar{1}.9206$	$\bar{1}.9211$	$\bar{1}.9216$	$\bar{1}.9221$	$\bar{1}.9226$	$\bar{1}.9231$	1	2	3	3	4
57	$\bar{1}.9236$	$\bar{1}.9241$	$\bar{1}.9246$	$\bar{1}.9251$	$\bar{1}.9255$	$\bar{1}.9260$	$\bar{1}.9265$	$\bar{1}.9270$	$\bar{1}.9275$	$\bar{1}.9279$	1	2	2	3	4
58	$\bar{1}.9284$	$\bar{1}.9289$	$\bar{1}.9294$	$\bar{1}.9298$	$\bar{1}.9303$	$\bar{1}.9308$	$\bar{1}.9312$	$\bar{1}.9317$	$\bar{1}.9322$	$\bar{1}.9326$	1	2	2	3	4
59	$\bar{1}.9331$	$\bar{1}.9335$	$\bar{1}.9340$	$\bar{1}.9344$	$\bar{1}.9349$	$\bar{1}.9353$	$\bar{1}.9358$	$\bar{1}.9362$	$\bar{1}.9367$	$\bar{1}.9371$	1	1	2	3	4
60	$\bar{1}.9375$	$\bar{1}.9380$	$\bar{1}.9384$	$\bar{1}.9388$	$\bar{1}.9393$	$\bar{1}.9397$	$\bar{1}.9401$	$\bar{1}.9406$	$\bar{1}.9410$	$\bar{1}.9414$	1	1	2	3	4
61	$\bar{1}.9418$	$\bar{1}.9422$	$\bar{1}.9427$	$\bar{1}.9431$	$\bar{1}.9435$	$\bar{1}.9439$	$\bar{1}.9443$	$\bar{1}.9447$	$\bar{1}.9451$	$\bar{1}.9455$	1	1	2	3	3
62	$\bar{1}.9459$	$\bar{1}.9463$	$\bar{1}.9467$	$\bar{1}.9471$	$\bar{1}.9475$	$\bar{1}.9479$	$\bar{1}.9483$	$\bar{1}.9487$	$\bar{1}.9491$	$\bar{1}.9495$	1	1	2	3	3
63	$\bar{1}.9499$	$\bar{1}.9503$	$\bar{1}.9506$	$\bar{1}.9510$	$\bar{1}.9514$	$\bar{1}.9518$	$\bar{1}.9522$	$\bar{1}.9525$	$\bar{1}.9529$	$\bar{1}.9533$	1	1	2	3	3
64	$\bar{1}.9537$	$\bar{1}.9540$	$\bar{1}.9544$	$\bar{1}.9548$	$\bar{1}.9551$	$\bar{1}.9555$	$\bar{1}.9558$	$\bar{1}.9562$	$\bar{1}.9566$	$\bar{1}.9569$	1	1	2	2	3
65	$\bar{1}.9573$	$\bar{1}.9576$	$\bar{1}.9580$	$\bar{1}.9583$	$\bar{1}.9587$	$\bar{1}.9590$	$\bar{1}.9594$	$\bar{1}.9597$	$\bar{1}.9601$	$\bar{1}.9604$	1	1	2	2	3
66	$\bar{1}.9607$	$\bar{1}.9611$	$\bar{1}.9614$	$\bar{1}.9617$	$\bar{1}.9621$	$\bar{1}.9624$	$\bar{1}.9627$	$\bar{1}.9631$	$\bar{1}.9634$	$\bar{1}.9637$	1	1	2	2	3
67	$\bar{1}.9640$	$\bar{1}.9643$	$\bar{1}.9647$	$\bar{1}.9650$	$\bar{1}.9653$	$\bar{1}.9656$	$\bar{1}.9659$	$\bar{1}.9662$	$\bar{1}.9666$	$\bar{1}.9669$	1	1	2	2	3
68	$\bar{1}.9672$	$\bar{1}.9675$	$\bar{1}.9678$	$\bar{1}.9681$	$\bar{1}.9684$	$\bar{1}.9687$	$\bar{1}.9690$	$\bar{1}.9693$	$\bar{1}.9696$	$\bar{1}.9699$	1	1	2	2	2
69	$\bar{1}.9702$	$\bar{1}.9704$	$\bar{1}.9707$	$\bar{1}.9710$	$\bar{1}.9713$	$\bar{1}.9716$	$\bar{1}.9719$	$\bar{1}.9722$	$\bar{1}.9724$	$\bar{1}.9727$	0	1	1	2	2
70	$\bar{1}.9730$	$\bar{1}.9733$	$\bar{1}.9735$	$\bar{1}.9738$	$\bar{1}.9741$	$\bar{1}.9743$	$\bar{1}.9746$	$\bar{1}.9749$	$\bar{1}.9751$	$\bar{1}.9754$	0	1	1	2	2
71	$\bar{1}.9757$	$\bar{1}.9759$	$\bar{1}.9762$	$\bar{1}.9764$	$\bar{1}.9767$	$\bar{1}.9770$	$\bar{1}.9772$	$\bar{1}.9775$	$\bar{1}.9777$	$\bar{1}.9780$	0	1	1	2	2
72	$\bar{1}.9782$	$\bar{1}.9785$	$\bar{1}.9787$	$\bar{1}.9789$	$\bar{1}.9792$	$\bar{1}.9794$	$\bar{1}.9797$	$\bar{1}.9799$	$\bar{1}.9801$	$\bar{1}.9804$	0	1	1	2	2
73	$\bar{1}.9806$	$\bar{1}.9808$	$\bar{1}.9811$	$\bar{1}.9813$	$\bar{1}.9815$	$\bar{1}.9817$	$\bar{1}.9820$	$\bar{1}.9822$	$\bar{1}.9824$	$\bar{1}.9826$	0	1	1	1	2
74	$\bar{1}.9828$	$\bar{1}.9831$	$\bar{1}.9833$	$\bar{1}.9835$	$\bar{1}.9837$	$\bar{1}.9839$	$\bar{1}.9841$	$\bar{1}.9843$	$\bar{1}.9845$	$\bar{1}.9847$	0	1	1	1	2
75	$\bar{1}.9849$	$\bar{1}.9851$	$\bar{1}.9853$	$\bar{1}.9855$	$\bar{1}.9857$	$\bar{1}.9859$	$\bar{1}.9861$	$\bar{1}.9863$	$\bar{1}.9865$	$\bar{1}.9867$	0	1	1	1	2
76	$\bar{1}.9869$	$\bar{1}.9871$	$\bar{1}.9873$	$\bar{1}.9875$	$\bar{1}.9876$	$\bar{1}.9878$	$\bar{1}.9880$	$\bar{1}.9882$	$\bar{1}.9884$	$\bar{1}.9885$	0	1	1	1	2
77	$\bar{1}.9887$	$\bar{1}.9889$	$\bar{1}.9891$	$\bar{1}.9892$	$\bar{1}.9894$	$\bar{1}.9896$	$\bar{1}.9897$	$\bar{1}.9899$	$\bar{1}.9901$	$\bar{1}.9902$	0	1	1	1	1
78	$\bar{1}.9904$	$\bar{1}.9906$	$\bar{1}.9907$	$\bar{1}.9909$	$\bar{1}.9910$	$\bar{1}.9912$	$\bar{1}.9913$	$\bar{1}.9915$	$\bar{1}.9916$	$\bar{1}.9918$	0	1	1	1	1
79	$\bar{1}.9919$	$\bar{1}.9921$	$\bar{1}.9922$	$\bar{1}.9924$	$\bar{1}.9925$	$\bar{1}.9927$	$\bar{1}.9928$	$\bar{1}.9929$	$\bar{1}.9931$	$\bar{1}.9932$	0	0	1	1	1
80	$\bar{1}.9934$	$\bar{1}.9935$	$\bar{1}.9936$	$\bar{1}.9937$	$\bar{1}.9939$	$\bar{1}.9940$	$\bar{1}.9941$	$\bar{1}.9943$	$\bar{1}.9944$	$\bar{1}.9945$	0	0	1	1	1
81	$\bar{1}.9946$	$\bar{1}.9947$	$\bar{1}.9949$	$\bar{1}.9950$	$\bar{1}.9951$	$\bar{1}.9952$	$\bar{1}.9953$	$\bar{1}.9954$	$\bar{1}.9955$	$\bar{1}.9956$	0	0	1	1	1
82	$\bar{1}.9958$	$\bar{1}.9959$	$\bar{1}.9960$	$\bar{1}.9961$	$\bar{1}.9962$	$\bar{1}.9963$	$\bar{1}.9964$	$\bar{1}.9965$	$\bar{1}.9966$	$\bar{1}.9967$	0	0	0	1	1
83	$\bar{1}.9968$	$\bar{1}.9968$	$\bar{1}.9969$	$\bar{1}.9970$	$\bar{1}.9971$	$\bar{1}.9972$	$\bar{1}.9973$	$\bar{1}.9974$	$\bar{1}.9975$	$\bar{1}.9975$	0	0	0	1	1
84	$\bar{1}.9976$	$\bar{1}.9977$	$\bar{1}.9978$	$\bar{1}.9978$	$\bar{1}.9979$	$\bar{1}.9980$	$\bar{1}.9981$	$\bar{1}.9981$	$\bar{1}.9982$	$\bar{1}.9983$	0	0	0	0	1
85	$\bar{1}.9983$	$\bar{1}.9984$	$\bar{1}.9985$	$\bar{1}.9985$	$\bar{1}.9986$	$\bar{1}.9987$	$\bar{1}.9987$	$\bar{1}.9988$	$\bar{1}.9988$	$\bar{1}.9989$	0	0	0	0	0
86	$\bar{1}.9989$	$\bar{1}.9990$	$\bar{1}.9990$	$\bar{1}.9991$	$\bar{1}.9991$	$\bar{1}.9992$	$\bar{1}.9992$	$\bar{1}.9993$	$\bar{1}.9993$	$\bar{1}.9994$	0	0	0	0	0
87	$\bar{1}.9994$	$\bar{1}.9994$	$\bar{1}.9995$	$\bar{1}.9995$	$\bar{1}.9996$	$\bar{1}.9996$	$\bar{1}.9996$	$\bar{1}.9996$	$\bar{1}.9997$	$\bar{1}.9997$	0	0	0	0	0
88	$\bar{1}.9997$	$\bar{1}.9998$	$\bar{1}.9998$	$\bar{1}.9998$	$\bar{1}.9998$	$\bar{1}.9999$	$\bar{1}.9999$	$\bar{1}.9999$	$\bar{1}.9999$	$\bar{1}.9999$	0	0	0	0	0
89	$\bar{1}.9999$	$\bar{1}.9999$	0.0000	0.0000	0.0000	0.0000	0.0000	0.0000	0.0000	0.0000					
90	0.0000														

LOGARITHMS OF COSINES

°	0′ 0.0°	6′ 0.1°	12′ 0.2°	18′ 0.3°	24′ 0.4°	30′ 0.5°	36′ 0.6°	42′ 0.7°	48′ 0.8°	54′ 0.9°	Subtract 1′	2′	3′	4′	5′
0	0.0000	0.0000	0.0000	0.0000	0.0000	0.0000	0.0000	0.0000	0.0000	$\bar{1}$.9999	0	0	0	0	0
1	$\bar{1}$.9999	$\bar{1}$.9999	$\bar{1}$.9999	$\bar{1}$.9999	$\bar{1}$.9999	$\bar{1}$.9999	$\bar{1}$.9998	$\bar{1}$.9998	$\bar{1}$.9998	$\bar{1}$.9998	0	0	0	0	0
2	$\bar{1}$.9997	$\bar{1}$.9997	$\bar{1}$.9997	$\bar{1}$.9996	$\bar{1}$.9996	$\bar{1}$.9996	$\bar{1}$.9996	$\bar{1}$.9995	$\bar{1}$.9995	$\bar{1}$.9994	0	0	0	0	0
3	$\bar{1}$.9994	$\bar{1}$.9994	$\bar{1}$.9993	$\bar{1}$.9993	$\bar{1}$.9992	$\bar{1}$.9992	$\bar{1}$.9991	$\bar{1}$.9991	$\bar{1}$.9990	$\bar{1}$.9990	0	0	0	0	0
4	$\bar{1}$.9989	$\bar{1}$.9989	$\bar{1}$.9988	$\bar{1}$.9988	$\bar{1}$.9987	$\bar{1}$.9987	$\bar{1}$.9986	$\bar{1}$.9985	$\bar{1}$.9985	$\bar{1}$.9984	0	0	0	0	0
5	$\bar{1}$.9983	$\bar{1}$.9983	$\bar{1}$.9982	$\bar{1}$.9981	$\bar{1}$.9981	$\bar{1}$.9980	$\bar{1}$.9979	$\bar{1}$.9978	$\bar{1}$.9978	$\bar{1}$.9977	0	0	0	0	1
6	$\bar{1}$.9976	$\bar{1}$.9975	$\bar{1}$.9975	$\bar{1}$.9974	$\bar{1}$.9973	$\bar{1}$.9972	$\bar{1}$.9971	$\bar{1}$.9970	$\bar{1}$.9969	$\bar{1}$.9968	0	0	0	1	1
7	$\bar{1}$.9968	$\bar{1}$.9967	$\bar{1}$.9966	$\bar{1}$.9965	$\bar{1}$.9964	$\bar{1}$.9963	$\bar{1}$.9962	$\bar{1}$.9961	$\bar{1}$.9960	$\bar{1}$.9959	0	0	0	1	1
8	$\bar{1}$.9958	$\bar{1}$.9956	$\bar{1}$.9955	$\bar{1}$.9954	$\bar{1}$.9953	$\bar{1}$.9952	$\bar{1}$.9951	$\bar{1}$.9950	$\bar{1}$.9949	$\bar{1}$.9947	0	0	1	1	1
9	$\bar{1}$.9946	$\bar{1}$.9945	$\bar{1}$.9944	$\bar{1}$.9943	$\bar{1}$.9941	$\bar{1}$.9940	$\bar{1}$.9939	$\bar{1}$.9937	$\bar{1}$.9936	$\bar{1}$.9935	0	0	1	1	1
10	$\bar{1}$.9934	$\bar{1}$.9932	$\bar{1}$.9931	$\bar{1}$.9929	$\bar{1}$.9928	$\bar{1}$.9927	$\bar{1}$.9925	$\bar{1}$.9924	$\bar{1}$.9922	$\bar{1}$.9921	0	0	1	1	1
11	$\bar{1}$.9919	$\bar{1}$.9918	$\bar{1}$.9916	$\bar{1}$.9915	$\bar{1}$.9913	$\bar{1}$.9912	$\bar{1}$.9910	$\bar{1}$.9909	$\bar{1}$.9907	$\bar{1}$.9906	0	1	1	1	1
12	$\bar{1}$.9904	$\bar{1}$.9902	$\bar{1}$.9901	$\bar{1}$.9899	$\bar{1}$.9897	$\bar{1}$.9896	$\bar{1}$.9894	$\bar{1}$.9892	$\bar{1}$.9891	$\bar{1}$.9889	0	1	1	1	1
13	$\bar{1}$.9887	$\bar{1}$.9885	$\bar{1}$.9884	$\bar{1}$.9882	$\bar{1}$.9880	$\bar{1}$.9878	$\bar{1}$.9876	$\bar{1}$.9875	$\bar{1}$.9873	$\bar{1}$.9871	0	1	1	1	2
14	$\bar{1}$.9869	$\bar{1}$.9867	$\bar{1}$.9865	$\bar{1}$.9863	$\bar{1}$.9861	$\bar{1}$.9859	$\bar{1}$.9857	$\bar{1}$.9855	$\bar{1}$.9853	$\bar{1}$.9851	0	1	1	1	2
15	$\bar{1}$.9849	$\bar{1}$.9847	$\bar{1}$.9845	$\bar{1}$.9843	$\bar{1}$.9841	$\bar{1}$.9839	$\bar{1}$.9837	$\bar{1}$.9835	$\bar{1}$.9833	$\bar{1}$.9831	0	1	1	1	2
16	$\bar{1}$.9828	$\bar{1}$.9826	$\bar{1}$.9824	$\bar{1}$.9822	$\bar{1}$.9820	$\bar{1}$.9817	$\bar{1}$.9815	$\bar{1}$.9813	$\bar{1}$.9811	$\bar{1}$.9808	0	1	1	1	2
17	$\bar{1}$.9806	$\bar{1}$.9804	$\bar{1}$.9801	$\bar{1}$.9799	$\bar{1}$.9797	$\bar{1}$.9794	$\bar{1}$.9792	$\bar{1}$.9789	$\bar{1}$.9787	$\bar{1}$.9785	0	1	1	2	2
18	$\bar{1}$.9782	$\bar{1}$.9780	$\bar{1}$.9777	$\bar{1}$.9775	$\bar{1}$.9772	$\bar{1}$.9770	$\bar{1}$.9767	$\bar{1}$.9764	$\bar{1}$.9762	$\bar{1}$.9759	0	1	1	2	2
19	$\bar{1}$.9757	$\bar{1}$.9754	$\bar{1}$.9751	$\bar{1}$.9749	$\bar{1}$.9746	$\bar{1}$.9743	$\bar{1}$.9741	$\bar{1}$.9738	$\bar{1}$.9735	$\bar{1}$.9733	0	1	1	2	2
20	$\bar{1}$.9730	$\bar{1}$.9727	$\bar{1}$.9724	$\bar{1}$.9722	$\bar{1}$.9719	$\bar{1}$.9716	$\bar{1}$.9713	$\bar{1}$.9710	$\bar{1}$.9707	$\bar{1}$.9704	0	1	1	2	2
21	$\bar{1}$.9702	$\bar{1}$.9699	$\bar{1}$.9696	$\bar{1}$.9693	$\bar{1}$.9690	$\bar{1}$.9687	$\bar{1}$.9684	$\bar{1}$.9681	$\bar{1}$.9678	$\bar{1}$.9675	1	1	2	2	2
22	$\bar{1}$.9672	$\bar{1}$.9669	$\bar{1}$.9666	$\bar{1}$.9662	$\bar{1}$.9659	$\bar{1}$.9656	$\bar{1}$.9653	$\bar{1}$.9650	$\bar{1}$.9647	$\bar{1}$.9643	1	1	2	2	3
23	$\bar{1}$.9640	$\bar{1}$.9637	$\bar{1}$.9634	$\bar{1}$.9631	$\bar{1}$.9627	$\bar{1}$.9624	$\bar{1}$.9621	$\bar{1}$.9617	$\bar{1}$.9614	$\bar{1}$.9611	1	1	2	2	3
24	$\bar{1}$.9607	$\bar{1}$.9604	$\bar{1}$.9601	$\bar{1}$.9597	$\bar{1}$.9594	$\bar{1}$.9590	$\bar{1}$.9587	$\bar{1}$.9583	$\bar{1}$.9580	$\bar{1}$.9576	1	1	2	2	3
25	$\bar{1}$.9573	$\bar{1}$.9569	$\bar{1}$.9566	$\bar{1}$.9562	$\bar{1}$.9558	$\bar{1}$.9555	$\bar{1}$.9551	$\bar{1}$.9548	$\bar{1}$.9544	$\bar{1}$.9540	1	1	2	2	3
26	$\bar{1}$.9537	$\bar{1}$.9533	$\bar{1}$.9529	$\bar{1}$.9525	$\bar{1}$.9522	$\bar{1}$.9518	$\bar{1}$.9514	$\bar{1}$.9510	$\bar{1}$.9506	$\bar{1}$.9503	1	1	2	3	3
27	$\bar{1}$.9499	$\bar{1}$.9495	$\bar{1}$.9491	$\bar{1}$.9487	$\bar{1}$.9483	$\bar{1}$.9479	$\bar{1}$.9475	$\bar{1}$.9471	$\bar{1}$.9467	$\bar{1}$.9463	1	1	2	3	3
28	$\bar{1}$.9459	$\bar{1}$.9455	$\bar{1}$.9451	$\bar{1}$.9447	$\bar{1}$.9443	$\bar{1}$.9439	$\bar{1}$.9435	$\bar{1}$.9431	$\bar{1}$.9427	$\bar{1}$.9422	1	1	2	3	3
29	$\bar{1}$.9418	$\bar{1}$.9414	$\bar{1}$.9410	$\bar{1}$.9406	$\bar{1}$.9401	$\bar{1}$.9397	$\bar{1}$.9393	$\bar{1}$.9388	$\bar{1}$.9384	$\bar{1}$.9380	1	1	2	3	4
30	$\bar{1}$.9375	$\bar{1}$.9371	$\bar{1}$.9367	$\bar{1}$.9362	$\bar{1}$.9358	$\bar{1}$.9353	$\bar{1}$.9349	$\bar{1}$.9344	$\bar{1}$.9340	$\bar{1}$.9335	1	1	2	3	4
31	$\bar{1}$.9331	$\bar{1}$.9326	$\bar{1}$.9322	$\bar{1}$.9317	$\bar{1}$.9312	$\bar{1}$.9308	$\bar{1}$.9303	$\bar{1}$.9298	$\bar{1}$.9294	$\bar{1}$.9289	1	2	2	3	4
32	$\bar{1}$.9284	$\bar{1}$.9279	$\bar{1}$.9275	$\bar{1}$.9270	$\bar{1}$.9265	$\bar{1}$.9260	$\bar{1}$.9255	$\bar{1}$.9251	$\bar{1}$.9246	$\bar{1}$.9241	1	2	2	3	4
33	$\bar{1}$.9236	$\bar{1}$.9231	$\bar{1}$.9226	$\bar{1}$.9221	$\bar{1}$.9216	$\bar{1}$.9211	$\bar{1}$.9206	$\bar{1}$.9201	$\bar{1}$.9196	$\bar{1}$.9191	1	2	3	3	4
34	$\bar{1}$.9186	$\bar{1}$.9181	$\bar{1}$.9175	$\bar{1}$.9170	$\bar{1}$.9165	$\bar{1}$.9160	$\bar{1}$.9155	$\bar{1}$.9149	$\bar{1}$.9144	$\bar{1}$.9139	1	2	3	3	4
35	$\bar{1}$.9134	$\bar{1}$.9128	$\bar{1}$.9123	$\bar{1}$.9118	$\bar{1}$.9112	$\bar{1}$.9107	$\bar{1}$.9101	$\bar{1}$.9096	$\bar{1}$.9091	$\bar{1}$.9085	1	2	3	4	5
36	$\bar{1}$.9080	$\bar{1}$.9074	$\bar{1}$.9069	$\bar{1}$.9063	$\bar{1}$.9057	$\bar{1}$.9052	$\bar{1}$.9046	$\bar{1}$.9041	$\bar{1}$.9035	$\bar{1}$.9029	1	2	3	4	5
37	$\bar{1}$.9023	$\bar{1}$.9018	$\bar{1}$.9012	$\bar{1}$.9006	$\bar{1}$.9000	$\bar{1}$.8995	$\bar{1}$.8989	$\bar{1}$.8983	$\bar{1}$.8977	$\bar{1}$.8971	1	2	3	4	5
38	$\bar{1}$.8965	$\bar{1}$.8959	$\bar{1}$.8953	$\bar{1}$.8947	$\bar{1}$.8941	$\bar{1}$.8935	$\bar{1}$.8929	$\bar{1}$.8923	$\bar{1}$.8917	$\bar{1}$.8911	1	2	3	4	5
39	$\bar{1}$.8905	$\bar{1}$.8899	$\bar{1}$.8893	$\bar{1}$.8887	$\bar{1}$.8880	$\bar{1}$.8874	$\bar{1}$.8868	$\bar{1}$.8862	$\bar{1}$.8855	$\bar{1}$.8849	1	2	3	4	5
40	$\bar{1}$.8843	$\bar{1}$.8836	$\bar{1}$.8830	$\bar{1}$.8823	$\bar{1}$.8817	$\bar{1}$.8810	$\bar{1}$.8804	$\bar{1}$.8797	$\bar{1}$.8791	$\bar{1}$.8784	1	2	3	4	5
41	$\bar{1}$.8778	$\bar{1}$.8771	$\bar{1}$.8765	$\bar{1}$.8758	$\bar{1}$.8751	$\bar{1}$.8745	$\bar{1}$.8738	$\bar{1}$.8731	$\bar{1}$.8724	$\bar{1}$.8718	1	2	3	4	6
42	$\bar{1}$.8711	$\bar{1}$.8704	$\bar{1}$.8697	$\bar{1}$.8690	$\bar{1}$.8683	$\bar{1}$.8676	$\bar{1}$.8669	$\bar{1}$.8662	$\bar{1}$.8655	$\bar{1}$.8648	1	2	4	5	6
43	$\bar{1}$.8641	$\bar{1}$.8634	$\bar{1}$.8627	$\bar{1}$.8620	$\bar{1}$.8613	$\bar{1}$.8606	$\bar{1}$.8598	$\bar{1}$.8591	$\bar{1}$.8584	$\bar{1}$.8577	1	2	4	5	6
44	$\bar{1}$.8569	$\bar{1}$.8562	$\bar{1}$.8555	$\bar{1}$.8547	$\bar{1}$.8540	$\bar{1}$.8532	$\bar{1}$.8525	$\bar{1}$.8517	$\bar{1}$.8510	$\bar{1}$.8502	1	2	4	5	6

LOGARITHMS OF COSINES (continued)

°	0′ 0.0°	6′ 0.1°	12′ 0.2°	18′ 0.3°	24′ 0.4°	30′ 0.5°	36′ 0.6°	42′ 0.7°	48′ 0.8°	54′ 0.9°	Subtract 1′	2′	3′	4′	5′
45	$\bar{1}$.8495	$\bar{1}$.8487	$\bar{1}$.8480	$\bar{1}$.8472	$\bar{1}$.8464	$\bar{1}$.8457	$\bar{1}$.8449	$\bar{1}$.8441	$\bar{1}$.8433	$\bar{1}$.8426	1	3	4	5	6
46	$\bar{1}$.8418	$\bar{1}$.8410	$\bar{1}$.8402	$\bar{1}$.8394	$\bar{1}$.8386	$\bar{1}$.8378	$\bar{1}$.8370	$\bar{1}$.8362	$\bar{1}$.8354	$\bar{1}$.8346	1	3	4	5	7
47	$\bar{1}$.8338	$\bar{1}$.8330	$\bar{1}$.8322	$\bar{1}$.8313	$\bar{1}$.8305	$\bar{1}$.8297	$\bar{1}$.8289	$\bar{1}$.8280	$\bar{1}$.8272	$\bar{1}$.8264	1	3	4	6	7
48	$\bar{1}$.8255	$\bar{1}$.8247	$\bar{1}$.8238	$\bar{1}$.8230	$\bar{1}$.8221	$\bar{1}$.8213	$\bar{1}$.8204	$\bar{1}$.8195	$\bar{1}$.8187	$\bar{1}$.8178	1	3	4	6	7
49	$\bar{1}$.8169	$\bar{1}$.8161	$\bar{1}$.8152	$\bar{1}$.8143	$\bar{1}$.8134	$\bar{1}$.8125	$\bar{1}$.8117	$\bar{1}$.8108	$\bar{1}$.8099	$\bar{1}$.8090	1	3	4	6	7
50	$\bar{1}$.8081	$\bar{1}$.8072	$\bar{1}$.8063	$\bar{1}$.8053	$\bar{1}$.8044	$\bar{1}$.8035	$\bar{1}$.8026	$\bar{1}$.8017	$\bar{1}$.8007	$\bar{1}$.7998	2	3	5	6	8
51	$\bar{1}$.7989	$\bar{1}$.7979	$\bar{1}$.7970	$\bar{1}$.7960	$\bar{1}$.7951	$\bar{1}$.7941	$\bar{1}$.7932	$\bar{1}$.7922	$\bar{1}$.7913	$\bar{1}$.7903	2	3	5	6	8
52	$\bar{1}$.7893	$\bar{1}$.7884	$\bar{1}$.7874	$\bar{1}$.7864	$\bar{1}$.7854	$\bar{1}$.7844	$\bar{1}$.7835	$\bar{1}$.7825	$\bar{1}$.7815	$\bar{1}$.7805	2	3	5	7	8
53	$\bar{1}$.7795	$\bar{1}$.7785	$\bar{1}$.7774	$\bar{1}$.7764	$\bar{1}$.7754	$\bar{1}$.7744	$\bar{1}$.7734	$\bar{1}$.7723	$\bar{1}$.7713	$\bar{1}$.7703	2	3	5	7	9
54	$\bar{1}$.7692	$\bar{1}$.7682	$\bar{1}$.7671	$\bar{1}$.7661	$\bar{1}$.7650	$\bar{1}$.7640	$\bar{1}$.7629	$\bar{1}$.7618	$\bar{1}$.7607	$\bar{1}$.7597	2	4	5	7	9
55	$\bar{1}$.7586	$\bar{1}$.7575	$\bar{1}$.7564	$\bar{1}$.7553	$\bar{1}$.7542	$\bar{1}$.7531	$\bar{1}$.7520	$\bar{1}$.7509	$\bar{1}$.7498	$\bar{1}$.7487	2	4	6	7	9
56	$\bar{1}$.7476	$\bar{1}$.7464	$\bar{1}$.7453	$\bar{1}$.7442	$\bar{1}$.7430	$\bar{1}$.7419	$\bar{1}$.7407	$\bar{1}$.7396	$\bar{1}$.7384	$\bar{1}$.7373	2	4	6	8	10
57	$\bar{1}$.7361	$\bar{1}$.7349	$\bar{1}$.7338	$\bar{1}$.7326	$\bar{1}$.7314	$\bar{1}$.7302	$\bar{1}$.7290	$\bar{1}$.7278	$\bar{1}$.7266	$\bar{1}$.7254	2	4	6	8	10
58	$\bar{1}$.7242	$\bar{1}$.7230	$\bar{1}$.7218	$\bar{1}$.7205	$\bar{1}$.7193	$\bar{1}$.7181	$\bar{1}$.7168	$\bar{1}$.7156	$\bar{1}$.7144	$\bar{1}$.7131	2	4	6	8	10
59	$\bar{1}$.7118	$\bar{1}$.7106	$\bar{1}$.7093	$\bar{1}$.7080	$\bar{1}$.7068	$\bar{1}$.7055	$\bar{1}$.7042	$\bar{1}$.7029	$\bar{1}$.7016	$\bar{1}$.7003	2	4	6	9	11
60	$\bar{1}$.6990	$\bar{1}$.6977	$\bar{1}$.6963	$\bar{1}$.6950	$\bar{1}$.6937	$\bar{1}$.6923	$\bar{1}$.6910	$\bar{1}$.6896	$\bar{1}$.6883	$\bar{1}$.6869	2	4	7	9	11
61	$\bar{1}$.6856	$\bar{1}$.6842	$\bar{1}$.6828	$\bar{1}$.6814	$\bar{1}$.6801	$\bar{1}$.6787	$\bar{1}$.6773	$\bar{1}$.6759	$\bar{1}$.6744	$\bar{1}$.6730	2	5	7	9	12
62	$\bar{1}$.6716	$\bar{1}$.6702	$\bar{1}$.6687	$\bar{1}$.6673	$\bar{1}$.6659	$\bar{1}$.6644	$\bar{1}$.6629	$\bar{1}$.6615	$\bar{1}$.6600	$\bar{1}$.6585	2	5	7	10	12
63	$\bar{1}$.6570	$\bar{1}$.6556	$\bar{1}$.6541	$\bar{1}$.6526	$\bar{1}$.6510	$\bar{1}$.6495	$\bar{1}$.6480	$\bar{1}$.6465	$\bar{1}$.6449	$\bar{1}$.6434	3	5	8	10	13
64	$\bar{1}$.6418	$\bar{1}$.6403	$\bar{1}$.6387	$\bar{1}$.6371	$\bar{1}$.6356	$\bar{1}$.6340	$\bar{1}$.6324	$\bar{1}$.6308	$\bar{1}$.6292	$\bar{1}$.6276	3	5	8	11	13
65	$\bar{1}$.6259	$\bar{1}$.6243	$\bar{1}$.6227	$\bar{1}$.6210	$\bar{1}$.6194	$\bar{1}$.6177	$\bar{1}$.6161	$\bar{1}$.6144	$\bar{1}$.6127	$\bar{1}$.6110	3	6	8	11	14
66	$\bar{1}$.6093	$\bar{1}$.6076	$\bar{1}$.6059	$\bar{1}$.6042	$\bar{1}$.6024	$\bar{1}$.6007	$\bar{1}$.5990	$\bar{1}$.5972	$\bar{1}$.5954	$\bar{1}$.5937	3	6	9	12	14
67	$\bar{1}$.5919	$\bar{1}$.5901	$\bar{1}$.5883	$\bar{1}$.5865	$\bar{1}$.5847	$\bar{1}$.5828	$\bar{1}$.5810	$\bar{1}$.5792	$\bar{1}$.5773	$\bar{1}$.5754	3	6	9	12	15
68	$\bar{1}$.5736	$\bar{1}$.5717	$\bar{1}$.5698	$\bar{1}$.5679	$\bar{1}$.5660	$\bar{1}$.5641	$\bar{1}$.5621	$\bar{1}$.5602	$\bar{1}$.5583	$\bar{1}$.5563	3	6	10	13	16
69	$\bar{1}$.5543	$\bar{1}$.5523	$\bar{1}$.5504	$\bar{1}$.5484	$\bar{1}$.5463	$\bar{1}$.5443	$\bar{1}$.5423	$\bar{1}$.5402	$\bar{1}$.5382	$\bar{1}$.5361	3	7	10	13	17
70	$\bar{1}$.5341	$\bar{1}$.5320	$\bar{1}$.5299	$\bar{1}$.5278	$\bar{1}$.5256	$\bar{1}$.5235	$\bar{1}$.5213	$\bar{1}$.5192	$\bar{1}$.5170	$\bar{1}$.5148	4	7	11	14	18
71	$\bar{1}$.5126	$\bar{1}$.5104	$\bar{1}$.5082	$\bar{1}$.5060	$\bar{1}$.5037	$\bar{1}$.5015	$\bar{1}$.4992	$\bar{1}$.4969	$\bar{1}$.4946	$\bar{1}$.4923	4	8	11	15	19
72	$\bar{1}$.4900	$\bar{1}$.4876	$\bar{1}$.4853	$\bar{1}$.4829	$\bar{1}$.4805	$\bar{1}$.4781	$\bar{1}$.4757	$\bar{1}$.4733	$\bar{1}$.4709	$\bar{1}$.4684	4	8	12	16	20
73	$\bar{1}$.4659	$\bar{1}$.4634	$\bar{1}$.4609	$\bar{1}$.4584	$\bar{1}$.4559	$\bar{1}$.4533	$\bar{1}$.4508	$\bar{1}$.4482	$\bar{1}$.4456	$\bar{1}$.4430	4	9	13	17	21
74	$\bar{1}$.4403	$\bar{1}$.4377	$\bar{1}$.4350	$\bar{1}$.4323	$\bar{1}$.4296	$\bar{1}$.4269	$\bar{1}$.4242	$\bar{1}$.4214	$\bar{1}$.4186	$\bar{1}$.4158	5	9	14	18	23
75	$\bar{1}$.4130	$\bar{1}$.4102	$\bar{1}$.4073	$\bar{1}$.4044	$\bar{1}$.4015	$\bar{1}$.3986	$\bar{1}$.3957	$\bar{1}$.3927	$\bar{1}$.3897	$\bar{1}$.3867	5	10	15	20	24
76	$\bar{1}$.3837	$\bar{1}$.3806	$\bar{1}$.3775	$\bar{1}$.3745	$\bar{1}$.3713	$\bar{1}$.3682	$\bar{1}$.3650	$\bar{1}$.3618	$\bar{1}$.3586	$\bar{1}$.3554	5	11	16	21	26
77	$\bar{1}$.3521	$\bar{1}$.3488	$\bar{1}$.3455	$\bar{1}$.3421	$\bar{1}$.3387	$\bar{1}$.3353	$\bar{1}$.3319	$\bar{1}$.3284	$\bar{1}$.3250	$\bar{1}$.3214	6	11	17	23	28
78	$\bar{1}$.3179	$\bar{1}$.3143	$\bar{1}$.3107	$\bar{1}$.3070	$\bar{1}$.3034	$\bar{1}$.2997	$\bar{1}$.2959	$\bar{1}$.2921	$\bar{1}$.2883	$\bar{1}$.2845	6	12	19	25	31
79	$\bar{1}$.2806	$\bar{1}$.2767	$\bar{1}$.2727	$\bar{1}$.2687	$\bar{1}$.2647	$\bar{1}$.2606	$\bar{1}$.2565	$\bar{1}$.2524	$\bar{1}$.2482	$\bar{1}$.2439	7	14	20	27	34
80	$\bar{1}$.2397	$\bar{1}$.2353	$\bar{1}$.2310	$\bar{1}$.2266	$\bar{1}$.2221	$\bar{1}$.2176	$\bar{1}$.2131	$\bar{1}$.2085	$\bar{1}$.2038	$\bar{1}$.1991	8	15	23	30	38
81	$\bar{1}$.1943	$\bar{1}$.1895	$\bar{1}$.1847	$\bar{1}$.1797	$\bar{1}$.1747	$\bar{1}$.1697	$\bar{1}$.1646	$\bar{1}$.1594	$\bar{1}$.1542	$\bar{1}$.1489	8	17	25	34	42
82	$\bar{1}$.1436	$\bar{1}$.1381	$\bar{1}$.1326	$\bar{1}$.1271	$\bar{1}$.1214	$\bar{1}$.1157	$\bar{1}$.1099	$\bar{1}$.1040	$\bar{1}$.0981	$\bar{1}$.0920	10	19	29	38	48
83	$\bar{1}$.0859	$\bar{1}$.0797	$\bar{1}$.0734	$\bar{1}$.0670	$\bar{1}$.0605	$\bar{1}$.0539	$\bar{1}$.0472	$\bar{1}$.0403	$\bar{1}$.0334	$\bar{1}$.0264	11	22	33	44	55
84	$\bar{1}$.0192	$\bar{1}$.0120	$\bar{1}$.0046	$\bar{2}$.9970	$\bar{2}$.9894	$\bar{2}$.9816	$\bar{2}$.9736	$\bar{2}$.9655	$\bar{2}$.9573	$\bar{2}$.9489	13	26	39	52	65
85	$\bar{2}$.9403	$\bar{2}$.9315	$\bar{2}$.9226	$\bar{2}$.9135	$\bar{2}$.9042	$\bar{2}$.8946	$\bar{2}$.8849	$\bar{2}$.8749	$\bar{2}$.8647	$\bar{2}$.8543	16	32	48	64	80
86	$\bar{2}$.8436	$\bar{2}$.8326	$\bar{2}$.8213	$\bar{2}$.8098	$\bar{2}$.7979	$\bar{2}$.7857	$\bar{2}$.7731	$\bar{2}$.7602	$\bar{2}$.7468	$\bar{2}$.7330	Differences untrustworthy here				
87	$\bar{2}$.7188	$\bar{2}$.7041	$\bar{2}$.6889	$\bar{2}$.6731	$\bar{2}$.6567	$\bar{2}$.6397	$\bar{2}$.6220	$\bar{2}$.6035	$\bar{2}$.5842	$\bar{2}$.5640					
88	$\bar{2}$.5428	$\bar{2}$.5206	$\bar{2}$.4971	$\bar{2}$.4723	$\bar{2}$.4459	$\bar{2}$.4179	$\bar{2}$.3880	$\bar{2}$.3558	$\bar{2}$.3210	$\bar{2}$.2832					
89	$\bar{2}$.2419	$\bar{2}$.1961	$\bar{2}$.1450	$\bar{2}$.0870	$\bar{2}$.0200	$\bar{3}$.9408	$\bar{3}$.8439	$\bar{3}$.7190	$\bar{3}$.5429	$\bar{3}$.2419					
90	$-\infty$														

°	0′ 0.0°	6′ 0.1°	12′ 0.2°	18′ 0.3°	24′ 0.4°	30′ 0.5°	36′ 0.6°	42′ 0.7°	48′ 0.8°	54′ 0.9°	1′	2′	3′	4′	5′
45	0.0000	0.0015	0.0030	0.0045	0.0061	0.0076	0.0091	0.0106	0.0121	0.0136	3	5	8	10	13
46	0.0152	0.0167	0.0182	0.0197	0.0212	0.0228	0.0243	0.0258	0.0273	0.0288	3	5	8	10	13
47	0.0303	0.0319	0.0334	0.0349	0.0364	0.0379	0.0395	0.0410	0.0425	0.0440	3	5	8	10	13
48	0.0456	0.0471	0.0486	0.0501	0.0517	0.0532	0.0547	0.0562	0.0578	0.0593	3	5	8	10	13
49	0.0608	0.0624	0.0639	0.0654	0.0670	0.0685	0.0700	0.0716	0.0731	0.0746	3	5	8	10	13
50	0.0762	0.0777	0.0793	0.0808	0.0824	0.0839	0.0854	0.0870	0.0885	0.0901	3	5	8	10	13
51	0.0916	0.0932	0.0947	0.0963	0.0978	0.0994	0.1010	0.1025	0.1041	0.1056	3	5	8	10	13
52	0.1072	0.1088	0.1103	0.1119	0.1135	0.1150	0.1166	0.1182	0.1197	0.1213	3	5	8	11	13
53	0.1229	0.1245	0.1260	0.1276	0.1292	0.1308	0.1324	0.1340	0.1356	0.1371	3	5	8	11	13
54	0.1387	0.1403	0.1419	0.1435	0.1451	0.1467	0.1483	0.1499	0.1516	0.1532	3	5	8	11	13
55	0.1548	0.1564	0.1580	0.1596	0.1612	0.1629	0.1645	0.1661	0.1677	0.1694	3	5	8	11	14
56	0.1710	0.1726	0.1743	0.1759	0.1776	0.1792	0.1809	0.1825	0.1842	0.1858	3	5	8	11	14
57	0.1875	0.1891	0.1908	0.1925	0.1941	0.1958	0.1975	0.1992	0.2008	0.2025	3	6	8	11	14
58	0.2042	0.2059	0.2076	0.2093	0.2110	0.2127	0.2144	0.2161	0.2178	0.2195	3	6	9	11	14
59	0.2212	0.2229	0.2247	0.2264	0.2281	0.2299	0.2316	0.2333	0.2351	0.2368	3	6	9	12	15
60	0.2386	0.2403	0.2421	0.2438	0.2456	0.2474	0.2491	0.2509	0.2527	0.2545	3	6	9	12	15
61	0.2562	0.2580	0.2598	0.2616	0.2634	0.2652	0.2670	0.2689	0.2707	0.2725	3	6	9	12	15
62	0.2743	0.2762	0.2780	0.2798	0.2817	0.2835	0.2854	0.2872	0.2891	0.2910	3	6	9	12	16
63	0.2928	0.2947	0.2966	0.2985	0.3004	0.3023	0.3042	0.3061	0.3080	0.3099	3	6	10	13	16
64	0.3118	0.3137	0.3157	0.3176	0.3196	0.3215	0.3235	0.3254	0.3274	0.3294	3	6	10	13	16
65	0.3313	0.3333	0.3353	0.3373	0.3393	0.3413	0.3433	0.3453	0.3473	0.3494	3	7	10	13	17
66	0.3514	0.3535	0.3555	0.3576	0.3596	0.3617	0.3638	0.3659	0.3679	0.3700	3	7	10	14	17
67	0.3721	0.3743	0.3764	0.3785	0.3806	0.3828	0.3849	0.3871	0.3892	0.3914	4	7	11	14	18
68	0.3936	0.3958	0.3980	0.4002	0.4024	0.4046	0.4068	0.4091	0.4113	0.4136	4	7	11	15	18
69	0.4158	0.4181	0.4204	0.4227	0.4250	0.4273	0.4296	0.4319	0.4342	0.4366	4	8	12	15	19
70	0.4389	0.4413	0.4437	0.4461	0.4484	0.4509	0.4533	0.4557	0.4581	0.4606	4	8	12	16	20
71	0.4630	0.4655	0.4680	0.4705	0.4730	0.4755	0.4780	0.4805	0.4831	0.4857	4	8	13	17	21
72	0.4882	0.4908	0.4934	0.4960	0.4986	0.5013	0.5039	0.5066	0.5093	0.5120	4	9	13	18	22
73	0.5147	0.5174	0.5201	0.5229	0.5256	0.5284	0.5312	0.5340	0.5368	0.5397	5	9	14	19	23
74	0.5425	0.5454	0.5483	0.5512	0.5541	0.5570	0.5600	0.5629	0.5659	0.5689	5	10	15	20	24
75	0.5719	0.5750	0.5780	0.5811	0.5842	0.5873	0.5905	0.5936	0.5968	0.6000	5	10	16	21	26
76	0.6032	0.6065	0.6097	0.6130	0.6163	0.6196	0.6230	0.6264	0.6298	0.6332	6	11	17	22	28
77	0.6366	0.6401	0.6436	0.6471	0.6507	0.6542	0.6578	0.6615	0.6651	0.6688	6	12	18	24	30
78	0.6725	0.6763	0.6800	0.6838	0.6877	0.6915	0.6954	0.6994	0.7033	0.7073	6	13	19	26	32
79	0.7113	0.7154	0.7195	0.7236	0.7278	0.7320	0.7363	0.7406	0.7449	0.7493	7	14	21	28	35
80	0.7537	0.7581	0.7626	0.7672	0.7718	0.7764	0.7811	0.7858	0.7906	0.7954	8	16	23	31	39
81	0.8003	0.8052	0.8102	0.8152	0.8203	0.8255	0.8307	0.8360	0.8413	0.8467	9	17	26	35	43
82	0.8522	0.8577	0.8633	0.8690	0.8748	0.8806	0.8865	0.8924	0.8985	0.9046	10	20	29	39	49
83	0.9109	0.9172	0.9236	0.9301	0.9367	0.9433	0.9501	0.9570	0.9640	0.9711	11	22	34	45	56
84	0.9784	0.9857	0.9932	1.0008	1.0085	1.0164	1.0244	1.0326	1.0409	1.0494	13	26	40	53	66
85	1.0580	1.0669	1.0759	1.0850	1.0944	1.1040	1.1138	1.1238	1.1341	1.1446	16	32	48	64	81
86	1.1554	1.1664	1.1777	1.1893	1.2012	1.2135	1.2261	1.2391	1.2525	1.2663	Differences untrustworthy here				
87	1.2806	1.2954	1.3106	1.3264	1.3429	1.3599	1.3777	1.3962	1.4155	1.4357					
88	1.4569	1.4792	1.5027	1.5275	1.5539	1.5819	1.6119	1.6441	1.6789	1.7167					
89	1.7581	1.8038	1.8550	1.9130	1.9800	2.0591	2.1561	2.2810	2.4571	2.7581					

LOGARITHMS OF TANGENTS

°	0′ 0.0°	6′ 0.1°	12′ 0.2°	18′ 0.3°	24′ 0.4°	30′ 0.5°	36′ 0.6°	42′ 0.7°	48′ 0.8°	54′ 0.9°	1′	2′	3′	4′	5′
0	−∞	3̄.2419	3̄.5429	3̄.7190	3̄.8439	3̄.9409	2̄.0200	2̄.0870	2̄.1450	2̄.1962	Differences untrustworthy here				
1	2̄.2419	2̄.2833	2̄.3211	2̄.3559	2̄.3881	2̄.4181	2̄.4461	2̄.4725	2̄.4973	2̄.5208					
2	2̄.5431	2̄.5643	2̄.5845	2̄.6038	2̄.6223	2̄.6401	2̄.6571	2̄.6736	2̄.6894	2̄.7046					
3	2̄.7194	2̄.7337	2̄.7475	2̄.7609	2̄.7739	2̄.7865	2̄.7988	2̄.8107	2̄.8223	2̄.8336					
4	2̄.8446	2̄.8554	2̄.8659	2̄.8762	2̄.8862	2̄.8960	2̄.9056	2̄.9150	2̄.9241	2̄.9331	16	32	48	64	81
5	2̄.9420	2̄.9506	2̄.9591	2̄.9674	2̄.9756	2̄.9836	2̄.9915	2̄.9992	1̄.0068	1̄.0143	13	26	40	53	66
6	1̄.0216	1̄.0289	1̄.0360	1̄.0430	1̄.0499	1̄.0567	1̄.0633	1̄.0699	1̄.0764	1̄.0828	11	22	34	45	56
7	1̄.0891	1̄.0954	1̄.1015	1̄.1076	1̄.1135	1̄.1194	1̄.1252	1̄.1310	1̄.1367	1̄.1423	10	20	29	39	49
8	1̄.1478	1̄.1533	1̄.1587	1̄.1640	1̄.1693	1̄.1745	1̄.1797	1̄.1848	1̄.1898	1̄.1948	9	17	26	35	43
9	1̄.1997	1̄.2046	1̄.2094	1̄.2142	1̄.2189	1̄.2236	1̄.2282	1̄.2328	1̄.2374	1̄.2419	8	16	23	31	39
10	1̄.2463	1̄.2507	1̄.2551	1̄.2594	1̄.2637	1̄.2680	1̄.2722	1̄.2764	1̄.2805	1̄.2846	7	14	21	28	35
11	1̄.2887	1̄.2927	1̄.2967	1̄.3006	1̄.3046	1̄.3085	1̄.3123	1̄.3162	1̄.3200	1̄.3237	6	13	19	26	32
12	1̄.3275	1̄.3312	1̄.3349	1̄.3385	1̄.3422	1̄.3458	1̄.3493	1̄.3529	1̄.3564	1̄.3599	6	12	18	24	30
13	1̄.3634	1̄.3668	1̄.3702	1̄.3736	1̄.3770	1̄.3804	1̄.3837	1̄.3870	1̄.3903	1̄.3935	6	11	17	22	28
14	1̄.3968	1̄.4000	1̄.4032	1̄.4064	1̄.4095	1̄.4127	1̄.4158	1̄.4189	1̄.4220	1̄.4250	5	11	16	21	26
15	1̄.4281	1̄.4311	1̄.4341	1̄.4371	1̄.4400	1̄.4430	1̄.4459	1̄.4488	1̄.4517	1̄.4546	5	10	15	20	24
16	1̄.4575	1̄.4603	1̄.4632	1̄.4660	1̄.4688	1̄.4716	1̄.4744	1̄.4771	1̄.4799	1̄.4826	5	9	14	19	23
17	1̄.4853	1̄.4880	1̄.4907	1̄.4934	1̄.4961	1̄.4987	1̄.5014	1̄.5040	1̄.5066	1̄.5092	4	9	13	18	22
18	1̄.5118	1̄.5143	1̄.5169	1̄.5195	1̄.5220	1̄.5245	1̄.5270	1̄.5295	1̄.5320	1̄.5345	4	8	13	17	21
19	1̄.5370	1̄.5394	1̄.5419	1̄.5443	1̄.5467	1̄.5491	1̄.5516	1̄.5539	1̄.5563	1̄.5587	4	8	12	16	20
20	1̄.5611	1̄.5634	1̄.5658	1̄.5681	1̄.5704	1̄.5727	1̄.5750	1̄.5773	1̄.5796	1̄.5819	4	8	12	15	19
21	1̄.5842	1̄.5864	1̄.5887	1̄.5909	1̄.5932	1̄.5954	1̄.5977	1̄.5998	1̄.6020	1̄.6042	4	7	11	15	18
22	1̄.6064	1̄.6086	1̄.6108	1̄.6129	1̄.6151	1̄.6172	1̄.6194	1̄.6215	1̄.6236	1̄.6257	4	7	11	14	18
23	1̄.6279	1̄.6300	1̄.6321	1̄.6341	1̄.6362	1̄.6383	1̄.6404	1̄.6424	1̄.6445	1̄.6465	3	7	10	14	17
24	1̄.6486	1̄.6506	1̄.6527	1̄.6547	1̄.6567	1̄.6587	1̄.6607	1̄.6627	1̄.6647	1̄.6667	3	7	10	13	17
25	1̄.6687	1̄.6706	1̄.6726	1̄.6746	1̄.6765	1̄.6785	1̄.6804	1̄.6824	1̄.6843	1̄.6863	3	7	10	13	16
26	1̄.6882	1̄.6901	1̄.6920	1̄.6939	1̄.6958	1̄.6977	1̄.6996	1̄.7015	1̄.7034	1̄.7053	3	6	10	13	16
27	1̄.7072	1̄.7090	1̄.7109	1̄.7128	1̄.7146	1̄.7165	1̄.7183	1̄.7202	1̄.7220	1̄.7238	3	6	9	12	15
28	1̄.7257	1̄.7275	1̄.7293	1̄.7311	1̄.7330	1̄.7348	1̄.7366	1̄.7384	1̄.7402	1̄.7420	3	6	9	12	15
29	1̄.7438	1̄.7455	1̄.7473	1̄.7491	1̄.7509	1̄.7526	1̄.7544	1̄.7562	1̄.7579	1̄.7597	3	6	9	12	15
30	1̄.7614	1̄.7632	1̄.7649	1̄.7667	1̄.7684	1̄.7701	1̄.7719	1̄.7736	1̄.7753	1̄.7771	3	6	9	12	15
31	1̄.7788	1̄.7805	1̄.7822	1̄.7839	1̄.7856	1̄.7873	1̄.7890	1̄.7907	1̄.7924	1̄.7941	3	6	9	11	14
32	1̄.7958	1̄.7975	1̄.7992	1̄.8008	1̄.8025	1̄.8042	1̄.8059	1̄.8075	1̄.8092	1̄.8109	3	6	8	11	14
33	1̄.8125	1̄.8142	1̄.8158	1̄.8175	1̄.8191	1̄.8208	1̄.8224	1̄.8241	1̄.8257	1̄.8274	3	5	8	11	14
34	1̄.8290	1̄.8306	1̄.8323	1̄.8339	1̄.8355	1̄.8371	1̄.8388	1̄.8404	1̄.8420	1̄.8436	3	5	8	11	14
35	1̄.8452	1̄.8468	1̄.8484	1̄.8501	1̄.8517	1̄.8533	1̄.8549	1̄.8565	1̄.8581	1̄.8597	3	5	8	11	13
36	1̄.8613	1̄.8629	1̄.8644	1̄.8660	1̄.8676	1̄.8692	1̄.8708	1̄.8724	1̄.8740	1̄.8755	3	5	8	11	13
37	1̄.8771	1̄.8787	1̄.8803	1̄.8818	1̄.8834	1̄.8850	1̄.8865	1̄.8881	1̄.8897	1̄.8912	3	5	8	10	13
38	1̄.8928	1̄.8944	1̄.8959	1̄.8975	1̄.8990	1̄.9006	1̄.9022	1̄.9037	1̄.9053	1̄.9068	3	5	8	10	13
39	1̄.9084	1̄.9099	1̄.9115	1̄.9130	1̄.9146	1̄.9161	1̄.9176	1̄.9192	1̄.9207	1̄.9223	3	5	8	10	13
40	1̄.9238	1̄.9254	1̄.9269	1̄.9284	1̄.9300	1̄.9315	1̄.9330	1̄.9346	1̄.9361	1̄.9376	3	5	8	10	13
41	1̄.9392	1̄.9407	1̄.9422	1̄.9438	1̄.9453	1̄.9468	1̄.9483	1̄.9499	1̄.9514	1̄.9529	3	5	8	10	13
42	1̄.9544	1̄.9560	1̄.9575	1̄.9590	1̄.9605	1̄.9621	1̄.9636	1̄.9651	1̄.9666	1̄.9681	3	5	8	10	13
43	1̄.9697	1̄.9712	1̄.9727	1̄.9742	1̄.9757	1̄.9772	1̄.9788	1̄.9803	1̄.9818	1̄.9833	3	5	8	10	13
44	1̄.9848	1̄.9864	1̄.9879	1̄.9894	1̄.9909	1̄.9924	1̄.9939	1̄.9955	1̄.9970	1̄.9985	3	5	8	10	13

AREAS OF CIRCLES

Diam.	0.0	0.1	0.2	0.3	0.4	0.5	0.6	0.7	0.8	0.9
0	0.0	0.0079	0.0314	0.0707	0.1257	0.1963	0.2827	0.3848	0.5027	0.6362
1	0.7854	0.9503	1.1310	1.3273	1.5394	1.7671	2.0106	2.2698	2.5447	2.8353
2	3.1416	3.4636	3.8013	4.1548	4.5239	4.9087	5.3093	5.7256	6.1575	6.6052
3	7.0686	7.5477	8.0425	8.5530	9.0792	9.6211	10.179	10.752	11.341	11.946
4	12.566	13.203	13.854	14.522	15.205	15.904	16.619	17.349	18.096	18.857
5	19.635	20.428	21.237	22.062	22.902	23.758	24.630	25.518	26.421	27.340
6	28.274	29.225	30.191	31.172	32.170	33.183	34.212	35.257	36.317	37.393
7	38.485	39.592	40.715	41.854	43.008	44.179	45.365	46.566	47.784	49.017
8	50.266	51.530	52.810	54.106	55.418	56.745	58.088	59.447	60.821	62.211
9	63.617	65.039	66.476	67.929	69.398	70.882	72.382	73.898	75.430	76.977
10	78.540	80.118	81.713	83.323	84.949	86.590	88.247	89.920	91.609	93.313
11	95.033	96.769	98.520	100.29	102.07	103.87	105.68	107.51	109.36	111.22
12	113.10	114.99	116.90	118.82	120.76	122.72	124.69	126.68	128.68	130.70
13	132.73	134.78	136.85	138.93	141.03	143.14	145.27	147.41	149.57	151.75
14	153.94	156.15	158.37	160.61	162.86	165.13	167.42	169.72	172.03	174.37
15	176.72	179.08	181.46	183.85	186.27	188.69	191.13	193.59	196.07	198.56
16	201.06	203.58	206.12	208.67	211.24	213.82	216.42	219.04	221.67	224.32
17	226.98	229.66	232.35	235.06	237.79	240.53	243.28	246.06	248.85	251.65
18	254.47	257.30	260.16	263.02	265.90	268.80	271.72	274.65	277.59	280.55
19	283.53	286.52	289.53	292.55	295.59	298.65	301.72	304.80	307.91	311.03
20	314.16	317.31	320.47	323.65	326.85	330.06	333.29	336.54	339.79	343.07
21	346.36	349.67	352.99	356.33	359.68	363.05	366.44	369.84	373.25	376.68
22	380.13	383.60	387.08	390.57	394.08	397.61	401.15	404.71	408.28	411.87
23	415.48	419.10	422.73	426.38	430.05	433.74	437.44	441.15	444.88	448.63
24	452.39	456.17	459.96	463.77	467.59	471.44	475.29	479.16	483.05	486.95
25	490.88	494.81	498.76	502.73	506.71	510.71	514.72	518.75	522.79	526.85
26	530.93	535.02	539.13	543.25	547.39	551.55	555.72	559.90	564.10	568.32
27	572.56	576.80	581.07	585.35	589.65	593.96	598.28	602.63	606.99	611.36
28	615.75	620.16	624.58	629.02	633.47	637.94	642.42	646.92	651.44	655.97
29	660.52	665.08	669.66	674.26	678.87	683.49	688.13	692.79	697.47	702.15
30	706.86	711.58	716.31	721.07	725.83	730.62	735.42	740.23	745.06	749.91
31	754.77	759.65	764.54	769.45	774.37	779.31	784.27	789.24	794.23	799.23
32	804.25	809.28	814.33	819.40	824.48	829.58	834.69	839.82	844.96	850.12
33	855.30	860.49	865.70	870.92	876.16	881.41	886.68	891.97	897.27	902.59
34	907.92	913.27	918.63	924.01	929.41	934.82	940.25	945.69	951.15	956.62
35	962.12	967.62	973.14	978.68	984.23	989.80	995.38	1000.98	1006.6	1012.2
36	1017.9	1023.5	1029.2	1034.9	1040.6	1046.3	1052.1	1057.8	1063.6	1069.4
37	1075.2	1081.0	1086.9	1092.7	1098.6	1104.5	1110.4	1116.3	1122.2	1128.2
38	1134.1	1140.1	1146.1	1152.1	1158.1	1164.2	1170.2	1176.3	1182.4	1188.5
39	1194.6	1200.7	1206.9	1213.0	1219.2	1225.4	1231.6	1237.9	1244.1	1250.4
40	1256.6	1262.9	1269.2	1275.6	1281.9	1288.2	1294.6	1301.0	1307.4	1313.8
41	1320.3	1326.7	1333.2	1339.6	1346.1	1352.7	1359.2	1365.7	1372.3	1378.9
42	1385.4	1392.0	1398.7	1405.3	1412.0	1418.6	1425.3	1432.0	1438.7	1445.5
43	1452.2	1459.0	1465.7	1472.5	1479.3	1486.2	1493.0	1499.9	1506.7	1513.6
44	1520.5	1527.5	1534.4	1541.3	1548.3	1555.3	1562.3	1569.3	1576.3	1583.4
45	1590.4	1597.5	1604.6	1611.7	1618.8	1626.0	1633.1	1640.3	1647.5	1654.7
46	1661.9	1669.1	1676.4	1683.7	1690.9	1698.2	1705.5	1712.9	1720.2	1727.6
47	1734.9	1742.3	1749.7	1757.2	1764.6	1772.1	1779.5	1787.0	1794.5	1802.0
48	1809.6	1817.1	1824.7	1832.2	1839.8	1847.5	1855.1	1862.7	1870.4	1878.1
49	1885.7	1893.4	1901.2	1908.9	1916.7	1924.4	1932.2	1940.0	1947.8	1955.6
50	1963.5	1971.4	1979.2	1987.1	1995.0	2003.0	2010.9	2018.9	2026.8	2034.8

Answers

ANSWERS TO CHAPTER 1

Exercise 1

1) 13   2) 10   3) 57   4) 7
5) 35   6) 15   7) 45   8) 74
9) 13   10) 20   11) 5   12) 10
13) 7   14) 7   15) 14   16) 21
17) 17   18) 13

Exercise 2

1) (a) $2 \times 12, 4 \times 6, 8 \times 3, 24 \times 1$
  (b) $2 \times 28, 4 \times 14, 7 \times 8, 56 \times 1$
  (c) $2 \times 21, 3 \times 14, 6 \times 7, 42 \times 1$
2) 2, 3, 4, 6, 12; 12, 6, 18, 24
3) 12, 15, 18, 21, 24, 27, 30, 33, 36, 39
4) (a) $2 \times 2 \times 2 \times 3$ (b) $2 \times 2 \times 3 \times 3$
  (c) $2 \times 2 \times 2 \times 7$ (d) $2 \times 2 \times 3 \times 11$
5) 23 and 29
6) (a) 24   (b) 60   (c) 12   (d) 24
  (e) 40   (f) 100   (g) 160   (h) 120
  (i) 420   (j) 5040
7) (a) 32   (b) 81   (c) 125   (d) 36   (e) 512
8) (a) 4   (b) 12   (c) 5   (d) 13   (e) 6   (f) 14

Exercise 3

1) 192, 768   2) 13, 16
3) 29, 35   4) 6, 2
5) 48, 96

Self-Test 1

1) b   2) a   3) b
4) c   5) c   6) a
7) b   8) b   9) d
10) c   11) d   12) b
13) d   14) c

ANSWERS TO CHAPTER 2

Exercise 4

1) $\frac{21}{28}$ 2) $\frac{12}{20}$ 3) $\frac{25}{30}$ 4) $\frac{7}{63}$
5) $\frac{8}{12}$ 6) $\frac{4}{24}$ 7) $\frac{24}{64}$ 8) $\frac{25}{35}$

Exercise 5

1) $\frac{1}{2}$ 2) $\frac{3}{5}$ 3) $\frac{1}{8}$ 4) $\frac{3}{5}$
5) $\frac{7}{8}$ 6) $\frac{3}{4}$ 7) $\frac{5}{7}$ 8) $\frac{18}{35}$
9) $\frac{2}{3}$ 10) $\frac{2}{3}$

Exercise 6

1) $3\frac{1}{2}$ 2) 2   3) $2\frac{1}{5}$ 4) $1\frac{1}{11}$
5) $2\frac{5}{8}$ 6) $\frac{19}{8}$ 7) $\frac{51}{10}$ 8) $\frac{26}{3}$
9) $\frac{127}{20}$ 10) $\frac{31}{7}$

Exercise 7

1) 12   2) 30   3) 12   4) 24
5) 40   6) 100   7) 160   8) 120
9) 420   10) 5040

Exercise 8

1) $\frac{1}{2}, \frac{7}{12}, \frac{2}{3}$ and $\frac{5}{6}$ 2) $\frac{3}{4}, \frac{6}{7}, \frac{7}{8}$ and $\frac{9}{10}$
3) $\frac{11}{20}, \frac{3}{5}, \frac{7}{10}$ and $\frac{13}{16}$ 4) $\frac{3}{5}, \frac{5}{8}, \frac{13}{20}$ and $\frac{3}{4}$
5) $\frac{9}{14}, \frac{11}{16}, \frac{7}{10}$ and $\frac{3}{4}$ 6) $\frac{3}{8}, \frac{2}{5}, \frac{5}{9}$ and $\frac{4}{7}$

Exercise 9

1) $\frac{5}{6}$ 2) $\frac{13}{10} = 1\frac{3}{10}$ 3) $1\frac{1}{8}$ 4) $\frac{11}{20}$
5) $2\frac{1}{8}$ 6) $1\frac{47}{120}$ 7) $4\frac{15}{16}$ 8) $14\frac{4}{15}$
9) $13\frac{23}{56}$ 10) $10\frac{2}{3}$ 11) $11\frac{5}{16}$ 12) $10\frac{13}{15}$

Exercise 10

1) $\frac{1}{6}$ 2) $\frac{2}{15}$ 3) $\frac{1}{6}$ 4) $\frac{1}{2}$
5) $\frac{1}{24}$ 6) $\frac{7}{8}$ 7) $2\frac{2}{7}$ 8) $1\frac{1}{5}$
9) $2\frac{19}{40}$ 10) $\frac{51}{160}$ 11) $\frac{41}{80}$

Exercise 11

1) $1\frac{3}{8}$ 2) $\frac{7}{20}$ 3) $6\frac{7}{8}$ 4) $\frac{2}{3}$
5) $8\frac{13}{80}$ 6) $12\frac{9}{40}$ 7) $2\frac{21}{80}$ 8) $8\frac{23}{32}$
9) $3\frac{7}{8}$ 10) $3\frac{31}{100}$

Exercise 12

1) $\frac{8}{15}$ 2) $\frac{15}{28}$ 3) $\frac{10}{27}$ 4) $1\frac{19}{36}$
5) $4\frac{9}{10}$ 6) $6\frac{2}{3}$ 7) $1\frac{32}{45}$ 8) $2\frac{53}{56}$

Exercise 13

1) $1\frac{1}{3}$ 2) 4   3) $\frac{7}{16}$ 4) $1\frac{1}{2}$
5) $\frac{1}{24}$ 6) 4   7) $6\frac{3}{4}$ 8) $8\frac{1}{4}$
9) 12   10) 100   11) 3   12) 2

Exercise 14

1) $\frac{3}{5}$ 2) 8   3) $1\frac{1}{3}$ 4) $1\frac{1}{2}$
5) $\frac{2}{3}$ 6) $\frac{25}{26}$ 7) $1\frac{1}{5}$ 8) $3\frac{5}{6}$

Exercise 15

1) $3\frac{13}{14}$ 2) 5   3) $2\frac{1}{2}$ 4) $\frac{5}{6}$
5) $\frac{2}{3}$ 6) $2\frac{1}{2}$ 7) $1\frac{2}{5}$ 8) $\frac{2}{3}$
9) $\frac{1}{6}$ 10) $\frac{3}{25}$

Self-Test 2

1) b   2) a and e   3) c   4) a
5) d   6) a   7) c and d   8) e
9) b   10) d   11) b   12) c
13) c   14) b, c   15) b

Exercise 16

1) 0.7	2) 0.37	3) 0.589
4) 0.009	5) 0.03	6) 0.017
7) 8.06	8) 24.0209	9) 50.008
10) $\frac{2}{10}$	11) $4\frac{6}{10}$	12) $3\frac{58}{100}$
13) $437\frac{25}{100}$	14) $\frac{4}{1000}$	15) $\frac{36}{1000}$
16) $400\frac{29}{1000}$	17) $\frac{1}{1000}$	18) $\frac{329}{10000}$

Exercise 17

1) 3	2) 11.5	3) 24.04	4) 58.616
5) 54.852	6) 4.12	7) 15.616	8) 0.339
9) 0.812	10) 5.4109		

Exercise 18

1) 41, 410, 4100
2) 24.2, 242, 2420
3) 0.46, 4.6, 46
4) 3.5, 35, 350
5) 1.486, 14.86, 148.6
6) 0.017 53, 0.175 3, 1.753
7) 48.53
8) 9
9) 1700.6
10) 5639.6

Exercise 19

1) 0.36, 0.036, 0.003 6
2) 6.419 8, 0.641 98, 0.064 198
3) 0.007, 0.000 7, 0.000 07
4) 51.04, 5.104, 0.5104
5) 0.035 2, 0.003 52, 0.000 352
6) 0.054 7) 0.002 05 8) 0.004
9) 0.000 008 6 10) 0.062 742 8

Exercise 20

1) 743.026 6	2) 0.951 534	3) 0.288 8
4) 7.411 25	5) 0.001 376	

Exercise 21

1) 1.33	2) 0.016	3) 189.74
4) 4.106 6	5) 43.2	

Exercise 22

1) 24.865 8, 24.87, 25
2) 0.008 357, 0.008 36, 0.008 4
3) 4.978 5, 4.98, 5
4) 22
5) 35.60
6) 28 388 000, 28 000 000
7) 4.149 8, 4.150, 4.15
8) 9.20

Exercise 23

1) $200 \times 0.005 = 1$
2) $32 \times 0.25 = 8$
3) $0.7 \times 0.1 \times 2 = 0.14$
4) $80 \div 20 = 4$
5) $0.06 \div 0.003 = 20$
6) $30 \times 30 \times 0.03 = 27$
7) $\dfrac{0.7 \times 0.006}{0.03} = 0.14$
8) $\dfrac{30 \times 30}{10 \times 3} = 30$

Exercise 24

1) 0.25	2) 0.75	3) 0.375	4) 0.687 5
5) 0.5	6) 0.666 7	7) 0.656 3	8) 0.453 1
9) 1.833 3	10) 2.437 5	11) 0.333	12) 0.778
13) 0.133	14) 0.189	15) 0.356	16) 0.232
17) 0.525	18) 0.384	19) 0.328	20) 0.567

Exercise 25

1) $\frac{1}{5}$	2) $\frac{9}{20}$	3) $\frac{5}{16}$	4) $2\frac{11}{20}$
5) $\frac{3}{400}$	6) $2\frac{1}{8}$	7) 0.000 1	8) 0.001 875

Self-Test 3

1) b	2) b	3) d	4) a
5) c	6) d	7) c	8) d
9) c	10) a	11) a	12) e
13) d	14) c	15) b	

ANSWERS TO CHAPTER 4

Exercise 26

1) 362.2	2) 14.438	3) 10.474
4) 70	5) 71.9	6) 2.627
7) 1.82	8) 0.000 375	9) 0.000 018 9
10) 76.2	11) 6.6	12) 0.020
13) 136.5	14) 28 467 000	

ANSWERS TO CHAPTER 5

Exercise 27

1) 38 p, 63 p, 58 p
2) 216 p, 359 p, 1768 p
3) £0.35, £0.78, £0.06, £0.03
4) £2.46, £9.83, £265.32
5) (a) £10.06 (b) £215.58 (c) £5.41
   (d) £2.35 (e) £1.99
6) (a) £2.24 (b) £7.93 (c) £68.62
   (d) £0.78 (e) £2.09

Exercise 28

1) £1.80	2) £5.95	3) £16.77	4) £168.72
5) 13 p	6) 22 p	7) £1.32	8) £2.17

Self-Test 5

1) b	2) a	3) a	4) e	5) e
6) c	7) d	8) b		

ANSWERS TO CHAPTER 6

Exercise 29

1) $\frac{8}{3}$	2) $\frac{2}{3}$	3) $\frac{3}{1}$	4) $\frac{3}{5}$
5) $\frac{2}{3}$	6) $\frac{3}{20}$	7) $\frac{25}{4}$	8) 150 m
9) £192	10) $\frac{6}{1}$		

Exercise 30

1) £500 and £300   2) £64 and £16

3) £50, £40 and £30　　　　4) £280
5) 15, 22.5 and 37.5 kg　　　6) 84, 294, 462 mm
7) £6258 and £4470　　　　8) £3.60

Exercise 31

1) £4.80　　　　　　　　　2) £4.24
3) 87 p, £47.85　　　　　　4) £1.75
5) 33.2 litres　　　　　　　6) $18\frac{1}{3}$, $36\frac{2}{3}$, 2, 40, 1
7) £224　　　　　　　　　 8) 7 hours

Exercise 32

1) $13\frac{1}{2}$ days　　　2) $3\frac{1}{3}$ days　　　3) 160 rev/min
4) 6　　　　　　　　5) 20 men

Exercise 33

1) 54.90　　　　　2) 5075　　　　　3) 38.40
4) 185.83　　　　　5) 3.96　　　　　6) 7250
7) 31.56　　　　　 8) 11.46　　　　 9) SK10.84 = £1
10) (a) 4200 francs　　(b) 3896 francs
　　 (c) 304 francs　　　(d) £29.51

Self-Test 6

1) c　　　　2) d　　　　3) a　　　　4) (a) c　　(b) a
5) a　　　　6) c　　　　7) a　　　　8) d

ANSWERS TO CHAPTER 7

Exercise 34

1) 70　　　2) 55　　　3) 36　　　4) 80
5) 62　　　6) 25　　　7) 70　　　8) 95

Exercise 35

1) 70　　　2) 73　　　3) 68　　　4) 81.3
5) 92.7　　6) 33.3　　7) 81.9

Exercise 36

1) 0.32　　　2) 0.78　　　3) 0.06　　　4) 0.24
5) 0.315　　6) 0.482　　7) 0.025　　8) 0.012 5
9) 0.039 5　10) 0.201

Exercise 37

1) (a) 10　　　　(b) 24　　　　(c) 6
　　 (d) 2.4　　　(e) 21.315　　(f) 2.516
2) (a) 12.5　　 (b) 20　　　　 (c) 16
　　 (d) 16.3　　(e) 45.5
3) 60%; 27　　4) 115 cm　　　5) $88\frac{2}{3}$ cm
6) (a) £7.20　　　(b) £13.20　　　(c) £187.50
7) (a) 2.083% are bad
　　 (b) 3.077% are absent
　　 (c) 87.76% eat lunches
8) 39 643　　9) 150 kg　　10) 600

Exercise 38

1) 25%　　　　2) (a) 20%　　(b) $16\frac{2}{3}$%
3) (a) $13\frac{1}{3}$%　(b) 9.95%
4) 10%　　　　5) 20%　　　　6) $33\frac{1}{2}$%
7) $12\frac{1}{2}$%　　　8) 17.65%

Exercise 39

1) £12.60　　　2) £85.50　　　3) 54 p
4) £8.50　　　 5) £530.10

Exercise 40

1) (a) £6.00　　　(b) £4.35
2) (a) £16.00　　 (b) 56 p
3) £12.00
4) (a) £3.40　　　(b) £59.20
5) £64.00　　　6) £2.85　　　7) £3.00
8) £20.00　　　9) £1500　　 10) £12 150

Self-Test 7

1) a, b, d　2) b　　　3) c, d　　4) d　　　5) c
6) b　　　7) c　　　8) c　　　9) a　　 10) d
11) c　　 12) (a) b　　(b) b　　(c) c
13) b　　 14) b　　　15) c

ANSWERS TO CHAPTER 8

Exercise 41

1) 22.24　　　　2) $12\frac{1}{8}$ kg　　　3) 16 p
4) 8.57 p　　　5) 97.6　　　　6) 2000
7) $14\frac{1}{2}$ years　　8) 9.13 p　　　9) 40
10) 76　　　　 11) 63　　　　 12) £32.90; 65.8 p

Exercise 42

1) 75 km/h　　　2) 4 hours　　　3) 350 km
4) 26 km/h　　　5) 75 km/h　　　6) 80 km/h
7) 5 hours　　　8) 38.4 km/h

Self-Test 8

1) d　　　2) b　　　3) a　　　4) b　　　5) d
6) a　　　7) a　　　8) c　　　9) c　　 10) b

ANSWERS TO CHAPTER 9

Exercise 43

1) £67.20　　2) £89.70　　3) £57.72　　4) £110.40
5) £2.24　　 6) £1.50　　 7) £1.60　　 8) £1.84

Exercise 44

1) £65.28　　　　　2) £144　　　　3) £162.44
4) £3.86 per hour　 5) 6 hours　　　6) 6 hours

Exercise 45

1) £26　　　　　　2) £111
3) £26; £94　　　 4) £245

Exercise 46

1) £360　　　　2) £262　　　　3) £476
4) £600　　　　5) £846

Exercise 47

1) £296　　　　　　2) £180
3) 90 p　　　　　　4) 31.25 p in the £1
5) £1 161 000　　　6) 9.1 p in the £1

7) £85 000   8) £87 960; 55 p
9) £391 000   10) 2.9 p in the £1

Exercise 48

1) £420   2) £800   3) £1864.50
4) £931.50   5) £1105.50

Exercise 49

1) £204.70   2) £80   3) £16

Exercise 50

1) £24.75   2) £71.68   3) 12%
4) £23.96   5) £272.40; £32.40   6) £10.09
7) £25.83

Exercise 51

1) £94.27   2) 730   3) £36.45
4) 345   5) £153.67   6) Method (b)
7) £85.82   8) £45.34   9) 400

Exercise 52

1) £47.77   2) £42.74   3) £146.40
4) £56.40   5) £111.43

Self-Test 9

1) b   2) c   3) a   4) d   5) b   6) c
7) a   8) d   9) b   10) d

ANSWERS TO CHAPTER 10

Exercise 53

1) £126   2) £20   3) 4 years
4) 5 months   5) $2\frac{1}{2}$ years   6) 7%
7) 9%   8) £320   9) £0.30
10) £66   11) £14.56
12) (a) £189   (b) £275   (c) £3200
    (d) £10 010   (e) £1701

Self-Test 10

1) d   2) b   3) a   4) c   5) d
6) b   7) d   8) a   9) a   10) c

ANSWERS TO CHAPTER 11

Exercise 54

1) £117.20   2) £331   3) £2567
4) £9461   5) £2506   6) £432; £542
7) £2765   8) $3011

Exercise 55

1) £175.35   2) £342.50   3) £1572
4) £9471   5) £1230

Exercise 56

1) £6655   2) £3271   3) £5260
4) £2440   5) £1007

Self-Test 11

1) c   2) c   3) c   4) c   5) a

ANSWERS TO CHAPTER 12

Exercise 57

1) (a) £1256   (b) £351   (c) £165.20
2) (a) £174.60   (b) £304.50   (c) £573.30
3) (a) £24   (b) £81   (c) £637.50
4) (a) £22.50   (b) £125   (c) £96
5) (a) 10.8%   (b) 2.35%   (c) 6.12%
6) £80; 10.67%   7) £738; £63; 8.54%
8) 32 p   9) £1125   10) 4.4%
11) 46.4%   12) £11 800

Exercise 58

1) (a) £400   (b) £362.32   (c) £583.33
2) (a) £28   (b) £60   (c) £20
3) £681.82; £40.91; 6.82%
4) £240   5) £300
6) £218.18   7) £29.63 less
8) (a) £1515   (b) £2561   (c) £78

Exercise 59

1) (a) 40 p in the £1   (b) 9.1 p in the £1
   (c) 33.57 p in the £1
2) (a) £2100   (b) £510.24   (c) £2978.82
3) 44.68 p in the £1   4) 20.32 p in the £1
5) £3589

Self-Test 12

1) d   2) b   3) a   4) b
5) a   6) c   7) c   8) b

ANSWERS TO MISCELLANEOUS EXERCISE

Exercise 60

1) 88%   2) £225   3) 441
4) (a) 91   (b) 50
5) 6   6) $1\frac{1}{2}$ 7) 7
8) $19\frac{1}{3}$ 9) £153.75   10) 17.3 kg
11) 55   12) 57.6 km/h   13) 11 811
14) $5\frac{5}{9}$ 15) 16.3   16) 27.3 m
17) £8   18) 24%   19) £13
20) (a) 0.049 5   (b) 0.049
21) 18.75%; £1690   22) £65.25   23) 10%
24) £1203.75   25) £72   26) $4\frac{1}{2}$ hours
27) (a) £400   (b) £480
28) £9.60   29) 45 km/h
30) (a) $\frac{1}{12}$ (b) 15.33
31) 7   32) 1100   33) £1.88
34) 24 seconds   35) £178   36) £1.35
37) 62   38) $\frac{1}{16}$ 39) £17.50
40) 39 km/h   41) £60   42) £32.50

43) (a) 0.167   (b) 0.027
44) 1976   45) £900   46) 2.52
47) 28%   48) £12   49) $5\frac{1}{2}$
50) £90.10
51) (a) £202.70   (b) £40.80   (c) 20.1%
52) £24 600   (a) £144   (b) 80 p   (c) 3.9%
    (d) £656 000
53) £35 000, 8%, 48 p
54) (a) 64 km/h   (b) 12.40 p.m.   (c) 16 km
    (d) 82 km/h; 8 min
55) (a) £3.50   (b) £4.20   (c) £3.78   (d) £1.80
    (v) 7.9%
56) (a) £2450   (b) £1440; $\dfrac{5000p}{7q}$
57) £96, £124.80, £19.20; 13%; 60%
58) £4600; (a) £6700, £7725, £8575   (b) 45.7%; £19 500
59) (a) £2222   (b) £3700   (c) £5525
60) (a) £835 000   (b) 10.40%   (c) £21 040 000; £12.70

ANSWERS TO CHAPTER 13

Exercise 61

1) 2.25   2) 4.41   3) 73.96
4) 9.923   5) 58.98   6) 27.35
7) 18.18   8) 62.67   9) 64.27
10) 75.76   11) 529   12) 1648
13) 9 566 000 14) 12 610   15) 9628
16) 0.000 361 17) 0.531 7   18) 0.000 017 80
19) 0.080 32   20) 0.000 000 334 6   21) 9.87
22) (a) 25   (b) 16   (c) 0.015 63   (d) 0.003 6

Exercise 62

1) 1.844   2) 2.862   3) 2.294
4) 3.039   5) 2.649   6) 1.735
7) 5.916   8) 9.445   9) 7.292
10) 9.110   11) 8.901   12) 7.072
13) 30   14) 26.94   15) 84.51
16) 298.3   17) 62.81   18) 29 890
19) 0.392 1   20) 0.041 21   21) 0.198 7
22) 0.027 98   23) 0.044 47

Exercise 63

1) 10   2) 15   3) 49   4) 24
5) 120   6) 30   7) 336   8) 2520

Exercise 64

1) $\frac{2}{3}$ 2) $\frac{3}{4}$ 3) $\frac{5}{7}$ 4) $\frac{2}{3}$
5) $\frac{9}{10}$ 6) $\frac{2}{3}$ 7) $\frac{5}{8}$ 8) $\frac{5}{7}$
9) $\frac{4}{5}$ 10) $\frac{1}{6}$ 11) 13   12) 12
13) 3   14) 9   15) 6

Exercise 65

1) 1.311   2) 1.960   3) 2.934
4) 3.551   5) 8.730   6) 9.508

Exercise 66

1) 0.294 1   2) 0.122 1   3) 0.190 0
4) 0.108 2   5) 0.142 6   6) 0.028 57
7) 0.011 21   8) 0.018 81   9) 0.001 111
10) 0.000 14   11) 6.506   12) 588.9
13) 25.34   14) 1277   15) 505.6

Exercise 67

1) 0.004 283   2) 53.12   3) 0.000 016
4) 0.344 9   5) 0.231 1   6) 7.458
7) 0.001 023   8) 0.005 163   9) 5.801
10) 9.881   11) 0.223 0   12) 0.346 5
13) 13.73   14) 0.065 4   15) 2.342 9
16) 0.273 67

Self-Test 13

1) c   2) a   3) b   4) b
5) a   6) c   7) b   8) c
9) a   10) b   11) b   12) b
13) d   14) d   15) b   16) a
17) c   18) b   19) b   20) c

ANSWERS TO CHAPTER 14

Exercise 68

1) 15   2) −12   3) −32   4) 14
5) −24   6) 26   7) −18   8) 23

Exercise 69

1) −5   2) −9   3) 5   4) 5
5) −1   6) 0   7) −4   8) 7

Exercise 70

1) 2   2) 3   3) 14   4) 4
5) 1   6) −5   7) −5   8) 16

Exercise 71

1) −42   2) −42   3) 42   4) 42
5) −48   6) 4   7) 120   8) 9

Exercise 72

1) −3   2) −3   3) 3   4) 3
5) −2   6) −1   7) 2   8) −1
9) −2   10) 12   11) −1   12) −2
13) −12   14) −3

Exercise 73

1) 5 and 198
2) −9
3) Rational: 1.57, $\frac{1}{4}$, −5.625, $\sqrt{9}$, 6.76 and −$3\frac{1}{2}$
   Irrational: $\sqrt{15}$
4) 9.578 2, −7.38, $\sqrt{8}$ and $7\frac{2}{3}$

Exercise 74

1) 13, 16   2) 29, 35
3) −6, −8   4) 3, 5
5) $\frac{1}{108}$, $\frac{1}{324}$ 6) 64, 81
7) 2, −2   8) 2.073 6, 2.488 32
9) 0.187 5, −0.093 75   10) −1.464 1, 1.610 51

Self-Test 14

1) b   2) a   3) d   4) d
5) b   6) d   7) b   8) c

ANSWERS TO CHAPTER 15

Exercise 75

1) $7x$ 2) $4x - 3$ 3) $5x + y$ 4) $\dfrac{x + y}{z}$

5) $\dfrac{x}{2}$ 6) $8xyz$ 7) $\dfrac{xy}{z}$ 8) $3x - 4y$

Exercise 76

1) 9 2) 3 3) 3 4) 18
5) 45 6) 6 7) 45 8) 30
9) 23 10) 38 11) 33 12) 33
13) 28 14) 1 15) $\frac{3}{4}$ 16) 5
17) 5 18) 7.7

Exercise 77

1) 4 2) 81 3) 54
4) 32 5) 1152 6) 74
7) 20 8) 3024 9) 3
10) 18.96

Exercise 78

1) $18x$ 2) $2x$ 3) $-3x$
4) $-6x$ 5) $-5x$ 6) $5x$
7) $-5a$ 8) $12m$ 9) $5b^2$
10) ab 11) $14xy$ 12) $-3x$
13) $-6x^2$ 14) $7x - 3y + 6z$
15) $9a^2 b - 3ab^3 + 4a^2 b^2 + 11b^4$
16) $1.2x^3 + 0.3x^2 + 6.2x - 2.8$
17) $9pq - 0.1qr$
18) $-0.4a^2 b^2 - 1.2a^3 - 5.5b^3$
19) $10xy$ 20) $12ab$ 21) $12m$
22) $4pq$ 23) $-xy$ 24) $6ab$
25) $-24mn$ 26) $-12ab$ 27) $24pqr$
28) $60abcd$ 29) $2x$ 30) $-\dfrac{4a}{7b}$

31) $-\dfrac{5a}{8b}$ 32) $\dfrac{a}{b}$ 33) $\dfrac{2a}{b}$
34) $2b$ 35) $3xy$ 36) $-2ab$

37) $2ab$ 38) $\dfrac{7ab}{3}$ 39) a^2

40) $-b^2$ 41) $-m^2$ 42) p^2
43) $6a^2$ 44) $5X^2$ 45) $-15q^2$
46) $-9m^2$ 47) $9pq^2$ 48) $-24m^3 n^4$
49) $-21a^3 b$ 50) $10q^4 r^6$ 51) $30mnp$
52) $-75a^3 b^2$ 53) $-5m^5 n^4$

Exercise 79

1) $3x + 12$
2) $2a + 2b$
3) $9x + 6y$
4) $\dfrac{x}{2} - \dfrac{1}{2}$
5) $10p - 15q$
6) $7a - 21m$
7) $-a - b$
8) $-a + 2b$
9) $-3p + 3q$
10) $-7m + 6$
11) $-4x - 12$
12) $-4x + 10$
13) $-20 + 15x$
14) $2k^2 - 10k$
15) $-9xy - 12y$
16) $ap - aq - ar$
17) $4abxy - 4acxy + 4dxy$
18) $3x^4 - 6x^3 y + 3x^2 y^2$
19) $-14P^3 + 7P^2 - 7P$
20) $+2m - 6m^2 + 4mn$
21) $5x + 11$
22) $14 - 2a$
23) $x + 7$
24) $16 - 17x$
25) $7x - 11y$
26) $\dfrac{7y}{6} - \dfrac{3}{2}$

27) $-8a - 11b + 11c$ 28) $7x - 2x^2$
29) $3a - 9b$ 30) $-x^3 + 18x^2 - 9x - 15$

Self-Test 15

1) True 2) True 3) False 4) True
5) True 6) False 7) True 8) True
9) True 10) False 11) True 12) True
13) True 14) False 15) False 16) True
17) False 18) True 19) True 20) False
21) True 22) True 23) True 24) True
25) False 26) False 27) True 28) False
29) False 30) True 31) True 32) False
33) True 34) True 35) False 36) True
37) False 38) False

ANSWERS TO CHAPTER 16

Exercise 80

1) $4(x + y)$ 2) $5(x - 2)$ 3) $2x(2 - 3y)$
4) $m(x - y)$ 5) $5(a - 2b + 3c)$ 6) $3y(1 - 3y)$
7) $ab(b^2 - 1)$ 8) $3x(x - 2)$ 9) $7(a - 2b)$
10) $9a(4a - 1)$

Exercise 81

1) $p^2 q$ 2) ab^2 3) $3mn$ 4) b 5) $3xyz$
6) $xy(xy - a + by)$ 7) $5x(x^2 - 2xy + 3y^2)$
8) $3xy(3x^2 - 2xy + y^4)$ 9) $\dfrac{1}{3}\left(x - \dfrac{y}{2} + \dfrac{z}{3}\right)$
10) $I_0(1 + \alpha t)$ 11) $a(2a - 3b) + b^2$ or $(2a - b)(a - b)$
12) $x(x^2 - x + 7)$ 13) $\dfrac{m^2}{pn}\left(1 - \dfrac{m}{n} + \dfrac{m^2}{pn}\right)$
14) $\dfrac{xy}{a}\left(\dfrac{x}{2} - \dfrac{2y}{5a} + \dfrac{y^2}{a^2}\right)$ 15) $\dfrac{l^2 m}{5}\left(\dfrac{m}{3} - \dfrac{1}{4} + \dfrac{lm}{2}\right)$
16) $\dfrac{a^2}{2x^3}\left(a - \dfrac{b}{2x} - \dfrac{c}{3}\right)$

Exercise 82

1) $x^2 + 4x + 3$ 2) $2x^2 + 11x + 15$
3) $10x^2 + 16x - 8$ 4) $a^2 - 3a - 18$
5) $6x^2 - 13x - 5$ 6) $x^2 - 5x + 6$
7) $8x^2 - 14x + 3$ 8) $x^2 - 1$
9) $4x^2 - 9$ 10) $2x^2 - 3x - 20$

Exercise 83

1) $(x + y)(a + b)$ 2) $(p - q)(m + n)$
3) $(ac + d)^2$ 4) $(2p + q)(r - 2s)$
5) $2(a - b)(2x + 3y)$ 6) $(x^2 + y^2)(ab - cd)$
7) $(mn - pq)(3x - 1)$ 8) $(k^2 l - mn)(l - 1)$

Exercise 84

1) $(x + 2)(x + 3)$ 2) $(x + 4)(x + 2)$
3) $(x - 2)(x - 5)$ 4) $(x - 5)(x - 6)$
5) $(x + 1)(x - 2)$ 6) $(x + 3)(x - 5)$
7) $(x - 2)(x + 4)$ 8) $(x + 4)(x - 3)$
9) $(2x - 5)(x - 1)$ 10) $(2x + 3)(x + 5)$
11) $(3x - 2)(x + 1)$ 12) $(x + 2)(3x - 14)$
13) $(2x + 1)(x - 3)$ 14) $(5x - 3)(2x + 5)$
15) $(3x - 7)(2x + 5)$

Exercise 85

1) $(x + 1)^2$ 2) $(x - 1)^2$
3) $(x + 2)^2$ 4) $(3x + 1)^2$
5) $(5x - 2)^2$ 6) $(x - 2)^2$
7) $(2x + 1)(2x - 1)$ 8) $(a + b)(a - b)$
9) $(1 + x)(1 - x)$ 10) $(11x + 8)(11x - 8)$
11) $(x - 3)$ 12) $(x - 7)$
13) $(2x + 5)$ 14) $(5x - 3)$
15) $(x + 1)^2$ 16) $(x - 1)^2$
17) $(3p - 5)$

Exercise 86

1) $(a - b)(a - b - 2x)$ 2) $(x + y)(3 + x + y)$
3) $5(3m - n)(3m - n - a)$ 4) $(x - y)(x + y + 1)$
5) $(a + b)(a - b - 3)$ 6) $(x + y)[3(x - y) - 2]$
7) $2[(m + n)(m - n + 2)]$ 8) $\pi R(R + 2h)$
9) $y(2y + 3a)(2y - 3a)$ 10) $\pi l(R + r)(R - r)$
11) $5x(2x + 3y)(2x - 3y)$ 12) $\frac{1}{3}\pi r^2(2r + h)$
13) $(a + c)(a - 2b)$ 14) $(x - 1 - 2y)(x - 1 + 2y)$
15) $y(2p - 3)(x - 1)$ 16) $(a + b)(a - b - 1)$
17) $2p(3p + 1)(3p - 1)$ 18) $(x - y)[3(x + y) + 2]$
19) $4(x - y)[2(x - y) + 1]$ 20) $(a - b)(a + b + 3)$

Self-Test 16

1) True 2) False 3) True 4) True
5) False 6) True 7) True 8) False
9) False 10) True 11) False 12) True
13) False 14) True 15) True 16) False
17) True 18) False 19) True 20) True
21) True 22) False 23) True 24) True
25) True 26) True 27) False 28) True
29) True 30) True

ANSWERS TO CHAPTER 17

Exercise 87

1) $\dfrac{b}{c}$ 2) $\dfrac{9s^2}{2t}$ 3) $\dfrac{8acz}{3y^3}$

4) $\dfrac{9qs}{pr}$ 5) $\dfrac{21b^2}{10ac}$

Exercise 88

1) $\frac{3}{5}$ 2) $\frac{5}{6}$ 3) $\dfrac{16(a + 2b)}{9(a + b)}$

4) $\frac{3}{2}$ 5) $\dfrac{1}{x + 2y}$ 6) $\dfrac{5x}{4(x + 4)}$

7) $a - b$ 8) $\dfrac{1}{3a - 2b}$ 9) $\dfrac{1}{4x + 5}$

10) $\dfrac{1}{2x - 3}$ 11) $\dfrac{1}{x + 3}$ 12) $a + b$

13) $a(a - 3x)$ 14) $2x - y$

Exercise 89

1) $\dfrac{47x}{60}$ 2) $\dfrac{a}{36}$ 3) $\dfrac{1}{2q}$

4) $\dfrac{32}{15y}$ 5) $\dfrac{9q - 10p}{15pq}$ 6) $\dfrac{9x^2 - 5y^2}{6xy}$

7) $\dfrac{15xz - 4y}{5z}$ 8) $\dfrac{40 - 11x}{40}$ 9) $\dfrac{19m - n}{7}$

10) $\dfrac{a + 11b}{4}$ 11) $\dfrac{8n - 3m}{3}$ 12) $\dfrac{5x - 2}{20}$

13) $\dfrac{x - 14}{12}$ 14) $\dfrac{13x - 21}{30}$

Exercise 90

1) $12x$ 2) $6xy$
3) $12ab$ 4) abc
5) $36m^2 n^2 p^2 q$ 6) $10a^2 b^4$
7) $(m - n)^2$ 8) $(x + 1)(x + 3)^2$
9) $x^2 - 1$ 10) $9a^2 - b^2$
11) $\dfrac{1}{x - 5}$ 12) $\dfrac{4x + 3}{(2x + 1)(2x - 1)}$
13) $\dfrac{3}{x - 3}$ 14) $\dfrac{3}{x(x + 5)}$
15) $\dfrac{-2x}{x^2 - 9}$ 16) $\dfrac{2x^2 + 4xy - 3x + 3y}{(x + y)^2(x - y)}$

Self-Test 17

1) a 2) a and c 3) b 4) a and d
5) c 6) b 7) d 8) d
9) b 10) c 11) c 12) a

ANSWERS TO CHAPTER 18

Exercise 91

1) 7 2) -4 3) $\frac{1}{2}$
4) 25 5) 12 6) 4
7) 12 8) 1 9) 14 884
10) 19

ANSWERS TO CHAPTER 19

Exercise 92

1) $x = 5$ 2) $t = 7$ 3) $q = 2$
4) $x = 20$ 5) $q = -3$ 6) $x = 3$
7) $y = 6$ 8) $m = 12$ 9) $x = 2$
10) $x = 3$ 11) $p = 4$ 12) $x = -2$
13) $x = -1$ 14) $x = 4$ 15) $x = 2$
16) $x = 6$ 17) $m = 2$ 18) $x = -8$
19) $d = 6$ 20) $x = 5$ 21) $x = 3$
22) $m = 5$ 23) $x = -\dfrac{29}{5}$ 24) $x = 2$
25) $x = \dfrac{45}{8}$ 26) $x = -2$ 27) $x = -15$
28) $x = \dfrac{50}{47}$ 29) $m = -1.5$ 30) $x = \dfrac{15}{28}$
31) $m = 1$ 32) $x = 2.5$ 33) $t = 6$
34) $x = 4.2$ 35) $y = -70$ 36) $x = \dfrac{5}{3}$
37) $x = 13$ 38) $x = -10$ 39) $m = \dfrac{25}{26}$
40) $y = \dfrac{9}{7}$

Exercise 93

1) $(x - 5)$ years 2) $(3a + 8b)$ pence

3) $(5x + y + z)$ hours   4) $2(l + b)$ mm

5) $£(a - x)$; $£(b + x)$ 6) $(120 + x)$ minutes

7) $£Y + \dfrac{nX}{100}$ 8) $£\dfrac{nx}{100m}$

9) $6a + 4b + c$ 10) $£(Mx + Ny + Pz)$

Exercise 94

1) 15   2) 10 and 5

3) 30 m by 33 m   4) 10 and 8

5) 3   6) 15, 16, 17

7) £118 and £262   8) 4 and 5

9) 16, 12 and 18 cm   10) $20°$, $50°$ and $110°$

Self-Test 19

1) True	2) False	3) True	4) True
5) False	6) False	7) False	8) False
9) True	10) True	11) False	12) True
13) False	14) False	15) False	16) True
17) False	18) False	19) True	20) False
21) True	22) False	23) False	24) False
25) False	26) a	27) c	28) b
29) b	30) a, b	31) c, d	32) d
33) b	34) d	35) c, d	36) b
37) c	38) c	39) b	40) c

ANSWERS TO CHAPTER 20

Exercise 95

1) 17   2) 160   3) 18.852   4) 252

5) 0.2   6) 400   7) 21   8) 180

9) 1875   10) 6

Exercise 96

1) $\frac{1}{2}$ 2) 5   3) 3   4) 4

5) 100   6) 8.593   7) 2.546   8) 6

Exercise 97

1) $\dfrac{c}{\pi}$ 2) $\dfrac{S}{\pi n}$ 3) $\dfrac{c}{P}$

4) $\dfrac{A}{\pi r}$ 5) $\dfrac{v^2}{2g}$ 6) $\dfrac{I}{PT}$

7) $\dfrac{a}{x}$ 8) $\dfrac{E}{I}$ 9) ax

10) $\dfrac{PV}{R}$ 11) $\dfrac{0.866}{d}$ 12) $\dfrac{ST}{s}$

13) $\dfrac{33\,000H}{PAN}$ 14) $\dfrac{4V}{\pi d^2}$ 15) $p + 14.7$

16) $\dfrac{v - u}{a}$ 17) $\dfrac{n - p}{c}$ 18) $\dfrac{y - b}{a}$

19) $5(y - 17)$ 20) $\dfrac{H - S}{L}$ 21) $\dfrac{b - a}{c}$

22) $\dfrac{B - D}{1.28}$ 23) $\dfrac{R(V - 2)}{V}$ 24) $C(R + r)$

25) $\dfrac{S}{\pi r} - r$ 26) $\dfrac{H}{wS} + t$ 27) $2pC + n$

28) $D - \dfrac{TL}{12}$ 29) $\dfrac{Vr}{V - 2}$ 30) $\dfrac{SF}{S - P}$

31) $\dfrac{V^2}{2g}$ 32) $\dfrac{w^2}{k^2}$ 33) $\dfrac{t^2 g}{4\pi^2}$

34) $\dfrac{4\pi^2 W}{gt^2}$ 35) $\dfrac{Pr}{V^2 + gr}$ 36) $\dfrac{Z^2 y}{1 - Z^2}$

37) $\dfrac{2 - k}{k - 3}$ 38) $\dfrac{3 - 5a}{4a}$ 39) $\dfrac{2ka}{aV^2 + 2k}$

40) $\dfrac{2S - dn(n - l)}{2n}$ 41) $\dfrac{c^2 + 4h^2}{8h}$ 42) $\dfrac{xD}{x + h}$

43) $\dfrac{p(D^2 + d^2)}{D^2 - d^2}$

Self-Test 20

1) b	2) d	3) a	4) b	5) d
6) b	7) d	8) a, c	9) b	10) c
11) c	12) b, d	13) c, d	14) a, b	15) d
16) c	17) d	18) c	19) b	20) c, d

ANSWERS TO CHAPTER 21

Exercise 98

1) 1, 2   2) 4, 5   3) 4, 1

4) 7, 3   5) $\frac{1}{2}$, $\frac{3}{4}$ 6) 3, 2

7) 4, 3   8) 3, 4   9) -1.5, 1

10) $-1, -2$ 11) 6, 3   12) $2, -1.5$

Exercise 99

1) 15 and 12   2) 16   3) £120 and £200

4) 9 and 7   5) 40 and 75   6) 300

7) 48, 64; 40   8) 30 p   9) 15, 21

10) 12

Self-Test 21

1) c	2) a	3) b	4) d
5) c	6) a	7) a	8) c
9) a, b	10) b	11) b, c	12) b, c

ANSWERS TO CHAPTER 22

Exercise 100

1) ± 5 2) ± 2.828 3) ± 4

4) ± 4 5) ± 4 6) ± 1.732

7) 5 or 2   8) $\frac{4}{3}$ or -3 9) 0 or -7

10) 0 or 2.5   11) -8 or 4   12) -5 or -4

13) 3   14) -9 or 8   15) $\frac{1}{3}$ or 2

16) $\frac{4}{7}$ or $\frac{3}{2}$ 17) $-\frac{4}{3}$ or $\frac{7}{3}$ 18) 0 or 3

19) 0 or -8 20) $-\frac{1}{2}$ or $\frac{3}{2}$

Exercise 101

1) 1.175 or -0.425 2) 1.618 or -0.618

3) 0.573 or -2.907 4) 0.211 or -1.354

5) 1 or -0.2 6) 3.886 or -0.386

7) -3.775 or 0.442   8) -9.18 or 2.18

9) -11 or 6   10) 3.303 or -0.303

Exercise 102

1) $x = 1, y = 2,$ or $x = 2, y = 1$
2) $x = -17, y = -20$ or $x = 9, y = 6$
3) $x = 6, y = 3$ or $x = 8.5, y = 0.5$
4) $x = 9, y = 3$ or $x = 4, y = 8$
5) $x = 3.2, y = -0.4$ or $x = 4, y = -2$
6) $x = 2.2, y = 5.4$ or $x = 3, y = 5$
7) $x = 4, y = 0.5$ or $x = \frac{1}{3}, y = 6$
8) $x = 1.5, y = -10.5$ or $x = -5, y = -30$

Exercise 103

1) 6 or -7 2) 9 m and 8 m   3) 15 cm
4) 4 m $\times$ 1 m   5) 13.35 m   6) 5, 6 and 7
7) 14 cm   8) $\frac{2}{5}$ 9) 8.83 m or 3.17 m
10) $d(d-2) + (d-4)^2 = 148; d = 11$ cm
11) (a) $\dfrac{100}{x}$ (b) $\dfrac{100}{x+1.5}; x = 2.87$
12) $\dfrac{15\,600}{x}; x = 12$
13) $\dfrac{240}{x}; \dfrac{240}{x+4}; x = 16; 2$ m

Self-Test 22

1) d   2) a   3) b   4) c
5) c   6) c   7) b   8) b
9) d   10) a   11) b   12) c, d

ANSWERS TO CHAPTER 23

Exercise 104

1) 3^{14} 2) b^{19} 3) 5^5
4) 2^7 5) 7^6 6) $81x^8 y^{12}$
7) $a^{10} b^{15} c^5$ 8) $\dfrac{5^7 a^{21}}{2^7 b^{14}}$ 9) $\frac{1}{10}, \frac{1}{32}, \frac{1}{81}, \frac{1}{25}$
10) 2, 2, 2   11) $3^4, 3^{12}, 3^{12}$ 12) $x^{\frac{1}{3}}, x^{\frac{3}{5}}, x^{\frac{4}{7}}$
13) 30   14) $1, \frac{1}{5}, 100$ 15) 12
16) $m = 2$ 17) $x = 1$ 18) $x = -12$
19) $p = 3$ 20) $x = 1$

Exercise 105

1) 8×10^3 2) 9.25×10^4
3) 8.93×10^2 4) 5.6×10^6
5) 3.5×10^{-2} 6) 7×10^{-1}
7) 3.65×10^{-4} 8) 7.12×10^{-3}

Exercise 106

1) 0.861 1   2) 0.913 7   3) 1.801 0
4) 2.855 2   5) 3.260 8   6) 4.895 6
7) 1.845 2   8) 5.246 3   9) $\bar{1}.251\,9$
10) $\bar{3}.802\,2$ 11) $\bar{2}.838\,3$ 12) $\bar{4}.856\,2$
13) 415.2   14) 54.43   15) 4.254
16) 1276   17) 0.171 6   18) 0.039 88
19) 0.000 428 4   20) 0.003 595

Exercise 107

1) 343.1   2) 564.5   3) 123.1
4) 0.010 38   5) 6.674   6) 26.36
7) 394.2   8) 0.005 390   9) 0.134 3
10) 0.000 189 3   11) 9085   12) 19 990
13) 0.178 6   14) 0.000 175 6   15) 1.585
16) 4.218   17) 92.61   18) 2.603
19) 1.066   20) 0.395 4   21) 0.947 1
22) 0.092 16

Exercise 108

1) 3.437   2) 3.614
3) 8.298   4) 224.8
5) 0.695 5   6) 0.768 9
7) 0.643 7   8) 3.966
9) 25.90   10) $I = \dfrac{Wl^3}{48Ey}; 37.54$
11) (a) 1000   (b) 3.162   (c) 1.585
12) (a) 1.252 7   (b) 0.666 7   (c) 4.321   (d) 100
(e) 100
13) 1.25   14) 5.623   15) 4.242

Self-Test 23

1) a   2) b   3) d   4) a   5) d
6) d   7) a   8) c   9) b   10) c
11) c   12) b   13) c   14) d   15) a
16) b   17) c   18) d   19) c   20) d
21) a   22) c   23) d   24) c   25) b

ANSWERS TO CHAPTER 24

Exercise 109

1) 28   2) 47   3) -4 4) 117
5) 16   6) 12, 17, 22, 27, 32 and 37
7) 215   8) 702   9) 490   10) 10

Exercise 110

1) 640, 40 960   2) 12 288   3) 2.144
4) 5.091   5) 80.76   6) 65.98
7) 10.76, 12.59, 14.73, 17.24, 20.17 and 23.60
8) 30.78   9) 215.4   10) 495.8

Self-Test 24

1) d   2) c   3) c   4) b   5) d

ANSWERS TO CHAPTER 25

Exercise 111

1) $4x^4 - 8x^3 - 10x^2 + 14x + 12$
2) $4x^4 + 18x^3 - 3x^2 + 32x - 15$
3) $2x^2 - 3x + 5$ 4) $3x^3 - 2x^2 + 7x - 3$
5) 723   6) 523
7) -1 8) $x - 1$
9) $p = q = 1$ 10) $(x - 4)$ and $(x - 1)$

Exercise 112

1) $A = 1, B = 3, C = 7$
2) $A = 2, B = -5$
3) $A = -3, B = 2$
4) $A = 6, B = -5, C = -21, D = 0$
5) $A = 2, B = -10, C = -1$

ANSWERS TO MISCELLANEOUS EXERCISE

Exercise 113

1) 3.57×10^{-2} 2) $2\pi r(r - 3h^2)$

3) (a) 0 or -4 (b) ± 2 4) $\frac{7}{5}$

5) $x = 2, y = -1$ 6) (a) 7.071   (b) 707.1

7) $\pm \frac{2}{3}$ 8) $x = \dfrac{y - c}{m}$

9) 5.3

10) (a) $3(x^2 + 4)$ (b) $3x(x + 4)$ (c) $3(x + 1)(x + 3)$

11) 25   12) 1.69

13) $n = \dfrac{Ir}{E - IR}$ 14) (a) -11.2 (b) 25.5

15) (a) $x^2 + 2xy + y^2$ (b) 6   16) (a) 343   (b) 0.11

17) (a) 3.5   (b) $4\pi r^2$ 18) $\dfrac{2}{x^2 - 1}$

19) 1042   20) 3 p

21) $\dfrac{k^2}{p^2}$ 22) 6 or -1

23) 0.841   24) $K = \dfrac{p^2 + 1}{1 - p^2}$

25) 2.39 or 0.28

26) $y = \pm 2, x = 5$ or -3 27) 342.3

28) $16\frac{1}{32}$ 29) $(x - 3)(x - 1)(2x - 1)$

30) $\dfrac{1}{x + 1}$ 31) 2 or -1

32) $(3x + 7)(3x + 1)$ 33) $\frac{7}{16}$

34) 10   35) $2(1 - 6x)(1 + x)$

36) 44   37) -2

38) 3   39) 0.2

40) $\dfrac{w + 2}{2w + 3}$ 41) $x - \dfrac{x}{x + d}$

42) 5.7×10^{-2}

43) $y = -6, x = -7; y = 1.75, x = 24$

44) $\dfrac{3x - 7}{(x^2 - 1)(x - 1)}$ 45) (a) 16   (b) 4   (c) 1

46) (a) $3(3 + x)(3 - x)$ (b) $(3 - 4x)(1 + 2x)$

47) 32   48) $\dfrac{2}{2x - 3}$

49) $x = \dfrac{y - p}{yp + 1}$ 50) (a) $\frac{3}{2}$ (b) 0.3 (c) 125

51) d   52) e

53) (a) e   (b) c   (c) d   54) d

55) b   56) e

57) d   58) e

59) d   60) e

61) a   62) c

63) c   64) d

65) c

66) $\dfrac{60}{x}, \dfrac{60}{x + 4}, x = 12$ or $-16, 224$

67) (a) (iii), $-2\frac{1}{2}$ (b) (i), $-\frac{1}{4}$ (c) -435 (d) -47

68) (a) $1\frac{1}{11}$ (b) 0.8977   (c) $\dfrac{5}{(x - 1)(2x + 3)}$

    (d) 9.3 or -0.8

69) (a) 3.078   (b) $a = \frac{1}{2}, b = 4; 100\frac{1}{2}; \pm 0.433\,0$

70) (a) $(x - 5)$ pence   (b) $\dfrac{3750}{x - 5}$

(c) $\dfrac{4000}{x}; \dfrac{3750}{x - 5} - \dfrac{4000}{x} = 50; x = 20$

71) (a) $4p - 4q = 20; p^2 - q^2 = 110; p = 13.5; q = 8.5$

    (b) $\dfrac{x^2 + 5}{x + 2} = 10; 11.3$

72) (a) $y = \dfrac{6 - x}{2x + 3}$ (b) $\dfrac{15}{2y + 1}$ (c) $\frac{3}{4}$ or -2

73) (a) $x = 3, y = -2$ and $x = \frac{19}{10}, y = \frac{13}{10}$

    (b) A $= -1$, B $= -1$

74) (a) 0.380 2

    (b) (i) 0.778 15   (ii) 0.954 24   (iii) 0.176 09

    (c) 8

75) (a) $x = -\frac{1}{5}$ or 5, $y = \frac{37}{15}$ or -1

    (b) $k = -\frac{2}{3}$ or 1; $(2x + 3)$ or $(2x - 2)$

ANSWERS TO CHAPTER 26

Exercise 114

1) (a) 5630   (b) 680   (c) 17 698

   (d) 5.92   (e) 0.68   (f) 6.895

   (g) 0.073   (h) 45.97   (i) 0.798

   (j) 0.005

2) (a) 9.753   (b) 0.259   (c) 0.058

   (d) 0.029 85   (e) 0.790 685

3) (a) 468   (b) 78.2   (c) 516 000

   (d) 389.7   (e) 8.8

4) (a) 1234   (b) 580 000   (c) 258

   (d) 3890   (e) 52

5) (a) 0.530   (b) 35   (c) 0.002 473

   (d) 0.597 600

6) (a) 56   (b) 0.096   (c) 8 630

   (d) 81   (e) 0.584

7) 18.2 tonnes   8) 19 400 kg

Exercise 115

1) 8 km   2) 15 Mg

3) 3.8 Mm   4) 1.891 Gg

5) 7 mm   6) 1.3 μm

7) 28 g   8) 360 mm

9) 64 mg   10) 3.6 mA

11) 5.3×10^4 m   12) 1.8×10^4 g

13) 3.563×10^6 g   14) 1.876×10^{10} g

15) 7×10^{-2} m   16) 7.8×10^{-2} g

17) 3.58×10^{-10} m   18) 1.82×10^{-5} m

19) 2.706×10^{14} m   20) 2.53×10^{-4} g

Exercise 116

1) 8.8 mm   2) 0.012 8 m²

3) (a) 1200 mm²   (b) 275 mm²   (c) 259.5 mm²

   (d) 774 mm²   (e) 1050 mm²   (f) 1094 mm²

4) 22.1 cm²   5) 13.42 cm²

6) 9.62 cm²   7) 143 cm²

8) 53.7 m²   9) 28 cm²

10) 2.12 m   11) 3062 mm²

12) 15.7 cm

13) (a) 11 200 mm²   (b) 3.02 cm²

14) (a) 22.0 mm   (b) 86.8 m   (c) 26.4 cm

15) (a) 10.94 mm   (b) 5.900 cm   (c) 62.1 m

16) 6.2 cm²   17) 3.41 cm

18) 2 592 mm²   19) 909

20) (a) 1.047 cm   (b) 2.29 cm
21) (a) 119.6°   (b) 10.16°
22) 8.92
23) (a) 4.71 m²   (b) 5.08 cm²   (c) 76.2 cm²
24) 288.6 mm²

Exercise 117

1) 5×10^6 cm³
2) 8×10^7 mm³
3) 1.8×10^{10} mm³
4) 0.83 m³
5) 8.5×10^{-4} m³
6) 0.078 5 m³
7) 5 m³
8) 0.002 5 ℓ
9) 827 000 ℓ
10) 8.275 ℓ

Exercise 118

1) 76.19 m
2) 10.61 m
3) 0.008 75 m³
4) 91.67 mm
5) 2 475 m
6) 128 300 mm³
7) 6.543 cm
8) 1.768×10^6
9) $V = t\left(\dfrac{\pi D^2}{4} - l^2\right)$; 2.46 cm³
10) (a) 37.14 m²   (b) 24.57 m²   (c) 383 201
11) 40 cm
12) (a) 47.19 cm   (b) 4303 cm²
13) 2.56 cm
14) 55 800 kg
15) 55 mm; 13.5 mm
16) (a) 6877 litres   (b) 15.82 m²   (c) 5.107 m²
17) 22.54 cm; $\frac{1}{2}$
18) 52 kg
20) 3.832 cm; 4.69 cm; 214.1 cm²
21) $93\frac{1}{3}$ cm³
22) 35 cm³; 11.14 m

Exercise 119

1) 5180 kg
2) 38.48 kg
3) 48.78 kg
4) 2.56 m²; 78.85 kg
5) 360.45 cm³; 8.04 g/cm³
6) 3.78 g/cm³
7) 577.5 kg
8) 29 g
9) 18 mm
10) 22.68 kg; 10.96

Exercise 120

1) 0.053 m³/s
2) 6.365 cm/s
3) 5 h
4) 0.4 m; $266\frac{2}{3}$ s
5) 3.82 cm/min
6) 7977 s
7) 5.941 m; 127.3 m/s
8) 238 m³; 2.11 m/s

Exercise 121

1) 113 cm³; 524 cm³
2) 27 cm³
3) 9.35 cm
4) 66 900 mm²; 10 500 mm²
5) 46.1 cm³
6) 22.7 kg; 13.10 kg
7) 560 kg; 16 cm
8) 3.5 cm; 3.18 cm
9) 41 900 mm³; 41 570 mm³
10) $\frac{1}{1000}$

Self-Test 26

1) c   2) d   3) b   4) d
5) d   6) c   7) b   8) a, c
9) b, d   10) b   11) c   12) b, d
13) d   14) a   15) b   16) b
17) d   18) b   19) a, d   20) a
21) d   22) c, d   23) a   24) a, c
25) b   26) c   27) b   28) b, d
29) a, c   30) a   31) b, d   32) a
33) a, d   34) b   35) c

ANSWERS TO CHAPTER 27

Exercise 123

2) 7.5; 3.7   3) 254.3 cm²   4) 45   5) 2.3 min

Exercise 124

5) 1, 3
6) $-3, 4$
7) $-5, -2$
8) $4, -3$
9) $m = 4, c = 13$
10) $m = 2, c = -2$
11) $y = 2x + 1$
12) $y = 3x - 2$
13) $y = -2x - 3$
14) $y = 4 - 3x$
15) $y = 5x + 7$
16) $y = 3x + 4$
17) $P = 4.74Q + 1.0$
18) $E = 0.51W + 3$
19) 1.29; 20
20) $E = 4I$

Exercise 125

1) (a) $a = 4.38, b = 28.49$ (b) 5.8 s   (c) 39.43 m
2) $a = 1.285, b = 3.714$ (a) 13.4   (b) 180%
3) (a) $a = 0.22, b = 1045$ (b) 45.5 km/h   (c) 35%
4) (a) $a = 7.19, b = 2.22$ (b) 0.56 kg   (c) 25%

Exercise 126

6) $x = 3$ or 4
7) $x = 4$
8) $x = \pm 3$
9) $x = -5.4$ or 3.7
10) (a) $x = -6.54$ or -0.46 (b) $x = -7.28$ or 0.28
   (c) $x = -6$ or -1
11) (a) $x = -1$ or $\frac{1}{3}$ (b) $x = -1.39$ or 0.72
   (c) $x = -1.21$ or 0.55
12) (a) $x = \pm 3$ (b) $x = \pm 2.24$ (c) No solution

Exercise 127

1) (a) ± 1.15 (b) -0.72 or 1.39   (c) 0 or 2.33
2) -6.16 or 0.16   3) $x = 4, y = 1$
4) $x = 7, y = 3$ 5) $x = 3, y = 2$
6) -0.54 or 1.40
7) 0, 3, 11.25   (a) 0 and 2   (b) 0.84; $2x^3 - 8x = 0$
8) 4, 4.75, 5, 3.85 or 0.65   9) $x^2 - x - 11 = 3.85$
10) $1, -1.75, -2, \dfrac{x^2}{4} + \dfrac{24}{x} - 12 = \dfrac{x}{3} - 2$, 2.6, 5.4

Self-Test 27

1) True   2) True   3) False   4) True
5) True   6) False   7) True   8) True
9) False   10) False   11) True   12) False
13) False   14) True   15) True   16) True
17) False   18) False   19) True   20) True
21) b   22) b   23) a   24) c
25) b   26) b   27) c   28) b
29) d

ANSWERS TO CHAPTER 28

Exercise 128

1) (a) $y = kx^2$ (b) $U = k\sqrt{V}$ (c) $S = \dfrac{k}{T^3}$
   (d) $h = \dfrac{k}{\sqrt[3]{m}}$
2) (a) $\frac{81}{8}$ (b) $\frac{4}{3}$ (c) $\frac{8}{9}$
3) 4.5   4) 36   5) $\sqrt{2} : 1$

Exercise 129

1) 4 mm
2) $1\frac{7}{9}$
3) 5.4
4) $p = 12$
5) 62
6) 4
7) -15 or 9
8) $v = 84t - 16t^2$; $5\frac{1}{4}$
9) 1930
10) $\frac{4}{25}$

Self-Test 28

1) True
2) True
3) False
4) True
5) True
6) False
7) True
8) False
9) False
10) True
11) True
12) True
13) True
14) False
15) False
16) c
17) b
18) a
19) c
20) d
21) d
22) c
23) a
24) b

ANSWERS TO CHAPTER 29

Exercise 130

1) $x > 2$
2) $x > 7$
3) $x > 2$
4) $x \leqslant 2$
5) $x \leqslant 2$
6) $x \geqslant 8$
7) $x = 2$
8) No solution
9) $x = 4, 5, 6$ or 7
10) $x = 0, 1, 2, 3, 4, 5, 6$ or 7

Exercise 132

6) $0 > x > 5$

Self-Test 29

1) c
2) d
3) c
4) c
5) c

ANSWERS TO CHAPTER 30

Exercise 133

1) $-5, 19$
2) $-4, 8$
3) 3
4) 5.52 or -6.52
5) $-4, 6, 1.25$
6) 8

Exercise 134

1) $2x$
2) $7x^6$
3) $12x^2$
4) $30x^4$
5) $1.5t^2$
6) $2\pi R$
7) $\frac{1}{2}x^{-\frac{1}{2}}$
8) $6x^{\frac{1}{2}}$
9) $x^{-\frac{1}{2}}$
10) $2x^{-\frac{1}{3}}$
11) $-2x^{-3}$
12) $-x^{-2}$
13) $-\frac{3}{5}x^{-2}$
14) $-6x^{-4}$
15) $-\frac{1}{2}x^{-\frac{3}{2}}$
16) $-\frac{2}{3}x^{-\frac{4}{3}}$
17) $-7.5x^{-\frac{5}{2}}$
18) $\frac{3}{10}t^{-\frac{1}{2}}$
19) $-0.01H^{-2}$
20) $-5x^{-2}$
21) $8x - 3$
22) $9t^2 - 4t + 5$
23) $4u - 1$
24) $20x^3 - 21x^2 + 6x$
25) $21t^2 - 6t$
26) $\frac{1}{2}x^{-\frac{1}{2}} + \frac{5}{2}x^{\frac{3}{2}}$
27) $-3x^{-2} + 1$
28) $\frac{1}{2}x^{-\frac{1}{2}} - \frac{1}{2}x^{-\frac{3}{2}}$
29) $3x^2 - 1.5x^{-\frac{3}{2}}$
30) $1.3t^{0.3} + 0.575t^{-3.3}$
31) $\frac{9}{5}x^2 - \frac{4}{7}x - \frac{1}{2}x^{-\frac{1}{2}}$
32) $-0.01x^{-2}$
33) $46.5x^{0.5} - 1.44x^{-0.4}$
34) $\frac{3}{2}x^2 + 5x^{-2}$
35) $-6 + 14t - 6t^2$

Exercise 135

1) -1
2) 6
3) $-\frac{1}{4}$
4) $x = 3$
5) $(\frac{1}{3}, -4\frac{5}{27}) ; (1, -3)$
6) 16
7) 12

Exercise 136

1) $-3\frac{1}{3}$
2) $13\frac{1}{4}$
3) $9, -23$
4) (a) -2.25 (b) 3.3 or -0.3 (c) 2.4 or -0.4
5) $2\frac{1}{4}$
6) $\frac{7}{2}, -\frac{1}{2}, +\frac{1}{2} ; -1\frac{13}{24}, \frac{5}{6}$
7) 262
8) $7.36 \times 7.36 \times 3.68$
9) $x = \frac{2}{3}, k = \frac{1}{3}$
10) $625 ; 38.23 \times 11.77$

Exercise 137

1) (a) 11 (max), -16 (min)   (b) 4 (max), 0 (min)
   (c) 0 (max), -32 (min)
2) (a) 54   (b) $x = \frac{5}{2}$ (c) $x = -2$
3) $(3, -15), (-1, 17)$ 4) (a) -2 (b) 1 (c) 9
5) (a) 12   (b) 12.48   6) $x = 1.5$
7) $x = 10$ 8) $r = 4$
9) 108   10) radius $=$ height $= 4.57$ m

Self-Test 30

1) True
2) False
3) True
4) True
5) True
6) True
7) False
8) True
9) True
10) False
11) True
12) True
13) False
14) True
15) True
16) True
17) False
18) True
19) True
20) True
21) False
22) True
23) True
24) True
25) False
26) a
27) b
28) c
29) c
30) c
31) c
32) d
33) b
34) d

ANSWERS TO CHAPTER 31

Exercise 138

1) $\frac{x^3}{3} + c$
2) $\frac{x^9}{9} + c$
3) $\frac{x^2}{2} + c$
4) $\frac{x^5}{5} + c$
5) $\frac{2x^3}{3} + c$
6) $x^5 + c$
7) $\frac{3x^5}{5} + c$
8) $\frac{5x^9}{9} + c$
9) $\frac{x^3}{3} + \frac{x^2}{2} + 3x + c$
10) $\frac{x^4}{2} - \frac{7x^2}{2} - 4x + c$
11) $\frac{x^3}{3} - \frac{5x^2}{2} + 2x + c$
12) $x^3 - x^2 + 3x + c$
13) $\frac{x^3}{3} - \frac{3x^2}{2} + 2x + c$
14) $\frac{x^3}{3} + 3x^2 + 9x + c$
15) $\frac{4x^3}{3} - 14x^2 + 49x + c$

Exercise 139

1) $y = \frac{x^2}{2} + 1$ 2) $46\frac{2}{3}$
3) $y = 10 + 3x - x^2 ; 10 ; 12.25$
4) $y = \frac{2x^3}{3} + \frac{3x^2}{2} + 2x - \frac{1}{6}$
5) $p = \frac{t^3}{3} - 3t^2 + 9t - \frac{17}{3}$

464

Exercise 140

1) $2\frac{1}{3}$
2) 8
3) $8\frac{2}{3}$
4) 4
5) $\dfrac{19}{6}$
6) $12\frac{2}{3}$
7) $2\frac{1}{3}$
8) $\dfrac{2}{3}$

Exercise 141

1) 136
2) 13
3) $5\frac{1}{6}$
4) $18\frac{2}{3}$
5) $3\frac{3}{4}$

Exercise 142

1) 25.6π
2) 6π
3) $\dfrac{26\pi}{81}$
4) $69\frac{1}{3}\pi$
5) $164\frac{2}{3}\pi$
6) $30\frac{8}{15}\pi$
7) 156π
8) 18π
9) $\dfrac{81\pi}{10}$
10) $\dfrac{187\pi}{35}$

Self-Test 31

1) b
2) b
3) d
4) c
5) a
6) b
7) b, c
8) d
9) a
10) b
11) c, d
12) a
13) c
14) a
15) d

ANSWERS TO CHAPTER 32

Exercise 143

1) 60 km/h
2) 5 hours
3) 300 km
4) 50 km/h
5) 36.4 km/h
6) 10.6 km/h
7) 22.1 km/h

Exercise 144

1) 10.20 a.m.; 20 km from A
2) (a) 21.24   (d) 18.00, 195 km from London
3) (a) 6 m/h   (b) 20 min   (d) 6 km/h
   (e) 10 km/h
4) (a) 48 km/h   (b) 344 km   (c) 95 km
   (d) 3.5 hours
5) (a) 19 hours 10 min.   (b) 70 km
   (c) 24.4 km/h   (d) 19.34 and 18.48 hours

Exercise 145

1) (a) 60 m   (b) 6 m   (c) 80 m
   (d) 120 m   (e) 300 m
2) (a) 5 m/s^2 (b) $\frac{1}{2}$ m/s^2 (c) 1.5 m/s^2
   (d) 2.5 m/s^2
3) 150 m
4) (a) 0.2 m/s^2 (b) 4 m/s   (c) 210 m
5) (a) 1 m/s^2 (b) 3 m/s^2 (c) 5 m/s
   (d) 250 m
6) (a) 1 m/s^2 (b) 2 m/s^2 (c) 0.5 m/s^2
   (d) 30 m/s   (e) 875 m
7) (b) 2 m/s^2 (c) 1.6 m/s^2 (d) 384 m
8) (b) 239 m
9) (b) (i) 2.5 m/s^2 (ii) 10 m/s^2
10) (a) 3.2 m/s^2 (b) 12.4 s   (c) 135 m

Exercise 146

1) 42 m/s
2) 6 m/s^2
3) (a) 9   (b) 0 or 2   (c) 6   (d) 1
4) 18, 6
5) (a) 5   (b) 17   (c) 4

Exercise 147

1) 7.5 m
2) 20.5 m/s; 48 m
3) $s = 7.5t^2 + 10t$; 160 m
4) 14.75 m
5) 60 m/s; 112 m
6) 136 m

Self-Test 32

1) a
2) a
3) c
4) c
5) b
6) c
7) c
8) d
9) b
10) c
11) c
12) d

ANSWERS TO MISCELLANEOUS EXERCISE

Exercise 148

1) (a) 42 860 cm^2 (b) 796 l
2) 35; 321.9 m^2
3) $\frac{15}{16}$
4) $5\frac{1}{4}$ cm; $16\frac{1}{2}$ cm
5) 22 cm $\times$ 13 cm
6) 8×10^{-2} mm
8) c
9) c
10) d
11) $M = \dfrac{LWTD}{100}$
12) (a) 4   (b) 1
13) (a) $-0.5 < x < 1.2$ and $x > 3.4$ (b) $-3\frac{1}{2}$
14) (a) 10 000 cm^2 (b) 100 cm^3
16) 7 cm
17) 60
18) 3 m, 112 m^2, 128 m^3
19) 288π
20) $A = \pi r^2$; $\dfrac{dA}{dr} = 2\pi r$
21) $y = 1.5x^2 + 4x - 5.5$
22) 10.63 cm
23) $\frac{1}{2}$
24) 4224 g
25) $14x - 35x^{-6}$
26) 10.4
27) 31
28) 12 cm
29) $v = 40 - 10t$; 40 m/s
30) 4
31) (a) $a = -2, b = 8$ (b) $4, -4$ (c) $(2, 2)$ (d) 8
32) 2.8, 4.2; first machine: 5.4 newtons
33) (a) 267.75 cm^2 (b) 324 cm^2
34) (a) $a = 18.7; b = 27$ (b) 27.5 h   (c) 24.8%
35) $2x + 2y = 31; x^2 + y^2 = (12.5)^2$; $3\frac{1}{2}$ cm; 12 cm
36) $A = 20, B = 8$ (a) 52 m/s^2 (b) 162 m
37) (a) 36 000 cm^3 (b) 7200 cm^2 (c) 146%
    (d) 82.25%
38) $0, -0.5, 0, -1.6, x = 0.70$ or 4.30
39) (a) 16   (b) 36   (c) 20 m
40) 750 m^3 (a) 200 m^2 (b) $\frac{1}{3}$
41) (a) 706.95 cm^2 (b) 21.45%   (c) 0.785 5 : 1
42) (a) $V = x^2 h; A = 2x^2 + 4hx$ (c) $x = 20$ cm
43) (a) 3.37   (b) $y = x + 5; (-5, 0)$ (c) $11\frac{1}{3}$
44) $x = (2, -2)$ (min); $x = (0, 2)$ (max)   (a) 9   (b) $(0, -25)$
45) $(0, 3), (0, -3)$
46) (a) 3.078   (b) $a = 0.5, b = 4; 100.5; \pm \dfrac{\sqrt{3}}{4}$
47) 27.7 cm^2
48) 14.4, 5.6
49) (a) $-\sqrt{7} \leqslant x \leqslant \sqrt{7}$ (b) 2.30 and -1.30
    (c) $-1.30 \leqslant x \leqslant 2.30$
50) (a) $x = 4, y = -\frac{1}{3}$ (b) $W = \dfrac{kV^2}{l}$
    (i) $\frac{4}{5}$ (ii) 57.6 cm   (iii) 220 V

ANSWERS TO CHAPTER 33

Exercise 149

1) 135°
2) 54°
3) 60°
4) 63°
5) 18°
6) 135°
7) 288°
8) 288°

9) 108°　　10) 90°　　　11) 28° 37′　　12) 69° 23′
13) 14° 22′ 34″　　14) 62° 48′ 11′　　15) 179° 11′ 25″
16) 21° 3′　　　　17) 22° 48′　　　18) 7° 43′ 56″
19) 5° 54′ 50″　　20) 36° 58′ 11″

Exercise 150

1) (a) 3.206　　(b) 3.130
2) (a) 286° 29′　　(b) 99° 7′　　(c) 9° 7′
3) (a) 1.449　　(b) 3.299　　(c) 5.149　　(d) 0.091

Exercise 151

1) 20°　　　　　　　　2) 100°　　　3) 35°
4) 70°, 110°, 110°, 70°　　5) 65°　　　6) 80°
7) c　　　　　　　　　8) c　　　　9) 54°
10) 130°　　　　　　　11) 65°　　　12) 230°, 32°
13) b, d

Self-Test 33

1) d　　　2) a　　　3) b　　　4) a　　　5) b, d
6) b, d

ANSWERS TO CHAPTER 34

Exercise 152

1) $x = 49; y = 131$　　　2) $x = 77; y = 81$
3) $x = 63; y = 98$　　　4) $x = 37; y = 127$
5) $x = 140; y = 60$　　　6) $x = 80, y = 70$

Exercise 153

1) $a = 10$　　2) $b = 22.4$　　3) $c = 2.65$
4) (a) 3.87　　(b) 4.24　　(c) 5.29
5) (a) 7.42　　(b) 3.71　　(c) 6.54
6) (a) 60　　(b) 40　　(c) 40
7) (a) $x = 70, y = 40, z = 35$
　 (b) $x = 110, y = 70, z = 70$

Exercise 154

1) c　　　2) b, c, d
3) RQ = 7; SX = 4; ∠ SXP = 97
4) PY = 6
5) BC = 5; ∠ BCA = 42
6) ADF ≡ DFE ≡ FEC ≡ BED
　 DGH ≡ GJE ≡ HGJ ≡ HJF

Exercise 155

1) {AFI}{CK}{BDM}{HJ}{GL}
2) b　　　3) b, d　　　4) d
5) a, d　　6) c　　　7) a, b
8) b　　　9) BC = 32　　10) EC = $4\frac{1}{2}$, AB = $8\frac{1}{3}$

Exercise 156

1) 72 cm²　　2) 36 cm²　　3) b
4) b　　　5) b　　　6) c

Exercise 157

1) $\frac{4}{5}$　2) $3\frac{1}{3}$　3) $\frac{3}{1}$　5) 7.5 cm²
6) (a) 3 cm　(b) 24 cm　7) $\frac{5}{8}$; 10 cm²
8) BP = 2.5 cm; PQ = 7.5 cm

Exercise 158

4) 74°　　6) $\frac{3}{4}$　　8) $\frac{5}{3}, \frac{3}{8}, \frac{3}{8}, \frac{9}{64}$
9) (a) 5 cm; 4 cm; $\frac{4}{25}$　　11) 3.2 cm
12) 29°　　　　　　13) 1.8 cm
15) $\frac{3}{4}$, 9 cm², 4 cm²

Self-Test 34

1) b, c　　2) c　　　3) d　　　4) a
5) b　　　6) b　　　7) a, b, c　8) d
9) b　　　10) a　　　11) c　　　12) a, c
13) b　　14) a, c　　15) b　　　16) b, d
17) d　　18) a, d　　19) c　　　20) a, b
21) b　　22) a, b, c　23) b　　　24) d
25) b　　26) c　　　27) a　　　28) c
29) c　　30) a　　　31) b　　　32) b
33) d　　34) b　　　35) d

ANSWERS TO CHAPTER 35

Exercise 159

1) $x = 143$　　　　2) $x = 93$
3) $x = 39, y = 105$　　4) d
5) a　　　　　　　　6) a
7) b　　　　　　　　8) 65
9) 100　　　　　　　10) Yes, Yes, Yes
11) 32°　　　　　　 12) 100°; 20°
14) 7.5 cm

Exercise 160

1) (a) 6　　(b) 12　　(c) 16　　(d) 20 right-angles
2) (a) 108°　(b) 135°　(c) 144°　(d) 150°
3) 131°　　　　4) 12　　　　5) 6°
6) 24　　　　　7) 7　　　　8) 132°, 75°
9) 72°, 108°　　10) 36°, 10　　11) $n = 30$
12) 12

Exercise 161

1) 28 cm²　　　　2) 84.84 cm²　　3) $6\frac{2}{3}$ cm
4) 12 cm　　　　5) 40 cm²　　　6) 240 cm²
7) (a) 14 cm²　(b) $2\frac{2}{3}$ cm²　　8) $5\frac{1}{3}$ cm

Self-Test 35

1) d　　　2) a　　　3) b　　　4) a
5) b　　　6) c　　　7) b　　　8) a
9) c　　　10) a, d　　11) c

ANSWERS TO CHAPTER 36

Exercise 162

1) 38　　　2) 120　　3) 61　　4) 50
5) D = 75, C = 110　　6) $x = 27, y = 58$
7) $x = 83, y = 70$　　8) 9.75
9) $a = 32, b = 42$　　10) $x = 110, y = 20$
11) 5.83

Exercise 163

1) 3.32　　2) 11.49　　3) 9.24　　4) $8\frac{1}{3}$
5) 1.35　　6) 1.24　　7) 40　　8) 1.53

Exercise 164

1) 59.89 2) 24 3) 57.0 4) 11.2
5) $x = 108, y = 43$ 6) 204
7) $a = 75, b = 105$ 8) $a = 202, b = 90$
9) $x = 60, y = 50$ 10) $a = 55, b = 57, c = 70$
11) $8\frac{1}{3}$ 12) 4.8

Exercise 165

1) 22.22 cm 2) 46.5 mm
3) 1.5 cm 6) $55°, 62\frac{1}{2}°, 125°, 117\frac{1}{2}°$
7) $38°, 33°$ 9) 24 cm
10) 10 cm, 12 cm 12) $\sqrt{x(x-2r)}$

Self-Test 36

1) b 2) d 3) c 4) a
5) b, d 6) d 7) c 8) a
9) d 10) b 11) c 12) b
13) d 14) b 15) a

ANSWERS TO CHAPTER 37

Exercise 166

1) Square 4. Rhombus 2. Isosceles
 trapezium 1. Isosceles triangle 1.
 Equilateral triangle 3. Regular hexagon 6.
2) Line symmetry: b, e, g, h, i
 Point symmetry: b, d, g, h.
3) (b) 2 (d) 2 (g) 8 (h) 4
4) (a) 6 (b) 5 (c) 8
5) (a) 9 (b) ∞ (c) ∞ (d) 4
6) (a) 1, 1, 1, 2, 0, 0, 0, 1, 2
 (c) 0, 0, 0, 2, 0, 2, 0, 0, 2

ANSWERS TO MISCELLANEOUS EXERCISE

Exercise 170

1) (a) 2 (b) none 2) parallelogram
3) (a) 210 cm² (b) 29 cm 4) 60°
5) 105° 6) 40°
7) 4.3 cm, 9.0 cm 8) 11.4 cm
9) 156° 10) 40°
11) 135° 12) (a) 18° (b) 93°
13) 73° 14) 80°
15) 61° 16) 30°
18) There are 2 lines of symmetry
19) 43° 20) 5 cm
21) 12.35 cm
23) $\triangle$ s CAB and CBD; CA = 9, BD = $4\frac{2}{3}$
26) 6.7 cm 28) 27°
29) 54°, 36° 30) 7.55 cm
31) 4 cm, 12 cm
33) (a) 4.668 cm (b) 9.877 cm (c) 2.363 cm
34) $x°, x°, \frac{1}{2}x°, \frac{3}{2}x°$; (a) $\frac{9}{25}$ (b) $\frac{3}{5}$ (c) $9\frac{3}{8}$ cm
35) (a) (i) 4 cm (ii) $\frac{25}{16}$; $2\frac{1}{2}$ cm (b) 8.318 cm
36) (a) 24 cm (b) 1 : 8 (c) $3\frac{1}{5}$ cm (d) 7 cm
 (e) 1.14 : 1
37) $y°$; $2y°$; $(90-2y)°$; $3y + x = 90°$; 5.28 cm
38) (a) 9.49 cm (b) 3.12 cm

ANSWERS TO CHAPTER 40

Exercise 171

1) (a) 0.5 (b) 0.7071 (c) 0.9272
2) (a) 19.5 (b) 48.6 (c) 46.1
3) (a) 0.2079 (b) 0.3123 (c) 0.9646
 (d) 0.1285 (e) 0.9990 (f) 0.0032
4) (a) 9° (b) 66° (c) 81° 6'
 (d) 4° 36' (e) 78° 55' (f) 47° 41'
 (g) 2° 52' (h) 15° 40'
5) (a) 3.381 (b) 10.13 (c) 25.94
6) (a) 41.8 (b) 40.8 (c) 22.4
7) 28.3 8) 0.794 9) 21.6
10) 7.47 11) 44.7, 44.7, 90.6

Exercise 172

1) (a) 0.965 9 (b) 0.911 4 (c) 0.201 1
 (d) 1.000 (e) 0.286 3 (f) 0.766 3
2) (a) 24 (b) 70 (c) 14° 42'
 (d) 64° 36' (e) 16° 32' (f) 89° 31'
 (g) 74° 52' (h) 61° 58'
3) (a) 9.33 (b) 2.64 (c) 5.29
4) (a) 60.7 (b) 69.3 (c) 53.3
5) 66.1°, 66.1°, 47.8°, 3.84
6) 2.88
7) 1.97
8) $\angle$ BAC = 92°, BC = 8.74
9) BD = 4.53, AD = 2.11, AC = 2.39, BC = 5.65

Exercise 173

1) (a) 0.324 9 (b) 0.634 6 (c) 1.361
 (d) 0.822 9 (e) 0.200 4 (f) 2.658
2) (a) 24 (b) 73 (c) 4° 24'
 (d) 21° 42' (e) 19° 38' (f) 39° 34'
 (g) 62° 33' (h) 0° 56'
3) (a) 4.35 (b) 9.29 (c) 4.43
4) (a) 59° (b) 15.9 (c) 22.7°
5) 7.70 6) 2.78 7) 33.3
8) 2.86 9) 2.09

Exercise 174

1) (a) $\bar{1}.679\,4$ (b) $\bar{1}.983\,7$ (c) $\bar{1}.995\,8$
 (d) $\bar{1}.959\,9$ (e) $\bar{1}.992\,7$ (f) $\bar{1}.094\,3$
2) (a) 57° 2' (b) 22° 25' (c) 75° 7'
 (d) 11° 42' (e) 80° 2' (f) 88° 24'
3) (a) 45° 42' (b) 18° 30' (c) 58°
4) 9.29 5) 46° 12'
6) 17° 42' 7) 5.81

Exercise 175

1) 0.948 4, 0.334 4 2) $\frac{3}{5}, \frac{4}{5}$
3) $\frac{5}{13}, \frac{5}{12}$ 7) 0.743 1
8) 0.454 0 9) (a) $\frac{3}{4}$ (b) $\frac{1}{3}$ (c) $\frac{3}{4}$
10) (a) 0.569 6 (b) 0.206 1 (c) 2.561 1
11) 41° 49' 12) 48° 35'

Exercise 176

1) 11.55 m 2) 9.60 m 3) 51°
4) 110 m 5) 10.63 m 6) 24.8 m
7) 1287 m 8) 38° 40' 9) 189 m

10) 74.88 m, 20° 42'   11) 2.97 m   12) 11.78 m
13) (a) 70.0 m   (b) 30 m   (c) 32.6 m
14) 53.26 m
15) (a) 4848 m   (b) 8746 m   (c) 4746 m
    (d) 45° 36'   (e) 6784 m

Exercise 177

1) (a) 92.62 km   (b) 151.5 km   2) 43.3 km; 25 km
3) 326° 19'   4) 11.55 km; 10.774 km
5) 44.4 m, S 64° 16' E   6) 24.72 km; 338° 51'
7) 24.41 km; 14.00 km   8) 127 km; 49° 34'
9) 11.5 km; N 61° 46' E   10) 15.23 km; 66° 48'

Exercise 178

1) 3.624 cm   2) 10.84 cm
3) 1.04 cm; 3.46 cm   4) 14.34 cm
5) 15° 20'; 0.553 cm   6) 71.62 cm

Exercise 179

1) (a) (3.606, 33° 41')   (b) (9.434, 58°)
   (c) (8.944, 116° 34')   (d) (5.831, 239° 2')
   (e) (7.211, 326° 19')   (f) (7.211, 236° 19')
   (g) (10.63, 318° 49')   (h) (3.162, 108° 26')
2) (a) (4.330, 2.500)   (b) (2.958, 6.344)
   (c) (−0.749, 1.854)   (d) (−3.392, 2.120)
   (e) (−6.657, −2.163)   (f) (−0.261, −2.989)
   (g) (2.270, −4.455)   (h) (2.598, −1.500)
3) (a) (2.5, 4.330)   (b) (0, 4)
   (c) (−4.243, 4.243)   (d) (5, −8.660)
4) (a) (2.236, 0.464)   (b) (5.831, 2.111)
   (c) (4.472, 4.249)   (d) (4.472, 5.819)
5) (a) (3.214, 90°)   (b) (4.397, 46° 58')

Self-Test 40

1) a	2) c	3) b	4) b	5) c
6) d	7) c	8) c	9) a	10) a
11) a	12) c	13) c	14) c	15) c
16) b	17) c			

ANSWERS TO CHAPTER 41

Exercise 180

1)
θ	$\sin \theta$	$\cos \theta$	$\tan \theta$
108°	0.9511	−0.3090	−3.078
163°	0.2924	−0.9563	−0.3057
207°	−0.4540	−0.8910	0.5095
320°	−0.6428	0.7660	−0.8391
134°	0.7193	−0.6947	−1.036
168°	0.2079	−0.9781	−0.2126
225°	−0.7071	−0.7071	1.000
286°	−0.9613	+0.2756	−3.487
300°	−0.8660	0.5000	−1.732
95°	0.9962	−0.0872	11.43

2) 14° 34'   165° 26'
3) 105° 42'
4) 31° 5'   148° 55'
   12° 31'   167° 29'
              204° 1'   335° 59'
   28° 9'   331° 51'
          139° 34'   220° 26'
           94° 41'   265° 19'
   58° 4'   238° 4'
   39° 9'   219° 9'
          166° 58'   346° 58'

5) $y = 28° 40'$ or $331° 20'$
   $x = 34° 40'$ or $145° 20'$
6) $\tan A = \frac{12}{5}$ $\cos A = \frac{5}{13}$ 7) $-\frac{7}{25}$ 8) $\frac{15}{17}$; $\frac{8}{15}$
9) $\frac{11}{60}$

Exercise 181

1) C = 71°, b = 5.90, c = 9.985
2) A = 48°, a = 71.52, c = 84.18
3) B = 56°, a = 3.741, b = 9.527
4) B = 46°, b = 13.61, c = 5.845
5) C = 67°, a = 1.508, c = 2.362
6) C = 63° 32', a = 9.485, b = 11.56
7) B = 135° 38', a = 9.394, c = 14.44
8) B = 81° 54', b = 9.948, c = 3.609
9) A = 53° 39', b = 2390, a = 2125
10) A = 13° 52', B = 144° 1', b = 17.17
11) C = 49° 57', A = 44° 46', a = 10.69
12) C = 36° 52', B = 93° 49', b = 30.26
13) B = 48° 32', C = 26° 24', c = 4.244
14) 21.74   15) 117.5   16) 11.25
17) 9.046   18) 21.78

Exercise 182

1) c = 10.15, A = 50° 10', B = 69° 50'
2) a = 11.81, B = 44° 36', C = 79° 24'
3) b = 4.987, A = 82° 33', C = 60° 9'
4) A = 38° 13', C = 60°, B = 81° 47'
5) A = 24° 42', B = 44° 55', C = 110° 23'
6) A = 34° 33', B = 18° 2', C = 127° 25'
7) c = 18.07, A = 35° 54', B = 26° 6'
8) a = 18.34, B = 18° 55', C = 29° 5'

Exercise 183

1) 540.4 cm²
2) 737.5 cm²
3) (a) 7.547 cm²   (b) 8.071 cm²
4) (a) 143   (b) 53.7   (c) 43.61
5) (a) 16.90 cm²   (b) 31.49 cm²   (c) 15.72 cm²
6) 89.15 cm²   7) 66.81 cm²   8) 19.31

Self-Test 41

1) a	2) b	3) c	4) c	5) c
6) a	7) c	8) b	9) d	10) c
11) a	12) a, c	13) b, d	14) c, d	15) a, c

ANSWERS TO CHAPTER 42

Exercise 184

1) (b) 13   (d) 15.26
2) (a) 4   (c) 71° 34'   (d) 12.65   (e) 50.6
   (f) 266.4
3) 12.73
4) 4.528
5) 14, q = 25° 23'
6) (a) 34° 56'   (b) 33°   (c) 31° 18'
7) (a) 17.32 cm   (b) 60°   (c) 61° 31'   (d) 19.71 cm
8) (a) 61° 56'   (b) 12 000
9) (a) 55° 9'   (b) 58° 54'
10) (a) 1524 m   (b) 43° 57'

ANSWERS TO CHAPTER 43

Exercise 185

1) 1 km   2) 28 km   3) 0.5 km
4) 1 : 500 000   5) 1 : 10 000 000   6) 80 km
7) 75 cm   8) 1.6 cm   9) 2.075 km
10) 5.6 km

Exercise 186

1) 120 000 m²   2) 80 000 m²
3) 0.25 cm²   4) 700 km²
5) (a) 13.41 cm²   (b) 538.6 m   (c) 0.1341 km²
6) 10.4 km²   7) 35.5 hectares

Exercise 187

1) $\frac{1}{25}$ 2) $\frac{1}{40}$ 3) 100 m   4) 30 m
5) 7° 11′   6) 1 : 4.81   7) 15 m   8) 1200 m

Exercise 188

1) 39° 48′   2) 1 : 2.85   3) 17° 21′
4) (a) 100 m   (b) 2 km   (c) 1 in 20.02
5) (a) (i) 100 m   (ii) 236 m
    (b) (i) 1.65 km   (ii) 2.05 km
    (c) 14° 56′

ANSWERS TO CHAPTER 44

Exercise 189

1) 6115 km   2) 2001 km   3) 4447 km
4) 5517 km   5) 2224 km
6) (a) 3335 km   (b) 94° E   7) 2.123 cm
8) 35° 13′W, 22° 42′N   9) 1556 km, 28° 34′ W
10) 47° 35′, 4799 km

Exercise 190

1) 13.20 hours   2) 53 minutes
3) 4 hours 16 min   4) 8 hours
5) 6.12 a.m.   6) (a) 16.20   (b) 6.40   (c) 65° W

ANSWERS TO CHAPTER 45

Exercise 192

1) 7.0 at 16° to N   2) 19.2 at 51° to N
3) 11.9 at 31° to N   4) 7.0 at 12° to N
5) 17.2 at 58° to N

Exercise 193

1) (a) **b**   (b) −**a**   (c) **a** + **b**
2) (a) 2**a**   (b) −3**a**
3) (a) **a** + **b**   (b) −$\frac{1}{2}$(**a** + **b**)   (c) $\frac{1}{2}$(**b** − **a**)
4) (a) **c**   (b) −2**c**   (c) −**a** + **c** or −(**b** + **c**)
5) (a) **a** − **b**   (b) **b** − **a**   (c) −**c**
    (d) 2**a**   (e) −**b**   (f) 2**b**
    (g) **a**

6) (a) **a** + **b**   (b) 2**b**   (c) **b** − **a**
7) (a) −(**a** + **b** + **c**)   (b) 2**a**   (c) 3**a** + **b** + **c**
8) (a) −**a**   (b) −**b**   (c) **c**
    (d) 2**b** or **a** + **b** + **c** (e) 2**a** + **b**   (f) 2**c** or **b** + **c** − **a**

Exercise 194

1) 7.81 at 33.7° to 4 vector   2) 12.2 at 21.6° to 6 vector
3) 20.0 at 36.9° to 16 vector   4) 7.85 at 73.2° to 5 vector
5) 20.7 at 18.1° to 12 vector

Exercise 196

1) 340 km/h 277°   2) 500 km/h 095°
3) 400 km/h 157°   4) 400 km/h 308°
5) 270 km/h 035°   6) 50 km/h 305°
7) 110 km/h 090°   8) 150 km/h 286°
9) 155 km/h 228°   10) 89 km/h 146°
11) 250 km/h 081°   12) 410 km/h 146°
13) 360 km/h 202°   14) 295 km/h 300°
15) 240 km/h 000°

Exercise 197

1) Upstream at 60°   2) 113° 35′
3) 14 km/h, 87° 30′   4) 23° 30′, 35 m
5) (a) 123° 30′   (b) 048°

Self-Test 45

1) c   2) d   3) b   4) c, d   5) a
6) d   7) c   8) a   9) c   10) d
11) b   12) b   13) d   14) b   15) c
16) c   17) d   18) c   19) a   20) b
21) c   22) b, d   23) d   24) a

ANSWERS TO MISCELLANEOUS EXERCISE

Exercise 198

1) (a) 1 cm   (b) $\frac{4}{1}$ 2) (a) 8.7 cm   (b) 6.2 cm
3) 15 cm
4) (a) 11.92 cm   (b) 3.420 cm
5) 38.30 m   6) 14.4 cm
7) 64° 9′   8) 83.14 cm²
9) $\frac{8}{15}$ 10) 3.871 cm
11) 31°
12) (a) (3, 90°)   (b) (5, 36° 52′)
13) (a) 17 cm   (b) 60 cm²
14) 31.6 m   15) 4.358 cm
16) 11.5 cm   17) 66° 15′
18) 38° 39′   19) 13.48 m
20) (a) 5.736 cm   (b) 34.416 cm²
21) (a) 400 m, 742 m   (b) 828 m
    (c) 153° 39′ (S 26° 21′ E)
22) (a) 54.72 m   (b) 20° 02′   (c) 128.6 m   (d) 90°
23) (a) 21.7 cm   (b) 51°   (c) 43.3 cm   (d) 758 cm
24) (a) 56° 18′   (b) 38° 40′   (c) 35° 13′
25) 7.506 cm; 6.633 cm   26) 120°
27) (a) 98.13 m   (b) 48.01 m   (c) 333° 55′; 34° 49′
28) (a) 20.92 km   (b) 11.02 km   (c) 122 min
29) (a) 2.938 km   (b) 2 h 48 min (14 h 48 min)
    (c) 18.28 km
30) (a) 200.3 cm²   (b) 33.42 cm; 6.871 cm; 41.2 cm²
31) (a) 66° 26′ N or S   (b) 22° 40′ S, 60° 20′ E
32) (a) 3°   (b) 198 m   (c) 57.9 m   (d) 30.3 m
33) (a) 5.853 m   (b) 46° 34′   (c) 3.808 m

Exercise 199

1) $A = \{5, 7, 9, 11, 13, 15\}$
2) $X = \{\text{Tuesday, Thursday}\}$
3) $B = \{2, 4, 6, 8, 10\}$
4) $P = \{2, 3, 5, 7, 11, 13, 17, 19, 23\}$
5) $Q = \{3, 6, 9, 12, 15, 18, 21, 24, 27, 30, 33\}$
6) $\{\text{multiples of 5 less than 26}\}$
7) $\{\text{family}\}$
8) $\{\text{prime numbers greater than 2 but less than 18}\}$

Exercise 200

1) infinite   2) finite   3) infinite
4) finite   5) infinite   6) null
7) finite   8) null   9) $n(A) = 4$
10) $n(B) = 10$

Exercise 201

1) $P = \{2, 4, 6, 8, 10\}, 7 \notin P$
2) $Q = \{1, 4, 9, 16, 25, 36\}, 18 \notin Q$
3) $R = \{17, 14, 11, 8, 5, 2\}, 9 \notin R$
4) $S = \{a, b, c, d, e, f\}, \phi \notin S$
5) $T = \{5, 7, 11, 13, 17, 19, 23, 29\}, 9 \notin T$
6) True   7) True   8) True
9) False   10) False

Exercise 202

1) (a) $\{3, 5, 9, 11, 13, 15\}$ (b) $\{6, 8, 12\}$
   (c) $\{3, 5, 11, 13\}$ (d) $\{6, 8, 12\}$
2) 16   3) c and d
4) No. $A \subset C \subset B$
5) $\{a\}, \{b\}, \{c\}, \{d\}, \{a, b\}, \{a, c\}, \{a, d\}, \{b, c\}, \{b, d\},$
   $\{c, d\}, \{a, b, c\}, \{a, c, d\}, \{a, b, d\}, \{b, c, d\}$
6) $g \subset a; h \subset b; e \subset c; f \subset d$
8) a, d, g   9) 32   10) 256

Exercise 203

1) (a) $\{a, e, i, o, u\}$
   (b) $\{u, v, w, x, y, z\}$
   (c) $\{b, c, d, f, g, h, j, k, l, m, n, p, q, r, s, t, v, w, x, y, z\}$
2) $\{\text{triangle, quadrilateral, pentagon, hexagon, heptagon, octagon}\}$
3) (a) $\{2, 3, 5, 7, 11, 13, 17, 19\}$
   (b) $\{3, 6, 9, 12, 15, 18\}$
   (c) $\{2, 3, 5, 7\}$
4) (a) $\{\text{Nov, Dec, Jan, Feb}\}$
   (b) $\{\text{Sept, Oct}\}$
5) $\{1, 4, 9, 16, 25\}$

Exercise 204

1) $\{2, 3, 4, 5, 6, 7, 8, 9, 11\}$ 2) $\{2, 4, 7, 8\}$
3) $\{5, 6, 7, 8\}$ 4) $\{3, 5, 6, 9, 11\}$
5) $\{2, 3, 4, 9, 11\}$ 6) $\{7, 8\}$
7) $\{2, 4, 5, 6, 7, 8\}$ 8) $\{3, 9, 11\}$
9) $\notin$ 10) $\cap, =$
11) $\in$ 12) $=$

13) $\subset$ 14) $\supset$
15) $\neq$ 16) $\subset, \subset$
17) $\notin$ 18) $\subset$
19) $\supset$ 20) $\subset$
21) $\{3, 4, 6, 7, 8, 9, 10\}$ 22) $\{6, 8\}$
23) $\{3, 4, 6, 7, 8, 9, 10\}$ 24) $\{6, 8\}$
25) $A \supset B$
26) $\{2, 3, 4, 5, 6, 7, 8, 9, 10, 11, 12, 13, 14, 15, 16\}$
27) $\{3, 4, 6, 8\}$ 28) $\{10, 12, 13, 14, 15\}$
29) ϕ
30) $\{3, 4, 6, 8, 10, 12, 13, 14, 15\}$
31)   32)

33)   34)

35)

36) (a) B (b) $A \cap B$ (c) $(A \cup B)'$ or $A' \cap B'$
   (d) $A' \cap B$ (e) $A \cup B$
   (f) $(A \cap B)'$ or $A' \cup B'$ (g) $A \cap B'$
37)

Exercise 205

1) $\{2\}$ 2) $\{2\}$ 3) $\{2, 3, 4, 5, 6, 7\}$
4) $\{2, 3, 4, 5, 6, 7\}$ 5) $\{2, 3, 6\}$ 6) $\{2, 3, 4, 5, 7, 8\}$
7) $\{4, 5, 7, 8\}$ 8) ϕ 9) $\{1, 2, 3, 6, 9\}$
10) $\{1, 2, 3, 4, 5, 6, 9\}$

Exercise 206

1) (a) 12   (b) 17   (c) 5   (d) 24
2) (a) 9   (b) 23   (c) 23   (d) 37
3) 40   4) 8   5) 7
6) (a) 34   (b) 36   (c) 40   (d) 9   (e) 10
   (f) 8   (g) 3   (h) 86
7) (a) 3   (b) 66   (c) 57   (d) 58   (e) 13
   (f) 11   (g) 10
8) 20   9) 140
10) (a) 3   (b) 25   (c) 7

Exercise 207

1) $A \Leftrightarrow Z; B \Leftrightarrow V; C \Leftrightarrow X; D \Leftrightarrow W; E \Leftrightarrow Y$
2) (a) true   (b) false $\Leftrightarrow$ (c) true   (d) true   (e) false $\Leftrightarrow$

3) (a) many to many   (b) many to one
  (c) many to many   (d) many to one
  (e) many to one   (f) many to one
  (g) many to one   (h) many to one
  (i) many to many   (j) one to one

ANSWERS TO CHAPTER 47

Exercise 208

1) (a) 10111   (b) 101010
  (c) 111101   (d) 111001
2) (a) 22   (b) 57   (c) 90   (d) 55
3) (a) 0.8125   (b) 0.4375   (c) 0.1875
4) (a) 0.011   (b) 0.0101   (c) 0.111
5) (a) 0.0010101   (b) 10010.0111011
  (c) 1101100.1011010
6) (a) 1110   (b) 100110
  (c) 111000   (d) 1100100
  (e) 1.0011   (f) 1.10100
  (g) 1101.0010   (h) 10010.00
7) (a) 101   (b) 100   (c) 1110
  (d) 1.110   (e) 10.001
8) (a) 110   (b) 100011
  (c) 1101110   (d) 101011111
  (e) 100011110
9) (a) 11   (b) 100   (c) 101
  (d) 1010   (e) 1101
10) (a) 10111.101   (b) 10011.00001
  (c) 10.0001   (d) 1.00101

Exercise 209

1) (a) 111_3 (b) 1120_3 (c) 11211_3
  (d) 1242_5 (e) 435_6 (f) 1213_4
  (g) 161_8 (h) 1304_6
2) (a) 100_3 (b) 3_4 (c) 1100_3
  (d) 13_4 (e) 4422_8 (f) 134_4
3) (a) 125   (b) 69   (c) 134
  (d) 313   (e) 187
4) (a) 1032_8 (b) 122_3
  (c) 11110_3 (d) 120_8

Exercise 210

1) (a) 1   (b) 2   (c) 3   (d) 4   (e) 4
  (f) 3   (g) 2   (h) 4
2) (a) 2   (b) 0   (c) 6   (d) 6   (e) 1
  (f) 2   (g) 6   (h) 0
3) (a) 6   (b) 6   (c) 6   (d) 3
4) 6, 10, 12, 15, 20, 30, 60
5) (a) 4   (b) 4   (c) 4
6) (a) 2   (b) 5   (c) 2   (d) 2 and 6
7) 4 or 3

Exercise 211

1) (a), (c)   2) No   3) Yes
4) (a), (d)   5) No

Exercise 212

1) (a) g   (b) Yes   (c) (i) d   (ii) f   (e) Yes
2) (a) No   (b) 1   (c) 3   (d) No

3)

−	0	1	2	3	4
0	0	4	3	2	1
1	1	0	4	3	2
2	2	1	0	4	3
3	3	2	1	0	4
4	4	3	2	1	0

(a) 4

4) (a) 11   (b) 1   (c) 0   (d) $-\frac{2}{3}$ (e) Yes   (f) Yes

5) (a) Set not closed under +
  (b) Every element does not have an inverse
  (c) Not associative
  (d) Every element does not have an inverse

6)

×	1	5	7	11
1	1	5	7	11
5	5	1	11	7
7	7	11	1	5
11	11	7	5	1

(a) 1   (b) Yes   (c) Yes

7) (a)

*	2	4	6	8
2	4	8	2	6
4	8	6	4	2
6	2	4	6	8
8	6	2	8	4

(b) (i) 2   (ii) 2 and 8   (iii) 6   (iv) 2, 4, 6 and 8
(c) (ii) 6   (iii) 2

8)

×	1	2	3	4	5	6
1	1	2	3	4	5	6
2	2	4	6	1	3	5
3	3	6	2	5	1	4
4	4	1	5	2	6	3
5	5	3	1	6	4	2
6	6	5	4	3	2	1

(a) 2 and 6   (c) (i) 4   (ii) 4

9) (a)

*	A	B	C	D	E
A	A	E	F	A	B
B	E	B	E	B	E
C	F	E	C	C	D
D	A	B	C	D	E
E	B	E	D	E	E

(b) Yes   (c) *D and E*; no   (d) $\{B, D, E\}$

10) (a) 1   (b) 5   (c) $\{1, 3, 5, 7\}$ (d) No solution

11)

○	I	P	Q
I	I	P	Q
P	P	Q	I
Q	Q	I	P

+	0	1	2
0	0	1	2
1	1	2	0
2	2	0	1

12)

●	I	X	Y	Z
I	I	X	Y	Z
X	X	I	Z	Y
Y	Y	Z	I	X
Z	Z	Y	X	I

×	1	3	5	7
1	1	3	5	7
3	3	1	7	5
5	5	7	1	3
7	7	5	3	1

13)

○	I	Y	X	H
I	I	Y	X	H
Y	Y	H	I	X
X	X	I	H	Y
H	H	Y	X	I

×	1	2	3	4
1	1	2	3	4
2	2	4	1	3
3	3	1	4	2
4	4	3	2	1

14) (a)

	P	Q	R	S	T	U
P	P	Q	R	S	T	U
Q	Q	R	P	U	S	T
R	R	P	Q	T	U	S
S	S	T	U	P	Q	R
T	T	U	S	R	P	Q
U	U	S	T	Q	R	P

(b) The inverse of P is R
The inverse of Q is R
The inverse of R is Q
The inverse of S is S
The inverse of T is T
The inverse of U is U

15)

×	1	3	5	7
1	1	3	5	7
3	3	1	7	5
5	5	7	1	3
7	7	5	3	1

$$
\begin{array}{cccc}
a & b & c & d \\
\updownarrow & \updownarrow & \updownarrow & \updownarrow \\
1 & 3 & 5 & 7
\end{array}
$$

16) 1, 3, 1, 5, 1, 7

17) (a) Yes
(b)
$$
\begin{array}{cccc}
A & B & C & D \\
\updownarrow & \updownarrow & \updownarrow & \updownarrow \\
P & Q & R & S
\end{array}
$$

ANSWERS TO CHAPTER 48

Exercise 213

1) (a) $\{(1, 6), (3, 10), (5, 14), (7, 18), (9, 22)\}$
   (b) $\{(1, 6), (3, 18), (5, 30), (7, 42), (9, 54)\}$
2) (a) 9   (b) 36   3) (a) 11   (b) $x \to 3x - 1$
4) (a) $\{(2, 0), (3, -2), (4, -4), (5, -6)\}$
   (b) $\{(2, 4), (3, 8), (4, 16), (5, 32)\}$
5) (a) $x \to 4x + 1$ (b) $(4, 17); (8, 33)$
6) $\{(0, 2), (1, 0), (2, 0), (3, 2), (4, 6)\}$
7) $x \to 2x$

Exercise 214

1) (a) 4   (b) 2   (c) 44   (d) $\frac{1}{4}$
2) (a) 17   (b) -23 (c) -7
3) (a) 1   (b) 21   (c) 0   (d) 5   (e) 33
4) $-1, 53, -1$
5) $6\frac{1}{2}, -3\frac{1}{2}$
6) $1\frac{1}{2}, \frac{1}{4}, -3\frac{1}{2}$
7) (a), (c), (d)

Exercise 215

4) $y = (3x + 5)^2$
5) (b) (i) $-\frac{10}{9}^\circ$ C   (ii) 68° F

Exercise 216

1) $f: x \to \dfrac{1}{3}x$ 2) $f: x \to \dfrac{x + 3}{2}$ 3) $f: x \to 2x + 3$

4) $f: x \to \dfrac{x + 15}{6}$ 5) $x \to \dfrac{2x + 5}{2 - x}$ 6) (a) 0   (b) $\frac{5}{6}$

7) $\frac{10}{3}, 2$ 8) $\frac{10}{4}, \frac{5}{4}$
9) (a) 9   (b) -2 (c) -27 (d) -131 (e) -8
10) $\dfrac{x - 9}{15} ; \dfrac{x + 1}{15}$ 11) 13   12) $\frac{16}{17}$

ANSWERS TO CHAPTER 49

Exercise 217

1) $L = 3, M = -1$

2) $\begin{pmatrix} 26 & 35 \\ 14 & 19 \end{pmatrix}$

3) (a) $\begin{pmatrix} 7 & 0 \\ 4 & 3 \end{pmatrix}$ (b) $\begin{pmatrix} 1 & 5 \\ 2 & -6 \end{pmatrix}$

   (c) $\begin{pmatrix} 14 & 0 \\ 8 & -2 \end{pmatrix}$ (d) $\begin{pmatrix} 10 & 4 \\ 12 & 2 \end{pmatrix}$

4) (a) $PQ = \begin{pmatrix} 2 & 1 \\ 3 & 1 \end{pmatrix}$

   $RS = \begin{pmatrix} -6 & 3 \\ 1 & -2 \end{pmatrix}$

   $PQRS = \begin{pmatrix} -11 & 4 \\ -17 & 7 \end{pmatrix}$

   $P^2 - Q^2 = \begin{pmatrix} 6 & 3 \\ 9 & 3 \end{pmatrix}$

   (b) $a = -2, b = 5$

5) $A^2 = \begin{pmatrix} 16 & -9 \\ -12 & 13 \end{pmatrix}$

   $B = \begin{pmatrix} -18 & 12 \\ 16 & -14 \end{pmatrix}$

6) $\begin{pmatrix} 9 \\ -1 \end{pmatrix}$

7) $p = 5, q = -1$

8) (a) $\begin{pmatrix} 3 & 1 \\ 2 & 2 \end{pmatrix}$ (b) $\begin{pmatrix} 1 & 3 \\ 2 & 3 \end{pmatrix}$ (c) $\begin{pmatrix} -1 & 2 \\ 1 & -1 \end{pmatrix}$

9) (a) (i) $\begin{pmatrix} 7 & 3 \\ 3 & 4 \end{pmatrix}$ (ii) $\begin{pmatrix} 1 & -1 \\ 4 & 12 \end{pmatrix}$ (iii) $\begin{pmatrix} 13 & 6 \\ 12 & 4 \end{pmatrix}$

   (b) (i) $\begin{pmatrix} 6 & 4 & 2 \\ 3 & 6 & 1 \end{pmatrix}$

   (ii) $\begin{pmatrix} 150 \\ 120 \\ 375 \end{pmatrix}$ (iii) $\begin{pmatrix} 2130 \\ 1545 \end{pmatrix}$

   (iv) The number of passengers that each airline can carry

10) (a) $\begin{pmatrix} 12 \\ 8 \\ 15 \\ 12 \\ 8 \end{pmatrix}$

   (b) $AB = \begin{pmatrix} -7 & 11 \\ 2 & -6 \end{pmatrix}$ $BA = \begin{pmatrix} -9 & -1 \\ -16 & -4 \end{pmatrix}$

   (c) $x = 4, y = -1$

11) (a) $x = 1, y = 2$ (b) $x = 3, y = 4$
    (c) $x = 2, y = 1$

Exercise 218

1) (a) $\sqrt{10} = 3.162; 18°\,26'$ (b) $\sqrt{74} = 8.602; 54°\,28'$
    (c) $\sqrt{73} = 8.544; 69°\,27'$

2) $R = \begin{pmatrix} 4 \\ 6 \end{pmatrix}$; 7.211 at $56°\,18'$

3) $R = \begin{pmatrix} 6 \\ 8 \end{pmatrix}$; 10 at $53°\,8'$

4) $M = \begin{pmatrix} 5 \\ 2 \end{pmatrix}$; 5.385 at $21°\,48'$

5) (a) 31.7   (b) 18.9   (c) -5.21
   (d) 1.55   (e) 0   (f) -5
   (g) -14.8 (h) 7.66

6) (a) 29, $4°\,40'$ (b) -14, $121°\,20'$
   (c) -25, $142°\,46'$ (d) 9, $55°\,18'$

7) 9.22 at $40°\,36'$ to the horizontal.

8) $\mathbf{p} = \begin{pmatrix} 3 \\ 1 \end{pmatrix}$, $\mathbf{q} = \begin{pmatrix} -1 \\ 3 \end{pmatrix}$ (a) $\mathbf{p} - \mathbf{q} = \begin{pmatrix} 4 \\ 4 \end{pmatrix}$ (b) $26°\,54'$

Exercise 219

1) (a)
$$\begin{array}{cccc} A' & B' & C' & D' \end{array}$$
$$\begin{pmatrix} 0 & 2 & 2 & 0 \\ -1 & -1 & -3 & -3 \end{pmatrix}$$

(b)
$$\begin{array}{cccc} A' & B' & C' & D' \end{array}$$
$$\begin{pmatrix} 0 & -2 & -2 & 0 \\ 1 & 1 & 3 & 3 \end{pmatrix}$$

(c)
$$\begin{array}{cccc} A' & B' & C' & D' \end{array}$$
$$\begin{pmatrix} -1 & -1 & -3 & -3 \\ 0 & -2 & -2 & 0 \end{pmatrix}$$

(d)
$$\begin{array}{cccc} A' & B' & C' & D' \end{array}$$
$$\begin{pmatrix} 1 & 1 & 3 & 3 \\ 0 & 2 & 2 & 0 \end{pmatrix}$$

(e)
$$\begin{array}{cccc} A' & B' & C' & D' \end{array}$$
$$\begin{pmatrix} 1 & 3 & 3 & 1 \\ 4 & 4 & 6 & 6 \end{pmatrix}$$

2)
$$\begin{array}{ccc} A & B & C \end{array}$$
$$\begin{pmatrix} 8 & 6 & 7 \\ 1 & -1 & 0 \end{pmatrix}$$

3) (a) $(-1, 7)$ (b) $(0, 5)$ (c) $(-6, 1)$
   (d) $(-4, 9)$ (e) $(5, 4)$

4)
$$\begin{array}{ccc} A' & B' & C' \end{array}$$
$$\begin{pmatrix} -1 & 2 & 2 \\ -6 & -6 & -3 \end{pmatrix}$$

5) (a)
$$\begin{array}{ccccc} A' & B' & C' & D' & E' \end{array}$$
$$\begin{pmatrix} 0 & 2 & 3 & 1 & -1 \\ -4 & -2 & 0 & 2 & 3 \end{pmatrix}$$

(b)
$$\begin{array}{ccccc} A' & B' & C' & D' & E' \end{array}$$
$$\begin{pmatrix} 1 & 3 & 4 & 2 & 0 \\ 2 & 0 & -2 & -4 & -5 \end{pmatrix}$$

(c)
$$\begin{array}{ccccc} A' & B' & C' & D' & E' \end{array}$$
$$\begin{pmatrix} -1 & -3 & -4 & -2 & 0 \\ -2 & 0 & 2 & 4 & 5 \end{pmatrix}$$

(d)
$$\begin{array}{ccccc} A' & B' & C' & D' & E' \end{array}$$
$$\begin{pmatrix} 2 & 0 & -2 & -4 & -5 \\ -1 & -3 & -4 & -2 & 0 \end{pmatrix}$$

(e)
$$\begin{array}{ccccc} A' & B' & C' & D' & E' \end{array}$$
$$\begin{pmatrix} -2 & 0 & 2 & 4 & 5 \\ 1 & 3 & 4 & 2 & 0 \end{pmatrix}$$

6)
$$\begin{array}{cccc} A' & B' & C' & D' \end{array}$$
$$\begin{pmatrix} -0.889 & -0.370 & 0.027 & 2.571 \\ 2.052 & 4.226 & 7.810 & 3.064 \end{pmatrix}$$

7)
$$\begin{array}{cccc} W' & X' & Y' & Z' \end{array}$$
$$\begin{pmatrix} -0.520 & 1.012 & -0.273 & -1.805 \\ 2.175 & 3.460 & 4.992 & 3.707 \end{pmatrix}$$

8)
$$\begin{array}{ccc} A' & B' & C' \end{array}$$
$$\begin{pmatrix} -1 & -3 & -2 \\ 6 & 8 & 10 \end{pmatrix}$$

9) (a) $\begin{pmatrix} 9 & 4 \\ 18 & 8 \end{pmatrix}$ (b) $(-31, -62)$

10) (a) $\begin{pmatrix} 1 & 4 \\ 0 & -1 \end{pmatrix}$

(b)
$$\begin{array}{ccc} A' & B' & C' \end{array}$$
$$\begin{pmatrix} 50 & 80 & 95 \\ -10 & -15 & -20 \end{pmatrix}$$

11) $(-6.84, 0.68)$

12) $(-2, -3), (-2, -1), (-4, -1), (-4, -3)$

13) (a) $(6, 2)$ (b) $(6, 2)$ (c) $(4, -1)$
   (d) $(-1, -1)$ (e) $(1, 2)$ (f) $(9, 4)$ (g) $(7, 1)$

14) $A(3, 2)$; $B(5, 2)$; $C(4, 3)$.

Exercise 220

2) (a) $(0, 0)$ (b) $(4, 2)$ (c) $(0, 0)$ (d) $(0, 0)$

3) $(-\frac{3}{2}, -\frac{5}{2})$

4) (a) $\begin{pmatrix} 0 & 2 & 8 & 6 \\ 0 & 0 & 2 & 2 \end{pmatrix}$ (b) $\begin{pmatrix} -2 & 1 & 7 & 4 \\ 0 & 0 & 2 & 2 \end{pmatrix}$

   (c) $\begin{pmatrix} 11 & 14 & 19 & 16 \\ 2 & 2 & 4 & 4 \end{pmatrix}$ (d) $\begin{pmatrix} 5 & 9 & 15 & 12 \\ 1 & 1 & 3 & 3 \end{pmatrix}$

5) (a) $\begin{pmatrix} 4 & 4 & 8 & 8 \\ 4 & 0 & 0 & 4 \end{pmatrix}$ (b) $\begin{pmatrix} -6 & -6 & -12 & -12 \\ 4 & 0 & 0 & 4 \end{pmatrix}$

   (c) $\begin{pmatrix} 2 & 2 & 4 & 4 \\ 6 & 0 & 0 & 6 \end{pmatrix}$ (d) $\begin{pmatrix} 2 & 2 & 4 & 4 \\ -2 & 0 & 0 & -2 \end{pmatrix}$

6) (a) $\begin{pmatrix} 0 & 4 & 4 & 0 \\ 0 & 0 & 3 & 3 \end{pmatrix}$ (b) $\begin{pmatrix} 0 & -1 & -1 & 0 \\ 0 & 0 & 2 & 2 \end{pmatrix}$

   (c) $\begin{pmatrix} 0 & 1 & 1 & 0 \\ 0 & 0 & 4 & 4 \end{pmatrix}$ (d) $\begin{pmatrix} 0 & 3 & 3 & 0 \\ 0 & 0 & -1\frac{1}{2} & -1\frac{1}{2} \end{pmatrix}$

ANSWERS TO CHAPTER 51

Exercise 221

1) $x = 6$; $y = 7$
2) Private motoring 15.7%; rail 39.3%; other 45%
3) Unskilled workers 52.9%; craftsmen 29.4%; draughtsmen 5.9%; clerical staff 11.8%
8) Clothing 81°; furniture 108°; stationery 27°; sports equipment 54°; household goods 90°

Exercise 222

1) (a) 40   (b) 11   (c) 35
6) (a) 12 000   7) 800 items   8) 16 000 articles

Exercise 223

5) (a) 15.015 and 14.985 mm
   (b) 0.03 mm   (c) 14.96–14.98 mm
6) Discrete: (b), (d), (g)

Exercise 224

1) £28   2) 175 cm   3) £41.20
4) 199.92 mm   5) 163.1 cm   6) 5
7) 4.5   8) 57   9) 5
10) no mode   11) 3, 5, 8   12) 4
13) 199.95 mm   14) 163 cm
15) $\bar{x} = 6$ mean deviation $= 2$
16) $\bar{x} = 3.175$ mean deviation $= 0.575$
17) $\bar{x} = 169$ cm mean deviation $= 0.794$
18) $\bar{x} = 5.5$ passes mean deviation $= 1.27$
19) $\bar{x} = 38.6$ cm mean deviation $= 1.44$
20) $\bar{x} = 8$ mean deviation $= 1$

ANSWERS TO CHAPTER 52

Exercise 225

1) (a) $\frac{1}{6}$ (b) $\frac{1}{2}$ (c) $\frac{1}{3}$ (d) $\frac{1}{2}$
2) (a) $\frac{1}{5}$ (b) $\frac{1}{2}$ (c) $\frac{33}{40}$ (d) $\frac{3}{40}$
3) (a) $\frac{1}{52}$ (b) $\frac{1}{13}$ (c) $\frac{4}{13}$ (d) $\frac{1}{26}$
4) (a) $\frac{1}{9}$ (b) $\frac{2}{9}$ (c) $\frac{1}{3}$
5) (a) $\frac{1}{5}$ (b) $\frac{9}{20}$ (c) $\frac{13}{20}$
6) (a) $\frac{1}{6}$ (b) $\frac{5}{18}$ (c) $\frac{5}{18}$
7) (a)
8) $\frac{37}{40}$

Exercise 226

1) $\frac{5}{52}$
2) (a) $\frac{1}{12}$ (b) $\frac{1}{4}$
3) (a) $\frac{4}{25}$ (b) $\frac{9}{25}$ (c) $\frac{12}{25}$
4) $\frac{9}{400}$
5) (a) 0.32   (b) 0.03
6) (a) $\frac{1}{13}$ (b) $\frac{1}{17}$
7) (a) $\frac{4}{27}$ (b) $\frac{5}{27}$
8) (a) $\frac{1}{3}$ (b) $\frac{5}{12}$ (c) (i) $\frac{1}{24}$ (ii) $\frac{1}{12}$
9) (a) $\frac{1}{6}$ (b) (i) $\frac{1}{18}$ (ii) $\frac{1}{36}$ (c) $\frac{1}{6}$
10) (a) $\frac{1}{6}$ (b) $\frac{1}{2}$ (d) (i) $\frac{1}{9}$ (ii) $\frac{5}{18}$
11) (a) $\frac{1}{4}$ (b) $\frac{5}{8}$ (c) $\frac{1}{28}$ (d) $\frac{9}{14}$
12) (b) (i) $\frac{1}{36}$ (ii) $\frac{1}{6}$ (iii) $\frac{25}{36}$ (c) $\frac{1}{12}$
13) (a) A $= \frac{10}{24}$ (or $\frac{5}{12}$); B $= \frac{10}{23}$; C $= \frac{14}{23}$; D $= \frac{9}{23}$ (b) $\frac{15}{92}$
14) (b) 0; $\frac{1}{25}$; $\frac{2}{25}$; $\frac{1}{5}$; $\frac{1}{25}$ (c) (i) 4   (ii) 9   (iii) 16

ANSWERS TO CHAPTER 53

Exercise 227

1) 14   2) 11, -5
3) 60 of Sure-clean, 20 of Quick-wash, £7.20
4) 16 Type P, 16 Type Q, £1120
5) (a) 10 hectares   (b) 5 of wheat, 4 of kale   (c) £56
6) A(0, 1), B(2, 3), C(5, 0); 13
7) 6 van journeys, 3 lorry journeys; £39
8) (b) 28   (c) 19   (d) 7
9) (b) 1 of ham, 4 of beef   (c) £1.80
10) 22

ANSWERS TO MULTI-CHOICE QUESTIONS

Exercise 228

1) c	2) d	3) b	4) a	5) c
6) e	7) c	8) e	9) c	10) b
11) b	12) c	13) c	14) c	15) c
16) a	17) b	18) c	19) e	20) b
21) d	22) b	23) a	24) a	25) e
26) b	27) d	28) c	29) e	30) d
31) d	32) b	33) a	34) a	35) a
36) e	37) b	38) c	39) none	40) c, e

ANSWERS TO MISCELLANEOUS EXERCISE

Exercise 229

1) $\begin{pmatrix} 0 \\ -4 \end{pmatrix}$ 2) (a) 2   (b) 3   3) 57_8

4) (a)

(b) $R = \{$even numbers which are multiples of 3$\}$
   $= \{6, 12, 18 \ldots\}$
   $= \{$multiples of 6$\}$

5) (a)

(b) $\begin{pmatrix} -1 & 0 \\ 0 & -1 \end{pmatrix}$

6) (a) 1   (b) 2   (c) 2.5
7)

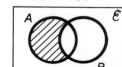

8) 2   9) $\{(0, 1), (1, 3), (2, 9)\}$

10)

11) $n = 3$ 12) $1\,1\,0\,1\,1_2$ 13) (a) 4   (b) 2, 3

14) (a) $\{7\}$ (b) $\{\ \}$

15) (a) not possible   (b) $\begin{pmatrix} 9 \\ 12 \end{pmatrix}$ (c) $\begin{pmatrix} 1 & -\frac{2}{3} \\ 0 & \frac{1}{3} \end{pmatrix}$

16) (a) 100_8 (b) 17_8

17) (a) $\begin{pmatrix} 2 \\ -7 \end{pmatrix}$ (b) $\begin{pmatrix} 7 \\ 8 \end{pmatrix}$

18) (a) 4   (b) 1

19) $\begin{pmatrix} 2 & -1 \\ -5 & 3 \end{pmatrix}$

20) (a) $\{3, 4, 5, 6, 7, 8, 9\}$ (b) 2

21) (a) Reflection in the y-axis   (b) $\begin{pmatrix} 0 & -1 \\ 1 & 0 \end{pmatrix}$

22) (a) $\{12, 13, 14, 16, 17, 18\}$ (b) 6

23) (a) -1 (b) $\frac{3}{5}$ 24) $\begin{pmatrix} 1\frac{1}{2} \\ -\frac{1}{4} \end{pmatrix}$ 25) $(-4, 0)$

26) $1\,0\,1\,1\,0\,0$ 27) $\{(0, 3), (1, 0), (2, -1), (3, 0)\}$

28) $W - 90^\circ, P - 150^\circ, S - 120^\circ$ 29) -8°

30) $\begin{pmatrix} 1 & -2 \\ -0.5 & 1.5 \end{pmatrix}$

Index